SECOND EDITION

An Introduction to

COMPUTERS AND
INFORMATION PROCESSING

Wiley Series in Computers and Information Processing Systems for Business

The Wiley Series in Computers and Information Processing Systems
Nancy Stern—Hofstra University
Advisory Editor

The Wiley Series in the Management Information Systems for Business
Hugh J. Watson—University of Georgia-Athens
Advisory Editor

SECOND EDITION

An Introduction to
COMPUTERS AND
INFORMATION PROCESSING

Robert A. Stern / Nancy Stern

John Wiley & Sons

New York   Chichester   Brisbane   Toronto   Singapore

Library of Congress Cataloging in Publication Data:

Stern, Robert A.
   An introduction to computer and information
processing.

   Includes index.
      1. Electronic data processing.   2. Electronic digital
computers.   I. Stern, Nancy B.   II. Title.
QA76.S745   1985   OC1.64   84-7422
ISBN 0-471-87687-9

Printed in the United States of America

10 9 8 7 6

Cover and Text design: Sheila Granda
Cover photo: © Joel Gordon 1983
Production Supervisor: David Smith
Copy Editor: Susan Giniger
Photo Editor: Elyse Rieder

To Melanie and Lori

About the Authors

Robert A. Stern is an attorney and a Professor of Mathematics and Computer Processing at Nassau Community College in Garden City, New York. He holds a B.S. in Industrial Engineering and a B.S. in Business Administration, both from Lehigh University, an M.S. in Operations Research from New York University, and a J.D. from St. John's University School of Law. He is the coauthor of several other information processing texts including *Structured COBOL Programming,* 4th ed., *370/360 Assembler Language Programming,* and *RPG II and RPG III Programming.* Mr. Stern has had diverse business experience as a systems analyst, an industrial engineer, and an attorney.

Dr. Nancy Stern is currently Professor and Chairperson of the Business Computer Information Systems Department at Hofstra University in Hempstead, New York. She holds an A.B. degree from Barnard College, an M.S. from New York University, and a Ph.D. from the State University of New York at Stony Brook. She is the coauthor of the texts mentioned above and is the author of *Flowcharting: A Self-Teaching Guide.* Dr. Stern is advisory editor of the Wiley series on Information Processing Systems, as well. One of her major interests is the history of computing; she has written several articles and books on computing history and is currently Assistant Editor-in-Chief of the *Annals of the History of Computing.*

Preface

OBJECTIVES

The primary purpose of this text is to provide the student with an understanding of hardware and software concepts and how they are used in information systems.

This book presents a realistic account of computer processing, unlike other texts, which often give an idealistic view. We stress the major problems in this field as well as the major advantages of computerization. Topics highlighted in this edition are:

A. The Need for Improved Communication Between the User and the Computer Professional

In the first edition, we emphasized the need for better communication between the user and the computer professional. Nonetheless, many schools believe that communication skills are not emphasized enough in their courses. This edition focuses on the reasons why communication problems exist in business and on techniques that may be used for minimizing these problems. Improving communication skills will help students become better computer professionals and managers.

Throughout the text, a case study is provided that not only integrates the subject matter in a meaningful way but asks questions of students in an effort to help them improve their communication skills as well as their analytical ability. Similarly, end-of-chapter applications that highlight state-of-the-art developments and controversial aspects of computing are followed by questions that test the student's ability to understand the concepts presented and to communicate that understanding. Term paper assignments are provided in appendix D in an effort to enhance students' skills in writing papers.

Each chapter has a chapter outline, objectives, summaries, and so on, that are designed to demonstrate how concepts can be effectively communicated in a user-friendly way. In summary, a primary focus is on improving skills.

B. Social, Ethical, and Legal Implications of Computing

Social issues relevant to the computing field are emphasized throughout the text, not just in isolated chapters. These issues are also reinforced in many of the applications.

We believe strongly that computer professionals should be cognizant of their social responsibilities, and should play a role in helping to more effectively integrate computers in today's society.

C. Systems and Management Concepts

This book has become more systems and management oriented, as seen in the text as well as the applications. There is a developmental case study added to the end of each chapter. The case study evolves throughout the text, with questions at the end of each chapter pertaining to the case and drawing on material presented in the text.

There is more of a focus on assessing and evaluating information processing technology, software, and systems, which are tasks frequently required of computer professionals and managers. Charts, graphs, and diagrams provide information to assist in assessing products. Attention is also given to evaluating computer advertisements and other marketing tools in an effort to help future professionals assess new products.

D. New and Timely Applications

Each application in the text provides useful state-of-the-art information relevant to each chapter; in addition, all applications test the student in four areas:

1. Understanding of key terms.
2. Software, hardware, and systems concepts.
3. Management concepts—relevant to the application.
4. Social, legal, or ethical implications pertaining to the application.

E. Improved Pedagogic Approach

Emphasis has been placed on a sound approach to teaching the subject, one that has been tested on a broad cross-section of college and university students. Because of the book's focus, it can be effectively used in a standard introductory course. It can also be used by interested readers who simply wish to learn more about the computing field.

Our pedagogic approach, used so successfully in the previous version of the book, has been enhanced with the following elements:

1. Clear and concise chapter outlines and chapter objectives that highlight the key concepts covered in each chapter.
2. A realistic, up-to-date, highly readable approach to each topic.
3. Self-evaluating quizzes with solutions provided that help students test their understanding of important concepts and ideas. There are self-evaluating questions throughout each chapter after major concepts have been presented. There is also a chapter self-evaluating quiz that tests students on the entire chapter's contents. These have solutions that indicate the page numbers where the material is discussed, for ease of reference.
4. An emphasis on illustrations, figures, and tables to highlight concepts and ideas.
5. Chapter summaries to reinforce the material presented in each chapter.
6. Review questions that can be assigned by the instructor as homework.
7. A key terms list at the end of each chapter highlighting items introduced and defined within the chapter. An end-of-text glossary contains formal definitions for all key terms specified.

8. An application at the end of each chapter, with key questions, to reinforce material presented and to provide some understanding of the major issues currently facing the computer field.

9. A developmental case study at the end of each chapter that integrates material presented in the text.

10. A marketing ad at the end of each chapter designed to provide some insight into how computer products are marketed.

F. Specific Attention to the Requirements of Major Curricula

This text covers course requirements specified in the DPMA and ACM curricula, and those for AACSB schools. The instructor's resource manual provides a chapter-by-chapter analysis of how this book conforms to the above standards.

G. Supplemental Packages

The following supplementary materials make *An Introduction to Computers and Processing Information*, 2nd ed., a truly unique package.

1. *Using Personal Computer Software.* This supplement focuses on teaching students to use word processing, data base management, and electronic spreadsheet packages.

2. *Study Guide.* This highly successful combined study guide and workbook approach includes chapter outlines, which the student can use for review, definitions of key terms, a broad spectrum of questions and answers, and key summaries and reviews. We have written this study guide ourselves to ensure that it is totally consistent with the text.

3. *Transparencies.* This is a four color transparency package that is coordinated with each chapter. There are two types of transparencies: (1) key illustrations from the text and (2) tables and illustrations *not* in the text that are designed both to maintain student interest and to highlight key concepts.

4. *Instructor's Resource Manual.* This comprehensive instructor's manual includes course outlines, chapter summaries, hints for classroom discussion, additional teaching aids, resource guides to films and software, guides to DPMA, ACM, and AACSB curricula, and many other features.

5. *Test Manual.* A test bank of more than 3000 questions is available.

6. *Microtest-bank.* A computerized version available for use on micros.

7. *Selecting and Evaluating Micros: A Manual, Slide, and Audio/Cassette Package.* A manual and a set of over 125 slides highlighting the selection and evaluation of micros is available; a cassette tape is also provided for use as an oral presentation to accompany the slides.

8. *Software Consists of* (1) A *Microstudy* version of the *Study Guide* for the IBM PC's and Apple IIe and IIc. (2) *A Software Tool for Programming and Debugging BASIC* with data sets for practice problems in the text and debugging exercises for teaching students how to find and correct errors. (3) A wide variety of software for use on many different micros accompanies the text.

THE UNIQUENESS OF THIS BOOK

1. Organization, User-Friendly Approach, and Emphasis on Human Factors in Computing

The presentation is ideally suited for college students. In particular, information systems are discussed from an applications-oriented point of view throughout the text and again as a unit near the end of the book; this effectively brings together the major concepts presented.

Our style of writing has been developed for introductory information processing students. It is highly readable and user-friendly, without compromising the conceptual level of the presentation.

2. A Thorough Guide to BASIC Programming

The chapter and appendix on BASIC explain the fundamentals of this languge in a clear manner. After reading Chapter 12 and discussing it in class, students will be able to write simple and intermediate-level programs without the need for a supplemental text. Reviewers have indicated that because of its organization and clear style, this BASIC chapter could well be a stand-alone text on the subject. Appendix A on BASIC programming provides additional material for higher-level applications.

3. Emphasis on Micros and Minis

This text does not simply append micros and minis as a supplement to the mainframe orientation; rather, they are a focus throughout the book. We emphasize how micros and minis can be used as alternatives and supplements to larger systems. Chapter 9 specifically focuses on micros and minis and places them in the proper perspective vis-à-vis mainframes.

4. An Emphasis on the Computer in Today's Society

The book begins with a comprehensive discussion about how computers are used today. In Chapter 17 we explore in depth some of the legal, social, and ethical issues relating to computers. Chapter 19 provides a look to the future, based on our own perception. We have included these comprehensive chapters both at the beginning and the end to alert students to some of the major issues still facing the computer profession today.

5. A Chapter on the Computer Professional

This chapter provides students with insight into the current job market, both for entry-level positions and more advanced ones as well. It is a realistic approach that provides numerous hints on writing resumes, preparing for interviews, taking interviews, and so on.

6. An Appendix Entitled "A Guide to Resources and Journals in the Computing Field"

Unlike a chapter-by-chapter bibliography, which is often obsolete before it is published, this guide in Appendix D will help students identify key associations and journals in the computing field. This knowledge will help them better prepare for term papers and will also serve them well as computer professionals.

7. A Focus on Data Communications

Because of the prevalence and great potential for data communications, this topic is emphasized throughout the text. In addition, Chapters 8 and 14 explore in depth the uses of data communications for word processing, point-of-sale systems, electronic funds transfer systems, and numerous other applications.

8. An Emphasis on Management Information Systems Concepts

Here, again, the applications orientation of the text is emphasized with a unit on information systems, one that examines decision support systems, cost-benefit analysis, equipment selection criteria, distributed data processing, and so on.

9. Included Are Many Test Questions and Applications Designed to Test Students' Understanding and to Reinforce the Material

The application, case study, and marketing ad at the end of each chapter not only reinforce the concepts presented in the chapter, but provide "real world" illustrations, highlight innovations in the computing field and point to social issues that exist.

The self-evaluating questions at the end of each chapter and at the end of each unit within a chapter also reinforce the concepts presented and provide an excellent method for students to assess how well they have understood the material.

At the end of each chapter there are review questions without solutions that instructors can assign as homework.

The study guide has approximately 1300 questions that include matching, true-false, multiple-choice, fill-ins, and application questions, of which 650 have solutions (the other 650 are answered in the instructor's manual). The instructor's manual has additional questions of this kind, which can be distributed and assigned as homework, or used in the preparation of tests. The test bank can be used in this way as well. In summary, the instructor has numerous resources for assigning homework and term paper topics, and for preparing tests.

We would like to express our appreciation to the following people at John Wiley and Sons for their extraordinary support in the development of this manuscript: Sheila Granda, design; Suzanne Ingrao, production manager; David Smith, production supervisor; Susan Giniger, copy editor; Elyse Rieder, photo editor. Our very special thanks goes to our editor Nina R. Lewis for her total commitment and dedication to this project. She has added a dimension to this book for which we are truly grateful.

We would also like to thank Carol Eisen for her outstanding contributions in preparing and reviewing the manuscript, and Carol Grimm for her work on the *Instructor's Resource Manual*.

Prior to writing this book, we performed an exhaustive survey of the needs of college professors and their students. We believe that this textbook will meet, and may even surpass, those needs and expectations.

This book will be updated every two to three years to provide users with a state-of-the-art guide to computing. For this, we welcome your comments and suggestions. Please feel free to contact us:

Professor Robert A. Stern
Professor of Mathematics and
  Computer Processing
Nassau Community College
Garden City, NY 11530
(516) 222-7383

Dr. Nancy Stern, Chairperson
Department of Business Computer
  Information Systems
Hofstra University
Hempstead, New York 11550
(516) 560-5716

Acknowledgments

We would like to take this opportunity to thank the following reviewers for their extremely helpful suggestions and comments throughout the development of this project.

Pete J. Aleman
Washington University in St. Louis

Bonnie H. Bailey
Morehead State University

Anthony Basillico
Community College of Rhode Island

Gordon Bassen
Kingsborough Community College

Robert H. Blissmer
Systems Consultant

Robert L. Carmichael
University of California-Los Angeles

Myron H. Goldberg
Pace University

Carol Grimm
Palm Beach Junior College

Joyce Hamilton
Henry Ford Community College

James Hunter
Western Carolina University

Bev Jameson
Johnson County Community College

Richard Klinger
Cayuga Community College

Charles R. Litecky
University of Missouri-Columbia

Richard Manthei
Joliet Junior College

Herbert C. Mayer
University of Wisconsin at Parkside

Chadwick H. Nestman
University of South Alabama

James Payne
Kellogg Community College

Carol Rowey
Community College of Rhode Island

Susan Van Sickle
Washburn University

Contents

MODULE 2   Mainframes, Minis, Micros, and More

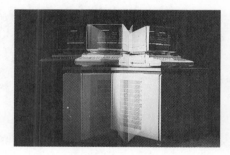

MODULE 3   Communicating with Computers in Today's World

MODULE 4   Understanding, Evaluating, and Using Software

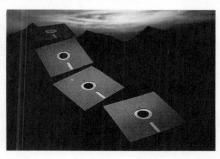

16 Management Information Systems 618

MODULE 6   The Human Factor in Computing

17 Obstacles to Overcome: Making the Computer Secure, Private, and User-Friendly 648

18 The Computer Professional 684

APPENDIXES

SECOND EDITION

An Introduction to
COMPUTERS AND
INFORMATION PROCESSING

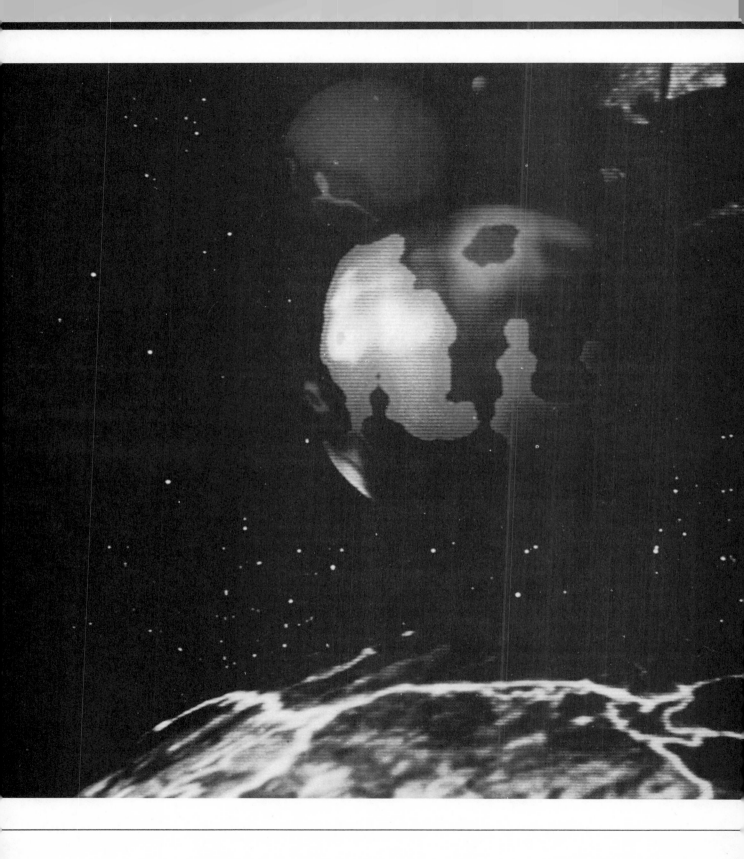

MODULE
1

COMPUTERS IN SOCIETY

CHAPTER 1

COMPUTERS
TODAY

CHAPTER OBJECTIVES

To familiarize you with:

- The elements of a computer system.
- Types of computers.
- The pros and cons of computerization.
- The ways in which computers are currently being used in society.
- Some of the concerns people have and social issues raised regarding the widespread use of computers.

I. A BRIEF NOTE ON THE FOCUS OF THIS BOOK

Welcome to the exciting world of computers and information processing! This book is designed to familiarize you with the ways in which computers may be used, but will *not* dwell on a host of terms and complex concepts. In a word, this book is meant to be **user-friendly**—this is your first computer term. Computers themselves should be ''user-friendly,'' which means that they are specifically designed to be understandable, useful, and nonthreatening to the user. The person who actually relies on computer results for achieving some objective is referred to here as the ''user.'' We hope you find our approach to computers to be a user-friendly one.

The book focuses on the use of computers in business but considers many other application areas as well.

The concepts presented fall into three basic categories.

Hardware—computer devices.

Software—sets of instructions that tell computer devices what operations to perform.

Information systems—broad application areas that integrate the use of hardware and software to accomplish specific goals.

This is *not* a book aimed at glorifying the computer. We do not focus on the virtues of computational devices, nor do we present an overly optimistic and unrealistic view of the current and future uses and impact of computers. Instead, our aim is to familiarize you with how computers are *actually used*. We will include examples of *effective* computerization as well as examples of applications that are regarded as failures.

This text does, however, have one optimistic point to convey: we believe that to achieve effective computerization and to minimize problems, computer users and computer professionals must work closely together.

Some of the general problem areas we focus upon include the following:

1. The need for control and security procedures to minimize computer crimes and errors.
2. The need for better computer techniques and standards to help develop and assess information systems.
3. The need for better communication between computer users and computer professionals to achieve improved results. This implies that users will need to better understand what computers can and cannot do. It also implies that computer professionals must be better able to understand user needs and to be more aware of, and sensitive to, appropriate ways of responding to those needs.

Still another orientation of this book focuses on the impact of computers not only on organizations but on individuals as well. We consider the widespread use of personal computers for individual use in the home, classroom, and office. This text, then, will include a ''people-oriented'' approach as well as an organizational one, with the newest phase of the computer revolution— that of the personal computer—being an integral part of our discussion.

But, above all, this book is designed to *teach*—not preach, nor serve as a reference manual or dictionary. It is our goal to actually explain computer concepts in a step-by-step, clear, and concise manner. Concepts and applications that are considered have been fully tested in a classroom setting. They are illustrated here with examples, diagrams, and photographs.

We include numerous teaching aids designed to help you understand computers and information processing and to reinforce your learning. These teaching aids include the following:

At the Beginning of Each Chapter

Chapter Outline—highlights the major topics to be considered and their relationships to each other.

Chapter Objectives—provides a brief overview of what you are expected to learn from the chapter.

Throughout the Chapters

Self-Evaluating Quizzes—these appear throughout each chapter to help you test your own understanding of the material presented. Solutions are provided so that you can test yourself.

End-of-Chapter Aids

Chapter Summary—provides a summary in outline form of the chapter's contents, for review purposes.

Chapter Self-Evaluating Quiz—includes a comprehensive set of questions with solutions that also include the page number indicating where the relevant material is discussed.

Key Terms List—lists all terms defined in the chapter for ease of reference; all key terms are introduced as boldfaced words within the chapter and are also defined in the glossary in Appendix F.

Review Questions—these may be assigned by your instructor for homework; if not, it is a good idea to answer them and ask questions about those with which you are having difficulty.

Applications—these are "real-world" examples of how computers are used and some of the problems associated with their use.

The Computer Ad—we include illustrative ads that use innovative and entertaining techniques to sell a computer product. They will help you understand how vendors view their products, how they view the intended market, and how they believe they can interest potential users in acquiring these products.

Case Study—this is a developmental hypothetical computer application that helps you to "build" an information system in a step-by-step fashion from chapter to chapter.

II. SOME BASIC FACTS ABOUT COMPUTERS

A. The Three Components of Computerization: Input/Processing/Output

The main purpose of using computers, regardless of the application, is to process data quickly and efficiently so that the information obtained is timely, meaningful, and accurate. Thus, computers are said to read incoming data, called **input**, process it, and produce outgoing information called **output**.

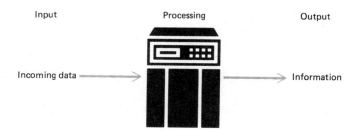

Input	Processing	Output
Incoming data →		→ Information

Data itself is defined as raw facts that need to be processed so that information is produced. **Information** is defined as processed, structured, and meaningful data.

Example 1

The grades that all students have received on a final exam constitute data or facts that need to be further processed. Processing of these facts can yield meaningful information such as the overall class average on the exam and the distribution of grades.

Example 2

The charges made by customers with department store credit cards represent data that must be processed to produce information such as each customer's account balance, the names of customers who have exceeded their credit limits, revised inventory records, and so on.

Example 3

Payroll data such as the hours worked by each employee and the corresponding hourly rates of pay can be processed to yield many types of information. In addition to being used to produce individual paychecks, this data can yield information on how much overtime pay was earned in total, how many employees earned more than a specified amount, and so on.

The operations that a computer can perform consist of the following:

IN A NUTSHELL

COMPUTER OPERATIONS

1. INPUT
   Read incoming data.
2. STORAGE and PROCESSING
   Store data, perform arithmetic operations and comparisons, and retrieve data for producing output.
3. OUTPUT
   Produce outgoing information.

Information processing refers to the set of operations and procedures required to process data and produce meaningful information. Sometimes the term **Electronic Data Processing** (EDP) is used to describe the processing of data by computer.

B. How Computer Systems Operate

1. The Computer System Defined

A **computer system** is a group of machines that together perform electronic data processing (EDP) or information processing functions. That is, the actual reading of incoming data, the processing, and the creating of output are performed by not one, but several machines that constitute a computer system. Thus when people use the term *computer,* they are really referring to an integrated group of devices or a *system.*

The actual devices that comprise a computer system at a given organization depend on the needs of the user. Generally a computer system includes the following elements:

Elements of a Computer System

1. Input devices
   Machines used for reading or entering data.
2. Central Processing Unit (CPU)
   The machine that actually performs the required operations.
3. Output devices
   Machines that produce information.

All these devices are linked by cables or communication lines so that the computer can operate as an integrated entity or system.

Note that there are numerous input and output devices, as well as storage devices, that can be used as part of a computer system. The following is a sample list of common devices:

Sample List of Common I/O (Input/Output) Media

Device	Representative Uses
Printer	Used for preparing internal reports for a company; also used for external forms of output sent to individuals, such as customer statements, payroll checks, W-2 payroll forms, and so on.
Terminal	A terminal is usually both an input and an output device. Typically, input is entered using a keyboard device, and information is either displayed on a terminal screen or printed on a typewriter-like device. There are, however, numerous other input/output components that can be part of a terminal. Sample uses of terminals include an airline reservation system, where an agent can (1) determine the seat availability on a particular flight by keying in the flight number and (2) have the computer print the ticket on the terminal itself. Another common use of terminals includes a brokerage system, where the latest stock quotations can be obtained from the computer by keying in the stock's code on a terminal.
Magnetic Tape and Magnetic Disk Drives	Tapes and disks are used for storing information that will be needed for future processing. Tapes and disks are two of the most common media used in computer installations for storing data—from inventory data to payroll data. Tapes and disks can also serve as both input and output from a computer system.

2. The Stored-Program Concept

Before a computer can actually read data, process it, and produce information, it must read in a set of instructions called a **program,** which actually indicates what processing is to be performed. Programs, like data, are stored in the computer. We say, then, that computers are **stored-program** devices, since they require a set of instructions to be stored before data can be processed.

Computer professionals called **programmers** prepare these instructions or programs for each application. The total set of programs that enables the computer system to process data is referred to as **software.**

In order for the computer to perform particular operations, an appropriate program must be entered into the **Central Processing Unit** or **CPU,** which is the main unit of the computer system. We can thus modify our schematic of a computer system as shown at the top of page 10.

A computer system at a company, for example, may have hundreds of different programs for use in a variety of application areas such as payroll, accounting, inventory control, and sales forecasting. A computer system in a home may have dozens of programs for typing reports, playing games, balancing the checkbook, and so on.

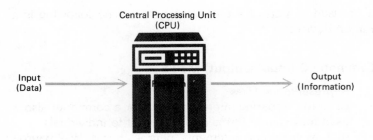

Central Processing Unit
(CPU)

Input
(Data)

Output
(Information)

Schematic of a computer
system.

Most large computer systems have the capability of storing more than one program in the CPU at the same time, thereby permitting several different jobs to be run concurrently. This concept is known as **multiprogramming.** Some large computers are also shared by numerous users who access the computer using terminals at remote locations—a concept known as **time-sharing.** These concepts will be considered in detail later on.

3. Information Systems: A Synthesis of Hardware and Software to Meet the Needs of Business Organizations

To actually obtain information from a computer, we need two things:

1. **Hardware**—the devices in the computer system.
2. **Software**—the set of programs that will read input, process it, and produce meaningful information.

But in order for the software and the hardware to produce useful results in a business environment, they must be part of an **information system.** An information system is the organized, structured, and integrated computerization of a business application. Such information systems require an efficient flow of data in order to operate effectively, to produce timely and correct output, and to provide management with the necessary facts to improve its decision-making ability. More and more business systems are being computerized in an effort to improve this flow of information and, in the end, to increase the profits of the company.

C. Types of Computers

This text considers the following types of computers:

1. Supercomputers. Used for vast "number crunching" applications mostly in scientific areas such as weather forecasting, medical research, and the space program.
2. Mainframes. Used predominantly by large- and medium-sized organizations for centralized processing of data.
3. Minicomputers. Used primarily in two ways: (1) by small organizations as the primary computer system and (2) by larger organizations for specific tasks that take some of the load off the mainframe.
4. Microcomputers. Used extensively in the home, in the office as a professional workstation, in small businesses for traditional commercial applications, and in educational institutions for teaching students about computers.

III. WHY COMPUTERIZE?

The primary reasons why organizations and individuals decide to use computers are as follows.

a. Computers Are Very Fast   Most modern computers can perform operations such as addition, subtraction, and so on, in speeds measured in **nanoseconds**— that is, billionths of a second. Some computers can operate at even faster speeds measured in **picoseconds,** which are trillionths of a second.

This means that the average computer can read thousands or hundreds of thousands of items, process them, and produce information in a relatively short time—minutes or, at most, hours.

b. Computers Are Very Accurate   Electronic technology is so advanced that when a computer is programmed correctly and when input is entered properly, the accuracy of the output is virtually guaranteed.

c. Computers Have Very Large Storage Capacities   The largest computers are capable of storing billions of items of data. Even the very smallest computers can store thousands of items. We will see that computers can be programmed to store information and programs on such media as magnetic tapes and disks, which can store millions of items of data and hundreds of programs. As a result, information previously stored manually in a room full of file cabinets can be compactly stored on just a few computer devices and accessed electronically as needed.

d. The Overall Cost of Computerization Is, In General, Far Less Than Comparable Manual Processing Costs for Large-Volume Jobs   Consider a company with 100,000 employees. A manual payroll procedure would be far more expensive to maintain than a computerized one. Cost savings is one of the advantages of computerization whenever a large volume of data is to be processed.

e. Computers Perform Tasks That Would Not Otherwise Be Feasible or Cost-Effective   Consider, for example, NASA's space program, which began in the 1950s when the first generation of computers was manufactured. The ability of the U.S. government to embark on the space program was directly related to the availability of computers for "number crunching"—solving millions of long, tedious equations. It is inconceivable to imagine the size of the labor force that would have been necessary to perform the same calculations manually.

Today, there are many tasks performed in a variety of applications that would not be feasible without a computer. Advanced weather forecasting, oil exploration projects, genetic research, and molecular studies are just a few of the more prominent examples. Moreover, businesses would not have been able to grow at the rates they have without computers to perform the repetitive, clerical tasks. The cost of labor necessary to do these tasks manually would have slowed the growth considerably.

f. Intangible Benefits   There are numerous reasons why organizations and people use computers; many of these reasons are not directly related to tangible factors such as greater speed, lower cost, and so on.

For organizational use, some of the intangible benefits of computerization include the following:

1. Providing managers and workers with greater flexibility by assisting them in the decision-making process and by delivering information in a timely manner.

2. Enabling the organization to move forward and compete effectively with other firms.

3. Providing customers and clients with immediate responses to inquiries about bills, services rendered, and so on.

In addition, personal use of computers has resulted in one very important intangible benefit: improving the overall quality of life. For home users, computers improve the quality of life by providing hours of entertainment, assisting with record keeping, providing teaching aides, enabling people to access centralized data on hotel and airplane availability, obtaining stock information, and so on.

For office workers, computers improve the quality of life by eliminating the need to retype documents over and over again, by electronically transmitting messages to other people in the organization, by performing tedious calculations, and so on.

This last benefit—that of improving people's lives—is the one that continues to have the most potential for computers. We can look to the future for even more benefits that will serve to further reinforce the fact that computerization is truly a revolutionary phenomenon in society today.

IV. WHY COMPUTERS SOMETIMES DISAPPOINT USERS

Despite the growing list of benefits that computers can bring to both organizations and individuals, we are all aware of numerous cases in which computers have failed to accomplish their goals to the satisfaction of those who use computer-produced information. If computer equipment is so fast and accurate, why should some results be disappointing?

Computers, today, are built with a great deal of precision so that the likelihood that the machine itself will produce erroneous output is small indeed.

Most problems with computerization, then, are attributable to the following factors.

a. Input Errors   When data is entered into a computer it must be relatively error free if it is to be processed correctly. The overwhelming majority of so-called "computer errors" result from erroneously entered input.

Suppose, for example, you call an airline and purchase an airplane ticket over the telephone. If the ticket that is mailed contains an error, the most probable cause is that the agent taking the order made an incorrect entry.

b. Errors in Instructing a Computer   Computers operate on data using a set of instructions called a program. The programmer writes this set of instructions, which is used to read data, process it, and produce output. At times, programs contain errors that do not become evident until a specific set of circumstances arises. Programming errors can result in serious problems for the user if they go undetected.

c. Overly Optimistic Projections of What an Information System Can Achieve, How Much It Will Cost, and When It Will Be Ready

In their enthusiasm, computer professionals sometimes underestimate job requirements and fail to provide for unanticipated delays and obstacles. Such optimism, in the end, can be extremely disappointing to an organization with a fixed budget and a projected schedule for computer use.

d. Misunderstandings Between Users and Computer Professionals

One main reason why computerized procedures frequently fail to meet their required objectives is because computer professionals and the people who will actually utilize the information, called **users** in this text, do not always understand each other's needs. That is, users do not adequately understand what computers can and cannot do; on the other hand, computer professionals sometimes do not understand how best to computerize a business application where guidelines have been established by the user. One primary aim of business programs in many colleges and universities is to bridge this communication gap between users and computer professionals.

e. Improper Controls and Security

As the use of computers for wide-ranging applications continues to grow, the need for proper control and security measures increases dramatically. Moreover, because terminals and microcomputers at remote locations are being linked with increasing frequency to central computers, the need for such control and security is even greater. Measures need to be taken to prevent unauthorized use of terminals and computers, if the integrity of data is to be maintained.

But many organizations have neglected this area or minimized its importance. The result has been an increase in errors, some resulting from innocent mistakes, others caused by deliberate attempts to defraud by computer or to sabotage an organization.

In addition, depending on the application area, improper controls can lead to an invasion of privacy. The government, the banking industry, and hospitals are examples of institutions that must take special measures to prevent the potential invasion of an individual's privacy by unauthorized access of computerized files.

f. Lack of Standards and Established Methods for Assessing Information Systems

Because the computer field is still relatively new, the ways in which computer professionals interact with users, design computerized systems, and write programs are diverse; that is, there are very few established practices and techniques that would help to formalize and standardize the process. Even hardware and software are not well standardized. Some software, for example, is only compatible or usable with a specific category of computer.

The result is that the tasks of the computer professional are less systematic and scientific than they should be. Similarly, the user has limited ability to assess the value and impact of a newly computerized system if there are no established techniques for evaluation.

g. The Changing Nature of Job Requirements   As organizational needs and social issues change over time, computerized systems may sometimes be unable to satisfy new and changing goals and objectives as they arise.

h. Fear and Resistance on the Part of the User   Unless users have been actively involved in the design and implementation of a computerized system, it is likely that they will face a newly computerized system with some resistance. Without user cooperation, information systems will almost always fail to meet their expectations. This is yet another reason why users and computer professionals must pool their resources and communicate better if effective computerization is to be achieved.

V. COMPUTERS IN SOCIETY

In this section, we consider some of the major social uses of computers today.

A. Computers in Education

There are two major objectives of utilizing computers in education. One is to teach people about computers; this means making people "computer literate." The other objective is to teach traditional subject areas with the aid of the computer. This is broadly defined as **computer-assisted instruction.** Both objectives are frequently met with the extensive use of microcomputers, although time-shared facilities could also be used. We will consider both these objectives of computers in education.

1. Computer Literacy

Until recently, learning about the computer was a choice that college students made if they were interested in working with these machines as computer professionals or if they hoped to apply a knowledge of information processing to their major field, such as accounting or finance.

While this remains the primary motivation of many college students who enroll in computer programs, computer literacy is currently being viewed as a prerequisite for *all* students. **Computer literacy,** broadly defined, implies an understanding of how the computer, in general, operates and how it may be used for specific applications. Almost everyone today can be classified as a computer user, since we are all affected by automation in banking, shopping, billing, and so on. If we are to effectively understand the ways these machines function and their impact on our everyday lives, we must become computer literate.

Consider the following discernible trends that have taken place in recent years, demonstrating how computer literacy is increasing in significance:

a. Computers Are No Longer an Educational Tool Utilized Exclusively or Even Predominantly on the College Level Secondary schools as well as elementary schools are acquiring computers at an ever-increasing rate. It is estimated that 60% of all public schools in the United States have at least one microcomputer that has been successfully integrated into the school's curriculum. In 1986 there will be close to 1 million computers in public schools in the United States. There is evidence to suggest that this trend will not only continue but will grow rather dramatically in the next few years. If pending legislation permits computer companies the write-offs they request for donating computers to schools, the use of computers at the elementary and secondary school levels will not only increase significantly, but will most probably result in sweeping changes in the way children are taught.

Advanced placement tests now make it possible for high school students to receive college credit for their computer expertise.

b. Many Colleges and Universities Have Begun to Require Their Students to Purchase a Specific Microcomputer This trend began in 1983 when Carnegie-Mellon University required all of its computer science majors to purchase IBM Personal Computers. These machines were sold to students at substantial discounts. The purchase price was spread out over four years and was built into the tuition cost.

Shortly after Carnegie-Mellon instituted its requirement, other schools began requiring its students to acquire a specific microcomputer. Currently many schools including Carnegie-Mellon are considering going substantially further: all students in all disciplines—not just computer majors—will eventually be required to obtain personal computers. Computer literacy on the college level, then, is seen in many institutions of higher education as an important university-wide goal.

c. Many Departments Are Offering and/or Requiring Computer Courses In addition to the traditional computer science and computer information processing departments, many other departments are offering computer courses. Some even require such courses for their majors.

Education majors in many schools are required to take a computer course. Similarly, art and music students are sometimes required to learn how to use computers in their discipline. English majors are frequently offered linguistics courses that consider how computers can "understand" text through manipulation of natural language elements.

The trend, then, is very clearly toward computer literacy at all levels in all disciplines. Many boards of education have begun to mandate that computer literacy be a requirement of all high school graduates.

Similarly, many colleges require all students to take at least one computer literacy course. In the education field, today, computer literacy appears to be viewed as the "fourth R"—taking its place alongside reading, 'riting, and 'rithmetic as an absolutely essential element in the learning process. The reason for this is clear: computers have begun to impact virtually all areas of our environment and understanding how they can be used is fast becoming a necessity.

2. Computer-Assisted Instruction (CAI)

Computers are also utilized in education to help students learn a wide variety of subjects from spelling, music, and geography to math and science. In almost all cases, the computer is a "programmed learning" tool. Short, well-conceived modules of instruction are displayed on a terminal screen, followed by questions to which students are asked to provide immediate responses. These responses are evaluated and a computer-produced response follows, which lets the student know immediately whether he or she is grasping the fundamentals. There is no need to wait for traditional periodic class tests.

The computer-assisted instruction or CAI field has grown significantly in recent years. Courseware, which is CAI software, was a $70 million industry in 1983; it is estimated that the total market for courseware will exceed $1 billion by 1987. Figure 1.1 illustrates microcomputers used in the education field.

Computer-assisted instruction has had the most success using the following techniques.

Figure 1.1
Microcomputers used for CAI. (Courtesy Apple Computer, Inc.)

a. Drill-and-Practice   After a subject has been introduced by a teacher, the computer can be used to reinforce the learning through practice problems. Practice problems in math, spelling, and geography are frequently provided by computers.

Using the computer for drill-and-practice saves the teacher time it would ordinarily take for providing and grading practice exercises. Moreover, many students find the novelty of the computer and its innovative displays a pleasant antidote to the tedium of traditional drill-and-practice exercises.

This CAI technique has become so successful that many vendors of CAI course materials actually guarantee results. One company that packages a drill-and-practice module for the Scholastic Aptitude Test (SAT), for example, will return the cost of the package if the student's SAT scores are not increased by a minimum of 70 points.

CAI has also proven useful in helping youngsters practice their spelling with computerized devices such as Speak 'N Spell (see Figure 1.2).

Figure 1.2
Speak 'N Spell:
computerized learning for
preschoolers. (Mark
Perlstein/Black Star.)

b. Tutorial   Computers also teach course material with the use of a tutorial, which is a subject module designed to allow students to learn at their own pace. The module frequently uses a computer's graphic and sound systems to make the learning experience as exciting as possible.

After a student completes the module, a series of questions are provided to test the learning. If the questions are answered properly, the student proceeds to the next module. If not, an alternative tutorial module on the same subject is provided.

In this way the student gets the advantage of a number of different teaching techniques. If one technique does not help the student to learn, others are available.

Many students, some who might even be classified as slow or unmotivated learners, find computer-assisted instruction to be stimulating and challenging. As a result, they often learn more, and at a quicker pace. Since students at a terminal can proceed at their own pace and not feel threatened by peer pressure, this type of education has had considerable success.

There are virtually thousands of such modules available in all subject areas. Moreover, there are organizations that specialize in providing computer-assisted instruction. PLATO, for example, is a system developed at the University of Illinois at Urbana, Illinois. There are thousands of lessons available in hundreds of subject areas for use on independent microcomputers or in a time-sharing mode where a remote terminal accesses a central computer. Figure 1.3 illustrates a touch panel where children can use the PLATO system to learn to read and to generate their own sentences.

TOUCH PANEL

In additional to using the keyboard, users can enter information into the computer with the touch panel. The touch panel is a transparent plastic film on the CRT, containing a 16 by 16 grid of electrodes that defines 256 touch-sensitive areas. When a lesson activates the touch panel, the user can respond to a question by touching a particular area of the screen instead of typing the answer on the keyboard. The touch panel detects the location, sends that information to the computer, and sounds a tone to acknowledge the touch.

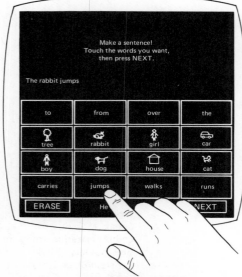

An elementary lesson in sentence building.

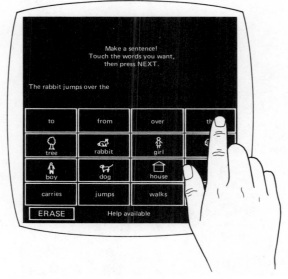

The student touches the words in the boxes to make a sentence.

A grammatically correct sentence results in an animation of the sentence.

Figure 1.3
Touch panel CAI lesson. (Courtesy Control Data Corp.)

c. Simulation   Computers are excellent tools for simulating experiments that would otherwise be too costly, take too long to produce results, or that might prove dangerous. Lessons in the physical and biological sciences are also available in which simulated experiments are performed (see Figure 1.4). Students may be asked, for example, to hypothesize about the results of a particular experiment

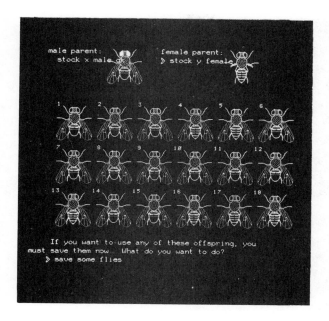

Figure 1.4
Sample CAI display for teaching genetics. (Courtesy Control Data Corp.)

before it is simulated. Social science modules with simulated population trends, polling techniques, and so on, are also available. Chemistry students can perform simulated experiments without putting themselves into physical danger.

Medical students can use simulation packages for testing their diagnostic skills. A simulator portrays a hypothetical patient with a set of symptoms. The medical student questions the patient, requests a series of tests from the simulator, and makes a diagnosis based on the simulated results. Such a procedure is a good way of helping medical students learn to make diagnoses without jeopardizing the welfare of actual patients.

Aircraft simulators are also used for teaching prospective pilots to fly under a variety of different circumstances. Figure 1.5 illustrates a flight simulator and

Figure 1.5
Overview of a DC-9 flight simulator. (Courtesy CAE Electronics.)

Figure 1.6
Computerized flight
simulator. (James R. Sugar/
Black Star.)

Figure 1.6 illustrates the instrument panel available in a typical flight simulator. Simulators are also available for teaching air traffic controllers how to respond to different hypothetical crisis situations.

d. Helping the Handicapped   Visually and hearing-impaired students can use computers with special adapters for learning at home or even in a classroom setting. Handicapped students with other physical handicaps may be able to use special joysticks, wands, or touch-sensitive screens instead of keying devices for entering answers (see Figure 1.7). These devices are easier to manipulate and require less manual dexterity than a typewriter-like device.

Advantages and Disadvantages of CAI

The overall advantages of computer-assisted instruction include the following:

1. Access to computers for learning when teachers are unavailable. The computer can provide virtually unlimited availability for teaching in schools, at home, in libraries, and so on.
2. Individualized instruction. Both slow and advanced students benefit from individualized instruction because they can proceed at their own pace. Shy

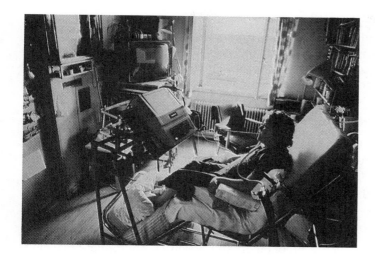

Figure 1.7
The computer as a tool for
the handicapped. (Courtesy
Apple Computer, Inc.)

students and those who do not respond well to teachers find individualized learning to be far less threatening.

3. Modules have been developed with numerous teaching techniques, many of which utilize dynamic and interesting graphics and sound effects. These help to make learning more interesting.

Potential problems of computer-assisted instruction include the following:

1. Reduced socialization. Students who spend a good deal of their time interacting with computers are reducing their overall interaction with teachers and peers in a group setting. Their learning of social values, norms, and patterns of group behavior may be reduced. Some people see this reduced socialization as a potential problem in terms of a student's overall learning of social norms.

2. Is CAI learning as effective as classroom learning? There have been numerous studies undertaken to determine how well computer-assisted instruction actually teaches students. As in all studies of this type, the results are not always conclusive nor are they consistent with one another. There is evidence to suggest that some students do very well with CAI modules and that overall learning time is reduced. But other studies seem to suggest that while most students tend to learn faster with CAI, they tend to forget more quickly as well. There is still need for further investigation of the long-term effects of CAI before a definitive evaluation of its merits can be made.

3. Resistance of some teachers to CAI. Some teachers still feel threatened by the computer; as a result, many are unwilling to utilize it as a teaching tool. If these machines are to supplement classroom learning, the teachers themselves must be willing and able to use them and to encourage their use by students. If teachers do not realize the potential benefits of computers both for themselves and for their students, the available packages and equipment will never be effective as teaching tools.

4. Good, inexpensive software is sometimes hard to find. Many teachers have found that the software that is available in their subject area is inadequate;

to use the computer effectively, they need to write their own programs. Although there are numerous languages such as Logo, Pilot, and Coursewriter designed specifically for this purpose, writing computer-assisted instruction modules can be very time consuming. Moreover, writing modules that display graphics or generate sound effects is even more difficult.

Computer-Managed Instruction (CMI)

In conjunction with CAI, **computer-managed instruction** (CMI) is a technique used by instructors to monitor the overall effectiveness of computer-assisted instruction. CMI can provide the following as a method for evaluating CAI and its teaching effectiveness:

CMI Elements

1. Test the student's level of preparation and assign an appropriate teaching module.
2. Based on pretests, determine the most effective learning techniques for each individual student.
3. Maintain records on student progress.
4. Determine the reliability of test questions themselves.
5. Determine the overall effectiveness of each learning module.

B. Computers in Health

Computers used in the health field have actually resulted in better medical diagnosis and have enhanced physicians' ability to save lives. The following are general application areas for computers in the health field:

1. Diagnosing Illness

a. The CAT Scanner   The CAT scanner, which utilizes a technique referred to as computed-axial tomography, was one of the first sophisticated devices designed to diagnose specific illnesses. See Figure 1.8 for an illustration of a CAT scanner.

Figure 1.8
CAT scanner. (Bill Pierce/Leo de Wys.)

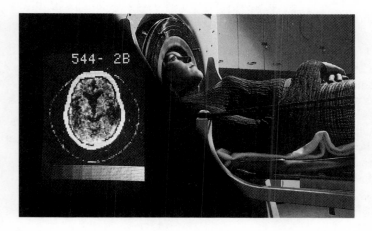

Figure 1.9
Radiation therapy treatment planner. (Courtesy J. Graham Brown Cancer Center and NKC, Inc., Louisville, Ky.)

The scanner rotates an X-ray tube around a specific body organ and produces a detailed photograph "slice" of the organ called a cross-sectional picture or tomogram. A computer then processes the data and projects an image of the organ on a display screen. This technique provides physicians with the ability to examine organs in a manner that would otherwise require surgery.

The CAT scanner has become an extremely effective diagnostic tool and has been particularly effective in diagnosing brain tumors, cancer of the pancreas, and strokes.

Despite their success as a diagnostic tool, not every hospital has a CAT scanner, mainly because they are very expensive devices. Initially the device sold for over $1 million; like other computerized systems it has decreased significantly in price, but it is still prohibitively expensive for smaller hospitals.

Currently, there are also radiation treatment planning computers that develop plans for radiation therapy. These plans are based on the diagnosis obtained from the CAT scanner (see Figure 1.9).

b. Other Computerized Diagnostic Machines   Considerable research is currently being undertaken to enable computerized devices to effectively and efficiently diagnose other physical ailments. Ultrasound images created by computer are currently available for diagnosing abdominal, obstetric, and gynecological problems. There are automated chemical analyzers available for evaluating blood and diagnosing certain deficiencies as illustrated in Figure 1.10.

Figure 1.10
Automated chemical analyzer. (Courtesy Baker Instrument Corp. and McNeil Pharmaceutical.)

2. Computerized Multiphasic Screening

In many hospitals as well as some doctors' offices, computers are used as a preliminary tool for taking a patient's history, determining the patient's symptoms, and making routine recommendations for laboratory tests and treatment. This is referred to as multiphasic screening.

The computer can collect, store, and transmit patient data, traditionally obtained by a doctor or a nurse. Benefits of computerized multiphasic screening include:

1. Saving staff time.
2. Enabling non-English-speaking people to more effectively communicate their symptoms and medical histories to a computer that "understands" or can interpret responses in foreign languages.
3. Making it easier to describe symptoms. Computers can display various parts of the body on a terminal screen. A patient can then point to the part that hurts and the computer can make preliminary diagnoses. In some situations, communicating with an inanimate device like a computer is less threatening and less embarrassing for the patient than communicating with a doctor.
4. Providing physicians with a "second opinion"—in case the doctor inadvertently fails to recommend a test or does not consider a specific course of treatment.

3. Monitoring a Patient's Vital Signs

After surgery and in cases of critical illness, patients can be hooked up to a computer that continuously monitors their vital signs and alerts appropriate personnel in the event of any abnormality. Computerized devices are far more effective than round-the-clock nurses and better able to determine even slight changes in a patient's vital signs. The possibility of a machine malfunction, however, is a disturbing thought to many patients and their families.

4. Computerized Devices in Medical Treatment

Great strides have been made in using computers to enable handicapped people to function more efficiently. Many hearing-impaired people use computerized devices for converting external sounds into electrical signals that can be carried to the inner ear. These people learn to correlate the vibrations they receive from the computer with actual sounds, thereby enabling them to interpret these sounds.

Similarly, visually impaired individuals can make use of a computerized device to help them "see" visual signals. A computer interprets light patterns and uses electrical signals to activate the cornea. In this way, sightless people can then correlate various signals with actual images.

Some paraplegics are currently using special computers for transmitting electrical impulses to the body, thereby enabling them to move around without a wheelchair (see Figure 1.11).

Stuttering is sometimes diagnosed as a psychological disorder that relates to a person's inability to communicate with others. For some stutterers, communicating with a computer has none of the intrinsic problems associated with

Figure 1.11
Helping the handicapped to walk with computer assistance. (Courtesy Dr. Jerrold Petrofsky, Wright State University, Dayton, Ohio.)

Figure 1.12
Linear accelerator that destroys cancerous growths. (Courtesy J. Graham Brown Cancer Center and NKS, Inc., Louisville, Ky.)

communicating with a therapist. Computers have been effectively used for analyzing a stutterer's speech patterns and systematically reinforcing the person when he or she speaks properly.

There are also computerized devices used in the treatment of illnesses such as cancer. Figure 1.12 illustrates a linear accelerator that bombards a malignant tumor with radiation that can destroy a cancerous growth.

5. Hospital Information Systems

A hospital information system is designed to automate as much of the information processing function in a hospital as is possible. The files that are typically maintained with such a system include the following:

Items Integrated in a Hospital Information File

Current patient file	Laboratory file
Medical staff file	Pharmaceuticals file
Nursing staff file	Dietary file

The interrelationship of these files can provide the following:

⫸ Interrelationship of Data

1. Medical and accounting data on each patient maintained from the time of admission until discharge.
2. Drug records that can monitor inventory, determine the overall effectiveness of specific drugs, determine which drugs have adverse side effects, and so on.
3. Laboratory records which ensure that patients taking a given test receive the appropriate pretest meals and medication, that they are billed properly, and so on.
4. Statistical records to assist researchers in diagnosing, preventing, and curing a wide range of illnesses.
5. Auditing of hospital records and procedures.
6. Traditional billing, payroll, accounts receivable, and accounts payable functions.

Figure 1.13 illustrates a nurse accessing a medical information and communications system.

With the use of an integrated hospital information system, all facets of hospital services and support are monitored.

Figure 1.13
Medical information and communication system. (Courtesy NCR.)

C. Artificial Intelligence

Artificial intelligence is a field of study that attempts to use computers for tasks traditionally considered to require some form of human intelligence.

Some application areas of artificial intelligence include the following:

1. Game Playing

Computers have been programmed by artificial intelligence researchers to play chess, checkers, and other games that have always been associated with "thinking." In 1957, a computer was programmed to play a passable game of chess; today chess-playing machines are available for home use that can play an expert game of chess. As of this writing, however, the computer still has not been able to beat the chess champions, prompting many to believe that although artificial intelligence has been successful, it cannot surpass human intelligence even in limited areas such as game playing.

2. Problem Solving

Artificial intelligence researchers have also produced a number of programs designed to solve problems such as brain teasers and mathematical problems. These problem solvers include methods designed to:

1. Determine the best "strategy" in a given situation.
2. Evaluate and analyze a pattern to determine its category, classification, or name.
3. Improve its own performance—mechanisms are built into the program to help improve its problem-solving ability based on previous experiences.
4. Solve specific problems in a wide variety of fields.

Several general problem solvers have been developed that can solve a number of mathematical problems and prove several difficult theorems, in both traditional and innovative ways.

3. Pattern Recognition for Scientific Analysis

Artificial intelligence is used to identify and classify shapes, forms and relationships. Programs that simulate human thinking, for example, have been written that analyze fingerprints. The ability of some computers to read a photograph of chromosome patterns and identify any abnormality is based on artificial intelligence techniques. Similarly, the pattern recognition ability of computers to scan satellite photographs and pinpoint the location of a hurricane was developed by artificial intelligence researchers (see Figure 1.14).

4. Education

Artificial intelligence has become an integral ingredient in making educational software more useful. That is, programs designed to simulate the human thought process are better able to teach and anticipate student responses than more traditional courseware.

5. Robotics

We will consider robots in industry in a later section; note, however, that the field of robotics, like education, utilizes artificial intelligence concepts. The objective in this instance is to create machines with human attributes such as sight, speech, perception, movement, and decision-making ability.

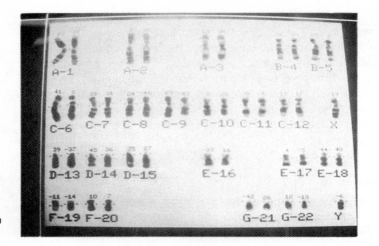

Figure 1.14
Chromosomes being matched by computer. (Dan McCoy/Black Star.)

Figure 1.15
The good life: a robot can do your housework. (Dan McCoy/Black Star.)

Some robots can analyze visual patterns using a TV camera. Some have pressure-sensitized "fingers" that can lift or move objects. These devices use artificial intelligence techniques to simulate human behavior. They have great potential for performing household tasks as well as industry-related jobs (see Figure 1.15).

6. Language Translation

In the past, machine translation had very limited success. The artificial intelligence community experimented with computerized translations from English to Russian; they then translated the results from Russian back to English to test their programs. In these experiments, the phrase "Out of sight, out of mind," for example, ended up as "The person is blind, and is insane." Similarly, the phrase "The spirit is willing but the flesh is weak" was translated back again as "The wine is good but the meat is raw."

Despite continuing problems in translating idioms and unusual phrases and deciphering sentence structures, machine translators have become useful tools, and their quality continues to improve.

Major artificial intelligence centers in the United States include MIT, Carnegie-Mellon University, and Stanford University; many professors and researchers at these centers have developed their own businesses for the purpose of selling software that utilizes the most sophisticated artificial intelligence techniques.

LOOKING AHEAD

Commercial interest in artificial intelligence has begun to focus on:

1. Vision systems
   a. To enable computers to interpret satellite photos.
   b. To enable industrial robots to identify objects on an assembly line.
2. Natural language systems
   To enable people to extract information from a computer using English rather than a sophisticated programming language.

3. Expert systems
   To enable computer programs to diagnose nuclear power plant accidents and interpret medical and scientific data in fields such as petroleum engineering, genetic engineering, and so on.

D. Computers in Art and Music

Computers, particularly microcomputers, have become enormously successful and popular tools for professional as well as amateur artists and musicians. There are even hand-held computer-controlled devices manufactured by Casio and Yamaha that function as electronic organs for both professional and personal use.

Computers in the art field are used for developing graphic designs and displays, testing variations of the displays, and teaching specific artistic techniques. The computer typically has either a graphics color terminal or a printer to display the design. There are software packages available that enable the user to enter or key in specific function keys on a terminal that will then generate a design. The keys used can designate a specific graphic form, pattern, or color. The user can also easily instruct the computer to alter the display by rotating it, modifying it, magnifying specific sections, changing specific colors, and so on.

When used as an artist's tool or by the amateur, the computer can be programmed to:

1. Produce a totally machine-generated display by using randomizing functions. A machine-generated artistic display is a frequent source of entertainment and interest to the amateur. Many professionals use a computer in this way to (a) see if the output generated has any artistic quality and/or (b) to analyze the components of that output in an effort to better understand the nature

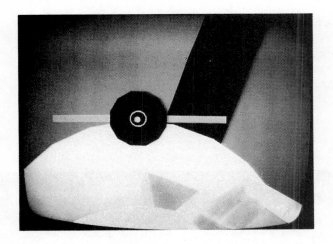

Figure 1.16
Computer-generated art.
(Courtesy NASA.)

of artistic creations. Many designs totally generated by computer have been displayed and sold as original works of art (see Figure 1.16).

2. Combine the artistic skills of the user with randomizing and digitizing capabilities of the computer. The digitizing operation can help an artist analyze the components of existing art. See Figure 1.17 for an illustration of a digitizer used for graphics displays.

Sometimes artists enter specific patterns and use the computer's randomizing and digitizing capabilities to alter the original work. Figure 1.18 illustrates

Figure 1.17
Digitizer. (Courtesy Bausch and Lomb.)

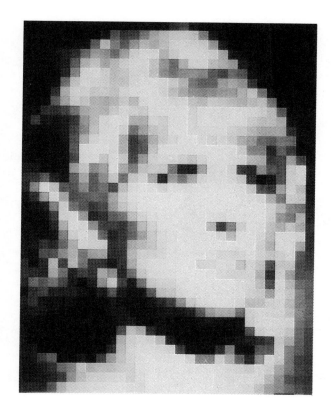

Figure 1.18
Digitized art. (Courtesy Blocpix.)

a digitized computer-generated picture that uses a familiar painting as its base. This coordinated effort of artist and digitizer can produce even more interesting artistic creations.

Advertising design is frequently created using a computer for entering an original advertisement and for modifying the ad to determine if different colors, a different focal point, or a different emphasis works better.

Similarly, computers can be used by amateur and professional musicians to compose music, or to play and refine existing musical compositions. Typically, a music synthesizer is necessary for converting electronic signals into sounds. Some synthesizers serve as electronic organs with the capability of simulating literally dozens of instruments and producing a sound that is practically symphonic in quality. The user can enter notes via a keyboard that has musical symbols as keys or special codes for representing the notes.

Because many microcomputer enthusiasts are interested in generating art and music with their microcomputers, there are many devices available for these purposes at relatively reasonable costs (see Figure 1.19).

Overall advantages of computers used for art and music include:

1. Complete flexibility in controlling a musical sound or artistic design.
2. Immediate feedback when testing a design or musical composition.
3. The ability to teach fundamentals of music or art.
4. The ability to play back music or display art with a minimum amount of distortion.

E. Computers in Other Humanities and in the Social Sciences

Computers can also be used in subjects such as English literature, sociology, archaeology, political science, and most other "liberal arts" subjects for tasks that have been traditionally performed by the professional:

1. Data handling and manipulation. There are programs available that can analyze archaeological data entered as input and provide the archaeologist with best estimates of the cultural background of a specific item, the estimated date of original use, cultural influences on its design, and so on. These programs have been developed to assist archaeologists by saving research time and providing some fast responses to queries on subjects with which the scholar may not be familiar.

    There are English literature and history software packages available that can estimate the period in history when a particular literary work was written. Some packages will even hypothesize as to who the author was!

    With increasing frequency, humanists and social scientists are finding that such packages can provide significant insight into research material.

2. Development of models. There are models available that a political scientist can use to test a specific hypothesis. Using an established model, a political scientist can ask the computer to predict who will win a given election if a series of hypothetical events occur. For example, the political scientist can enter the candidates who he or she believes will be running, the anticipated state of the economy at the time of election, the expected status of pending world disarmament treaties, and so on.

    The ability of the computer to predict any outcome is, of course, subject to a series of variables and there is a wide margin for error. But many social scientists find that existing models are useful and that newer versions are even better at making predictions.

3. Retrieving source material from a library or data base. Humanists and social scientists often spend a large amount of time in libraries doing research. Computers with access to general library data bases and to specific subject data bases can provide professionals with citations to library sources that

might otherwise take hours or days to locate. Some systems can actually provide the *entire source*, such as a journal article, rather than simply a reference to the source.

F. Computers in Industry

1. Manufacturing Applications

Computers have been effectively used in many instances to control the overall production process (see Figure 1.20).

Figure 1.20
Computer-controlled production process. (Courtesy Eli Lilly and Co.)

2. Air Traffic Control

Without computers, the ability of traffic controllers to monitor air traffic would be severely limited. Figure 1.21 illustrates a computer used to control air traffic.

Figure 1.21
Computerized air traffic control. (Courtesy Sperry Corp.)

3. Robots in Various Production Processes

The term "robot" is usually associated with humanoid-type creations that walk and talk like those in science fiction and futuristic movies. In actuality, the growing field of **robotics,** which is the design and use of robots, tends to be far more widespread in industry but not quite as humanistic as one might expect.

An industrial robot is a computer-controlled machine typically used for performing tasks that:

1. Are repetitive.
2. Require a great deal of precision.
3. Can be somewhat dangerous.

Although robots have been in existence for industrial applications since 1959, they became widespread only in the late 1970s, when computer technology made it possible to program robots for repetitive tasks that require considerable precision.

Most industrial robots have huge arm-like structures with claws capable of grasping items and with sensory feedback mechanisms designed to automatically stop the machine if a malfunction is detected. Industrial robots are used extensively as the following:

Uses of Robots

Assemblers in automotive and other assembly plants

Welders

Spray painters

Material handlers

Packagers

Die casters

Mixers of dangerous chemicals

Fire fighters

Bomb deactivators

Figure 1.22 shows a composite of several robots in use for specific applications.

In addition to their mechanical ability to lift, paint, operate equipment, and so on, some robots have laser beams for locating objects and TV cameras for "eyes."

Some robots have computer components that enable them to perform a single function, while others are multifunctional. Still other robots can be reprogrammed to perform a variety of different tasks.

The advantages of using robots in industry include the following:

1. The ability to have machines perform boring, repetitive, and sometimes dangerous tasks.
2. The ability to re-allocate the existing labor force for more interesting jobs that require human abilities and sensitivities.
3. Cost and upkeep: it costs approximately $5.00 per hour to operate and maintain the average robot.
4. Robots can operate on a 24-hour, seven-day-a-week basis and not suffer from fatigue, although they do, on occasion, break down or malfunction.

Although there are clear advantages to using robots in industry, the labor force in the United States is somewhat resistant to their use. There is considerable fear that robots will lead to mass unemployment. This fear exists despite the fact that, thus far, more jobs in total have been generated building and maintaining robots than have been lost by robots taking over existing jobs. Moreover, many industrial organizations have negotiated with labor unions on this very issue and agreed not to fire any employee because of robots; the agreement is based on the belief that the work force can be effectively reduced through the natural process of attrition—employees voluntarily leaving, retiring, and so on.

Nonetheless, the eventual impact of robots on the labor force is a matter of some concern. Companies claim they can retrain workers displaced by ro-

(a)

(b)

(c)

Figure 1.22
Robots in industry. *(a)* Robots welding automobile bodies at an assembly plant. (Courtesy Cincinnati Milacron.) *(b)* A robot drilling holes in an aircraft fuselage panel. (Courtesy Cincinnati Milacron.) *(c)* Robot for handling nuclear materials. (Georg Fischer/ Woodfin Camp.)

bots, but union leaders respond that many workers do not wish to change their jobs. Partly as a result of this and other issues, the widespread use of robots has not yet been realized to the extent originally anticipated. Japanese companies that *guarantee* jobs to their employees have thus far had considerably more success using robots in industrial settings.

Although the great majority of robots are strictly mechanical types used in industry, the human-like type has also become available. Some organizations use human-like robots with voice capability as:

Receptionists.

Mail deliverers.

Advertisers—alerting customers in a store to special sales and pointing to the location of various products.

Hospital aides—making coffee, bringing magazines and books to patients, and so on.

Entertainers—in movies, computer shows, children's hospitals, and so on.

LOOKING AHEAD

The Robotics Industry: Will It Measure Up?

For many years, the symbol of a fully integrated computer revolution was a robot with the intelligence and physical capability to be virtually at our "beck and call." Yet not only has such a robot remained largely futuristic, but more modest predictions for robots performing simple mechanical tasks have only recently begun to be realized. What about the future?

First, there is likely to be a shakeout in the robotics industry, with mergers and bankruptcies leaving far fewer companies than are currently in the field.

Second, the industry remains largely optimistic. Evidence suggests that the market for these devices will increase dramatically in the years ahead. In fact, some companies are preparing for this increase by designing robots to build robots!

Third, the greatest immediate challenge to the industry is likely to come from abroad. The United States currently leads the Japanese, but the lead is not an unsurmountable one.

4. Computer-Aided Design and Manufacturing: CAD/CAM

In recent years, computer-aided design and manufacturing systems have increased in power, decreased in cost, and have been effectively used in a number of applications. Originally, CAD/CAM was used for assisting an engineer or draftsperson in designing a device for a manufacturing firm. Today, CAD/CAM is used for a wide range of design applications. Figure 1.23 shows an automated inspection system designed by a CAD/CAM system.

A CAD/CAM system utilizes sophisticated graphics hardware and software, digitizing and plotting techniques, and simulation or modeling methods. Prices of such systems range from several thousand dollars to over $750,000 for a very advanced system.

Typical applications of CAD/CAM include the following:

Applications of CAD/CAM

- Mechanical design and drafting.
- Manufacturing and numerical control of machines.

Figure 1.23
Automated inspection system. (Courtesy Battelle Columbus Laboratories.)

- Plant design.
- Integrated circuit design.
- Cartography—drawing of maps.

Architectural, engineering, automotive, and aerospace industries are among the major users of CAD/CAM. There are even CAD/CAM services available for firms that are too small to acquire their own system.

CAD/CAM has also found its way into some more humanistic aspects of technology. A great deal of research has been undertaken in human rehabilitation using these devices. For example, scientists and engineers use CAD/CAM for designing artificial limbs and wheelchairs and for testing their design with simulators to see how they will perform under different degrees of stress and other environmental conditions. Figure 1.24 shows a composite of CAD/CAM systems and generated designs.

VI. CONCERNS ABOUT THE SOCIAL IMPACT OF COMPUTERS

We have considered some of the primary uses of computers in society today. Although the benefits of such applications may be readily apparent, there are many social issues that are raised by the use of machines in these areas, including:

1. The potential of computers to have a dehumanizing effect on people and society in general. When we find ourselves dealing with voice recordings instead of people, and suffering frustrations from our inability to correct so-called computer errors, we are reminded that machines frequently reduce interpersonal relationships and can impact our day-to-day lives in adverse ways.

2. The potential of computers to replace workers and increase unemployment. Most studies suggest that although unemployment has indeed occurred in some areas as a result of computerization, the need for computer professionals has, in total, more than compensated for this unemployment. None-

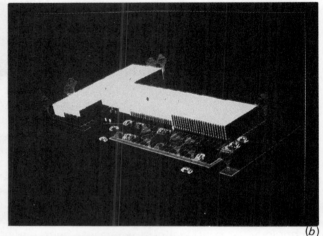

(a)

(b)

Figure 1.24
(a) CAD/CAM system featuring an interactive terminal, pen plotter, and digitizer. (Courtesy Computervision.) (b) Architectural design created by CAD/CAM system. (Courtesy Computervision.) (c) Aircraft design created by CAD/CAM system. (Courtesy Lockheed-California Co.)

(c)

theless, most computerized procedures have the potential for reducing the size of the work force, particularly in cases where robots replace humans. Computer professionals and users must work closely to avoid mass unemployment and displacement of employees. Retraining programs can prove most useful as a preventative measure to minimize the effects of reduced labor needs.

3. The potential of computers to invade our privacy. A recent poll indicated that 54% of the American public considers the present widespread use of computers to be a threat to personal privacy. The growing concern for an individual's right to privacy has raised numerous philosophical and legal questions about limits that should be placed on the use of computers in society. This is especially true in light of the increasing number of computerized data banks that are being maintained throughout the country by various organizations such as credit bureaus, governmental agencies (the IRS, FBI, etc.), and the health insurance industry.

   Although information in a particular data bank may be accurate and relevant for the purpose of the organization maintaining that data bank, it may be misinterpreted or taken out of proper context when entered into another organization's data bank. Moreover, most individuals believe that data of a personal nature should not be disseminated without their express approval.

   To illustrate how the issue of privacy can be involved with the maintenance of data banks, consider the following case. Recently, government researchers investigating the long-term effects of abortions examined the medical records of 48,000 women, without seeking prior consent. Inadvertently, the names of some of the women were disclosed in a preliminary report. This is a clear violation of an individual's right to privacy.

   There are numerous government committees studying the problems associated with privacy and the computer and several laws relating specifically to these issues have been passed both on a national and statewide level. This is discussed further in Chapter 17.

4. The potential of computers to be used in the commission of a crime. If an unauthorized user breaks a computer code and steals money from an individual's bank account, this could cause serious problems since it might be difficult to prove. With the increasing use of computers in society, such risks become more prevalent. Chapter 17 focuses on how such problems may be minimized.

5. The changing nature of the workplace and the home environment may have profound effects on society in general. The ability of workers to perform their jobs at home using a terminal may mean that working conditions and working relationships will be dramatically affected. The ability of a housewife to order necessities and obtain banking services and other information while at home may change the nature of household tasks and have an effect on interpersonal relationships as well. Similarly, the extensive use of computers by school children may reduce their peer relationships and encourage them to respond and think in more "computerized" ways.

   There is still no way of knowing whether these and other social changes will ultimately occur and whether or not they will prove to be beneficial. It is advisable to pay close attention to developments in this area so that we are better able to assess the social impact of the computer. We will be considering social issues in more depth throughout the text.

CHAPTER SUMMARY

I. Computerization consists of
   A. Hardware—devices.
   B. Software—programs.
   C. Information systems—the integration of hardware and software to accomplish specific goals.

II. Computer systems consist of
   A. Input devices.
   B. Central Processing Unit (CPU).
   C. Output devices.
   D. A program must be in the CPU in order for input data to be processed and converted to meaningful information.

III. Why use a computer?
   A. Speed.
   B. Accuracy.
   C. Storage.
   D. Low cost.
   E. More operations than can be effectively performed manually.
   F. Assists with decision-making.
   G. Accommodates growth.
   H. Provides immediate access to data.
   I. Can improve the overall quality of life.

IV. Pitfalls to be avoided
   A. Input errors.
   B. Program errors.
   C. Poor cost estimates.
   D. Inadequate communication between user and professional.
   E. Poor controls and security.
   F. Lack of standards.
   G. Systems that cannot accommodate changing user needs.
   H. Fear and resistance.

V. Computer-assisted instruction (CAI)
   A. This refers to computers used as tools in the educational process.
   B. Advantages.
      1. Reduces teaching load and frees the teacher from drill-and-practice work.
      2. Students can learn at their own rate.
      3. Instruction is individualized.
      4. Problems caused by interpersonal relationships between students and their peers or between students and teachers are minimized.
      5. Graphics ability of computers makes learning more interesting.
   C. Disadvantages.
      1. High cost.
      2. The teaching effectiveness of CAI has not been definitively proven.
      3. Creativity may be inhibited.

    D. Computer-managed instruction: an additional feature of CAI.
      1. This refers to the use of computers to help teachers evaluate student performance and the overall teaching effectiveness of each CAI unit.
      2. Can be an integral part of CAI.
VI. Computers in health.
    A. Diagnosing illness.
      1. Computers can maintain updated information on patterns of existing illnesses, new illnesses, and new findings.
      2. Computers can then assist the physician in diagnosing a specific illness.
    B. Monitoring a patient's vital signs.
    C. Assisting medical students in diagnosing hypothetical illnesses on simulated patients.
    D. Hospital information systems.
      1. Maintain medical and accounting data on patients.
      2. Maintain drug records to monitor inventory and determine the overall effectiveness of specific drugs.
      3. Maintain statistical records to assist researchers in diagnosing, preventing, and curing a wide range of illnesses.
VII. Artificial intelligence—the use of computers for solving problems that are frequently described as requiring human intelligence, judgment, insight, or experience.
VIII. Computers in the humanities and social sciences
    A. Used for data handling and manipulation.
    B. Used to develop models.
    C. Used to retrieve written material from a library or data base.
    D. Used to create computer-generated art and music.
IX. Computers in industry—used for a variety of applications including robotics and computer-aided design and manufacturing (CAD/CAM)
X. Concerns about the social impact of computers
    A. The potential to have a dehumanizing effect.
    B. The potential to replace workers.
    C. The potential to invade our privacy.
    D. The potential to be used in the commission of a crime.
    E. The effects on working conditions and working relationships.

Chapter Self-Evaluating Quiz

At the end of each chapter in this text, and sometimes at the end of a subsection, there is a series of self-evaluating questions. These questions are followed by solutions. The purpose of these quizzes is to provide you with a method of evaluating your understanding of the chapter. The solutions also specify the page numbers on which the specific topic is discussed.

1. Computers take incoming data called _____, process it, and produce outgoing information called _____.

2. The main unit of a computer system is called the _____.

3. The set of instructions that specifies what operations a computer is to perform is called a _____.

4. Most modern computers can perform operations at speeds measured in _____.

5. The overwhelming majority of so-called "computer errors" result from _____.

6. The communication gap that frequently results in poorly designed computer applications relates to poor communication between _____ and _____.

7. The teaching of traditional subject areas with the aid of the computer is defined as _____.

8. (T or F) Besides cost, there are no major disadvantages associated with CAI.

9. _____ is a field of study that attempts to use computers for tasks that traditionally require some form of human intelligence.

10. (T or F) Computers have found little use in the humanities and social sciences.

Solutions

1. input / page 7
   output / page 7

2. Central Processing Unit (CPU) / page 9

3. program / page 9

4. nanoseconds—billionths of a second / page 11

5. erroneously entered input / page 12

6. users / page 13
   computer professionals / page 13

7. computer-assisted instruction (CAI) / page 14

8. F—Potential problems include reduced socialization and the resistance of some teachers to CAI. / page 21

9. Artificial intelligence / page 26

10. F—They have been used in many applications such as data handling, the development of models, and the retrieval of source material from a library or data base. / page 32

Key Terms

Note: Key terms are specified at the end of each chapter. When these terms are defined in the chapter, they appear in boldface. They may also be found in the Glossary at the end of the text.

Artificial intelligence
Central Processing Unit (CPU)
Computer-assisted instruction (CAI)
Computer literacy
Computer-managed instruction (CMI)
Computer system
Data

Electronic data processing (EDP)
Hardware
Information
Information processing
Information system
Input
Multiprogramming

Nanosecond
Output
Picosecond
Program
Programmer
Robotics

Software
Stored-program concept
Time-sharing
User
User-friendly

Review Questions

1. Find an article from a local newspaper that describes a computerized system that failed to meet its objectives. Describe the circumstances and see if you can provide some reasons why the failures occurred. What recommendations would you make for avoiding similar problems in the future?

2. Find an article from a local newspaper that describes direct and substantive benefits derived from a specific computerized system.

3. Indicate major reasons why some people have negative reactions to the use of computers.

4. Discuss some of the important social issues that have arisen as a result of the widespread use of computers.

5. Discuss some of the pros and cons for using computer-assisted instruction.

6. How are computers used in the health field?

7. What are some of the reasons for resistance to computers in the health field?

APPLICATION

ALL I WANTED WAS TO BUY A BAG OF GROCERIES

by Terril J. Steichen

The other day I wrote out a check to pay for groceries. The clerk told me, while looking over my check, that in the near future, the store was starting a new computerized check-approval system. I would have to make a new application if I wanted to keep paying for food with a check.

After over five years of biweekly or triweekly visits to this particular store, I didn't understand why I had to make out a brand-new application. But curious, I asked for a blank application.

The old system simply kept track of bad checks. If a person wanted to continue to cash checks, he had better not write checks he couldn't cover. It was simple. Apparently, it was too simple.

New Form

The new application form demanded that I tell them my social security number (are they going to attach my old-age pension?), my drivers license number (which is the same), how old and fat I am, who is silly enough to employ me and where that silly employer does business—all of that in addition to the normal address and phone numbers.

Why, I asked, did I have to give out all this information just to continue to buy groceries as I have been doing for five years? "Because the old system didn't work well enough," the manager explained. I persisted a bit, though the manager looked increasingly uneasy and exasperated. "But why pick on me? I've never written a bad check?"

"You don't seem to understand," he said (this phrase became pretty familiar the more I pursued the matter). "The old system let too many bad check writers write bad checks."

New Check Approval

Now that, of course, makes sense. Because of the normal float and other delays, unscrupulous or careless people can go on for a long time before their bad check records catch up with them. I'm sure that the new computerized check approval system will be more effective at catching bad checks than the old one was. All that data about how old and fat I am could be useful in tracking me down, if need be. And to store and retrieve that extra information only takes a few more fields on the computer record—pretty trivial, from the technical standpoint.

There is only one problem. It takes me—a person with an unblemished record of trustworthiness (at least from the standpoint of my checking account)—and dumps me into a pot with the worst thieves in the country. For the store's ease of screening out crooks, I am presumed to be a crook until proven otherwise. That's just fine for the store and for the data processing processors. But what about me?

I don't like the mistrust and presumption of guilt that seems to come with so many computerized applications.

Why does a store clerk have to presume every customer is in the credit companies' bad-credit listing, forcing me and all the other customers to wait while the clerk proves that is not so? In my case, I could have told him so if only he had asked me.

America is the world's great melting pot. That's a great concept because it means that we take the best the rest of the world has to offer, put it all together and come out with something even better—or that's what I thought it meant. But with the way that businesses are computerizing that melting pot, it seems as though something is changing, something quite important.

That's not logical, I know. It won't compute. But it bothers me.

Source: Computerworld, January 16, 1984, page 34. Copyright © 1984 by CW Communications/Inc., Framingham, MA 01701. Reprinted with permission.

Questions
1. Understanding Key Terms
   (*Note:* There are no key terms specific to the computer field in this article, but there are terms that have some significance in computer applications.)
   a. System.
   b. Float.
   c. Computerized check approval.
   d. Bad-credit listing.
2. Software, Hardware, and Systems Concepts
   a. Explain why a new application form had to be completed by customers.
   b. How will the new system minimize the risk of bad checks being accepted by the store?
3. Management Considerations
   a. If you were the manager of the store and a customer complained about this new procedure, how would you handle the situation?
   b. Can you think of any way that the inconvenience to the customers could be minimized?
4. Social, Legal, and Ethical Implications
   a. What are some of the potential social problems that can develop if a new system causes inconvenience to customers?
   b. What are some of the potential legal problems that could occur if a new system as described in the application were implemented improperly?

CASE STUDY: McKing's Superburgers, Inc.

Objectives of the Case Study
One educational tool that often proves successful in helping students understand the techniques practiced in a given field is called "the case study approach." Using this approach, the student is often asked to apply the tools of a particular specialty to either a hypothetical or "real-world" situation.

In this book, we use the case study approach to illustrate how a computer specialist actually determines the components to be used in computerizing a set of business operations. We will study a hypothetical company called McKing's Superburgers, Inc., which is considering the acquisition of a computer.

We will provide details about McKing's at the end of each chapter in a section called "Case Study." You will then be asked to answer questions about the McKing enterprise and make recommendations regarding the computerization of its operations.

The objectives of this case study are as follows.

1. To provide you with an illustration of factors to consider when deciding (1) whether to computerize, and (2) the type of computerized design that would be most suitable.
2. To provide you with a vehicle for testing your knowledge of how computers can be effectively used in a typical business setting.
3. To provide a step-by-step approach for determining the hardware, software, and systems design features that should be utilized for a specific application.
4. To help you better communicate your ideas and recommendations in written form.

This material can be used both as a preview, as well as a review, of concepts included within each chapter.

The Approach Used
Each chapter will include a brief description of some of the basic operations of McKing's Superburgers, Inc. This description will typically be followed by:

1. A series of general discussion questions about the case.
2. A series of specific questions asking you to recommend how McKing's might best computerize its operations.

Both types of questions will require you to draw on material presented in the respective chapter in order to provide answers or to make recommendations. The general questions are designed to make you think about the case as a whole and can be used for classroom discussion. The specific questions ask for actual recommendations about the computerization of McKing's. Each recommendation should include an explanation or justification indicating why you made a specific decision.

Note that there are no answers or recommendations that are absolutely correct or incorrect. Instead, different recommendations and answers made by different students could all be correct if they have a proper foundation and can be justified.

A Guide to Answering Questions on the Case Study
You should answer each question as if you are a computer specialist or a user responding to a management request for information. As you gain more understanding of computer hardware and software, and as you become more aware of management's needs, your answers will become more meaningful and more professional.

Consider the ad entitled "There's a Concerto in Your Computer" that appears in Figure 1.25.

1. Define the following terms and phrases as they are used in the ad:
   a. Music synthesizer system.
   b. The "Compu-Music system is software based."
   c. "Allows for virtually infinite hardware expansion."
   d. "Programming the Compu-Music."
2. Is Compu-Music intended for the musician or the computer professional? Explain your answer.
3. The ad states that Compu-Music "can never become obsolete." Explain why this claim is made. Do you agree with the claim? Explain your answer.
4. Suppose you have a personal computer and were considering the purchase of Compu-Music. Prepare a list of questions you would need to ask of a computer dealer.
5. Compu-Music cannot be used with all computers. Do you think this fact will limit its sales? Explain your answer.

Particular attention should be given to answering questions in a clear, concise, and well-organized way. The ability to communicate well is very important for computer professionals and businesspeople if they are to effectively design integrated computerized systems.

The Systems Study

After reading all the chapters and answering the questions about the case study, you will be able to draw on your answers to prepare a full **systems study,** which specifies a formal recommendation about the computerization of McKing's Superburgers. Your instructor may ask for this systems study at the end of the semester to satisfy a course requirement. If so, he or she will provide you with guidelines for preparation of the systems study and with the precise format you should follow.

Figure 1.25 Marketing computer products. (Courtesy Roland Corp.)

Case Description

McKing's Superburgers, Inc. consists of 12 fast-food restaurants located in Chicago, Illinois. McKing's has been experiencing a growth of 15% per year in gross sales, despite the economic problems faced by the retail industry in general and by the Midwest region in particular. But management at Mc-King's is concerned because profits increased only 10% last year and 8% this year. Since the increase in profits has not kept pace with the increase in sales, McKing's has begun to realize that there are inefficiencies in their operations that are having a negative impact on profit margins.

McKing's has already undertaken a study to determine if computerization of the processing of orders will help profits keep pace with sales. Management realizes that the initial start-up cost of a computer system may mean an actual decrease in profits for the first few years; but if it can be demonstrated that the long-term effect will be to increase profits and to decrease inefficiencies, management would be inclined to computerize.

Several computer vendors have been asked to evaluate McKing's procedures and to make presentations on their equipment. The vendors selected were those that produce the most comprehensive computerized retail systems called point-of-sale systems. A **point-of-sale system** generally operates in the following manner. Each product sold is identified on special electronic cash registers at the ordering counter (see Figure 1.26). The cash registers are linked to a central computer. The checker keys in the item purchased and the computer "looks up" or finds the price of that item. The price appears on the register display for consumer reference. The stored prices can be changed at a central location to reflect special promotional sales and discounts, increases in prices, and corrections to erroneously stored data.

Figure 1.26
Point-of-sale cash register.
(Bob Hahn/Taurus.)

The computerized system can perform the following functions:

1. Provide electronic ordering that will do the following:
   a. Accumulate totals.
   b. Allow discounts for coupons and promotionals.
   c. Compute sales tax.
2. Provide managers with inventory reports so that:
   a. Preparation of items that are selling well can begin when the current quantity on hand falls below a predetermined level. This improves efficiency, decreases waiting time, and leads to improved customer satisfaction.
   b. Efficient reordering of raw materials can be accomplished.
   c. The effects of various promotionals and pricing policies can be assessed.
   d. Customer preferences at various restaurant locations can be assessed.
3. Reduce errors associated with ordering by:
   a. Minimizing arithmetic errors.
   b. Making it easier to train order takers.
   c. Improving job satisfaction.
4. Enable price changes to be easily effected by storing the new prices in the computer, without requiring order takers to keep track of them.

Questions

1. Effects of Automation

    Suppose McKing's Superburgers, Inc. has decided to computerize its order-taking procedures. You realize that some of the employees—both order takers and managers—may be very concerned about how the changes might affect them.

    a. What are some of the reasons why employees at McKing's might be concerned?

    b. What steps would you take to minimize their concerns?

2. Privacy and Security

    When an application is computerized, there is an added risk that unauthorized use of the system may result. An employee or a customer, for example, may gain access to the central computer and inadvertently or deliberately change the prices of some items.

    a. Besides the changing of prices, what other changes might be made by unauthorized use of the system at McKing's?

    b. What steps would you take to minimize these risks?

3. Consumer Reaction

    Many consumers fear computers for a wide variety of reasons. Some of these reasons are justified and some of them are based on misconceptions about how computers are utilized.

    a. What are some of the consumer fears that might arise when McKing's computerizes its order-taking procedures?

    b. What steps would you take to minimize these consumer fears?

CHAPTER 2

COMPUTERS IN BUSINESS: AN OVERVIEW

CHAPTER OBJECTIVES

To familiarize you with:

- How businesses are typically organized and how they utilize information.
- The basic reasons for computerizing business functions.
- How business procedures are computerized.
- The structure of computer facilities within a company's organizational structure.
- The staffing of a computer facility.

In Chapter 1 we considered the various ways in which computers are used in our society. The main emphasis of this book, however, is on information processing—the use of computers to produce meaningful output for business-people.

I. COMPUTERS IN BUSINESS

The basic goals of business are to maximize profits and minimize costs. Computers are most effective when they assist in achieving these objectives. Some ways in which computers function to meet these goals are as follows:

IN A NUTSHELL

FUNCTIONS OF COMPUTERS IN A BUSINESS ENVIRONMENT

1. To reduce the need for human record keeping by automating clerical functions.
2. To reduce the number of errors produced in record-keeping operations.
3. To store data efficiently.
4. To make information readily available to businesspeople who need it.
5. To assist management by providing information that is helpful in making critical decisions.

II. BUSINESS ORGANIZATION

A. Typical Departments Within a Business Organization

There are numerous ways in which computers can provide the above types of services to a company. First, companies are typically divided into departments, where each department has specific objectives that must be met. Figure 2.1 illustrates some of these departmental objectives. Although there may be an overlap in the goals or objectives of individual departments, each has very specific tasks to perform.

The department that is responsible for computerizing many of these tasks is commonly referred to by one of the following names:

EDP—Electronic Data Processing

MIS—Management Information Systems

CIS—Computer Information Systems

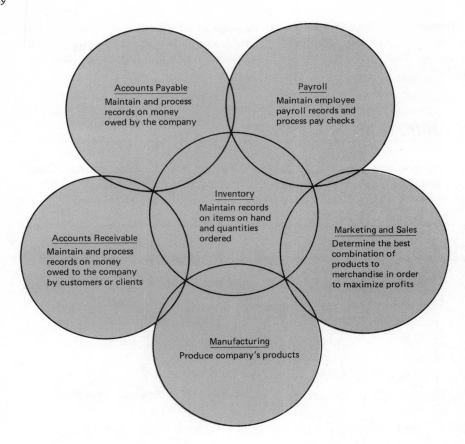

Figure 2.1
Typical business
applications.

There are two ways in which business objectives are met.

▐▐▐▶ **Meeting Business Objectives**

1. Each department performs a specified set of functions.
2. All of the departments' operations must be *integrated* so that a meaningful total structure is obtained.

Similarly, computers are used in two ways within an organization.

▐▐▐▶ **How Computers Function in Business Organizations**

Function	*Purpose*
1. The traditional systems approach	The major objective is to satisfy the needs of each user department—on both an operations and a managerial level. Each department stores its collection of data in individual files.
2. The Management Information Systems (MIS) or top-down approach	A primary objective is to integrate the functions of each department so that top-level management can be provided with a total picture of companywide functions. A store of data called a **data base** is used for maintaining companywide records.

B. How Departments Interact

Each department within an organization has its own personnel and its own set of objectives that must be met in order for the company to function properly. An organization chart depicts the departmental levels of responsibility for employees within a company. Figure 2.2 illustrates a typical organization chart.

But what an organization chart does *not* illustrate and what the above discussion omits is the *interdependence* of functions within an organization. No department stands alone; each is integrally related to the company as a whole. To think of each department as an independent entity, rather than as an element within the larger structure, is both narrow and misleading. Figure 2.3 illustrates how some departments interact.

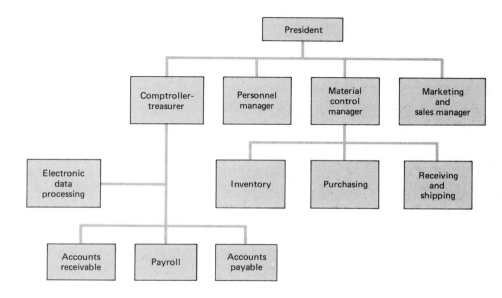

Figure 2.2
Sample organization chart for a retail firm.

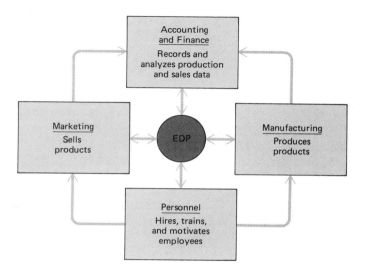

Figure 2.3
The interdependency of business functions.

C. The Staff Within These Departments

The computer facility of a company, regardless of its name, serves all departments. The computer staff must work closely with the following types of departmental employees to achieve desired goals:

1. Operations Staff

Computers provide the operating staff with fast and accurate record-keeping information. That is, computers are used to perform repetitive functions that would otherwise be performed by clerks, except that these machines are faster and more accurate if programmed properly. The operations staff typically use computers to:

1. Enter data.
2. Inquire about the status of computerized files.
3. Update files.
4. Type letters, reports, and documents.

2. Management

Computers provide management with information that is used to help make decisions. That is, these electronic devices make information available to management that would otherwise take extensive manual computation and integration of data. This information enables company executives to make more timely decisions based on a more thorough picture of the company's overall operations. Figure 2.4 describes the levels of management and the basic responsibilties of these levels. There is software available that can help each level of manager perform all of the responsibilities listed.

Figure 2.5 provides a more detailed description of typical EDP functions performed for each level of management.

There is a general procedure employed for using computers to assist in decision-making. It is called the information-feedback cycle and is illustrated in Figure 2.6. Note that the process is cyclical so that decisions made initially can be used to take action that ultimately affects the way in which new data is collected. This new data is then used to generate information that provides the basis for more effective decisions.

Figure 2.4
Levels of management
utilizing computers.

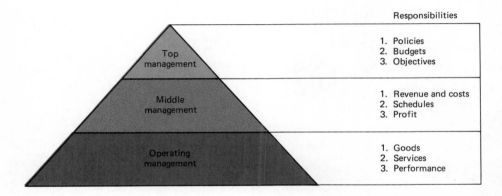

Information-Feedback Cycle

1. Data is processed to produce information.
2. Information is used to make required decisions.
3. Decisions result in appropriate action.
4. The action taken produces more data that again needs to be processed and the cycle is repeated.

User Level	Range of Managerial Decisions	Uses of EDP	Examples of Decisions Made
Upper management	Long-range	• Policy making • Resource allocation • Strategic planning • Assistance in identifying problems • Decision-making analyses	• Should we market a new product? • Should we go international? • Should we acquire Japanese devices?
Middle management	Relatively short-range	• Policy implementation • Tactical planning • Operational planning and control	• What should we produce for the holidays? • How many parts should we keep in inventory? • How many units should be stocked on the store floor? • How much should we order next year?
Lower management	Short-range	• Status inquiries • Processing of orders, shipments, etc. • Preparation of accounts receivable • Preparation of payroll checks every two weeks	• What customers' accounts are delinquent? • What inventory should be moved from the warehouse to the store floor?

Figure 2.5
Typical EDP functions performed for management.

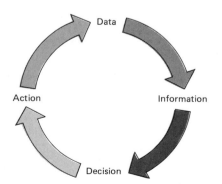

Figure 2.6
Information-feedback cycle.

III. HOW BUSINESS PROCEDURES ARE COMPUTERIZED

Figure 2.7 provides an analysis of which departments generally make the most use of computers.

Each set of procedures within a department is designed to satisfy specific objectives. This set of procedures is referred to as a **business system.** When a business system is not functioning satisfactorily, it must be redesigned so that it more effectively meets the needs of the department and the organization as a whole. Among the reasons for dissatisfaction with business systems are the following.

Figure 2.7
Analysis of computer usage by department.

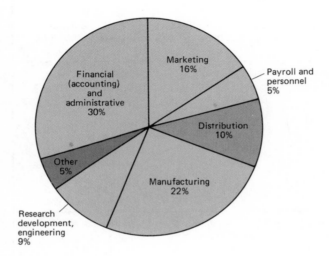

Reasons for Redesigning Existing Business Systems

1. Inability to provide timely information.
2. Costly and inefficient procedures.
3. High error rate.
4. Inability to accommodate growth.
5. Inability of management to make appropriate decisions because information provided is insufficient, inaccurate, or late.

When a manager of a business department or an executive of the company decides that a business system needs to be revised, he or she calls on a systems analyst to determine why the current set of operations is not satisfactory and how the objectives of the system can be better met. Basically, the systems analyst performs the following functions.

IN A NUTSHELL

TASKS OF A SYSTEMS ANALYST

1. Analyzes the existing business procedures to determine the basic problem areas.
2. Designs a new, more efficient business system if required.
3. Provides specifications to programmers so that the required programs can be written.
4. Implements the new system so that it functions smoothly and effectively.

Because systems analysts have expertise in computer applications, their recommendations for a new business system usually include the use of computers for processing data. They are responsible for establishing specifications that enable programmers to write adequate programs. Computerized collections of data called files are created and kept up to date by the data processing department.

Systems analysts, then, work closely with department employees within the business, called users, to determine how the present system functions, what the basic problems are, and how a new design might alleviate some of the problems.

Note that one major reason why computerized business systems fail to meet their objectives is a lack of proper communication between user groups within a company and systems analysts. Computer professionals and businesspeople, in general, must learn to work closely and to understand each other's respective needs if this communication gap is to be bridged. That is, (1) users or businesspeople must be made more aware of how computers can be effectively utilized, and (2) computer professionals must be more aware of the needs of each system and of the company as a whole, if computerization is to achieve its stated objectives.

The analyst is a computer professional who might be one of the following:

1. *A staff employee within the organization.* Companies with computer facilities hire systems analysts who are called on to analyze and design business systems for specific departments within the firm.

2. *An outside consultant.* A company might hire, on a consulting basis, an external analyst or consultant who can objectively evaluate the organization's needs and requirements.

In either case, the systems analyst is a computer professional called on to analyze existing procedures and to make recommendations for new, usually computerized, systems. Thus the analyst must understand and be able to integrate knowledge of the following elements:

IN A NUTSHELL

SYSTEMS CONSIDERATIONS

1. HARDWARE
   A business system should make appropriate use of computer equipment.

2. SOFTWARE
   Programming support, necessary for achieving specific computerized output, must be understood and properly utilized.

3. INFORMATION SYSTEMS
   The main task is to combine hardware and software considerations so that properly functioning and integrated information systems are achieved.

The text focuses on the above three units in the sequence indicated. Computer professionals must possess a detailed knowledge of each. See Figure 2.8 for sample allocation of a typical computer department's budget in terms of personnel, hardware, and other costs.

Figure 2.8
Sample allocation of a computer department's budget.

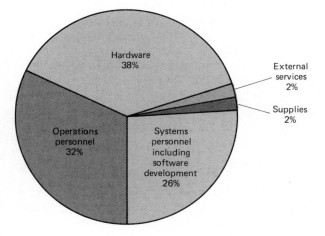

Self-Evaluating Quiz

1. (T or F) If a computerized business system will not result in decreased cost, it should not be implemented.
2. Computers used on the operations level should result in _____.
3. Computers used on the management level should result in _____.
4. EDP is an abbreviation for _____.

5. Explain why an integrated approach to systems analysis is so important.

6. MIS is an abbreviation for _____. Explain the main differences between MIS and a traditional systems approach.

7. Explain the major aspects of a systems analyst's job.

8. Systems analysts may be _____ employees or _____.

9. A systems analyst must have knowledge of devices, called _____, and knowledge of programs, called _____. The integration of these two elements into meaningful computerized designs requires knowledge of _____.

10. Indicate why organizations computerize business procedures.

Solutions

1. F—Sometimes there are other justifications besides money for a computerized business system—reduced error rates, greater capacity for growth, etc.

2. automated record keeping that is more timely and results in fewer errors

3. information that improves the decision-making process

4. Electronic Data Processing

5. Without an integrated approach, each system will be designed as an independent entity, with no consideration for its relationship to other systems. The result can be individual systems that function properly, but these systems may not provide top management with the information they need for evaluating the company's overall activities.

6. Management Information Systems
   MIS focuses on the *integrated* approach to systems analysis. It also views the needs of top management as its main priority.

7. analyze an existing system
   design a new, computerized system
   provide specifications to programmers
   implement the new design

8. staff (within the organization)
   outside consultants

9. hardware
   software
   information systems

10. to decrease cost
    to increase efficiency
    to minimize errors
    to improve the decision-making process

IV. TYPES OF COMPUTER FACILITIES WITHIN A COMPANY'S ORGANIZATIONAL STRUCTURE

There are numerous ways in which computer facilities can be organized within a company's overall structure. The three most commonly used methods are as follows.

IN A NUTSHELL

TYPES OF COMPUTER FACILITIES

Centralized
There is one central computer facility, which provides computer services to all users.

Decentralized
Each department has its own computer facility, which functions autonomously with its own equipment and support staff.

Distributed
There is a central computer facility to control, coordinate, and monitor the activities of independent computers or workstations in each department.

We discuss each type of facility in detail. Note that the last two types of organizations evolved from the first. Until recently, almost all computer facilities within organizations were centralized. With the growing capability and decreasing cost of minicomputers and microcomputers, first decentralized and then distributed facilities have become very popular.

Figure 2.9 illustrates how the three types of computer facilities might be integrated into the overall organization.

The last method of organization, the distributed approach, is the one that is most likely to provide a more integrated systems perspective, one that will not only achieve each department's need, but those of the organization as a whole. In companies that have as their goal an integrated management information system, distributed computer facilities are most often used.

A. Centralized Data Processing

When there is one computer facility that services the company as a whole, this usage is referred to as **centralized data processing.** A centralized facility may appear within the organization in one of several ways:

1. A Subdivision of the Accounting or Finance Department

When computers were first used in business organizations, they were initially employed to satisfy accounting and financial needs. Thus it was quite natural for EDP to become a subdivision of one of these departments. Even today, the primary function of a computer facility in many organizations is to service these departments. Hence, it is not uncommon to find EDP as a subdivision of accounting or finance, or some related department.

The main disadvantage of a computer facility being contained within a department such as accounting or finance is that the specific department always has priority, even when numerous other systems require computerization. That is, an accounting application is apt to receive more attention than other applications because of the organizational structure, even if other applications require more immediate attention.

1. Centralized computer facility

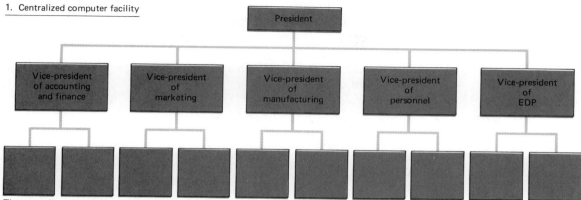

There usually exists a lack of integration from department to department.

2. Decentralized computer facilities

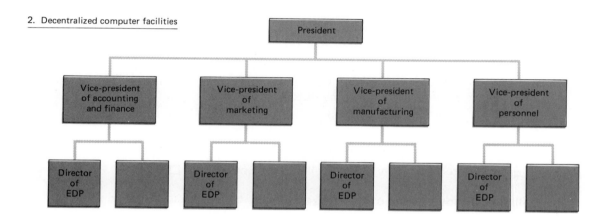

3. Distributed computer facilities

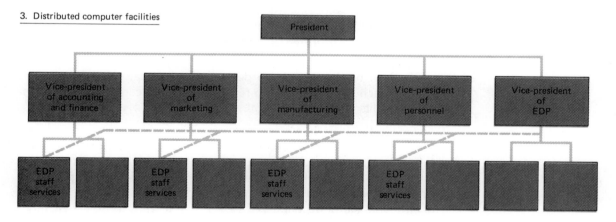

Figure 2.9
Comparison of centralized,
decentralized, and
distributed computer
facilities.

2. A Separate Department

When data processing is a separate department, the position of EDP director is typically a corporate-level management job. The director reports to either an executive vice-president or the president. The following chart illustrates some of the ways in which centralized EDP may fit into many organizational structures, based on a recent survey.

⫸ The Relationship of EDP to Other Areas

Person to Whom EDP Officer Reports	Percent of Companies
Senior VP or executive VP	35
Controller	33
VP finance	17
President	15

3. A Time-Sharing Facility

Computer time and computer support is supplied to the company from an outside firm, using a time-sharing arrangement. In this way, the company can minimize its need for hardware and computer professionals and rely either solely or predominantly on some outside source.

B. Decentralized EDP

There are several problems inherent in centralized EDP.

⫸ Disadvantages of Centralized EDP

1. A single, often overworked computer staff is required to service all departments. Each computer professional, then, will have only limited knowledge of individual user needs. Since computer professionals do not work with any one department long enough to fully understand its needs, the communication gap between user departments and the computer staff is a recurring problem.

2. It is difficult, if not impossible, to determine the actual computer costs to attribute to each department. As a result, a company cannot effectively assess the benefits of computerization.

To alleviate these problems, many companies have established separate computer facilities for each department. This is called **decentralized data processing.** In this way, each department can obtain the precise equipment it needs, hire a staff of computer professionals with knowledge of its specific requirements, and be responsible for its own computer costs.

The disadvantage of decentralized EDP is that it tends to isolate each department so that there is no integration or coordination of a company's hardware, software, and systems support. Frequently, duplication of effort and duplication of equipment purchases result. Decentralization also reduces the ability of management to obtain information on the company as a whole.

The growth of micros and minis has made it possible for many companies to use small computers as independent devices to fulfill their information processing needs on a department-by-department basis.

C. Distributed Data Processing

Distributed data processing (DDP) is a relatively new concept designed to maximize the advantages of both centralized and decentralized data processing while minimizing the disadvantages. In a DDP environment, each department has its own computer capability. The equipment may consist of terminals, micros, or minis linked to a centralized large-scale system. The local needs of each department are met with the equipment at each department's station. In addition, control and coordination is maintained by the main processing unit. With the proliferation of minis, micros, and terminals, there has been a tremendous growth in DDP systems that use a network of devices controlled by one central computer. Figure 2.10 gives a well-known application of a distributed processing network.

The main advantages of the distributed approach are as follows:

Advantages of Distributed Data Processing

- Each department's needs can be met on an individual basis.
- Control and centralization can still be obtained.
- Duplication of effort can be minimized.
- It is easier to assess the cost of each department's computer needs.
- It is easy for a company to accommodate growth by simply linking additional minis or micros to the system as needed.

The trend in the computer industry currently favors distributed data processing. In the past, expanding a centralized system had limitations and tended to be costly. Today, it is relatively easy and inexpensive to expand a DDP system. With the growth of micros, many companies add these personal computers as professional workstations for independent tasks such as word processing, budgeting, sales analysis and forecasting, and so on; in addition, these micros can be linked to a central computer in a distributed network.

For a breakdown of the types of computer facilities used in business, see Figure 2.11. Figure 2.12 provides an overview of the advantages and disadvantages of each type of facility.

Figure 2.10
The New York Stock Exchange: an example of a highly sophisticated distributed data processing network. (Robert McElroy/ Woodfin Camp.)

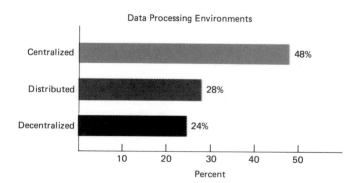

Data Processing Environments

Centralized — 48%
Distributed — 28%
Decentralized — 24%

Percent (10 20 30 40 50)

Figure 2.11
The prevalence of centralized, decentralized, and distributed computer facilities.

Figure 2.12
Advantages and
disadvantages of different
types of computer facilities.

	Advantages	Disadvantages
Centralized DP	1. Results in standardized equipment and procedures, for the company as a whole. 2. Computer specialists work as a group—DP procedures become more professional; supervision of activities is improved. 3. Reduces duplication of effort.	1. It is difficult to assess each user's DP needs, costs, and the effectiveness of DP for that user. 2. It is difficult to determine priorities for computer use. 3. Management-level resistance to DP exists because control of activities is in the hands of the DP manager.
Decentralized DP	1. Direct control by users minimizes the traditional communication gap; computer professionals better understand department's needs. 2. Response to user needs is more direct; pressure from other departments is minimized. 3. Assessing the effectiveness of each DP facility is easier.	1. There is duplication of files, processing, and reporting. 2. Lack of standardization exists. 3. Costs are usually more. 4. Management control is more difficult.
Distributed DP (DDP)	1. Combines the advantages of centralized and decentralized data processing. 2. Employs an integrated approach to systems. 3. Represents the best method for accommodating growth.	1. Requires sophisticated hardware and software control. 2. Requires strict adherence to standards.

V. THE ORGANIZATION OF A CENTRALIZED COMPUTER FACILITY

A director of EDP or MIS may have various titles depending on the organization. Titles such as director, manager, or vice president of MIS, Information Services, Computer Information Systems, Data Processing, and so on are common. Regardless of the title, he or she is responsible for the entire computer facility. The director usually has responsibility for the following staff.

A. Staff

1. Systems Manager and Systems Analysts

The systems manager supervises the activities of an organization's systems analysts. You will recall that the **systems analyst** is the person responsible for analyzing existing business procedures, determining the basic problem areas or inefficiencies, and designing a more efficient computerized set of procedures or system. The systems manager assigns specific tasks to individual analysts and evaluates their progress.

TABLE 2.1   Sample Average Salaries for Computer Professionals

Title	Cleveland	Denver	New York	San Francisco
Systems analyst				
Up to 4 years experience	$21,600	$27,200	$34,800	$32,100
Over 4 years experience	27,200	31,500	41,300	35,200
Programmer				
Up to 2 years experience	21,300	21,800	26,000	23,100
Over 4 years experience	24,400	29,700	37,600	35,400
Operator				
Up to 2 years experience	15,700	14,500	18,700	19,900
Over 4 years experience	18,000	17,300	21,600	22,800
EDP auditor				
Up to 2 years experience	23,200	23,900	28,400	24,400
Over 4 years experience	40,500	33,000	45,800	38,100
Data base administrator				
Up to 2 years experience	22,700	25,500	30,100	29,200
Over 4 years experience	34,200	37,300	46,100	45,400

Source: Source EDP.

2. Programming Manager and Programmers

The programming manager directs the activities of an organization's programmers. The **programmer** receives the job requirements from a systems analyst and is responsible for *writing* and *testing* programs that will integrate into the business system as a whole. The programming manager is the individual who supervises the activities of programmers.

Smaller companies sometimes cannot afford a full computer staff. .They may hire an additional category of computer professional called a **programmer analyst,** who not only designs business systems but writes all the necessary programs as well. In this way, the programmer analyst is responsible for the entire design, including all the programming and implementation.

3. Operations Manager and Operators

An operations manager is responsible for the overall operations of the computer center. He or she supervises the data entry procedures, control procedures, and equipment operations at the center. He or she is held accountable for the efficient and effective utilization of computer equipment. An operations manager must see to it that computer errors are kept to a minimum and that the computer system is relatively secure from breakdown, fire, power outages, unauthorized use, and inadvertent misuse.

4. EDP Auditors

EDP auditors are accounting and computer specialists who are responsible for assessing the *effectiveness* and *efficiency* of the computer system and for ensuring its overall integrity.

5. Data Base Administrator

The **data base administrator** is responsible for the structure, design, and control of all data processing files. A data base administrator is responsible for organizing and designing the data base and associated computer files used by the organization. The data base administrator is held accountable for the efficient design of the data base and for implementing proper controls and techniques necessary for accessing the data base.

Table 2.1 on page 67 shows sample salaries for computer professionals. Chapter 18 provides an in-depth analysis of careers in computing.

LOOKING AHEAD

Shortage of Computer Professionals to Continue Over the Next Five Years

Although the United States is the world leader in the electronics and computer-related industries, it continues to suffer from a shortage of professionals in those fields.

Job categories with the highest projected growth over the next five years include computer programmers and analysts (103% growth).

The American Electronics Association, Palo Alto, California, recommends that each U.S. company in the electronics industry contribute 2% of its research and development budget to electronics and computing education.

Figure 2.13
(a) A general overview of a computer facility. (b) A detailed breakdown of a typical computer facility.

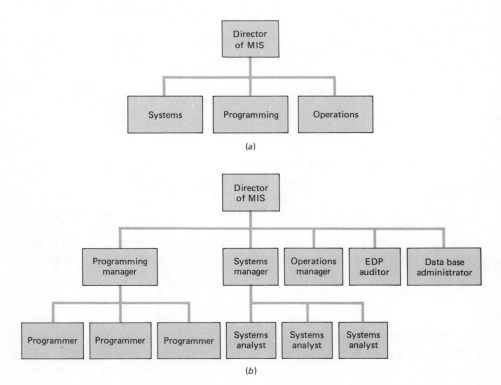

B. The Structure Within a Computer Facility

There are numerous ways in which a computer facility can be organized. Figure 2.13 illustrates an organization where programmers and analysts report to different supervisors. In this type of organization, programmers and analysts work together in the design of programs for a new system but there is no supervisor-subordinate relationship between the two groups. This type of organization may mean that analysts have less actual control over the programmers working on a specific application, but there will be a freer exchange of ideas between the two groups.

Figure 2.14 illustrates an organization where programmers report directly to systems analysts. In this type of organization, analysts are in a supervisory position where they assign programs to be coded for new systems to members of their staff and then monitor and assess the progress of their programmers. In this instance there is one manager of both systems and programming.

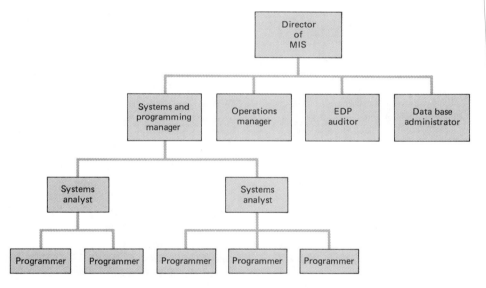

Figure 2.14
An organization chart where programmers report to analysts.

CHAPTER SUMMARY

   I. Why computerize business functions?
      A. For record keeping.
      B. To reduce errors.
      C. To store data efficiently.
      D. To facilitate decision making.
  II. Business organization
      A. Departments within a company have specific objectives, which must be met on two levels.

      1. Operations level.

      2. Management level.

  B. Information-feedback cycle—each department performs the following:

      1. Processes data.

      2. Provides information based on data.

      3. Makes decisions based on information.

      4. Takes appropriate actions based on decisions; these actions result in the processing of data and the information-feedback cycle is repeated.

  C. Departments must function independently and on an integrated basis to meet companywide objectives. Thus both of the following approaches are necessary.

      1. Traditional systems approach
A business system or set of procedures is designed to function independently to achieve departmental objectives.

      2. Management Information Systems (MIS) approach
All procedures are treated as part of an integrated whole so that top-level management can obtain information about the entire company.

III. Computerizing business systems

  A. Systems analyst—evaluates an existing system, makes recommendations for a new design, provides specifications to programmers, and implements the new design.

  B. The systems analyst must have knowledge of:

      1. Hardware.

      2. Software.

      3. Information systems.

  C. The analyst may be employed by the company or be an outside consultant.

IV. Types of computer facilities

  A. Centralized—one computer installation services the entire company.

  B. Decentralized—each department has its own independent computer installation; this arrangement usually uses minicomputers, microcomputers, or workstations in each department.

  C. Distributed—each department has access to a computer for its own processing needs; in addition, there is a centralized facility that integrates the data and its processing on a companywide basis.

V. Staff of a centralized computer facility

  A. The overall director of the computer facility typically reports to the executive VP or to the controller, depending on the organization.

  B. Staff:

      1. Systems analysts—report to a systems manager.

      2. Programmers—report to either a programming manager or to individual systems analysts.

      3. Operations manager—supervises the computer and data entry operators.

4. EDP auditor—evaluates the overall efficiency of the computer facility.
5. Data base administrator—responsible for the structure, design, and control of all data processing files.
6. Programmer analyst—some organizations, mostly smaller ones, have a programmer analyst responsible for both the systems design and the programming of an entire business system.

Chapter Self-Evaluating Quiz

1. A(n) _____ chart depicts the departmental levels of responsibility for employees within a company.
2. The set of procedures within a department that is designed to satisfy specific objectives is referred to as a(n) _____.
3. A major reason why computerized business systems fail to meet their objectives is a lack of proper communication between _____ and _____.
4. With a (centralized, decentralized) computer facility, it is difficult to determine the actual computer costs to attribute to each department.
5. A (centralized, decentralized) computer facility enables each department to have its own independent computer facility.
6. A Management Information System that attempts to satisfy the needs of each department as well as the needs of the company as a whole is likely to use a _____ computer facility.
7. The growth of micro- and minicomputers that can be linked to large-scale computer systems increases the prevalence of _____ computer facilities.
8. A programmer analyst is a computer professional who _____.
9. A person responsible for the structure, design, and control of data processing files is called a _____.
10. In some computer organizations, programmers report to _____. In other organizations, programmers report to _____.

Solutions

1. organization / page 55
2. business system / page 58
3. user groups / page 59
   systems analysts / page 59
4. centralized / page 64
5. decentralized (or even distributed) / page 64
6. distributed / page 65
7. distributed / page 65

8. designs a system and writes all the programs as well (This is usually the case in smaller organizations.) / page 67
9. data base administrator / page 68
10. a programming manager / page 69
    systems analysts / page 69

Key Terms

Business system
Centralized data processing
Data base
Data base administrator
Decentralized data processing
Distributed data processing (DDP)

EDP auditor
Management Information System (MIS)
Programmer
Programmer analyst
Systems analyst

Review Questions

I. True-False Questions

1. (T or F) Electronic Data Processing, often abbreviated EDP, is defined as the use of automated procedures to enter data, to operate on it, and to produce desired results.

2. (T or F) Distributed data processing facilities have become very popular, partly because of the growing capability and decreasing cost of micro- and minicomputers.

3. (T or F) It is important for computer professionals to have a general understanding of how the business in which they work is organized and functions.

4. (T or F) The title "data base administrator" is another name for the position of "director of EDP."

5. (T or F) It is possible for a centralized data processing facility to use a time-sharing arrangement with an outside firm.

6. (T or F) It is possible for some companies to utilize computerized operations without having a data processing staff.

7. (T or F) With a decentralized data processing facility, there is duplication of files, processing, and reporting.

8. (T or F) Once a system has been designed, the programming staff is then called on to write the set of computer instructions that is required within the system.

9. (T or F) The programming staff always reports directly to the data processing manager.

10. (T or F) An organization chart depicts the interdependence of functions within an organization.

II. Fill in the Blanks

1. Departments within a company do not function as independent entities because _____.

2. The major objectives of an accounts receivable department are _____.

3. MIS is an abbreviation for _____.

4. The four elements of the information-feedback cycle are _____, _____, _____, and _____.

5. A pictorial representation most often used to evaluate the overall structure in an organization is called a(n) _____.

6. From an organization chart, we can determine the relationship of each _____ to the company as a whole.

7. A data processing organization usually has three main components: a(n) _____ staff, a(n) _____ staff, and a(n) _____ staff.

8. The _____ analyzes the elements of the present system, determines the requirements of the job, and decides if a computerized set of procedures is economically justifiable.

9. Major disadvantages of centralized EDP are _____ and _____.
10. A major disadvantage of decentralized EDP is that it _____.

APPLICATION

DEMAND SURGES FOR HIGH-LEVEL MIS EXECS

by Rutrell Yasin

NEW YORK—As the economy began to improve late last year pent-up demand for high-level MIS executives was suddenly released and many executive search firms indicated that the demand will continue well into this year according to recruiters interviewed by MIS Week.

However, the call is for a new breed of high-level MIS manager—a business manager who understands how the MIS function can be used as an effective tool to keep his or her firm competitive. According to executive recruiters this new breed of MIS talent—often in their 30s and 40s—is reporting more and more to the CEO or chief operating officer and the industry leading the way is the financial services sector.

In addition, although many do not have hard statistics, executive recruiters cited the movement of women into many of these high level positions, a trend that they welcome as they search for top talent in a field that is in short supply.

Herbert Halbrecht, president of Halbrecht Associates, Stamford, Conn., a MIS executive search firm, is involved with searches from coast to coast. About 40 percent of his business is in the banking or financial services area. There were trends that became pronounced in '83, particularly in the banking and financial services industries which have continued into '84 and beyond.

Salaries "Delightfully" Going Up

In '84, the demand for MIS executives has not diminished and the salaries have continued to "delightfully" go up, Halbrecht noted. Because of decentralization one will increasingly find that the vice president of retail systems or wholesale systems no longer reports to the vice president of information services but rather to the executive in charge of retail banking.

At one time, line managers did not want the information function under them, but now there is a younger breed of managers who are not afraid of the information function and more importantly understand how to use it. Since banking executives are using MIS and demand-

ing more and more control of the resources that enable them to put a product in the field, the information systems executive working for the line officer has to contribute to the bottom line or he or she can get killed, Halbrecht asserted.

"I anticipate that the trend will accelerate substantially," Halbrecht noted. Halbrecht explained that he keeps hearing about the matrix environment but is not "terribly sanguine" about how well it is working with the executives involved. "If the VP of retail systems reports to the VP of information services and the VP of information services is not in sync with the VP of retail banking, then the likelihood of being successful is remote," he explained.

Salary-wise, Halbrecht explained that positions that used to pay $75,000 to $85,000 are now in the range of $85,000 to $100,000. "And these are not necessarily the No. 1 guys of the computer function," Halbrecht noted, adding that in some cases a senior VP of retail systems can be making $150,000, depending on how much importance the bank puts on the function, while at a bank of comparable size, the head of the information function does not even make that much.

Traditionally, MIS functions reported to the financial officer. But, to the extent that the technology has an impact on one's marketing strategy, then they should report to the CEO or chief operating officer.

John Johnson, vice president of Lamalie Associates, Cleveland, also linked the demand for MIS executives with the economy. From his perspective, MIS executives "probably outpaced the marketplace in '84." Johnson noted that the demand for executives in general was up 51 percent in 1984 and speculated that the demand for MIS executives was up over that.

Describing the type of executive his clients have been seeking, Johnson said, "What we are seeing is that clients are requiring that the senior MIS executives be more global thinkers, as opposed to narrower MIS thinkers." That requirement has led some organizations to seek someone over another with more business experience, he noted.

Larger Systems Sought

Michael Rottblatt, vice president of Korn/Ferry International in Stamford, Conn., noted that the firms that have controlled the movement of money and thus needed control of information with greater real-time speed, have always sought larger, more sophisticated systems. "This held true five years ago and it holds true today," Rottblatt explained. With the move for greater sophistication and greater power, there was a greater need for that individual who could handle it—a corporate manager of MIS.

Rottblatt said that he is also seeing cases wherein some MIS executives are being promoted out of MIS. He explained that he just placed an individual in an insurance firm who is senior vice president of MIS and administration and also a member of the executive committee, which puts him in the position to assist in the decision-making and strategic planning process. In addition, he reports directly to the president of the company.

The more forward-thinking companies are taking on this perspective because the MIS executives support the business objectives, and companies such as insurance firms cannot even offer new products without the assistance of MIS, Rottblatt noted.

Halbrecht, of Halbrecht and Associates, noted that with the importance of telecommunications, salaries in this function are really "zooming up." He cited the example of a woman that he placed in a job who wound up being paid $20,000 more than the company had thought they would pay for that position.

Source: Management Information Systems Week, January 25, 1984, page 27. Reprinted with permission.

Questions
1. Understanding Key Terms
   Define the following terms as they are used in the application:
   a. MIS manager.
   b. Information systems.
   c. Line manager.
   d. CEO.
   e. Distribution company.
2. Software, Hardware, and Systems Concepts
   a. Based on the article, what are some of the criteria for an effective MIS manager?
   b. Is it necessarily true that a person with the most knowledge of hardware, software, and systems concepts will make the best MIS manager?
3. Management Considerations
   Based on the application, explain some of the ways in which an MIS organization can function within a company.
4. Social, Legal, and Ethical Implications
   a. What training or education would be helpful in assisting a potential MIS executive to be more of a "global thinker, as opposed to a narrower MIS thinker"?
   b. Based on the article, are women suited for top-level MIS positions? Explain your answer.

CASE STUDY: McKing's Superburgers, Inc.

1. Computer Staff
   If computerization at McKing's Superburgers is to be achieved, a Director of Management Information Systems will need to be hired.
   a. Prepare a job description for this director.
   b. Suppose you were the president of McKing's but you had very little familiarity with computers. What methods would you use for evaluating the progress of the Director of MIS after he or she was hired?
2. Type of System
   a. Do you think a distributed, centralized, or decentralized system would be most appropriate in this case study? Explain your answer.

b. For each type of system considered, to whom should the Director of Management Information Systems report?
3. Information-Feedback Cycle
   Suppose a customer places an order at McKing's. Trace the effects of this order through the various phases of the information-feedback cycle.

THE COMPUTER AD: A Focus on Marketing

Consider the ad entitled "Sometimes, you need a solution before you know the problem" that appears in Figure 2.15.

1. Define the following terms as they appear in the ad:
   a. End user.
   b. Hardware, software, and networking tools.
   c. Strict standards for accountability, documentation, support, and cost effectiveness.
2. The claim is made that Control Data Business Information Services can provide an alternate resource for computer support. In your own words, explain what that means.
3. This is an ad that offers solutions to people before they know the problem. Would the user therefore tend to be well versed in information processing or not? Explain your answer.
4. Would a small business beginning to think about the ways in which computers can save time and money benefit from the services described above? What about a large organization with a major computer organization already in place? Be specific in your answers.

Sometimes, you need a solution before you know the problem.

End users don't always know exactly *what* they need, but they usually know precisely *when* they need it. Typically, it's yesterday.

They don't do it to complicate your life, but to uncomplicate theirs. All too often, the need for fast solutions exceeds their understanding of the problems. Theirs and yours. After all, your responsibilities are to meet the data processing requirements of the entire organization. That's why you've established the need for clear definitions, defined parameters and realistic priorities. But to someone with an urgent need, your rules and procedures may seem more like obstacles than answers.

That's when Control Data Business Information Services can help you *and* your end users. Even when they don't know exactly what they need (their problems are urgent and important, but ill-defined, evolving, or both), we can help them create their own prototype systems. In a fraction of the normal development time.

We provide the hardware, software and networking tools. More important, we provide people trained, experienced and dedicated to helping end users arrive at prompt, responsible solutions. But just because we help show them the light, we don't keep you in the dark. We share and adhere to your strict standards for accountability, documentation, support and cost effectiveness. Which is why we keep you informed.

You maintain control. And you decide when or if these new applications should be integrated into your own system. Either way, you've helped provide your end users with sound solutions

without burdening or diverting any of your energies and resources.

Today, data processing managers in hundreds of the nation's largest companies are benefiting from Control Data Business Information Services . . . we're the alternate resource.

When you have to provide a solution before you know the problem, let us help you and your end users. They get the answers they want. You keep the control you need.

For more information, write:
C. J. Brown, Senior Vice President
Control Data
Business Information Services
500 West Putnam Avenue
Greenwich, CT 06830

© 1982 Control Data Corporation

CD CONTROL DATA CORPORATION

Figure 2.15
Marketing computer products. (Courtesy Control Data Business Information Services.)

CHAPTER

3

THE HISTORY OF COMPUTERS AND INFORMATION PROCESSING

CHAPTER OBJECTIVES

To familiarize you with:

- The rich heritage that culminated in the Computer Revolution.
- The pioneers in computing.
- The major computing innovations.
- The nature of technological innovation and development.

I. THE HISTORY OF COMPUTERS

The electronic digital computer has had, and continues to have, a profound impact not only on business but on society in general. Historical studies are extremely useful in evaluating that impact and understanding the process of change that leads to even more advanced technologies.

But before **digital computers** became popular, most computational devices were **analog.** An analog device is one that measures or processes data in a continuous form. A traditional watch or clock, as opposed to a digital timepiece, is an analog device. Time is represented in a continuous fashion. A slide rule, as opposed to a calculator, is an analog device. Quantities are represented on a continuous scale. Similarly, fuel gauges are usually analog devices.

Physical quantities are best measured in a continuous fashion and thus are ideally suited for analog computation. Voltage, temperature, and pressure, for example, are frequently computed using analog devices. Hence voltmeters, thermometers, and barometers are additional examples of analog devices.

A disadvantage of analog computation is that when data is represented in continuous form, readouts can only approximate actual results.

A digital device is one that measures and represents quantities as discrete digits. On an analog device, 1.5 is represented as the midpoint between 1 and 2. On a digital device, 1.5 is represented as two digits, 1 and 5, with a decimal point between them. Note the difference between the representation of time on analog and digital devices as follows:

Analog clock   Digital clock

The study of history can help to explain what can and cannot be reasonably expected from technological developments. How various computational devices affected past societies will undoubtedly shed some light on how computers currently impact society and how they are likely to affect our society in the future. In the words of the philosopher George Santayana:

Those who do not learn from history are destined to repeat it.

That is, without a keen understanding of past developments, we will find ourselves continually "reinventing the wheel." Moreover, we will fail to learn from past mistakes and be less successful in guiding our own destinies.

We consider the history of computers at this point in the text because we believe that a historical analysis will help provide an understanding of the current significance of the computer and its impact on society. This chapter, then, provides a discussion of how and why computer technology evolved as it did.

Figure 3.1
Abacus—a major calculating
instrument from ancient
time through the present.
(Courtesy IBM.)

What Is History? Let us begin with a statement about what history is not: it is not simply the study of dates, events, and places despite the fact that many texts treat it as such. Providing a string of facts is not the study of history but tedious data collection.

History is the study of specific events in the context of the eras in which they evolved. Historical study should shed light on each event and inventor in an effort to better understand each achievement and its impact on developments today.

Thus, we consider key computational devices and discuss their relevance to the specific era in which they evolved, their relevance to our era, and the overall impact of the innovation on society in general. In this analysis we emphasize the fact that technological developments are really responses to social forces. They tell us something about societies themselves and how they respond to change.

A. The Pre-Modern Era

The concept of counting and calculating dates back to the beginnings of civilization. In order to trade, "buy" or "sell" in the modern sense, it was necessary for a society to be able to compute. One of the earliest devices invented for this purpose was the **abacus** used in Babylonian, Arabic, Chinese, and Roman civilizations.

The abacus was not only used by ancient civilizations but has been prevalent throughout the centuries, and was particularly popular in Europe in the 1500s and 1600s when international trading became fundamental to society. It is still used in some societies today such as Russia, China, and Japan. Indeed, in many Chinese communities in the United States one can find businesspeople still using the abacus (see Figure 3.1).

B. The Scientific Revolution, 1543–1687: The Modern Age of Science Begins

The Scientific Revolution is a period in history that resulted in a new orientation toward science and technology, one that was so radically different from what existed before that the term "revolution" is deemed appropriate. This period begins in the mid-sixteenth century with the discovery that the sun, not the earth, is really the center of the universe. With humankind replaced as the central force in the universe, a whole host of religious, political, and social changes resulted. The Scientific Revolution that resulted culminated with the formal definition of the laws of nature as specified by Isaac Newton in 1687.

With these laws of nature, scientific principles became the basis for uncovering life's secrets for many people.

As you might expect, the Scientific Revolution fostered an interest in computation and computational devices. Society came to value any tools or instruments that could help the scientist perform experiments and uncover more advanced laws of nature and science. Thus, for the first time, technology became a discipline closely allied to science. Instrument makers and technologists, once considered artisans, began to work closely with scientists to help uncover nature's laws and to apply those laws to the development of machines that would improve the quality of life.

This focus on science and technology helps to explain the interest in computational devices that evolved during the sixteenth and seventeenth centuries. Another reason for an increased interest in computation was the growth of commerce and the evolution of a middle class of tradespeople and merchants who performed many calculations. Businesspeople as well as scientists found a need for devices that could count quickly and accurately.

With the emerging values of modern scientists and the growing need for computational tools, it is not surprising that some of the most important people in the Scientific Revolution were inventors of calculating equipment as well as influential scientists.

1. Blaise Pascal (1623–1662)

Blaise Pascal (Figure 3.2) was a French mathematician and experimental physicist who was one of the first modern scientists to develop and build a calculator. In 1645, he devised a calculating machine that was capable of adding and subtracting numbers. It was one of the first calculating machines ever developed. The machine was operated by dialing a series of wheels. Around the circumference of each wheel were the numbers 0 to 9. Sums or totals appeared above the dials in indicators (see Figure 3.3).

Although he received a patent for his device, Pascal did not have much success in marketing it. Perhaps the most plausible explanation for the lack of interest in this device is that it was difficult to repair and many people remained skeptical as to its ability to save time.

The programming language Pascal, which is discussed in Chapter 10, was named for this inventor.

Figure 3.2
Blaise Pascal (1623–1662). (Courtesy IBM.)

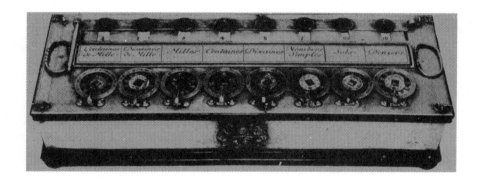

Figure 3.3
Pascal's calculator. (Courtesy IBM.)

Figure 3.4
Gottfried Leibniz
(1646–1716). (Courtesy IBM.)

Figure 3.5
The calculator designed by
Leibniz. (Courtesy IBM.)

2. Gottfried Leibniz (1646–1716)

Like Pascal, **Gottfried Leibniz** (Figure 3.4) was a seventeenth-century scientist who recognized the value of building machines that could do mathematical calculations and save labor too.

In 1694, Leibniz completed his calculator, which is shown in Figure 3.5. It utilized the same techniques for addition and subtraction as Pascal's device but could also perform multiplication and division. However, as was the case with Pascal's device, Leibniz's machine was somewhat ahead of its time. Society, for the most part, was not yet ready to use calculating devices designed to save labor.

C. The Industrial Revolution, 1760–1830: The Modern Age of Technology Begins

Whereas the Scientific Revolution, for the most part, shaped people's ideas toward science, the Industrial Revolution had a far greater social impact on the average person.

The Industrial Revolution began in England around 1760, and by 1830 British society was so dramatically changed that a "revolution" was said to have occurred. The changes accompanying the Industrial Revolution, which quickly spread in the nineteenth century to other Western European countries and to the United States, include the following:

Changes Produced by Technological Growth

1. Transition from rural to urban society.
2. Transition from hand products to mechanized manufacturing.
3. Transition from regional or local commerce to a wide-area system utilizing mass transportation.
4. Attention to labor-saving machinery.
5. Development of a working class.

Whereas the Industrial Revolution brought with it many civilizing influences, there are those who still maintain that the negative effects of technology far outweigh its virtues. The anti-technological view that many people express today is often associated with the belief that labor-saving machinery, and computers particularly, will result in mass unemployment. Such unemployment characterized many towns in nineteenth-century England and was a direct result of new technological devices that were introduced. Yet the Industrial Revolution produced several inventions that were to have a profound impact on the computing field.

1. Jacquard's Weaving Loom

Joseph Marie Jacquard (Figure 3.6) was a French inventor in the earliest years of the French Industrial Revolution. In 1804, he developed a method for controlling the operation of a weaving loom with the use of holes punched into cards. With holes punched into appropriate positions on the card, a weaving loom could be mechanically "programmed" to weave specific patterns and to use specific colors (see Figure 3.7). Jacquard's device was to become the prototype of the punched card machines used for processing data at the end of the nineteenth century and into the first half of the twentieth century. Such machines are still in use today.

Because Jacquard developed his machine during the Industrial Revolution, he did not encounter the resistance that Pascal and Leibniz faced. Instead, his device was very successful. By 1812, as many as 11,000 Jacquard looms were used in France alone. Jacquard became a successful inventor largely because

Figure 3.6
Joseph Marie Jacquard
(1752–1834). (Courtesy IBM.)

Figure 3.7
Jacquard's weaving loom.
(Courtesy IBM.)

his machine was developed during an era in which labor-saving machinery was in high demand.

It is also interesting to note that inventors during the nineteenth century, for the first time, began to be recognized as "heroes." Jacquard, for example, was honored by the Napoleonic government and given a pension as well. The time had finally come when governments felt the need to support and even reward inventors. The hope was that such support would lead to other developments that would continue to benefit society as a whole.

2. Babbage's Analytical Engine

Charles Babbage (Figure 3.8) was a nineteenth-century Englishman who is frequently considered the father of the modern computer. Although he did not actually build an operational computer himself, his ideas became the very basis for modern computational devices.

In 1822, Babbage began work on a device called the **Difference Engine,** which was designed to automate a standard procedure for calculating the roots of polynomials (see Figure 3.9). The calculations were used for producing astronomical tables, required by the British Navy for navigational purposes.

Despite his foresight and his keen ideas, Babbage did not complete his original project. Instead, he abandoned the Difference Engine to work on a more powerful device, the **Analytical Engine,** which was remarkably similar in concept to twentieth-century digital computers (see Figure 3.10).

The Analytical Engine was designed to use two types of cards: one, called

Figure 3.8
Charles Babbage
(1791–1871). (Courtesy IBM.)

Figure 3.9
Babbage's Difference
Engine. (Courtesy IBM.)

Figure 3.10
Babbage's Analytical
Engine. (Courtesy IBM.)

operation cards, to indicate the specific functions to be performed by the device, and the other, called variable cards, to specify the actual data. The cards were similar to the ones Jacquard had used. This idea of entering a program, or set of instructions, on cards, followed by data cards, is one method used by modern computers for implementing the stored-program concept.

Babbage conceived of two main units for his Analytical Engine:

1. An area he called a *store* within the device, in which instructions and variables would be placed; today we call this the memory of the computer.
2. An area he called a *mill* within the device, in which arithmetic operations would be performed. Today we call this the arithmetic-logic unit.

It is interesting to note that Lady **Ada Augusta** Byron (Figure 3.11), the Countess of Lovelace and daughter of the poet Lord Byron, worked closely with Babbage in the design of programs for the Analytical Engine. She wrote a demonstration program for the Analytical Engine, prompting many to refer to her as the first programmer. The programming language Ada, discussed in Chapter 10, was named for her.

Babbage was a mathematician with a considerable interest in invention inspired by the industrialization that characterized his society. He began by applying science to technology in a new and exciting way. Yet he never accomplished his goal; that is, his machines were never built. The reasons why are the subject of considerable controversy. Some suggestions are:

1. The technology was not advanced enough to render his machines practical.
2. Babbage was not able to obtain the resources necessary to fund his projects. He received an unprecedented grant from the British government to fund the Difference Engine but when it was not completed within the specified period of time, the government rejected further requests for funds.
3. Babbage's own, idiosyncratic personality placed more emphasis on the development of an idea than on the construction of operable devices.

Figure 3.11
Ada Augusta (1815–1853).
(Courtesy *Annals of the
History of Computing*.)

In summary, it is clear that, despite Babbage's insights, the time was not ripe for the invention of a digital computer. Many of his ideas, however, were later incorporated in modern computers.

D. "Yankee Ingenuity": The Growth of American Technology

From the mid-nineteenth century on, America's technological achievement came to mean something more than simply machine development. The term "Yankee ingenuity" as it applies to the American ideal signified a society in which technology came to be seen as a positive social force. In other countries, labor-saving devices meant mass unemployment, abuse of child labor, and so on. Americans, however, always viewed such machinery as beneficial, since the early years of industrialization were characterized by labor shortages, not unemployment.

1. Herman Hollerith

Herman Hollerith (Figure 3.12a) is characteristic of the kind of inventor who influenced American industrialization toward the end of the nineteenth century.

In the 1880s, Hollerith was employed by the Census Bureau, which was falling far behind in its ability to provide census reports. As we will see in Chapter 4, Hollerith, who was trained in engineering and had an understanding of industrial needs as well, developed a punched card that would contain census data coded in the form of punched holes (see Figure 3.12b). Hollerith then built tabulating equipment that could read the cards and process the data (see Figure 3.13). Hollerith's Tabulating Machine Company merged with another firm to form a company that would eventually be known as IBM.

(a)

Figure 3.12
(a) Herman Hollerith (1869–1926). (b) Hollerith's punched card compared in size to a dollar bill. (Courtesy IBM.)

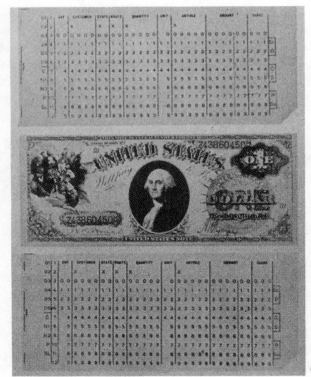

(b)

Figure 3.13
Hollerith's tabulating
machine. (Courtesy IBM.)

2. Electrical Accounting Machines

Based on the work of Hollerith and others, electrical accounting machines, called EAM devices, were developed to perform data processing functions within business organizations. These devices, which can still be found at some companies, could sort, reproduce, and merge punched cards and perform limited arithmetic and printing operations. Figure 3.14 illustrates two electrical accounting machines.

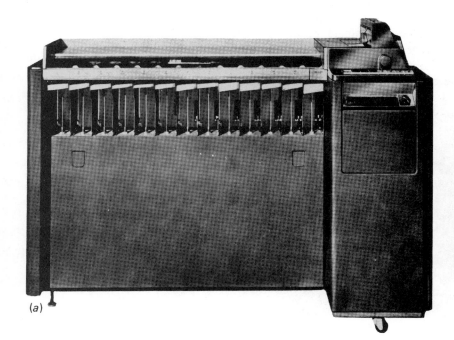

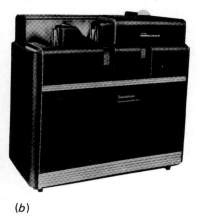

Figure 3.14
Electrical accounting
machines. (a) Sorter. (b)
Reproducer. (Courtesy IBM.)

(a)

(b)

Figure 3.15
Sample control panels wired for different EAM devices. (Courtesy IBM.)

The machines were capable of handling only one form of input—the punched card. There was no memory capability and basically each device had to be *wired* to perform a given procedure. Figure 3.15 shows sample control panels wired for use in punched card devices.

A major limitation of electrical accounting machines was that each device was designed to perform a given function, such as sorting or merging cards, thus necessitating the use of several machines to complete a particular data processing job.

3. World War II and Computers

Many historians have suggested that wartime is a particularly fertile period for technological invention. The case of the electronic digital computer clearly supports that point of view. World War II saw the development of **Howard Aiken**'s **Mark I,** the first electromechanical relay computer, developed at Harvard, with engineering assistance from IBM, during the period 1939 to 1944 (*see* Figure 3.16 for photographs of Aiken and his machine). At about the same time, **George Stibitz** (Figure 3.17) was developing a relay computer for Bell Telephone Laboratories. The fact that both inventions were developed independently of one another suggests that the time was indeed ripe for technolog-

(*a*)

Figure 3.16
(*a*) Howard H. Aiken (1900–1973). (*b*) Mark I. (Courtesy IBM.)

(*b*)

ical advance in computational equipment and that wartime helped to spur these developments.

During World War II, the U.S. government actively sought to support numerous projects that might assist in solving its diverse problems. Largely as a result of these wartime needs, the government funded a group of young engineers working at the Moore School of Electrical Engineering of the University of Pennsylvania, who developed the first fully electronic digital computer to solve ballistics problems. Under the direction of **J. Presper Eckert, Jr.,** and **John Mauchly,** the **ENIAC** was constructed during the period 1943 to 1946. It was an electronic digital computer consisting of 18,000 vacuum tubes and requiring the manual setting of switches to achieve the desired programming (see Figures 3.18 and 3.19).

Figure 3.17
George R. Stibitz (1904–).
(Courtesy Bell Labs.)

Figure 3.18
ENIAC accumulators.
(Courtesy Sperry Corp.)

Figure 3.19
ENIAC with its developers—
J. Presper Eckert, Jr. (left)
and John Mauchly (center).
(Courtesy Moore School.)

4. After World War II

Following the war, Eckert and Mauchly and their associates at the Moore School began work on the **EDVAC,** the first stored-program computer. This machine was built with the assistance of the distinguished mathematician **John von Neumann,** who provided the logical structure for the stored-program concept. Von Neumann went on to build his own computer at the Institute for Advanced Study at Princeton, a device that became the prototype for numerous computers developed at many universities and for the IBM 701 (see Figure 3.20).

Eckert and Mauchly's EDVAC was not finished until 1951 but in 1949, the first stored-program computer called the **EDSAC** was completed at Cambridge, England. The EDSAC was built under the direction of **Maurice V. Wilkes,** who had been influenced by the Moore School's work on EDVAC.

In 1946, Eckert and Mauchly left the University of Pennsylvania to form their own company to build commercial computers. The first such commercial computer, which was completed in 1951, was called the **UNIVAC I** (see Figure 3.21). This machine was delivered to the Census Bureau and shortly thereafter became available to business organizations as well. One of the first major tasks performed by the UNIVAC I was prediction of the 1952 Presidential election—correctly! Figure 3.22 shows the UNIVAC I being used to predict the 1952 election.

Eckert and Mauchly's company was taken over in 1950 by Remington Rand, which later merged to become Sperry Rand. IBM became a competitor of Sperry in the manufacturing of commercial computers in the early 1950s and a great new industry was formed.

E. The Micro: A New Phase in the Computer Revolution

With the widespread use of micros today, you may find it difficult to believe that its history began only about a decade ago.

In 1975, a small company called MITS, Inc. marketed the Altair, which was a personal computer that was delivered as a kit. The user had to assemble the product and then connect it to a display, printer, or other device, as needed.

This micro was followed quickly by Tandy Corporation's first Radio Shack computer in 1976. The Radio Shack micro quickly overtook the market with its ready-to-use packaging and available software. In addition, Tandy already had outlets for sales and maintenance with its Radio Shack stores. As a result, the first Radio Shack computer became a huge success.

In 1977, Apple introduced its microcomputer for home, business, and school use. It also enjoyed a great deal of success, particularly in elementary, junior, and senior high schools.

During the next several years, virtually thousands of companies, large and small, went into the microcomputer business, selling both hardware and software. The market then increased dramatically when IBM introduced its first personal computer in the fall of 1981. In the first year, IBM acquired 23% of an ever-increasing market. Although predictions of a shake-out in the market are frequently made, and although many computer companies have lost money or gone bankrupt, there is no doubt that the micro market will continue to thrive in the years ahead.

Figure 3.20
John von Neumann
(1903–1957). (Courtesy IBM.)

Figure 3.21
UNIVAC I. (Courtesy Sperry
Corp.)

Figure 3.22
UNIVAC I correctly predicts
the outcome of the 1952
presidential election.
(Courtesy Sperry Corp.)

II. THE COMPUTER GENERATIONS

Since the 1940s, *four generations* of computers have evolved. Table 3.1 gives a brief history of these four generations. From the first generation to the fourth, the trend has been to produce more powerful, less expensive, smaller, and more reliable computers. We see that this trend continues even today.

TABLE 3.1 Computer Generations

	First (1951–58)	Second (1958–64)	Third (1964–74)	Fourth (1974+)
Technology	Vacuum tubes; mercury delay lines; card-oriented	Transistors; magnetic cores; tape-oriented	Integrated circuits; time-sharing; disk-oriented	Very-large-scale integrated circuits; bubble memory; cache memory; minicomputer oriented
Software	Machine level	Low-level symbolic languages	High-level symbolic languages; operating system introduced	Virtual memory and network processing
Operation time	Milliseconds (thousandths of a second)	Microseconds (millionths of a second)	Nanoseconds (billionths of a second)	Nanoseconds or picoseconds (trillionths of a second)
Applications	Mostly scientific (some accounting)	Batch-oriented business data processing	On-line processing with integrated data bases, and data communications	Distributed data processing, MIS, decision support systems
Cost	$5/function	50¢/function	5¢/function	1¢ to .01¢/function
Processing speed	2000 instructions/second	1 million instructions/second	10 million instructions/second	100 million to 1 billion instructions/second
Time between failures	Minutes to hours	Days	Days to weeks	Weeks
Business focus	Accounting	Accounting, marketing, payroll, manufacturing	Data communications	Information systems

The first generation of computers (1951–1958) began with the introduction of the UNIVAC I in 1951. This computer, as well as others of the same generation, used vacuum tubes to control operations. Vacuum tubes were somewhat unreliable and generated a significant amount of heat.

The second generation of computers (1958–1964) was a direct result of the invention of the transistor by Bell Labs in 1947. Transistors were much faster, more reliable, and much smaller than vacuum tubes. This generation of computers also used magnetic cores for representing data in a computer. As a result of transistors and cores, a significant increase in the speed and processing capability of computers was achieved. Businesses began to use computers in increasing numbers and new programming languages were developed to accommodate commercial applications.

The third generation of computers (1964–1974) was also characterized by a continuing trend in decreasing the size of components. The integrated circuit containing numerous components fused on a single silicon chip marked the technology achievement of this era.

Fourth-generation computers (1974+) were a direct result of the micro-processor. The Intel Corporation was the company that first developed the **microprocessor,** or computer on a **chip.** This microprocessor, which had virtually no market in 1973 when it was first made commercially available, now represents a multi-billion-dollar industry. Microprocessors are not only used in fourth-generation computers, but for a wide variety of products including automobiles, sewing machines, microwave ovens, electronic games, and so on.

The invention of the microprocessor has resulted in a tremendous widening of the computer revolution; indeed, some have even called the microprocessor the start of a second revolution. Microprocessors have already profoundly affected our everyday lives and will undoubtedly continue to do so far into the future.

Fourth-generation computers continue to be characterized by chips that can contain increasing numbers of items. Currently, the technology has advanced to the point that 256,000 items can be stored on a single microchip and predictions are that by the end of the decade over 1 million items will be able to be stored. This further miniaturization of components, commonly referred to as very-large-scale integration (VLSI), results in increased speed, greater reliability, and enormous storage capacities for current computers.

The fifth generation of computers is close at hand and will be characterized by advances in artificial intelligence that will minimize the need for complex programming. The Japanese, who are currently at the forefront in the development of fifth-generation computers, refer to them as truly "intelligent machines." Chapter 19 provides a discussion of the future potential of these machines.

Figure 3.23 illustrates how technology has decreased the cost and processing time of computers over the last 30 years.

	1955	1960	1965	1975	1985
Cost	$14.54	$2.48	47¢	20¢	7¢
Processing time	375 seconds	47 seconds	29 seconds	4 seconds	1 second

Figure 3.23
How technology has decreased cost and processing time.

CHAPTER SUMMARY

I. Pre-Modern Era
   A. Very little emphasis on technology for labor-saving purposes.
   B. Abacus—ancient invention—widely used for mechanical calculations.
II. Scientific Revolution: 1543–1687
   A. Science and technology begin to become focal points in society.

B. Mechanical calculators.
   1. Pascal's calculator.
   2. Leibniz's calculator.
III. Industrial Revolution: 1760–1830
   A. Technology comes to be viewed as a measure of civilization.
   B. Emphasis on labor-saving devices.
      1. Jacquard's weaving loom.
      2. Babbage's Analytical and Difference Engines.
      3. Hollerith's tabulating equipment.
IV. Twentieth-century computational equipment
   A. Electrical accounting machines.
   B. World War II ushers in the age of computers.
      1. Aiken's Mark I.
      2. Eckert and Mauchly's ENIAC, EDVAC, and UNIVAC.
      3. Wilkes' EDSAC.
   C. The micro.
      1. Developed in 1975.
      2. Radio Shack was the first successful micro, followed by Apple.

Chapter Self-Evaluating Quiz

1. A pre-modern calculating device with a history of several thousand years that is still in use today is the _____.

2. Pascal and Leibniz were unsuccessful in marketing their calculators because _____.

3. Jacquard's device was to become the prototype of the _____ for processing data.

4. The person most often referred to as the father of the modern computer is _____.

5. Even though the Analytical Engine was never built, it is nevertheless significant because _____.

6. Babbage's Analytical Engine was designed to use two types of cards: _____ and _____.

7. The nineteenth-century figure who worked closely with Babbage and is often considered the world's first programmer is _____.

8. Major limitations of Electrical Accounting Machines are _____, _____, and _____.

9. The first electronic digital computer built in the United States was called the _____ and was developed during the years 1943 to 1946.

10. The stored-program concept was first conceived for a post-World War II machine called the _____. The inventors of this concept were _____.

11. The UNIVAC I was designed by _____.

12. Eckert and Mauchly sold their company to an organization that is today called the _____ Corporation.

Solutions

1. abacus / page 80

2. society was not yet ready for calculating devices designed to save labor / page 82

3. punched card machine / page 83

4. Charles Babbage / page 84

5. Babbage's ideas were later incorporated in modern computers / page 85

6. operation cards to enter instructions / page 85
variable cards to enter data / page 85

7. Ada Augusta, the Countess of Lovelace / page 85

8. they handle only punched cards / page 88
they have no memory capability / page 88
they generally must be wired to perform a given procedure / page 88
each machine performs a different function / page 88

9. ENIAC / page 89

10. EDVAC / page 90
Eckert, Mauchly, and von Neumann / page 90

11. Eckert and Mauchly / page 90

12. Sperry / page 90

Key Terms

Abacus
Aiken, Howard
Analog computer
Analytical Engine
Augusta, Ada
Babbage, Charles
Chip
Difference Engine
Digital computer
Eckert, J. Presper
EDSAC
EDVAC

ENIAC
Hollerith, Herman
Jacquard, Joseph
Leibniz, Gottfried
Mark I
Mauchly, John
Microprocessor
Pascal, Blaise
Stibitz, George
UNIVAC
von Neumann, John
Wilkes, Maurice

Review Questions

Part I

1. What is the relevance of the history of computers?

2. Why did the Scientific Revolution foster an interest in computation and computational devices?

3. Why were Pascal and Leibniz unsuccessful in having their calculating devices widely accepted by society?
4. What is the significance of Jacquard's weaving loom in the history of computers?
5. Although Babbage was unsuccessful in completing his Difference Engine and the Analytical Engine, why is he frequently considered the father of the modern computer?
6. What are electrical accounting machines?

Identify the following people and devices and indicate why they are significant.

7. Blaise Pascal
8. Gottfried Leibniz
9. Jacquard weaving loom
10. Charles Babbage
11. Analytical Engine
12. Ada Augusta
13. Herman Hollerith
14. ENIAC
15. EDVAC
16. John von Neumann
17. UNIVAC
18. EDSAC
19. Mark I
20. Microprocessor

Part II
Identify the technological advances that categorized the four generations of computers.

CASE STUDY: McKing's Superburgers, Inc.

1. The computer vendors selected to make proposals for computerization of McKing's all offer sophisticated point-of-sale systems. Your supervisor asks you to prepare a brief review of the past performance of each vendor.
   a. What sources would you use for obtaining this information?
   b. What actual information would you provide that would best highlight the vendors' past performance?
2. Suppose one of the vendors has been in business since 1900 and the others are relatively new, having been founded within the last decade. Would you regard the vendor with a longer history to have a competitive edge? Explain your answer.
3. Suppose one of the vendors manufactures its own chips, while the others purchase chips from various suppliers. Would you consider this to be a factor in evaluating the vendors?
4. Suppose one of the vendors was a major manufacturer of computer equipment in the 1950s and 1960s, but has lost some of its competitive advantage in the last decade. There are reasons why such a vendor might provide you with *better* services as a result of this decline. There are also reasons why such a vendor might *not* provide you with better services as a result of this decline. Discuss both positions.

THE COMPUTER AD: A Focus on Marketing

The following ad appeared in a June 1963 issue of *Datamation*. We consider it here from a historical point of view.

OTHER COMPUTERS WERE DESIGNED FOR
BUSINESS MEN!
THE LGP-30 WAS CREATED FOR ENGINEERS
AND SCIENTISTS

What does an engineer or a scientist respect most? Answer—sheer brainpower. The LGP-30 packs more brainpower than any computer in its class. 4096 word memory—2,000 more than its nearest competitor. And alphanumeric input-output via keyboard or punched paper tape. Then comes—independence. The LGP-30 is the easiest computer to program and operate. If you know algebra—you can achieve programming competence in hours or days. Even nontechnical personnel can master it. You'll never have to be dependent upon computer programming specialists. And you can set it up right in your own office or any other point of use. No expensive installation—just plug it into a conventional outlet. Right now—scientists and engineers, in addition to businessmen, in hundreds of universities and corporations are using the LGP-30. Therefore, the LGP-30 is able to offer you the use of the most

extensive Program Library in its class. No doubt, the program you need is ready now—and that's a big saving in time and money. You also benefit from membership in the computer industry's largest, most active information-swapping pool of users. Cost? Well, let the businessmen in your organization worry about that. And there's mighty little worrying to do, for a computer with comparable capacity would cost twice as much. The LGP-30—a complete system—rents for only $1,100 per month.

Questions
1. What implications are made in the ad about the differences between business computing and scientific computing? Be specific.
2. Describe the input, output, and CPU of the LGP-30 as best you can.
3. Most modern computers are used for both business as well as scientific use. That is, there are no longer machines that are, in general, marketed for only one segment of the population. What are the advantages and disadvantages of this modern approach?
4. Explain the implications of the statement: "Cost? Well, let the businessmen in your organization worry about that."

MODULE
2

**MAINFRAMES,
MINIS, MICROS,
AND MORE**

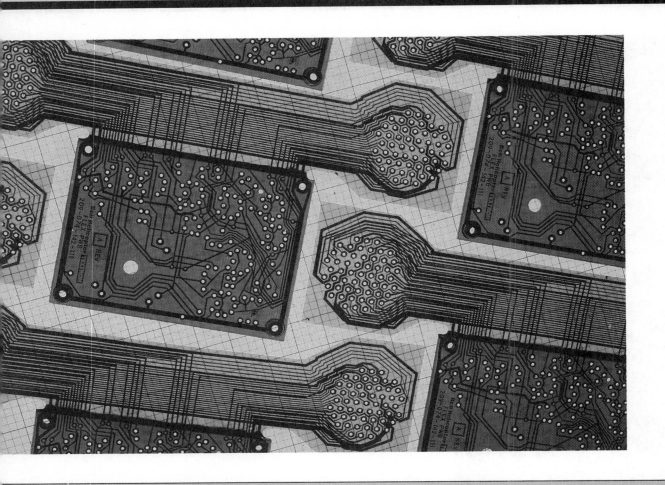

CHAPTER

4

PROCESSING OF DATA
BY COMPUTER

CHAPTER OBJECTIVES

To familiarize you with:

■ Elements of a computer system.
■ How computers operate on input data to produce output.
■ Types of computer systems.
■ Methods of processing data.
■ Internal machine representation of data.
■ Technologies used for storage.

I. THE COMPUTER SYSTEM

A series of devices that together operate as an integrated unit is called a computer system. A computer system consists of separate components or units that include the following elements:

IN A NUTSHELL

ELEMENTS OF A COMPUTER SYSTEM

1. **INPUT UNITS**
   Read input data and transmit it to the central processing unit.
2. **OUTPUT UNITS**
   Produce processed data as output.
3. **CENTRAL PROCESSING UNIT (CPU)**
   Controls all operations of a computer system; contains primary storage; runs or executes computer instructions.
4. **AUXILIARY OR SECONDARY STORAGE UNITS**
   Provide additional storage for data and programs.

The schematic in Figure 4.1 illustrates the integration of the basic elements in a computer system. Figure 4.2 shows a typical computer system with these four elements.

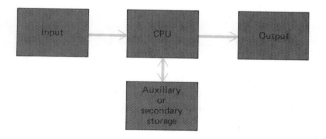

Figure 4.1
The basic elements in a computer system.

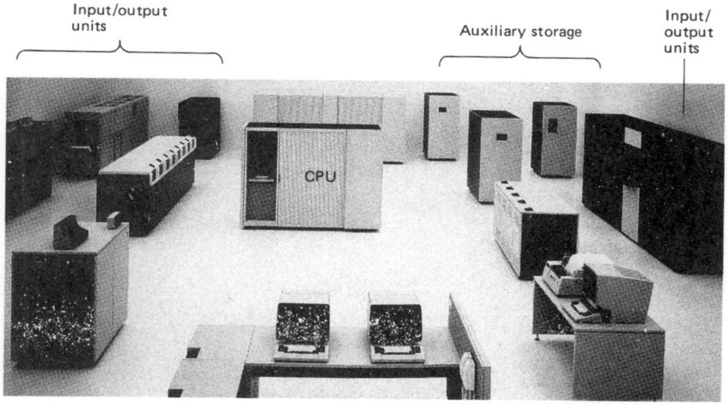

Figure 4.2
IBM 3081 computer system.
(Courtesy IBM.)

A computer system consists of a series of independent machines or hardware that function in an integrated manner to produce desired output. Thus, computer systems have a wide variety of input/output (I/O) units that can be linked to the CPU.

In this chapter we discuss the basic characteristics of the central processing unit of a computer system and how it processes data. Keep in mind that in order to operate on data at any given time, a computer must be under the control of a program, or set of instructions indicating what the inputs are and precisely what processing is required to produce the desired output. The program, written by a programmer, must be read into the CPU using an input unit before processing can begin.

A. Input Units

Each input unit of a computer system reads data from a specific input form. Disk drives read disk input; terminals read keyed input; and so on. The input device then converts the data into electronic pulses that are transmitted to an input storage area of the CPU for processing.

Each organization acquires a computer system consisting of a set of input units that are applicable for its specific needs. Thus every installation has specific input as well as output "configured" to satisfy its own unique requirements. Some systems, for example, will contain only terminals and tape drives as input units; others may include disk devices as well as numerous other input and output devices. Figure 4.3 illustrates the most common input forms and the devices that can read data from these forms.

We will consider the most common input units in Chapter 5. Note that some computer devices have both input and output components making them input/output units. A terminal, for example, typically has a keyboard that serves as input and a screen or printer that serves as output.

B. Output Units

Each output unit of a computer system accepts information from the CPU and converts it to an appropriate output form. A printer, for example, is an output unit that prints reports or graphs based on information processed and produced by the CPU. Figure 4.4 on page 106 illustrates the most common output forms and units. These are considered in detail in Chapter 6.

C. Central Processing Unit

1. How It Operates

The **central processing unit,** or **CPU,** is the unit of the computer system that controls all computer operations as follows:

CPU Operations

1. Reading of input from an input device into storage.
2. Processing of input data according to program specifications.
3. Producing information by activating an output unit.

Device	Form of Input	Description
Keyboard terminal	Data entry via keyboard 	Data is entered from remote locations.
Magnetic disk or floppy disk drive	Magnetic disk  Floppy disk 	Data is recorded as magnetized spots or bits.
Magnetic tape drive	Magnetic tape 	Data is recorded as magnetized spots or bits.
Bar code reader	Bar code 0 43000 11460	Data is recorded as a series of bars with different widths.
Optical reader	Typed or handwritten characters 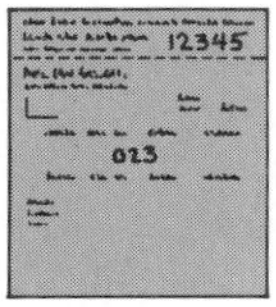 12345 013	Data is recorded on printed or handwritten forms.
Card reader	Punched card 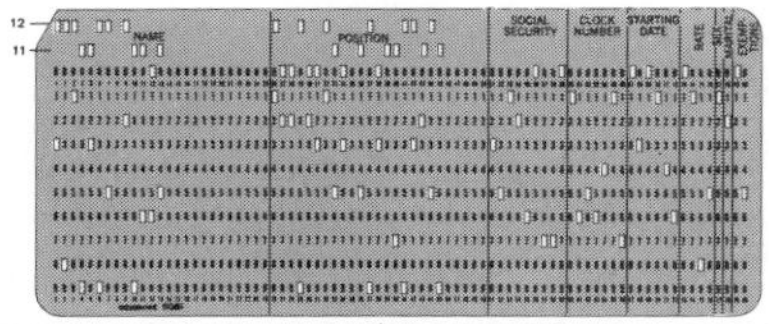	Data is recorded as punched holes.
Magnetic ink character recognition reader	Bank checks 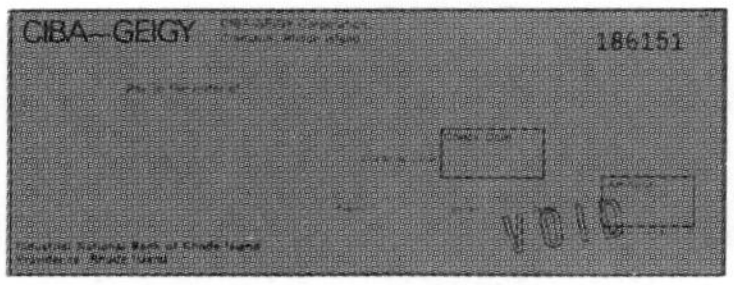 CIBA—GEIGY 186151 VOID	Data is recorded in magnetic ink on the bottom of the checks.

Figure 4.3
Sample input devices of a computer system.

Device	Form of Output	Description
Printer	**Printed report** 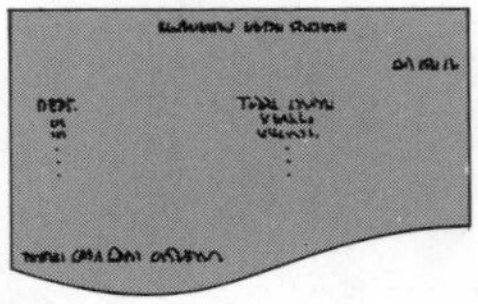	Produces a printed report.
Cathode ray tube	**Terminal display** 	This is an output device that can be used to obtain computer-produced information on a screen.
Magnetic disk or floppy disk drive	**Hard disk  Floppy disk** 	Data may be recorded on magnetic disk or a floppy disk as output.
Magnetic tape drive	**Magnetic tape** 	Data may be recorded on magnetic tape or cassette tape as output.
Plotter	**Graphic data** 	Graphs, figures, and pictures may be produced as output.
Card punch	**Punched card** 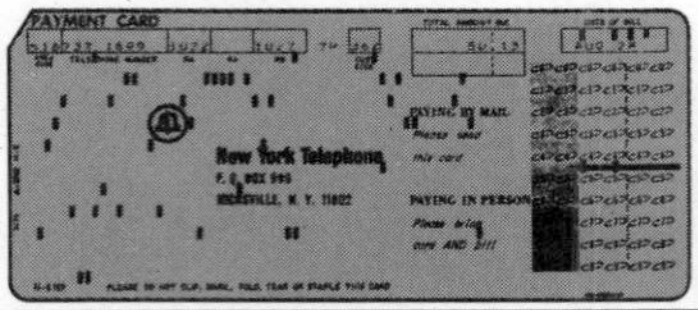	Punches cards as output.
Computer output microfilm	**Microfilm** 	Produces output as miniaturized microfilm records.

Figure 4.4
Sample output devices of a computer system.

The CPU must be linked by either cables or communication lines to all input and output units that comprise the computer system. The program, or set of instructions to process data, is read into the CPU before input can be entered and output produced.

2. The Data Processing Cycle

All data processing operations require the reading of input, the processing of input data, and the creation of output information. The data processing cycle thus means "input/process/output" for one data item; this sequence is then repeated until there is no more data to process. Let us consider a simple illustration as in Figure 4.5.

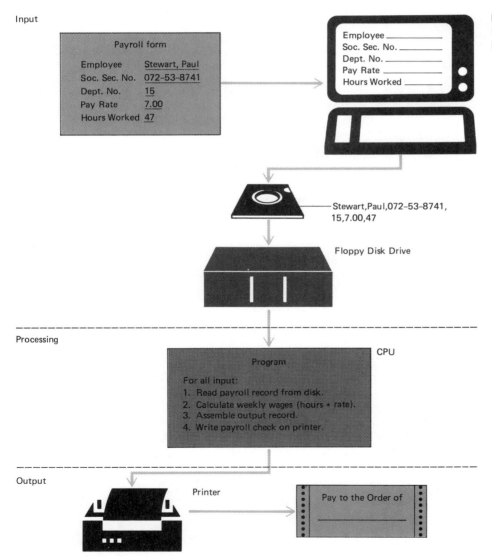

Input

Payroll form

Employee   Stewart, Paul
Soc. Sec. No.   072–53–8741
Dept. No.   15
Pay Rate   7.00
Hours Worked   47

Employee _____
Soc. Sec. No. _____
Dept. No. _____
Pay Rate _____
Hours Worked _____

Stewart,Paul,072–53–8741,
15,7.00,47

Floppy Disk Drive

Processing

CPU

Program

For all input:
1. Read payroll record from disk.
2. Calculate weekly wages (hours * rate).
3. Assemble output record.
4. Write payroll check on printer.

Output

Printer

Pay to the Order of

_____

Figure 4.5
Example of the data processing cycle.

In our illustration, the payroll form is a source document that must be translated into a machine-readable form; that is, the data must be entered using an input unit of a computer system. In our illustration, a keyboard with a cathode ray tube display was originally used for keying the data onto a mini or floppy disk. The floppy disk, then, is the input form to be read by the computer.

The central processing unit contains the program that will (1) read the data from the floppy disk, (2) store the data in the CPU, (3) process the data according to the instructions specified in the program, and (4) produce the desired output form by activating the appropriate output unit of the computer system.

The data processing cycle, then, consists of the following operations:

1. An *input* operation that activates an input unit. The input unit physically reads the data from the floppy disk and transmits it to the program's input area of the CPU.

2. A *processing* operation that can include: (a) basic arithmetic, (b) moving of data from one area within the computer to another (e.g., from an input area to an output area), or (c) logical control procedures that test for various conditions such as: is hourly rate greater than 5, has the employee worked overtime (more than 40 hours), and so on.

3. An *output* operation that transmits information from the program's output area of the CPU to an output unit that writes or records the information.

SUMMARY: Operations Performed by the CPU

1. Controls the Reading of Input
   Data is read by an input unit.
   Input data is transmitted to the CPU for processing.
2. Processes Data According to Programmed Instructions
   Data can be added, subtracted, multiplied, or divided.
   Data can be transferred from one area within the CPU to another.
   Logical tests can be performed on the data.
3. Controls the Preparation of Output
   Information is transmitted from the CPU to an output unit.
   Information is written by the output unit.

3. Components of the CPU

There are three components of the CPU:

IN A NUTSHELL

COMPONENTS OF THE CPU

1. Primary storage.
2. Control unit.
3. Arithmetic-logic unit.

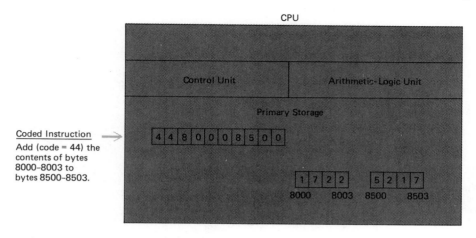

Figure 4.6
Example of data and
instructions in primary
storage.

a. Primary Storage   **Primary storage,** sometimes referred to as main memory, holds instructions and data needed for processing. Primary storage consists of storage positions within the CPU, each of which is identified with a storage address.

Each character of an instruction or each character of a data item is read into a storage position. A single storage position is called a **byte** of storage. Figure 4.6 illustrates data and instructions located in primary storage.

We will see that the primary storage capacity of very small computers like microcomputers may be as few as 4000 addressable locations or bytes. The letter K is often used as an abbreviation for approximately 1000 storage positions or bytes (it is actually equivalent to 1024 bytes). Thus we say that the **memory size** or primary storage capacity of the smallest micros is 4K.

Larger systems have primary storage capacities measured in terms of **megabytes** or millions of bytes, abbreviated MB. These systems, with primary storage capacities in the megabyte range, can process very large and complex programs with extensive input/output requirements. They can also process numerous programs concurrently, a concept known as multiprogramming.

Most businesses use computers that are classified as micros, minis, and mainframes. The primary storage capacities of these three classifications have the following basic ranges:

Primary Storage

Computer	Basic Range (can be expanded)
Micro	4K to 128K
Mini	256K to 512K
Mainframe	256K to 50+MB

Figure 4.7 illustrates some examples of mainframe capacities.

A Cross-Section of IBM Mainframes			
System	Average Storage Capacity (MB = megabytes)	System	Average Storage Capacity (MB = megabytes)
3084	64 MB	4300	16 MB
3083	32 MB	S/38	4 MB

Note: In contrast, Digital Equipment Corporation's VAX 11/780 supermini has an 8-MB average storage capacity.

Figure 4.7
Examples of mainframe
capacities.

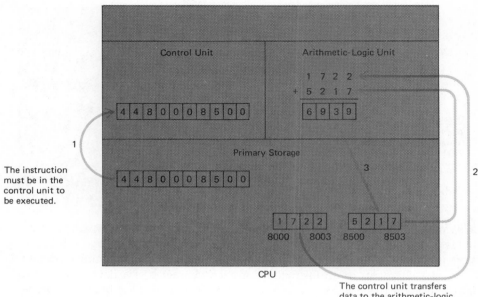

Figure 4.8
How the control unit
functions.

b. Control Unit   The **control unit** of the CPU monitors the operations performed by the entire computer system. A special program called the **supervisor** oversees all computer operations that are handled by the control unit. The supervisor is usually supplied along with the computer or is acquired from a separate vendor. It determines when each user program is to be executed and activates the appropriate input and output units as needed.

Each instruction of a user program is transferred by the supervisor from main memory to the control unit where it is executed. The control unit will also fetch any data needed for computation and place that data in the arithmetic-logic unit, as required.

The control unit handles the transfer of data from main memory to the arithmetic-logic unit and back again. Figure 4.8 illustrates this procedure.

c. Arithmetic-Logic Unit   Whenever an instruction requires an arithmetic operation or a comparison to be made, the control unit activates the **arithmetic-logic unit.**

The following list provides a summary of CPU functions:

SUMMARY: CPU Functions

1. The *control unit* fetches each instruction from *primary storage* and executes it.

   In Figure 4.8, the coded instruction will add the contents of storage positions 8000–8003 to storage positions 8500–8503.

2. If an arithmetic or logic operation is to be performed, the control unit transmits the required data to the *arithmetic-logic unit*.

   In Figure 4.8, the contents of storage locations 8000–8003 and the contents of storage locations 8500–8503 are placed in the arithmetic-logic unit for addition.

3. If an arithmetic operation or a comparison is required, the arithmetic-logic unit will operate on the data.

   In Figure 4.8, the addition of the two areas is performed in this unit.

4. The control unit returns all results to primary storage.

   In Figure 4.8, the control unit transmits the sum to primary storage.

D. Auxiliary Storage Units

Despite the large storage capacities of many CPUs, there is usually a need for **auxiliary** or secondary **storage** that is not part of the CPU which makes additional storage available as required. This auxiliary storage contains programs and data that will be called into the CPU when needed.

The most common auxiliary storage media are magnetic disks and sometimes magnetic tapes that can store millions or even billions of bytes of data, and hundreds of programs. Other mass storage devices are also sometimes used for auxiliary storage as will be seen in Chapter 7.

Auxiliary storage increases the total storage capacity of the computer system in a way that is far cheaper than increasing primary storage. The access of data and programs from auxiliary storage is very fast, although not as fast as main memory access time.

II. TYPES OF COMPUTER SYSTEMS

It is virtually impossible to definitively categorize computers by size, cost, or scope. Even computer manufacturers do not always agree on what distinguishes a minicomputer from a microcomputer, for example.

This lack of any standard method of categorizing computers has resulted in a significant amount of confusion for the user. In addition, any textbook's effort to categorize computers is, to some extent, arbitrary. We will use the categories discussed in this section simply as guidelines.

Note that these categories are designed to serve as typical ranges only. The user is apt to find, for example, that one manufacturer markets its computer as a ''mini'' when it might fit into another manufacturer's category as a mainframe.

Note, too, that even the terms used for defining these categories are not standardized. Some manufacturers, for example, subdivide their mainframes into ''large scale,'' ''medium'' and ''small''; others use terms like ''maxi'' and ''midi.''

Similarly, some micros may be marketed as home computers, personal computers, or small business computers.

With these limitations in mind, we will now provide an analysis of each category of computer.

IN A NUTSHELL

A COMPARISON OF COMPUTERS

Category	Memory Size	Basic Cost
Supercomputer	Hundreds of mega-bytes	$10 million +
Mainframe	256K–50 + MBs	Several hundred thousand dollars–$5 million
Minicomputer	256K–512K (expandable to several MBs)	$10,000–$150,000
Microcomputer	4K–128K in basic form (add-on memory is available)	Under $100–$10,000

A. Supercomputers

Supercomputers are the fastest, largest, and costliest computers available. Their speed, for example, is in the 100 million instructions-per-second range (sometimes abbreviated as MIPS). This speed begins to approach the fastest measurable speed of any machine. Supercomputers are usually too expensive and too large for typical business applications. They tend to be used primarily for scientific applications in weather forecasting, aircraft design, nuclear research, and seismic analysis. Commercially, supercomputers are sometimes used as *host* processors in large networks that process data from thousands of remote stations. Supercomputers are sometimes used for time-sharing as well. In total, there are less than several hundred of these computers in use in the entire United States.

Only the very large computer manufacturers such as IBM, Control Data, Amdahl, and Burroughs build supercomputers. One company, Cray Research, specializes in supercomputers and offers extremely sophisticated hardware and processors. Figure 4.9 shows a supercomputer. Figure 4.10 provides an analysis of how supercomputers are used in the United States.

B. Mainframes

Mainframes are the traditional medium and large-scale computer systems used in most business organizations for (1) information processing in a centralized or distributed mode and (2) data communications applications where terminals at remote locations transmit data to a central processing unit.

A mainframe typically has an advanced control system and is capable of linking up with dozens of input/output units, and even minis for additional computer power. It can perform usually up to 10 MIPS, that is, 10 million instructions per second. Figure 4.11 gives an example of a mainframe.

Figure 4.9
The Cray-1 Supercomputer.
(Courtesy National Center
for Atmospheric Research.)

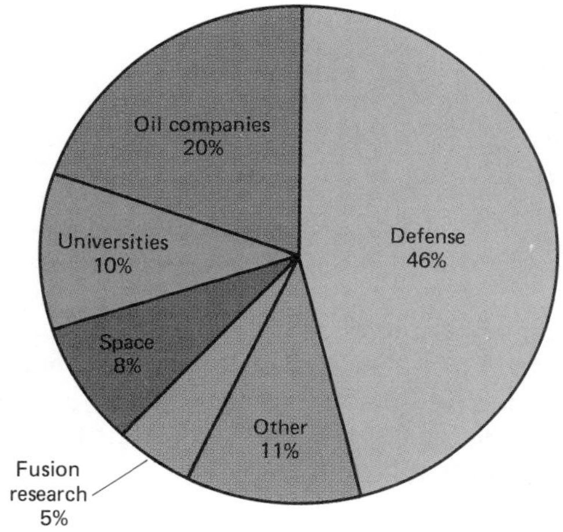

Figure 4.10
An analysis of how
supercomputers are used in
the United States.

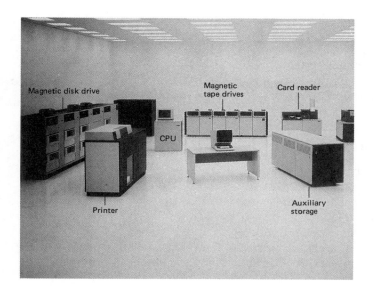

Figure 4.11
IBM 4341 computer system.
(Courtesy IBM.)

Most computer manufacturers provide a family of "upgradable" or upwardly compatible mainframes. The lowest number in the family represents the smallest computer. Higher-number machines within the family are fully compatible with lower numbers so that a company can upgrade without fear of incompatibility in terms of software and hardware. For example, NCR has an 8000 series of computers; the 8200 is a smaller model within the series and the 8600 is a larger model in that same series. If a user trades in the NCR 8200 for the larger 8600, it can be relatively assured that all current software and hardware will be compatible. Similarly, an IBM 4331 is a computer within the 4300 line that is smaller than, but compatible with, the IBM 4341.

The largest mainframe manufacturers and some of their series of computers are listed as follows.

⫸ Examples of Series of Computers

Manufacturer	Family
IBM	4300 Series
	3300 Series
Honeywell	700 Series
NCR	8000 Series
Burroughs	700 Series
	800 Series
	900 Series
Sperry	1100 Series

There are many other computers manufactured by the above companies and by a wide variety of other manufacturers as well. In addition, many manufacturers offer one-of-a-kind models designed for specific small business or office automation applications. The following sample list illustrates the different categories of mainframes that are available.

⫸ Categories of Mainframes

Type of Mainframe	Example
Small business computer	IBM s/34
"Midi" business computer system	IBM s/38
Medium-sized general purpose system	NCR 7050
Large-sized general purpose system	NCR 8600

C. Minicomputers

Minicomputers have become very popular in business, either to replace or supplement existing computer power. Minis are frequently used to add computer power in a company that has an existing mainframe. When a mainframe's capacity or power is no longer adequate, the user has the choice of *upgrading*, that is, replacing the mainframe, or adding computer power, typically with the use of minis. Minis can easily be made to interact with mainframes for a wide variety of business applications by adding hardware interfaces and some appropriate software.

Sometimes an organization decides to decentralize or distribute its computer power to various stations or locations within user departments. Minicomputers are ideal for processing data in a decentralized mode since they are small, yet powerful enough for many applications. Indeed, some companies have eliminated their mainframes entirely and depend solely on minis. In addition, minis can be useful for distributed functions, taking some of the load off the mainframe. Moreover, minis have also made it possible for many smaller organizations to afford a computer for the first time.

The minicomputer category, like the mainframe category, varies widely. There are "superminis" manufactured by companies like the Digital Equipment Corporation, Prime, and Wang that are competitive with mainframes in terms of size, speed, and applicability, yet they can cost thousands of dollars less. Figure 4.12 illustrates Digital Equipment Corporation's supermini called the VAX.

Figure 4.12
Example of a supermini.
Inset is close-up of CPU.
(Courtesy Digital Equipment Corp.)

D. Microcomputers

The increasing use of micros for home, school, business, or professional offices has been even more revolutionary. Although these computers have limited memory and speed, their cost makes them very attractive for applications that would otherwise not find computerization feasible. Moreover, micros, like minis, are frequently used to provide additional computer power for companies that already have mainframes or minis.

Initially, smaller firms (such as Radio Shack, Commodore, and Apple) dominated the microcomputer market. When the huge marketing success of these machines became evident, many major manufacturers such as IBM and Digital Equipment Corporation began to manufacture micros that have also become highly competitive.

Because of the huge growth in the mini and microcomputer field, we will consider these computers and their associated input/output units in Chapter 9. The next two chapters consider hardware more commonly associated with mainframes.

Most companies have a mix of different sized computers and I/O units called "peripherals" that can be accessed by these computers. See Figure 4.13 for an analysis of the average computer equipment used by a medium-sized company.

E. Plug-Compatible Input/Output Equipment to Accompany a CPU

A computer system is typically identified by the name or number of its CPU. A VAX 11/780, for example, manufactured by the Digital Equipment Corporation, will have the number "11/780" on its CPU. Separate input, output, and auxiliary storage units are then configured for this CPU to provide a computer system that will satisfy each user's needs. Thus a disk drive used with a VAX 11/780 system might be the same drive manufactured by DEC or other vendors for numerous systems.

Until two decades ago, a computer manufacturer was able to sell *as a package* a fully configured system with all peripherals. This meant the user typically bought or leased an entire computer system from the same vendor as a packaged product. Now, vendors are required to offer hardware that is *unbundled,* meaning that each unit must be made available as a separate item with an individual unit price. As a result, there are independent vendors that specialize in providing specific input/output units which are **plug-compatible** with numerous CPUs. Thus the user need not utilize only Burroughs hardware with a Burroughs CPU. Instead, an organization is free to acquire the most efficient input/output units that can be found which will satisfy its needs.

F. Evaluating Computer Systems

Computer systems are assessed in terms of the following criteria.

IN A NUTSHELL

CRITERIA USED FOR EVALUATING COMPUTER SYSTEMS

1. Memory size.
2. Cost.
3. Speed.
4. Number and type of I/O units.
5. Software availability.
6. Upward compatibility.
7. Ease of using plug-compatible input/output units with the computer system.
8. Unique or special features that make the system ideal for particular applications.
9. Maintenance costs.

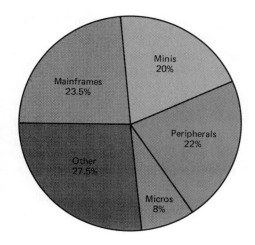

Figure 4.13
Analysis of an average
hardware budget for a
medium-sized company.

After deciding which category of computer would best satisfy a user's needs, the actual system to be acquired must be determined. This is usually a committee decision in which users and computer professionals participate.

Note that *time-sharing* is always an alternative to acquiring one's own system. That is, an organization can always rent or lease CPU time from a company that specializes in providing computer services to user organizations. An organization can also contract with a consultant or service bureau to provide all its computational needs.

Self-Evaluating Quiz

1. (T or F) All IBM 3033 systems have the same CPU and the same input/output units.

2. (T or F) The reading of input data by an input unit of a computer system is performed under the control of a CPU.

3. Another term for a CPU's primary storage is _____.

4. A single storage position is called a _____ of storage.

5. K is a letter used to represent approximately _(no.)_ bytes of storage; the designation MB is used to represent _(no.)_ bytes of storage.

6. The _____ of the CPU monitors the operations performed by the computer system.

7. The program that controls the overall operations of the CPU is called the _____.

8. Arithmetic or logic operations are performed by the _____ unit of the CPU.

9. Results of an arithmetic operation are transmitted to primary storage by the _____ unit.

10. Magnetic _____ and _____ are commonly used as auxiliary storage media.

11. (T or F) Most large companies use supercomputers.

12. (T or F) Centralized computer systems used by most large organizations are classified as mainframes.

13. (T or F) An IBM 4331 is fully compatible with an IBM 4341 within the IBM 4300 series.
14. (T or F) IBM was the first manufacturer of microcomputers.
15. If a company cannot afford its own mainframe, it can rent or lease computer time from a(n) _____ company.

Solutions

1. F—Each computer is configured with input/output units to satisfy its own individual needs.
2. T
3. main memory
4. byte
5. 1000 (actually 1024) one million (one megabyte)
6. control unit
7. supervisor
8. arithmetic-logic
9. control
10. disk
    tape
11. F—Most large companies use mainframes; supercomputers are used for specific scientific functions and by a very small number of companies.
12. T
13. T
14. F—IBM manufactures micros, but there were numerous smaller companies like Apple, Commodore, and Radio Shack who manufactured them first.
15. time-sharing (or service bureau)

III. METHODS OF PROCESSING DATA

A CPU may be used to process data in a variety of ways. We consider the most common methods as follows:

▐▐▐➡ Methods of Processing Data

1. Batch processing.
2. Immediate processing.

A. Batch Processing

Batch processing means that data is collected in groups or batches and entered into the computer in large volumes. Using this method, data is *not* processed immediately as it is transacted. Instead, data is collected and processed in large groups at fixed intervals.

For example, invoices of items received by a company's warehouse may be collected from the inventory staff at the end of the day. These invoices may be used on a daily basis to update, or make current, the quantity on hand for each part number stocked by the company. Similarly, a key-to-disk device may be used to key the inventory data and store it on a disk in a key-to-storage procedure; the disk is then used at a later date for future batch processing.

If this key-to-disk procedure for storing inventory data is performed by a device not directly under the control of the mainframe, it is called an **off-line operation.** Figure 4.14 illustrates a batch processing procedure that (1) uses a key-to-disk operation for storing data and (2) then processes the disk in a batch mode.

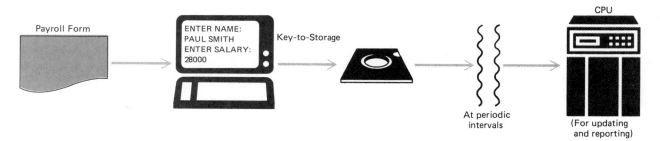

Figure 4.14
Example of a batch processing procedure.

A batch operation is ideal for applications that do not require immediate processing. It is easier and cheaper to process data in batch mode than if immediate processing were required.

Batch processing is, however, suitable only if there is no urgency about processing records as soon as the data is transacted or entered. To wait a fixed period of time to process data means that for a period of time, the master file or data base is not as current as it could be. Many payroll applications, for example, use batch processing. Data such as time cards and payroll change reports can be used to alter a payroll file once a week just before paychecks are produced. Immediate processing may simply not be required in this instance since the payroll file needs to be current only once a week, when paychecks are produced.

But consider as an example a master accounts receivable file, which contains all customer data. Each time a customer makes a purchase, a record of the transaction is created. If the transaction records are used to update the accounts receivable master file at the beginning of each day, then the master file is only current once a day. It does not contain transactions that have been made during the course of the day, that is, since the last batch update procedure. This may be acceptable for some organizations, but may not be suitable in all instances, especially if it is desirable to check whether a customer's credit limit has been exceeded at the time each sale is made.

In addition, if a customer service department exists to answer customer inquiries, for example, a master file that is batch processed cannot be counted on to contain current information. In short, for some accounts receivable systems where cost is a major factor, batch processing is used; for others, alternative methods of processing are employed.

Despite the disadvantages of batch processing, it is widely used for many applications where (1) records can easily be collected in groups and (2) a master file or data base need not be current all the time.

In summary, batch operations frequently process data that has been stored on floppy disk or magnetic tape in a key-to-disk or key-to-tape procedure; moreover, older, punched card systems process data in batch mode. All such operations are referred to as **key-to-storage procedures** and they are usually performed off-line, that is, not directly under the control of the main CPU.

Tapes and disks are ideally suited for processing high-volume files in a batch mode. The data stored on the tape or disk may be manually transported or electronically transmitted to the CPU where it is periodically processed.

B. Immediate Processing

Sometimes, however, data must be processed *immediately* as soon as it is transacted. In this case, *terminals* are used at the point where the data is generated. As transactions are made, the data is entered using the terminal. That data is then immediately transmitted to the CPU, typically with the use of either telephone lines or direct cables.

In short, **immediate processing** of data requires on-line operations, where an **on-line operation** is one that uses devices directly connected to the CPU either for data entry or for inquiring about the status of a file. With a terminal,

Figure 4.15
An example of an on-line hotel reservation system. This Holiday Inn Holidex nationwide reservation system utilizes keyboard display terminals. (Courtesy Teletype Corp.)

we can either enter data, or ask questions about some record or file that is stored by the computer. Figure 4.15 gives an example of immediate processing.

Real-Time Processing: When Immediate Processing Is Quick Enough to Enable Users to Make Decisions   We have seen that immediate processing usually requires data entry using a terminal. That data can be used to update a file immediately on entry or to inquire about the status of existing records. If the processing of transactions or changes is performed immediately, and inquiries into the updated file can then be made quickly enough to enable the user to make decisions, this is called **real-time processing.** Real-time processing then is one type of high-speed immediate processing. Figure 4.16 illustrates a real-time application.

Airline reservation systems, for example, that use a network of terminals require high-speed immediate processing in a real-time environment. Each time

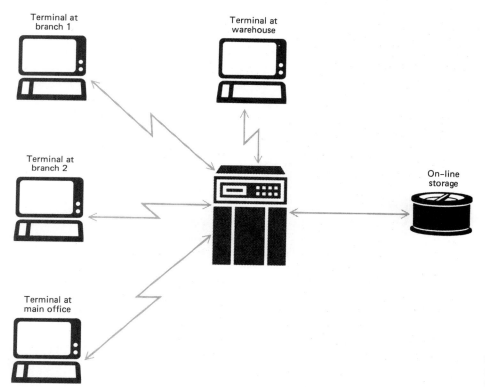

Figure 4.16
Illustration of a real-time inventory system.

a ticket is issued or canceled, or a plane's schedule is altered, the data must be immediately entered into a computer, processed, and made available very quickly so that users can make appropriate decisions about which flight to book. Even though hundreds of airline data-entry operations are performed concurrently throughout the world, they all must be processed quickly enough to enable each user to decide on an immediate course of action. This is categorized as real-time processing.

Figure 4.17 compares the major methods of processing data. Note that real-time processing implies the use of immediate processing with on-line procedures.

Figure 4.17
Comparison of the major
methods of processing data.

Batch Processing
1. Periodic processing.
2. Input data usually sequenced.

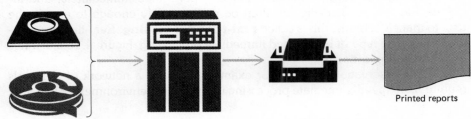

Printed reports

Immediate Processing

1. Input can be entered at point of transaction.
2. Input data is usually not sequenced.
3. Responses to inquiries are made immediately.

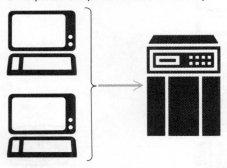

Real-Time Processing

1. Immediate processing of data entered.
2. Results can be produced quickly enough to affect decision making.

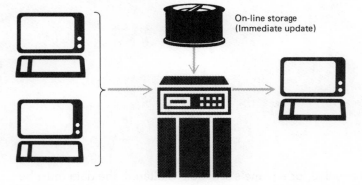

On-line storage
(Immediate update)

SUMMARY: Batch Versus Immediate Processing

Batch
1. Data is read into the computer at fixed intervals rather than immediately.

Immediate
1. As data is collected, it is entered into the computer with the use of terminal devices that are directly connected to the CPU.

Batch

2. Files are not always current since data used to update them is not immediately entered.

3. We will see that tape, cards, and sometimes disks can be batch processed.

4. Terminals or other devices may be used for data entry; the data would then usually be stored on tapes or disks for future batch processing.

Immediate

2. As data is entered on-line into the computer, it may be immediately used to update files and thus keep them current at all times. If the updating process is performed quickly enough to enable a user to then inquire about the status of the file after it has been updated, this is called real-time processing.

3. We will see in Chapter 7 that magnetic disks are usually up-dated immediately and tape is usually updated in batch mode.

4. Terminals are usually used to enter data in an immediate mode.

Self-Evaluating Quiz

1. (T or F) Terminals may only be used for on-line processing.

2. When a terminal is used to enter data directly on a disk that is not connected to a CPU, this is called a(n) _____ operation.

3. (T or F) When terminal data is processed immediately, this is always a real-time procedure.

4. Suppose payroll changes need to be processed by a computer before pay-checks are printed each week. These payroll changes are best processed in a(n) (batch/on-line) mode. Explain your answer.

5. Suppose an accounts receivable system has terminals at each cash register for entering charge account sales. The terminals may be directly connected to a CPU in a(n) (batch/on-line) mode if immediate updating of the ac-counts receivable customer file is required. If, however, the file needs to be updated only once a day, the terminals can be used for entering data on a disk that is processed at a later time in a(n) (batch/on-line) mode.

6. (T or F) Suppose you are a customer at Lacy's Department Store and you call to inquire about the status of your account. You would like to determine how much money you need in your checking account to pay your bill. If the customer account representative tells you that your balance due is $550 and you know that this balance does *not* include today's purchases, then this system would be called a real-time system.

7. (T or F) Suppose a bank maintains customer accounts in a centralized file. If a teller uses a touch-tone phone to key in data pertaining to withdrawals and deposits, then the system must be real-time.

8. Off-line processing usually uses _____ devices for entering terminal data and storing it on tapes or disks.

9. When records are processed at fixed intervals (i.e., once a day or once a week), we call this _____.

10. (T or F) Real-time processing of data always involves immediate accessibility to a CPU.

Solutions

1. F—A terminal can be used in an off-line procedure to store data on a tape or disk using a key-to-storage device (key-to-tape or key-to-disk).

2. off-line (or key-to-storage)

3. F—If the terminal data is used for inquiry only, or if it is queued and used to update a master file only when there is time, this is not real-time processing.

4. batch—There is no need for immediate or on-line accessibility to a CPU or to a payroll file.

5. on-line
   batch

6. F—It does *not* include immediate updating of records.

7. F—It may be on-line but it is not necessarily real-time (e.g., keyed entries may go to a disk that is used to update the customer accounts file *every* hour).

8. key-to-storage (key-to-tape and key-to-disk)

9. batch processing

10. T

IV. INTRODUCTION TO COMPUTER TECHNOLOGY

A. Data Representation

People commonly communicate with one another using data consisting of letters of the alphabet (A to Z), digits (0 to 9), and special symbols such as $, ., -, and so on. Computers are capable of reading such characters into primary storage but this data must be converted into a form that permits high-speed internal processing.

All computers use some variation of the **binary numbering system** for representing every character, where a **character** is defined as a letter, digit, or special symbol.

In the binary numbering system, there are only two possible digits: 0 and 1. This system is ideal for computer processing because the "1" is used to denote the presence of an electrical pulse or signal in the computer circuitry, and a "0" is used to denote the absence of such a signal. Figure 4.18 illustrates how the computer utilizes the binary numbering system.

We begin by considering how binary and decimal numbers can be converted one into the other. Then we focus on how the computer actually stores characters internally, using a form of binary representation.

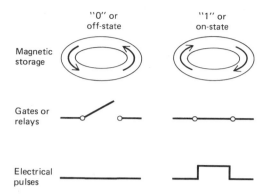

Figure 4.18
How the computer utilizes
the binary numbering
system.

1. Binary Representation

Most numbering systems are called "positional," because the physical location
or position of a digit within the number affects the value. For example, in a
positional numbering system, the number 23 has a different value than the
number 32 even though the digits are the same. In positional numbering systems, the *place value* is critical.

Recall that the decimal or base 10 system has the following positional
values:

. . .	10^3	10^2	10^1	10^0	Exponential value of position
	1000	100	10	1	Decimal value of position

A 1 in the second or tens position and a 0 in the units position (10) is the
number following 9. After we reach 9, there are no more single digits; thus we
proceed to the next position, the tens position, initializing the units position with
0. 10, then, is the decimal number following 9.

In the base 10 or decimal system, each position has a value that is a factor
of 10. The first position has a value of 10^0 or 1, the second has a value of 10^1
or 10, . . .; the seventh position would have a value of 10^6 or 1,000,000, and
so on.

The binary numbering system has a base of 2. Thus each position has a
place value that is a factor of 2. We have then:

. . .	2^4	2^3	2^2	2^1	2^0	Exponential value of position
	16	8	4	2	1	Decimal value of position

Any number raised to the zero power is 1; therefore, the units position has
a place value of 2^0 or 1. The second position has a value of 2^1 or 2 (any number
raised to the first power is the number itself). The third position has a value of
2^2 or $2 \times 2 = 4$; and so on.

In the binary numbering system, we have only two digits, 0 and 1. To represent the number 2 in binary we have already, in effect, run out of digits; hence we must initialize the units position and proceed with the position adjacent to the units position—the 2's position. That is, 10 in binary is 2 in decimal.

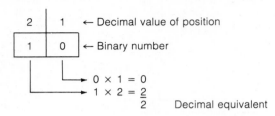

We say, then, that 10_2 (10 in base 2) $= 2_{10}$ (2 in base 10). In our illustration the subscript represents the base. A 3 in base 2 would be 11; to represent a 4 we must initialize the two rightmost positions and place a 1 in the next or 4's position. Thus 100 in binary is a 4 in decimal. A 5 would be 101. Notice that the sequence is 0, 1, then proceed to the next position and initialize the previous one (10, 11, 100, and so on).

Binary	Decimal	Binary	Decimal	Binary	Decimal	Binary	Decimal
0	0	100	4	1000	8	1100	12
1	1	101	5	1001	9	1101	13
10	2	110	6	1010	10	1110	14
11	3	111	7	1011	11	1111	15

Using the binary numbering system, the computer can represent any decimal number with a series of on-off circuits, where "on" is represented by a binary 1 and "off" is represented by a binary 0.

2. Determining the Decimal Equivalent of a Binary Number

All positional numbering systems have similar structures. To obtain the decimal equivalent of a number in any base, multiply the digits by their positional values and add the results.

Example 1

$1001_2 = (?)_{10}$. Find the decimal equivalent of 1001 in binary (represented as 1001_2, where the subscript denotes the base).

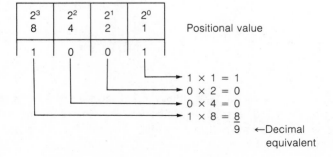

Thus, $1001_2 = 9_{10}$. We can simplify this calculation by eliminating all multiplications where 0 is a factor. Thus we have:

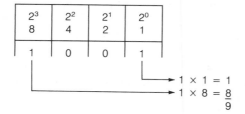

In short, the binary digit with a positional value of 8 and the binary digit with a positional value of 1 are "on"; the others are "off." That is, the 8-bit and the 1-bit are on, where **bit** is an abbreviation for *binary digit*.

Example 2

$1110_2 = (?)_{10}$.

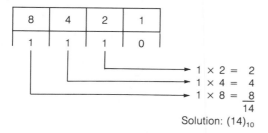

Solution: $(14)_{10}$

Example 3

$11101_2 = (?)_{10}$.

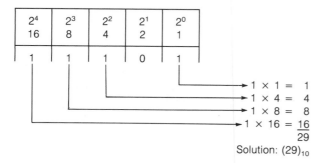

Solution: $(29)_{10}$

Given any binary number we can find its decimal equivalent by the following technique.

Given a Binary Number—Find the Decimal Equivalent

1. Determine the positional or place value of each digit.
2. Add the place values for all positions that contain a 1.

3. Determining the Binary Equivalent of a Decimal Number

Computers generally represent numeric data in binary form or some variation of this form, where digits are indicated by a series of on-off switches, circuits, or magnetized bits. Keep in mind that numeric data is entered, as input, in standard decimal form and then converted by the computer itself to a binary representation. Before the data is produced as output it is again converted to decimal form for readability.

Thus far, we have focused on the way in which binary numbers are converted into decimal numbers. In this section, we will consider the manner in which the binary equivalent of a decimal number may be determined.

This conversion process is a relatively simple task when small numbers are used. We merely employ the positional values of binary numbers to find the right combination of digits.

Example 1

$10_{10} = (?)_2$. This example focuses on determining what combination of 1, 2, 4, 8, 16, 32, . . . will equal 10.

It is clear that we do not need to use more than four binary digits to represent 10_{10}, since the fifth positional value is 2^4 or 16, which is greater than 10_{10}. Hence, we must determine what combination of 8, 4, 2, 1 will equal 10.

There is only one such combination. The numbers $8 + 2 = 10$. Thus our binary equivalent is:

8	4	2	1
1	0	1	0

In order to represent the decimal number 10 in binary form, the 8-bit (or *binary digit*) and the 2-bit are "on" while the others are off.

Thus, $10_{10} = 1010_2$.

Example 2

$(14)_{10} = (?)_2$. Here, again, we use four binary digits since the next position has value 16, which exceeds the required quantity. Again, we must determine what combination of 8, 4, 2, 1 will produce 14.

There is only one such combination: the 8-, 4-, 2-bits are "on" ($8 + 4 + 2 = 14$), while the 1-bit is "off."

Thus, $(14)_{10} = (1110)_2$.

Example 3

$(23)_{10} = (?)_2$. Here, we must use a combination of the numbers 16, 8, 4, 2, 1 that will produce 23. We must determine which bits are "on." The 16-bit must be on, since the 8-, 4-, 2-, 1-bits can produce a maximum decimal number of 15. Thus the 16-bit must be "on" to obtain a number larger than 15. The 8-bit is "off" since 16-8 produces 24, which exceeds the required number. Thus the 16-4-2-1-bits are "on" and only the 8-bit is "off." We have, then,

$$(23)_{10} = (10111)_2$$

The method we have been using to determine the combination of positional values that produces the required number is useful only with small numbers. Consider the task of finding the combination of binary numbers for the decimal number 1087, for example. In short, the above method is rather cumbersome for larger decimal numbers. When larger numbers are to be converted, the remainder method described in Appendix C is used. (Appendix C provides a more thorough discussion of conversion procedures, binary arithmetic, and other numbering systems that are used for computer processing.)

Self-Evaluating Quiz

1. The decimal system has a base of _(no.)_ while the binary system has a base of _(no.)_ .

2. Since numbers are frequently represented within the computer as a series of on-off switches, the _____ numbering system is exceedingly well suited to computer processing.

3. (T or F) All numbers must be fed into the computer in binary form.

4. (T or F) There are numbers that can be expressed in base 2 that cannot be expressed in base 10.

5. (T or F) In general, more binary digits are necessary to represent a number than are necessary in the decimal numbering system.

6. $2^2 =$ _____.

7. $2^5 =$ _____.

8. $2^3 =$ _____.

9. $10^2 =$ _____.

10. Find the decimal equivalent for each of the following:
    a. 11011_2
    b. 1101_2
    c. 1111_2
    d. 11001_2
    e. 11111_2

11. The binary numbering system uses _(no.)_ digits.

12. The digits used in the binary numbering system are _____ and _____.

13. The binary numbering system is ideally suited to computer processing because the digit _____ represents the on-state and the digit _____ represents the off-state.

14. The term "bit" is an abbreviation for _____ _____ .

15. The decimal and binary numbering systems are called _____ numbering systems because the location or position of each digit is significant.

16. (T or F) Any number raised to the zero power is 1.

17. The binary number 1011 is equivalent to the decimal number _____.

18. The binary number 110110 is equivalent to the decimal number _____.

19. The binary number 11101 is equivalent to the decimal number _____.

20. The largest decimal number that can be represented by four binary digits is _____.

21. The binary equivalent of the decimal number 86 is _____.

22. The binary equivalent of the decimal number 101 is _____.

Solutions

1. 10; 2

2. binary or base 2

3. F—Decimal numbers as well as binary numbers can be entered as input. Decimal numbers will, however, be converted into binary form or some variation of binary form before they are processed.

4. F

5. T—For example, 16 in base 10 uses two digits but requires five in binary (10000).

6. $2^2 = 2 \times 2 = 4$

7. $2^5 = 2 \times 2 \times 2 \times 2 \times 2 = 32$

8. 8

9. 100

10.

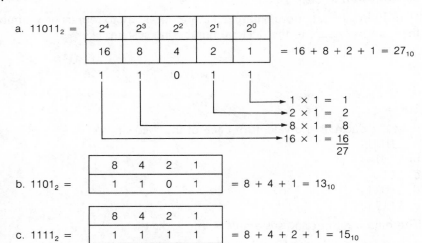

a. $11011_2 =$	2^4	2^3	2^2	2^1	2^0	
	16	8	4	2	1	$= 16 + 8 + 2 + 1 = 27_{10}$
	1	1	0	1	1	

$1 \times 1 = 1$
$2 \times 1 = 2$
$8 \times 1 = 8$
$16 \times 1 = \underline{16}$
27

	8	4	2	1	
b. $1101_2 =$	1	1	0	1	$= 8 + 4 + 1 = 13_{10}$

	8	4	2	1	
c. $1111_2 =$	1	1	1	1	$= 8 + 4 + 2 + 1 = 15_{10}$

	16	8	4	2	1	
d. $11001_2 =$	1	1	0	0	1	$= 16 + 8 + 1 = 25_{10}$

	16	8	4	2	1	
e. $11111_2 =$	1	1	1	1	1	$= 16 + 8 + 4 + 2 + 1 = 31_{10}$

11. two

12. 0; 1

13. 1
    0

14. *binary digit*

15. positional

16. T

17. 11:

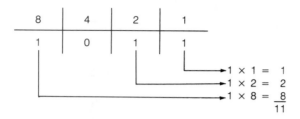

18. 54:

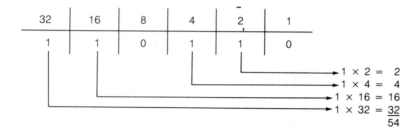

19. 29:

16	8	4	2	1
1	1	1	0	1

16 + 8 + 4 + 1 = 29

20. 15 ($1111_2 = 15_{10}$)
21. $(1010110)_2$
22. $(1100101)_2$

4. Representation of Characters in Storage

We have seen that, through a combination of on-off pulses, it is possible to represent any decimal digit. These on-off pulses are called bits, where a bit is an abbreviation for binary digit.

Recall that each storage position in main memory is called a byte. If each byte contained four digit bits, representing the decimal numbers 8-4-2-1, it would be possible to represent any of the decimal digits 0 to 9. That is, with 8-4-2-1 we can represent the decimal digits 0 to 9, as well as numbers 10 to 15 (see Figure 4.19).

In short, four bits in each byte are used to represent a single decimal digit. An "on" bit means that an electric current is present and an "off" bit means that no current is present.

But what about the representation of alphabetic characters or special symbols? How can they be represented using binary digits or bits? To accommodate these characters, the computer frequently uses an 8-bit code with four *zone bits* as well as four *digit bits:*

The four leftmost bits are called *zone bits.*

The four rightmost bits are called *digit bits.*

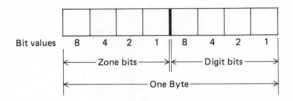

Thus each storage position or byte consists of eight data bits; four are used for zone representation and four are used for digit representation. One computer code frequently used to represent letters, digits, and special symbols is called **EBCDIC,** which is an abbreviation for *Extended Binary Coded Decimal Interchange Code.* The four zone bits are used to indicate codes for letters, unsigned numbers, positive numbers, negative numbers, and special characters. The digit bits can be used to represent the numbers 0 to 9 using four bits. For example, 1111 in the zone bits designates a character as an unsigned number; 1100 in the zone bits indicates that the character will be one of the letters A–I. If 1100 appears in the four zone bits, the digit bits then will indicate which specific letter from A–I is being represented. Figure 4.20 illustrates the EBCDIC code.

Figure 4.19
The binary equivalents of decimal digits 0 to 15.

Decimal Digit	Bits			
	8	4	2	1
0	0	0	0	0
1	0	0	0	1
2	0	0	1	0
3	0	0	1	1
4	0	1	0	0
5	0	1	0	1
6	0	1	1	0
7	0	1	1	1
8	1	0	0	0
9	1	0	0	1
10	1	0	1	0
11	1	0	1	1
12	1	1	0	0
13	1	1	0	1
14	1	1	1	0
15	1	1	1	1

EBCDIC uses a ninth bit called a check or *parity bit* that minimizes the risk of transmission errors. On *even parity* computers, there must always be an even number of bits on in one storage position at any time. The parity bit is turned on in order to ensure that there is an *even* number of bits on at all times. Consider the digit 2, for example, which is represented as follows:

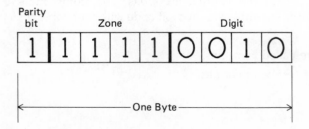

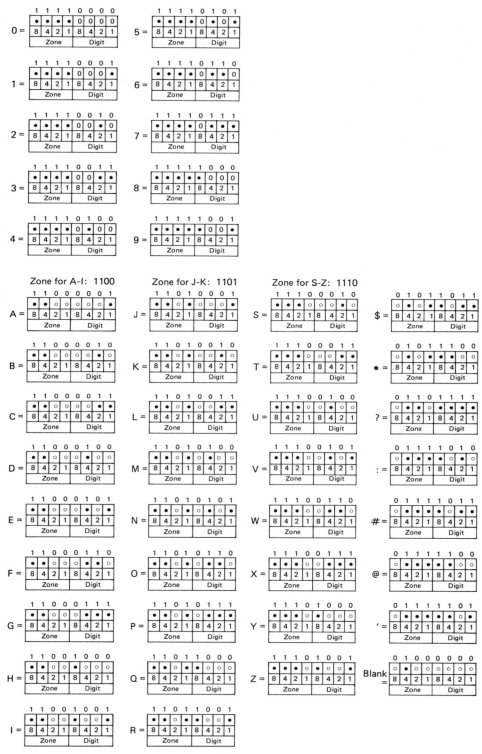

Figure 4.20

The EBCDIC code for numbers,

letters, and selected special characters.

The parity bit would be turned on because without it there are an odd number of bits on. If a character results in an even number of bits on, the parity bit remains off. In this way, the loss or gain of a single bit in transmission would be easily detected by the computer itself since that would result in an odd number of bits on. There are also odd parity computers, as well, which require an odd number of bits on at all times.

Figure 4.21 (at right) provides an example of how this 9-bit code, including the parity bit, is used to represent specific data in storage for even parity computers. Each character is stored in one byte or storage location, which consists of 9 bits.

EBCDIC is not the only computer code, although it is used by many computers. BCD or Binary Coded Decimal is an older code for internal computer representation. **ASCII** is another common computer code. ASCII is an ab-

Figure 4.22
The bit configurations of the EBCDIC, 8-bit ASCII, and 7-bit ASCII codes.

Character	EBCDIC	8-bit ASCII	7-bit ASCII	Character
0	1111 0000	0101 0000	011 0000	0
1	1111 0001	0101 0001	011 0001	1
2	1111 0010	0101 0010	011 0010	2
3	1111 0011	0101 0011	011 0011	3
4	1111 0100	0101 0100	011 0100	4
5	1111 0101	0101 0101	011 0101	5
6	1111 0110	0101 0110	011 0110	6
7	1111 0111	0101 0111	011 0111	7
8	1111 1000	0101 1000	011 1000	8
9	1111 1001	0101 1001	011 1001	9
A	1100 0001	1010 0001	100 0001	A
B	1100 0010	1010 0010	100 0010	B
C	1100 0011	1010 0011	100 0011	C
D	1100 0100	1010 0100	100 0100	D
E	1100 0101	1010 0101	100 0101	E
F	1100 0110	1010 0110	100 0110	F
G	1100 0111	1010 0111	100 0111	G
H	1100 1000	1010 1000	100 1000	H
I	1100 1001	1010 1001	100 1001	I
J	1101 0001	1010 1010	100 1010	J
K	1101 0010	1010 1011	100 1011	K
L	1101 0011	1010 1100	100 1100	L
M	1101 0100	1010 1101	100 1101	M
N	1101 0101	1010 1110	100 1110	N
O	1101 0110	1010 1111	100 1111	O
P	1101 0111	1011 0000	101 0000	P
Q	1101 1000	1011 0001	101 0001	Q
R	1101 1001	1011 0010	101 0010	R
S	1110 0010	1011 0011	101 0011	S
T	1110 0011	1011 0100	101 0100	T
U	1110 0100	1011 0101	101 0101	U
V	1110 0101	1011 0110	101 0110	V
W	1110 0110	1011 0111	101 0111	W
X	1110 0111	1011 1000	101 1000	X
Y	1110 1000	1011 1001	101 1001	Y
Z	1110 1001	1011 1010	101 1010	Z

breviation for *American Standard Code for Information Interchange*. Some computers and terminals use a 7-bit ASCII code; others use an 8-bit ASCII code similar to EBCDIC. All three codes are illustrated in Figure 4.22 (at left). In all codes, combinations of binary digits 0 and 1 represent characters.

For a more detailed discussion of data representation and computer numbering systems, *see* Appendix C.

Figure 4.21
Example of data represented in an even parity EBCDIC computer.

SUMMARY: Data Representation

1. Computers use some form of the binary numbering system.
   a. Combinations of 0's and 1's represent all characters
   b. 0 = "off"-state
   c. 1 = "on"-state
2. Computers frequently use eight bits (binary digits) to represent each character.
   a. Each storage position or byte consists of eight bits:
   Four bits for a zone
   Four bits for a digit (8-4-2-1)
   b. An additional parity bit is used to minimize data transmission errors.
3. Common computer codes
   a. EBCDIC—Extended Binary Coded Decimal Interchange Code
   b. ASCII—American Standard Code for Information Interchange (may be 7- or 8-bit code)

Self-Evaluating Quiz

1. EBCDIC is an abbreviation for _____.
2. In an 8-bit EBCDIC code, four bits are referred to as _____ bits and the other four are called _____ bits.

3. The digits 0 to 9 can be represented using <u>(no.)</u> digit bits.

4. The term "bit" is an abbreviation for _____.

5. Each _____ of storage in EBCDIC computers consists of eight bits.

Find the EBCDIC representation for each of the following. Use Figure 4.22 as a reference. There is no need to memorize the table.

6. A

7. 8

8. 5

9. T

10. K

Solutions

		ZONE	DIGIT
1. Extended Binary Coded Decimal Interchange Code	6.	1100	0001
2. zone; digit	7.	1111	1000
3. four (8-4-2-1)	8.	1111	0101
4. binary digit	9.	1110	0011
5. byte or location	10.	1101	0010

B. Types of Storage Technology

1. Magnetic Core Memory: An Historical Perspective

Until recently, many CPUs used magnetic cores to represent data and instructions in memory. A **magnetic core** is a tiny doughnut-shaped ferrite element, about the size of a grain of salt.

A magnetic core can be magnetized in one of two directions—clockwise or counterclockwise. A core that is magnetized in the clockwise direction is said to be "off." A core that is magnetized in the counterclockwise direction is "on." "On" cores represent the binary digit 1 and "off" cores represent the binary digit 0. Planes or groups of cores are stacked to form binary digits that represent characters in memory, usually eight binary digits (bits) to one storage position (byte) (see Figure 4.23 for an illustration of magnetic core memory.)

Figure 4.24
A computer chip compared to a petal of a flower. (Courtesy NCR.)

2. Integrated Circuits

In most modern computers, core memories have largely been replaced by integrated circuits. **Integrated circuits** consist of hundreds of electronic components that have been etched on a thin silicon wafer. Current flowing through a circuit represents an "on"-state, used to specify the binary digit 1; when current does not flow, this represents a binary digit of 0.

Thousands of integrated circuits can be placed on a single **chip** no larger than a petal of a flower (see Figure 4.24). Chips have resulted in smaller-sized computers with very large memories. Indeed, there are single chips available that have the memory capacity of large-scale systems of a decade ago. One chip can typically store from 64,000 to 256,000 bytes of memory on a single board. Moreover, the use of chips makes servicing of computers easy and efficient. When errors occur, the chips can be tested and the malfunctioning ones easily removed and replaced. In addition, the memory size of a computer can be supplemented with ease by simply adding chips or boards, where a board

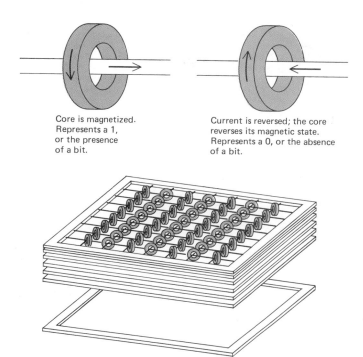

Core is magnetized.
Represents a 1,
or the presence
of a bit.

Current is reversed; the core
reverses its magnetic state.
Represents a 0, or the absence
of a bit.

Cores in a plane.

Figure 4.23
Magnetic core storage.

can contain numerous chips. Figure 4.25 illustrates boards containing 64K and 256K bytes of memory.

Integrated circuits are made from semiconductor materials. There are two main types of semiconductor memories: bipolar and metal oxide semiconductor (MOS), the latter being far more prevalent.

Integrated circuits represent the major form of memory in current computers, but there have been major innovations in memory technologies that have enhanced the capabilities of semiconductor devices. Figure 4.26 illustrates how the cost of semiconductor storage is decreasing at the same time that capacity is increasing. We can therefore expect that semiconductors will remain a useful type of storage technology in the years ahead.

LOOKING AHEAD

Chips That Fix Themselves

If an individual component of a conventional computer logic chip malfunctions, then the defective chip must be located and replaced. To make computers more resilient, some manufacturers are attempting to develop chips that can diagnose a defective component and compensate for the malfunctioning part.

Trilogy Systems is currently designing large wafers on which can be placed two or three times the number of circuits that are actually needed to perform a specific function. In this way, the wafers can diagnose a problem and perhaps even repair themselves. Adding such self-diagnosis and self-repair capabilities to chips could well revolutionize the semiconductor business.

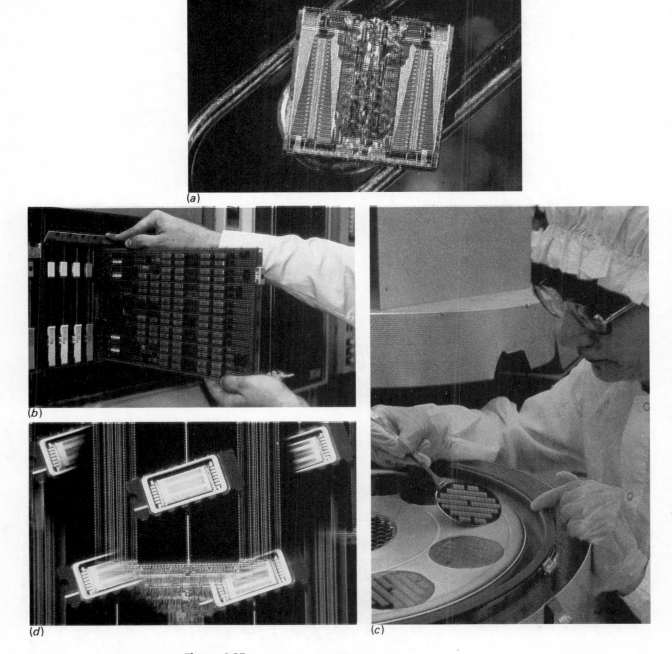

Figure 4.25
(a) 64K chip. (Courtesy IBM.) (b) A 14 × 8 inch circuit pack that provides memory for a computer. The pack contains 80 devices, each capable of storing 64K bytes of data. (Courtesy Bell Labs.) (c) Manufacturing 64K devices. (Courtesy Bell Labs.) (d) 256K chips shown against an enlarged photo of the circuitry that is used. (Courtesy NEC.)

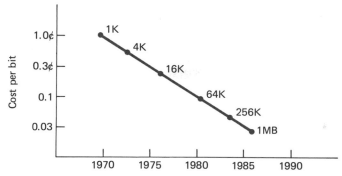

Since 1970, as the storage capacity of a chip has quadrupled every three years, the cost per bit of storage has been cut in half.

Figure 4.26
The development of semiconductor storage.

3. Magnetic Bubble Memory

One major innovation in storage technology is called magnetic bubble memory. **Magnetic bubble memory** consists of magnetized spots on a thin film of semiconductor material (see Figure 4.27 for an illustration of magnetic bubble technology).

The speed with which data in magnetic bubble memory can be accessed is not as great as that of integrated circuits, but it has one major benefit: data

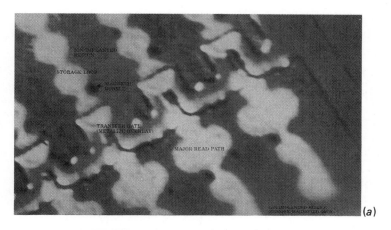

(a)

(b)

Figure 4.27
(a) An ion-implanted bubble memory magnified 300 times. (Courtesy Bell Labs.) (b) An integrated communication system that incorporates up to eight magnetic bubble memories on each mass storage card, for a combined storage capacity of 8 million bits of data per card. (Courtesy Intel Corp.)

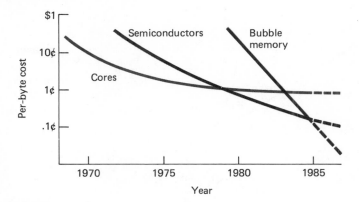

Figure 4.28
Cost comparison of core, semiconductor, and bubble memories.

can be retained in memory even if the power is shut off. This factor is called "nonvolatility." Magnetic bubble memory's non-volatile nature is particularly important in an era when problems with energy and power supplies can mean frequent blackouts, brownouts, or power surges, all of which can have serious effects on computer processing.

Because of the non-volatility of bubble memory, it is frequently used within temporary storage units of input/output devices such as terminals.

Figure 4.28 provides a historical cost comparison of core, semiconductor, and bubble memories. From this chart, you can see that semiconductor memories are currently the most cost-effective, but by 1990 bubble memory may be less costly and thus may compete more effectively with semiconductor devices.

4. Cache Memory

Cache memory is at the high end of the performance spectrum. That is, access to cache memory is much faster than access to traditional main memory. As a result, using cache memory can double the speed of a computer. But because cache memory is expensive, it is used for relatively small memories. Typically it is used for storing the most frequently referenced data and instructions (see Figure 4.29).

Cache memories are used extensively in minicomputers; moreover, cache memory has great potential for supercomputers and larger mainframes as well.

Figure 4.29
Memory device with cache memory. (Courtesy Cipher Data Products, Inc.)

5. Laser and Optical Memories

Additional experiments with integrated circuits as well as with optical and laser memories have resulted in even more efficient memories, which will undoubtedly be of great significance in the future. **Optical** and **laser memories** provide nonmagnetic alternatives for storage using light energy rather than magnetic fields to store characters. Figure 4.30 shows an example of a holographic disk that may some day replace traditional disk devices for auxiliary storage.

Figure 4.30
Holographic disk used for auxiliary storage. (Courtesy IBM.)

LOOKING AHEAD

Optical Disk: Will It Replace Magnetic Disk for Auxiliary Storage?

Optical disks have a large storage capacity, like magnetic disks, but until recently were not erasable, and hence not reusable. Now that erasable optical disks have been developed, there is evidence that they may replace not only magnetic disks but filing cabinets, microfilm, and perhaps even books as places to store information.

In an erasable disk system, a laser records information by changing the reflectivity of tiny spots on the disk, a change that can be reversed by another laser.

A single erasable, optical disk eight inches in diameter resembles a 45-rpm record and can store 10,000 to 15,000 documents or pictures. It costs approximately $20. There are larger versions as well.

C. Features of Primary Storage

There are two main types of primary storage, one that can store and access data and instructions and the other that can only access pre-recorded or pre-programmed instructions or functions.

1. Random-Access Memory (RAM)

Random-access memory (RAM) is the part of memory that is used for storing programs and data. RAM can be accessed or altered as needed by each program.

2. Read-Only Memory (ROM)

Read-only memory (ROM) is the part of computer memory that contains prewired functions. This part of memory *cannot* be altered by programmed instructions.

ROM might contain, for example, a square root procedure, eliminating the need for the programmer to write a set of instructions to determine square roots. Including such a function in the hardware is frequently cheaper, faster, and more efficient than requiring the programmer to code it. Similarly, instructions necessary to interpret user programs are frequently stored on ROM.

Functions in read-only memory are permanently stored and cannot be altered by a program. "Read-only" means that this area of storage can only be accessed; it cannot be used for storing instructions or data. ROM can only be changed by rewiring the circuits.

In short, ROM is part of the CPU hardware that actually contains a set of instructions, or program. Thus, the traditional distinction between hardware (devices) and software (programs) is slowly eroding. Another name for ROM is **firmware.**

In small systems where main memory is limited, the use of ROM is very popular. Whereas programs occupy bytes of main memory, ROM can be built into the system and thus not utilize any user memory. ROM can contain operating system features that would otherwise need to be programmed and would use up memory space.

There are two variations of ROM that are available.

IN A NUTSHELL

TYPES OF ROM

PROM—programmable read-only memory
> ROM that can be programmed by the user or vendor. This chip allows flexibility for users who would like to produce their own ROM.

EPROM—erasable programmable read-only memory
> A chip is not only programmable to include a set of functions but the program can be "erased" or overlaid with another program through a microcode procedure.

CHAPTER SUMMARY

I. Computer system
   A. Consists of input units, output units, central processing unit (CPU), and auxiliary or secondary storage units.
   B. Data processing cycle.
      The sequence "input/process/output" is performed for each data item.
   C. Components of the CPU.
      1. Primary storage—the main memory of a computer system.
         a. Each storage position is called a byte.
         b. Memory size is described in terms of K (thousands of bytes) or MB (megabytes, or millions of bytes).
      2. Control unit—monitors the operations of the entire computer system with the use of a special program called the supervisor.
      3. Arithmetic-logic unit.
II. Types of computer systems
   A. Major categories are supercomputers, mainframes, minicomputers, and microcomputers.

    B. Most computer manufacturers provide a family of upwardly compatible mainframes.

    C. Plug-compatible input/output units are available for use with numerous CPUs.

III. Methods of processing data

    A. Batch processing—data is collected in groups and entered into the computer in large volumes.

    B. Immediate processing—data is processed as soon as it is transacted; requires on-line operations, that is, terminals directly connected to the CPU.

    C. Real-time processing—when immediate processing is quick enough to enable users to make decisions.

IV. Computer technology

    A. Data representation.

        1. Computers use some form of binary (base 2) numbering system.

            a. 0 = "off"-state.

            b. 1 = "on"-state.

        2. Computers frequently use eight bits (binary digits) to represent each character.

        3. Common computer codes.

            a. EBCDIC.

            b. ASCII (7- or 8-bit code).

    B. Types of storage technology.

        1. Magnetic core: an historical perspective.

            a. Tiny, doughnut-shaped ferrite rings.

            b. Magnetized in one direction to represent "on"-state; magnetized in the other direction to represent "off"-state.

            c. Older form of memory; still used in some computers.

        2. Integrated circuits on a chip.

            a. Made from semiconductor material.

            b. Consists of thousands of electronic circuits on a thin silicon wafer.

            c. Two types: bipolar and metal oxide semiconductor (MOS); the latter is more prevalent.

            d. Widely used in most computers today.

            e. Very easy to service—when a chip malfunctions, it can easily be replaced.

        3. Magnetic bubble memory.

            a. Consists of magnetized spots on a thin semiconductor film.

            b. Relatively low access speed.

            c. Non-volatile: data remains in storage even if power is shut off.

            d. Used with very small computers.

        4. Cache memory.

            a. Very fast access.

            b. Very expensive.

5. Laser and optical memories for external memory—some already exist; perhaps these will be the wave of the future.
C. Features of memory.
   1. ROM—read-only memory.
      a. Accessible by a program, but cannot be altered.
      b. Contains prewired functions such as square root procedures.
      c. Because of ROM, the traditional separation between hardware and software is disappearing.
      d. Another name for ROM or preprogrammed hardware is firmware.
   2. RAM—random-access memory.
     Memory that is used for storing programs and data.

Chapter Self-Evaluating Quiz

1. The term CPU is an abbreviation for _____.
2. The component of a computer system that transmits data to the CPU is called the _____.
3. The two types of storage available in most computer systems are called _____ and _____ storage.
4. The form of storage located in the CPU is called _____ storage.
5. One function of the CPU is to _____.
6. The three components of the CPU are _____, _____, and _____.
7. Another name for a storage position is a(n) _____.
8. The storage capacity of a computer system is called its _____.
9. (T or F) The basic primary storage capacity of a typical microcomputer is one megabyte.
10. A special program called the _____ oversees all computer operations that are handled by the control unit of the CPU.
11. (T or F) Most major computer manufacturers provide a family of upwardly compatible mainframes.
12. (T or F) Minicomputers are frequently used as supplements to a mainframe.
13. Data that is collected in groups and then entered at fixed intervals is said to be processed in _____ mode.
14. Describe some differences between batch processing and immediate processing.
15. When a keyboard is used to enter data onto a tape or disk we call this a _____ operation.
16. A banking system enables depositors to inquire about the status of their

accounts at any given time. For such a system to work properly, transactions would need to be entered in a(n) _____ operation.

17. The type of memory that consists of tiny ferrite rings magnetized to indicate on-off states is called _____ memory.

18. The most common form of computer memory in use today is the _____.

19. A small unit consisting of integrated circuits is sometimes called a _____.

20. Integrated circuits are made from a _____ material.

21. If data is not retained in a computer when the power is shut off, this is referred to as _____.

22. The computer memory type that has the advantage of nonvolatility is called _____.

23. RAM is an abbreviation for _____.

24. The term used to describe memory that is accessible by a program but that cannot be altered by that program is called _____.

25. The term used to describe hardware that includes built-in functions or procedures is _____.

Solutions

1. central processing unit / page 104

2. input unit / page 104

3. primary / page 109 auxiliary or secondary / page 111

4. primary / page 109

5. control the operations of the computer system / page 110 provide primary storage / page 109 perform arithmetic and logic operations / page 110

6. primary storage / page 109 control unit / page 110 arithmetic-logic unit / page 110

7. byte / page 109

8. memory size / page 109

9. F—It is 4K to 128K in basic form. / page 112

10. supervisor / page 110

11. T / page 114

12. T / page 114

13. batch / page 118

14. Batch processing is performed at intervals, whereas immediate processing operates on data as it is transacted. With batch processing, major files are not always current. / page 122

15. key-to-tape or key-to-disk or key-to-storage / page 120

16. on-line or immediate / page 120

17. magnetic core / page 136

18. integrated circuit / page 136

19. chip / page 136

20. semiconductor / page 137

21. volatility / page 140

22. magnetic bubble / page 140

23. random-access memory / page 141

24. ROM—read-only memory / page 141

25. firmware / page 142

Key Terms

Arithmetic-logic unit
ASCII
Auxiliary storage
Batch processing
Binary numbering system
Bit
Byte
Cache memory
Central processing unit (CPU)
Character
Chip
Computer system
Control unit
EBCDIC
Firmware
Immediate processing
Input unit
Integrated circuit
Key-to-storage procedure

Laser memory
Magnetic bubble memory
Magnetic core
Mainframe
Megabyte (MB)
Memory size
Microcomputer
Minicomputer
Off-line operation
On-line operation
Optical memory
Output unit
Plug-compatible
Primary storage
RAM (random-access memory)
Real-time processing
ROM (read-only memory)
Supercomputer
Supervisor

Review Questions

I. True or False

1. (T or F) A computer system consists of independent machines that function in an integrated manner to produce the desired output.
2. (T or F) All operations performed by the computer system are controlled by the CPU.
3. (T or F) All data processing centers have the same basic computer equipment.
4. (T or F) Most computer systems utilize auxiliary storage.
5. (T or F) The three main classifications of equipment at a computer center are hardware, software, and the operating system.
6. (T or F) The primary storage unit of the CPU contains the stored program.
7. (T or F) Storage is composed of locations or addressable positions.
8. (T or F) The memory size of most current computers usually does not exceed 128K.
9. (T or F) The supervisor of a computer system is itself a program.
10. (T or F) When a system can defer the process of making a file of data current, then batch processing is utilized.

II. Fill in the Blanks

1. The data processing cycle consists of three phases called _____, _____, and _____.
2. The three sections of the central processing unit are _____, _____, and _____.
3. The number of storage positions available in a computer is called its _____.
4. The program responsible for controlling the operations of the totally integrated computer system is called the _____.

5. The main type of memory used in computers is _____.

6. A major advantage of magnetic bubble memory is _____.

7. The term used to describe hardware that has prewired instructions is _____.

8. The area of memory not available for storing instructions is called _____.

9. The binary numbering system is ideally suited for computer processing because _____.

10. The decimal equivalent of the binary number 110111 is _____.

11. The decimal equivalent of the binary number 10011 is _____.

12. The binary equivalent of the decimal number 253 is _____.

13. The binary equivalent of the decimal number 177 is _____.

14. Any number raised to the zero power is _____.

15. The EBCDIC code consists of __(no.)__ zone bits, __(no.)__ digit bits, and __(no.)__ parity bits.

APPLICATION

'COMPATIBILITY' MAY BE IN EYE OF THE VENDOR

by Johanna Ambrosio

Compatibility fever has reached the office systems marketplace, it seems, with most of the major vendors promising to link their gear to equipment from IBM and Wang Laboratories Inc.

This type of compatibility between different manufacturers' systems will be the buzz phrase of the new year, industry watchers say.

However, at issue, observers add, is how each vendor defines the term and to what degree compatibility is achieved. "Just because you plug two things together and they don't blow up doesn't mean they're compatible," says Thomas Billadeau, president of The Office Systems Consulting Group, Cambridge, Mass. "Most of the vendors use the term and don't define it."

Instead, Billadeau adds, vendors promise compatibility and leave users to define it however they wish. "What the vendors mean is 'we'll work to get to whatever level we can get to.' "

Compatibility among systems has mushroomed recently beyond the traditional mainframe-to-mainframe linking concept, to encompass all types of emulation, communication and actual box-for-box replacement.

On an office-systems level, most experts define compatibility as the ability to exchange information—which includes but is not restricted to programs and files—between different vendors' machines. Once accessed, the information should be able to be read, edited and printed.

Also, the experts add, compatibility means transparency—users should neither know nor care where the file is, as long as they are able to get it from wherever it resides.

Although compatibility among many vendors' computers is important, almost everyone agrees on the critical need to hook into IBM's machines. "IBM compatibility is a necessity . . . vendors are scrambling to get it," says Michele S. Preston, vice president of the New York-based L.F. Rothschild, Unterberg, Towbin.

IBM's protocols for intersystem document transfer are Document Interchange Architecture (DIA) and Document Content Architecture (DCA), and it is important for other vendors to provide support for both, observers say. DIA is a protocol that allows documents to be transmitted between IBM machines; DCA concerns the actual control codes governing the documents' composition.

But understanding the need to adopt IBM's protocols is only the first hurdle. This implementation can be difficult for other vendors, primarily because IBM is just beginning to publish the specifications for DIA and DCA. And just because a vendor supports DIA and DCA does not make the machines automatically compatible, according to Joseph A. Ramellini, vice president of consulting services for Office Sciences International Inc., Iselin, N.J.

Another age-old obstacle to achieving compatibility with IBM rests with IBM itself. Even IBM has not licked the problem internally. And, for example, although the firm has brought its 8100, 5520 and Displaywriter office computers all under the umbrella of the Distributed Office Support System (Disoss) software, its Professional Office System (Profs) was left out of the scene.

"Even IBM hasn't gotten its act together. It hasn't implemented what it announced," says John Murphy, vice president for Advanced Office Concepts Corp., Bala Cynwyd, Pa.

Observers predict compatibility problems will be eased, but never completely solved. "You'll never get higher than 70- to 80-percent compatibility; there are too many things pulling vendors apart," Ramellini adds.

Among possible factors working against the adoption of compatibility for some vendors is the need to keep their current installed base "hooked" with proprietary architecture, or with architectures that differ slightly from a standard.

Some observers attribute other factors besides thinking of users' welfare to companies promising compatibility. "It's a marketing ploy. Lesser vendors are announcing compatibility promises because the major vendors have," Walsh says.

Source: Information Systems News, January 9, 1984, page 23. Reprinted with permission.

Questions
1. Understanding Key Terms
   Define the following terms as they are used in the application.
   a. Emulation.
   b. Compatibility.
   c. Transparency.
   d. Protocols.
   e. Architecture.
2. Software, Hardware, and Systems Concepts
   In your opinion, does compatibility require software as well as hardware elements? Explain your answer.
3. Management Considerations
   As a manager, what criteria would you use for ensuring that a vendor's claim of compatibility was valid?
4. Social, Legal, and Ethical Implications
   If compatibility claims proved to be overly-optimistic or altogether misleading, do you think legal action would be warranted? Explain your answer.

CASE STUDY: McKing's Superburgers, Inc.

1. Would you recommend batch processing or immediate processing for McKing's for each of the following applications? Explain your answers.
   a. Entering orders.
   b. Making price changes.
   c. Obtaining status reports that indicate the quantities on hand of prepared items at the counter.
2. How would you determine whether each vendor's product had the latest computer components?
3. Suppose a point-of-sale system recommended by one vendor had 512K of RAM, while the others had one megabyte of RAM. What questions would you ask to determine whether the system with less storage capacity could adequately handle your requirements?

THE COMPUTER AD: A Focus on Marketing

Consider the ad entitled "Four Little Words That Strike Fear in the Heart of the 1980's" that appears in Figure 4.31.

1. Define the following terms as they are used in the ad:
   a. On-line.
   b. Downtime.
   c. Hardware self-checking.
   d. Four-megabyte system with 60-megabyte disk storage.
   e. Transaction processing.
2. Why do components have "partners"?
3. The ad clearly emphasizes the fact that the cost of service and the need for servicing computers is minimized. Do you think this is of major concern to computer users today? Explain your answer.

FOUR LITTLE WORDS THAT STRIKE FEAR IN THE HEART IN THE 1980'S.

"The computer is down."

Every day another business goes "on line." Every day the world becomes more dependent on computers. And every day it becomes more important for the world to have a computer that won't even skip a heartbeat.

Over the past decade there have been computers designed to eliminate downtime. However, all previous approaches depend heavily on software techniques to provide fault tolerance. A comparison of these old systems with the new Stratus/32 Continuous Processing™ System will illustrate how far we have come in one leap, by using advanced hardware technology instead of complex software.

How the Stratus Hardware Solution Supersedes the Software Solution.

Stratus's hardware design means that fault tolerance is invisible to your application programs and users. In contrast, the software-based systems require complex, performance-stealing software in order to implement fault tolerance. This

means that new programs are more difficult to develop, they run slower, and existing programs can't be run without major changes.

Hardware Self-checking Causes a Breakthrough in Service.

Each Stratus/32 tests itself EIGHT MILLION TIMES A SECOND while it executes your programs, so faults are detected BEFORE they corrupt your data. And when there is a failure, there's no need to rush to call your Stratus service technician. For one thing, the failed component has a partner that continues operations as usual (without slowing down the system), so there's NO DOWNTIME. In addition, repairs can be made WITHOUT STOPPING THE SYSTEM. It is so easy to repair a Stratus/32 that our service is provided at about one-half the average price charged by other computer manufacturers.

$140,000, Software Included.

$140,000 buys you a complete four megabyte 32-bit system with 60 megabytes of disk storage, magnetic tape drive, and system SOFTWARE. If you like our hardware, you will be even more impressed with our software. (A common reaction among our users.) Briefly, our software offering includes VOS (a virtual operating system), transaction processing, networking, IBM communications, data management system, interactive forms builder, symbolic debugger, COBOL, Basic, PL/I, Fortran, Pascal, word processing . . .

To get more information call us at 617-653-1466. The computer you can count on has arrived.

Stratus
CONTINUOUS PROCESSING™

Now that the world relies on computers it needs a computer it can rely on.

Figure 4.31
Marketing computer products. (Courtesy Stratus Computer, Inc.)

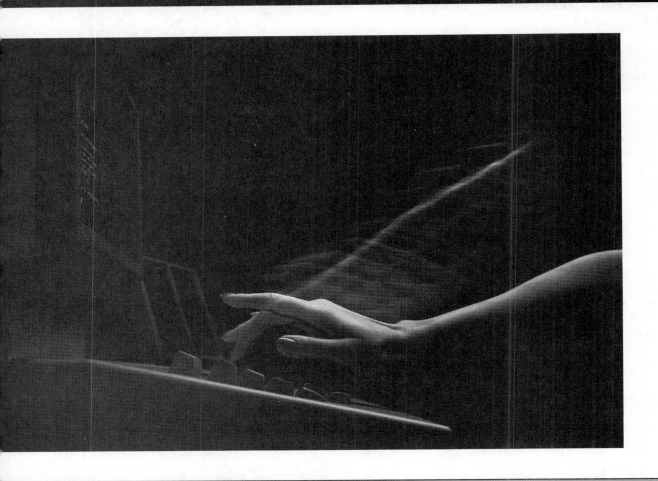

CHAPTER

5

ENTERING INPUT TO A COMPUTER

CHAPTER OBJECTIVES

To familiarize you with:

- How data is most commonly entered into a computer.
- Traditional data entry techniques used for converting a source document into a form that can be read by input units such as tape, disk, and card devices.
- Input units that collect data at the source of a transaction.
- Input units that read source documents directly, without requiring a conversion process to create a machine-readable form.
- How data is organized for file processing.
- Methods used to minimize input errors.

I. DATA ENTRY CONCEPTS

A. An Overview of Methods Used for Data Entry

Typical examples of input data for business applications include the following:

Examples of Input Data

Application	Data to Be Processed
Inventory	Purchase orders
	Shipping orders
Accounts receivable	Charge slips
	Credit slips
Payroll	Time cards
	Payroll change reports

Before any type of data can be entered into a computer, it must be in a form that can be read by an input unit. The input unit then transmits the incoming data to the central processing unit (CPU). Input data may be processed in one of two ways:

1. Immediately, as the data is generated.
   In this case the input unit transmits either to the CPU directly or over data communications lines, depending on whether the input unit is at the same location as the CPU.
2. In batch mode, after all data has been collected.
   Data entered on tape, disk, and cards is usually processed in batch mode.

Figure 5.1 illustrates both types of data entry techniques.

B. The Source Document: Data at the Point of Transaction

Input to a computer frequently comes from documents such as purchase orders, charge slips, or payroll change reports. These documents are prepared in the department where the data is transacted, that is, where a change in status actually occurs. Because they are prepared at the "source" of a transaction, they are called **source documents.** In order for data recorded on a source document to be processed by a computer, it must be in a form that can be read by an input unit. There are many types of input units and in this chapter we consider the major ones.

Some input units can read source documents directly. For computer systems with this capability, the data simply needs to be collected and transmitted to the computer. Figure 5.2 illustrates an input unit that can read source documents directly.

Note that while many source documents are printed forms such as sales slips, purchase orders, and so on, a source document could also be an inventory bar code tag, or a time card punched with holes, or some other non-printed form of input. Since these latter input forms are used for capturing data at the source, they too are called source documents, even though they may not be on printed paper. To read inventory bar code tags directly into a computer

1. Data entry for immediate processing.

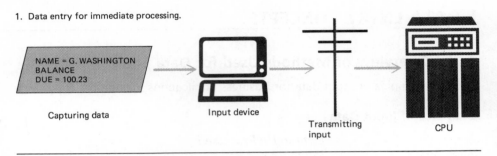

NAME = G. WASHINGTON
BALANCE
DUE = 100.23

Capturing data   Input device

Transmitting
input

CPU

2. Key-to-storage data entry for batch processing.

Figure 5.1
Comparison of data entry
techniques.

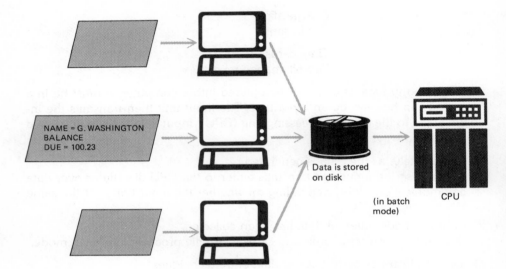

NAME = G. WASHINGTON
BALANCE
DUE = 100.23

Data is stored
on disk

(in batch
mode)

CPU

Figure 5.2
An optical character reader,
which can read source
documents directly.
(Courtesy IBM.)

system, we would need an input device called a bar code reader; to read time cards we would need a punched card reader, and so on.

C. Data Entry Devices: When Source Documents Must Be Converted to Machine-Readable Form

Frequently, source documents cannot be read *directly* by an input unit. Sometimes the document may not be in a standard format, or the acquisition of an input unit that reads the printed data directly is too expensive for the organization. In these cases, the source document would need to be *converted* into a form that could be accepted by some input unit available at the company.

Conversion of data from a source document to machine-readable form is performed with the use of **data entry devices.** Data entry devices typically involve either (1) keying data directly into the CPU in an on-line mode or (2) keying data onto some key-to-storage medium such as disk or tape (or in older applications, cards) for future batch processing. See Figure 5.3 for an illustration of an on-line data entry system. In this illustration, data that is keyed into the system is immediately processed by the CPU.

Data entry, then, refers to the collection and preparation of data so that it may be read by an input unit. The data is converted into machine-readable form for immediate processing, or stored on tape or disk for future processing. Data entry devices usually use keyboard units for actually entering the data, but other data entry components are also available.

Figure 5.3
Example of an on-line order entry system. This system manages and controls the entire order processing cycle, including order entry, inventory control, shipping control and receiving, invoicing, accounts receivable, sales analysis, and information inquiry. (Courtesy McAuto/ McDonnell Douglas- St. Louis.)

D. Transmitting Input Data to a Computer

Once the input data has been collected and prepared in some form that can be read by an input unit, it must be physically available to the input unit. This input unit transmits the data to the CPU either directly by cable or over data communications lines, depending on whether the device is located at the same site as the CPU.

There are two main ways in which incoming data can be transmitted to an input unit of a computer system.

1. Transmittal of Data to the Input Unit by Messenger

After data has been collected, it may be mailed or delivered by messenger to the site of the input unit. Since such manual transmittal is subject to delays, it is only used when there is no immediate need for the data.

Suppose, for example, that payroll change reports are prepared in five separate payroll offices of a large organization. Once a week, a messenger takes the payroll change reports from the five offices and brings them to the data entry center where they are keyed onto disk. The disk is then processed once a week. In this instance, the manual transmittal of data from the offices to the data entry center is acceptable because the data is only needed weekly.

2. Electronic Transmission of Input to a Computer
Using Data Communications

Data may be keyed into a terminal at the source and then transmitted directly over communication lines to a CPU for immediate processing. Communication lines include telephone lines, cables, and air waves transmitted from relay towers. These are discussed in detail in Chapter 8.

E. Summary and Applications of Data Entry Concepts

In summary, before data can be read by an input device of a computer system, it must be collected, prepared, and transmitted to the input device. There are numerous data entry techniques that may be used for capturing the data and converting it to machine-readable form or reading it directly by an input unit.

Let us consider several applications as follows:

Application 1.   Consider a large department store. Each time a charge customer makes a purchase, the sales clerk keys the account number and the amount of purchase using a keyboard device. In this instance, data is collected at the *point of sale* and is either immediately transmitted to the computer for processing or is saved for future batch processing (see Figure 5.4).

Application 2.   An insurance firm has 300 brokers or field representatives who sell insurance. Each time a policy is sold, the broker "dials up" a computer and verbally transmits data indicating the customer's identification, the type of policy, and the amount of the policy. The input unit is a voice recognition device that either processes the data immediately or stores it for future batch processing (see Figure 5.5).

Application 3.   Employees at a factory use a device for keying in shipments received as they are delivered to the factory. This data is entered onto a cassette tape. At the end of the day, the tape containing data on all shipments received is transmitted to the computer center where it is read by a tape cassette reader in batch processing mode. Figure 5.6 illustrates how this type of data is collected at the source.

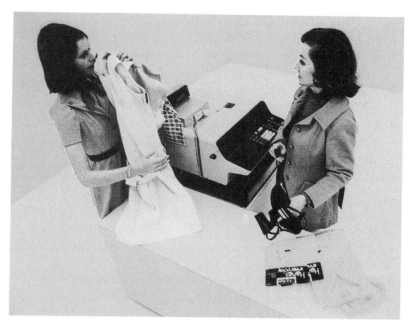

Figure 5.4
Example of a point-of-sale
system in a department
store. (Courtesy NCR.)

Figure 5.5
An insurance salesperson
using a voice recognition
device. (Courtesy Interstate
Electronics Corp.)

Figure 5.6
Collecting data at the
source. (Courtesy NCR.)

Self-Evaluating Quiz

1. Before data can be entered into a computer, it must be in _____ form.
2. If an input device is not at the same site as the CPU, input data is usually transmitted to the CPU over _____.
3. A _____ is an originating form containing data; examples of such forms include a purchase order, charge slip, and credit slip.
4. (T or F) A source document is always a printed document.
5. (T or F) It is always necessary to key a source document into a medium such as tape or disk to make it machine-readable.
6. To convert a source document to machine-readable form, a _____ device is used.
7. (T or F) A data entry device must be connected on-line to a computer system.
8. _____ refers to the collection and preparation of data so that it may be read by an input unit.
9. (T or F) It is possible to use a terminal for preparing a source document so that data may be transmitted directly to the CPU.
10. (T or F) Input units always transmit data to a CPU over data communications lines.

Solutions

1. machine-readable
2. data communications lines
3. source document
4. F—It can be a bar-coded tag, punched card, etc.
5. F—Sometimes a source document can be read directly by an input unit, so that a keying operation is not required.
6. data entry
7. F—Data may be keyed onto a tape, disk, or even cards for future batch processing.
8. Data entry
9. T
10. F—Frequently, input units are at the same site as the CPU and are connected by cable to the CPU.

II. INPUT UNITS OF A COMPUTER SYSTEM

In this section, we consider the most common input devices used in business applications. Below, we outline the devices to be discussed.

IIII➡ Common Input Units

1. Key-to-storage units
2. Punched card readers
3. Input from a terminal
   a. Keyboard

b. Light pen, mouse, or touch-sensitive screen
c. Voice recognition
d. Touch-Tone telephone
4. Optical scanners
 a. Optical character reader
 b. Bar code reader
 c. Optical mark reader
5. Specialized input units for data entry in banking
 a. Magnetic ink character reader
 b. Automatic teller machine

   While the above list may seem to be extensive, it actually represents only the most common units. There are many other input units used for specialized applications.

   Recall that input units may be *at the same site* as the CPU or they may be *at a remote location* linked to the CPU either by cable or by communication lines. Note, too, that input units may process data immediately as it is entered, or at fixed intervals in a batch mode.

A. Traditional Methods for Entering Input in Batch Mode

1. Key-to-Storage Systems

Many companies use a key-to-storage system for converting large numbers of source documents to disk or tape. Smaller companies use key-to-storage systems for converting source documents to floppy disk or to tape cassette. In each case, the concept is similar. Data entry operators key the data onto a high-speed medium for future batch processing by the computer.

Types of Key-to-Storage Systems

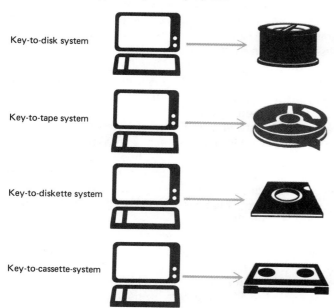

Key-to-disk system

Key-to-tape system

Key-to-diskette system

Key-to-cassette-system

Figure 5.7 illustrates a key-to-storage system.

The features of tape and disk that make them ideally suited for storing high-volume data are considered in Chapter 7.

2. The Punched Card

a. The 80-Column Card and Card Reader   The oldest input unit of a computer system is the punched card reader. Although cards have their limitations, they are still sometimes used in businesses. In addition, many colleges still use cards for entering computer programs, so that students need to know a little about them. Cards are typically processed in batch mode after they have been punched.

Data is usually entered on a punched card using a data entry device called a keypunch machine, illustrated in Figure 5.8. This is a manual machine that requires an operator to keypunch data on a card from a source document. The keypunch machine converts the keyed data to holes on a card.

A card reader accepts data recorded in the form of holes punched into a card, which is similar in size to a dollar bill. These punched cards may be familiar to the student because they are commonly used as school registration cards, stock dividend checks, and electric bills, just to name a few examples. You probably have been advised many times not to "bend, fold, staple, or mutilate" them, although many of you have probably been tempted to do just that, whenever a computer mistake has occurred!

The standard punched card holds 80 characters of data, one in each column (see Figure 5.9). Each card is considered a record or unit of data for a specific application. The record consists of characters of data, where a character is a letter, digit, or special symbol such as $, %, or *. This means that a typical record stored on a card is limited to 80 characters. If, however, a record consisted of more than 80 characters, multiple cards would be required.

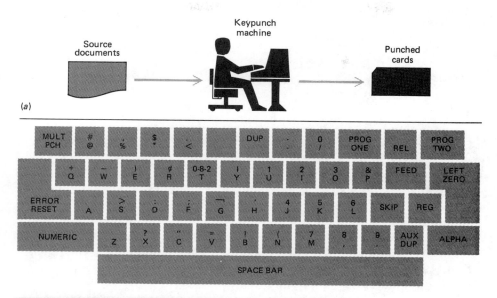

(a)

(b)

Figure 5.8
(a) Keypunching cards from source documents.
(b) Keypunch machine.
(Courtesy IBM.)

Punched cards are typically read by a **card reader** and processed by the computer in batch mode (see Figure 5.10).

Data is recorded on a card using a code for punching holes devised by Herman Hollerith. As indicated in Chapter 3, Hollerith invented a series of punched card devices for tabulating information in the late nineteenth century. The **Hollerith code** for representing data on cards is still widely used today.

To represent a digit in a specific column, a hole is punched in the corresponding digit row of the punched card. Thus to represent the number 123 in card columns 30 to 32, holes are punched in the 1-row of column 30, the 2-row of column 31, and the 3-row of column 32.

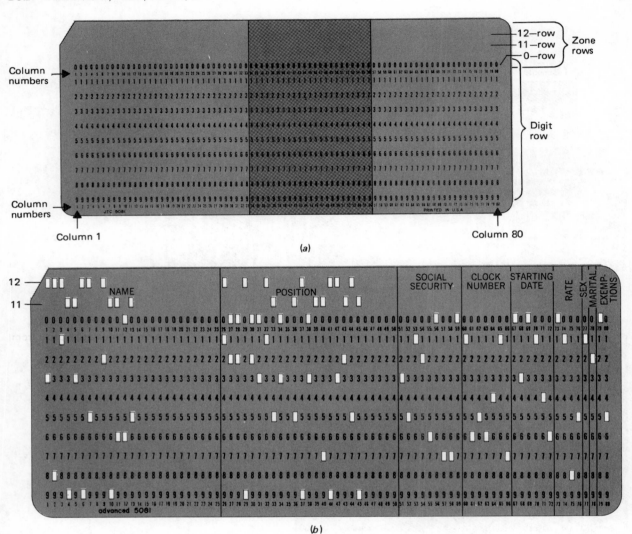

Figure 5.9
(a) Standard punched card with columns 34 to 56 shaded. *(b)* Example of a time card.

To represent *letters* on a punched card, a combination of two punches is used in a single column. Each letter requires two punches: a zone punch and a digit punch. That is, holes are punched in *two* rows of a *single* column for each letter:

1. Zone row (0-row, unnumbered 11- and 12-rows on top of card).
2. Digit row (0-9 rows).

Figure 5.11 illustrates the Hollerith code for digits, letters, and special characters. Note that this code is very similar to the ASCII and EBCDIC codes discussed in the previous chapter for internal storage representation of data.

It is not necessary for the user to memorize the Hollerith code; a keypunch machine will automatically convert keyed characters to punched holes.

A card reader uses either (1) mechanical components or brushes to sense punched holes, or (2) photoelectric or laser beam methods for electronically sensing holes without the use of brushes (see Figure 5.12 for illustrations of punched card mechanisms used in card readers).

Figure 5.10
Card reader. (Courtesy IBM.)

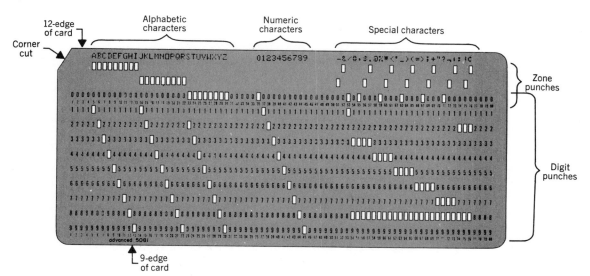

Figure 5.11
Punched card illustrating
the Hollerith code.

b. Other Forms of Punched Cards

(1) The 96-Column Card.   In addition to the standard 80-column card, there
is a 96-column card (Figure 5.13) developed much later (in 1969), which can
only be used with certain computer systems such as the IBM System/3.

Although it holds 20% more data, the 96-column card is physically smaller
than the standard 80-column card and is subdivided into three separate tiers
or punching areas, each capable of storing 32 characters of data. The code
used with this card is called BCD or *Binary Coded Decimal*. This BCD code is
very similar to the Hollerith code used to represent data on 80-column cards.
Note that holes punched on a 96-column card are round, as opposed to the
rectangular holes on standard punched cards.

Figure 5.12
Card reader mechanism.
(a) How a card reader
mechanically senses
punched holes.
(b) Photoelectric cells used
to scan a punched card.

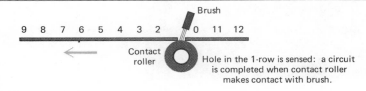

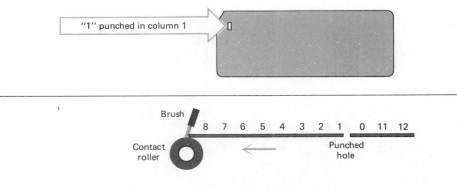

1. When card is first read by card reader.

2. When 1-punch is sensed.

(a)

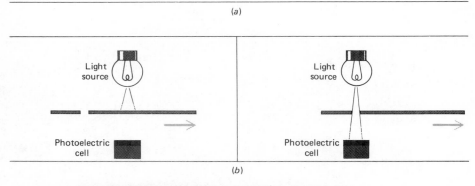

(b)

Figure 5.13
Sample 96-column card.

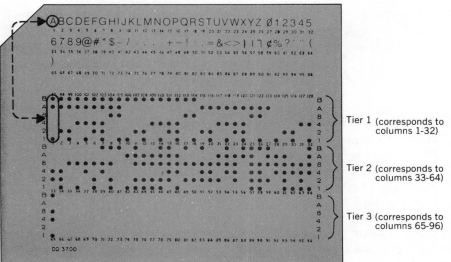

Tier 1 (corresponds to columns 1-32)

Tier 2 (corresponds to columns 33-64)

Tier 3 (corresponds to columns 65-96)

(2) Punched Card Output and Turnaround Documents.   As noted, a punched card can be created or keypunched from a source document to serve as *input* to a computer. In addition, a punched card can be produced as *output* from a computer using a card punch device.

When a card is created as output, it will sometimes be re-entered into the data processing flow at some later date as input. You may, for example, receive your utility bill in the form of a punched card. You would then be instructed to return the card with your payment. When returned, the card is entered into the computer, this time as input to indicate that a payment is to be credited to your account. A card that is created as output and then used at a later date as input is called a **turnaround document** (*see* Figure 5.14).

Figure 5.14
(a) Utility bill on a punched card that serves as a turnaround document.
(b) The processing of that bill.

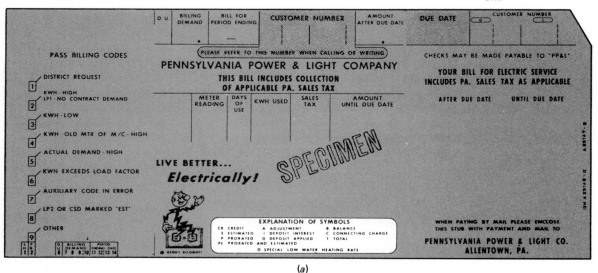

(a)

Computer System → Utility Bill   (Output)

To customer

Returned to DP with payment

Same Utility Bill   (Input)

Computer System

Updates amount now due from customer

(b)

The following list compares advantages and disadvantages of punched cards as input.

IIII➡ **Advantages and Disadvantages of Card Input**

Advantages
1. Cards are inexpensive.
2. Cards can be read by people as well as machines.
3. A card may be used effectively to represent a unit of data consisting of up to 80 (or 96) characters.
4. A card may be used as a turnaround document. After being produced as output, it can then re-enter the cycle as input at a later date.

Disadvantages
1. Cards can be bent, stapled, folded, and mutilated, making them very difficult to maintain. Cards are also very sensitive to changes in heat and humidity.
2. Cards are read by a card reader, which is a very slow input unit.
3. Cards cannot be reused after they have been punched.
4. Card records are restricted to an 80-column (or 96-column) format.
5. Cards are bulky for representing a large volume of data.

B. Methods of Entering Input That Reduce Manual Labor

Key-to-storage and punched card input are typically created from a source document and processed by the CPU in batch mode after all data has been accumulated. In most instances, source documents are collected from the users and transported to a data entry department. There, they are converted by a staff of data entry operators to machine-readable form using key-to-storage systems or keypunch machines.

The process of collecting source documents and physically transporting them to another location requires manual intervention and can lead to errors if source documents are misplaced or lost.

One method for reducing the manual transmittal of data and its associated errors is to use a remote terminal at the point where a source document is created. The terminal may then be used for entering input that is immediately transmitted to the CPU without the need for collecting data and physically transporting it.

1. Input from a Terminal

A terminal is a computer device that is used for interacting or communicating with a CPU. Most terminals can be used for entering data as well as receiving messages from the CPU. Messages from the computer are usually either printed on paper or displayed on a screen. We will focus on the most common input components of terminals.

a. Keyboard The most common terminals are those with a keyboard, on which a user or data entry operator types or *keys* data into the system. Frequently, the data is entered at the source by keying it on a terminal linked via communication lines to a CPU.

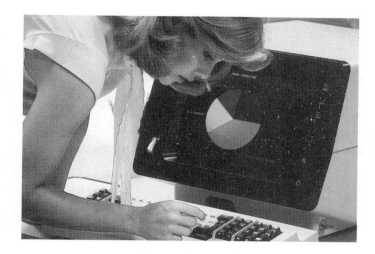

Figure 5.15
Keyboard-CRT terminal.
(Courtesy IBM.)

Keep in mind that terminals with keyboards usually have either a typewriter component for printing or a CRT screen for (1) displaying the data being transmitted and (2) receiving responses or queries from the CPU. Both the typewriter and CRT are output components that will be considered in the next chapter.

Most point-of-sale systems in department stores use keyboard terminals for entering a customer's charge account number and amount of purchase. There are also hand-held portable keyboard terminals available for entering data and storing it on a mini-medium such as cassette tape or floppy disk. Figure 5.15 illustrates a keyboard-CRT terminal.

b. Light Pen, Mouse, or Touch-Sensitive Screen   Instead of keying data into a terminal, an operator may use a **light pen** to enter data on a CRT screen (see Figure 5.16). The device uses a laser beam for transmitting signals to the CPU. A light pen is used to reduce manual labor by enabling input to be entered

Figure 5.16
Use of a light pen for entering data. (Courtesy IBM.)

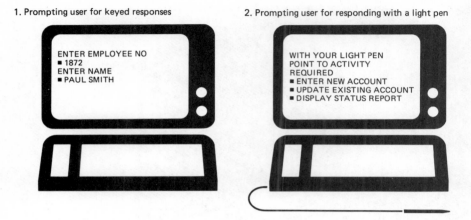

1. Prompting user for keyed responses

ENTER EMPLOYEE NO
■ 1872
ENTER NAME
■ PAUL SMITH

2. Prompting user for responding with a light pen

WITH YOUR LIGHT PEN
POINT TO ACTIVITY
REQUIRED
■ ENTER NEW ACCOUNT
■ UPDATE EXISTING ACCOUNT
■ DISPLAY STATUS REPORT

Figure 5.17
Prompts for data entry.

as a series of responses to "prompts" or questions asked by the computer (see Figure 5.17). Similarly, a light pen can be used for making modifications to an existing layout displayed on a screen. Because light pens require the user to simply write on a screen or point to desired functions, they are considered to be very "user-friendly." There are many other similar devices for interacting with a screen in this way. Chapter 6 considers the various tools for making interaction between a user and a screen more user-friendly.

A **mouse** is a device used mostly with microcomputer systems to point to a specific requirement or to select a specific function displayed on a screen. A mouse enables a user to move a prompt or pointer on the CRT to a specific place on the screen for indicating which elements are required for processing. We will discuss the mouse in Chapter 9.

Some CRTs enable a user to simply touch the screen and point to a desired item or response.

c. Voice Recognition Unit   A **voice recognition unit** enables the user or data entry operator to verbally transmit input to a CPU. This unit interprets the spoken word and transmits the input as electronic signals to the computer. Such units are relatively new and still have problems with high error rates. Nonetheless, they are currently being used for on-site order entry and inventory control. When an order is made, a user can "call up" the computer using a standard telephone and place the order electronically by speaking into a voice recognition unit. Voice recognition units also have great potential for handicapped people who cannot key in data or use a light pen. Figure 5.18 illustrates a voice recognition unit used in a laboratory setting.

Before the device transmits the data to the CPU it usually verifies the input by repeating the message back to the user; this reduces the possibility of errors. Existing computer systems may be modified to accept voice input with the use of a "plug-in" voice recognition unit. Figure 5.19 illustrates a computer board that contains the circuitry for voice recognition.

d. Touch-Tone Telephone and/or Portable Keying Device   It is possible to use a telephone and/or a portable keying device for both accessing a computer and for actually transmitting input to a CPU (see Figure 5.20). A bank teller, for example, may "call up" the computer using a Touch-Tone telephone or

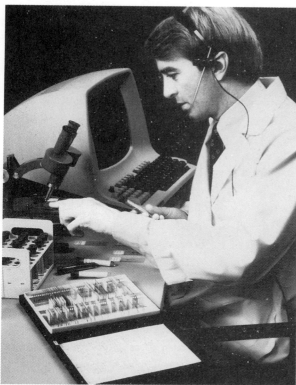

Figure 5.18 (left)
Voice recognition in a laboratory setting. (Courtesy Interstate Electronics Corp.)

Figure 5.20 (left)
Portable keying device for entering data using a standard telephone. (Mathew Naythons/Black Star.)

Figure 5.19
Voice recognition device that can interpret a vocabulary of 100 words. (Courtesy Interstate Electronics Corp.)

portable keying device. Using the same device, the teller can then enter an account number, a code indicating whether the transaction to be entered is a withdrawal or a deposit, and the amount of the transaction. The computer must be programmed to accept these digital signals and to determine, for example, if there is enough money in the account when a withdrawal is requested. The response to the teller may be an audio signal or a verbal response obtained by the computer from a series of stored messages. To minimize the potential for unauthorized use, access to a computer must be carefully monitored when telephone equipment is utilized.

LOOKING AHEAD

1. Touch panel screens called "plasma displays" will gain in popularity. A user need only touch a menu for the input to be transmitted.

2. CRTs will continue to be more compact in size.

3. Speech recognition devices will become increasingly popular as input units.

Self-Evaluating Quiz

1. (T or F) An input unit of a computer system is always at the same site as the CPU.
2. (T or F) Data is always entered on a terminal using a keyboard.
3. (T or F) A standard Touch-Tone telephone may be used as a terminal.
4. (T or F) Most terminals can be used for entering data as well as receiving information from a computer.
5. Terminals with keyboards usually have a _____ component for printing or a _____ screen for displaying data being transmitted and for receiving messages from the CPU.
6. To change data displayed on a screen, a _____ pen may be used.
7. A _____ enables the user or data entry operator to verbally transmit input.
8. The standard punched card can store (no.) characters of data.
9. The code used for punching data on an 80-column card is called the _____ code.
10. The data entry device typically used for entering data from a source document onto a card is called a _____ machine.
11. To represent an alphabetic character or letter on an 80-column punched card, we use a combination of (no.) punches in a single column.
12. A _____ document is one that is created by the computer system to be later entered as input again.

Using the illustration in Figure 5.11, indicate the Hollerith code representation for the following:

13. V
14. B
15. Q

Solutions

1. F—It may be located remotely and linked by data communication lines.
2. F—Other devices such as a light pen, voice recognition unit, or telephone may be used in place of a keyboard.
3. T
4. T—This chapter focuses on the input component of a terminal that enables it to transmit to a CPU.
5. typewriter
   CRT (cathode ray tube)

6. light
7. voice recognition unit
8. 80
9. Hollerith
10. keypunch
11. two (zone punch [0, 11, 12] and digit punch [0–9])

12. turnaround
13. 0-5
14. 12-2
15. 11-8

Thus far, we have seen that a remote terminal can be used at the point where a source document is created. By eliminating the need for collecting data and physically transporting it to the computer center, the use of terminals can effectively reduce manual labor and the potential errors associated with misplaced or lost documents.

A second major method for reducing manual intervention is to eliminate the need for the conversion procedure altogether. In this way, a source document need not be keyed or converted to a machine-readable form.

In some instances, a terminal can eliminate this source document conversion procedure. Consider, for example, a clerk in an inventory department who uses a voice recognition device for entering inventory data into a computer. A conversion procedure is not required to make the input machine-readable. Instead, the clerk can read inventory data directly from labels on products and verbally transmit it to a CPU. In this instance, then, a terminal not only enables data to be collected at the source but it eliminates source document conversion as well.

The following are input devices specifically designed to reduce manual labor by either (1) reading source documents directly or (2) enabling users to eliminate the need for the source document itself.

2. Optical Scanners

Optical scanning devices or **scanners** can "read" or scan data from a source document itself and process the data immediately, or store the data on a magnetic medium for future batch processing. Scanners eliminate the need for keying data onto a terminal, a key-to-disk machine, a keypunch machine, and so on; they use the source document as input directly.

Most optical scanners use a laser or photoelectric device. The data is read by a light source that converts characters or codes into electronic signals.

The most common optical scanners are the following.

a. Optical Character Recognition (OCR) Devices   **Optical character recognition devices** can read data that has been typed or handwritten on a source document. One type of optical character reader is a high-speed page reader that can read printed or handwritten data from receipts, bills, purchase orders, and so on. The device eliminates the process that would otherwise be necessary to convert source documents to machine-readable form (see Figure 5.21). Most OCR devices require printed data to be in a special type or *font* (see Figure 5.22). Similarly, an OCR device that reads handwritten data requires precise hand lettering (see Figure 5.23).

Figure 5.21
OCR device. (Courtesy
Kurzweil Computer
Products.)

Figure 5.23
Typical rules for making
handwritten characters
readable by OCR devices.

Figure 5.22
Sample type font required
by some OCR devices.

ABCDEFG
HIJKLMN
OPQRSTU
VWXYZ,.
$/*-123
4567890

Rule	Acceptable	Unacceptable
1. Make letters big.	REDFORD	REDFORD
2. Use block letters.	ROBERT	Robert
3. Carefully connect lines.	571	571
4. Close loops.	9086	9086
5. Do not link characters.	ROBERT	ROBERT

Traditional optical character readers vary in speed from 50 characters per second, for devices that read handwritten characters, to 3000 characters per second for devices that read typed characters. Some high-speed OCR document readers, designed for specific source documents, can read from 200 to 1200 documents per minute.

Optical character page readers can be somewhat expensive, ranging in price from $20,000 to $300,000 for larger units. Thus for most applications that process fewer than 10,000 documents per day, it would be cheaper to key source documents into machine-readable form than to acquire an OCR device. Moreover, this equipment has a relatively high error rate resulting from typographical errors, erasures, misprinting, and misalignment, commonly found on source documents. As the reliability of these devices improves and the cost decreases, they will have even greater potential for the future.

Hand-held **wand readers** are also becoming popular in department stores, libraries, hospitals, and factories for reading optical characters that contain inventory data (see Figure 5.24).

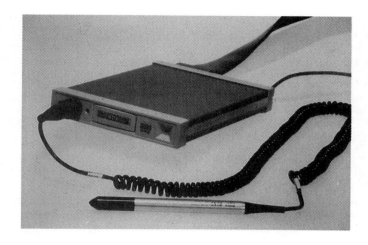

Figure 5.24
Hand-held wand reader.
(Courtesy Intermec Corp.)

b. Bar Code Reader The black and white bars that you see on grocery items at your local supermarket, for example, are read by a **bar code reader.** They identify each product and manufacturer. The code is called the **Universal Product Code (UPC)** and has been the standard for the grocery industry since 1973 (see Figure 5.25).

The bar code reader has a scanning device that translates black and white (or light and dark) bars of different widths into electrical impulses. Thus, there is no need to manually use a data entry device such as a cash register to key the data into the computer. When using a bar code reader, data is already in machine-readable form.

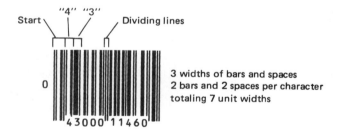

3 widths of bars and spaces
2 bars and 2 spaces per character
totaling 7 unit widths

Figure 5.25
Example of the Universal Product Code, which can be read by a bar code reader.

At supermarket checkout counters, a bar code reader scans the bar code, transmits it to the CPU for a price look-up, and then records the item description and price on a register receipt.

Some industries use bar code readers for inventory control purposes as shown in Figure 5.26. In addition to supermarkets, many assembly lines, warehouses, and distribution centers have devices that read bar codes on individual items to maintain control of inventory.

Even people may be identified with bar codes. For the last several years, runners in the New York City Marathon have been issued identifying bar codes to wear on their jerseys. As each runner finishes the marathon, a scanning device records the runner's name and order of finish from the bar-coded jersey.

Figure 5.26
Bar code reader used in
inventory systems. (Courtesy
Intermec Corp.)

Figure 5.27
Portable mark-sense reader.
(Courtesy HEI, Inc.)

In general, optical character readers are considered to be more "user-friendly" than bar code readers because they can scan letters and digits, including handwritten characters, as opposed to bar codes. Bar code readers, however, have the following advantages.

IIII➡ Advantages of Bar Code Readers

1. Bar code readers are cost-effective units for a wide variety of inventory applications.
2. Readers can scan bar codes with a relatively high accuracy rate.
3. In supermarket applications, an item that is put on sale can simply have the price in the CPU changed, without the necessity of re-marking each item that day. (Note, however, that some states do, in fact, require each item to have a price stamped on it; in other states, it is sufficient to have the price marked on the shelf where the item is stocked.)

c. Optical Mark Reader   An **optical mark reader,** sometimes called a mark-sense reader, detects the presence of pencil marks on predetermined grids (see Figure 5.27). Students are very familiar with one type of source document that is

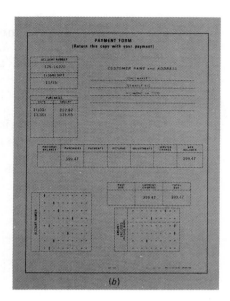

Figure 5.28

Examples of forms that can be read by an optical mark reader. *(a)* Answer sheet.
(b) Payment form that serves as a statement to the customer. When this form is returned
with payment, the account number and amount enclosed (marked at the bottom of the
form) serve as input to an optical mark reader.

mark-sensed: the computer-scored test paper. Answers are placed in specific grids
clearly marked for each question, typically as the letters A–E. In addition to tests,
payment forms and invoices may be mark-sensed and read by a computer with
the use of an optical mark reader (see Figure 5.28 for an illustration of forms
generally read by an optical mark reader).

Because marks must be specifically coded in grids without any stray pencil
marks, these devices have limited versatility and therefore limited use.

IN A NUTSHELL

REVIEW OF OPTICAL SCANNING DEVICES

1. Optical character recognition device.
   Reads typed or handwritten data. Can be high-speed, large devices
   or hand-held wand readers.
2. Bar code reader.
   Used extensively in supermarkets to read grocery items. Also used
   for inventory control in many other industries.
3. Optical mark reader.
   Used extensively for scoring tests and also for payment forms and
   invoices.

3. Specialized Input Units for Data Entry in Banking

a. Magnetic Ink Character Reader Figure 5.29 illustrates magnetic ink digits that are encoded on the bottom of bank checks. When the check is distributed to the bank's customer, it contains data that identifies the account. After the check has been used in a transaction and returned to the bank, it is encoded with the amount of the check.

Large batches of checks are then accumulated and read by a high-speed **magnetic ink character reader (MICR)** device, which reads, sorts, and transmits the magnetic ink characters to a device such as tape or disk (see Figure 5.30).

In the United States, more than 100 million checks are processed with MICR devices each day. Note that these units can only read *digits*.

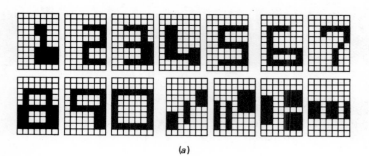

(a)

Figure 5.29
(a) Magnetic ink digits. *(b)* Bank check showing the use of magnetic ink digits.

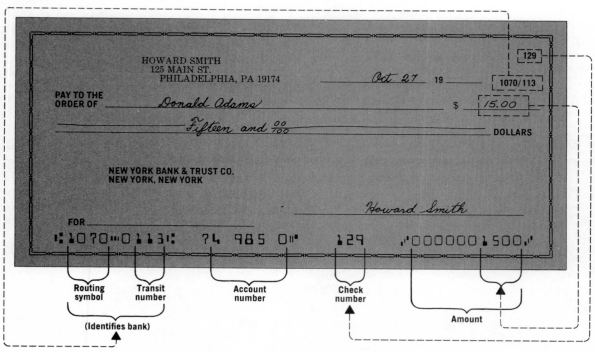

(b)

Figure 5.30
MICR reader/sorter used in a
banking operation.
(Courtesy Honeywell.)

b. Automatic Teller Machine   Electronic funds transfer (EFT) systems are on-line banking systems in which data entered at the point of transaction automatically and immediately updates banking records. Fully integrated and interactive electronic funds transfer systems are in the process of being designed (see Chapter 14), but have not yet been fully realized.

One aspect of an EFT system, however, that has become highly successful in many banks throughout the United States is the **automatic teller machine.**

Automatic teller machines found at bank branch offices serve as data entry terminals for the processing of deposits and withdrawals (see Figure 5.31).

These devices provide 24-hour banking service to customers. The customer inserts a plastic bank identification card and is then usually required to key in a personal identification number, sometimes referred to as a password, for security purposes. If the card and password are valid, the customer indicates the nature of the transaction. In this way, a deposit or withdrawal may be made. For withdrawals, cash is provided immediately to the customer, assuming there are sufficient funds in the account.

Figure 5.31
Automatic teller machine.
(Courtesy IBM.)

Self-Evaluating Quiz

1. Data read by an input device may be processed in two ways: _____ or in _____ mode.
2. A(n) _____ is a device that can read printed or handwritten data using a light source to convert characters into electronic signals.
3. The bar code used on grocery items is called the _____.
4. (T or F) A bar code reader at a supermarket reads product data and the price from each item.
5. A point-of-sale terminal in a department store typically uses a _____ device to enter charge account data at the point where the charge is made.
6. (T or F) Applications that use optical scanners do not need to convert source documents into a machine-readable form because the document itself can be read.
7. A device that can read pencil marks used to answer multiple choice test questions is called a(n) _____.
8. The device that reads specially recorded characters on the bottom of bank checks is called a _____.
9. (T or F) Bank checks can be coded with magnetized letters or digits.
10. A(n) _____ is a computer input unit found at bank branch offices for processing deposits and withdrawals.
11. (T or F) Data entry devices may be used for entering data directly into a CPU or for storing data on tape and disk.
12. If a data entry device is used to key data onto a tape, the tape will usually be processed in a _____ mode.

Solutions

1. immediately
   batch
2. optical character reader or optical scanner
3. Universal Product Code
4. F—Price is usually stored in the computer.
5. keyboard
6. T—That is the main advantage of optical scanners.
7. optical mark reader or mark-sense reader
8. magnetic ink character reader
9. F—Digits only.
10. automatic teller machine
11. T
12. batch

III. PREPARING INPUT DATA

A. Hierarchy of Data

When input is collected and stored for processing, it is usually organized using the following concepts.

Organization of Input

Character—The smallest unit of data consisting of a letter, digit, or special symbol such as $, %, and so on.

Field—One or more consecutive characters representing a data item (e.g., NAME field, AMOUNT field, and so on).

Record—Groups of fields pertaining to a specific application (e.g., a sales slip or a credit slip is an example of a record).

File—A major collection of records for given systems such as payroll, inventory, sales, and so on.

Figure 5.32 shows a schematic of the relationships among characters, fields, records, and files.

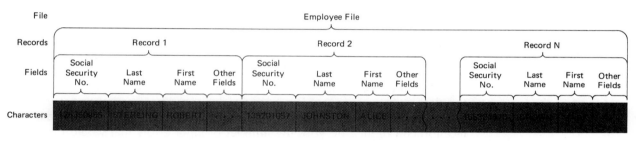

Figure 5.32
Illustration of a tape file showing the hierarchy of data.

B. File Design Considerations

The actual design of input records in a file is performed by a systems analyst with the advice of the user. That is, if a sales slip, for example, is to be keyed on a terminal, the format of that record must be efficient for computer processing as well as acceptable to the user. Several rules are followed for effective computerization.

1. Data should be entered in a concise format. Extraneous characters such as dollar signs and commas are not typically included in input data. Decimal points can also be eliminated without affecting decimal alignment.

2. Each record in a file has a key field that uniquely identifies the record. This key should be positioned as the first field, so that each record is clearly identified. A sales record, for example, would be entered with account number first; a payroll record could be entered with Social Security number as its key field, and so on.

3. Codes should be used to make data concise. That is, Marital Status could be an eight-character field to accommodate entries such as "DIVORCED," "MARRIED," "WIDOWED," and so on. But a more efficient system would be to code the field so that it consists of a single character code, where D = Divorced, M = Married, and so on.

C. Detecting Data Entry Errors

Murphy's law has specific relevance to data entry operations: if something can possibly go wrong, it eventually will go wrong. To ensure a reliable data entry procedure, data should be checked and rechecked to minimize errors before input is processed by the computer.

Data entry and keying errors are the major type of input errors and account for 10% of all computer processing mistakes. A 10% error rate is a relatively high one and cannot be tolerated for most applications. The following discussion provides an insight into several methods that are used to reduce these data entry errors. In this section we briefly consider the systems design features used to detect and minimize data entry errors. (Chapter 15 discusses these and other controls in more depth.)

1. Data Verification for Key-to-Storage Operations

For many applications, data is keyed and then stored on some storage medium such as a disk or tape. For verification purposes, a second data entry operator re-keys the same data but this time the device used does not actually create input; instead, it checks to see that the data entered this second time matches the data originally entered. If the two keying operations do not match, the data entry operator determines whether the data was incorrectly entered the first time and what corrections, if any, are necessary.

Data verification is a costly procedure because it essentially duplicates the data entry procedure. But because data validity is so important in most applications, the cost is frequently considered a worthwhile expense. Data verification can reduce by 90% the number of input errors that would otherwise occur.

2. Control Listings and Totals That Are Checked by the User Organization

A second method used to minimize data entry errors is by producing a listing of all input called a **control listing.** A total of the number of records processed is also supplied to ensure that some records were not inadvertently left out. The user department typically assigns a clerk the task of checking these control listings and totals to ensure that all data was in fact entered and that there are no errors.

3. Programmed Checks

Programs that are written to minimize data entry errors usually include control procedures. Suppose a specific application requires payroll data to be entered. It is possible to include tests in a program to ensure that (1) each hourly rate entered falls within pre-established limits, (2) name and Social Security number are included for each record, (3) the hours worked field is reasonable, and so on. Other programmed checks include procedures to ensure that data entered is in the appropriate format.

As previously noted, each group of characters used to represent a unit of data is called a *field.* **Numeric fields** are checked to make certain they have only numeric data; alphabetic fields are checked to make certain they have only letters or blanks. **Alphanumeric fields** can contain any type of data (either alphabetic, numeric, or special characters); they need not be checked to ensure proper data format, since any characters are acceptable.

Programmed checks reduce the risk of mistakes; they also reduce the risk of an employee deliberately trying to cheat the system by entering a high hourly rate or hours worked entry in a payroll procedure. Programmed checks cannot eliminate all input errors but they can help to minimize them.

4. Using Sequence Numbers for Data Records

For some applications that use purchase orders or invoice numbers, data records must be numbered consecutively. A program can check to see that all input data has been entered with consecutive numbers. If the program detects missing numbers in a purchase order file, for example, it would print an error message that would require a user to check the file.

D. Evaluating Data Entry Devices

How do computer professionals determine the type of data entry procedure to use for a specific application? The answer will, of course, depend on the input devices to be used. There are many factors that influence the selection of input forms; moreover, these factors are dependent on intangible components such as overall company preferences, specific user preferences, and current equipment on hand. The tangible factors influencing selection and evaluation of data entry devices include the following.

IN A NUTSHELL

FACTORS INFLUENCING SELECTION OF INPUT DEVICES

1. Cost of (a) data entry procedures and (b) the input device.
2. Speed of the input device.
3. Nature of the source document (can conversion be eliminated?).
4. Reliability of the input device.
5. User-friendliness and ease of operation of the input device.
6. Physical size of the input device.
7. On-site requirements for installing the input device.
8. Is there a need to capture data at the source?

CHAPTER SUMMARY

I. Data entry
  A. How data becomes input.
    1. Data may be keyed from a source document to some machine-readable form such as a tape, disk, or punched cards.

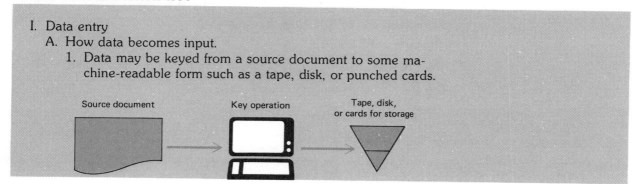

Source document   Key operation   Tape, disk,
                                                or cards for storage

2. Data may be read directly by an input device capable of reading source documents.

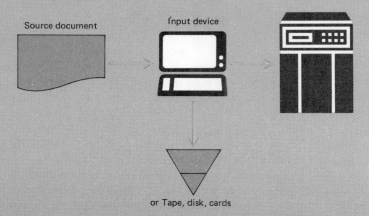

Source document   Input device

or Tape, disk, cards

B. When data is entered as input:
 1. It may be immediately processed by a CPU.
 2. It may be stored on a tape, disk, or cards for future batch processing by the CPU.
II. Input units of a computer system
 A. Terminal input.
  1. Keyboard—for keying input data.
  2. Light pen, mouse, or touch-sensitive screen—for making changes to a CRT or selecting items from a menu.
  3. Voice recognition unit—for entering verbal input.
  4. Touch-Tone telephone—for keying numeric input from remote locations.
 B. Card reader.
  1. The punched card is an older input form that is still sometimes used.
  2. Punched card data can be read by people as well as machines.
  3. Standard punched card data is restricted to an 80-column format.
  4. Cards are difficult to maintain—they can be bent, stapled, folded, etc.
 C. Optical scanners.
  1. Optical character readers can read handwritten and printed data directly from source documents.
  2. Bar code readers can read the Universal Product Codes on grocery products.
  3. Optical mark readers are used for computerized test scoring.
 D. Input for banking.
  1. Magnetic ink character readers can read and sort numeric data coded on the bottom of bank checks.
  2. Automatic teller machines at bank branches are used for entering deposits and withdrawals.

E. Tape and disk.
Tapes and disks are used for high-volume, high-speed data entry.
Tape and disk processing are discussed in Chapter 7.
III. Input design
  A. Data is typically stored as fields within records. The collection of records is called a file.
  B. Input should be carefully designed.
    1. Key fields are coded first.
    2. Sequence numbers for input records should be used where appropriate.
IV. Minimizing input errors
  A. Check input by duplicating the data entry procedure for verification.
  B. Control listings that print all input and totals should be checked by the user.
  C. Programs should include control procedures for minimizing errors.

Chapter Self-Evaluating Quiz

1. A purchase order used as input to a computer system would be called a _____.

2. If a purchase order is handwritten, there would be two ways of inputting it into the computer system: _____ and _____.

3. (T or F) Some input units can read source documents directly; others require source documents to be converted to some machine-readable form.

4. (T or F) An inventory tag that contains a bar code could be an example of a source document.

5. Converting from source documents to machine-readable form usually requires an operator to enter data by _____ it.

6. (T or F) If input data is prepared 50 miles from the computer center, the fastest method for transmitting it is by special messenger.

7. (T or F) If a payroll record required 100 characters of data, and the form used for the record was punched cards, then two cards would be required for each payroll record.

8. Representing digits on a punched card requires (no.) hole(s) per column; representing letters on a punched card requires (no.) hole(s) per column.

9. (T or F) All punched cards have 80 columns.

10. (T or F) A turnaround document must be converted to machine-readable form before it can be processed.

11. A _____ is usually connected to a CRT for entering data into the CPU.

12. One way to enter data on a CRT is to use a _____ to touch specific grids on the screen to indicate functions desired.

13. (T or F) A Touch-Tone telephone must be used in conjunction with a voice recognition device to enter data into a CPU.

14. Input devices that can read printed characters directly from a source document are called _____.

15. At supermarket checkout counters, a bar code reader _____ each item's universal product code, looks up the price of the item in the _____, and records the item description and price on a register receipt.

16. (T or F) Automatic teller machines reduce the need for human tellers; moreover, they enable people to bank 24-hours a day.

17. The smallest unit of data consisting of a letter, digit, or special symbol is called a _____.

18. Files of data consist of units of data called _____.

19. (T or F) The entire group of sales slips read by a computer system would be called a data file.

20. A _____ field is one that uniquely identifies the record within a file.

21. (T or F) Most data entry errors are a result of transmission errors from an input device to the CPU.

22. (T or F) It is necessary to have a program check an alphanumeric field to ensure that data is in the proper format.

Solutions

1. source document / page 153
2. using an optical character reader that can scan handwritten data / page 171 converting to machine-readable form using a key device / page 155
3. T / page 155
4. T / page 153
5. keying / page 155
6. F—The fastest method is to transmit the data over communications lines. / page 156
7. T—A standard card can contain only 80 characters. / page 160
8. one / page 161 two—one zone and one digit / page 162
9. F—Most punched cards have 80-columns. Some, however, have 96-columns. / page 163
10. F / page 165
11. keyboard / page 166

12. light pen (or even your finger if it is a touch-sensitive screen) / page 167
13. F—Touch-Tone phones may be used with voice recognition devices but they do not always need to be; the operative word in the question is "must." / page 168
14. optical character readers or optical scanners / page 171
15. scans or reads / page 173 CPU or storage / page 173
16. T / page 177
17. character / page 179
18. records / page 179
19. T / page 179
20. key / page 179
21. F—Most data entry errors are a result of keying or manual errors. / page 180
22. F—Any character is acceptable in an alphanumeric field. / page 180

Key Terms

Alphanumeric field
Automatic teller machine
Bar code reader
Card reader
Control listing
Data entry device
Data verification
Field
File
Hollerith code
Light pen
Magnetic Ink Character Reader (MICR)
Mouse

Numeric field
Optical character recognition (OCR)
  device
Optical mark reader
Optical scanning device (optical
  scanner)
Record
Source document
Turnaround document
Universal Product Code (UPC)
Voice recognition unit
Wand reader

Review Questions

1. (T or F) Source documents must be converted to machine-readable form with the use of key-to-storage devices.

2. Input that is on printed paper would be read by an input device called a(n) _____.

3. Banks use _____ for reading magnetized digits on checks.

4. Tests that are to be computer-scored are read by an input device called a(n) _____.

5. (T or F) Card readers are still used to read input data at some organizations, but they are slower than tape or disk drives.

6. (T or F) Input can only be entered on a terminal with the use of a keyboard.

7. (T or F) It is not yet possible for devices to interpret verbal messages.

8. (T or F) A file of data consists of data records.

9. A(n) _____ field is one that can contain any type of data—letters, digits, or special characters.

10. (T or F) An address field is an example of an alphabetic field.

11. The most common cause of data entry errors is _____.

12. (T or F) Data that is entered on a terminal may be immediately transmitted to a CPU or stored on tape or disk for future batch processing.

13. The code used for representing data on a punched card is called the _____ code.

14. Using a _____, a user can make changes directly to a CRT screen.

15. The code used for representing product information on grocery items is called the _____.

16. (T or F) A telephone may be used as a terminal.

17. (T or F) Most terminals can both transmit messages to a CPU and receive responses from the CPU.

18. A system that is used for keying data and storing it on tape or disk is called a _____ system.

19. Processing data at fixed intervals rather than immediately as it is transacted is called _____.

20. Verification of data refers to the process of _____.

APPLICATION

SPEECH RECOGNITION: AN IDEA WHOSE TIME IS COMING

by George M. White

Someday machines that recognize speech will be commonplace. People will talk to computers, typewriters, toys, TV sets, household appliances, automobile controls, door locks, and wristwatches. Each of these speech-recognition applications is currently being explored; some early forms are already on the market, while other forms are proving to be beyond our current capabilities. In this article, I'll examine some of the theory and market prospects for this exciting and elusive technology.

Having our lives filled with machines that obey verbal commands can transform our views of machines. Mechanical devices can take on a subtle lifelike quality when given the ability to respond to speech. This lifelike quality is further amplified when coupled with the machine intelligence that emanates from personal computers, arcade games, robotics, and household automation systems. We continue to be fascinated by the evolution of such intelligent products, and we probably could not reverse this trend, even as visionaries warn that we'll lose our freedom to new mechanical life forms.

Automatic speech recognition is generally considered to be the most difficult and complex problem in the field of voice processing. Voice synthesis, compression, analysis, encryption, and transmission are all more narrowly defined, and all contribute to the solution of the speech-recognition problem. Some of the world's largest companies (AT&T, IBM, Exxon), the U.S. Department of Defense, and several universities have been developing speech-recognition technology for years without the hoped-for degree of success. But despite difficulties, steady progress is being made.

In the past 10 years, at least a dozen start-up companies have been founded explicitly to develop and market speech-recognition products. Although several have gone out of business, about a dozen companies plan to be in the market with new products in 1984.

Philosophical Issues

The specter of Big Brother may not be of concern in Western society today, but the evolution of distributed intelligence among machines with speech-recognition capability certainly provides the technical base for monitoring our activities. In fact, the U.S. National Security Agency has developed what may be the world's most advanced speech-recognition algorithms. This system spots keywords in intercepted verbal transmissions from "unfriendly" nations. Currently, it is not likely that such techniques would be used for domestic surveillance. But speech technologists as well as the public must be aware of the potential loss of privacy.

Speech recognition is not a typical engineering problem. It is a scientific Gordian knot. It draws on LSI (large-scale integration) and VLSI (very large-scale integration) chip design, signal processing, acoustic-phonetics, natural-language theory, linguistics, mathematics of stochastic (probability) processes, and computer science techniques. Because of its multidisciplinary nature and because many competent minds have pondered the problem for years, we should not expect a breakthrough in speech-recognition capability. Progress will be made, but it will be evolutionary, not revolutionary. Naive enthusiasm from novices in the field sometimes leads to proclamations that dramatic progress is imminent. Such views fail to consider the interdependence of disciplines required to produce a commercially viable product.

Nearly 15 years ago, a number of companies and engineering organizations predicted near-term success in speech recognition. This prompted a prominent scientific leader, John Pierce, to say that automatic speech recognition was the domain of "untrustworthy engineers" and that we would not have speech recognition until we had true artificial intelligence (AI).

Pierce based his critique on the observation that normal speech contains many words that are acoustically ambiguous, and it is only through contextual information and knowledge of linguistic constraints that we are able to remove the ambiguity. Because only humans have demonstrated sufficient understanding of the language constructs of spoken sentences to use them in a way that is unambiguous, Pierce's conclusion that fluent speech recognition requires human-like intelligence is understandable.

Today we do have elemental speech-recognition systems that recognize short utterances. However, this does not nullify Pierce's argument; it is a matter of the type of speech to be recognized. When fluent conversational speech is involved, a "model of the domain of discourse" must be employed, and the recognition process is called "understanding." This is, by definition, in the domain of AI. Recognition of short utterances using only template pattern-matching techniques is, in current vernacular, "pattern recognition," not "understanding."

In a broader sense, even the simplest forms of speech recognition are a part of AI, and AI is spread out in the technologies that make up modern society. The maturation of speech recognition and AI has not been by intellectual tour de force but by a broad-based industrial/technical evolution. Key events in this evolution include the appearance of the mass market for home computers, VLSI, mass-production techniques, and, perhaps, even Pac-Man. Although these are not usually thought of in the same context as machine intelligence and speech recognition, they play a significant role in the development of such capabilities, and they cannot be ignored by forecasters and planners who hope to tell us what products will materialize in the next few years.

Success is slowly materializing. Today we have adequate machine intelligence to achieve elemental automatic speech recognition (ASR), but we are a long way from conversational speech understanding.

Source: BYTE, January 1984, page 213. Reprinted with permission.

Questions
1. Understanding Key Terms
   Define the following terms as they are used in the application:
   a. Machine intelligence.
   b. Automatic speech recognition.
   c. VLSI technology.
2. Software, Hardware, and Systems Concepts
   What problems have been encountered that have kept speech recognition devices from being widely used?
3. Management Considerations
   What application areas can you see for speech recognition devices that have not been mentioned in the application?
4. Social, Legal, and Ethical Implications
   Suppose a bank enables users to make deposits and withdrawals via a speech recognition device. What controls would be necessary to minimize unauthorized use of the system?

CASE STUDY: McKing's Superburgers, Inc.

1. Data Entry
   Computer vendors have recommended a variety of devices for the order-entry process at McKing's. The list of devices includes the following:
   1. Voice recognition unit.
   2. CRT screen with a light pen.
   3. Keyboard terminal with keys designating menu items and system functions.
   4. An optical character recognition device to read order forms completed by customers.
   5. An optical mark reader to read order forms completed by customers that have digits to represent specific items.
   a. What factors would you consider in determining which data entry device to select?
   b. Based on the above list, what would be your recommendations for input devices for McKing's? Explain your answer in detail.

Figure 5.33
Example of a terminal for restaurant use. (Courtesy NCR.)

2. Examine the terminal in Figure 5.33 and indicate if it would be appropriate for McKing's. Indicate the pros and cons of this device.

3. Inventory File
   A major file that will be maintained in connection with the order entry system is a prepared food file. The purpose of this file is to keep records on the quantity on hand at the counter of each item that is prepared in the kitchen.
   a. Indicate the fields you would expect to find in this file for McKing's.
   b. Would you use any coded fields? Explain your answer.
   c. Indicate which field you would recommend as the key field for this file.
   d. What procedure would you recommend for entering price changes or new items to this file?

THE COMPUTER AD: A Focus on Marketing

Consider the ad entitled "The All American Keyboard" that appears in Figure 5.34.

1. The Cherry Keyboard is marketed as a "detached" keyboard. What are the advantages of such a device?
2. Indicate the advantages of "nonglare keycaps."

3. What message do you believe the manufacturers are attempting to convey with the physical design and colors of the keyboard?
4. ASCII code is provided with this keyboard. What other codes might be available?

Cherry's new DIN-compatible foam pad capacitive keyboard:

° Low enough in profile to meet 1985 European ergonomic standards.

° Low enough in price to be your most cost-efficient spec.

Now, Cherry's proven foam pad capacitive technology is available in a low profile, linear feel, full travel keymodule. A keymodule that's ideal for detached encoded keyboards. With a uniquely simple design requiring only five parts and a snap-in angled foam pad for hysteresis to prevent teasing. New ergonomic cylindrical button set with non-glare keycaps.

Another Cherry first is our new hex sense amplifier with six inputs that allow horizontal rows of keys to be attached with minimal printed circuit complexity... requires only six I/O lines from a microprocessor for operation. An inexpensive microprocessor that provides ASCII or other codes, N-key rollover, serial output and bi-directional serial interfaces.

Send today for complete technical and application data.

Just .704" (17.88mm) from PC board to keycap top of home row!

CHERRY KEYBOARDS

CHERRY ELECTRICAL PRODUCTS CORP. 3600 Sunset Avenue, Waukegan, IL 60087 • 312/578-3500

Figure 5.34
Marketing computer products. (Courtesy Cherry Electrical Products Corp.)

CHAPTER

6

COMPUTER-PRODUCED OUTPUT

CHAPTER OBJECTIVES

To familiarize you with:

■ The most common output units and media used with computers.
■ The format of printed output.
■ The format of output displayed on a screen.
■ The use of graphics, audio responses, and microfilm as alternatives to traditional printed or displayed output.
■ Methods used for displaying or printing output in user-friendly ways.

I. INTRODUCTION

A computer reads data from some input form that can be accepted by the system and processes it according to the specifications provided in a program. If the procedure runs smoothly, the result of this operation is output information that is timely, meaningful, user-friendly, and in a useful format.

In the past, computer-produced output was prepared almost exclusively as a printed report. This form is still widely used but there are numerous alternative methods of providing information.

We will consider the following output media and the corresponding devices that generate the output form:

Output Medium	Device Used
Printed reports	Printer or hard-copy terminal
Terminal response—displayed	Cathode ray tube (CRT) or video display terminal
Graphs—bar charts, pie charts, line drawings	Graphics display terminal or plotter
Verbal response	Audio response unit
Microfilm	Computer output microfilm (COM) unit

Note that although there are numerous other output media and devices, the above represent the most commonly used.

The type of output to be provided for any given application is determined by the systems analyst in conjunction with the user. Factors affecting the type of output that will be required for any application include the following:

Factors Influencing the Output Form Selected

1. Current equipment at the company.
2. Specific needs of the user. For example, is printed or displayed output needed? Is graphic or typed data more appropriate?
3. What the user regards as "user-friendly" output.
4. Processing requirements of the application. For example, will batch or immediate processing be required?

Output can typically be produced (1) at the computer site and then distributed or (2) at remote locations by using terminals. Output can also be produced on a regularly scheduled basis, or "on demand," as needed. Some printers can display graphics as well as printing typed characters, both in color.

II. COMMON OUTPUT UNITS

A. The Printer and Hard-Copy Terminal

A traditional printer is an output unit that produces printed output, usually in batch mode. A hard-copy terminal is a type of printer that is usually used in an on-line mode to provide immediate responses to inquiries or to provide reports at remote locations. Both units provide **hard-copy** or printed output.

We will consider the following three major types of printers.

⫸ Types of Printers

Category	Primary Application	Speed
Serial printer	Hard-copy terminal or printer for micro	Slow-speed (measured in characters per second)
Line printer	Used mostly as the main printer for computers in the mini to mainframe range	Medium-speed (measured in lines per minute)
Page printer	Used mostly for large mainframes	Fast-speed (measured in pages per minute)

The following discussion focuses on the types of serial, line, and page printers currently available.

1. Serial Printer

Serial printers are most commonly used as terminals or as printers for microcomputers. Like typewriters, these devices print one character at a time, which produces a relatively slow form of output. Figure 6.1 illustrates a serial printer. Because they are slow, serial devices are primarily terminals or printers for minis and micros; that is, they are rarely used as primary printers for mainframes.

As we will see, serial printers can print characters using either (1) a pattern of dot-matrices or (2) standard, fully formed characters using a device such as a daisy wheel.

a. The Dot-Matrix Printer The **dot-matrix** or wire-matrix **printer** is one of the most common serial printers, and is frequently used with line printers as well. Each print position consists of a rectangular grid of pins. A character is represented by activating a specific combination of pins that are pressed against a carbon ribbon to imprint it. See Figure 6.2 for an illustration of characters formed with dot-matrix printers.

Figure 6.1
Example of a serial printer. (Courtesy IBM.)

The grid size for dot-matrix printers varies, but 5 × 7, 7 × 5, and 9 × 7 grids are common.

Dot-matrix printers tend to be faster and more versatile than printers that print fully formed characters, like typewriters. One reason they are more versatile is because dot-matrix printers can provide greater graphics capability; they can use a gridlike structure for forming a wide variety of characters.

Speeds of dot-matrix printers vary widely, but the typical range is from 50 to 1000 or more characters per second. Prices vary as well, with a typical range of from several hundred dollars to $5000 or more. The slower devices are, of course, cheaper than the faster ones.

b. The Daisy Wheel Printer   The most popular mechanism for printing fully formed characters with serial printers is the **daisy wheel**. A daisy wheel is a flat disk with petal-like projections on which print characters appear, as illustrated in Figure 6.3. These devices provide better quality printing than dot-matrix printers. They are sometimes referred to as "letter-quality printers," although some dot-matrix printers can produce high quality output as well. Daisy wheel printers also provide versatility, since print wheels can be easily replaced to provide for different type fonts, foreign alphabets, and numerous special characters such as mathematical symbols. Most daisy wheels, however, do not have as much graphics capability as can be provided by dot-matrix printers.

Daisy wheel printers are usually slower than dot-matrix devices. Speeds for daisy wheel printers tend to vary from 10 to 100 characters per second, with prices ranging from several hundred dollars to $3000 or more. The following chart provides a basic comparison of dot-matrix and daisy wheel printers.

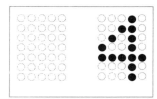

5 × 7 dot pattern

ABCDEFGH
IJKLMNOP
QRSTUVWX
YZ012345
6789—.,;8
/✦$*#%@=
(+)

Figure 6.2
Sample dot-matrix characters.

Figure 6.3
Daisy wheel mechanism. (Courtesy AGT Computer Products, Inc.)

IN A NUTSHELL

DOT-MATRIX AND DAISY WHEEL SERIAL PRINTERS

Printer	Features	Advantages	Limitations	Speed[1]	Cost
Dot-matrix	Characters represented by activating a combination of pins on a grid	Fast; can have good graphics	Does not always provide high-quality print	50 to 1000 cps	Several hundred dollars to $5000 +
Daisy wheel	Flat disk contains characters that rotate and strike paper	Wheels can easily be changed for representing different type fonts, different alphabets, and mathematical symbols	Slow; very little graphics	10 to 100 cps	Several hundred dollars to $3000 +

[1]In characters per second (cps).

Figure 6.4
Ink-jet printer. (Courtesy
Taylor Instruments and
Printacolor.)

Note that dot-matrix mechanisms are still the most popular type for serial printers.

In summary, for high-volume, interoffice documents where the quality of printing is not as important as speed, dot-matrix printers would probably be used. Where "letter-quality" printing is the major consideration for producing letters and documents to be mailed to customers, a daisy wheel printer would probably be used.

c. Nonimpact versus Impact Printers   Serial printers are usually either dot-matrix or daisy wheel devices. These printers can also use impact or nonimpact mechanisms. An **impact printer** operates mechanically with a hammer striking a key in a manner similar to a typewriter. **Nonimpact printers** use a newer technology.

Most serial and line printers are impact devices. Nonimpact serial printers used as terminals are usually thermal or ink-jet devices. As we will see later, the fastest printers almost always use some high-speed nonimpact technology, such as a laser or xerographic mechanism.

Some serial printers, such as thermal printers, use special paper sensitive to heat. Characters are formed by selectively heating the print head. Other serial printers, such as ink-jet printers, use electrostatically charged characters to hit the paper. Ink-jet printers are often used for producing printed output in color, or for printing graphics (see Figure 6.4).

Figure 6.5 shows an analysis of the types of serial printers that are currently used.

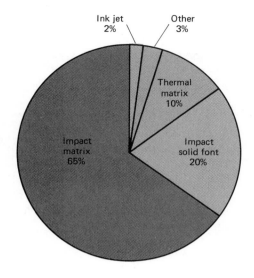

Figure 6.5
Analysis of types of serial printers that are currently used. (*Source*: GML Corp.)

Self-Evaluating Quiz

1. (T or F) A terminal may be used as a printer if it can produce hard-copy output.
2. Most printers used with microcomputers or as hard-copy terminals are (serial/line/page) printers.
3. Most printers used for moderate to high-volume printing with minis and mainframes are (serial/line/page) printers.
4. The fastest type of printer in use today is called the (serial/line/page) printer.
5. Printers with speeds measured in characters per second are (serial/line/page) printers.
6. A printer that forms characters out of a wire-matrix grid is called a _____ printer.
7. The most common mechanism used for printing fully formed characters for serial printers is the _____.
8. (T or F) Dot-matrix printers are usually classified as letter-quality printers.
9. A(n) _____ printer operates mechanically with a hammer striking a key in a manner similar to a typewriter.
10. (T or F) Nonimpact devices are used for high-speed as well as serial printers.

Solutions

1. T
2. serial
3. line
4. page
5. serial

6. dot-matrix
7. daisy wheel
8. F
9. impact
10. T

2. Line Printer

Most minis and mainframes use **line printers** for moderate- to high-volume information processing applications. These devices print one line of output at a time. If you are working with a micro in a classroom environment, you are apt to be using a serial printer. If you use terminals linked to a mainframe or mini, your output is likely to be produced by a line printer.

a. Print Mechanism for Line Printers: Band, Chain, or Drum   Most line printers are classified as follows:

1. Band printer.
2. Chain printer.
3. Drum printer.

The following is a discussion of the technical features of these types of line printers, for those of you with an interest in printer technology.

(1) Band Printer.   A **band printer** uses a flexible stainless steel print band that is photo-engraved with print characters as in Figure 6.6. The band rotates horizontally until the characters to print are properly aligned.

Band printers are new devices that have become the most popular type of line printer in a relatively short time. They are inexpensive, with removable bands that allow type fonts to be changed easily. They also provide high-quality printing.

(2) Chain Printer.   With a **chain printer,** there is one print hammer for each print position on the line. The characters are printed when the hammer presses the paper against the inked ribbon, as in Figure 6.7.

The chain revolves horizontally past all print positions. As a character on the chain passes the position in which it is to print, the hammer presses the paper against the ribbon. This produces a character image. Two major disadvantages of chain printers are that they are relatively high priced, and some have chains that are difficult to change.

Figure 6.7
Print chain mechanism.

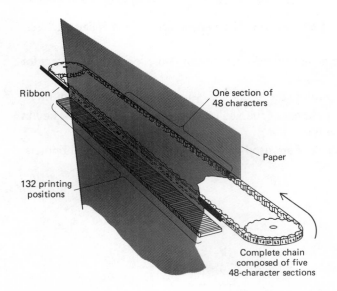

Ribbon

One section of
48 characters

Paper

132 printing
positions

Complete chain
composed of five
48-character sections

(a)

(b)

Figure 6.6
(a) Band printer. (b) Ribbons and bands are easily accessible for changing. (c) Boards are easily replaceable in case of malfunction. There are extra slots in the board for adding functions. (Courtesy Control Data Corp.)

(c)

(3) Drum Printer. A **drum printer** uses a cylindrical steel drum embossed with print characters. Each column on the drum contains all the characters; each array of characters corresponds to a single print position on the line. As the drum rotates at high speed, the character that is to print reaches the appropriate position and a hammer then strikes that character (see Figure 6.8).

Number of bands corresponds
to number of printing positions

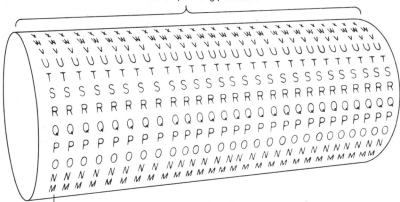

Print position 1

Figure 6.8
Print drum.

Drum printers are being replaced by newer band printers, which are more versatile and tend to last longer.

In summary, the line printer at most companies is likely to be a band printer. Line printers, in general, vary in speed between 100 and 2000 or more lines per minute. Prices vary too, from a few thousand dollars to $50,000 and up.

Most serial and line printers are typically categorized as impact printers because they operate by using a hammer to strike a character against an inked ribbon; the impact causes an image of the character to be printed. The impact mechanism used is similar to that of a typewriter.

The main disadvantage of impact over nonimpact printers is that they are usually slower, noisier, and subject to mechanical breakdown. Yet because they are relatively inexpensive, they remain the most popular type of printer.

In short, most printers used for moderate- to high-volume operations are *impact line printers* that use *band technology*. Figure 6.9 shows typical speeds for line printers and the types of technology used for these devices.

3. Page Printer

A **page printer** is a *nonimpact printer* that uses electronic components for producing very high-speed output. Two common types of high-speed nonimpact page printers are:

1. Laser.
2. Xerographic.

Figure 6.10 illustrates a laser printer that can print up to 21,000 lines per minute.

Figure 6.11 provides an in-depth view of the physical characteristics of all types of nonimpact printers.

Figure 6.9
Typical speeds for line printers, and the types of technology used. (*Source:* Digital Associates Corp.)

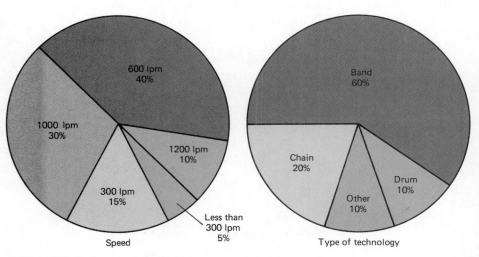

Notes: 1. lpm - lines per minute
2. Percentages are based on the total number of line printers in use.

Figure 6.10
Laser printer. (Courtesy
DatagraphiX, Inc.)

Figure 6.11
Features of nonimpact
printers.

Type	Major Use	Technology	Advantages	Disadvantages	Typical Speed	Approximate Cost
Thermal	Low-speed terminals	Temperature sensitive; paper changes color when treated; characters are formed by selectively heating print head	Quiet; relatively inexpensive	"Special purpose" paper required; cannot use pre-printed form; paper fades (print quality is poor)	Several dozen to several hundred characters per second	Under $10,000
Electrosensitive	High-speed terminals	Paper has metallic coating; voltage is applied to print mechanism, which burns away metallic coating	Low cost; high speed	Black printing on silver paper is not very attractive; print quality is poor; paper wrinkles	160 to 6600 characters per second	Under $5000 on the average
Ink-jet	High-quality printing	Electrostatically charged drops hit the paper	High-quality printing	Relatively slow	Several hundred characters per second	Under $30,000 on the average
Electrostatic	High-speed printing and plotting	Dielectric paper moves past a stylus; voltages are applied selectively; paper then passes through a toner	Very high speed	Requires special paper; requires messy preparation	Several hundred to 6000 lines per minute	Tens of thousands of dollars to over $100,000
Laser	High speed	Laser beam directed onto a drum; paper then passes through a toner	Very high speed; excellent quality; the most promising high-speed print technology	High cost; requires a preparatory phase	Several hundred *pages* per minute	Several hundred thousand dollars
Xerographic	High speed	Uses printing method similar to that used in copying machines	Prints on standard 8½ × 11 paper	Complex copying process subject to breakdown	5000 lines per minute	Several thousand dollars

4. Evaluating Printers

a. Impact versus Nonimpact   The following list summarizes the major differences between impact and nonimpact printers.

||||> **Impact versus Nonimpact Printers**

	Impact		Nonimpact
For	*Against*	*For*	*Against*
1. Inexpensive	1. Slow	1. Can be used for high-speed output	1. Costly
2. Can produce numerous carbon copies, as needed	2. Noisy	2. Can produce high-quality printed output	2. Paper is sometimes expensive
	3. Subject to mechanical breakdown		3. Cannot produce carbon copies

b. Factors to Consider When Selecting a Printer   The factors used for selecting printers will vary depending on the needs of the user organization. The following list represents some of the factors to be considered when evaluating printers.

IN A NUTSHELL

FACTORS USED FOR SELECTING PRINTERS

1. Speed.
2. Cost.
3. Print mechanism.
4. The number of characters per line.
5. Type of characters or "type font" required—can the printer handle different type fonts?
6. Is a printer needed to produce graphics?
7. Is a printer needed to print in color?
8. Are lower- as well as uppercase letters needed?

LOOKING AHEAD

Trends in Printer Technology

1. Serial printer technology is moving more toward dot-matrix methods and away from fully formed characters.
2. Thermal printers are losing popularity as serial printers.
3. Electrostatic printing still suffers from low quality and high paper costs.
4. Ink-jet printing is still expensive but holds promise for the future.
5. Sales of serial printers is increasing in large part because they are used with micros, while sales of impact line and nonimpact page printers are decreasing.

Self-Evaluating Quiz

1. Most mainframes use (serial/line/page) printers for moderate to high-volume information processing applications.
2. A line printer prints one _____ at a time.
3. The three most common print mechanisms used with line printers are _____, _____, and _____, with _____ being the most popular.
4. Most serial and line printers are typically categorized as _____ printers because they operate by using a hammer to strike a character against an inked ribbon.
5. (T or F) The major disadvantage of impact printers over nonimpact printers is that they are usually slower and noisier.
6. Page printers use some type of (impact/nonimpact) technology for printing output.
7. (T or F) Page printers tend to be the slowest type of printers available.
8. (T or F) All printers print characters using a similar type face.
9. (T or F) Some printers can print output in color.
10. (T or F) Graphics capability can be provided with some printers.

Solutions

1. line
2. line
3. band
   chain
   drum
   band
4. impact
5. T
6. nonimpact
7. F—They are the fastest.
8. F—There are different type fonts available.
9. T
10. T

B. Cathode Ray Tube (CRT)

The **cathode ray tube (CRT)** is a video display unit similar to a television screen, as illustrated in Figure 6.12. This output unit displays information from the computer on the screen.

Typically, a keyboard is used with a CRT for entering data. The screen displays the data entered by the user so that it can be checked before it is transmitted. Similarly, CPU messages are displayed to the user on the CRT.

A light pen can also serve as an input tool by the user for making graphic corrections or additions to the display on the cathode ray tube. An operator uses the pen to modify data on the screen or to point to the options required. These modifications or options are then transmitted to the CPU. See Figure 6.13 for an illustration of a light pen used in conjunction with a CRT.

CRT units are widely used where output from a computer is desired at remote locations and where hard-copy or printed output is not required. Airline terminals, for example, use cathode ray tubes to display flight information. Changes to the data displayed on the screen can be made by the CPU instan-

Figure 6.12
CRT display terminal.
(Courtesy IBM.)

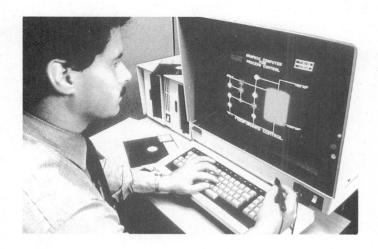

Figure 6.13
CRT with light pen.
(Courtesy CalComp.)

taneously. Similarly, stock brokerage firms use CRTs with keyboards for requesting the latest stock quotations. The user keys in the stock for which information is required. The computer displays the responses on the screen. Such CRT output is called **soft copy,** that is, a visual display with no permanent record.

If hard-copy versions of CRT output are necessary, then display devices can be equipped with additional features such as a printer or a display copier.

C. Graphics Display Terminal and Plotter

Many people believe that using graphs for business applications provides managers with more information and more decision-making capability than can be accomplished with a traditional report. Those who advocate the use of graphics for displaying output believe strongly in the old adage that "a picture is worth a thousand words."

There are two categories of output devices that can provide graphics capability: (1) a soft-copy or CRT graphics display terminal and (2) a hard-copy plotter or graphics printer.

A **graphics display terminal** is a CRT with the ability to display a wide variety of graphic, pictorial, and even animated data on a screen, often in color, as in Figure 6.14. **Plotters** and graphics printers are hard-copy output devices that can print graphic data, as in Figure 6.15.

A graphics printer is usually adequate for providing graphics ability to businesses; however, such a unit is not always capable of printing the intricate and

Figure 6.14
Graphics display terminal.
(Courtesy McAuto/
McDonnell Douglas-
St. Louis.)

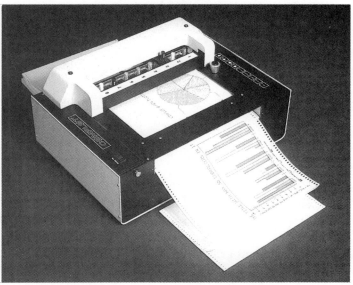

Figure 6.15
Eight-pen plotter. (Courtesy
Hewlett Packard.)

complex designs that might be needed for computer-aided design and other sophisticated applications for which a plotter would be more appropriate.

Plotters were originally used for automotive design, aircraft design, and architecture, but now that they are cheaper and faster, they are sometimes used for business graphics as well.

For those of you with an interest in the technical features of plotters, the following provides a basic overview of the most frequently used types.

⮞ Types of Plotters

	Description	*Advantages*	*Disadvantages*
Flatbed plotter (Figure 6.16a)	The paper is held in place, usually by a vacuum. A writing instrument that can move in two directions draws the image.	Can be used to add to existing drawings.	Large drawings need large machines.
Drum plotter (Figure 6.16b)	The paper moves over a rotating cylinder to accomplish one direction of movement; the writing instrument moves in the opposite direction.	A large design can be drawn by a relatively compact unit.	Cannot produce very wide drawings.
Electrostatic plotter (Figure 6.16c)	The paper moves in one direction and the writing instrument in another. But instead of a single pen, there is a row of styluses that move across the width of the paper.	Very fast.	Limited choice of media on which writing can occur; single-color images.

The following list summarizes some of the main uses of graphic units.

⮞ Some Uses of Graphics Units

1. Design Work
   To assist engineers in the design of machinery, military equipment, architectural drawings, etc.
   The design is displayed on a screen; programs that simulate "real-world" tests prove the viability of the design; the design can then be altered with a light pen as necessary.
2. Business Graphs for Management Decision-Making
   To help managers make decisions by displaying comprehensive data in graphic form.

3. Medical Diagnosis and Evaluation

Patients use a picture of a human body displayed on a screen to point to various pressure points or areas of pain. The computer provides physicians and other diagnosticians with possible illnesses corresponding to the symptoms.

Figure 6.17 provides an analysis of the computer graphics market.

(a)

(b)

Figure 6.16
(a) Flatbed plotter. (b) Drum plotter. (c) Electrostatic plotter. (Courtesy CalComp.)

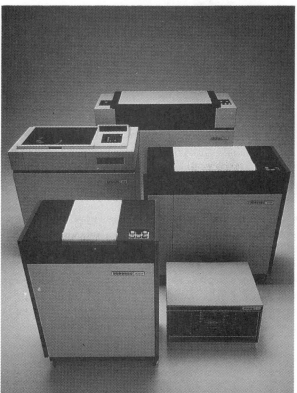

(c)

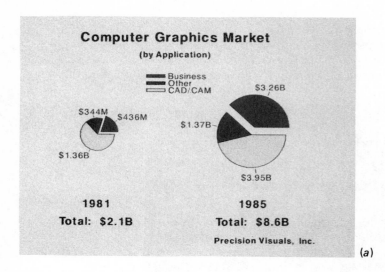

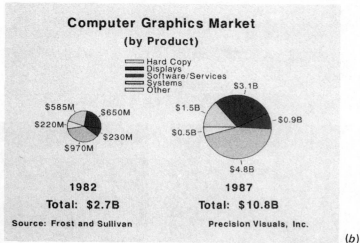

Figure 6.17
The computer graphics market. (Courtesy Precision Visuals, Inc.)

D. Audio Response Unit

An **audio response unit** is an output unit that can provide the user with a verbal response rather than a printed or displayed one. The computer can be equipped with various prerecorded phrases, words, and messages that are extracted from a file, as required, for answering a specific request. The verbal messages are transmitted using an audio response unit.

Many banks use telephone equipment along with audio response units. Suppose a customer wishes to cash a check at a branch office. The teller keys in the customer's account number and the amount of his or her check using a Touch-Tone telephone. The computer then determines if the account has sufficient funds on hand. The appropriate verbal response is then transmitted to the teller via the telephone using an audio response unit to provide verbal responses. The teller will then either cash the check or politely refuse, depending on the computer's response. See Figure 6.18 for an illustration of an audio response unit.

Figure 6.18
A bank teller uses a Touch-Tone telephone to call a remote computer and request the status of an account. After keying the account number and a code for the information desired, the teller receives a voice response.

Customers can interact with audio response units in a similar manner for carrying out "pay-by-phone" services in certain banks. Basically, bank customers can indicate by phone those creditors who should be paid automatically by the bank. An audio response unit can be programmed to verbally verify the user's request over the telephone.

Audio response units also have great potential for enabling visually impaired people to interact with a computer. In addition, many order-entry systems enable salespeople to telephone the computer and (1) obtain verbal information concerning current inventory status or (2) place orders and receive verbal confirmation by the computer.

Audio responses to the user may be made as a result of (1) a typed request or (2) a spoken inquiry that can be interpreted by a voice recognition device. Voice recognition units in conjunction with audio response units enable a user with a telephone at virtually any location to access a computer and receive a verbal message. Such voice systems are considered highly user-friendly and are likely to be used with increasing frequency in the future as the technology develops and the cost decreases.

E. Computer Output Microfilm Unit

Microfilm and microfiche have had a long and successful history primarily as noncomputerized storage media. These are photographed records or documents in miniature requiring special devices to be read by users. They are exceedingly useful methods of producing high-volume information quickly and storing it in a relatively small space. Figure 6.19 illustrates the space-saving feature of microfilm. Hundreds or even thousands of records can be stored on a single unit, and easy-access microfilm readers are capable of accessing specific records in a relatively short period of time. *Microfilm* stores data on rolled film. *Microfiche* stores data on frames within a rectangular unit (see Figure 6.20).

Libraries are the most common users of microfilm, storing many editions of a journal or newspaper on a single unit and making this material accessible to readers with the use of microfilm or microfiche readers.

Figure 6.19
Before and after microfilming. (Courtesy Kodak.)

Figure 6.20
Miniaturized X-rays stored on microfiche. (Courtesy Anacomp.)

1. Computers and Microfilm or Microfiche

In recent years, the computer industry has come to recognize the distinct advantages of microfilm. Because the storage of a large number of records or printed reports has proven cumbersome, computer devices capable of creating and retrieving documents on microfilm have become increasingly popular.

There are microfilmers available that can assign a microfilm location or address to each document as it is being microfilmed. A terminal can be used to retrieve a particular document, which can be viewed on a microfilm reader. See Figure 6.21 for an example of a microfilmer and a microfilm reader.

Computer output microfilm (COM) units include those that, when linked to a CPU, can create output on microfilm or microfiche at very great speeds (see Figure 6.22). Keep in mind that to access these COM reports, microfilm readers are used.

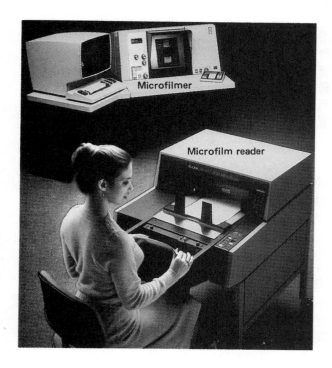

Figure 6.21
Microfilmer and microfilm
reader. (Courtesy Kodak.)

Figure 6.22
COM recorder. (Courtesy
DatagraphiX, Inc.)

Microform is a general term used to describe all miniature output including microfiche and microfilm. COM units can produce the following microforms (Figure 6.23):

Microforms

1. Microfiche card: each frame stores one printed document; requires microfiche reader to access; most prevalent form of COM.
2. Aperture card: standard punched card with provision for filmed report, picture, graph, etc.; requires a microfiche reader to access; punched data on card can be read by card machines.
3. Microfilm: rolled film—16 mm, 35 mm, or 105 mm—requires microfilm reader to access.

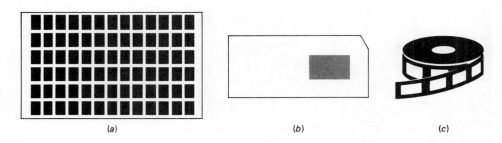

Figure 6.23
Examples of microforms.
(*a*) Microfiche card. (*b*)
Aperture card. (*c*) Roll
microfilm.

(*a*)   (*b*)   (*c*)

2. Advantages of Computer Output Microfilm

The use of microfilm as output in place of standard printed reports has the following advantages:

IIII▶ **Advantages of COM**

1. Output is produced at very great speeds: microfilm output can be created at speeds in excess of 120,000 characters per second or 21,800 lines per minute.
2. Output is in miniaturized, compact form: this small size can typically save the user 98% of the storage space otherwise required for output.

In short, COM is sometimes used by companies for storing output that would otherwise require a significant number of printed reports. COM is used primarily for in-house applications.

The following list summarizes the major advantages and disadvantages of COM:

IN A NUTSHELL

COMPUTER OUTPUT MICROFILM

Advantages

1. Concise Storage
   Output on microfiche or microfilm is easier to store than printed output.
2. Speed
   Output can be produced on microfiche or microfilm at great speeds.
3. Saving of Paper Costs
   Microfiche or microfilm is much cheaper as a medium than paper.

Disadvantages

1. COM Cannot Be Manually Read; It Must Be Read by Machine
   Since microfiche or microfilm cannot be read manually, COM readers are necessary—these devices are subject to breakdown, and because data cannot be read directly, they may generate some resistance by users.
2. COM Devices Are Costly

Self-Evaluating Quiz

1. The _____ is a video display device similar to a television screen.
2. (T or F) A video display device may or may not have high-speed graphics capability.
3. (T or F) A video display unit usually has a keyboard for transmitting data from the CPU to the user.
4. Output from a screen is called _____ since no permanent record is provided.
5. (T or F) Graphics display units always display output in color.
6. When the computer selects a verbal message from a disk or tape and transmits it to a user, a(n) _____ output unit is required.
7. A _____ unit is used for creating a high volume of output data on microfilm very quickly.
8. (T or F) Computer-produced microfilm can be read manually without the use of a microfilm reader.
9. (T or F) Computer-produced microfilm can be used to save storage space since hard-copy reports need not be generated.
10. Microfilm and microfiche are collectively referred to as _____.

Solutions

1. cathode ray tube (CRT)
2. T
3. F—The keyboard transmits data from the *user* to the *CPU*.
4. soft-copy
5. F—Not always.
6. audio response
7. computer output microfilm (COM)
8. F—Microfilm readers are required.
9. T
10. microforms

III. CHARACTERISTICS OF OUTPUT

A. Printed or Typed Output

1. Features of Reports

A printed or typed hard-copy report, still the most common form of output, can be produced using either a printer or a terminal.

When a standard line or page printer is used to produce output, the report is typically prepared in batch mode on a regularly scheduled basis. Payroll checks, customer bills, and sales reports are examples of printed output produced in batch mode on a regularly scheduled basis.

When a terminal is used to produce hard-copy output, the report may also be prepared in batch mode, or it may be an on-line, immediate response to an inquiry.

In either case, a major requirement of hard-copy output is that it should be user-friendly, that is, easy to read and as clear as possible. The following three items help to make printed output user-friendly:

➡ Elements of Printed Output That Make It User-Friendly

1. Headings
   Headings generally supply identifying information such as report name, date, page number, and field names.

2. Alignment of Data
   Reports do not have fields adjacent to one another; instead, spaces always appear between fields for readability.

3. Edit Symbols as Part of Output
   Input records are designed to be as concise as possible. They do not always contain symbols such as dollar signs, commas, or even decimal points; these symbols are not necessary for processing input. Printed reports, however, must be as clear and readable as possible. While 124503 may be a typical AMOUNT field on an input record, it is more readable and user-friendly when printed as $1,245.03. An *edit symbol* is one that helps to make concise input fields more meaningful and user-friendly when displayed or printed as output information. Symbols such as dollar signs, commas, decimal points, and so on, make data more readable.

2. Continuous Forms

a. Feeding Continuous Forms Through a Printer   Reports that serve as computer output are printed on **continuous forms.** These are forms that are connected, separated only by perforations, as illustrated in Figure 6.24. They are fed into a printer as one continuous sheet so that constant feeding of forms is not required. After an entire report has been printed, it is separated or "burst" into individual sheets.

These individual pages are then bound to make one report, or they are transmitted to different people as necessary. Each page must have its own heading and usually a page number so that misplaced documents can be properly sequenced.

b. The Number of Characters per Line on a Continuous Form   The number of characters per line varies depending on the printing and the paper used. Some pages can contain 80, 100, 132, or 150 characters per line. Most printers can be adjusted to accept paper of varying widths.

c. Preparing Multiple Copies of a Continuous Form   Many continuous forms can be multiple part with carbon paper between each sheet. There are also carbonless continuous forms that can be used for obtaining extra copies. High-speed page printers, however, usually require a report to be printed several times to obtain extra copies; that is, these units frequently cannot make multiple copies.

d. Standard Stock Paper and Preprinted Forms   Reports can be printed either on blank paper called standard stock paper or on preprinted forms.

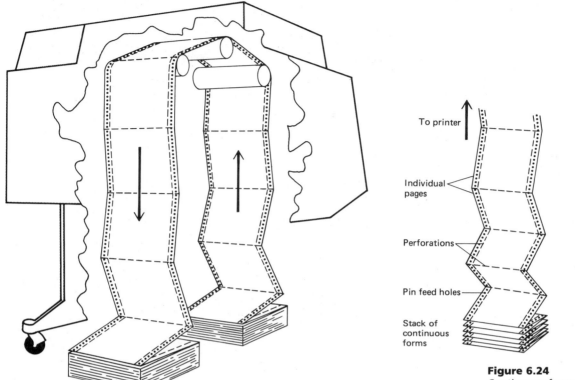

Figure 6.24
Continuous forms.

Standard stock continuous forms come in numerous lengths, with 11-inch and 12-inch forms being the most common. Usually, 6 lines of output can be printed per inch. This means that up to 66 lines of information can be printed on a standard 11-inch form. Sometimes, however, to condense a report, 8 lines per inch are utilized.

In addition to printing reports on standard plain, lined, or unlined sheets, reports can be prepared on special preprinted forms. A bank statement, commonly printed by a computer as output, is an example of a preprinted form. These forms that are sent by a company to customers, clients, and so on, usually have the company name and other identifying information preprinted on each page even before the computer prepares the output. Figure 6.25 illustrates an accounts receivable statement prepared by the computer on preprinted forms. Note that the heading and the vertical and horizontal lines are preprinted on the continuous form; that is, they are not printed by the computer.

Keep in mind that these preprinted forms must be ordered from a company specializing in forms and are usually used only for *external reports* that are mailed outside the organization. Bills, checks, and student transcripts, for example, are typically prepared on preprinted forms. Standard stock paper is used for *internal reporting* to company personnel.

e. The Use of Margins and Spacing on a Continuous Form Note, however, that reports do not usually have data on every line of a page. Generally, there are

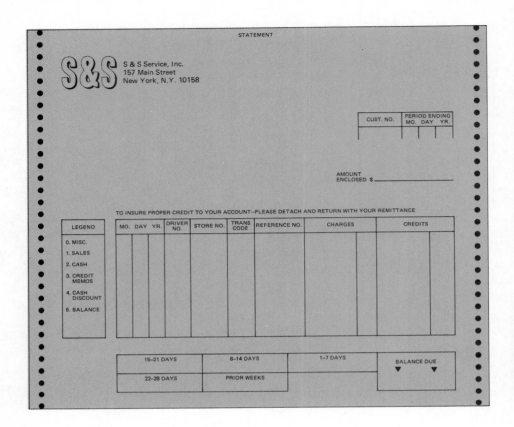

Figure 6.25
Example of a preprinted form.

both top and bottom margins; that is, several blank lines are included at the top and bottom of each form for readability. Similarly, many reports utilize double or triple spacing to separate heading and detail lines.

3. The Printer Spacing Chart for Designing Printed Output

A **Printer Spacing Chart,** illustrated in Figure 6.26, is a tool utilized by a systems analyst to help design the layout of information to be printed. It is used to align data across the page by indicating the specific print positions that will contain the computer-produced information. It is also used for specifying the exact headings to be printed, and the editing to be performed to make fields more readable.

4. Types of Reports

Hard-copy or printed reports are usually classified as follows.

Types of Reports

1. DETAIL OUTPUT—Each print line corresponds to an input record.
2. SUMMARY OUTPUT—Individual input records are processed collectively and printed in summary form.
3. EXCEPTION OUTPUT—Only individual input records that do not fall within pre-established guidelines are printed.

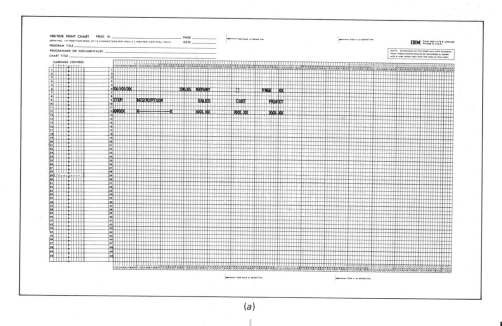

(a)

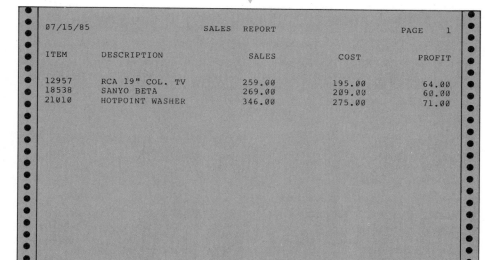

(b)

Figure 6.26
(a) Illustrative Printer Spacing Chart. (b) Sample printout based on the chart.

Detail reporting is the least efficient output form because it generates the most number of print lines. In some instances, such as the printing of a payroll check for each employee in a company, or a bill for each customer, detail printing is required. In other instances, we may find that such reports result in waste and inefficiency because they could easily be replaced by a summary report which would be more useful.

Exception reports print only those records that are exceptions to pre-established criteria. Sometimes this type of report is most appropriate. For example, printing a detail report of each customer and the amount due would be wasteful if all that was needed was an exception report of customers who owe more than $5000.

Self-Evaluating Quiz

1. A printed report should always include a _____ that supplies identifying information such as report name, date, and page number.
2. _____ symbols such as dollar signs, commas, and decimal points are used to convert concise input fields into more meaningful output.
3. Reports are printed on _____ that are connected, separated only by perforations.
4. (T or F) Printers always print 120 characters per line.
5. If a report is printed on paper that contains the company's trademark, the form is called a _____.
6. (T or F) Printers always use 11-inch paper.
7. A systems analyst uses a tool called a _____ to map out the print positions in which data is to be aligned across a page of a report.
8. If each customer record on a file is used to print a bill, we call this (detail/summary/exception) reporting.
9. If a report contains a list of all employees who will be 65 years old within the next year, we call this a(n) (detail/summary/exception) report.
10. (T or F) If feasible, summary reports should be generated in place of detail reports because they are cheaper, save paper, and may be more useful.

Solutions

1. heading
2. Edit
3. continuous forms
4. F—The number of characters per line varies depending on the size of the paper.
5. preprinted form
6. F—There is a wide variety of paper sizes.
7. Printer Spacing Chart
8. detail
9. exception
10. T

B. Displaying Information on a Screen and Entering User Responses Interactively

1. Features of Displayed Information

Displayed output on a CRT requires somewhat different design considerations than printed output. This is because output on a CRT is generally displayed *interactively,* with users entering data or inquiries, and the CPU responding with a message or with some specific information.

As with printed output, CRT output should include headings and fields that have been aligned and edited so that the information is as readable as possible.

However, because CRT output is usually displayed interactively, with the user or data entry operator and the computer communicating with one another, additional factors should be considered.

The primary consideration when displaying output and requesting a response from the user is to make the interaction as user-friendly as possible.

2. Techniques Used to Make Data Entry and Displayed Output User-Friendly

The following are common techniques for interactive processing with a CRT.

a. Menus   When a user or data entry operator interacts with a computer using a keyboard linked to a CRT, the CRT should display precise instructions, and should require an easily coded response from the user. Typically, a **menu** is displayed asking the user to select the specific application or program desired from a series of choices. See Figure 6.27 for an illustration of a menu that might be displayed on a CRT.

Suppose that the user keys the number 3 on the keyboard in response to the menu in Figure 6.27; this indicates that the ''receivables'' program is required. The next response from the computer or the CRT might be another menu, asking for additional data, as in Figure 6.28.

Thus, after one of the items from the main menu is selected, a more specific menu may be displayed from which the user makes other selections. This technique of employing menus from which users select required items makes it very easy to interact with the CRT using a keyboard or other device such as a light pen or mouse. No written manual need be consulted to determine what to do; the instructions are clearly displayed on the screen. In the illustrations above, the user need only key a single digit or letter response.

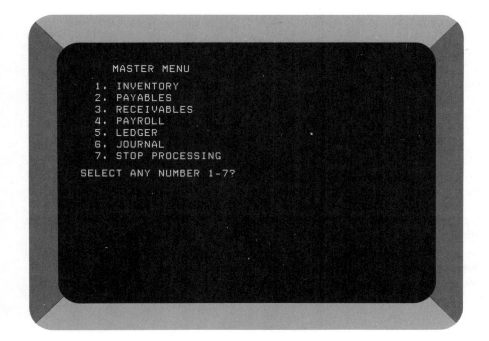

Figure 6.27
Example of a menu.

```
        MASTER MENU
    1.  INVENTORY
    2.  PAYABLES
    3.  RECEIVABLES
    4.  PAYROLL
    5.  LEDGER
    6.  JOURNAL
    7.  STOP PROCESSING
SELECT ANY NUMBER 1-7?
```

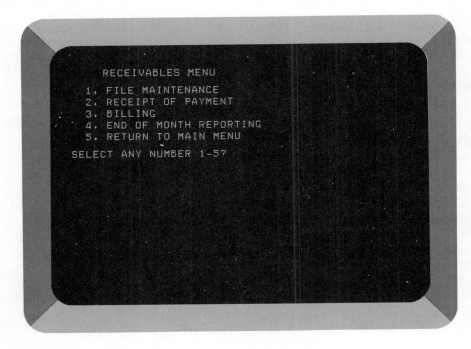

Figure 6.28
Example of a receivables menu.

Frequently, systems also include "HELP" menus that users can consult if they need additional information on how to proceed. Menus must be designed and programmed so that they anticipate most types of user requests for a given application.

b. Prompts Once an application is selected, a user will typically need to enter data at specific data entry points on the CRT screen. These points are indicated by a **prompt,** which highlights the items to be completed. Figure 6.29 shows how prompts can be designated with the use of shading on a screen. The shaded areas are those requiring user responses. Once the user keys in these entries, the computer will display a specific response on the screen. In the figure, the user is requesting flight information. The prompts indicate that the origin of the flight and the destination are to be keyed in by the user along with the desired time of departure; the computer then responds with information on available flights leaving at the approximate time specified.

Use of shaded areas on a screen is one technique for prompting a user. Another technique is to have a blinking "cursor" that "points to" the entry requiring a user response. The cursor could be a square, rectangle, triangle, or underline that blinks to indicate what item is required.

c. ENTER or RETURN Key on a Keyboard Most keyboards have an ENTER or RETURN key, or some comparable character key, that must be depressed before the data that has been entered is actually transmitted to the CPU. Using this key enables a user to take as long as necessary to enter data without fear of slowing down the CPU. Since the data is *not* transmitted until the ENTER key is depressed, CPU time is not being used and the user need not feel rushed. Moreover, an entry can be verified before it is transmitted to the CPU by checking it on the screen and making necessary corrections prior to depressing the ENTER key.

Figure 6.29
Example of prompts on a CRT screen.

d. Scrolling   Sometimes a user wishes to refer to some other portion of a CRT text, possibly to some data that was entered previously. Most keyboard-CRTs have arrows or cursors that allow the user to **scroll** forward or backward so that a different portion of the text can be displayed.

e. Function Keys on a Keyboard   A function key is a key on a keyboard that has been pre-programmed to perform some operation when keyed. That is, a function key when depressed can be used, for example, for loading a specific file, if it has been programmed for that purpose. A function key can also be programmed to perform a specific calculation. Sometimes a function key is used to automatically display a ''help'' menu or to scroll to a specific point on a display screen. By programming a function key to perform an operation that is frequently required, user time is saved because there is no need to make additional keystroke entries or to look up procedures for performing a function.

There are many other features that are either standard or available with CRTs and keyboards which can make interaction with a computer extremely user-friendly. The systems analyst, programmer, and user should work closely together when designing a data entry system or an inquiry-response system using a CRT. A primary objective is to ensure that features are utilized that ease the burden of the data entry operator or user.

3. Ergonomics

Ergonomics is broadly defined as the science of making the work environment safer and more comfortable for employees. Ergonomics has as its goal increased job satisfaction for users. CRTs are currently being designed with ergonomics in mind. Features have been added to CRTs to make them physically more comfortable for the user, as shown in the following list:

||||➡ **Ergonomic Features of CRTs**

1. Detached keyboard—can be moved to suit the user.
2. Tilt and swivel tubes—like a chair, the CRT can be adjusted to user requirements.
3. Larger characters.
4. Adjustable color or light intensity of the display.
5. Flickerless display.
6. Lead screens to reduce radiation.

LOOKING AHEAD

Many States Consider Regulations on the Use of Video Display Terminals

Concern about health problems associated with video display terminals has prompted many states to consider legislation regulating their use in offices. Provisions of some proposed laws range from furnishing pregnant women with anti-radiation jackets to requiring that vendors inform users of potential health hazards.

Computer equipment manufacturers are attempting to prove that claims of the harmful side effects of video display terminals are invalid. Although recent studies conducted by the U.S. Department of Health and Human Services and the National Academy of Sciences have concluded that radiation emissions from these devices are well below federal safety standards, there are many labor unions that are pushing for legislation both for safety and ergonomic reasons.

Self-Evaluating Quiz

1. (T or F) Headings and other identifying information are usually not necessary for CRT output.
2. (T or F) CRT output is usually produced in an interactive mode.
3. A _____ displayed on a CRT asks the user to select a specific choice from a series of alternatives.
4. (T or F) Frequently the response to one menu selection causes another, more detailed menu to be displayed.
5. Typically, a user responds to a menu by _____.
6. (T or F) Menus are infrequently used because they tend not to be user-friendly.
7. A _____ menu provides the user with additional information for interacting with the system.
8. A _____ highlights the field to be entered as input.
9. (T or F) A prompt could be designated with a shaded area or a blinking cursor.

10. (T or F) Each character of data is immediately transmitted to the CPU as it is entered.

11. A _____ is a key on a keyboard that has been pre-programmed to perform a specific operation.

12. The science of _____ focuses on making the work environment physically attractive; it has resulted in the use of CRTs with swivel tubes and adjustable display colors for ease of reading.

Solutions

1. F

2. T

3. menu

4. T

5. keying in a number or letter

6. F—Menus are considered to be highly user-friendly.

7. HELP

8. prompt

9. T

10. F—Usually data is transmitted only after the ENTER or RETURN key has been depressed.

11. function key

12. ergonomics

IV. EVALUATING OUTPUT MEDIA AND UNITS

The type of output to be generated and the output unit to be used, as with input, are determined by the systems analyst in conjunction with the user.

Many factors affect the decision, including the following.

Criteria for Selecting an Output Medium and Unit

1. Is hard copy or soft copy needed?
   (For example, is the data to be retained in hard-copy form for future reference or is a simple display all that is needed?)

2. Is distribution to remote locations required?

3. Cost of equipment.

4. Speed.

5. Availability of hardware.

6. Volume of output required.

7. User preference.

CHAPTER SUMMARY

I. Where is the output produced?
   A. At the computer site.
   B. Using terminals at remote locations where needed.

II. When is output produced?
  A. On a regularly scheduled basis.
  B. On demand.
III. Types of printers:
  A. Serial.
    1. Slow.
    2. Typewriterlike—printing one character at a time.
    3. Used with micros and terminals.
    4. Dot matrix is the most common mechanism.
  B. Line printer.
    1. Medium speed.
    2. Primary printer for minis and mainframes.
    3. Prints a line at a time.
    4. Band printer is the most common.
  C. Page printer.
    1. High speed.
    2. Prints a page at a time.
    3. Uses nonimpact technology.
IV. Other output units:
  A. CRT and graphics display unit.
  B. Plotter.
  C. Audio response unit.
  D. Computer output microfilm.
V. Formatting printed output:
  A. Continuous forms are used—preprinted or standard.
  B. Headings should be used.
  C. Data should be aligned with margins.
  D. Editing symbols should be used.
  E. A Printer Spacing Chart is a useful tool for planning printed output format.
VI. Displayed output:
  A. Should be designed to be user-friendly.
  B. Prompts and menus should be used.

Chapter Self-Evaluating Quiz

1. (T or F) In general, serial printers are slower than line printers.
2. A _____ printer represents characters by activating a combination of pins on a grid.
3. Letter-quality printers may use a flat disk called a _____ containing fully formed characters.
4. (T or F) In general, impact printers are faster than nonimpact devices.
5. (T or F) The most common mechanism used for line printers is a chain.
6. (T or F) Most page printers are nonimpact printers.
7. The major feature of a terminal is that it can access a computer from _____ .
8. (T or F) Output that is displayed on a CRT screen is referred to as soft copy.

9. (T or F) Plotters and graphics display terminals can be used for displaying data in graph form.

10. A device that can obtain verbal responses from a file and transmit them to a user is called a(n) _____.

11. _____ devices can create output on microfilm or microfiche.

12. (T or F) Microfiche records can be read manually.

13. _____ are needed on printed documents to ensure the proper identification of each page.

14. The term _____ is used to describe perforated paper that is fed into a printer for generating reports.

15. In addition to standard stock continuous forms, _____ forms containing information such as the company name may be used for printing particular reports.

16. (T or F) Reports generally contain top and bottom margins for readability.

17. A layout form called a _____ is used by programmers and analysts, and verified by users, to ensure that output data will be aligned properly.

18. A(n) _____ report is one that prints only those individual records that do not fall within pre-established guidelines.

19. A blinking cursor on a CRT screen is an example of a _____.

20. (T or F) Ergonomics is broadly defined as the science of making the work environment safer and more comfortable for employees.

Solutions

1. T / page 194
2. dot-matrix / page 194
3. daisy wheel / page 195
4. F / page 196
5. F—Band printers are the most common line printers. / page 198
6. T / page 200
7. any remote location, either at the same site as the CPU or at a different one / page 203
8. T / page 204
9. T / page 204
10. audio response unit / page 208

11. Computer output microfilm (COM) / page 210
12. F—A microfilm reader is necessary. / page 211
13. Headings / page 214
14. continuous form / page 214
15. preprinted / page 215
16. T / page 216
17. Printer Spacing Chart / page 216
18. exception / page 216
19. prompt / page 220
20. T / page 221

Key Terms

Audio response unit
Band printer
Cathode ray tube (CRT)
Chain printer

Computer output microfilm (COM)
Continuous form
Daisy wheel printer
Dot-matrix printer

Drum printer
Ergonomics
Graphics display terminal
Hard-copy output
Impact printer
Line printer
Menu
Microform (microfilm, microfiche)

Nonimpact printer
Page printer
Plotter
Printer Spacing Chart
Prompt
Scroll
Serial printer
Soft-copy output

Review Questions

I. True-False

1. (T or F) A detail report is a more efficient type of report than a summary report.

2. (T or F) Where possible, exception reports should be printed in place of detail reports because they highlight specific conditions and generate less paper.

3. (T or F) Most computer centers with mainframes use line printers.

4. (T or F) Page printers tend to be used by organizations requiring high-speed printed output.

5. (T or F) Most hard-copy terminals are line printers.

6. (T or F) A band printer is the most common type of line printer.

7. (T or F) A dot-matrix printer is typically used for letter-quality output.

8. (T or F) Printers for microcomputers cannot be purchased for less than $3000.

9. (T or F) Some printers can print 132 characters per line.

10. (T or F) A printer that prints a line at a time is called a serial printer.

11. (T or F) Menus are typically displayed on page printers because they are user-friendly.

12. (T or F) A CRT displays data that is either entered by the user or that is transmitted by the CPU to the user.

13. (T or F) When the CRT indicates to the user the item to be keyed in by displaying an underline or a flashing square, we call this a prompt.

14. (T or F) Data keyed in at a terminal by a user is not usually transmitted to the CPU until the ENTER or RETURN key is depressed.

15. (T or F) A CRT frequently has a keyboard connected to it for data entry purposes.

II. Fill in the Blanks

1. The two most common forms of computer output are _____ and _____.

2. When large volumes of data need to be stored in a small area, a _____ device may be used.

3. When a verbal message is transmitted from the CPU to the user, a(n) _____ unit is required as the output device.

4. A _____ is a design tool used to map out the format of data on a printed report.

5. A _____ is a type of continuous form that is fed through the printer with a company logo, headings, shaded areas, and so on already printed on it.

6. One way to make printed output user-friendly is to include _____ symbols such as dollar signs and commas.

7. A _____ form of output is one that may be kept as a permanent record; a _____ form of output is one that is simply displayed on a screen.

8. The line printer at most companies is likely to be a _____ printer.

9. A _____ is a CRT with the ability to display graphic, pictorial, and even animated data on a screen.

10. Microcomputers generally use _____ printers that print one character at a time like a typewriter.

APPLICATION

PRINTERS HANDLE OUTPUT FROM DIFFERENT CPUs

CALGARY, Alberta—A Canadian company with diversified interests in insurance, property management and resort operations solved a hardware problem from a hardcopy angle by installing a switching system that allows two printers to handle output from both an IBM and a Digital Equipment Corp. processor.

"Our IBM 4341 was using two high-speed printers [IBM 3203 Model 5]—a very costly operation, especially since the output need was really equivalent only to about 1½ printers," explained Vi Sadler, director of computer services for the Cascade Group here. "At the same time, our two DEC PDP-11/70s, one of which we knew would be phased out within 12 months and the other somewhat later, were functioning with two old 300 line/min printers, which were not operating at an efficient level."

Besides the IBM 4341—soon to be upgraded to an IBM 3033—Cascade's Computer Services Division uses an IBM 4331. The two PDP-11/70s will be eliminated in favor of a distributed data processing system using PDP-11/44s this year.

Confronting its output problem, Cascade's DP operations staff consulted with Southern Systems-Canada in Willowdale, Ont., which provides users with printer systems compatible with most computer processors. Cascade decided to use two 1,100 line/min Southern Systems QT 1100 printers together with Southern Systems' PS-10 switcher.

"The two Southern Systems printers take up far less space than the IBM 3203 printer," Sadler said. "The two actually fit into space that would be required for one IBM printer."

"The difficulty in achieving this versatility previously was that the electronic interfacing needs of the DEC and the IBM are so different that only very, very costly switching systems could have accomplished what the PS-10 does today, very inexpensively," added Steve Miller, vice-president of information systems for Cascade. "Having the two printers—switchable either to the DECs or the IBMs—also gives us a backup output system should one have any downtime."

The Cascade Group companies include Family Life Insurance Co., Soverign Life Insurance; Soverign-General; Merrett Management Ltd., a property management firm; and the Panorama Ski Resort. "Our DP operations serve all those companies," Miller said.

"The biggest applications are the administration of the insurance policies in the life and casualty business. These are large systems running on IBM," he said.

"The DEC equipment has been used for most of our noninsurance needs—the reservation system for Panorama Ski Resort, as well as property management functions for Merrett, plus general ledger and accounts payable for all those companies."

Because Cascade has to support such a diversity of applications, "we require a diverse set of tools—the necessity for having both DEC and IBM. It's been very cost-effective for us to use the two Southern Systems printers on the three computers. The alternative would have been two printers for the IBM and two for the DEC—a costly solution."

Source: Computerworld, November 14, 1983, page 38. Copyright © 1983 by CW Communications/Inc., Framingham, MA 01701. Reprinted with permission.

Questions
1. Understanding Key Terms
   Define the following terms as they are used in the application.
   a. Switching system.
   b. Electronic interfacing.
   c. Backup output system.
   d. Downtime.
2. Software, Hardware, and Systems Concepts
   What questions would you need to ask your computer vendors to determine if a single printer could be used by two different systems?

3. Management Considerations
   If the use of a printer were feasible with different CPUs, would you think it appropriate to investigate whether other input/output devices could be used in this way? Explain your answer.

4. Social, Legal, and Ethical Considerations
   Suppose you interfaced a single printer with two CPUs. For some reason, the systems went down and your accounts payable procedure was delayed. This resulted in interest charges that you had to pay to your creditors. Under what conditions should the vendor of the printer and/or CPUs be held accountable? Explain your answer.

CASE STUDY: McKing's Superburgers, Inc.

1. Output Devices
   McKing's management would like to provide each restaurant manager with an output device for obtaining printouts such as inventory reports, sales analysis reports, activity reports, and so on. Consider the following list of output devices:

   1. Band printer.
   2. Chain printer.
   3. CRT.
   4. Daisy wheel printer.
   5. Dot-matrix printer.
   6. Drum printer.
   7. Electrostatic printer.
   8. Electrosensitive printer.
   9. Graphics display terminal.
   10. Plotter.
   11. Ink-jet printer.
   12. Xerographic printer.
   13. Page printer.

   a. What questions would you ask of each restaurant manager to help you determine the best output device to acquire?
   b. What output devices would you reject as inappropriate for McKing's? Indicate your reasons.
   c. What factors would you consider to be most important when selecting output devices?
   d. Indicate which of the above output devices you would consider most appropriate for obtaining output for each restaurant manager.

2. Management Reports
   Management would like each restaurant manager to be able to obtain reports relating to sales activity, prepared food status, food costs, and so on. These reports would be generated "on demand," that is, whenever a manager needed them.
   a. What kinds of summary reports would you recommend be provided? Describe in as much detail as possible the kind of information that you think should be included in each type of report.
   b. What kinds of exception reports would you recommend be provided? Describe in as much detail as possible the kind of information that you believe should be included in each type of exception report.
   c. Suppose a restaurant manager insists that you provide him or her with a detail report. You believe that this detail report is really not necessary. That is, you believe a summary report provided to all the other managers would really serve this manager just as well. What questions would you ask to determine if the manager really needed the detail report? What arguments or strategies would you use to convince the manager that the detail report is really unnecessary?

THE COMPUTER AD: A Focus on Marketing

Consider the ad entitled "Bubble Breakthrough" that appears in Figure 6.30.

1. Define the following terms as they are used in the ad:
   a. Non-volatile.
   b. Bubble memory.
   c. Data integrity.
   d. Host computer.

2. Indicate how a color graphics terminal could benefit from bubble memory capability. Be specific.
3. A terminal with local computer power, that is, not totally dependent on the computer power of the host, would be called an intelligent terminal. Would you categorize the computer in the ad as intelligent? Explain your answer.

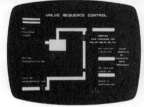 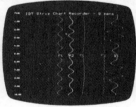 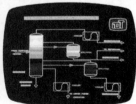

IDT 2200. First and only color graphics terminal with bubble memory!

The IDT 2200, with bubble memory storage in the terminal, establishes a new standard in color graphics capability and reliability. Non-volatile bubble memory allows you to retain permanent displays in the terminal, and ensures data integrity even in the harshest environment. Bubble memory unburdens your host computer of memory requirements and dramatically reduces transfer time to the terminal. With its increased megabit capacity, you can build and store permanently an entire library of pictures and subpictures in the terminal.

PLOT 10* software compatibility is now available. A new hardware vector generator draws vectors 10 times faster. New front access design permits easy maintenance, plus room for three full-color display memory planes.

IDT 2200 with bubble memory. The newest reason why we're earning a reputation for cost-effective performance in color graphics terminals.

Customer-configured...performance-proven.

*A Trademark of Tektronix, Inc.

 Industrial Data Terminals Corp.
173 Heatherdown Drive, Westerville, Ohio 43081 (614) 882-3282

Figure 6.30 Marketing Computer Products. (Courtesy Industrial Data Terminals Corp.)

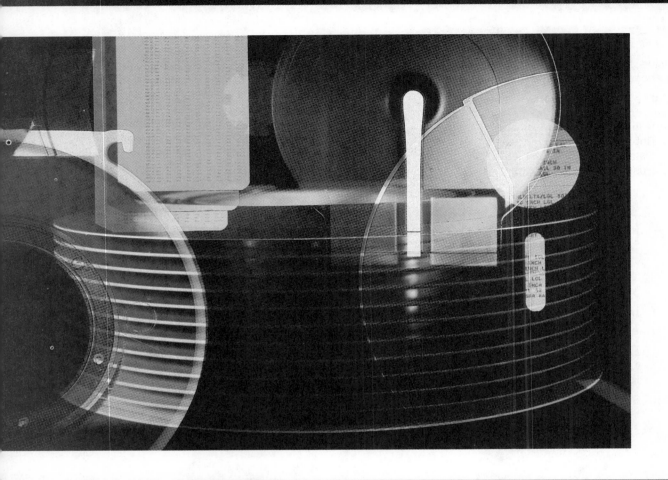

CHAPTER 7

TAPE AND DISK: FOR FILE PROCESSING AND AUXILIARY STORAGE

CHAPTER OBJECTIVES

To familiarize you with:

- File processing concepts.
- Physical features of magnetic tape and disk files and drives.
- Characteristics of tape and disk processing.
- Sequential file organization on a tape and methods of file organization on a disk.

I. FILE PROCESSING DEFINED

Thus far we have focused on input and output media in which individual data items are processed. A terminal, for example, may be the input device for entering purchase orders that are used to print a status report on a line printer.

The entire collection of data pertaining to any given application is called a *file*. If it is the major collection of data used for storing critical information, answering inquiries, and producing output such as bills and statements, then this file is called a *master file*.

For most business applications, then, a master file of data contains a major collection of information pertaining to that application. A payroll system, for example, would utilize a master payroll file containing all data necessary for processing paychecks and maintaining salary history information. Similarly, an accounts receivable system would utilize a master accounts receivable file containing all pertinent accounts receivable data.

Master files are typically stored on media such as magnetic tape and magnetic disk that can be processed at high speeds. Tape and disk devices are not only fast, but they are capable of storing large volumes of data in a relatively small area. Before we discuss tape and disk in more detail, we will review some major concepts of file processing, including the hierarchy of data.

Files are subdivided into *records* that are units of data pertaining to a given entity within the file. Thus an accounts receivable file may consist of debit records and credit records; an inventory file may consist of purchase order records and quantity-on-hand records.

Each record within a file has a specific format, indicating the layout of data contained within the record and the size and type of that data. A payroll record, for example, may be represented as shown in Figure 7.1. The entire collection of payroll records would be referred to as the payroll file.

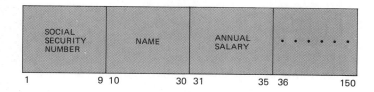

Figure 7.1
Example of a payroll record on magnetic tape.

Within each record, we have items called Social Security Number, Name, Salary, and so on. These are known as *fields* of data within the payroll record. A field is a consecutive group of *characters* representing a unit of data such as Name, Salary, and so on.

Each field, then, is a series of characters. Because Social Security Number is coded as the first field in the payroll record, it appears in record positions 1-9; Name is in record positions 10-30, and so on.

Thus within files, we have records containing fields that consist of characters. You will see that another reason why tape and disk are typically used for storing files is that they can store records of any size or format.

The design of all files for a given application is the responsibility of the systems analyst. Thus, systems analysts must determine (1) the specific files necessary for processing data in a system, (2) whether these files should be stored on tape, disk, or some other medium, and (3) the format of records within each file.

Because of the following features of tapes and disks, they are ideal media for storing master files or other high-volume data files.

Features of Tape and Disk Processing

1. Input/output capability of tape and disk drives.
   A tape or disk drive can serve as *both* an input and an output device for a given application. We can instruct a computer to read from a tape or write onto a tape that is mounted on a **tape drive;** similarly, we can program a computer to read from or write onto disks mounted on a **disk drive.**
2. High-speed processing.
   Disk drives and tape drives can read and write data at extremely fast rates.
3. Ability to store hundreds of thousands of records on one reel of magnetic tape or on one disk pack.
4. Ability to process any record size or format.

The foregoing features of tape and disk also make them ideal for secondary or auxiliary storage units to a CPU.

Tapes are typically used for storing a master file if processing is performed in a *batch* mode; disks are best used if master file processing is performed *immediately,* in an on-line or real-time environment. That is, if a terminal is to access information from a master airline reservation file, that master file would usually be stored on disk. Consider the following schematic as an illustration:

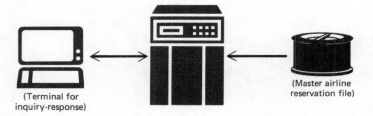

(Terminal for inquiry-response)

(Master airline reservation file)

Disks can be used for *either* batch or immediate processing. As a result, some computer centers use disks for all file processing and use tapes only for backup. Other computer centers have used tapes for batch processing for many years, and continue to do so.

We will now consider the specific features of tapes and disks and their corresponding drives.

II. MAGNETIC TAPE FILES AND TAPE DRIVES

A. Features of Magnetic Tape

A magnetic tape drive is a high-speed device that is very similar to a home cassette or tape recorder. It can read (play) data from a magnetic tape and can also write (record) data onto a tape.

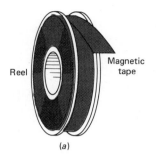

Reel   Magnetic tape

(a)

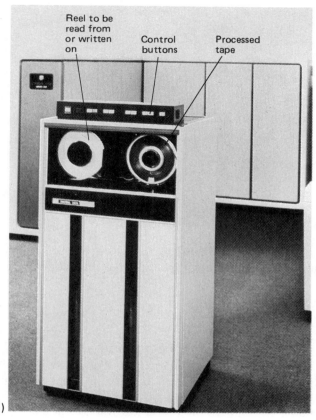

Reel to be read from or written on   Control buttons   Processed tape

(b)

Figure 7.2
(a) Magnetic tape reel.
(b) Magnetic tape drive.
(Courtesy Control Data Corp.)

The tape itself, then, is a file type that can serve as input to, or output from, a computer. It is one of the most common file types for storing high-volume data that is typically processed in a batch mode. See Figure 7.2 for an illustration of a magnetic tape and tape drive.

1. Physical Characteristics

A typical magnetic tape is generally 2400 to 3600 feet long, but larger and smaller sizes exist. Most tapes are ½ inch wide. The tape is made of plastic with an iron oxide coating that can be magnetized to represent data. The magnetized spots or bits are extremely small and not visible to the human eye. One main advantage of tape is that large volumes of data can be condensed into a relatively small area. Data that can be punched into an 80-column card or displayed on an 80-character line of a CRT, for example, can typically be stored in $\frac{1}{10}$ inch or less of magnetic tape. The average tape, which costs approximately $20, can store up to 100 million characters. After a tape file has been processed and is no longer needed, the same tape may be reused repeatedly to store other information by erasing and writing over the old file.

2. Representation of Data on a Magnetic Tape

a. Nine-Track Representation Data is represented on tape in a manner very similar to the CPU's internal code. There are nine longitudinal tracks or recording surfaces on a tape, each capable of storing magnetized bits:

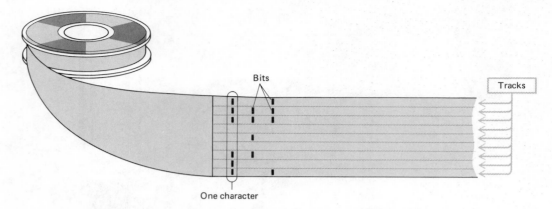

You will recall that the EBCDIC code used on many computers for internal representation of data uses a similar 9-bit code:

4 zone bits.

4 digit bits.

1 parity bit.

The **parity bit** is a check bit that is used to minimize the risk of transmission errors. On *even-parity* computers, there must always be an even number of bits on in one storage position at any time. Thus, the parity bit is turned on when the code for a character results in an odd number of bits on; otherwise the parity bit is turned off. In this way, the loss or gain of a single bit in transmission would be easily detected by the computer itself, since any time an odd number of bits is on an error is indicated. There are odd-parity computers as well, which require an *odd* number of bits to be on in each storage location. Figure 7.3 illustrates the representation of characters on a 9-track, even-parity tape.

The representation of the number 173 on a 9-track, even-parity tape would directly conform to the EBCDIC representation as follows:

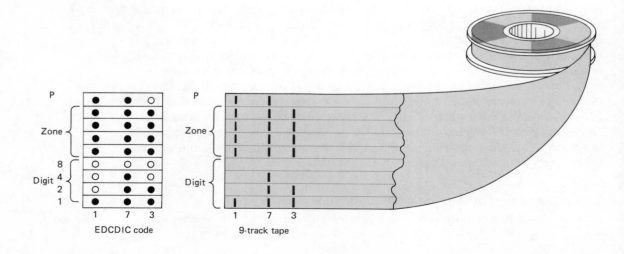

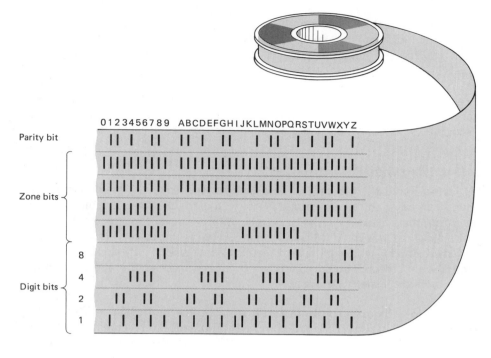

Figure 7.4 represents some other characters.

The representation of data on tape as magnetized bits results in two of the main advantages of tape:

1. Tapes can be written on, or read from, at high speeds.
2. Large volumes of data can be stored on a single tape.

Figure 7.3
Representation of characters on nine-track, even-parity tape.

b. Tape Density Note that millions of characters can be recorded as magnetized bits on a single magnetic tape. The primary reason for this storage capability is the fact that bits are exceedingly small so that hundreds of them can be placed on a very condensed area of tape. The actual number of characters that can be represented in an inch of tape is called the tape **density.** Since each character is

Figure 7.4
Representation of the characters 5, 7, A, and B on 9-track, even-parity tape.

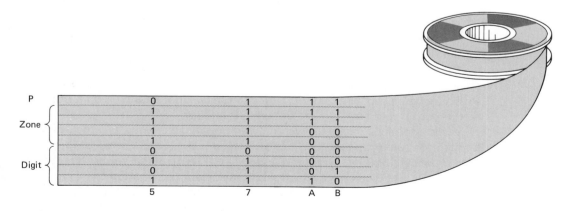

represented by a series of bits in a specific position, tape densities are measured in **bits per inch (bpi).** The term bytes per inch would be more appropriate since the density indicates the number of characters per inch of tape, where each character may require numerous "on" bits; despite the misnomer, the term bits per inch is still used. The most common tape densities are 800 bpi, 1600 bpi, or 3250 bpi, but some tapes have densities of 6250 or more characters per inch. Thus, on most tapes, 800 to 1600 characters of data or the equivalent of 10 to 20 cards of data can be represented in a single inch of tape. This high-storage capacity is a major reason why magnetic tapes are so frequently used at computer installations.

c. Specifying Tape Records

(1) Using Fixed-Length or Variable-Length Records.   As previously noted, a tape can have any record size; it is not restricted, like cards or a line entered on a terminal, to an 80-column format. Moreover, all tape records within a given file need not have the same length. That is, tapes can store (1) **fixed-length records,** where all records are the same size, or (2) **variable-length records,** where the lengths differ. We focus on fixed-length tape records because they are easier to process.

(2) Blocking Records to Minimize Wasted Space and to Save Time.   Between physical tape records the computer automatically reserves a fraction of an inch of blank tape called an **interblock gap (IBG).** Thus when a tape is created as computer output, it is created as indicated in Figure 7.5, with interblock gaps between physical records.

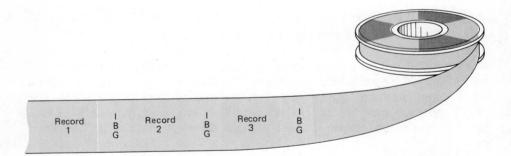

Figure 7.5
Physical tape records separated by interblock gaps (IBGs).

When a tape record is read at high speeds, it takes a fraction of a second for the drive to physically stop when it senses the end of the record. This delay is analogous to that of applying the brakes on a car: it takes several feet before the automobile physically comes to a halt. The interblock gap (IBG) is created so that, when a record is read, the mechanism will not pass over data from the next record in the time it takes to come to a halt.

This interblock gap is usually a fraction of an inch, being as large as 0.6 of an inch for some tape systems. Thus if small record sizes are used, there will be a significant amount of unused tape between each actual record. Figure 7.6 shows how interblock gaps can result in inefficient use of a tape.

To minimize wasted space and save access time, tape records are frequently blocked so that several actual or *logical* tape records are grouped together in a

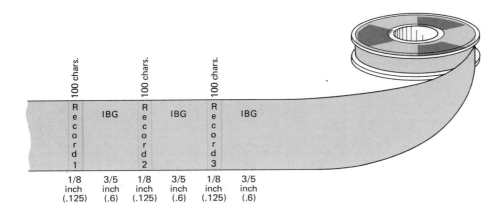

Figure 7.6
Representation of data showing unused tape (IBGs).

block as in Figure 7.7. **Blocking** of logical records maximizes the efficient use of the tape by increasing the speed at which data is transferred to or from the CPU.

In many programming languages, it is relatively simple to instruct the computer that there are, for example, 100-character logical records that are blocked 20. In that case, the computer will read in a block of 2000 characters (100 × 20), processing each logical record within the block in sequence. In short, blocking makes more efficient use of computer time; moreover, the handling of blocked tape files is relatively easy for the programmer.

d. Recording Data on a Magnetic Tape   There are two methods used for recording data on a tape.

(1) Magnetic Tape Drive.   A program can be written to read data from some input device such as a terminal and to produce, as output, a magnetic tape by activating the read/write head of the tape drive (see Figure 7.8). The **read/ write head** can be programmed to either read data or write data, depending on the job requirements.

(2) Key-to-Tape Encoder or Key-to-Tape System.   A key-to-tape encoder, as illustrated in Figure 7.9, is a device similar to a keypunch machine. It requires

Figure 7.7
Blocking of tape records.

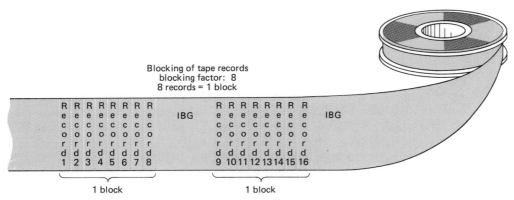

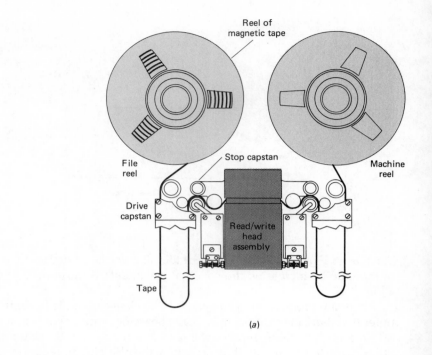

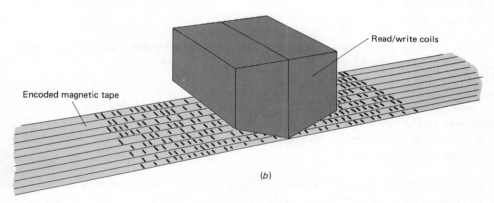

Figure 7.8
(a) Read/write head on tape drive. (b) A close-up of the read/write head.

an operator to manually key data onto the tape from a source document such as a purchase order or sales slip. When the operator depresses a key for a specific character, the device converts it to the appropriate magnetized coding. Frequently, the data keyed is also displayed on a screen so that the operator can check it for accuracy.

Key-to-tape encoders can also be used for verifying that data originally entered on a tape was entered correctly. The operator re-keys the same data and the machine checks to see that the re-entered data is the same as that previously encoded on the tape.

When numerous data entry devices share a processor that creates magnetic tape output, we call this a key-to-tape system.

Figure 7.9
Key-to-tape encoder.
(Courtesy Honeywell.)

B. Characteristics of Magnetic Tape Drives

1. A Tape Drive Is Like a Tape or Cassette Recorder

A magnetic tape drive functions like a home recorder in the following ways:

1. Data can be recorded or written onto a tape and stored for future processing.
2. Data can be read from the same tape at any time to produce output reports or be used for further processing, such as updating a master file.
3. When data is written on a tape, all previous data is written over or destroyed. For this reason, precautions must be taken to prevent the inadvertent destruction of important tape files. These precautions will be discussed later in the chapter.

2. Tape Drives Have High-Speed Capability

Tape drives process data at high speeds because (1) tape data is read electronically by sensing magnetized bits and (2) tape data is written electronically by actually magnetizing areas of tape. Data can be read or written at speeds of from 100,000 to 300,000 characters per second on the average, that is, approximately 200 inches per second.

C. Characteristics of Magnetic Tape Processing

1. Tapes Are Used for High-Volume Files

Because magnetic tapes can be processed very quickly and can store large amounts of data, they are frequently used for high-volume master files. The Internal Revenue Service, for example, stores taxpayer information on tapes that are accessed as needed to process tax returns.

2. Tapes Are Used for Sequential Processing

Processing records sequentially means that we begin with the first record on a tape, process it, then read the second record in sequence, process it, and so on.

To access a record with Transaction Number 254, for example, from a tape file that is maintained in Transaction Number sequence, we must read past the first 253 records. We instruct the computer to read a record, test if it contains Transaction Number 254, and, if it does not, read the next record. Thus, 254 records are read. There is no convenient method to instruct the tape drive to skip the first few inches of tape or to go directly to the middle of the tape. Because tapes are thread through a single read/write head, they must be processed *sequentially.*

This sequential feature of tape processing makes it ideally suited for batch processing. That is, if a master file is to be updated or made current with input records that have been collected into one file in sequence, batch processing is most appropriate and magnetic tape is best used as the file medium for the master file, as shown in the following schematic:

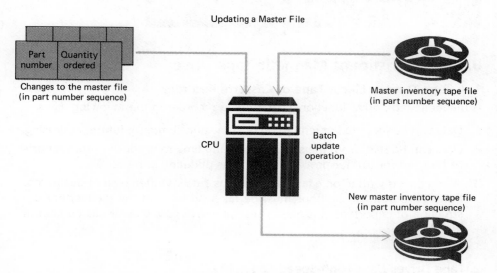

Updating a Master File

Part number | Quantity ordered

Changes to the master file
(in part number sequence)

CPU

Batch update operation

Master inventory tape file
(in part number sequence)

New master inventory tape file
(in part number sequence)

As a result of this sequential feature of tapes, they are not generally used for on-line processing. When a master file is to be accessed immediately in no specific sequence, it is unlikely that a tape drive would be fast enough to access the master file.

If an inventory file is created on tape with 100,000 records and only a handful of these are required to be printed in an on-line or immediate mode, then tapes would once again not provide the best file type. Processing time—and thus cost—would be excessive, since most of the file must be read even to process only a small number of records. Sequential processing is beneficial only when *most* records on a high-volume file are required for normal processing.

In short, tapes are well suited for batch processing but not for immediate processing. Since disks can be used for both batch and on-line processing, many organizations use disks for *all* their file processing.

3. It Is Not Practical to Rewrite or Alter Records on a Tape

If an input tape file is to be modified or altered so that it includes additional information, *two* tape files are required: one for the original file and one for the new file that will incorporate the changes. That is, the same tape cannot usually be read from and then written on with additions or changes. Consider the following schematic of an update procedure using tape.

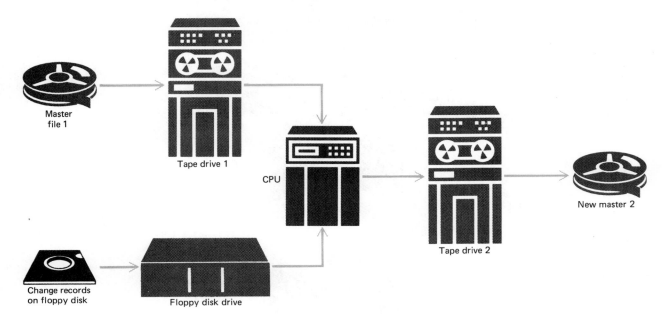

One advantage of this tape update procedure is that an *automatic backup tape* always exists after updating. The original tape that served as input can be used for re-creating a file in case the new tape is damaged, inadvertently erased, misplaced, or stolen.

4. The Need for Controls to Maintain the Integrity of Tape Files

Most medium- and large-sized organizations have hundreds or even thousands of magnetic tapes, each utilized for a specific application. These tapes are usually stored in a separate room called a tape library.

Because data recorded on these tapes is not "readable" or visible to the naked eye, it is often difficult to maintain control of all the tapes. If a master accounts receivable tape is inadvertently "written over," or used as output for some other job, for example, the result could be an expensive re-creation process. In this case, the writing of the output would destroy the existing accounts receivable information. Several control measures have been implemented at most installations to prevent such occurrences, or to reduce the extent of damage, should they occur.

a. Use of External Tape Labels   External gummed labels are placed on the face of each tape (see Figure 7.10), identifying it and indicating its *retention cycle,* which specifies how long it should be maintained. These labels are clearly visible to anyone, so that the chances of inadvertent misuse of a valuable tape are reduced. The problem with gummed labels, however, is that they sometimes become unglued. Their effectiveness is also directly related to the effort and training of the computer staff. If operators are negligent, then the labels are sometimes ignored.

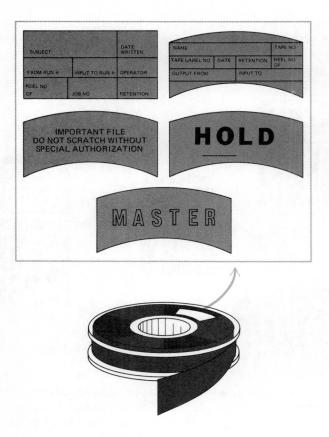

Figure 7.10
External tape labels.

b. Hiring a Tape or Media Librarian   Most medium- and large-sized companies have numerous tapes and disks that must be filed or stored and released
for reuse when no longer required. Such companies employ a tape or media
librarian to maintain control of the files in the library. If he or she performs the
job properly, there will be less misuse or misplacing of tapes and disks. See
Figure 7.11 for an illustration of a tape librarian and a tape library.

c. Programming Standard Tape Labels on the Tape   To make the identification of tapes more reliable, most programs include a built-in routine that creates
a tape label record on each output tape. This label is produced as the first tape
record, using magnetized bits. When the tape is entered as input, at some later
date, then this first label record, called a **header label,** is checked as part of the
program to ascertain that the correct tape is being used.

Thus the header labels are created on output tapes and later checked on
the tapes when they are used as input. This label creation for output and label
checking for input is a standard procedure in most programs. Since it uses the
computer to verify that the correct tapes are being used, there is less danger of
errors resulting from carelessness.

d. Use of a File Protection Ring   Those available tapes that may be written on,
or used as output, have a plastic **file protection ring** inserted in the back (see
Figure 7.12). The tape drive is electronically sensitized so that it will not create an

Figure 7.11
Tape library and librarian.
(Courtesy Honeywell.)

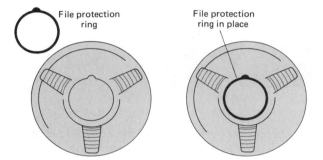

File protection
ring

File protection
ring in place

Figure 7.12
File protection ring. On
most systems, when the ring
is in place, both reading
and writing of tape records
can occur. When the ring is
removed, only reading can
occur.

output record unless this ring is in its proper place. For those tapes that are to be maintained and not "written over," the ring has been removed. This is similar to removing the tabs of a cassette tape when we wish to save its contents. Thus if an operator erroneously attempts to use a magnetic tape for an output operation, the computer prints a message that states, in effect, "NO RING—NO WRITE." If the operator is cautious, he or she will examine the external label and realize that the wrong tape is being used. Sometimes, however, an operator will merely place a ring on the tape (any file protection ring fits all tapes) and restart the job. Thus this method, alone, minimizes the misuse of tapes, but does not totally eliminate the problem.

e. Maintenance of Backup Tapes   As we have discussed, tapes can be inadvertently erased, damaged, misplaced, or stolen. It is therefore necessary to maintain backup tapes so that the re-creation process, should it become necessary, is not enormously costly and cumbersome.

Suppose a new master tape is created each month. After processing, it is best to store the old master tape and transactions used for updating, in case the new master tape needs to be re-created. In this way, if some mishap should befall the new master tape, it is a simple task to re-create it. Normally, operators maintain two previous "generations" of tapes in addition to the present one, in order to prevent any serious problem.

D. Other Types of Tapes

It is not practical to have large tape drives for small computer systems such as microcomputers and even some minicomputers. Instead, these systems use tape cassettes or tape cartridges (see Figure 7.13). These cassette and cartridge devices, miniature versions of the larger drives, are discussed in detail in Chapter 9.

(a)

(b)

Figure 7.13
(a) Tape cassette. (Courtesy Verbatim.) (b) Computer system with tape cartridge unit. (Courtesy IBM.)

E. The Future of Tapes

We will see in the balance of this chapter that disks have all the advantages of tape plus some very useful additional benefits for immediate processing. Consequently, many companies have begun to phase out tapes altogether and are focusing exclusively on disks for file processing and for auxiliary storage. In organizations where data bases are utilized in an on-line environment and where inquiries into the status of records require immediate responses, tapes are simply not adequate.

Self-Evaluating Quiz

1. Data is recorded on magnetic tape in the form of _____.
2. Most computer centers use _(no.)_ -track tapes.
3. _____ is the term used when an even number of bits must be on for any character.
4. The number of characters per inch of tape is called the _____.
5. To minimize the amount of tape that is wasted, logical records are often grouped or _____.
6. When records on a single tape file have different sizes depending on the format of each record, then the file uses _____ records.
7. Between tape records, the computer automatically reserves a fraction of an inch of blank tape called a(n) _____.
8. (T or F) A magnetic tape can serve as either input to or output from a computer system.
9. A magnetic tape drive resembles, in concept, a home _____.

10. (T or F) After a tape has been processed and is no longer needed, the same tape may be reused to store other data.

11. The three major advantages of tape processing as compared to card processing are: _____, _____, and _____.

12. Two methods of recording data onto a magnetic tape are with the use of a(n) _____ and a(n) _____.

13. Because of the sequential feature of tape processing, tapes are ideally suited for _____ processing.

14. A major disadvantage of tapes is that they can only be processed _____.

15. The sequential method of processing tape records is efficient when _____.

16. Because of the large number of magnetic tapes that are used in many installations, _____ often becomes a problem.

17. The creation of programmed _____ on an output tape is used for checking purposes when the tape will serve as input at a later date.

18. Most computer installations employ people called _____ to ensure proper handling of tapes.

19. Microcomputer systems use _____ instead of tape drives.

20. (T or F) Updating a master tape file requires the creation of a new master tape file.

Solutions

1. magnetized spots or bits
2. 9
3. Even parity
4. tape density
5. blocked
6. variable-length
7. interblock gap (IBG)
8. T
9. tape recorder
10. T
11. speed, ability to store large volumes of records, ability to store any size record

12. key-to-tape encoder or system magnetic tape drive
13. batch
14. sequentially
15. most of the records are required for processing, in sequence
16. control or identification
17. labels
18. tape librarians
19. tape cassette or cartridge drives
20. T

III. MAGNETIC DISK FILES AND DISK DRIVES

A. Features of Magnetic Disk

1. Physical Characteristics

Magnetic disk is another high-speed medium that can serve as either input to, or output from, a computer system. Like tape, the disk has an iron oxide coating

(a)   (b)

Figure 7.14
Two examples of disk
packs and disk drives. ([a]
Courtesy IBM. [b] Courtesy
Dept. of the Air Force.)

that can store millions of characters of data, typically 100 million or more. The
magnetic disk drive is used both for recording information onto the disk and
for reading information from it (see Figure 7.14).

The standard magnetic disk is really a **disk pack** consisting of a series of
platters or disks typically 14 inches in diameter, arranged in a vertical stack and
connected by a central shaft. The concept is similar to a group of phonograph
records stacked on a spindle. The actual number of disks in a pack varies with
the unit, but many have 11 disks as illustrated in Figure 7.15.

Data may be recorded on *both* sides of each disk. There are, however,
only 20 recording surfaces for an 11-disk unit, because the top surface of the
first disk and the bottom surface of the last disk do not contain data; these two
surfaces tend to collect dust and hence are not viable for data storage.

In an 11-disk pack, with 20 recording surfaces, the drive has 10 access
arms, each with its own read/write head that is used for reading and writing
data. Figure 7.16 illustrates these read/write heads, each of which reads the
bottom surface of one disk and the top surface of the next disk. One reason

Figure 7.15
Cross-sectional view of a
typical disk pack.

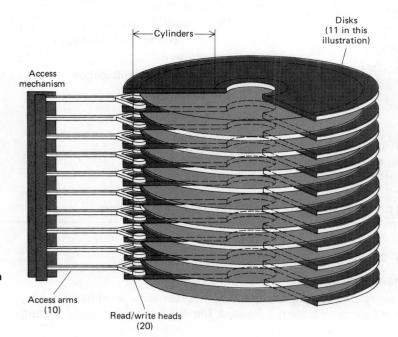

Figure 7.16
How data is accessed from a
disk pack. The read/write
heads move in and out
together as a function of
the access mechanism.

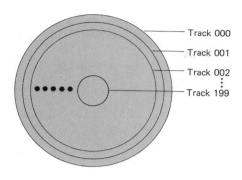

Figure 7.17
Tracks on a disk surface.

why access time for a disk is considerably shorter than for a tape is because disks have numerous read/write heads rather than just one.

Each disk surface records data as magnetized bits in concentric circles called **tracks** (see Figure 7.17). The number of tracks varies with the disk pack but 200 tracks per surface is common. Each track can store thousands of bytes of data. Although the surface area of tracks near the center is smaller than the surface area of external tracks, all tracks store precisely the same number of bytes. This is because data stored in the innermost tracks is stored more densely.

Disks vary widely in their storage capacity and their specifications. Individual records on most disks can be addressed by the following elements:

Addressing Disk Records

1. Surface number.
2. Track number.
3. Sector number (for some disks).

A sector is a pie-shaped subdivision of a disk.

Note that surface, track, and sector numbers begin at 0.

Many disks also use the cylinder concept for addressing disk records. In Figure 7.18, for example, all tracks numbered 050 on all surfaces constitute a

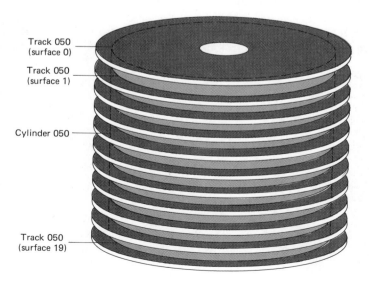

Figure 7.18
The cylinder concept on a magnetic disk pack.

cylinder that is accessible by a read/write mechanism. If there are 200 tracks per surface, there would thus be 200 cylinders (numbered 000 to 199) for the disk pack.

Figure 7.19 shows characteristics of several commonly used disks.

Characteristic	Model			
	IBM 3340	IBM 3350	IBM 3370	IBM 3380
Disk diameter	14 in.	14 in.	14 in.	14 in.
Storage capacity of drive (in megabytes)	35–70	317.5	571.4	1260.5
Tracks per surface	696	1110	1500	1770
Data surfaces	3–6	15	12	15
Transfer rate Data is transferred from the disk to main memory—measured in megabytes transferred per second	0.885	1.2	1.9	3
Access time Average time it takes to locate a disk record (measured in thousandths of a second)	35.1	33.4	30.1	24.3

Figure 7.19
Characteristics of several commonly used disks.

2. Representation of Data on a Magnetic Disk

Data is represented on a disk using a 9-bit code similar to the EBCDIC code discussed for tapes. Each byte or character is represented longitudinally along a disk track by a 9-bit configuration. As with tape records, disk records can be any length, can be fixed or variable, and can be blocked to maximize the efficient use of the disk. Figure 7.20 illustrates how data can be stored on a disk track.

3. Recording Data on a Magnetic Disk

There are two methods used for recording data on a disk.

a. Magnetic Disk Drive   A program can be written to read data from some input device such as a terminal and to produce, as output, a magnetic disk.

Figure 7.20
Storing data on a disk track.

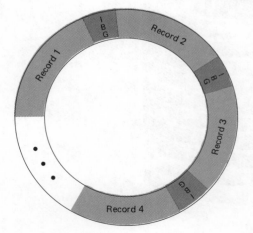

Figure 7.21
Key-to-disk system.
(Courtesy Honeywell.)

b. Key-to-Disk Encoder or Key-to-Disk System A key-to-disk encoder is similar to a keypunch machine or key-to-tape encoder. An operator codes data from a source document onto a magnetic disk using a typewriterlike keyboard. When two or more key devices share one processor for creating a magnetic disk, we call this a key-to-disk system (see Figure 7.21).

B. Characteristics of Magnetic Disk Drives

Magnetic disk drives are direct-access devices designed to minimize the access time required to locate specific records. Each drive has not one but a series of access arms that can locate records on specific surfaces. For disk drives with 10 access arms as indicated in Figure 7.16, the time it takes to locate specific records will be much less than that required by a tape drive with only one read/write mechanism.

There are several types of disk mechanisms.

1. Moving-Head Magnetic Disk

With a **moving-head disk,** all the read/write heads are attached to a single movable access mechanism. Thus the access mechanism moves directly to a specific disk address, as indicated by the computer.

Because all the read/write heads move together to locate a record, this type of mechanism has a relatively slow access rate as compared to other disks. The access time, however, is still considerably faster than for tape.

2. Fixed-Head Magnetic Disk

Since disks are generally used for high-speed access of records from a file (e.g., an airline reservation file), any method that can reduce access time will result in a substantial benefit. For this reason, **fixed-head disks** were developed. These devices do *not* have a movable access arm. Instead, each *track* has its own read/write mechanism that accesses a record as it rotates past the arm. The disks in this device are not removable and the capacity of each disk is somewhat less, but the access time is significantly reduced.

Still other disk devices combine the technologies of both moving- and fixed-head access to produce a high-capacity, rapid access device.

Figure 7.22
Winchester disk drive.
(Courtesy McNeil
Pharmaceutical.)

3. Winchester Disk

This is a new type of device with fixed disks that are not removable. The read/write head assembly and the disk are in a sealed container, making them less susceptible to contamination from dust, dirt, or smoke. Because they are inexpensive and have a smaller capacity than other disks, Winchester disks are used predominantly with smaller systems (see Figure 7.22).

4. Floppy Disk

As previously noted, minicomputer and microcomputer systems utilize small versions of magnetic tapes called cassettes or cartridges for processing with their tape units. Similarly, minicomputer and microcomputer systems utilize small versions of the standard 14-inch magnetic disks called *floppy disks* or diskettes. Floppies most frequently come in 8-inch, 5¼-inch, and a variety of 3-inch versions (with the 3-inch being the most common). Figure 7.23 illustrates one type of floppy disk. Figure 7.24 illustrates a key-to-floppy disk system. We discuss the features of floppy disks in depth in our discussion of micros in Chapter 9.

Figure 7.23
Color-coordinated floppy
disks. (Courtesy Cenna
Technology, Inc.)

Figure 7.24
Key-to-floppy disk system.
(Courtesy Sperry Corp.)

C. Characteristics of Magnetic Disk Processing

1. Disks Are Used for High-Volume Files

Because magnetic disks can be processed very quickly and can store large amounts of data, they are frequently used for high-volume files.

2. Disks Are Used for Either Direct-Access or Sequential Processing

A main advantage of using disks, as compared to tape, is its **direct-access feature**—the ability to directly access records in an on-line mode. Because a disk has numerous addressable recording surfaces and numerous read/write heads, records can be accessed directly without the need to search the entire file.

There are three common types of file organization for disks.

1. Sequential.
2. Indexed.
3. Direct.

As we will now see, the last two types of file organization are used for directly or randomly accessing records.

a. Sequential File Organization   When a disk stores and processes records in sequence, it is functioning exactly like a tape.

b. Indexed File Organization   The most common method for accessing magnetic disk records directly or randomly is with the use of an *index*. During the creation of records, the computer uses file-handling programmed routines to establish an index on the disk itself, thereby creating an **indexed file.** There are two methods of accessing an indexed file; they are called the **indexed sequential access method (ISAM)** and the **virtual storage access method (VSAM).**

The index on ISAM and VSAM files essentially indicates where each record is located. The concept is similar to that of the index found at the end of a book, which specifies the page where each item of information can be located.

The disk index stores the addresses or locations of records that are written on the disk. The address, in basic terms, refers to the surface number and track (and, on some systems, a sector number) where a particular record can be found. A *key* (or *control) field* in each record, as indicated by the programmer, is used by the computer as the basis for addressing records in the index. As an example, if a payroll file is stored on a disk, a key field would probably be Social Security Number or Employee Number, if this is to be used as a means of identification. The index will contain each employee or Social Security Number and the address of the corresponding record.

To access any disk record, then, the user need only supply a particular key data field, such as Employee Number 17537. The computer then "looks up" the corresponding disk address for this record in the index and seeks that record directly.

VSAM files have the following advantages over ISAM files.

IN A NUTSHELL

ADVANTAGES OF VSAM

1. VSAM is more efficient for accessing records.
2. VSAM records are organized more efficiently on an indexed file.
3. Alternate key fields may be used to access a VSAM file.
   A manager with access to a VSAM file has greater flexibility when inquiring about the status of individual records. For example, an employee payroll file that uses VSAM may have a Social Security Number as the primary key and Employee Name as an alternate key. The manager, then, can retrieve the record by keying in *either* the employee's Social Security Number or Name.

Records on an indexed file can be accessed both randomly and sequentially. That is, it is possible to make changes to the file directly whenever the changes occur and then later to print reports, bills, statements, checks, and so on, in sequence.

c. Direct File Organization   In a **direct file,** records may be accessed by converting a key field, through some arithmetic calculation, into an actual address that identifies the surface, track, and possibly sector or cylinder. As a simplified example, in a three-digit Account Number key field, the first digit provides the surface number and the last two digits provide the track number. This scheme would use 10 surfaces and 100 tracks, and is faster than indexed access, because there is no need to look up an address on an index. It sometimes requires more extensive programming because the programmer typically determines the best mathematical formula for converting key fields to addresses.

If the key fields are in sequence, however, and most of the records have consecutive key fields (e.g., 001, 002, 003, and so on), the key need not be converted to an address; that is, the record with a key of 001 is placed at the first disk location; the record with a key of 002 is placed at the second, and so on.

3. Disk Files May Be Easily Accessed and Modified as Needed

Disks have the added advantage over tapes of permitting updates or changes to existing records on the *same* disk. In this way, a new disk need not be created to incorporate the current changes, as is required with tape processing. That is, the same disk may be used for *both* input and output. We can read a record from a disk and make changes to that record on the same disk; we can add records to the disk; we can delete records from the disk. Figure 7.25 illustrates an update operation using a master disk file.

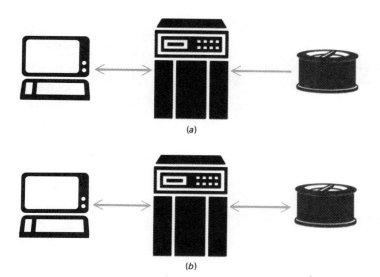

(a)

(b)

Figure 7.25
Querying and updating a master disk file. (a) Inquire about a flight. (b) Issue a ticket for a flight and update disk accordingly.

4. Maintaining Disk Files

Disks, like tapes, cannot be read manually and hence there is a need for appropriate controls to make certain that disk files are properly handled. As with tapes, the following controls are used for disks:

1. External labels are placed on disks for identification.
2. A programmed header label is created as the initial disk record, which is checked each time the disk is used to make certain that the correct disk is being processed.

Disks, however, have an added control problem that does not affect tape processing. Since tapes cannot be used as input and output during the same procedure, each tape update results in both a new tape and an old one, where the old one can be used for re-creation if necessary.

Since changes are made directly to an existing disk, the update procedure destroys previous file data; that is, there is no automatic backup file. To prevent the loss of master data resulting from erroneous processing, sabotage, or fire, disk files are usually copied onto a tape just for backup purposes. Thus a separate backup procedure is necessary after disks have been processed.

D. Mass Storage Devices

Although magnetic disks are the most common direct-access devices for file processing and auxiliary storage, there are other media and associated devices that can be used for direct access in an on-line environment. Figure 7.26 illustrates an IBM 3850 Mass Storage System, which utilizes a honeycomb apparatus for storing data. Other devices use cartridge units. Mass storage devices have great storage capability but they tend to be slow.

Figure 7.26
An IBM 3850 Mass Storage System. (Courtesy IBM.)

IV. COMPARING TAPE AND DISK AS FILE TYPES

Thus far in this chapter we have considered the two most common media for storing data files and the devices associated with them. Most medium and large computer systems utilize tape and disk files primarily, whereas some small systems such as the IBM System/3 still utilize card files. Table 7.1 indicates the physical characteristics of tape and disk file types. Table 7.2 provides a summary of these common file media.

TABLE 7.1 Physical Characteristics of Tape and Disk

Characteristics	Magnetic Tape	Magnetic Disk
Record length	Limited only by storage requirements of the system	Limited only by storage requirements of the system
Total capacity	1 to 10 million characters	Several hundred million to over a billion characters
Method of access	Sequential	Direct or sequential
Equipment used to create file	Key-to-tape system or tape drive	Key-to-disk system or disk drive
Reusable	Yes	Yes
Manually readable	No	No
Transfer rate (to CPU)	15,000 to 320,000 characters per second	100,000 to 5 million characters per second

TABLE 7.2   Summary of Tape and Disk

File	Features	Advantages	Disadvantages
Magnetic tape	1. Data recorded as magnetized bits on iron oxide coating	1. Very efficient for high-volume jobs in a batch-processing environment	1. Control problems exist because data is not manually readable
	2. Data recorded by key device or tape drive	2. Can store millions of characters on one reel	2. Mainly used for sequential processing
		3. Flexible record size	3. Cannot add data to an existing tape
Magnetic disk	1. Data recorded as magnetized bits on iron oxide coating	1. Very efficient for high-volume jobs in an on-line environment	1. Backup files must be created for control purposes
	2. Data recorded by key device or disk drive	2. Can store millions of characters on one disk pack	2. Read/write head crashes can destroy disk files
		3. Can add data onto an existing disk	3. More expensive than tape
		4. Flexible record size	

Let us consider some examples that illustrate how the computer specialist, in conjunction with the user, determines the most suitable file type for a specific application.

Example 1

A payroll system that services 75,000 employees produces weekly payroll checks in Social Security Number sequence. Two reports are also produced quarterly, both in Social Security Number sequence.

Since the volume of records is relatively large and the output must be produced as efficiently and in as timely a manner as possible, card processing would not be adequate. Since records in a payroll file would generally be processed in a fixed sequence (Social Security Number, usually), the direct-access feature of disk would not be applicable. Thus tape is the best medium for a payroll file, such as the one above, although disk could be used as well.

Example 2

A company with 5000 customers has a master file of all information used to produce customer bills once a month. The file is also used to answer inquiries from customers about the status of their account.

Since the file is accessed both sequentially for billing purposes and randomly for inquiry purposes, a disk file would be most appropriate.

Example 3

A small-scale company has 500 customers and wishes to maintain a single accounts receivable file that can be used by the computer to produce monthly bills and that can be used by the clerks to answer inquiries.

Since the volume is relatively small, a cassette tape or floppy disk used with a mini or micro would be a suitable medium.

LOOKING AHEAD

Disks are very versatile for file processing and auxiliary storage. They have replaced tapes in many organizations for handling *all* types of files and will continue to do so in the years ahead.

Yet disk storage tends to be one of the most expensive components of a computer system. Figure 7.27 gives a breakdown of disk storage costs by type of system. These figures suggest that disk will remain a relatively costly unit of a typical computer system.

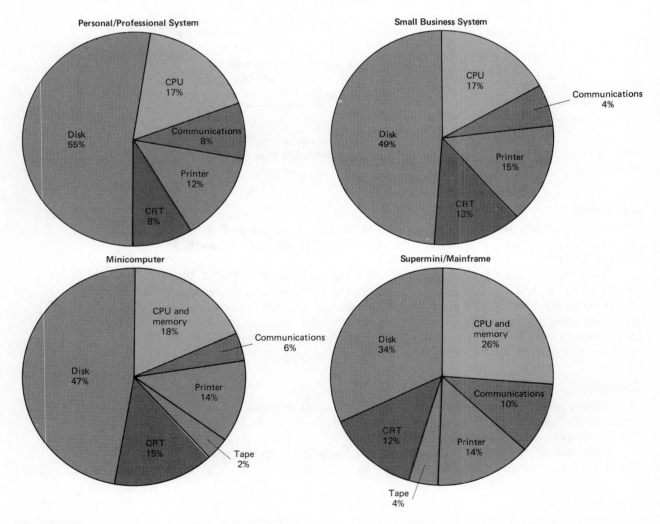

Figure 7.27
Analysis of disk storage costs.

CHAPTER SUMMARY

I. Primary uses for tape and disk
   A. To store high-volume files like master files.
   B. For auxiliary or secondary storage.
II. Common features of tape and disk
   A. Tapes and disks can be used as either input or output.
   B. Tape and disk drives can read and write data very quickly using their read/write heads.
   C. Tapes and disks can store millions of characters of data.
   D. Tapes and disks can store records of any size.
   E. Tapes and disks store data as magnetized bits.
   F. Tape and disk records may be blocked to maximize efficient use of the storage medium.
   G. Tape and disk files are identified with header labels.
   H. Tape and disk files may be created by key-to-storage systems, either key-to-tape or key-to-disk.
III. Distinctions between tape and disk
   A. Access mode:
      1. Tapes must be processed sequentially.
      2. Disks can be processed either sequentially or randomly. For random access capability, disks are typically organized as either indexed or direct files.
   B. Updating:
      1. Changes may not be made directly to a tape; for updating, an entirely new tape must be created.
      2. Changes may be made directly to a disk.
IV. Physical characteristics of magnetic tape
   A. 2400 to 3600 feet long, ½ inch wide, plastic tape with iron-oxide coating.
   B. Tape density (bpi) from 800 to 6250 characters per inch.
   C. Tape cassettes and cartridges may be used with micro systems.
V. Physical characteristics of magnetic disk
   A. Disk pack also has iron-oxide coating.
   B. Pack consists of a series of platters arranged in a vertical stack.
   C. Each platter—except for top and bottom—has two recording surfaces.
   D. Address of a disk record consists of a surface and track number, and sometimes a sector number.
   E. Floppy disks and Winchester hard disks are other types that are frequently used with micro and mini systems.

Chapter Self-Evaluating Quiz

1. (T or F) Tapes and disks are both capable of storing high-volume files.
2. (T or F) Tapes and disks are both capable of storing any size record.
3. A tape is best used for _____ processing, in a(n) _____ mode.
4. A tape uses magnetized _____ to represent data.
5. A disk pack has a series of platters or disks each of which has _(no.)_ recording surfaces.

6. Data is recorded on a disk in concentric _____.

7. (T or F) Because a disk has a series of recording surfaces and numerous read/write heads, it is possible to access disk records more quickly than tape records.

8. A _____ is a direct-access medium used with most microcomputers.

9. A disk is best used for _____ processing, in a(n) _____ mode.

10. For direct access of disk files, two methods of file organization are _____ and _____.

11. (T or F) Disks may not be processed sequentially.

12. (T or F) An existing indexed disk record may be altered and then rewritten onto the same physical space on the disk.

13. (T or F) Disks and tapes both usually have programmed labels.

14. (T or F) Maintaining control of disk files is easier than maintaining control of tape files.

15. (T or F) It is generally a good idea to copy a master disk file onto a tape for backup purposes.

Solutions

1. T / page 233
2. T / page 233
3. sequential / page 242
   batch / page 242
4. bits / page 236
5. two—except for the first and last disks, each of which has only one recording surface. / page 248
6. tracks / page 249
7. T / page 249

8. floppy disk / page 252
9. random or direct / page 253
   on-line / page 253
10. indexed / page 253
    direct / page 254
11. F / page 253
12. T / page 254
13. T / page 255
14. F / page 255
15. T / page 256

Key Terms

Blocking
Bpi (bits per inch)
Cylinder
Density
Direct-access feature
Direct file
Disk drive
Fixed-head disk
Fixed-length record
Header label
IBG (interblock gap)

Indexed file
Indexed sequential access method
   (ISAM)
Moving-head disk
Parity bit
Read/write head
Tape drive
Track
Variable-length record
Virtual storage access method (VSAM)

Review Questions

I. True or False

1. (T or F) Major files in most data processing installations are stored on cards.

2. (T or F) A tape file is generally used when most records from a large master file are required for sequential processing during each run.

3. (T or F) Punched cards are a high-speed medium that can serve as input to, or output from, a computer.

4. (T or F) A very small computer center could operate with just a terminal, CPU, and printer.

5. (T or F) Some devices are equipped to process records directly while others can only process them sequentially.

6. (T or F) Batch processing refers to the accumulation of data prior to its entry into the computer flow.

7. (T or F) Batch processing is most often utilized with direct-access files.

8. (T or F) Data recorded on a disk or tape can be read by a COM device.

9. (T or F) A record on a tape may be read by a computer system and additional information may then be added to that record.

10. (T or F) If a tape is used as output (i.e., "written over"), then information that was originally recorded on it will be destroyed.

11. (T or F) A file protection ring is used to ensure that a tape is not inadvertently destroyed.

12. (T or F) Information can be more densely stored on a magnetic tape than on a punched card.

II. Fill in the Blanks

1. The basic advantages of tape processing over card processing are _____ and _____.

2. A record on a tape may be any _____, as long as it is physically consistent with the area of primary storage reserved for the program that accesses it.

3. A _____ is a device that requires an operator to code data from a source document onto a magnetic tape via a typewriterlike keyboard.

4. When most records are required for processing in a specified sequence, then _____ is considered the most suitable file type.

5. Two disadvantages of tape processing are _____ and _____.

6. The creation of a header label record on a tape is required because _____.

7. A tape librarian is employed by many companies because _____.

8. A disk index is used to _____.

9. Two disadvantages of disk processing are _____ and _____.

10. The direct method of file organization on a disk requires a key field to be converted to a(n) _____.

APPLICATION

WHAT'S HOT AND WHAT'S NOT

What's Hot in Storage Technology
Boasting 4G bytes of storage and sometimes even more, one **optical disk storage** system can store the entire *Encyclopedia Britannica* if necessary. Optical disks grew out of the entertainment industry's marketing of movies to the home and, as a result, can store images as well as digital information.

While there are numerous applications for document storage already in place today, the future could well see a boom in erasable optical disks that are interchangeable with magnetic disk drives. "If there's a breakthrough in cost for erasable disks, they'll naturally take off," according to Hank Koehn, director of futures research for the Los Angeles-based Security Pacific Bank.

Vertical Recording technology strives to stand magnetic bits of information on end instead of side by side on a disk as they are today. According to Diebold's Dell, this would have a compacting effect, leading to 4 billion bytes on one disk by 1986 and 15 billion bytes on a disk by 1990. "They wouldn't look a lot different, but there would be 100 times the density [of information]," Dell said.

What's Not Hot
Last year at this time, microcomputer users were barraged with multiple sizes in disk drive offerings, and many wondered which one would end up being the standard. Now, it looks like the use of **8-in. disk drives** and **3½-in. disk drives** will not reach widespread use in the microcomputer market. With even advanced micros such as the Apple Computer, Inc. Lisa settling on 5-in. drives, the micro market has at least one standard by which to live.

Source: Computerworld Forecast '84, January 2, 1984, page 16. Copyright © 1984 by CW Communications/Inc., Framingham, MA 01701. Reprinted with permission.

Questions
1. Understanding Key Terms
   Define the following terms as used in the application:
   a. 4G bytes of storage. ("G bytes" is an abbreviation for "gigabytes"—see if you can find or guess at a definition of this term.)
   b. Optical disk storage.
   c. Vertical recording.
2. Software, Hardware, and Systems Concepts
   Indicate application areas where optical disks have great potential.
3. Management Considerations
   If you were a DP manager, what questions would you need answered before deciding to use optical disk storage technology?
4. Social, Legal, and Ethical Implications
   a. Do you think the fact that optical disk technology is still in its infancy should influence a person's decision to use it? Explain your answer.
   b. Do you think the fact that 5¼-inch floppy disks are more popular than 8-inch or 3-inch versions should influence a person's decision as to what type of disk drives to purchase? Explain your answer.

CASE STUDY: McKing's Superburgers, Inc.

1. File Type
   A master file of items sold and their current prices at each restaurant must be created. This master file may need to be accessed from numerous terminals concurrently.
   a. What device would you suggest for storing the master file? Explain your answer.
   b. Which of the following types of file organization would be the most likely to be used for the master file? Explain your answer.
      1. Sequential.
      2. Indexed.
      3. Direct.
2. Record Layout
   Provide a record layout showing the fields you would recommend and their relative positions in a record of the master file.
3. In addition to a master file, do you think there might be a need for a file to store historical or archival data for future reference? Explain your answer. What items would you store in an historical file?

Consider the ad entitled "Pack Up Your Troubled Packs and Cartridges in an Old Kit Bag" that appears in Figure 7.28.

1. What types of difficulties is Dysan alluding to when they say "troubled packs and cartridges"?

2. What questions would you need to ask Dysan before considering their offer?
3. What is meant by Dysan's claim that they have "precision magnetic media"?

DISCOVER THE DYSAN DIFFERENCE

Pack All Your Troubled Packs and Cartridges in an Old Kit Bag

And Save. Save. Save!

**SPECIAL
LIMITED OFFER.
DOUBLE
TRADE-IN VALUE:**

If you act now, you can receive twice the trade-in credit you normally earn toward the purchase of Dysan's superior quality disc packs and cartridges. So, pack up your old disused disc packs and contact Dysan by July 31, 1983.

Need more information? Call your nearby Dysan Representative or use our toll free 800-551-9000 number. Or simply fill in the coupon. Discover the difference Dysan's precision magnetic media can make. For your system *and* your budget.

 **Dysan** CORPORATION

Corporate Headquarters
5201 Patrick Henry Drive
Santa Clara, CA 95050
(800) 551-9000

**SPECIAL
LIMITED OFFER!**

☐ Yes, I'm interested in Dysan's Double Trade-In Value Offer.

☐ Yes, I'd like a free copy of your rigid media service brochure.

Name: _____
Company: _____
Address: _____
City: _____ State: _____ Zip: _____
Phone: (_____) _____

Figure 7.28
Marketing computer products. (Courtesy Dysan Corp.)

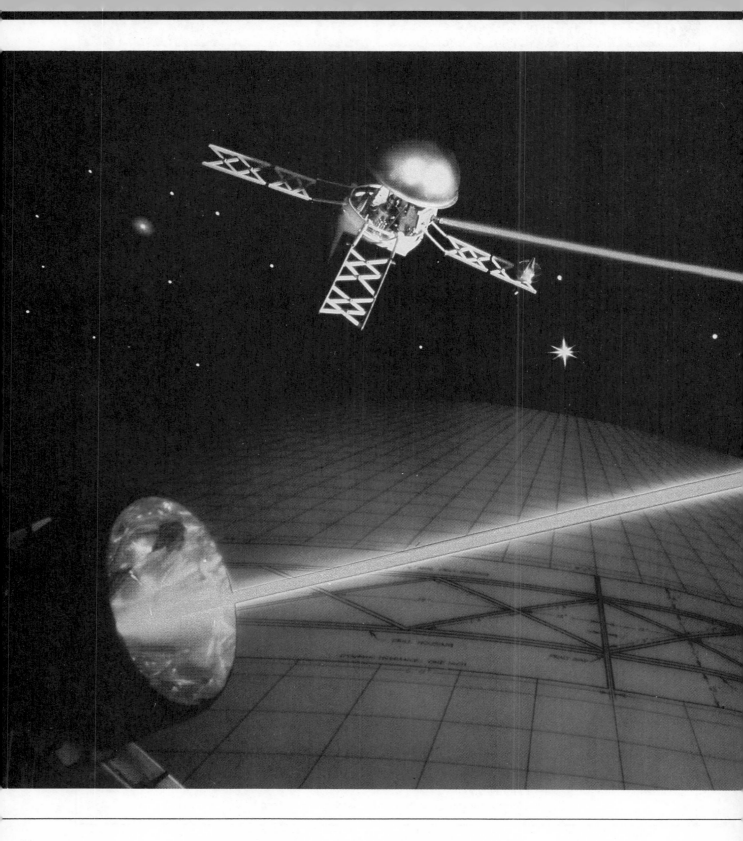

MODULE
3

COMMUNICATING
WITH COMPUTERS
IN TODAY'S
WORLD

CHAPTER 8

DATA COMMUNICATIONS: APPLICATIONS AND CONCEPTS

CHAPTER OBJECTIVES

To familiarize you with:

- Data communications applications.
- Elements of a data communications system.
- Conventional and innovative communication links.
- Organizations that supply communication lines.
- Types of transmission lines.
- Interfaces between terminals and communication lines.
- Network concepts.

I. DATA COMMUNICATIONS APPLICATIONS

A *terminal* is essentially any device that may be located some distance from a computer yet transmit and receive messages from the CPU. While keyboard devices and cathode ray tubes (CRTs) are most commonly used in this way, any input/output device at a location not specifically within the computer center can function as a terminal.

Data communications refers to the technology that allows electronic transmission of data from one location or site to another. We will see that data communications may consist simply of a cable connecting a terminal in one room to a CPU in another. Most frequently, however, data communications refers to terminals that interact with a CPU using telephone lines as a "communication channel" or linkage. More advanced data communications applications may involve the high-speed transmission of not only data but photographs, illustrations, and voice messages over long distances, using a network system. Network systems can transmit and receive messages according to programmed priorities and can use complex communication technologies that depend on microwave and satellite stations.

In this section we focus on the general applications of data communications systems for businesses. In the next section we explore the various types of technologies used to implement these systems. For now, we will think of a data communications system as one that has terminals at remote locations linked to a CPU using a communication facility such as a cable or a telephone line.

In summary, when there is a need to access a CPU from a location not physically at the computer site, we use terminals and data communications facilities. Because of advances in technology, we can enter or retrieve data from a CPU in virtually any form and from virtually any location. There are computers in all categories—mainframes, minis, and micros—that can be used for communications applications.

Following are the more common applications of such technology.

A. Remote Data Entry

Computers are very efficient at processing large amounts of data at high speeds. In many instances, however, manual procedures are used to transmit data to the computer site. This significantly reduces the overall efficiency of computers, as follows:

Typical Manual Procedures That Result in Decreased Efficiency of Computerization

1. Source documents are collected and *manually transported* to a data entry facility for keying into machine-readable form.
2. After it is prepared, the machine-readable input is *manually transported* to the CPU.
3. After the data has been processed, the computer-produced output is *manually transported* to users.
4. For each transmittal, control procedures are implemented to ensure that no

data is lost on its way to the data entry headquarters, computer center, or the user. People must *manually supervise* these control procedures.

Although one application may require only 30 minutes to actually process data by computer, the entire procedure beginning with the manual collection of input and ending with the manual transmittal of output to the user may take several days to complete. Moreover, the risk of loss of data and errors is increased because of the need for these manual procedures.

In many instances, this extensive time delay and the risk of errors are simply unacceptable. To alleviate transmittal bottlenecks, terminals may be used at locations where the data is actually transacted. When data is entered on a terminal at the point of transaction, we call this **remote data entry.** Figure 8.1 illustrates the various ways in which remote data entry may be implemented.

The use of terminals for remotely entering data has the following advantages.

Advantages of Using Terminals for Remote Data Entry

1. Data is entered at the point where it is actually transacted and transmitted electronically to the CPU. There is no need for manual transmittal of data.
2. Input errors can be corrected immediately in an on-line mode.
3. Input control and error correction can be handled by the computer, thereby eliminating manual intervention.
4. Depending on the type of terminal used (voice recognition unit, bar code reader, etc.), it is possible to eliminate a manual conversion procedure otherwise necessary to convert data into machine-readable form.

Remote data entry, then, involves the use of terminals in key locations that have access to a central computer for the primary purpose of entering input. These terminals may be placed in different departments, such as Payroll, Accounts Receivable, Inventory, and Accounts Payable. In this way, the Accounts Receivable Department, for example, can enter billing data into the computer with its terminal, and the Payroll Department can similarly enter salary changes with its terminal. Both departments, then, may have direct access to one central computer from different locations.

Several terminals may also be used within a *single* department. Suppose, for example, that the Inventory Department has *several* warehouses throughout the United States. To computerize inventory procedures *without* the use of terminals, these warehouses would be required to prepare inventory statements and send them to the computer center, where they would be logged in and then converted to a machine-readable form prior to computer processing. The transmittal of this data would be performed manually and could, therefore, become very inefficient. With the use of remote data entry, however, terminals can be placed at each warehouse. The inventory data can then be transmitted speedily and *directly* to the computer via the terminal. The computer can accumulate all warehouse data efficiently and effectively by minimizing manual intervention (see Figure 8.2).

Data entered at a remote location may be (1) processed immediately—this is called **transaction-oriented processing,** or (2) stored and then processed at fixed intervals in batch mode.

On-line data entry

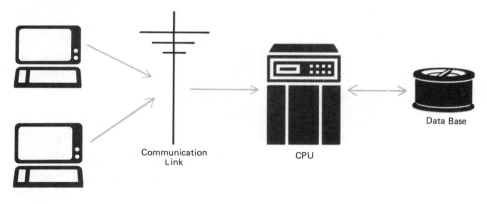

Batch data entry

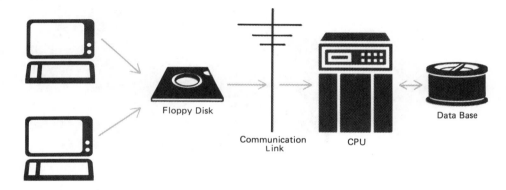

Figure 8.1
Ways of implementing
remote data entry.

Distributed data processing

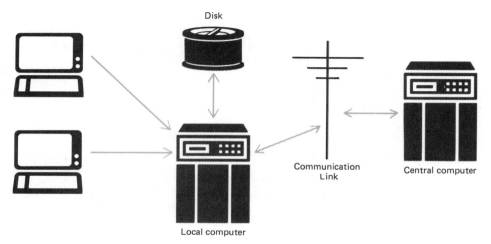

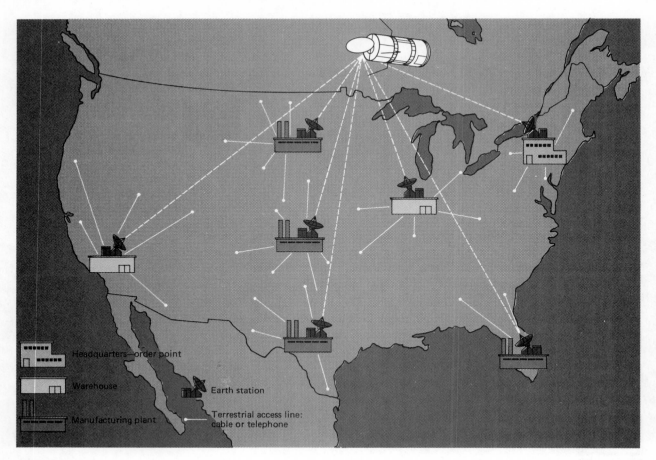

Figure 8.2
Remote data entry
inventory system.

Legend in figure:
Headquarters—order point
Warehouse
Manufacturing plant
Earth station
Terrestrial access line: cable or telephone

1. Transaction-Oriented Processing: Immediate Processing of the Data

When input data is entered from a terminal that is directly connected to the CPU, an *on-line* operation is being performed. The computer can process the input data as it is entered and alter or update the required files immediately. When terminal data is processed immediately, a magnetic disk is usually utilized for storing master files, since it provides the ability to access existing records randomly and make any required changes immediately. Sometimes this is referred to as "on-line real-time" processing, or, more commonly, as "interactive processing."

Point-of-sale systems in department stores, fast-food restaurants, and supermarkets, as well as Electronic Funds Transfer systems in banks are major users of transaction-oriented processing. Chapter 14 discusses these applications in depth.

2. Terminal or Key-to-Storage Operations for Future Batch Processing

Although terminals are frequently used when immediate access to a CPU is desired, it is also possible to use terminals for future batch processing. In some cases, data is keyed using a key-to-storage device, and directly transmitted to disk or tape.

When all the data has been entered and stored on tape or disk, the entire file that has been created can then be processed by the CPU at some later time in *batch mode.* This use of terminals for batch processing is more efficient than immediate processing for three reasons, as follows:

IN A NUTSHELL

ADVANTAGES OF TERMINALS FOR BATCH VERSUS TRANSACTION-ORIENTED PROCESSING

1. *Reduced communication time.* Transmission of data from a high-speed tape or disk to a CPU is much faster than using a terminal keyboard in an on-line mode.
2. *Reduced communication costs.* Data can be transmitted after standard working hours when the telephone or other communication rates are cheaper.
3. *The master file to be updated does not need to be on-line at all times.* Rather, the master file is called in only when the batch processing procedure is to be performed.

Keep in mind that transaction-oriented processing of data in an on-line mode is performed only when files must be kept current at all times. Consider the following example.

Suppose a department store chain, with several branches, wishes to computerize its Accounts Receivable system so that customers' charges can be automatically added to their accounts. When immediate updating of charge accounts is required, transaction-oriented processing is used to modify master files immediately in an on-line mode. In this way, inquiries from customers and managers about the current status of an account can be answered by accessing the Accounts Receivable customer file.

When, however, the Accounts Receivable customer file is not used for anything but weekly printing of bills and reports, charge account data can be keyed using a key-to-storage device and stored on tape or disk. Later on, perhaps after the store is closed, all charge data can be processed in a batch processing mode and used to update the Accounts Receivable customer file. Batch processing with the use of terminals can result in substantial savings of computer time and communication costs, since immediate, on-line processing is not a requirement. Figure 8.3 summarizes remote data entry for immediate processing and batch processing.

B. Making Inquiries from Remote Locations

A central computer with files of data stored on a random access medium such as a disk may be accessed by remote terminals for the purpose of requesting information. That is, the terminal at a remote location is used to make inquiries

IMMEDIATE PROCESSING

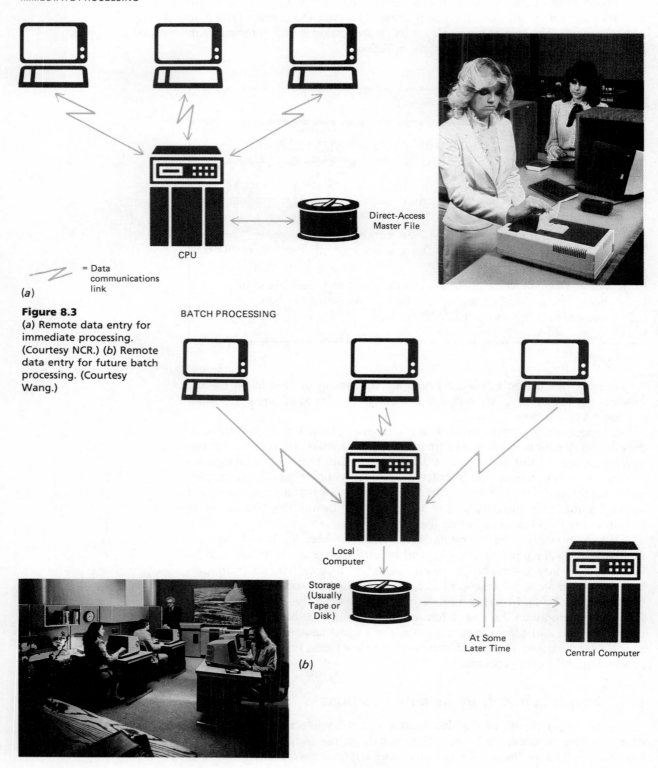

Direct-Access Master File

CPU

= Data communications link

(a)

Figure 8.3
(a) Remote data entry for immediate processing. (Courtesy NCR.) (b) Remote data entry for future batch processing. (Courtesy Wang.)

BATCH PROCESSING

Local Computer

Storage (Usually Tape or Disk)

At Some Later Time

Central Computer

(b)

Figure 8.4
Information display system
used for answering
inquiries. (Courtesy IBM.)

concerning the data on a disk file. Figure 8.4 shows an information display
system used for answering inquiries.

Various businesses use terminal devices for inquiry purposes. Brokerage
firms, for example, rely on such devices for quoting stock prices to their customers. A central file that can be accessed randomly is maintained. This file
contains stock prices that are updated on-line as new prices become available.
This file can be accessed by numerous stockbrokers who have terminals at their
desks. To obtain a price, the stock code is keyed in. The computer receives this
code immediately, accesses the price from the file, and transmits the information
back to the terminal. In this way, any stock price may be quoted within seconds.
The computer itself must be preprogrammed to accept the inquiry, seek the
appropriate information, and transmit it to the user.

Insurance firms also use terminals for inquiry purposes to quote insurance
rates to their customers. When inquiries such as these are made, the terminal
user may not always have the ability to alter central files; that is, the system
may be programmed so that the inquiry operation only permits accessibility.

The terminal is an efficient method of access or inquiry only when information must be immediately extracted from a file. When a request can be
delayed, the expense of utilizing terminals may not be justified. Thus, terminals
are generally used for inquiry purposes in the following situations:

Terminals Used for Inquiry

1. Customers need immediate replies to inquiries.
2. Managers or executives need immediate information for decision-making
   purposes.

Note that many data communications systems enable users to enter data
as well as make inquiries. For example, many brokerage houses have terminals
that enable brokers to enter an order as well as to inquire about a stock's price.

C. Remote Job Entry

In a **remote job entry (RJE)** application, terminals and other I/O devices are used for (1) programming the computer or (2) running existing programs. In remote job entry applications, a program is entered along with data. Output is produced at the same remote location where the input and the program were entered; thus, there is no need for manual transmittal of output back to the user.

Students who run programs from terminals located throughout a university or college are operating in a remote job entry environment. Users who enter program requirements and input data from their local stations are also operating in an RJE environment. Engineers who have terminals linked to a CPU for solving equations and obtaining other mathematical results are similarly operating in an RJE environment. Keep in mind that with remote *data* entry, the computer has been previously programmed to process the data. With remote *job* entry, the program is supplied *along with* the data.

An RJE station, for example, may consist of a disk drive and printer. A program and the corresponding data are entered from a disk at the remote location and processed by a mainframe which is at a different location. The output is then transmitted back to the user on the printer (see Figure 8.5).

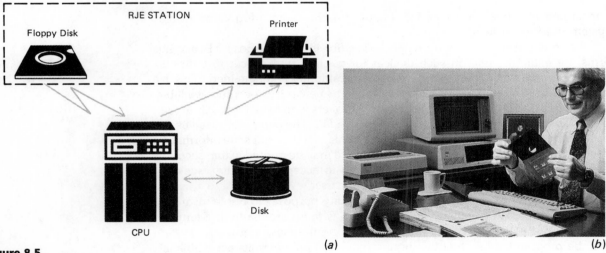

(a)　　　　　　　　　　　　　　　(b)

Figure 8.5
(a) Schematic of an RJE station. (b) Example of an RJE station. (Courtesy IBM.)

D. Time-Sharing

Time-sharing is the ability of a computer to be shared by more than one user organization for more than one application at the same time. Each user can independently access some partition or section of the CPU; processing of all programs is then handled by the supervisor or control program.

Time-sharing operations typically involve the use of terminals. Suppose a company has a large central computer that it makes available for time-sharing. Companies may rent or share the computer's time using terminals at their individual offices. The terminals may be used for entering programs and/or data to be processed. This sharing of computer time is quite advantageous for small companies that find the cost of acquiring and maintaining their own mainframes too expensive.

A school, for example, may have several terminals linked to a large mainframe that is shared by many schools in a time-sharing environment. Students are taught the BASIC language and can then write programs and enter data on the terminals to be transmitted to the time-shared CPU. Each student's results and/or any programming errors are immediately displayed on their respective terminal.

In a time-sharing system, there are various methods that can be used for allocating computer time and resources so that one user does not monopolize the system at the expense of other users. "Time-slicing" is one very popular method in which a small amount of computer time is allocated to each user. When the allotted time is up, the CPU transfers control to another user program and puts the first program in a "wait state" for a short time. Numerous programs may be executed concurrently in this interleaved manner. Since computers execute instructions in speeds measured in nanoseconds (billionths of a second) or picoseconds (trillionths of a second), this method of switching from one program to another will not usually be evident to the users who will be obtaining their output concurrently.

It should be recognized, however, that there are several potential disadvantages to time-sharing.

1. When the user wants to access the system, the computer may be too busy to handle the request, or it may be nonfunctional due to a mechanical breakdown, a power failure in the computer center, and so on.

2. There are potential problems with security and privacy that are particularly problematic in a time-sharing environment; these must be adequately taken into account.

3. Time-sharing can become expensive if usage is high. It must be remembered that total transmission costs and charges for CPU time depend on the amount of time the system is utilized, plus line costs.

We have thus seen that some companies can use time-sharing instead of an in-house computer system to satisfy their computing needs. The current availability of mini- and microcomputers provides a viable alternative to time-sharing for small organizations. Although these small systems do not have the capability of larger systems, they are far less expensive and can sometimes satisfy all the needs of smaller organizations.

Self-Evaluating Quiz

1. The term _____ refers to the use of electronic transmission of data from one location or site to another using telephones or other linkages.

2. (T or F) The use of terminals at remote locations saves manual transmittal of data, which can be very time-consuming.

3. (T or F) Data entered at a terminal may be directly transmitted to a CPU or stored on tape or disk.

4. Processing data in _____ mode means that it is first stored and then processed at fixed intervals.

5. The immediate processing of data in an on-line mode is required only when files must be kept _____ at all times.

6. The terminal is an efficient method of access or inquiry only when information must be extracted from a file _____.

7. (T or F) Rather than immediately updating the master file, a stock exchange would be likely to store incoming stock quotations on a tape or disk for future processing.

8. (T or F) A store that performs its updating once a day would be likely to store incoming transactions on a tape or disk for future processing.

9. Data communications systems used for inquiry purposes most often utilize _____ files, because they have the advantage of random accessibility.

10. Entering both a program and input from a disk at a remote location is called _____.

11. The term _____ is used to describe a technique that enables several businesses to rent computer time from a service organization; this is frequently advantageous for small companies that cannot afford their own computer.

12. (T or F) Minis and micros as well as mainframes may be used for data communications applications.

Solutions

1. data communications
2. T
3. T
4. batch (or off-line)
5. current
6. immediately or on-line
7. F—Stock exchanges require up-to-date information immediately.
8. T
9. disk or direct-access
10. remote job entry
11. time-sharing
12. T

II. ELEMENTS OF A DATA COMMUNICATIONS SYSTEM

The hardware required for any data communications application includes the following:

IN A NUTSHELL

ELEMENTS OF A DATA COMMUNICATIONS SYSTEM

1. Communication channel or link.
2. Terminal and appropriate communication interfaces.
3. Central processor.

A network may also be an element of a data communications system, as we will see later on.

In this section, we focus on the major types of communication channels currently available.

A. Communication Channels

When the distances between terminals and a CPU are not very great and the speed of transmission is not a critical factor, simple communication links or channels are used. For example, if a CPU and several terminals are located within the same building or in different buildings that are near one another, *conventional cables* or *standard telephone lines* are most frequently used for communication links. In fact, we will see that most data communications applications rely on these simple communication links.

1. Terminals May Be Linked to a CPU by a Conventional Cable

When terminals are directly and permanently linked to a CPU by cable, we say they are **hardwired.** This method of linkage is used when terminals are near the CPU and when the location of each terminal is not expected to change. If a hardwired terminal is moved, rewiring of the cable would be necessary. One main advantage of hardwired terminals is that they have immediate access to a CPU as soon as they are turned on. There is no need, as with a telephone line, to "dial up" or call the computer.

2. Terminals May Transmit and Receive Computer Messages over Standard Voice-Grade Telephone Lines

A standard telephone may be used for data communications between a terminal and a CPU. We will see that additional interface equipment is necessary to convert the digital computer signals so that they can be transmitted over the phone. This interface equipment is, however, readily available in many forms and is inexpensive.

The use of a standard telephone for data communications is far more flexible than hardwiring since terminals can be located virtually anywhere and still have access to a mainframe. This makes it possible, for example, for salespeople or field representatives to call in orders from any location and transmit transaction data directly to a CPU. When using a telephone for data communications, the user must dial up the computer's phone number or key it in using a Touch-Tone phone. If a computer line is free, the terminal will then have direct access to the CPU.

Most data communications applications make use of standard telephone lines for transmitting or receiving messages using a terminal, although other more sophisticated channels are also available. **Teleprocessing** (or tele-communications) is the term sometimes used to describe data communications using telephone lines. For many applications, the terms *data communications* and *teleprocessing* are frequently used interchangeably, although data communications may use other linkages besides a telephone.

Current Disadvantages of Standard Telephones

1. Relatively low speed.

2. Relatively high error rate because phones were designed for voice needs.

3. Long distance transmission is very expensive.

3. Other Communication Channels

Although the use of standard cables and standard telephones for data transmission are widespread in data communications applications, numerous other channels or links are commonly used. These other channels frequently have the following added advantages:

▌▌▶ Some Advantages of Alternative Communication Channels

1. Concurrent handling of numerous terminals at many locations.

2. Inexpensive access to a CPU from very great distances and numerous locations.

3. Ability to satisfy complex communication requirements such as error detection, priority scheduling, and networking.

Following are the most common alternatives to standard cables and standard telephone lines:

a. Leased Telephone Lines   A leased telephone line is a private line that is dedicated to a specific organization for its individual data communications needs. A leased line may have the ability to handle digital data only, or it may be able to handle both voice and data just like a standard telephone line.

Because leased lines have frequently been designed specifically for data transmission, they often have the following advantages:

IN A NUTSHELL

ADVANTAGES OF LEASED TELEPHONE LINES

1. Messages from one location to another are automatically switched.

2. The CPU is always accessible on a permanent line.

3. Phone lines are "conditioned" so that there is less static and fewer transmission errors.

4. The overall transmission charges are lower.

5. The lines are more secure from wiretapping and other security risks.

---

b. Microwave Stations   A microwave station permits the transmission of data, such as radio signals, without the need for lines or wires. Microwave stations are used primarily for transmitting data at high speeds over very long distances. You may be familiar with the dish-type antennas of microwave stations that are typically located on the roofs of buildings or on hilltop locations. Note that microwave transmission for data communications is fast but expensive. MCI is currently a major supplier of microwave communication channels.

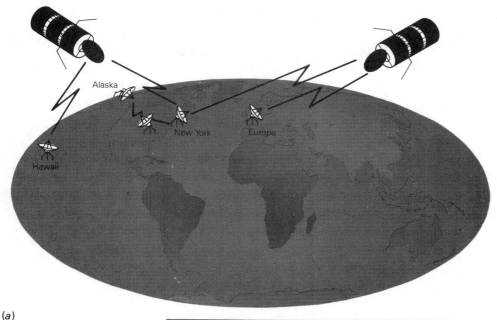

(a)

(b)

Figure 8.6
(a) The use of satellites for data communications. (b) Worldwide telecommunications service is provided between Earth-based transmitting stations, such as the one shown here in Indonesia, and satellites in space. (Courtesy ITT.)

c. Satellite Stations   A satellite is a relay station in stationary orbit located as many as 23,000 miles from Earth. It is used for high-volume data transmission as well as television broadcasting and telephone transmission. A satellite beams transmissions to other satellites, which relay them to stations on Earth. There are several dozen satellites currently in orbit. Figure 8.6 illustrates how satellite stations are used.

d. Coaxial Cables and Fiber Optics: New Technologies for Data Transmission over Wire

A **coaxial cable** is used in place of standard electrical wires for high-quality data transmission. It consists of a central cylinder surrounded by a series of wires that can carry data at very high speeds. Coaxial cables are laid for communication channels under the floor or in the ceiling of many computer centers. They are also used underground or undersea by telephone companies to provide high-quality phone transmission.

A **fiber optic cable** consists of thin glass fibers that can transmit a high volume of data at fast speeds. Approximately one-half the diameter of a strand of human hair, fiber optic tubes are connected as cables to make a light path. They are used for very high-speed data transmission and are relatively inexpensive as well. Fiber optics has been highly regarded as a technology that might replace more conventional methods of data communications entirely. Figure 8.7 illustrates fiber optic technology.

In summary, a wide variety of channels may be used for data communications applications. Simple applications typically make use of standard telephone lines as well as hardwiring of terminals, sometimes with the use of coaxial cables or fiber optics. Advanced data communications systems may use leased telephone lines, microwave stations, and even satellite stations.

LOOKING AHEAD

Study Predicts Fiber Optic Boom in Telecommunications Industry

The U.S. market for fiber optic systems will reach $2 billion by 1990 from only $4 million in 1973, according to a recently published study by International Resource Development Inc., a market research firm.[1]

The telecommunications industry spent $90–100 million on fiber optic systems in 1983, or 40% of the total market. The study predicts defense applications such as missile guidance and secure communications will account for fiber optic sales of $431 million by 1990.

[1] *Mini-Micro Systems*, October 1983, page 75.

4. Suppliers of Data Communications Facilities

The traditional source for obtaining communication channels is a **common carrier** like American Telephone and Telegraph (AT&T) Information Systems. Common carriers specialize in offering standard telephone lines called "switched lines" or leased, private lines. A switched line connects telephone lines to each other using central office switching equipment.

AT&T Information Systems also offers private lines and lines specifically designed for data transmission. These lines are of high quality and minimize the need for interfaces to convert signals to an appropriate form.

In addition to common carriers, there are special carriers that provide alternative communication channels. One category of special carrier is called the **value-added carrier.** A value-added carrier leases lines, typically from AT&T, and adds improvements such as error detection, faster response time, and compatibility among different types of hardware. The largest value-added carriers include RCA, GTE, as well as AT&T itself. Until 1982, the American Telephone

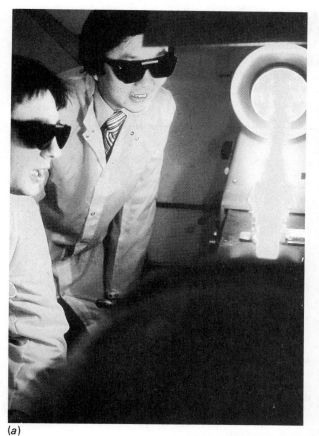

(a)

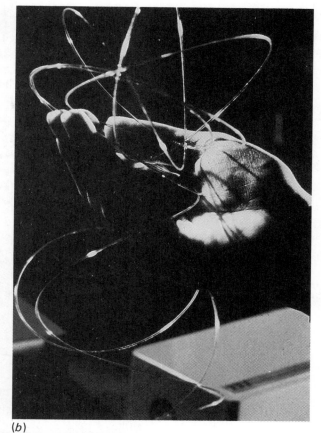

(b)

(c)

Figure 8.7
(a) Production of fiber optic
cable. An early step in the
production of an optical
fiber cable is to draw a thin
thread from a white-hot rod
of specially treated pure
silica. (Courtesy ITT.) (b)
Example of a fiber optic
cable that contains 320
separate fibers. (Courtesy
ITT.) (c) Fiber optic analyzer
for installing and
maintaining fiber optic
communications systems.
(Courtesy NCC.)

and Telegraph Company functioned primarily as a common carrier. As a result of eight years of antitrust litigation, the company was able to form its value-added subsidiary, AT&T Information Systems. In exchange, however, AT&T was required to divest itself of the Bell operating companies.

We will see later that value-added carriers can provide advanced communication facilities called networks to user organizations as well.

IN A NUTSHELL

FEATURES OF VALUE-ADDED NETWORKS

1. Leased telephone lines.
2. Added processing capabilities.
3. Higher speeds.
4. Reduced error rates.
5. Reduced transmission costs because many terminals share long distance lines.
6. Protocol conversion to enable terminals to communicate with incompatible computers.

---

5. Cost of Data Communications Lines

The cost of communication channels is typically charged in terms of (1) message units or packets of data or (2) a flat rate that varies depending on the distance the data is to be transmitted. AT&T, for example, offers WATS service, an acronym for Wide Area Telephone Service. With WATS, a business pays a flat rate for any number of transmissions within a given radius.

In general, the cost of using communication channels is decreasing while the speed of transmission continues to increase. Currently, for example, AT&T Information Systems can simultaneously transmit 280,000 messages over 72 fiber optic strands at a cost of $0.01 per mile.

LOOKING AHEAD

Trends in Data Communications

1. More favorable restructuring of rates and facilities.
2. More digital transmission facilities.
3. Increased use of communication satellites for long-distance transmission.
4. More widespread use of fiber optics for short- and long-distance transmission.
5. Increased competition between AT&T Information Systems and other companies for special services and value-added facilities.

6. Speed of Transmission Across Communication Channels

A summary of typical speeds of data transmission over communication channels follows. The band widths (narrow, baseband, and broadband) refer to the capacity of a channel to transmit data. The speed of a communication channel is sometimes referred to as the **baud rate.**

IN A NUTSHELL

SPEED OF TRANSMISSION LINES

Type of Line	Example	Characteristics	Range of Transmission Speed (bps = bits per second)
Narrow band (low speed)	Teletype	least costly, slow	up to 150 bps
Baseband (voice-grade or mid-range)	Telephone	common, some noise	1800 to 19,200 bps
Broadband (high speed)	Leased lines, microwave, satellite, fiber optics	more expensive, least noise	20,000 to 300,000 bps

---

7. Types of Transmission Lines

There are three types of transmission lines.

a. Simplex   A **simplex line** permits transmission of data in one direction only. A simplex line, then, might be used with a printer that *only receives* messages from a CPU. Because of the inability of simplex lines to transmit in two directions, they are not frequently used.

b. Half-Duplex   A **half-duplex line** permits transmission of data in two directions but not at the same time. When the line is being used to transmit data from a terminal to a CPU, it cannot be used simultaneously to transmit back from the CPU to the terminal. Thus exchanges must be performed consecutively, first one way, then the other, rather than at the same time. A CB radio is an example of a device that uses a half-duplex line.

c. Full-Duplex   Using a **full-duplex line,** data may be transmitted in both directions *at the same time.* A telephone is an example of a device that can make use of a full-duplex line. This type of transmission is only available with sophisticated data communications systems.

Figure 8.8 illustrates the three types of lines.

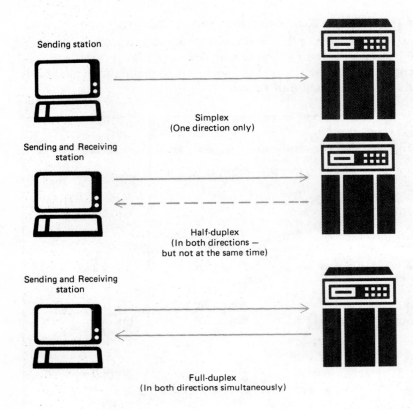

Figure 8.8
Types of transmission lines.

B. Hardware

1. Terminals

Terminal devices are typically located wherever large volumes of input data, inquiries, or jobs are anticipated. For maximum efficiency, it is important to position remote terminals at strategic locations where the data flow is the greatest.

In Chapters 5 and 6 we considered the various input/output devices that can be used with a computer. Virtually any of these can be used as a terminal if it is placed at a remote location.

The simplest type of terminal is a Touch-Tone phone. A user can access a computer with the phone, then key in a digital message. Touch-Tone phones are widely used in this way by sales representatives for transacting data (i.e., transmitting orders to the main office).

The most common terminals, however, are the typewriter terminal and the keyboard-CRT. Both are capable of transmitting messages to the CPU using a keyboard. A typewriter terminal receives hard-copy responses and a CRT receives soft-copy messages on a screen. In addition, point-of-sale systems make extensive use of bar code readers as terminals.

In a data communications system, a mini- or microcomputer may also serve as a terminal. We would call this an "intelligent" terminal because, in addition to being an input/output device, it has its own computing ability. In short, an **intelligent terminal** is programmable and generally has greater storage capacity than a non-intelligent terminal, sometimes called a "dumb" terminal.

Figure 8.9
(a) Modem. (Courtesy Rolm Corp.) (b) A modem being used with a terminal and a telephone. (Courtesy Rolm Corp.)

(a)   (b)

2. Modems and Couplers as Interfaces

Telephone lines were designed for transmitting voice messages in "analog" or continuous fashion. But terminals and CPUs transmit digital messages in terms of pulses or frequencies. To enable a telephone line to transmit and receive digital messages, a special interfacing device called a **modem** or coupler is required.

The word *modem* is an abbreviation for *modulator-dem*odulator. When linked to a terminal, this device converts digital messages to analog form for transmission over telephone lines (see Figure 8.9). At the other end, when linked to a CPU, a modem re-converts the transmitted analog signals back into digital form. Figure 8.10 shows how a modem operates.

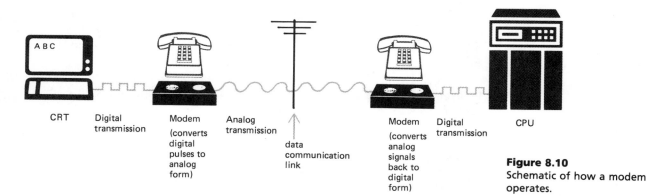

Figure 8.10
Schematic of how a modem operates.

An **acoustic coupler** is a special type of modem connected to a telephone for direct conversion of pulses. It is frequently part of a terminal itself (see Figure 8.11). Even when terminals are hardwired to CPUs, an interface is sometimes needed to ensure that all digital signals being transmitted are compatible.

3. Communication Controllers

In complex data communications systems where many terminals interact with a CPU, the cost of communication lines is high, often exceeding the actual

Figure 8.11
Terminal with a built-in
acoustic coupler. (William
Hubbell/Woodfin Camp.)

computer cost. Moreover, the need to coordinate terminal activity in such systems can be very great.

There are numerous types of controllers frequently used for minimizing communication costs and integrating the use of terminals, but we will focus on the two most common types.

a. Multiplexer A **multiplexer** is a device that can collect messages from numerous terminals and transmit them collectively at high speeds over one communication channel, as shown in Figure 8.12. Figure 8.13 illustrates the actual multiplexer itself.

The terminals are typically linked to the multiplexer by cable. Then, with a *single* modem and a *single* communication channel, the multiplexer transmits the collected data at high speeds to the CPU. There is no need for individual channels and individual modems for each terminal. In short, a multiplexer is used to improve the efficiency of a data communications application. Figure 8.14 illustrates how data is transmitted using a multiplexer.

Similarly, multiplexers can be used for *message switching;* that is, a multiplexer can receive collective responses from the CPU and transmit each response back to the appropriate terminal.

Figure 8.14
How data is transmitted
using a multiplexer.
(Courtesy MICOM.)

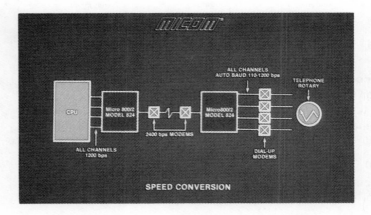

a. Transmission without a multiplexer.

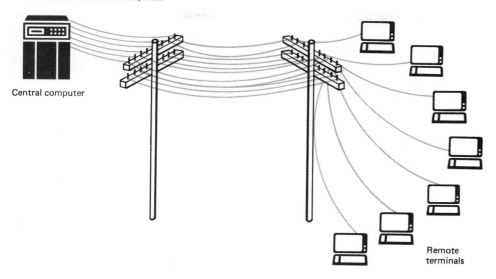

Central computer

Remote
terminals

b. Transmission with a multiplexer.

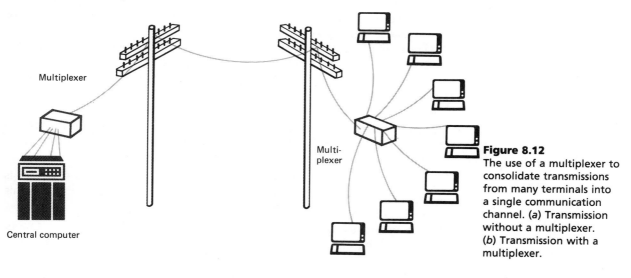

Multiplexer

Multi-
plexer

Central computer

Figure 8.12
The use of a multiplexer to
consolidate transmissions
from many terminals into
a single communication
channel. (a) Transmission
without a multiplexer.
(b) Transmission with a
multiplexer.

Figure 8.13
Multiplexer. (Courtesy
MICOM.)

b. Front-End Processor   Multiplexers are ideal for reducing communication costs and making transmission more efficient. Sometimes, however, a minicomputer in place of or in addition to a multiplexer is used for advanced control functions. The mini has the added advantage of performing computer functions as well as facilitating the flow of data to the mainframe. That is, the mini can format the data, edit it, test for errors, etc., *prior to processing by a mainframe.* A mini used in this way is called a **front-end processor.** A mini may also be used at the other end to format, edit, etc., messages from the mainframe before they are transmitted back to each terminal. In this instance, the mini would be called a "back-end processor."

C. Central Processor

1. CPU Requirements

A CPU used in conjunction with data communications equipment generally requires the following.

1. *Complex control features.* A highly sophisticated control system and supervisor capable of processing data from numerous stations are needed. Control capabilities typically include:
   a. The ability to query terminals, called **polling,** to determine if there are messages waiting to be sent.
   b. The ability to establish a queue or priority system if several messages are being transmitted simultaneously.
   c. The ability to maintain the security and integrity of the system by establishing and checking codes and passwords that provide access to authorized users only.
2. *Interrupt ability.* Because the CPU operates on data from various terminals concurrently, it must be able to incorporate priority scheduling and to interrupt programs if more important ones need processing.
3. *Interaction with direct-access devices.* High-speed random access of files is a very important aspect of data communications. Files to be accessed in this way are usually stored on disk.
4. *Multiprogramming capability.* Only computers with the ability to process more than one program concurrently can be used for processing data from numerous terminals.

There are many mainframes, minis, and micros specifically designed for functioning in a data communications environment. In general, the larger the computer, the more terminals it can employ for its data communications needs.

Note that although a CPU can be programmed to minimize security risks in a data communications environment, the threat of such risks remains high. Chapter 17 focuses on the methods used to reduce the risk of unauthorized users invading a data communications system for personal gain or for sabotage.

2. Communicating with the CPU

Methods used for interacting with a CPU vary widely. Typically, when telephones are used, the user dials a phone number assigned to the computer or keys the phone number using a Touch-Tone phone. If the computer cannot

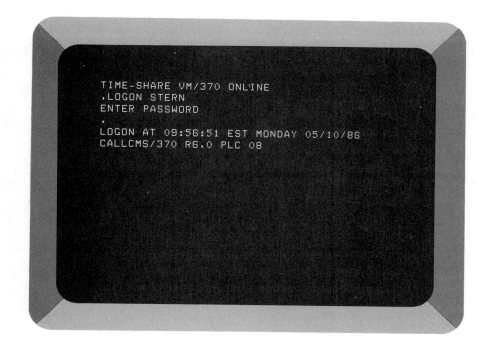

```
TIME-SHARE VM/370 ONLINE
.LOGON STERN
ENTER PASSWORD
.
LOGON AT 09:56:51 EST MONDAY 05/10/86
CALLCMS/370 R6.0 PLC 08
```

Figure 8.15
Sample log-on procedure.

handle the transmission at that time, a busy signal will usually be heard. If the computer is free, however, a high-pitched carrier wave will sound over the telephone. The user then places the handset of the phone on the coupler, which provides an interface between the terminal and the telephone line.

Regardless of whether the computer must be dialed up or whether it is hardwired to the terminal, users will be requested by the computer to log on, that is, to follow a given set of procedures to identify themselves. Typically a log-on procedure involves having to enter one or more authorization codes, sometimes referred to as account numbers or user numbers, and/or passwords. See Figure 8.15 for an example of a log-on procedure. If the codes and passwords are not properly entered, the computer will respond with a message such as INVALID PASSWORD—TRY AGAIN. It should be noted that on some systems a user must enter a log-on code in a precise way, or the computer will automatically break the connection with the terminal. This procedure is a security measure to thwart unauthorized users who break into a computer system through trial-and-error entry of log-on codes.

Once on-line communications have been successfully established, the computer indicates that it is ready. The user can then proceed, for example, to (1) run a program already stored in the computer system, (2) enter an entirely new program from the keyboard of the terminal, or (3) enter new or revised data to be stored in the computer system. The computer will respond with the appropriate results on the terminal.

Self-Evaluating Quiz

1. In a data communications system, a communication _____ or link is necessary for connecting a remote terminal to a CPU.

2. Most simple data communications systems use _____ or _____ as a data communications link.

3. Hardwired terminals can use standard electrical cables or newer _____ cables for data transmission.

4. A _____ is a private communication line offered by telephone companies for dedicated data communications use by an organization.

5. High-speed data communications can make use of wireless _____ stations and _____ stations.

6. A _____ cable consists of thin particles of glass that can carry a high volume of data at high speeds.

7. (T or F) All communication channels are obtained directly from AT&T.

8. The speed of a communication channel is called the _____ rate.

9. (T or F) Baseband transmission over telephone lines is faster than broadband transmission over leased lines.

10. When transmission is permitted both to and from a CPU over the same communication line—*but not at the same time*—the line is called a _____ line.

11. When transmission is permitted both to and from a CPU over the same communication line *at the same time*, the line is called a _____ line.

12. A(n) _____ is a device that converts terminal signals in digital form to analog form for transmission over telephone lines.

13. A _____ is a device that can collect messages from numerous terminals and transmit them collectively over a single communication line.

Solutions

1. channel
2. a standard voice-grade telephone line
   a cable
3. coaxial or fiber optic
4. leased or private line
5. microwave
   satellite
6. fiber optic
7. F—There are other carriers such as RCA and GTE.
8. baud
9. F—Baseband transmission is slower than broadband transmission.
10. half-duplex
11. full-duplex
12. modem or acoustic coupler
13. multiplexer

D. Networks

With the growth of data communications systems, the use of centralized computer centers has been expanded to include remote access from numerous terminals or other CPUs. This means that different branches within an organization can communicate with each other and that different organizations themselves can communicate with one another.

The term **network** is used to describe a coordinated system of linked terminals or minis and mainframes that may operate independently but also share data and other resources. The central CPU or mainframe is called the **host computer,** and the terminals or minis linked to it are called **nodes.** A network has both hardware and software components for providing required linkages and establishing the most efficient method of communication control for routing of messages.

1. Some Commercially Available Networks

There are two main types of commercially available communication networks that provide automatic coordination and compatibility among different types of hardware.

a. Private Branch Exchange (PBX)   Electronic private branch exchange switching systems utilize a computer-controlled switching mechanism for handling communications across phone lines.

Value-added carrier systems such as GTE's Telenet operate nationwide common carrier networks for communications between computers and terminals. Telenet, for example, uses minicomputer controllers, switches, and interfaces to organize these lines into a nationwide network. A user can simply dial into the nearest network node to gain access. Within the network, data is organized into packets of up to 128 characters each, and these packets are routed individually through the network toward their destinations. Figure 8.16 shows an electronic PBX system.

Along with a fixed network fee, the user is typically charged per 1000 packets transmitted, regardless of distance. This could result in a significant reduction in communication cost as compared to conventional telephone rates. Telenet provides local dialing capability to approximately 250 cities. Tymnet, Inc. is another value-added network carrier that provides data communications capability to businesses. In addition to 250 nationwide locations, Tymnet provides access to 35 international locations. AT&T Information Systems also offers a network called Advanced Information System/NET1 service.

b. Local Area Network   A **local area network** (LAN) is a transmission medium for terminals and host computers closely linked by a single facility or in

Figure 8.16
Example of an electronic PBX system that uses Intel's 8080 microprocessor chip. (Courtesy Intel Corp.)

nearby facilities. In general, the range of a local area network is approximately 50 miles. These network systems are designed, as the name implies, for local use and as alternatives to standard switching systems. Coaxial cables, rather than telephone lines, are used for most local area networks, but some use fiber optic cables as well.

The two basic types of local area networks are *baseband* (medium-speed) and *broadband* (high-speed). The basic difference between the two is the band width, which, in addition to speed, determines:

1. Cost.

2. The number of simultaneous transmissions.

3. The ability to handle voice and data interactively.

Broadband networks are based on cable television technology. They can handle data, voice, and video transmissions at very high transmission rates, much higher than baseband networks. Like a cable television network, the band width can be divided into numerous *channels*. In this way, each channel can be dedicated to a specific kind of equipment or application. Wang's Wangnet is probably the most popular broadband network available commercially.

Baseband networks are more limited but far less costly. They provide only one channel, and all the equipment attached to the cable must use this one channel. The most popular baseband network that is available commercially is Xerox's Ethernet, which uses coaxial cable. Currently, Ethernet can network up to 1024 workstations. Ethernet is supported by Intel and the Digital Equipment Corporation as well as by Xerox. For systems that do not require voice or video transmission but focus exclusively on data transmission, Ethernet is currently the least costly network.

2. General Categories of Networks

Large organizations such as banks, department stores, and brokerage houses make extensive use of networks. Figure 8.17 illustrates a network-based system.

There are several types of networks that may be used by an organization in a distributed data processing environment where each department has a

Figure 8.17
Example of a computer network. (Courtesy New York Power Pool.)

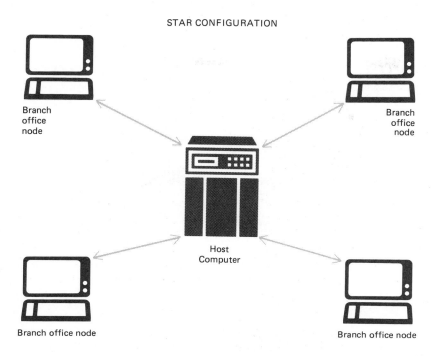

STAR CONFIGURATION

Branch
office
node

Branch
office
node

Host
Computer

Branch office node

Branch office node

1. Most common among early networks such as telephone systems.
2. Relies on the central node for control of operations.

Figure 8.18
Example of a star
configuration.

node—a mini or micro at a remote station—and they are all integrated under the control of a host or central mainframe. The type of network used depends on the geographic location of nodes, the degree of communication control necessary for messages, and the speed of transmittal. We will briefly examine the three most common methods of networking for companies with host computers and nodes used in a distributed environment.

a. Star Configuration   In this type of network, a central host computer receives all messages and routes responses to the appropriate node (see Figure 8.18). If one node becomes inoperable, it is simply bypassed. This technique of networking is often used by banks and for time-sharing in schools. In a star configuration, the reliability of the CPU is most critical, because if the central processor "goes down," the entire system is unusable.

b. Ring Configuration   In this type of network, CPUs and terminals or nodes are connected in *serial* fashion, where messages must pass through a consecutive chain. In this case, there is no host computer. Each node, which is usually a computer, handles its own applications and also shares resources over the entire network. The main disadvantage of this system is that if one node becomes inoperable, the entire system fails. Such a network is best for decentralized systems in which no priorities are required. Figure 8.19 illustrates a ring configuration.

c. Plex Configuration   This is a truly interactive network where each node has direct access not only to a host computer but to every other node as well. In a sense, each node can form its own star network. Organizations in which some

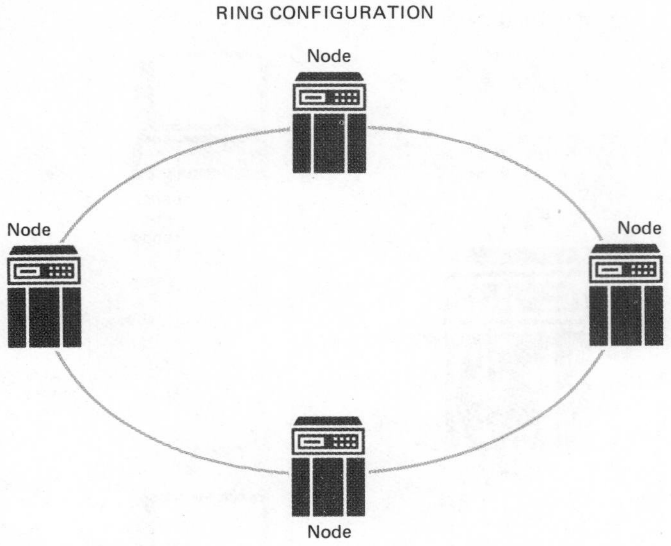

RING CONFIGURATION

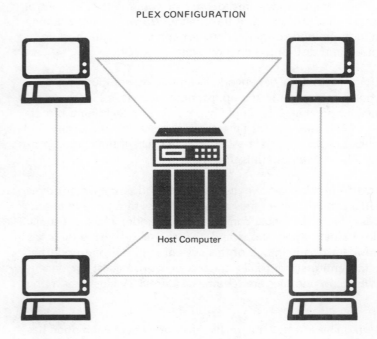

Figure 8.19
Example of a ring
configuration.

1. Circulates all messages.
2. A failure of any one node may interrupt the network operation.

data bases are decentralized and others are maintained by a central facility would use a plex system. In this way, any node can access any data base. Department stores often use plex networks; order entry information is collected at the point of sale and can then be passed along to regional offices. Figure 8.20 illustrates a plex configuration.

Figure 8.20
Example of a plex
configuration.

PLEX CONFIGURATION

Host Computer

1. Fully interactive.
2. Allows nodes to be added or removed without impairing the network.

LOOKING AHEAD

Efficient Local Area Nets to Grow

The use of local area networks will increase significantly during the 1980s, because they represent the most efficient way of interconnecting a growing population of data terminals. The growth of local area networks is being spurred by a growing awareness that data terminals can enable middle-level executives to do significantly more work in less time. Also spurring the use of local area networks is rising communication costs.

The predictions are that:

1. Local area networks will continue to employ ring-, star-, and plex-type networks.
2. Local area network costs will decrease as the technology improves.
3. Fiber-optic, cable-based local area networks will become very popular.

CHAPTER SUMMARY

I. Why Use Data Communications
  A. For remote data entry to process transactions immediately or in batch mode.
  B. For making inquiries from remote locations.
  C. For remote job entry.
  D. For time-sharing.
II. Data Communications Components
  A. Communication link.
    1. Cable—coaxial or fiber optic.
    2. Telephone lines—leased or voice-grade.
    3. Microwave or satellite transmission.
  B. Types of communication linkages.
    1. Simplex.
      a. In one direction only.
      b. For example, CPU-to-remote printer.
    2. Half-duplex.
      a. In both directions but not at the same time.
      b. Used where speed is not critical.
    3. Full-duplex.
      a. Data may be transmitted in both directions at the same time.
      b. Fastest, most sophisticated, and costliest.
  C. Interfaces.
    1. Modems or couplers.
      a. Interfaces between communication lines and CPU.
      b. Convert digital signals to analog form and back again.
    2. Communication controller.
      a. Integrates the use of terminals by collecting messages and transmitting them at high speeds, by prioritizing messages, and so on.
      b. Multiplexers and front-end processors are communication controllers.

III. Networks
   A. Provide sophisticated control and coordination of a series of systems and/or devices.
   B. Types.
      1. Private Branch Exchange uses switching mechanisms.
      2. Local area network—for transmission within a radius of 50 miles.
   C. General categories of networks.
      1. Star configuration.
         A central host computer receives messages and routes them to an appropriate remote station or node.
      2. Ring configuration.
         CPUs and nodes are connected in serial fashion where messages pass through a consecutive chain.
      3. Plex configuration.
         Interactive system where every node has direct access not only to a host but to each other.

Chapter Self-Evaluating Quiz

1. The term _____ means the use of terminals for entering data at remote locations.

2. When data is entered remotely from terminals, it may be stored on tape or disk for future _____ processing, or it may be processed _____.

3. The term _____ means the use of terminals for entering an entire application—data and program—from a remote terminal.

4. (T or F) Programs and data may be entered on disk from remote locations.

5. When several user organizations rent time from a company that specializes in providing computer services, the concept is called _____.

6. Data communications requires the use of a _____ to link terminals with a CPU.

7. (T or F) Telephone lines and conventional cables are the most commonly used linkages in simple data communications applications.

8. Two types of cables that are frequently used specifically for linking terminals to a CPU are _____ and _____.

9. (T or F) Broadband transmission of data using microwave and satellite stations is extremely fast.

10. A _____ line permits transmission of data in two directions but not at the same time.

11. To enable a telephone to transmit and receive digital messages, a special interface device called a _____ is required.

12. (T or F) Terminals may be linked directly to a CPU or may be linked to a multiplexer or other communication processor used for collecting messages and transmitting data.

13. (T or F) Networks may only connect terminals or CPUs within a single organization.

14. In a star network, a _____ is the main CPU for coordinating and interacting with all nodes.

15. When terminals or minis that serve as nodes are located relatively near a host computer, the most efficient type of network is called a _____.

Solutions

1. specific answer—remote data entry / page 270
   more general answer—data communications / page 269
2. batch / page 272
   immediately / page 272
3. remote job entry / page 276
4. T / page 276
5. time-sharing / page 276
6. communication channel or link / page 279
7. T / page 279
8. coaxial cables / page 282
   fiber optic cables / page 282
9. T / page 285
10. half-duplex / page 285
11. modem or coupler / page 287
12. T / page 288
13. F—A network can connect nodes from numerous organizations. / page 292
14. host computer / page 295
15. local area network / page 293

Key Terms

Acoustic coupler
Baud rate
Coaxial cable
Common carrier
Data communications
Fiber optic cable
Front-end processor
Full-duplex line
Half-duplex line
Hardwired
Host computer
Intelligent terminal

Local area network
Modem
Multiplexer
Network
Node
Polling
Remote data entry
Remote job entry (RJE)
Simplex line
Teleprocessing
Transaction-oriented processing
Value-added carrier

Review Questions

I. True or False Questions

1. (T or F) Data communications equipment is used to reduce the overall time it takes to make output available to users.
2. (T or F) Data communications equipment may only be used with mainframes.
3. (T or F) The use of data communications equipment decreases the need for manual transmittal of data.
4. (T or F) The use of data communications equipment eliminates the need for converting digital signals over telephones.

5. (T or F) A multiplexer can reduce the overall cost of communication lines.

6. (T or F) A major benefit of data communications is to facilitate the flow of data both into and out of a computer center.

7. (T or F) Remote terminals can be placed strategically at different locations but must be in the same building as the computer.

8. (T or F) Terminals enable users to have direct access to central files or to a data base.

9. (T or F) Users should know how to program data communications systems.

10. (T or F) Terminals can only be used for immediate processing.

11. (T or F) Key-to-storage processing is usually employed when data is to be processed in groups or batches at some later time.

12. (T or F) An Accounts Receivable system that utilizes a daily update procedure to make the master file current could use a key-to-storage device to process charge slips once a day rather than process the charges as they are transacted.

13. (T or F) A stock exchange could normally process changes in stock quotations once a day in a batch-processing mode.

14. (T or F) Most terminals can both transmit and receive data.

15. (T or F) CRTs display data in hard-copy form.

16. (T or F) Leased private telephone lines, while generally expensive, reduce noise and interference for data communications systems.

17. (T or F) A bank with hundreds of branch offices and the need to coordinate the activities of them all from one central location is likely to use a network.

18. (T or F) A local area network is typically used when a host computer and the associated nodes are relatively near each other.

19. (T or F) A plex network is generally regarded as most useful when nodes need to communicate actively with each other as well as with a host computer.

20. (T or F) Fiber optic cables have great potential for data communications applications.

II. Fill in the Blanks

1. Data communications systems utilize _____ placed strategically at key locations to enter input.

2. Data is transmitted to the CPU from terminals via _____ lines.

3. When input data is entered from a terminal for the purpose of directly altering the contents of records on a file, this is called a(n) _____ operation.

4. When terminal data is first converted to a separate medium, such as tape or disk, then _____ processing is usually utilized.

5. If an Accounts Receivable system utilizes terminals to enter all sales data for charge customers, and the system has the ability to provide up-to-the-minute charge information for customer inquiries, then _____ processing is required.

6. If, in the above system, customer inquiries are answered with data that is current only through the previous day's sales, then _____ processing is being used.

7. Small companies that have need of data processing equipment but find the cost of acquisition and maintenance prohibitive could benefit from renting terminals with access to a central processing unit. This concept is referred to as _____.

8. If a company utilizes a terminal for answering inquiries, then the data file is probably stored on _____.

9. A transmission line for both receiving and transmitting data at the same time is called a _____ line.

10. Communication channels may be obtained from _____ carriers as well as common carriers like AT&T.

11. The term _____ is used to describe a coordinated system of linked terminals or minis and CPUs that may operate independently but also share data and other resources from a central CPU.

12. In a network, the central processor is called the _____, and the terminals or minis linked to the CPU are called _____.

13. The network that uses a computer-controlled switching mechanism for handling communications over phone lines is called a _____.

14. A _____, abbreviated LAN, is a transmission medium for terminals and host computers linked by a single facility or in nearby facilities.

15. _____ networks are those that can handle data, voice, and video transmission and are based on cable television technology.

APPLICATION

FIBER OPTICS—THE LOGICAL CHOICE FOR USERS

by Richard J. Pybus

If a poll had been conducted in any company 10 years ago about the number of data terminals it would be using in 1983, the result probably would have been a number about one-eighth of the actual total.

The result of this poor planning is often a network consisting of almost every type of local data communications device on the market, communicating over a virtual tangle of data cables and borrowed intercom pairs. This approach has worked fine for many up to this time, but what does a company do for the next 10 years of growth now that all of its conduits are full and the building supervisor flatly refuses to let the firm hang cables out the window?

Data communications can be divided into three neat categories: remote DP, which uses telecommunications or other facilities; local point-to-point data transfer; and the local area network. In many cases, the bulk of the ongoing data transfer is between terminals and a processor.

Fiber optic systems have not yet evolved to the point where they should be considered for long-distance networks. Lease-based systems fare a bit better, as evidenced by AT&T's choice of this technology for its Northeast Corridor project.

Industry Niche
This niche of the industry has grown quite rapidly in the past couple of years, partly because some of the old problems associated with the handling of the fiber cable have been eliminated. Fiber cable manufacturers have developed their craft to the point where a user may buy a cable for any application.

Many data communications managers are looking at fiber optic systems because they are running out of cable space in their facilities. Faced with the dilemma of having to provide as much bandwidth as possible in as little space as possible, they may opt for fiber.

Source: Computerworld, January 31, 1983, page 5. Copyright © 1983 by CW Communications/Inc., Framingham, MA 01701. Reprinted with permission.

Questions
1. Understanding Key Terms
   Define the following terms in the context in which they are used in the application:
   a. Remote DP.
   b. Local point-to-point data transfer.
   c. Local area network.
   d. Bandwidth.
2. Software, Hardware, and Systems Concepts
   State the advantages of fiber optics as indicated, or implied, in the application.

3. Management Considerations
   If you were a manager of an organization, what criteria would you use for determining whether fiber optics could satisfy your data communications needs?

4. Social, Legal, and Ethical Implications
   What security precautions would be necessary for systems that use fiber optics? Explain your answer.

CASE STUDY: McKing's Superburgers, Inc.

One of the proposals submitted by a vendor recommends a distributed data processing system for McKing's. This proposal suggests that each individual restaurant should have its own computer system for local processing. In addition, the main office should have a central computer that would be accessible to management and would enable the restaurants to communicate with each other through a data communications system.

1. Type of Communication Channels
   Which of the following communication channels do you think might be appropriate for McKing's? Explain the reasons for your selections.
   a. Conventional cable.
   b. Voice-grade telephone line.
   c. Leased telephone lines.
   d. Microwave stations.
   e. Satellite stations.
   f. Coaxial cable.
   g. Fiber optics.

2. Type of Transmission Line
   Which of the following types of transmission lines do you think would be appropriate for McKing's? Explain your answer.
   a. Simplex line.
   b. Half-duplex line.
   c. Full-duplex line.

3. Type of Communication Network
   What questions would you need to ask the restaurant managers and the vendors to determine which of the following types of communication networks would be appropriate for McKing's?
   a. Private branch exchanges (PBX).
   b. Baseband local area network.
   c. Broadband local area network.

4. Type of Network Configuration
   What questions would you need to ask the restaurant managers to determine which of the following types of network configurations would be appropriate for McKing's?
   a. Star configuration.
   b. Ring configuration.
   c. Plex configuration.

THE COMPUTER AD: A Focus on Marketing

Consider the ad entitled "Why Install Cables for Data When There's A Network Right Under Your Nose?" that appears in Figure 8.21.

1. Define the following terms as they are used in the ad:
   a. Local area network.
   b. Cable.
   c. Modem.
   d. 9600 bps.
   e. Full-duplex.
   f. ASCII terminal.
2. In your own words, describe how you think this data carrier system works. How does it compare to a network that carries data exclusively?
3. Note that the ad specifies that this data carrier system can be used by specific computers only. Based on the ad itself, see if you can determine what the requirements of the compatible systems are.

Why install cables for data when there's a network... right under your nose?

If you're tired of the endless hassle of expanding your local area network—not to mention the expense of installing cable and limited distance modems—Teltone has some very good news for you.

It's called the DCS-2 Data Carrier System, and it lets you use existing PABX wires to carry both voice and data traffic *simultaneously.*

That's right. Up to 9600 BPS of dedicated-channel, full duplex asynchronous data can be transmitted or received by any ASCII terminal in your system—and the data won't interrupt phone service.

With the DCS-2 your PABX becomes a common communications network, where making a computer hookup is as easy as plugging in a phone. It's fast, FCC Part 68 registered, and it won't cost you the roof over your head.

So before you make another equipment move, find out how Teltone can help you keep it simple. Just call our toll-free hotline at 1-800-227-3800 Ext. 1122 (in California 1-800-792-0990 Ext. 1122) or write Teltone Corporation, PO Box 657, Kirkland, WA 98033. In Canada call (416) 475-0837 or write 91 Telson Road, Markham, Ontario L3R 1E4.

TELTONE®

For users of DEC, Prime, Data General, Tandem, IBM Series/1, H-P and other asynchronous computers.

Figure 8.21
Marketing computer products. (Courtesy Teltone Corp.)

CHAPTER 9

MICROS AND MINIS: THE SECOND PHASE OF THE COMPUTER REVOLUTION

CHAPTER OBJECTIVES

To familiarize you with:

- Microcomputer and minicomputer applications.
- Components of micros and minis.
- The most popular micros and minis and typical configurations.
- The most popular software and operating systems for micros.
- How to determine which micro or mini would be best for your specific application.
- What the future holds for micros and minis.

As we have seen, mainframes with their enormous capacity, high speed, and available software and hardware continue to provide large- and medium-sized companies with most of their computer power.

Yet despite the sustained growth and use of mainframes in industry, technological advances have made computer power available in smaller, less expensive machines. These micros and minis are typically used to:

1. Supplement current computer facilities in some companies.
2. Provide computer capability to small companies that would not otherwise be able to afford it.
3. Enable consumers, educators, and others to use computers for everyday activities.

As a result, the use of micros and minis in business in the last few years has been increasing at tremendous rates. Moreover, these machines have even wider applicability in professional offices, educational institutions, and the home. Thus, while mainframes continue to dominate in large organizations, the growth of microcomputers and minicomputers has become the second phase in the so-called computer revolution. Figure 9.1 shows how the use of minis and micros has grown over the past few years. Indeed, the expectation is that by 1990 there will be more total dollars earned from microcomputer sales than from mainframe sales!

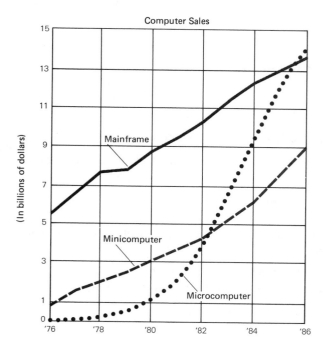

Figure 9.1
The growth of minis and micros. (*Source:* International Data Corp.)

This chapter focuses on the concepts relevant to micros and minis and also considers some of the primary ways in which these machines are being used now and the ways in which they are likely to be used in the future. The social impact of microcomputing is also explored.

I. MICROCOMPUTERS

A. Definition of a Micro

As indicated previously, there are no standard definitions that can be used to definitively distinguish one type of computer from another. In this book, we will define a **microcomputer** as a device with a basic internal storage capacity from 4K to approximately 128K, and with a basic cost from under $100 to several thousand dollars. Many computers that fit our category of "micro" can have storage capacities in excess of 128K if they include add-on memory boards; similarly, many micros cost more than several thousand dollars if they are purchased with numerous peripheral devices and sophisticated software. In summary, the range indicated here is not definitive, but it will provide a handy guide for determining which machines are typically classified as micros. In general, computers labeled in advertisements as personal computers, home computers, or small business computers are typically micros that sell for under $1000; those micros that cost more than $1000 in their basic configuration are typically designed for professional use in business or education.

B. Applications of Micros

The overwhelming majority of microcomputers are used for the following types of applications.

1. Medium- and Large-Scale Businesses

||||▶ **Major Objectives**

To take some of the burden off professional staffs as well as mainframes and to provide services that can facilitate business operations.

Many companies have made micros available to their staffs to serve in the following capacities:

1. Terminals that may access a companywide data base or be used to transmit messages.
2. Professional workstations for managers to perform calculations, answer inquiries, and analyze data.
3. Modules in a distributed data processing environment.
4. Stand-alone word processing units for secretaries and office managers.

Figure 9.2 shows a micro used in a medium-sized office.

2. Small Businesses and Professional Offices

||||▶ **Major Objective**

To perform the major information processing functions in small businesses and professional offices.

Figure 9.2
Micro used in a medium-sized office for Accounts Receivable. (Courtesy Radio Shack, a division of Tandy Corp.)

Like larger organizations, a small business or professional office such as a lawyer's, doctor's, or accountant's, can also use a micro as a professional workstation or as a word processor. But many small organizations utilize micros for their entire range of business applications as well, such as accounting, inventory, and payroll. This is particularly true because micros are relatively inexpensive, and because software packages are available for a wide variety of business applications. Figure 9.3 shows a micro in a professional office.

3. Education

Major Objectives

To teach students in elementary and secondary schools as well as in universities (1) how to program and (2) how to use software packages. In addition, com-

Figure 9.3
Use of a micro in a professional office. (Courtesy Radio Shack, a division of Tandy Corp.)

puters are used as a learning tool for introducing new topics in a variety of subject areas.

Most elementary and secondary schools, as well as universities, have micros available to teach students how to write programs. Computer literacy and computer programming are widely viewed as essential components of education today. Micros are used for (1) teaching students about computers and (2) teaching programming.

In addition, there are many software packages available that can be used to teach students in subjects ranging from spelling to architecture. Micros have been enormously successful in providing computer-assisted instruction, especially where drill-and-practice techniques are most useful. There are numerous programs available that drill students in multiplication, geography, and reading. Many of these programs include animated graphics displays that are entertaining and interesting to small children as well as older users. Moreover, experiments can be simulated with a computer that are effective in teaching students scientific subject matter without incurring risks and without requiring great cost. Figure 9.4 illustrates a micro used in the classroom.

Figure 9.4
Micro used in education.
(Courtesy Apple Computer, Inc.)

4. Consumers and Home Users

Major Objectives

For entertainment, accessing data bases, word processing, and improving efficiency in the home.

Although it may seem overstated to expect a microcomputer to improve the overall quality of life for the consumer, the increasing application areas available in the home make this objective a realistic goal for the near future. Among the more common application areas currently in use today are the following:

IN A NUTSHELL

HOME USES OF COMPUTERS

1. Financial and personal record keeping.
2. Word processing.
3. Entertainment and games.
4. Communication link to a time-shared data base.
5. Monitoring of energy use.
6. Serving as a security system.
7. Electronic mail.
8. Education.

Because the cost of micros is constantly decreasing while the number of application areas is increasing, it is now reasonable to expect that by the year 2000 virtually every home in the United States will have a microcomputer (see Figure 9.5).

Figure 9.5
Micro used in the home for entertainment. (Courtesy Apple Computer, Inc.)

5. Teletext and Videotex Services

Major Objective

To provide users with a wide variety of services from stock information to hotel reservations to mail order facilities.

When communicating with service or subscriber organizations, a microcomputer functions essentially as a terminal. A modem or other interface is typically necessary to enable the device to transmit and/or receive signals using a telephone.

There are two general categories of communications available from external organizations:

1. **Teletext**—A one-way system of transmitting graphics and text onto home and office screens. This is similar to cable television facilities.

2. **Videotex**—A two-way system that enables users to receive as well as transmit messages; for example, prices of items at a local store can be displayed on a screen and the user can then transmit an order directly to the store.

There are numerous subscriber services available that can provide either teletext or videotex services. The most common applications include the following:

Computerized Subscriber Services

1. Dow Jones retrieval of stock information.
2. News summary of *The New York Times.*
3. United Press International wire service information.
4. Airline schedules.
5. Hotel reservations.
6. Restaurant reservations.
7. Shop-at-home services.
8. Electronic mail.
9. Banking at home.

Some of the most common computerized subscriber service organizations are The Source, CompuServe, and the Dow Jones Retrieval System. Figure 9.6 lists typical subscriber costs. Since subscribers are typically logged on only for a few minutes each time, the actual cost per run is usually low.

Figure 9.6
Typical dollars and cents costs for subscriber services. Prices are approximate and for 300 baud service; prices for 1200 baud are higher.

```
The Source
Initiation fee:  $100
Connect time:  $21/hr from 7 A.M. to 6 P.M.
               $8/hr from 6 P.M. to midnight
               $6/hr from midnight to 7 A.M.

CompuServe
Initiation fee:  $25
Connect time:  $22/hr from 5 A.M. to 6 P.M.
               $5/hr from 6 P.M. to 5 A.M.

Dow Jones Retrieval System
Initiation fee:  $50
Connect time:  $60/hr for "prime time"
               $12/hr for "nonprime time"

Note: Telephone charges are additional.
```

Once subscribers pay an initiation fee, they receive a local telephone number, an appropriate account code, and a password. The user may then call the telephone number, link the terminal to the modem or interface, and access the data base using the account code and password. Typically an extensive menu is provided from which a specific service or data base may be selected. Individ-

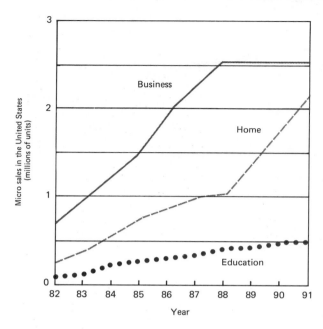

Figure 9.7
Projected sales in the United
States of microcomputers.

uals or businesses that subscribe to the same service can also send mail and messages to each other using the subscriber service as a switching network.

So far, we have discussed application areas for micros in businesses, homes, and the education field. Figure 9.7 shows an analysis of the projected sales of micros in the United States broken down into these three market segments. You will note that both home and business use of micros are expected to grow substantially, while the use of computers in education is expected to taper off.

It is significant that the average cost of these micros has been decreasing at the same time that computer power has been increasing. This trend is expected to continue in the near future (see Figure 9.8).

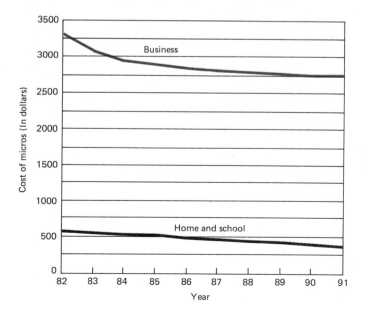

Figure 9.8
Average microcomputer
prices.

C. Components of a Microcomputer System

As previously noted, a basic microcomputer ranges in price from under $100 to several thousand dollars, depending on the hardware and software acquired. The minimum configuration consists of the following items.

1. Microprocessor

A microprocessor has random access memory (RAM) from 4K to 128K, which is used to store instructions and data. It also consists of read-only memory (ROM), which is memory that has been pre-programmed to facilitate the processing of data. A translator program that enables the user to write BASIC instructions, for example, may be pre-programmed as ROM on some micros. The amount of RAM and the quality and sophistication of ROM vary with each microprocessor.

2. Keyboard

A keyboard is the basic unit for entering data and for coding program instructions. The micros that sell for under several hundred dollars consist of a microprocessor and a keyboard only. Figure 9.9 illustrates an inexpensive portable TRS-80 computer. Many micros also include additional components, as discussed below.

3. Cathode Ray Tube or Monitor

A cathode ray tube (CRT) is a TV-like screen that is used to display user messages and computer responses. If a micro does not come equipped with a CRT, then a TV screen with an adapter may be used.

4. Auxiliary Storage

For most computer applications, a device is necessary to store programs or data for future processing. Typically, auxiliary storage for a micro is provided by:

1. A tape cassette or cartridge for sequential access.
2. A floppy disk or hard disk for random access.

Tape units can provide only sequential access and thus tend to be slow. That is, if a program has been stored in the middle of the tape, it would be necessary to read past the first half of the tape in an effort to read the program.

Figure 9.9
Radio Shack TRS-80 portable computer (Courtesy Radio Shack, a division of Tandy Corp.)

Disk units can be used for random access as well as sequential access. Although they are more expensive, disk units are far more popular than tape units for all sizes of computers.

a. Tape Cassette or Cartridge Device   **Tape cassettes** and **cartridges** (see Figure 9.10) are similar to mini-magnetic tapes. They are used to store not only programs, but data that is processed sequentially in a batch mode. Typically, the tape in a cassette is 285 feet long as compared to the standard magnetic tape, which is usually 2400 to 3600 feet long. The density, or number of characters stored per inch of tape, tends to be less than that of larger tapes, averaging 200 to 800 characters per inch.

Standard cassette devices that are used to play music may be employed to record data for a micro. But these devices were not really designed to provide quality data transmission; many micros, therefore, utilize specially developed cassette devices.

The rate at which the tape cassette device transmits data or receives data from the CPU, called the transfer rate, is usually very slow compared to standard magnetic tape drives. A typical range is from several hundred to several thousand characters per second. For a comparison of the physical characteristics of magnetic tapes and tape cassettes, see Figure 9.11.

Figure 9.11
Comparison of physical
characteristics of magnetic
tapes and tape cassettes.

	Magnetic Tapes	*Tape Cassettes*
Record length	Limited to its impact on the computer (2K is an acceptable limit on most systems)	80 to 720 characters
Total capacity	1 to 45 million characters	23,000 to 720,000 characters
Density	800 to 6000 characters per inch	200 to 800 characters per inch
Mode of access, method of creation, and handling features are similar.		

A tape cartridge device has features similar to those of a cassette device, except that it has been developed specifically for computer use and thus tends to be more reliable.

b. Floppy Disk and Hard Disk Drives   A **floppy disk,** like a standard magnetic disk, stores data and programs using direct-access methods of processing. Hence the access time of floppy disk drives is significantly faster than that of cassette or cartridge drives.

The transfer rate for floppy disks is much slower than that for traditional magnetic disks but is significantly faster than that for cassettes or cartridges. For some technical facts about floppy disks, see Figure 9.12. For a comparison of floppy disks to conventional magnetic disks, see Figure 9.13. For a comparison of cassettes, cartridges, floppies, and disks, see Figure 9.14.

Figure 9.12
Typical facts about floppy
disks.

- The number of concentric circular tracks per surface is 77 + .
- Each track has sectors (26 +).
- Each sector can store 128 or more bytes.
- Each surface can store 256K to approximately 1 million bytes.
- Diskette—a term frequently used to describe 2-sided floppies (150 tracks); used with drives that have two read/write heads.

	Hard Disks	Floppy Disks
Record length	Limited to its impact on the computer (2K is an acceptable limit on most systems)	1 to 1000 characters
Total capacity	1 to 100 million or more characters	256,000 to 1.2 million characters
Density	800 to 6250 characters per inch	1600 to 6250 characters per inch
Mode of access, method of creation, and handling features are similar.		

Figure 9.13
Comparison of physical characteristics of hard disks and floppy disks.

Disk drives, though more costly, are more efficient for storing programs and data. The two most popular types of disk media for micros are floppy disks and Winchester hard disks.

Floppy disks are the most popular external storage medium for micros. There are numerous sizes for floppies, but the most popular are 8-inch, 5¼-inch, and 3-inch versions (see Figure 9.15).

An 8-inch floppy in its basic form has a storage capacity of 256K characters. *Double-density* 8-inch floppies can store twice the number of bits on a disk and therefore have twice the storage capacity of single-density disks. *Double-sided*

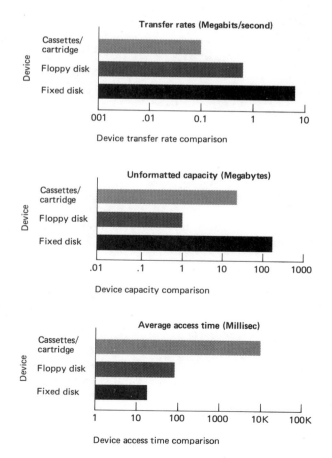

Figure 9.14
Comparison of cassettes, cartridges, floppies, and disks.

(a)

(b)

(c)

Figure 9.15
(a) Eight-inch floppy.
(Courtesy Maxell.) (b) Color-
coordinated 5¼-inch mini-
floppies. (Courtesy Cenna
Technology, Inc.) (c) Three-
inch micro-floppy disk and
disk drive. (Courtesy
Amdek.)

8-inch floppies read and record data on both sides of the disk; this, too, doubles the capacity. Thus a double-density, double-sided, 8-inch floppy has a storage capacity of over 1 million characters.

The 8-inch floppy tends to be used by businesses rather than home users. One main problem with floppies, in general, is their lack of compatibility, particularly if they are double-density disks. Most single-density, 8-inch floppies, however, can be read by a wide variety of computers.

The 5¼-inch mini-floppy disk can store 80K or more characters in single-density form, but there are double-density versions available that can store up to 300,000 or more characters. These 5¼-inch disks are not usually compatible, so that a disk created using an Apple computer, for example, could not be read by a TRS-80.

See Figure 9.16 for an analysis of which disks are currently most popular. The 3-inch category of micro-floppy actually comes in several sizes including 3-inch, 3¼-inch, and 3½-inch.

Sometimes users find that even 8-inch floppy disks do not have enough storage capacity. Even though some of these floppies can store over a million characters, this frequently does not suffice. Since a page of text uses typically

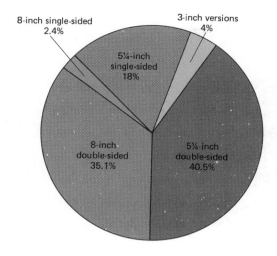

Figure 9.16
Analysis of floppies in use.
(*Source:* Venture
Development Corp.)

about two thousand characters, a floppy can store at most 500 pages of data, which may not be sufficient for some applications.

As a result, *hard disk drives* have recently been made available for micro-computers. An average hard disk for micro use can store between 5 and 100 million characters, but there are some with even greater capacities. Most of these hard disk drives make use of an IBM innovation referred to as Winchester technology. **Winchester disk drives** provide higher storage capacity and greater reliability than many other types of disk drives. Figure 9.17 illustrates a standard 5¼-inch disk drive mechanism and a Winchester disk drive.

Greater protection from environmental concerns such as dust is provided because Winchester disk technology seals the disk and the read/write head assembly into a single module. The read/write mechanism is very light, which provides a greater protection against "head crashes." Head crashes sometimes occur on disk devices when dust and other particles force the head to collide with the disk surface, resulting in loss of all data on the disk and damage to the unit.

Note that hard disks have a much greater capacity than floppies, but there is a price to pay for this benefit: hard disk drives cost two to ten times the price of floppy disk drives.

How Winchester Disk Drives Differ from Traditional Hard Disks

1. Drives have fixed, not removable, disks.
2. The disk and the read/write head assembly are in a sealed box.
3. The sealed box prevents dust, dirt, and smoke from contaminating the disk.
4. The read/write head remains much closer to the disk than the head of other disk drives.
5. Advantages:
   a. The access time is faster than for floppies.
   b. There is greater reliability because a sealed unit is used.
   c. Periodic maintenance is not required.

Winchester disk drives with about 10MB capacities cost between $1300 and $4500.

(a)

(b)

Figure 9.17
(a) Standard 5¼-inch disk drive mechanism. (Courtesy Qume Corp., a subsidiary of ITT Corp.) (b) 5¼-inch Winchester disk drive. (Courtesy Vertex Peripherals.)

There are numerous other technologies for disks, including pocket-sized hard disks:

LOOKING AHEAD

Will Removable Pocket-sized Hard Disk Cartridges Replace the Floppy?

Advantages:

1. Far more capacity per unit (6 megabyte compared to 1 megabyte floppies).
2. Cost per megabyte is decreasing.
3. Better performance.
4. Shorter access time.
5. Faster data transfer rate.
6. Better interchangeability between drives.
7. Smaller in size.

5. Printer

If hard copy is required from a micro, then a serial printer is typically used. If hard copy is to be used for producing formal reports or documents, then a **letter-quality printer** is required. The print produced by a letter-quality printer is very clear and easy to read because fully formed characters are used.

Although letter-quality devices produce high-quality output, they are usually much slower than high-speed, dot-matrix printers and more expensive as well. A typical letter-quality printer that prints 45 to 55 characters per second costs from several hundred dollars to about $1000. Most have a standard tractor-feed unit for feeding continuous forms, but they usually can be purchased with an adapter for inserting individual sheets that are printed using a friction-feed mechanism. Some micro users have two printers, a high-speed device, where the quality of print is not critical, and a letter-quality printer for generating reports that will be sent outside the company.

6. Other Data Entry Devices

In addition to using a keyboard, there are a series of devices available that enable a user to enter data by directly making contact with a CRT.

a. Mouse   A **mouse** is a push-button control device that eliminates the need to type computer commands. Instructions are given by the user to the computer by pointing an arrow on the screen to a picture or word and then pushing the button on the mouse. The user moves the arrow on the screen by sliding the mouse across the desktop.

Apple's Lisa and Macintosh computers make extensive use of the mouse to facilitate processing. This device makes micros far more *user-friendly* (see Figure 9.18). See Figure 9.19 for an illustration of Lisa's monitor screen.

b. Light Pen, Wand, or Touch-Sensitive Screen   A light pen or wand may similarly be used on a CRT screen to enter data by pointing to the menu items desired by the user. A touch-sensitive screen enables the user to simply touch the desired screen element.

Figure 9.18
Apple Lisa with mouse. (Courtesy Apple Computer, Inc.)

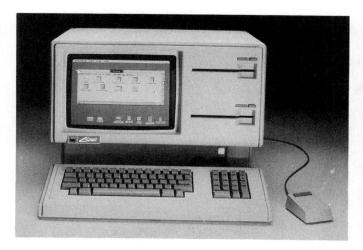

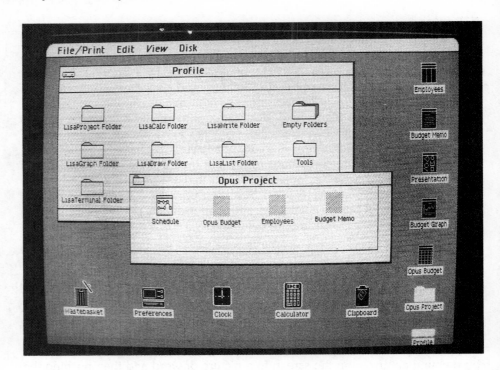

Figure 9.19
Example of Lisa's monitor screen. (Courtesy Apple Computer, Inc.)

c. Joystick A joystick is typically used for game playing but can also be used to enter user requests. This device enables the user to vary screen images by moving the stick to the right or left or up or down.

7. Additional Devices
There are many additional devices that are available with micros. They include the following:

1. Voice and music synthesizers—for audio output.
2. Modems or interfaces—for using the micro to transmit over data communication lines.
3. Additional RAM and ROM.

D. The Best-Selling Micros
The following micro manufacturers have sold the most units to date and have the greatest potential for continuing that trend:

1. IBM.
2. Apple.
3. TRS-80 (Tandy).
4. Commodore.

IBM is currently the frontrunner in the micro field. Figure 9.20 illustrates several current micros.

Note that other major computer manufacturers, including Wang, Hewlett-Packard, and the Digital Equipment Corporation have followed IBM into the

(a)

(b)

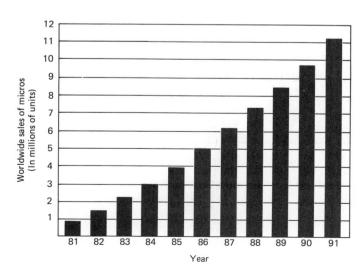

(c)

Figure 9.20
(a) IBM PC. (Courtesy IBM.)
(b) Portable micro. (Courtesy
Toshiba.) (c) Pocket
computer for student use.
(Courtesy Sharp Electronics
Corp.)

personal computer field. There are also numerous IBM-compatible micros on
the market. The expected total number of microcomputers that will be sold
during the next decade is indicated in Figure 9.21.

In short, personal computing has become a big business. There are currently over 1000 retail stores that sell computers, peripherals, and software to

Figure 9.21
Projected worldwide sales
of micros.

consumers and businesses. There are more than 400 clubs in the United States for personal computer users. There are more than 30 magazines, some with a circulation greater than 100,000, that focus on home computer uses. As the cost of technology decreases and as more and more software is made available, home computers will become increasingly popular. When microcomputers can offer word processing capability that can replace the electronic typewriter (a $250 savings) and can access an encyclopedia of information on a disk (a $400 to $600 savings), all for a few hundred dollars, then they become a viable alternative to existing home technology. At that point, virtually no home could afford to be without one.

E. Who Sells Microcomputers

Micros can be obtained from:

1. Computer stores.
2. Manufacturers.
3. Systems houses that can supply packaged systems with software; these houses may also have programmers available for providing services.
4. Mail-order houses.
5. Office-product suppliers.
6. Retail distributors, including department stores, electronic stores, and toy stores.

See Figure 9.22 for an analysis of the sources people typically use for purchasing micros. The following items should be considered when deciding from which vendor to purchase a system.

IN A NUTSHELL

FACTORS TO CONSIDER WHEN SELECTING A VENDOR

1. Cost.
2. Available software.
3. Service.
4. Reputation of the vendor.
5. Are personnel knowledgeable?
6. Warranties or guarantees.
7. Training provided.

For users with a vast amount of experience and knowledge, cost may be the primary consideration. For novices, the other factors may be more important.

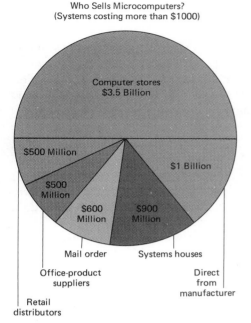

Who Sells Microcomputers?
(Systems costing more than $1000)

Computer stores
$3.5 Billion

$500 Million

$500
Million

$600
Million

$900
Million

$1 Billion

Mail order

Systems houses

Office-product
suppliers

Direct
from
manufacturer

Retail
distributors

Figure 9.22
Analysis of sources used for
obtaining micros. (*Source:*
Future Computing Corp.)

F. Operating Systems and Software

In order to effectively use any computer, it should have a series of control
programs or an **operating system** to facilitate the storing of files, program
execution, printing, and so on. Some micros have built-in operating systems.
Most computers, however, either provide their own operating system or enable
users to purchase one of the more popular operating systems. The IBM personal
computers, for example, have their own operating systems but they can also
utilize other, more sophisticated operating systems.

There are two types of operating systems that have become standards in
the industry and are available for use on a wide variety of micros: CP/M and
CP/M-86; PC-DOS and MS-DOS. These have the following features:

1. CP/M and CP/M-86

CP/M, which stands for Control Program for Microprocessors, is a disk operating system produced by the Digital Research Company. Versions of CP/M are
available for many micros on floppy or hard disk. CP/M-86, one version of
CP/M, is available for certain micros such as the IBM, while the standard CP/
M is more common for other micros. In addition, many computer manufacturers
are making one or the other version of CP/M available on mainframes for
interfacing with micros.

To utilize CP/M, the micro must have at least 16K of main memory and
some type of disk. Some basic commands in CP/M that facilitate the processing
of programs include:

ERA—erase a file.

DIR—list all file names.

STAT—indicate the number of storage positions used for specific programs.

SAVE—save memory contents on a disk file.

CP/M also has an edit command—ED—which permits the user to easily enter all files and programs. Where text editing or word processing is a major requirement of the system, however, more advanced editors are recommended.

There is also another version of CP/M called **MP/M,** which is an operating system that enables several users to run programs concurrently using one CPU. MP/M stands for Multiprocessing Monitor Control Program.

2. PC-DOS and MS-DOS

IBM personal computers are sold with an operating system called **PC-DOS,** which stands for personal computer disk operating system. Microsoft sells a very popular version of a disk operating system called **MS-DOS,** which is used on IBM and IBM-compatible personal computers.

Many people view CP/M and MS-DOS as the two operating system standards, although UNIX and many others are available.

3. Software Packages

Following are examples of the more popular software packages available for many micros.

||||➤ **Examples of Software Packages for Micros**

Package	Use
VisiCalc	Electronic spreadsheets:
Calcstar	1. For accounting applications.
SuperCalc	2. To perform "what if" analyses by changing variables and seeing how these changes might affect some overall outcome. See Figure 9.23 for a display produced by VisiCalc.
Easy Writer WordStar	For word processing.
dBase II & III Condor	To establish, access, and report from a data base.
Visi-on Multiplan LOTUS 1-2-3	Combines the features of all three—spreadsheets, word processing, and data base management.

Many of the more innovative packages provide screen images called "windows" in which text and other files can be viewed, moved, and changed around using a two-button, cursor controller (called a mouse), or other device. Windowing also may permit multiple packages to be run concurrently.

G. Technical Features to Look for When Buying Microcomputers

1. Speed

Most micros are capable of executing approximately 250,000 or more instructions per second.

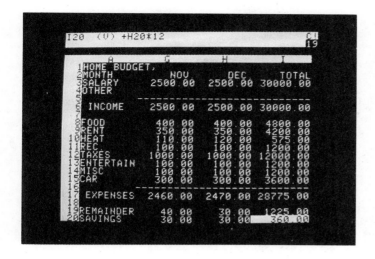

Figure 9.23
Sample VisiCalc display for preparing a budget. (Courtesy Apple Computer, Inc.)

2. Word Length

The capability of a micro depends not only on its speed but also on how much data it can handle in a single operation. The amount of data that a computer can handle in a given operation is called a word. Each word consists of a series of bits. The greater the word length, the faster the processing and the greater the capacity and handling ability of the computer. Most mainframes have a word length of 32 to 64 bits, but there are high-powered devices currently available with even greater word lengths.

When introduced, micros had 4-bit word lengths. This made them slow, somewhat inefficient, and difficult to program. Shortly thereafter, 8-bit word lengths became popular. The newer micros, such as the IBM personal computers (PC, XT), have 16-bit and even 32-bit word lengths.

3. Microprocessor

Each microcomputer has a different type of microprocessor or chip used for memory (see Figure 9.24). The most widely used chips include the following:

Chip	Illustrative Computers
Intel 8080	North Star, Heath
Intel 8088	IBM Personal Computers (PC, XT)
MOS 6502	Apple, Atari, PET
Zilog Z80	Radio Shack, Cromemco
MC 68000	Apple Lisa and Macintosh

CP/M, CP/M-86, MS-DOS, and UNIX (Xenix on micros) are widely available for many of these microprocessors.

4. Bus

The internal connection that is used to move data from one part of the computer to another is called a **bus.** Buses also transmit data from the microprocessor to input/output devices. One of the most common buses available is called the **S-100 bus.** If a micro has this bus, there are a wide variety of input/output devices available that can be used with it.

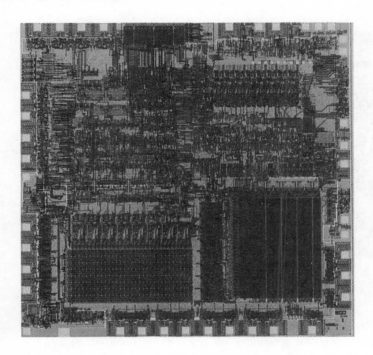

Figure 9.24
This chip represents a microprocessor. (Courtesy National Semiconductor.)

5. Software

There are numerous programming packages that can be run on micros, many of which have already been discussed. In addition, many programming languages can be run on micros. BASIC, for example, is available in numerous forms. CBASIC is a version specifically for commercial use, Tarbell BASIC is a fully interactive version that interprets each line of code as it is entered rather than after all instructions have been entered. Other programming languages available in numerous versions for micros are: COBOL, Forth, FORTRAN, Pascal, C, and so on. These are discussed in the next chapter.

6. Physical Characteristics

Users may be concerned with a variety of physical characteristics of the micro.

a. Weight and Size   Portability may be a criterion for some users. Some micros, such as the Compaq and KayPro, come in a briefcase to facilitate transporting of the device.

b. Power Supply   A built-in battery supply may be a criterion for some users, especially if portability is a desired feature. A battery also ensures that data will not be lost in the event of a power failure.

c. Size of Screen   The size of the CRT screen typically ranges from 3 inches to 12 inches, but there are other sizes as well.

7. Input/Output Units

A micro has a series of ports, which allow linkage with input/output units. The number of ports varies from system to system. Most micros can be linked to printers, graphics display devices, disk units, and so on.

H. The Social Impact of Microcomputing

The number of micros in homes, offices, and schools has been increasing at revolutionary rates. In 1982 *Time* Magazine awarded its "Man of the Year" designation to the personal computer! This was the first time in the magazine's history that a nonhuman was so designated. This award illustrated how important the personal computer became by 1982 and how highly regarded *Time* viewed its potential impact for the future. *Time* believes that personal computers will improve the quality of life and will help people be more productive at work and become more creative in general.

If, indeed, virtually every home, school, and business will have a microcomputer by 2000, as predicted, what impact might this have on our society? Among the more frequently discussed areas of social impact are the following three:

1. Education

In general, many schools have begun to make children computer literate at a very early age. If properly guided, these youngsters will be able to program and use computers to achieve results and to learn about their environment in exciting, new ways. Students, for example, may be required to use a disk at home to study certain topics and then answer questions that appear on the disk.

The educational community must, however, take great care to ensure that the process of socialization is not eroded by overutilization of computers for instructional purposes. That is, one primary purpose of education is to teach children to live, work, and cooperate with others in the world. This objective is still best accomplished by interacting with peers and teachers. Since the use of computers may reduce this interaction, great care must be taken in fostering socialization.

2. The Workplace

Microcomputers enable workers to communicate from remote locations with their colleagues. Thus, the need for the physical presence of workers at their workplace is diminished with the use of micros. Often, people can be just as effective working at home as working in an office. Employees who have on-line terminals in their homes, for example, can perform word processing and other jobs without having to be physically present in the office. This concept has been referred to as **telecommuting.**

Enabling workers to spend time at home may have an impact on the economy and society in general. For example, urban areas might benefit greatly since mass transportation and energy supplies could be better allocated. Moreover, job satisfaction of individual workers can be improved by enabling them to accomplish their duties in less restrictive ways.

Such far-reaching changes in worker interaction could have a profound effect on businesses as well. Sociologists have begun to study the potential effects of reduced worker interaction and communication not only on business but also on the mental well-being of employees. The emergence of a new type of "electronic cottage," that is, at-home jobs through electronics, is foreseen as a realistic development that can be expected in the near future. The concept has already been implemented in pilot projects with great success.

3. Activities at Home

The use of microcomputers enables individuals to perform a wide variety of functions from their home that would otherwise require traveling, such as shopping, banking, retrieving information, and so on. This affects not only the worker and the student, but handicapped people or those who might be confined because of inclement weather, illness, or conflicting responsibilities. The use of computers, then, could improve the quality of life for many people by providing more free time. It can also help to increase family interaction by enabling people to spend more time at home.

Once again, sociologists have begun to study the actual effects that increased time at home will have on people. Some sociologists have suggested that the reduced external interaction could stifle individuality and reduce communication skills.

Thus, although the potential benefits of microcomputers in homes, schools, and businesses have great promise, the social ramifications of widespread computer use could have some negative consequences as well.

Self-Evaluating Quiz

1. (T or F) Micros are frequently used for teaching BASIC to elementary school children.
2. (T or F) Micros currently do not have the capability for word processing applications.
3. (T or F) It is possible to use micros in a distributed data processing environment.
4. (T or F) Consumer use of micros has decreased in the last several years.
5. (T or F) Floppy disks are commonly used to provide micros with random access capability.
6. (T or F) The capacity of a floppy disk can exceed one million bytes.
7. (T or F) One 8-inch disk that has a program stored on it can be used by micros with $5\frac{1}{4}$-inch disk drives.
8. (T or F) Winchester disks are hard disks that generally provide micros with greater capacity than if floppies were used.
9. (T or F) All printers used with micros are letter-quality printers.
10. (T or F) It is possible to obtain up-to-the-minute stock prices by using a micro as a terminal.
11. (T or F) The major mainframe and minicomputer manufacturers have not chosen to build micros.
12. A push-button control device that allows users to enter instructions for the Apple Lisa and other computers is called a _____.
13. The most common method for entering data on a micro is a _____.
14. The two most common methods for displaying output from a micro are a _____ and a _____.
15. Two common operating systems for micros are _____ and _____.
16. (T or F) 16-bit micros are, in general, faster than 8-bit micros.
17. (T or F) All micros use the same type of microprocessor or chip.

18. (T or F) Disk units are more commonly used with micros than tape units because they provide random access capability.
19. The internal connection that is used to move data from one part of a computer to another is called a _____.
20. (T or F) Micros may be used for electronic mail.

Solutions

1. T
2. F
3. T
4. F
5. T
6. T
7. F
8. T—In general.
9. F—Sometimes dot-matrix printers are used.
10. T
11. F—IBM and DEC are two examples of companies that build micros.
12. mouse
13. keyboard
14. CRT
printer
15. CP/M
CP/M-86
PC-DOS
MS-DOS
MP/M
16. T
17. F—There are numerous chips that are popular.
18. T
19. bus
20. T

II. MINICOMPUTERS

As we have seen, the trend in the computing field is currently to "think small." Many organizations have traded in their mainframes for a series of minicomputers that collectively process data more efficiently and effectively and at a lower cost. If an organization has a mainframe that is not powerful enough, there are two alternatives: (1) trade in the mainframe for a bigger one, or (2) increase computer power by linking one or more minis to the current mainframe. Many companies choose the latter alternative and find that minis are very effective in accommodating growing computational needs.

A. Definition of a Mini

But just what is a minicomputer? As is the case with attempts to categorize micros, there is no real consensus. We will define a **minicomputer** (see Figure 9.25) to be a system that sells for as low as $50,000, on the average, in its basic form, with a memory size of from 256K to 2MB.

Figure 9.26 indicates the major differences between minis and micros. Note that smaller minis use equipment commonly part of micro systems while larger minis use full-scale equipment commonly part of mainframe systems.

Figure 9.25
Example of a minicomputer system. (Courtesy Sperry Corp.)

Figure 9.26
Major differences between micros and minis.

	Micro		Mini
	Personal Applications	*Business Applications*	*Business Applications*
CPU storage (bytes)	4 to 16K	16 to 128K	256K to 2MB
Maximum no. of terminals	1	2 to 8	8 to 64
Disk storage on-line (millions of bytes)	0.5 to 14	1 to 50	10 to 500
Printers	Character printers (30 to 165 characters per second)	Line printers (100 to 600 lines per minute)	Line printers (600 to 3000 lines per minute)
Other peripherals Card read/punch	Not usually available	Available	Available
Magnetic tapes	Cassette	Cassette	Full scale
Communications	None to limited	Limited to full scale	Full scale
Terminals	CRT or printer	CRT or printer	All types including cash register
Price range	$100 to $3000	$1,200 to $20,000	$15,000 to $800,000 (with all accessories)

Although we defined the basic memory size of minis as ranging from 256K to 2MB, add-on capability can be purchased in the form of integrated circuit chips that provide increased flexibility. Minis also range from desktop models common in small businesses to interactive and highly powerful superminicomputer systems such as the DEC VAX and the Harris supermini. See Figure 9.27 for an illustration of a supermini. The Digital Equipment Corporation (DEC), which manufactures the PDP computers, was the pioneer in the minicomputer field in the mid-1960s. The following is a list of the top 10 minicomputer manufacturers:

1. IBM.
2. Digital Equipment.
3. Burroughs.
4. Data General.
5. Hewlett-Packard.
6. Wang Labs.
7. Prime Computer.
8. Honeywell.
9. Gould.
10. Texas Instruments.

Figure 9.27
Examples of superminis.
(Courtesy Harris Corp.)

B. Applications of Minis

The many uses of minicomputers include the following.

1. Stand-Alone, General-Purpose Systems

Minicomputers may be used to perform a wide range of typical business functions such as payroll, billing, and inventory control for small- and medium-sized business users.

2. Special-Purpose, Turnkey, and Dedicated Systems

A minicomputer may be used as a **special-purpose system** designed by the manufacturer to satisfy the needs of a specific type of user. For example, a mini may be a computer-aided design tool for a manufacturing system as illustrated in Chapter 1. The system is specifically designed for that purpose.

In other instances, general-purpose computers are acquired, and software is written specifically for the user with no computer expertise. The user organization does not need to write any programs or possess any computer expertise at all. One simply "turns on" the general-purpose computer system and it will indicate what an operator should do to achieve the desired results. This is referred to as a **turnkey system**—no programming or computer expertise is required to utilize the system, which has been pre-programmed for specific applications.

In addition, many large organizations use **dedicated** minis that are specifically programmed for a single application. For example, minicomputers may be placed in individual warehouses to handle inventory control for that warehouse. Or, a minicomputer can be used to store, edit, and verify all transactions at a given branch office.

3. Modules in a Distributed Data Processing (DDP) System

Minicomputers can be used by large organizations for two primary purposes: to process data at a specific location and to feed data into a mainframe (see Figure 9.28).

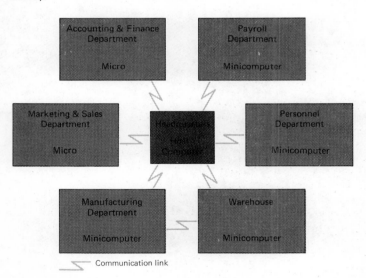

Figure 9.28
A network of computers linked to a mainframe.

4. Front-End Processors

A mini that is linked to a mainframe in some distributed network can alleviate some of the burdens of the main CPU, while providing computer power to remote locations. The separate centers process data locally, and the mainframe integrates the functions of all centers. Such use of minis can be significantly less expensive and often far more efficient than upgrading the mainframe itself.

A mini can, for example, organize, validate, and process data from a series of terminals. The output is then transmitted at high speeds to a large-scale system that integrates the data from a network of minis. In this way, the mini serves as a front-end processor. This use is a main application of minis in large organizations today. The network of minis relieves the main computer system of edit and control procedures and also facilitates the handling of communications. Micros may be used in this way as well.

In 1984, the number of minicomputer installations was well over 1 million units, constituting approximately one-fifth of the total computer market. Of the 1 million installations, about 60% were used as either stand-alone, general-purpose systems or as turnkey systems in small businesses. The rest were used either in decentralized data-processing organizations or as part of distributed systems.

C. Equipment

As noted, smaller minis use the same peripheral equipment as micros. That is, floppy disks, hard disks, and serial printers are common input/output media. Larger minis and superminis have far more sophisticated equipment, such as standard tape and disk drives, line printers, optical scanners, and so on.

III. PROBLEMS ASSOCIATED WITH ACQUIRING MICROS AND SOME MINIS

Keep in mind that there are some inherent difficulties associated with the acquisition of micros and some minis.

A. Lack of Compatibility and Standardization

Recall that many mainframes supplied by major vendors have some element of **compatibility.** That is, one could acquire a small-sized IBM 4331 computer and upgrade it to a larger version of the 4300 series as necessary. Moreover, many vendors supply plug-compatible hardware that can be used with any mainframe.

Minis or micros, however, tend to lack this element of compatibility. A floppy disk unit, for example, developed for one mini or micro is usually not compatible with another. Moreover, even the disks themselves are not standard. There are numerous, incompatible versions of disks, disk drives, and other media and devices.

B. Lack of Adequate Vendor Support

Larger computer systems are relatively expensive. Frequently they are leased and supplied with service contracts. Thus, when users acquire mainframes, they are likely to receive some support and service from the vendor. Problems encountered in implementing the system and maintaining it are handled by the vendors or their agents as necessary. But minis or micros are relatively inexpensive. They are frequently purchased outright. Typically, the vendors or their agents cannot afford to provide support for these less costly systems. Maintenance contracts can be obtained, but they are often very expensive.

CHAPTER SUMMARY

I. "Think small"

The current trend in the EDP industry is on the development of minis and micros for large and small business use and for the home market as well.

II. Distinction between mini and micro

A. There is no clear distinction between a mini and a micro. Different manufacturers use different terms.

B. Definition used in this chapter: A minicomputer is a system that sells for as low as $50,000, on the average, and has a memory size of 256K to 2 megabytes in its basic form. Microcomputers sell for several hundred dollars in their basic form and have basic memory sizes from 4K to 128K.

III. Applications of micros

A. Home entertainment.

B. Education.

C. Personal and financial applications.

D. Communication link to a time-shared service.

E. Workstations in small businesses and professional offices.

IV. Applications of minis

A. Stand-alone, general-purpose systems.

B. Special-purpose, turnkey, and dedicated systems.

C. Modules in a distributed data-processing system.

D. Front-end processors.

V. Units used with minis and micros

A. CPU—usually desk top.

B. Terminal—with keyboard and printer or CRT, or both.

C. Tape cassette or cartridge units—similar to tape drives.

D. Floppy disk unit or hard disk.

VI. Problems with minis and micros

A. Devices are not yet compatible with larger units or standardized within the industry.

B. Vendor support is frequently inadequate; there is not enough service provided with these systems.

Chapter Self-Evaluating Quiz

1. Another name for a microcomputer is _____.

2. (Teletext/Videotex) refers to a one-way system of transmitting graphics and text onto home and office screens.

3. (T or F) A microprocessor typically consists of RAM and ROM.

4. A cassette or cartridge is similar in principle to a _____.

5. A floppy disk is similar in principle to a _____.

6. (T or F) A Winchester disk drive is a kind of floppy disk unit.

7. (T or F) There are currently no standard operating systems available for use on micros.

8. (T or F) A micro with an 8-bit word length is generally slower than one with a 16-bit word length.

9. A computer system that requires no programming or computer expertise is referred to as a _____ system.

10. A dedicated mini is one that is _____.

11. Minis used for both processing local data and feeding data into a mainframe are usually being used for _____.

12. List two problems associated with minicomputers.

Solutions

1. personal, home, or small business computer / page 308

2. Teletext / page 312

3. T / page 314

4. magnetic tape / page 315

5. magnetic disk / page 316

6. F—It is a hard disk unit. / page 319

7. F—CP/M and MS-DOS are two that are available. / page 325

8. T / page 327

9. turnkey / page 334

10. programmed for a single application / page 334

11. distributed data processing / page 334

12. lack of compatibility and standardization / page 335
   lack of adequate vendor support / page 335

Key Terms

Bus
Compatibility
CP/M
Dedicated mini
Floppy disk
Letter-quality printer
Microcomputer
Minicomputer
Mouse
MP/M
MS-DOS

Operating system
PC-DOS
S-100 bus
Special-purpose system
Tape cartridge
Tape cassette
Telecommuting
Teletext
Turnkey system
Videotex
Winchester disk drive

Review Questions

1. (T or F) Minicomputers have become very popular as alternatives or supplements to mainframes.

2. (T or F) There exists no real standardized source that can be used to determine computer categories. That is, what one manufacturer calls a mini, another might call a micro.

3. What is the major difference between teletext and videotex services?

4. What is meant by an operating system?

5. (T or F) Minis do not generally have data communication capability.

6. (T or F) Minis are commonly used in distributed data processing systems.

7. A mini used to edit, format, and control data from a series of terminals before it is transmitted to the mainframe is called a _____.

8. Explain the basic similarities and differences between floppy disks and standard magnetic disks.

9. Explain the basic similarities and differences between cassette tapes and standard magnetic tapes.

10. Explain the basic similarities and differences between cassettes and floppy disks.

11. Is the lack of standardization in the minicomputer market unusual for the computer industry? Explain your answer.

12. Indicate some of the ways in which small businesses might use minis. Indicate some of the ways in which larger businesses might use minis.

13. Do you think microcomputers will continue to have a viable home market? Explain your answer.

14. State some of the elements you would use to determine whether Company ABC should acquire a mini or a micro.

15. Indicate the meaning of distributed data processing and explain why it has become so popular in recent years.

16. Does the emergence of plug-compatible machines increase or decrease the problems normally associated with standardization issues and the lack of compatibility? Explain your answer.

17. What are the differences between a hard disk and a floppy disk?

18. How are turnkey minicomputer systems used by small businesses?

19. Explain how microcomputers are currently used. How are they applicable for small businesses? Explain your answer.

20. Should cost be an overriding factor when one is deciding upon a computer system? Explain your answer.

21. (T or F) A dot-matrix printer is another name for a letter-quality printer.

22. (T or F) All floppy disks are dual-sided, dual-density media.

23. (T or F) Head crashes are very common with Winchester disk drives.

24. (T or F) A tape cassette unit is far more flexible than a floppy disk for micro users.

25. (T or F) Typically, 16-bit micros are faster and more efficient than 8-bit micros.

26. (T or F) CP/M is a commonly used operating system for micros.

27. (T or F) The internal connection that is used for moving data from one part of a computer to another is called a bus.

28. (T or F) Micros enable people to communicate with their office from home.

29. (T or F) Micros are used almost exclusively by consumers.

30. (T or F) MS-DOS is an operating system used with IBM and IBM-compatible micros.

APPLICATION

MICROS BREATHING NEW LIFE INTO DDP

by Eric Bender
and Tom Henkel

When the superminicomputer burst onto the DP scene in the late 1970s, industry pundits proclaimed the birth of a new concept in computing. In the future, they said, companies would scrap their massive central DP facilities in favor of smaller, regional superminis.

This concept of distributed data processing had merits. For example, a company could reduce its networking costs by using interactive remote processors linked, in a batch mode, to one central host mainframe. And the company could provide faster response time and boost flexibility, as well as prevent all corporate computer operations from coming to a grinding halt in the event of a system failure or disaster in the central computer room.

But there could also be problems with the concept. While superminis cost less than mainframes, their use in remote locations generally requires separate DP staffs, noted Frank Gens, an analyst with the Yankee Group consulting firm in Boston. As a result, DDP based on superminicomputers often proved expensive.

Now, with the explosion of microcomputers, the concept of DDP is making a comeback. Microcomputers recently introduced by AT&T, Digital Equipment Corp. and IBM, among others, appear suited for applications similar to those targeted by the supermini vendors about five years ago. But they are much less expensive than superminis and, generally, do not require highly trained personnel to run them.

"The first steps have been taken to start—and I emphasize *start*—solving the problems of distributed computing," said Jack Scanlon, vice-president of AT&T's Computer Systems Division. "Everyone's moving to glue his desktop into the mainframe. Nobody has the total solution. You have to make compatible systems out of incompatible parts."

Current DDP implementations are just beginning to fill in the gaps. Often, firms make the initial connection between mid-level machines, then establish links to low-end machines (personal computers) and, finally, make mainframe links.

Compared with traditional time-sharing, micro-based DDP offers users flexible processing and data storage strategies, adherents said. Another plus is modular expansion, said Nathan Kalowski, product group manager for the DEC Professional series. As one example, the Decnet local-area network permits a company to add computer systems "Erector-set fashion, allowing a constantly increasing number of systems that can get on the network without degrading performance," Kalowski said.

But microcomputers are not the cure-all for the problems associated with DDP. For example, difficulties continue to crop up in network management and in gaining access to the central data base, which will remain centralized for the foreseeable future, AT&T's Scanlon said.

Another issue of concern is security. By offering microcomputer users access to corporate data bases, "you've just increased the number of tentacles into that data base, and chances of inappropriate access or sabotage go up," Scanlon said.

And Steve P. Barnhart, director of marketing for NCR Corp.'s VRX operating system, pointed out that many groups within corporations that are heavily involved with microcomputers got that way because of dissatisfaction with the service provided by the central DP facility. As those departments became more adept at using micros, they began to appreciate the wealth of information stored in the corporate mainframes. Now, the renegade departments are running back to the DP department, seeking access to corporate data bases, Barnhart said.

Yet another problem with micro-based DDP is keeping multiple copies of the same data files up to date. "There are all kinds of heuristic approaches, but none of the solutions is very good," AT&T's Scanlon said.

Additionally, Kalowski noted, distributed networks may come at a cost premium compared with time-sharing systems for data entry or dedicated in-house applications. However, "there's no reason that a time-sharing environment can't be compatible with a distributed computing environment," he said.

DDP is slowed by technical difficulties and by a lack of demand, some who associate the concept with office automation said. "The idea of a multipurpose network has grown with extreme slowness," said Frederic Withington, vice-president for information systems at Arthur D. Little, Inc. in Cambridge, Mass.

"Most large companies generate a big data base and bring it into [a] central place for batch jobs," he said. "The data resides centrally most of the time. Despite what distributed data base and personal computer freaks say, most work is batch applications."

DDP, on the other hand, is more appropriate in situations in which many users are working with information and shipping it around, according to Withington. "In the real world, people work with paper documents and imprecise information and all sorts of unfinished material floating across the desk," he said. For large companies, the cost of putting this all on a computer typically is not justified—nor will it be justified until work habits change, he claimed.

"You need a decision support data base, a public data base that is easy to use and electronic mail in which every user can be reached before a lot of people go to workstations," Withington said.

Source: Computerworld, May 21, 1984, page 1. Copyright © 1984 by CW Communications/Inc., Framingham, MA 01701. Reprinted with permission.

Questions
1. Understanding Key Terms
   Define the following terms in the context in which they are used in the application:
   a. Distributed data processing.
   b. Networking.
   c. Central data base.
2. Software, Hardware, and Systems Concepts
   What are some of the disadvantages of using superminis in place of mainframes for DDP?
3. Management Considerations
   Why are micros making DDP more viable? Why is DDP not always the best solution to a company's DP needs?
4. Social, Legal, and Ethical Implications
   What are some of the social and legal concerns of companies that are considering DDP?

CASE STUDY: McKing's Superburgers, Inc.

1. One of the vendors has submitted a proposal to McKing's that calls for a distributed data processing system with minicomputers located in each restaurant. What would be the advantages and disadvantages of acquiring the following types of minis? Explain your answers.
   a. Stand-alone, general-purpose system.
   b. Special-purpose system.
   c. Turnkey system.
   d. Dedicated system.
   e. Front-end processor.

2. Recognizing that there are some inherent difficulties associated with the acquisition of minis, what are some specific questions you would ask the vendor that would help you evaluate the recommended equipment and minimize the inherent disadvantages?

3. Several restaurant managers have indicated that they will be purchasing their own micros to be used separately from the point-of-sale system.
   a. Would you recommend that McKing's Superburgers encourage or discourage such acquisitions? Explain your answer.
   b. What guidelines would you establish for acquisition of these micros?
   c. What advantages would be derived from each restaurant using the same type of micro? Do you regard these advantages as overriding— that is, would you suggest that management adopt a policy to ensure that all micros are the same make and model?

THE COMPUTER AD: A Focus on Marketing

Consider the ad entitled "Announcing the Accelerator II" that appears in Figure 9.29.

1. Indicate how the Accelerator II would be used.
2. Would you call this a machine dependent or machine independent piece of hardware? Explain your answer.
3. Do you think the Apple Corporation objects to another company marketing a product such as the Accelerator II? Explain your answer.

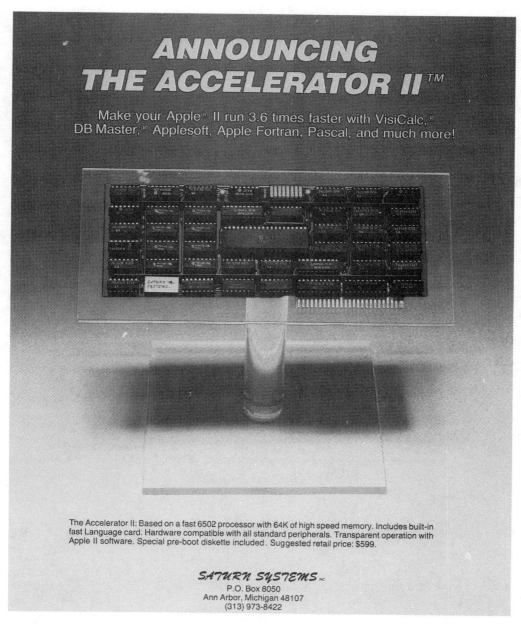

Figure 9.29
Marketing computer products. (Courtesy Saturn Systems, Inc.)

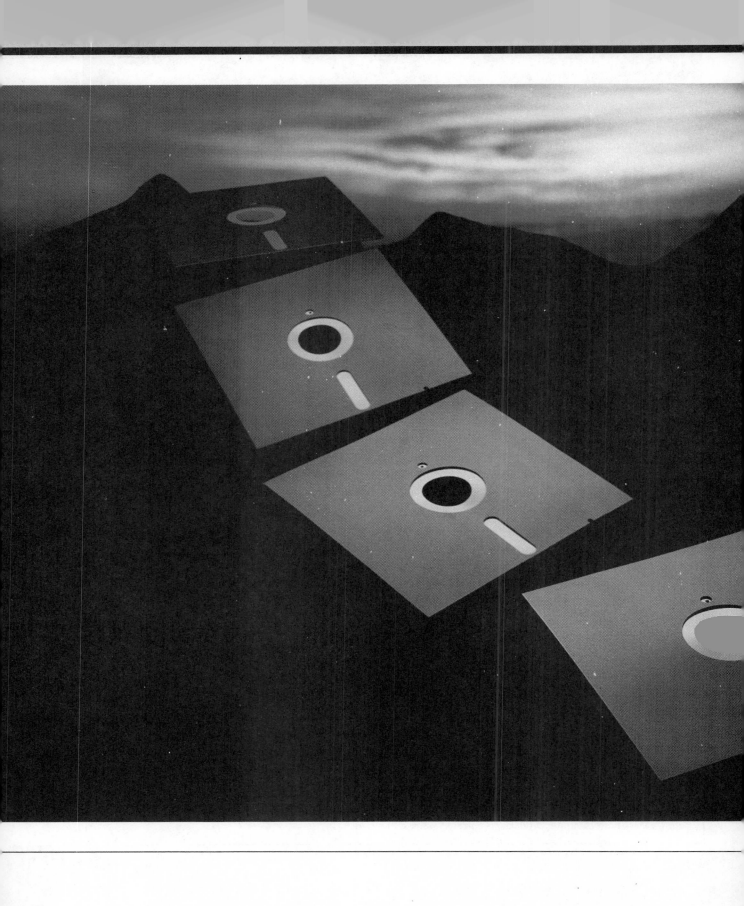

MODULE
4

UNDERSTANDING, EVALUATING, AND USING SOFTWARE

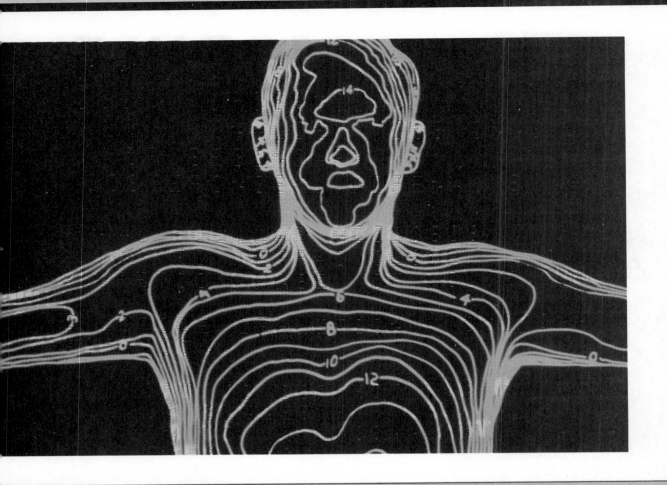

CHAPTER 10

A GUIDE TO
APPLICATION SOFTWARE

CHAPTER OBJECTIVES

To familiarize you with:

- The features of application software.
- Steps involved in planning, programming, debugging, implementing, and documenting application programs.
- An overview of program planning tools.
- The relationship between machine languages and symbolic languages.
- The most common application programming languages.
- The advantages and disadvantages of in-house versus outside sources of software.
- Methods used to evaluate application software.

I. REVIEW OF INFORMATION PROCESSING CONCEPTS

As we have stated many times before, this book focuses on three main aspects of computer processing that must be properly integrated to achieve effective computerization: computer hardware, computer software, and information systems.

A. Computer Hardware

Computer hardware consists of the input and output devices that, combined with the central processing unit, read data into the system, process it, and produce required information.

B. Computer Software

Hardware cannot effectively be utilized unless the system has been properly programmed. Computer software is the program support designed to maximize the efficient and effective use of the equipment.

The most common factors used to measure the effectiveness of both hardware and software include the following:

IN A NUTSHELL

FACTORS USED TO ASSESS THE EFFECTIVENESS
OF HARDWARE AND SOFTWARE

1. Cost.
2. Speed.
3. User-friendliness.
4. Ease of maintenance.
5. Vendor support.
6. Compatibility with the CPU and the overall computer system.

We have already seen that the distinction between hardware and software is becoming less clear. There are numerous chips and boards available that have been pre-programmed to perform required tasks. This combination of hardware and software is called firmware or read-only memory.

C. Information Systems

An information system integrates hardware and software so that a computerized application is achieved. This information system is designed so that it can be accessed by both management and operations personnel for producing required results and for assisting in the decision-making process.

The previous two units focused on computer hardware. This unit examines software in detail. There are basically two major types of software that organizations acquire. Each consists of programs designed to accomplish specific tasks as efficiently and effectively as possible.

II. TYPES OF SOFTWARE AND THE PEOPLE WHO DEVELOP IT

The two types of software are (1) application software and (2) operating system software.

A. Application Software

Application software refers to programs designed to computerize a given job; these programs are written to meet the needs of individual users. Following are some examples.

Examples of Application Programs

1. A payroll program to update a master file.
2. An accounts receivable program to print customer bills.
3. An inventory program to answer inquiries about the quantity on hand of each item in stock.

Depending on the needs of an organization, there are numerous sources for obtaining application programs:

Sources of Application Programs

1. Custom-designed Application Programs
   These may be prepared by:
   a. Programmers within the user organization.
   b. Consultants or freelance programmers hired by the user organization to write customized packages.
2. Pre-packaged Application Programs
   These are sold or leased by:
   a. Computer vendors.
   b. Freelance or self-employed programmers.
   c. Software houses.

Custom-designed programs are written specifically to meet an individual user's needs. These tend to have the greatest chance of achieving user satisfaction, but the price is usually high. On the other hand, pre-packaged or "canned" programs are written for general applications. They are far less costly but typically require a compromise—either users will need to modify the package or they must be willing to sacrifice their own specific needs to the specifications of the package.

In the past, most large-scale organizations with a programming staff would typically call upon that staff to write application programs. But because the cost of programming has increased considerably in recent years, many of these companies are willing to strike a compromise by acquiring a pre-packaged application even though it may require some modification. Small companies with a limited computer staff almost always elect to acquire packages or to contract with freelance programmers for their services. The decision to "make or buy" application software is an individual one that requires careful consideration.

As you have seen in the previous chapters, in addition to the availability of packages for mainframes, there is a wide variety of software for micros as well.

B. Operating System Software

Operating system software consists of the set of programs that are designed to optimize the efficient use of the computer system as a whole. The operating system includes a control program called the **supervisor,** which monitors all of the computer's operations. The operating system software also consists of a library of programs that can be called into the CPU by the supervisor as needed. Figure 10.1 shows how the operating system interacts with the CPU.

The operating system software is usually supplied by the following.

Suppliers of Operating System Software

1. Computer Manufacturers or Vendors
   For many computers, the operating system is supplied along with the hardware. In this way, it is tailored to the needs of each computer system.
2. Software Houses
   Many companies specialize in providing operating systems for specific types of hardware. Digital Research, for example, is a company that sells several operating systems such as CP/M and MP/M for microcomputers. Microsoft makes MS-DOS available for IBM and IBM-compatible microcomputers. Bell Labs makes UNIX available for mainframes, minis, and micros.

Systems commands such as those that enable a programmer to list a program, run a program, save a program, and so on, are part of operating system software.

This chapter focuses on application software and introduces application programming concepts. Chapter 13 gives a more thorough discussion of operating systems.

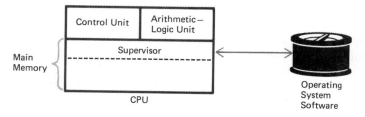

Figure 10.1
How an operating system interacts with the CPU.

C. Types of Programmers

Note that programmers, in general, fall into three categories.

1. **Application programmers**—these are the people who write the programs for a given application such as payroll, accounting, sales, etc. They must be familiar not only with programming concepts but also with business information processing needs.

2. **Maintenance programmers**—these are the people responsible for revising and updating existing programs as needed. They are like troubleshooters who are called upon to patch or modify existing projects.

3. **Systems programmers**—these are highly technical people who design programs to maximize the efficiency of the supervisor, existing software, and the overall operating system. Systems programmers, then, maintain manufacturer and other vendor-supplied systems software.

This chapter discusses application software written by application programmers and modified by maintenance programmers. Chapter 13 covers systems software written by systems programmers. Chapter 18 provides a description of the career opportunities for these types of programmers.

III. APPLICATION PROGRAMS

Figure 10.2 provides an overview of the steps involved in writing application programs. We will consider each of these steps in detail.

A. Systems Design Features: Ensuring That the Program Integrates Properly with the System

Application programs are usually part of a computerized business system; that is, they are *not* written independently to satisfy isolated user needs. Rather, most often a user department or division within an organization sets out to computerize *an entire set of procedures* or business system. Thus, in a business organization the accounts receivable system would typically be computerized *in its entirety* so that all procedures interrelate properly. This might require one program to print customer bills, another program to update the master accounts receivable file, a third program to provide management with required accounting information, and so on. Thus, application programs are typically written as part of an overall design for the entire computerized business system. This approach minimizes the risk of duplication of effort and ensures that programs within the system will be compatible with one another.

The systems analyst is responsible for the overall design of the business system. Once management approves the design, the analyst first determines the programs within the system that need to be written. Then he or she provides the programmer with a set of specifications that indicate the job requirements. Figure 10.3 shows a typical set of specifications that the analyst might give to the programmer. Before a programmer begins to plan the program, he or she must carefully review the overall objectives of the system and the set of program specifications provided by the analyst.

B. Program Planning

The first task of the programmer, then, is to understand the basic requirements of the system as a whole and to determine precisely how the program will be integrated into that system. Failure to plan properly can result in program errors. The two main programming errors that frequently occur are as follows:

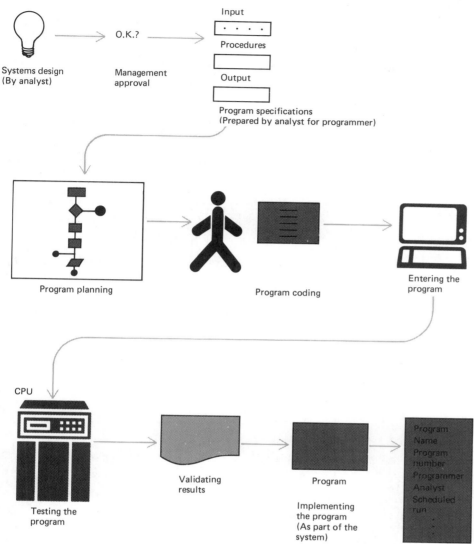

Input

Procedures

Output

Program specifications
(Prepared by analyst for programmer)

Systems design
(By analyst)

Management
approval

O.K.?

Program planning

Program coding

Entering the
program

CPU

Testing the
program

Validating
results

Program

Implementing
the program
(As part of the
system)

Program
Name
Program
number
Programmer
Analyst
Scheduled
run

Documenting
the program

Figure 10.2
Steps involved in writing
application programs.

IN A NUTSHELL

WHY PROGRAM ERRORS OCCUR

1. The programmer does not possess enough information to write a complete program.
   Typically, this occurs when the analyst did not provide the programmer with precise specifications.

2. The programmer is misinformed.
   The programmer did not obtain a totally accurate understanding of the program requirements.

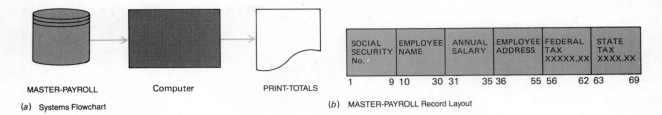

MASTER-PAYROLL   Computer   PRINT-TOTALS

(a) Systems Flowchart

SOCIAL SECURITY No.	EMPLOYEE NAME	ANNUAL SALARY	EMPLOYEE ADDRESS	FEDERAL TAX XXXXX.XX	STATE TAX XXXX.XX
1 9	10 30	31 35	36 55	56 62	63 69

(b) MASTER-PAYROLL Record Layout

Figure 10.3
Sample specifications for a programmer.

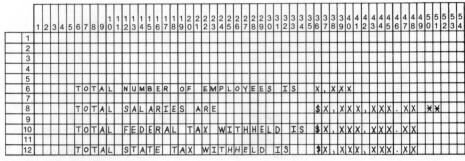

(c) PRINT-TOTALS Printer Spacing Chart

The following program specifications should be supplied to the programmer by the analyst during the program planning stage to minimize the above problems:

Program Specifications

1. Descriptions of input and output.
2. Error-control procedures required.
3. Arithmetic procedures required.
4. Logical control procedures required.
5. Control totals necessary to assist the user in verifying program output.

Planning a program is an extremely important phase in the programming process. Yet it is frequently ignored by programmers eager to begin coding. When the planning stage is omitted, there is a high risk that the program will require major modification later on—and modifying an existing program is far more time consuming and inefficient than getting it right initially.

A programmer who omits the planning stage of a program is similar to an architect who constructs a building without first preparing a blueprint. In either case, the risk of errors will be greatly increased. The main component of program planning consists of structuring the logical control procedures so that they are correct, efficient, and standardized. There are several standard planning tools that may be used by programmers.

Tools for Planning Program Logic

1. Program flowchart.
2. Pseudocode.
3. HIPO chart.

These planning tools will be discussed in detail in the next chapter. We simply provide an overview here so that you will have some idea of how they are used to plan program logic.

1. Program Flowchart

A **program flowchart** is a pictorial representation of the logic flow in a program. It includes, in block diagram form, the major program elements and how they are logically integrated.

The symbols in a flowchart are used to depict the logical flow of instructions in a program. Each symbol denotes a type of operation. The programmer writes a note inside each symbol that specifies the actual instruction to be incorporated in the program. Figure 10.4 illustrates a program flowchart.

A program flowchart is extremely useful for planning a program prior to coding because it helps the programmer clarify the instructions to be coded and the sequence in which these instructions should be executed.

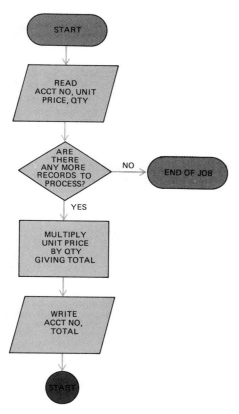

Figure 10.4
Sample flowchart.

2. Pseudocode

Pseudocode has become increasingly popular as a planning tool for *structured programs*. As we will see in the next chapter, a **structured program** is a standardized method for producing output, one which is easier to evaluate, test, and modify.

Pseudocode uses a programlike instruction code for depicting logic flow. Unlike a flowchart, it uses words rather than figures or symbols to indicate the sequence of steps to be performed. Certain logical control procedures are very easy to outline in pseudocode, making this a useful planning tool. Figure 10.5 illustrates a pseudocode that might be used for planning the logic to be used in a program.

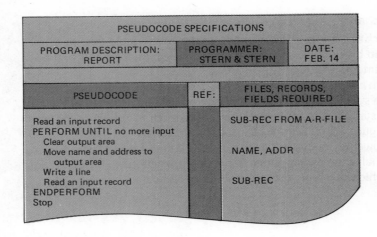

Figure 10.5
Sample pseudocode
specifications.

3. HIPO Chart

HIPO is an abbreviation for *hierarchy plus input-process-output*. A **HIPO chart** focuses on precisely how inputs to a program are processed to produce outputs. A top-down approach is used, where the main procedures precede less important procedures in the overall design. Like a flowchart, a HIPO chart contains pictorial representations; but HIPO focuses on input, processing, and output elements of structured designs (see Figure 10.6).

C. Coding the Program

Once the logic flow of a program has been planned using either a flowchart, pseudocode, or a HIPO chart, the programmer begins the step-by-step process

Figure 10.6
Sample HIPO chart.

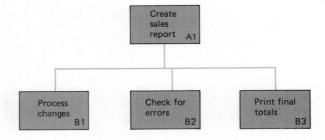

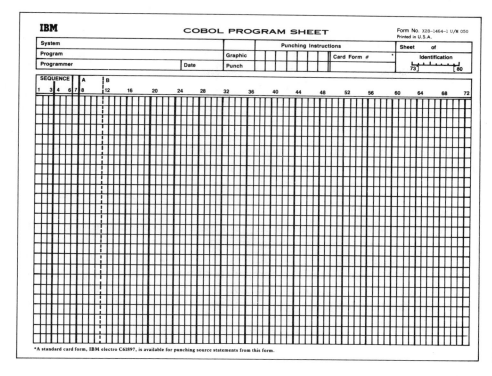

Figure 10.7
Sample coding sheet.

of writing the instructions in their appropriate sequence. Writing instructions is called **coding a program.** Programs are coded on paper called coding or program sheets (see Figure 10.7). The particular sheet in the figure is used for coding COBOL programs; COBOL is a major language to be discussed later on in this chapter.

After the program has been coded and the programmer has checked it for accuracy, it must be entered into the computer. Frequently, the programmer keys the program using a keyboard that is on-line to a computer system; sometimes, however, the programmer keys the program onto disk, tape, or cards for batch processing. If the program is entered using a terminal, one line of coding corresponds to one keyed line on the terminal. Figure 10.8 illustrates how programs are entered.

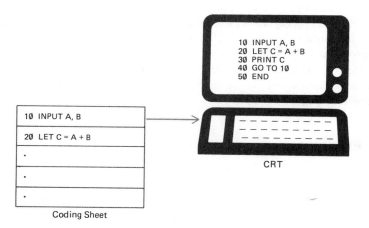

Figure 10.8
Example of how a program is entered into a computer.

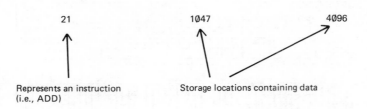

Figure 10.9
Example of machine language coding.

The programmer must be familiar with two broad categories of computer programming languages: (1) machine languages and (2) symbolic languages.

1. Machine Languages

In order to be run or executed, a program must be in **machine language.** Each computer has its own machine language. In each case, it is a complex language that uses actual machine addresses and cumbersome operation codes (see Figure 10.9). Because of the complexity of machine language, most programs are written in a symbolic language first, and then *translated* into the computer's machine language before they are executed or run.

2. Symbolic Languages

The overwhelming majority of programs are written in a symbolic programming language that is much easier than machine language for the programmer to learn and code. A **symbolic program** uses instructions such as ADD or + instead of complex operation codes, and symbolic addresses such as A1 or AMOUNT-IN, T or TOTAL, and S or SUM, to represent actual memory locations. Thus, to add two amounts in a symbolic language, we may say LET T = A1 + A2 instead of the machine language code, which may be something like 21 1047 4096.

A symbolic program, then, is one that is easier for the programmer to code. This program is not, however, executable. That is, it cannot be executed or run until it has been translated or converted into machine language. The computer itself performs this translation process. A computer program called a **translator** can interpret symbolic code and convert it into machine language. Thus a program written in a symbolic language requires two phases to be run: a translation phase and an execution phase (see Figure 10.10).

The symbolic program written by the programmer is called a **source program.** Source programs must be translated into machine language before they can be run. The translated or executable program in machine language is called the **object program** (see Figure 10.11).

D. Testing the Program

1. The Translation Phase

When a source or symbolic program is translated, there are three forms of output produced (see Figure 10.12). We will consider each form of output in detail:

IN A NUTSHELL

COMPUTER-PRODUCED RESULTS OF A TRANSLATION

1. Source Program Listing
   This is a printout of all symbolic instructions as they were keyed in by the programmer.

2. List of Errors or Diagnostics
   If any programming rules have been violated, they are listed along with the source program as **syntax errors.** Diagnostics specify the error made and sometimes indicate how it must be corrected. If a word is misspelled or improperly defined, for example, it will be listed as a syntax error.

3. Object Program
   This is the machine-language equivalent of the source program. If there are no syntax errors, the object program may be run immediately or saved for future execution.

Translation Phase: The computer converts the symbolic code into machine code.

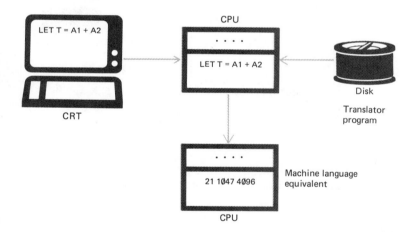

Execution Phase: After the entire program has been successfully translated, the computer runs or executes it.

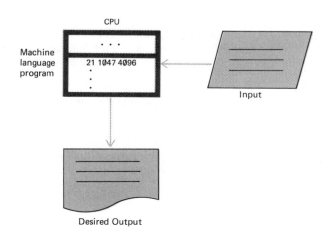

Figure 10.10
The two phases of running a program.

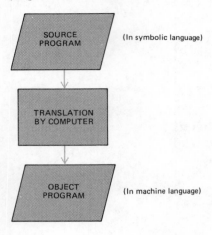

Figure 10.11
Translating a source program. Only object programs are executable.

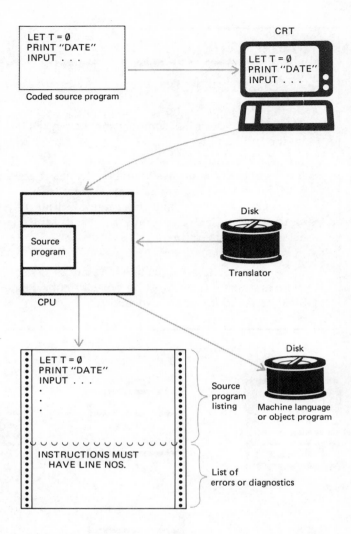

Figure 10.12 (at right)
Steps involved in translating a program.

There are three categories of translator programs used to convert source code to object code:

Program Translators

Name of Translator Program	Name of Translation Process	Description
Compiler	Compilation	The source program is *easy* to code; all instructions are read first and then translated in their entirety into object code.
Interpreter	Interpreted translation	The source program is *easy* to code; instructions are translated one line at a time into object code.
Assembler	Assembly	The source program is more *difficult* to code; it requires complex coding but produces an efficient, machinelike program.

a. The Compiler   Some symbolic programming languages, such as FORTRAN and COBOL, are called **high-level programming languages** because they are easy to code. A **compiler** takes a high-level source program, such as one in FORTRAN or COBOL, and translates it into machine language. Since the source program is relatively easy to learn and is not at all like machine language, the translation or compilation is a very complex process.

Each high-level programming language has a compiler for translating source code in that language into machine language. Thus there is a COBOL compiler, a FORTRAN compiler, etc., for each computer. Compilers are part of the operating system software and are called into the CPU when a program is to be translated. They are supplied by software houses or computer vendors.

b. The Interpreter   When a program is compiled, the entire source program is read first and then translated. An **interpreter** differs from a compiler in that it can translate one line of coding at a time. Thus, suppose a program has errors on lines 15, 18, and 35. If it is compiled, the errors will be printed at the end of the entire translation process. If it is interpreted, an error will print after line 15 is entered. The programmer may then be able to correct the line of coding interactively. Similarly, errors on line 18 and line 35 will be noted as soon as the lines are entered.

Both compilers and interpreters translate easy-to-code, high-level languages into machine language. There are, for example, BASIC compilers as well as BASIC interpreters. The instruction set would be the same; only the method of translation differs. A compiler is more efficient but less user-friendly in that the programmer must wait until after all instructions are entered to discover if any errors have occurred. An interpreter sacrifices efficiency for a user-friendly, interactive, or "conversational" translation. Interpreters are common for micros and on-line entry of programs from terminals.

IN A NUTSHELL

INTERPRETERS AND MICROS

Some micros have BASIC interpreters or compilers stored on auxiliary storage and read in as needed, just like larger systems. Other micros have BASIC interpreters or compilers stored in read-only memory. In this way, an interpreter is always available for translating a program without the need to call it in; moreover, the translator, as part of ROM, does not occupy storage that could be used for data and user programs.

---

c. The Assembler   An **assembler language** is a low-level symbolic programming language very similar to machine language. Some symbolic addresses are permitted for ease of coding, but because assembler language is so like machine language, the assembly process is not a very complex one. Programming, however, is more complex than in a high-level language. Thus, while the translation itself is fast and relatively simple, programming tends to be cumbersome.

Assembler languages are written for each machine's own internal language and thus are machine dependent. That is, while a BASIC program may be run with relatively few changes on virtually all computers with BASIC compilers, assembler language for IBM computers is vastly different from assembler language for DEC computers.

The operating system software for most computers usually includes numerous translators, enabling programmers to code in a wide variety of languages. A typical microcomputer, for example, is likely to have two or three translators while a mainframe may have dozens.

2. The Execution Phase

The translation phase produces an object or machine language program, a source listing, and a listing of rule violations or syntax errors. If syntax errors have occurred, they must be corrected; the source program is then translated again until an error-free object program is produced. The **execution** or running of a program cannot take place until this has been accomplished.

Programs that have no syntax errors are *not* necessarily correct. That is, the program may properly follow all rules but fail to produce the desired output. This would occur if a program had logic errors. **Logic errors** can occur from mistakes in the sequencing of instructions as well as from improperly coded instructions that do not contain syntax errors but nevertheless do not accomplish specifically what was desired. These errors will not be detected during the translation phase. Programs must be executed or tested to determine if they are producing the desired output. For example, if a program prints a line containing totals before all records for a given group have been accumulated, this would be a logic error that could be detected only during execution.

To detect logic errors in a program, the programmer prepares test or sample data for checking purposes. The program would be run with the test data, and the programmer would manually compare the computer-produced output with the output that should have been produced. If everything checks, then the program is considered **debugged,** or free from errors, and is ready to be run on a scheduled basis. If not, the errors must be found and corrected, and the program re-translated and re-executed.

Two techniques are required to minimize logic errors:

1. *The programmer should prepare test data with great care.* Test data must be carefully prepared to incorporate all possible types of input. If the program includes a test for a specific condition on input, then the test data should also include that condition. This ensures that the program procedure works properly and minimizes the risk of errors during regular production runs.

2. *The programmer should include numerous error control routines in the program.* If a program is to multiply an hours worked field by an hourly rate field, the program should first ensure that these fields are numeric and have reasonable values. That is, hourly rate should not be less than the minimum wage or greater than some pre-established guideline for the company (e.g., $15.00 per hour). If an error is detected, then typically a message is printed requiring the user to correct the mistake.

There is an adage in information processing that because of the large volume of data, anything that can possibly go wrong with input data will eventually go wrong. Testing a program with all types of input and including many error control routines will minimize the risks. When a logic error is detected, the programmer must fix the source program and have it re-translated. The program must then be executed again with test data to ensure that it is running properly.

In summary, debugging a program consists of the following steps:

Debugging a Program

Phase	Type of Error Detected	How to Correct the Error	How to Minimize Errors
Translation	Syntax	Re-key source code and translate program again.	Desk-check program for typos and other errors before translating.
Execution	Logic	Re-key source code; translate and execute program again.	1. Use planning tools (flowcharts, pseudocode, HIPO charts) to ensure correct logic. 2. Carefully prepare test data. 3. Include error control procedures.

E. Implementing the Program

Once all of the programs for a specific system have been written and completely debugged, the systems analyst, together with the programmer, must arrange for converting from the old system to the new, computerized one. The process of conversion is a very important one and must be carefully implemented to minimize errors and ensure a smooth transition from the old procedure to the new one. The programmer works closely with the entire operating staff to make certain that the following requirements are met:

Implementation Requirements

1. The conversion must be performed smoothly.
2. The operating staff must know precisely what to do.
3. The programs must run without errors.

Sometimes a program that is thought to be fully debugged produces errors during this conversion process. This may mean that the programmer did not fully provide for every contingency in the program. More critically, it may mean that the programmer did not fully understand the job requirements. In either case, the program would require modification.

Because some errors are likely to occur during a conversion process, it would be unwise, in most instances, for an organization to simply abandon the old system one day and then rely completely on the new system the next day.

Instead, conversion procedures are usually performed *in parallel* with the old system until everyone is satisfied that the new system is reliable.

F. Documenting the Program

After a program has been fully tested and implemented, the programmer must write up the full specifications for all users. This is called documenting the program.

Documentation typically consists of the following:

IIII➤ **Documentation Package Contains:**

1. A final source listing.
2. A list of control procedures incorporated.
3. A list of error tests that are included in the program along with the disposition of these errors.
4. Input/output specifications.
5. Flowcharts, pseudocode, or HIPO charts used to plan the program.
6. Test data used.
7. Schedules to be maintained.

These and all other items are maintained by the computer facility as well as by the user department. If all pertinent data is contained within the documentation package, then the program can be run and modified without requiring the original programmer's assistance. Careful documentation is beneficial to the programmer who otherwise would be called upon, as the need arises, to make whatever adjustments become necessary. Careful documentation is also beneficial to the organization as a whole, since the programmer may leave the company, or be unavailable when problems arise. With a complete documentation package, all important aspects of the program are specified in written form, and there should be no need to consult the programmer once the system has been implemented.

Self-Evaluating Quiz

1. Planning tools such as _____, _____ or _____ should be carefully prepared by the programmer before coding begins to ensure that his or her program will contain the appropriate sequence of instructions.
2. Once the steps of a program have been outlined and the programmer is satisfied that they logically integrate, the next step is to _____.
3. A program is written on _____.
4. After a program is written, it must be _____.
5. Computers can execute programs only if they are in _____ form.
6. A(n) _____ language is one which is far easier for the programmer to code but which requires a translation phase.
7. Errors listed during a translation procedure are called _____ errors.

8. High-level programming languages typically require a complex translation phase, called a(n) _____, while low-level programming languages require a simpler translation phase, called a(n) _____.

9. The operating system includes a control program called the _____, which monitors all of the computer's operations.

10. (T or F) Programs are coded on coding sheets, which are sometimes key-punched into cards or keyed on a terminal.

11. (T or F) Programs may be executed when they are in symbolic language.

12. (T or F) Machine language programming requires complex operation codes and actual machine addresses too cumbersome for the average programmer to utilize.

13. (T or F) A program in symbolic language requires both a translation and an execution phase.

14. (T or F) A program written in COBOL is called the object program.

15. A full description of a fully debugged program with all its specifications is provided to the computer staff and the user in the form of a _____ package.

Solutions

1. program flowcharts, pseudocode, HIPO charts
2. code the program
3. coding sheets
4. compiled or interpreted or assembled or translated
5. machine language
6. symbolic
7. syntax
8. compilation; assembly

9. supervisor
10. T
11. F—They must first be translated into machine language.
12. T
13. T
14. F—It is called the source program.
15. documentation

IV. MAJOR HIGH-LEVEL PROGRAMMING LANGUAGES

As noted, source programs written by the programmer must be translated into machine language before they can be executed. There are numerous programming languages that can be used on many computers for various business applications. In this section we describe most of the major languages in use today. We divide our discussion into (1) the three most common languages, (2) other major languages, and (3) specialized languages. Figure 10.13 lists all of the languages considered. Note that although our list includes the most common languages used today, it is not an exhaustive list. There are virtually hundreds of programming languages currently available.

High-Level Languages	Features
Ada APL BASIC C COBOL Forth FORTRAN LOGO Pascal PL/1 RPG II and RPG III	1. Easy to program. 2. More difficult for the machine to translate. 3. Usually independent of the specific computer.
Low-Level Languages	Features
Assembler languages	1. Similar to machine language. 2. More difficult to program. 3. Easier for the machine to translate. 4. Computer-dependent.

Figure 10.13
Features of programming
languages.

A. The Three Most Common Languages

1. BASIC

BASIC is the most widely used programming language for micro- and mini-computer use, and it is very popular for mainframe use as well. It was developed at Dartmouth College as an interactive language designed to make it easy for beginners and users to learn, debug, and correct syntax errors. Figure 10.14

Figure 10.14
Example of a BASIC
program.

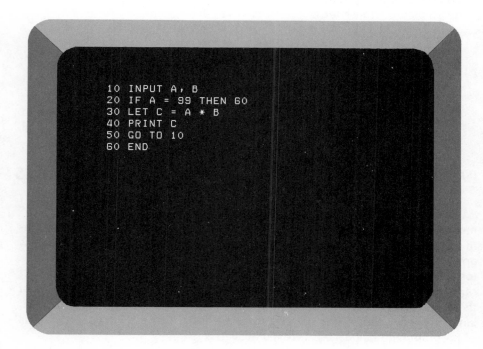

illustrates a simple BASIC program that reads in two numbers, calculates the product, and then prints the answer.

BASIC is an acronym for *Beginner's All-purpose Symbolic Instruction Code.* The term "beginner" means that it is ideally suited for teaching people with no previous programming background. As a result, it is very commonly used to teach students in introductory computer courses and to run programs at small businesses that have either a small programming staff or none at all. Because it uses simplified mathematical notation, BASIC is a popular language for engineers and scientists as well as for businesspeople and students.

A standard form of BASIC may be run on a wide variety of computers, but most systems have extended versions of the language that have far more capability. These extended versions are not, however, standardized and vary widely from system to system.

Chapter 12 provides an indepth discussion of BASIC; Appendix A focuses on advanced topics in BASIC.

2. COBOL

COBOL is an acronym for *COmmon Business Oriented Language.* As the name implies, COBOL is ideally suited for business information processing and file-oriented applications. It is also a "common" language in the sense that a standard form of COBOL can be run on many different makes and models of computers.

An agency called the American National Standards Institute (ANSI) with representatives from government, academia, and business is responsible for developing a standard version of COBOL. The government has stated that it will *not* use any computers from manufacturers who do not have COBOL compilers that adhere to the standards developed by the Institute. This virtually ensures compliance by major computer manufacturers.

COBOL is considered a self-documenting language because it is English-like, making it easy for users to read and easy for programmers to debug. Figure 10.15 illustrates a program excerpt that calculates each employee's net pay based on hours worked and hourly rate.

Since most business-oriented problems operate on vast amounts of data requiring high-speed processing, a business language must be capable of easily and effectively handling high-speed storage media such as magnetic tape and disk. COBOL uses instructions that make programming for these high-level devices a simple task. That is, we can perform disk header label routines, blocking functions, indexing of disk records, and so on, with relative ease in COBOL.

Since most business problems do not require complex mathematical routines, a business language would not usually need to include high-level mathematics. Hence, simple arithmetic operations are easily performed in COBOL; but mathematical functions such as square-root and trigonometric routines that can easily be coded in languages such as FORTRAN or APL are difficult to code in COBOL.

The Nature of Business-oriented Problems

In short, business-oriented problems generally require the processing of large amounts of high-level input and output but do not require very complex arithmetic. These problems are ideally suited for COBOL programming.

(a)

```
IDENTIFICATION DIVISION.
PROGRAM-ID. SAMPLE.
*
ENVIRONMENT DIVISION.
INPUT-OUTPUT SECTION.
FILE-CONTROL. SELECT EMPLOYEE-FILE ASSIGN TO TAPE-1.
              SELECT PAYROLL-REPORT ASSIGN TO PRINTER.
*
DATA DIVISION.
FILE SECTION.
FD  EMPLOYEE-FILE LABEL RECORDS ARE STANDARD.
01  EMPLOYEE-RECORD.
    05   EMPLOYEE-NAME        PICTURE A(20).
    05   HOURS-WORKED         PICTURE 9(2).
    05   HOURLY-RATE          PICTURE 9V99.
FD  PAYROLL-REPORT LABEL RECORDS ARE OMITTED.
01  PAYROLL-RECORD.
    05   FILLER               PICTURE X(5).
    05   NAME-OUT             PICTURE A(20).
    05   FILLER               PICTURE (5).
    05   HOURS-OUT            PICTURE 9(2).
    05   FILLER               PICTURE (5).
    05   RATE-OUT             PICTURE 9.99.
    05   FILLER               PICTURE (5).
    05   NET-PAY              PICTURE 999.99.
    05   FILLER               PICTURE (81).
WORKING-STORAGE SECTION.
01  EOF                       PICTURE 9          VALUE 0.
*
PROCEDURE DIVISION.
    OPEN INPUT EMPLOYEE-FILE
         OUTPUT PAYROLL-REPORT.
    MOVE SPACES TO PAYROLL-RECORD.
    READ EMPLOYEE-FILE AT END MOVE 1 TO EOF.
    PERFORM WAGE-ROUTINE UNTIL EOF = 1.
    CLOSE EMPLOYEE-FILE
          PAYROLL-REPORT.
    STOP RUN.
WAGE-ROUTINE.
    MOVE EMPLOYEE-NAME TO NAME-OUT.
    MOVE HOURS-WORKED TO HOURS-OUT.
    MOVE HOURLY-RATE TO RATE-OUT.
    MULTIPLY HOURS-WORKED BY HOURLY-RATE GIVING NET-PAY.
    WRITE PAYROLL-RECORD AFTER ADVANCING 2 LINES.
    READ EMPLOYEE-FILE AT END MOVE 1 TO EOF.
```

(b)

(Employee Name)	(HOURS)	(RATE)	(NET-PAY)
ROBERT REDFORD	40	5.50	225.00
PAUL NEWMAN	50	8.00	400.00
LINDA EVANS	30	6.50	195.00

Figure 10.15
A COBOL program excerpt with output. (a) COBOL program listing. (b) Sample output.

IN A NUTSHELL

THE CURRENT STATUS OF COBOL

Investment in COBOL programs is so great that it is difficult to turn our attention to more modern alternatives. The same is true of COBOL programmers, who continue to emerge from industry, academic, and government training programs in surprising numbers. COBOL, whatever its failings, is not yet dead.

COBOL and its contemporaries, however, address only a portion of today's programming language issue and provide even less of the solution to the total applications development problem. This is evident in most organizations committed to the development of progressive, on-line applications using data base management software and methodology.

Source: Computerworld/Extra!, "Integrated Fourth Generation Software Languages," by Richard L. Kaufman, Martin A. Goetz, and N. Adam Ron, September 1, 1983, page 38.

3. FORTRAN

The symbolic programming language **FORTRAN,** developed by IBM in the 1950s, is an abbreviation for *Formula Translator*. As the name implies, FORTRAN is a mathematical language ideally suited to setting down formulas. Figure 10.16 shows an excerpt of a FORTRAN program that calculates net pay for each employee from hours worked and hourly rate. Note that FORTRAN uses many of the same symbols as BASIC.

Figure 10.16
A FORTRAN program excerpt.

```
      DIMENSION NAME (5)
   5  READ (1,10) NAME, HOURS, RATE
  10  FORMAT (5A4, F2.0, F3.2)
      IF (HOURS .EQ. -1) GO TO 99
      WAGES = HOURS * RATE
      WRITE (3,20) NAME, HOURS, RATE, WAGES
  20  FORMAT ('0', 5X, 5A4, 5X, F3.0, 5X, F4.2, 5X, F6.2)
      GO TO 5
  99  STOP
      END
```

FORTRAN is most often used for scientific and engineering applications and for business problems that rely heavily on mathematical formulas. Although FORTRAN can easily handle complex mathematical problems, it is not as well suited for high-volume input/output operations as COBOL is, for example.

The Nature of Scientific Problems

Most scientific applications utilize numerous and sometimes complex mathematical operations with little input/output. That is, several numbers fed into a computer used to compute a rocket's trajectory can result in hours of computer calculations. For mathematical problems, we generally use many calculations and comparatively little input/output. FORTRAN, as a mathematical language, was created for handling complex calculations but sacrifices some of the ease with which high-volume input/output, such as disk, can be handled.

Note that FORTRAN is used predominantly in business applications where mathematics is required. Sales forecasting and inventory control are applications that most often use FORTRAN. In short, COBOL is a more effective language when dealing with business-oriented problems that include large amounts of input/output with relatively simple calculations. FORTRAN is a more effective language when dealing with scientific or business-oriented problems that include complex calculating routines with relatively simplified input/output. BASIC is most popular for smaller applications that, like FORTRAN, do not require extensive input/output capability.

B. Other Major Languages

1. Ada

Ada is a relatively new programming language that has been developed under the sponsorship of the Department of Defense. The language is named for Ada, the Countess of Lovelace, who designed what we would call ''programs'' for Charles Babbage's computing engines in the nineteenth century.

One main objective of Ada is to encourage good programming practice with control structures that are well developed. Structured design is a critical element of this language.

Ada was developed by the Department of Defense for military applications including communications and weapons control. Thus, Ada makes extensive use of real-time procedures, automatic error recovery, and fail-safe operations.

At present, Ada is the only high-level programming language to combine real-time features with structured programming capabilities. Hence it has great potential for commercial applications as well as military ones. For example, applications in process control, factory automation, word processing, and office automation would be ideal for Ada.

Currently, however, there are only a few available compilers. Ada's significance, then, rests in its potential rather than its current use.

2. APL

APL is an acronym for *A Programming Language*, not a very exciting name for a high-powered interactive programming language.

LOOKING AHEAD

Predictions About Ada

An increasing number of companies are looking to market Ada compilers as a result of the U.S. Department of Defense estimates that the market for them will total $10 billion by 1990.

Ada is expected by some to become the single computer language for all branches of the U.S. military.

Figure 10.17
The APL keyboard.

APL is best used with a terminal in an interactive mode. A special APL keyboard is required for programming in this language (see Figure 10.17). The need for special symbols makes APL somewhat difficult to learn and code. Despite this disadvantage, APL is ideally suited for handling complex problems in a free-form style of coding. IBM makes APL available to many of its minicomputer users as an alternative to the more commonly used BASIC. In addition, many mainframes support APL, particularly for time-sharing operations.

3. Pascal

Pascal is one of the more recently developed and more promising programming languages. It was developed by Niklaus Wirth during the years 1968 to 1971. Like Ada, the name "Pascal" is not an acronym or an abbreviation. Rather, Pascal was named for the mathematician and inventor Blaise Pascal (1623–1662), who developed one of the earliest calculating machines.

The Pascal programming language is considered to have a great deal of potential for computer users because it, like Ada, facilitates the use of structured programming techniques, which is discussed in Chapter 11. As noted, **structured programming** is a technique designed to standardize programming and make debugging easier. Pascal makes use of IF-THEN-ELSE and DO-WHILE control structures, which, as we shall see, are the very basis of structured programming techniques.

Pascal has been recently adopted as a primary programming language for many microcomputers. It promises to be one of the most important languages in the years ahead. Figure 10.18 shows a program excerpt in Pascal.

4. PL/1

PL/1, an abbreviation for *Programming Language/1*, is a symbolic language that is designed to meet the needs of both scientific and commercial computer users. That is, it is designed to combine the major advantages and features of COBOL and FORTRAN so that a user can employ it for scientific as well as commercial problems. There are other versions of PL/1, such as PL/C and PL/M, which are used on some systems.

PL/1 is a most effective language in organizations that require both scientific and commercial applications. An engineering firm, for example, that has one large computer used for engineering and business (e.g., payroll, accounts receivable, and accounts payable) applications might best employ PL/1 as its primary programming language. In this way, the company need not hire two

```
(*   BILLING PROGRAM
     VARIABLE NAMES:

     Q:   QUANTITY PURCHASED
     P:   UNIT PRICE
     A:   NET AMOUNT *)


PROGRAM PROGRAM1 (INPUT, OUTPUT);
VAR CH:CHAR; Q,P,A:REAL; I:INTEGER;
BEGIN
WHILE NOT EOF (INPUT) DO
BEGIN
FOR I: = 1 TO 3 DO
     BEGIN

          (*  READ AND WRITE NAME AND ADDRESS *)

          WHILE NOT EOLN DO
          BEGIN READ (CH);
          IF NOT EOF THEN WRITE (CH);
          END;
          IF NOT EOF (INPUT) THEN
               BEGIN READLN; WRITELN;
               END
     END;
     IF NOT EOF (INPUT) THEN
     BEGIN
                    (* READ QUANTITY AND PRICE *)
          READ (Q,P);
          A := Q * P;
          WRITE ('  NET = ',A);
          READLN;
          WRITELN;
          FOR I : = 1 TO 2 DO WRITELN;
     END
END
END.
```

Figure 10.18
A Pascal program excerpt.

types of programmers, those with knowledge of FORTRAN and those with knowledge of COBOL. Similarly, employee transfers between the scientific programming staff and the commercial programming staff can easily be made.

There are, then, many advantages to adopting a single programming language for companies that have scientific as well as commercial needs. In this way *both* high-level mathematics and high-volume input/output can be effectively handled using one language. The main disadvantage of PL/1 is that it is more complex than most other languages. See Figure 10.19 for a program excerpt in PL/1.

```
/*COMPUTE EMPLOYEE SALARIES*/
PAYROLL: PROCEDURE OPTIONS (MAIN);
        DECLARE NAME      CHARACTER (20);
        DECLARE RATE      FIXED DECIMAL (3,2);
        DECLARE HOURS     FIXED DECIMAL (2);
        DECLARE SALARY    FIXED DECIMAL (5,2);
        PUT PAGE LIST ('NAME','SALARY');
        PUT SKIP;
        ON ENDFILE END-OF-FILE=1;
        GET LIST (NAME,RATE,HOURS);
        DOWHILE (END-OF-FILE=0);
            IF HOURS > 40
            THEN SALARY = 40*RATE+1.5*RATE*(HOURS-40);
            ELSE SALARY = HOURS*RATE;
            PUT SKIP (1) LIST (NAME,SALARY);
            GET LIST (NAME, RATE, HOURS);
        END;
END PAYROLL;
```

Figure 10.19
A PL/1 program excerpt.

5. RPG II and RPG III

Many business organizations, particularly small-scale ones, or those that rely on minicomputers, do not need the extensive options available with COBOL or PL/1. Their needs could be satisfied with a simplified language that is most often used to print output from files stored on disk or even cards. There is usually very little complex programming involved to produce printed output.

RPG, an abbreviation for *Report Program Generator,* is a symbolic language ideally suited for creating printed reports from input media. Current versions of RPG include RPG II, the most commonly used version, and RPG III, designed with structured programming and data base techniques but thus far only available on a small number of computers.

A minimum of programming effort is required with RPG II and RPG III. That is, it is a very simple language. Page numbers, page headings, edited results, and final totals, for example, are printed in RPG with minimal programming effort.

Thus, it is relatively easy to train RPG II and RPG III programmers, since the various logical control options of COBOL, FORTRAN, PL/1, and other languages need not be learned. Because the primary purpose of this language is to create printed reports or other output, few logic problems are encountered. Thus, RPG II and RPG III are ideal languages for individuals with little or no programming expertise. Both are semi-standard languages, in that they may be used on some computers but not all. Many minicomputers rely heavily on RPG II and RPG III. See Figure 10.20 for a program excerpt in RPG II.

C. Specialized Languages

The following discussion includes those languages that have been in existence for some time but are used for special purposes only. It also includes languages

```
FPAYFILE  IP    F       80              READØ1 SYSIPT
FREPORT   O     F      132      OF      PRINTERSYSLST
IPAYFILE  NS    Ø1
I                                           1   20 NAME
I                                          21  22ØHOURS
I                                          23  252RATE
C     Ø1        HOURS        MULT RATE   WAGES   52H
OREPORT   H    2Ø1      1P
O         OR            OF
O                                          73 'PAYROLL  REPORT'
O         D    1        Ø1
O                          NAME        40
O                          HOURS  Z    60
O                          RATE   1    80
O                          WAGES  1   1ØØ
```

Figure 10.20
An RPG II program excerpt.

that are relatively new but have great potential. Thus, although the languages in this section are mentioned for reference only, many computer installations do, in fact, make extensive use of them.

1. C

An operating system has traditionally been written in an assembler language because assembler language is very efficient. This, however, makes the operating system machine-dependent.

UNIX is a major operating system written in C, a language developed at Bell Labs. **C** is used to write operating systems and application programs for research and business. As UNIX continues to attract businesses as a user-friendly operating system, C will gain even more popularity.

2. Forth

Forth, a language developed in the early 1970s, is ideal for real-time control applications and for a wide variety of engineering problems. It was originally called *Fourth* to signify its use as a fourth-generation language. The IBM 1130 on which it was initially run, however, allowed a maximum of five characters for a name; hence the name was changed to *Forth*.

Forth has the advantage of being both high-powered and available for small systems. It can be used to write operating systems and can also be used on personal computers.

Its main advantages include the following:

1. Speed of translation.
2. The need for very little computer memory.
3. Ease of extending the language to satisfy specific needs.
4. Logical control structures.

A Forth program has elements that are both compiled and interpreted.

3. LOGO

LOGO is a language developed in the 1970s specifically for teaching children how to interact with a computer. It is essentially a dialect of LISP, a list-oriented language. Both LISP and LOGO were developed by artificial intelligence researchers.

LOGO uses a graphic "turtle" that responds to simple commands and can be used for drawings and graphics. LOGO is commonly used in elementary schools and is also supported by several microcomputers. Figure 10.21 illustrates the LOGO language.

4. Simulation Languages

The **simulation languages** most commonly used for modeling or simulating applications are GPSS (*General Purpose System Simulator*) and Simula (*Simulation Language*). These languages enable the programmer to use the computer to simulate "real world" situations and make decisions based on the outcomes. Using a simulation language, for example, we could determine how many toll booths should be constructed at a particular bridge entrance based on anticipated traffic patterns.

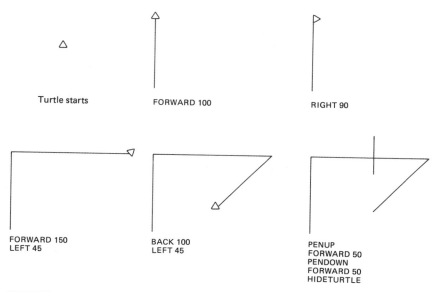

Figure 10.21
Sample LOGO commands used to move a graphic turtle.

Turtle starts   FORWARD 100   RIGHT 90

FORWARD 150
LEFT 45

BACK 100
LEFT 45

PENUP
FORWARD 50
PENDOWN
FORWARD 50
HIDETURTLE

FORWARD moves the turtle in the direction it is facing.
RIGHT and LEFT rotate the turtle.
PENUP and PENDOWN raise and lower the pen—the turtle leaves a trace when it moves with the pen down.

There are literally hundreds of other languages in use today, but 95% of all existing programs are coded in one of the languages discussed above.

Programming Languages and Micros

Virtually all of the above languages, in some form, can be run on micros. The price of compilers is typically several hundred dollars or less.

Languages such as BASIC, C, Forth, and LOGO are specifically well suited for microcomputer processing.

V. EVALUATING APPLICATION SOFTWARE

A. Assessment

As previously noted, there are three main methods for acquiring application software.

1. In-house or internal programmers.
2. Consultants or "third-party" software suppliers.
3. Pre-packaged applications sold by computer vendors or software suppliers.

Figure 10.22 summarizes the advantages and disadvantages of each.

Method of Acquisition	Advantages	Disadvantages
Internal programmer	1. Programmer possesses a more thorough knowledge of user's needs. 2. Maintenance and modifications are easily performed.	1. Cost of design and debugging is relatively expensive. 2. Programmer may not be very well informed of specific application.
Third-party software supplier	1. Supplier can provide an objective evaluation of user's needs. 2. Supplier can provide software support for users of minis and micros who do not have an in-house staff.	1. Less expensive than in-house programming (do not need to pay fringe benefits, etc.), but still expensive. 2. After program is complete, it is difficult to obtain support for maintenance and modification.
Packaged applications	1. Lowest cost—the actual cost of the package is absorbed by a *number* of users rather than one. 2. Programmers have a great deal of knowledge of the specific applications.	1. No flexibility. 2. Modifications are extremely costly. 3. The user organization has no control of procedures that are to be included.

Figure 10.22
Acquisition of application software.

Users and programming managers assess programs as follows.

IN A NUTSHELL

ASSESSING SOFTWARE

1. Overall user satisfaction.
2. Reliability.
3. Ease of implementation.
4. Ease of use.
5. Efficiency.
6. Ease of maintenance.
7. Documentation.
8. Simplicity.

Pre-packaged programs tend to be assessed as follows:

Assessing Pre-Packaged Software

1. Is the package designed for a firm of your size?
2. Does the package allow for growth?
3. How are changes and updates to the package handled?
4. Does the package provide flexibility?
5. Does the package actually do what you want it to do?
6. How much support will you get from the vendor?
7. Will the package run on your hardware?

Many computer journals and reference manuals such as Datapro and Data World rate software packages. These analyses can often prove quite helpful to the user.

B. Trends in Application Software

The cost of hardware is decreasing over time while the salaries that are paid to information processing employees continue to rise. Because salaries constitute such a large part of an information processing budget, many organizations find themselves in need of external software support even though they may have a staff of programmers and systems analysts. For an average information processing budget, see Figure 10.23. It should be noted that many organizations rely on internal programmers as well as third-party programmers and pre-packaged applications for their software support.

In short, many organizations are beginning to rely heavily on *external* software—third-party programs and pre-packaged applications. The federal government, however, has recently undertaken a study that indicates that external software contracts sometimes result in unsatisfactory products and can be very costly to the user as well (see Figure 10.24). Thus, the control and flexibility of internal software, though more expensive, may be more reliable in many instances.

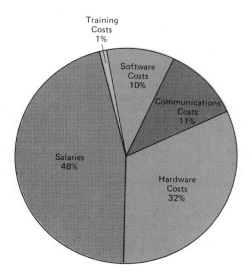

Figure 10.23
Average information processing budget.

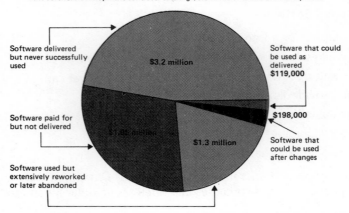

General Accounting Office: Federal Agencies Squandering
$$$ on Bids for Software Support

Nine software development contracts totaling $6.8 million—where the money went

Figure 10.24
Analysis of sample external
software contracts.

IN A NUTSHELL

THE NEED FOR INTEGRATED SOFTWARE

The application development backlog is overwhelming in many organizations. DP departments may be lagging three to four years behind in implementing user requests for new applications. In frustration, users are bypassing DP, installing their own microcomputers or turning to outside service vendors that offer high-level end-user languages in a time-sharing environment.

    These alternatives offer immediate benefits in rapid development of applications, but the benefits are often short term. The resulting multiple, incompatible, nonintegrated systems will bring long term problems of cost and chaos that far outweigh their short term benefits.

Source: Computerworld/Extra!, "The User Wave," by Clive Finkelstein," September 1, 1983, page 29.

Following is a list of popular generalized packages available specifically for micros to help users develop their own applications.

Examples of Standard Packaged Programs Available for Micros

1. VisiCalc, SuperCalc, Lotus 1-2-3

   Electronic spreadsheet designed for accounting applications and for manipulating numbers to determine the best course of action in different situations.

2. WordStar with:
   SpellStar
   MailMerge

   Word processing package that includes:
   A check on spelling.
   The ability to print mailing lists and personalized correspondences.

3. dBase II and III, Condor

   Enables user to establish, access, and update a data base.

CHAPTER SUMMARY

I. Types of software
   A. Application software—programs designed to computerize a given job.
   B. Operating system software—programs designed to optimize the efficient use of the computer system, as a whole.
      1. Includes a control program called the supervisor.
      2. Includes a library of programs, such as translators, that can be called into the CPU by the supervisor, as needed.
   C. Types of programmers.
      1. Application programmers—write programs for a given application such as payroll, accounting, etc.
      2. Maintenance programmers—revise and update existing programs as needed.
      3. Systems programmers—design programs to maximize the efficiency of the supervisor, existing software, and the overall operating system.

II. Writing application programs
   A. Program planning—use of program flowcharts, pseudocode, HIPO charts.
   B. Coding the program.
      1. The program is coded on coding or program sheets and then entered into the computer.
      2. The symbolic program is called a source program.
   C. Translating the program.
      1. Computer-produced results of the translation phase.
         a. Source program listing—printout of symbolic instructions as they were keyed in.
         b. List of syntax errors—violations of programming rules.
         c. Object program—machine-language equivalent of the source program.
      2. Types of program translators.
         a. Compilers.
         b. Interpreters.
         c. Assemblers.
   D. Testing the program for logic errors.
      1. Sample data is used for checking purposes.
      2. Debugging a program means finding and correcting the errors.

III. Major high-level programming languages
   See Table 10.1 for a review of these languages.

TABLE 10.1   High-Level Programming Languages

Name	Meaning	Main Uses	Features
Ada	Named for Ada, the Countess of Lovelace	1. Supported by the Department of Defense 2. Used primarily for military applications	1. Control structures are well developed 2. Combines real-time features with structured programming capabilities

TABLE 10.1 High-Level Programming Languages (continued)

Name	Meaning	Main Uses	Features
APL	A Programming Language	1. Used on minis 2. Used with time-sharing facilities	1. Interactive 2. Requires special graphics keyboard 3. Relatively complex 4. Scientifically oriented
BASIC	Beginner's All-purpose Symbolic Instruction Code	1. Used on mainframes and minis for some production runs 2. Used on numerous micro systems for teaching purposes	1. Interactive 2. Easy to learn 3. Uses mathematical notation 4. Can be used for business and scientific problems
COBOL	Common Business Oriented Language	Used on all computers, but primarily on mainframes and minis	1. Ideal for business applications 2. Easily handles disk and tape features 3. English-like
FORTRAN	Formula Translator	Used primarily on mainframes and minis	1. Ideal for scientific applications 2. Uses mathematical notation
Pascal	Named for the mathematician Blaise Pascal	Used on all types of computers	1. General-purpose language 2. Focuses on structured programming techniques
PL/1	Programming Language One	Used mostly on mainframes	1. Combines the features of COBOL and FORTRAN 2. Somewhat complex to code
RPG II and RPG III	Report Program Generator	Used primarily on IBM minicomputers but can be used on larger systems as well	1. Very simple language 2. Ideally suited for printing reports

Chapter Self-Evaluating Quiz

1. (T or F) The systems analyst provides the programmer with job requirements from which the programmer must create his or her program.
2. The program flowchart indicates _____.
3. The process of writing the actual computer instructions is called _____.
4. In order for programs to be executed, they must be in a _____.
5. Programs are rarely written in a _____ language because of its _____.
6. Programs are generally written in a _____ language, which must be converted or translated into machine language.
7. Symbolic programs must be _____ before they can be _____.
8. A source program is _____.

9. An object program is _____.
10. The output from a compilation consists of _____, _____, and _____.
11. A compiler is a _____.
12. _____ is a language that is similar to machine language with only minor variations to simplify programming effort.
13. After a program has been compiled successfully, with no errors, then the _____ phase is undertaken.
14. The execution phase will determine if there are _____ in the program.
15. COBOL is an acronym for _____.
16. COBOL is a common language in the sense that _____.
17. COBOL is a business language in the sense that _____.
18. COBOL is a(n) _____ -like language, which makes it easy to train programmers.
19. (T or F) Logarithmic functions and other complex mathematical routines can easily be handled in COBOL.
20. Business problems have need for _____ but usually do not involve complex _____.
21. FORTRAN is an abbreviation for _____.
22. Complex _____ routines can easily be performed in FORTRAN, while large amounts of _____ can best be handled in COBOL.
23. A scientific application usually requires (high/low) volume input/output with (high/low) volume mathematical operations.
24. A symbolic programming language designed for the Department of Defense's military applications that has potential use for business as well is _____.
25. A language that is ideally suited for implementing the structured programming technique is _____.
26. PL/1 combines the advantages of _____ and _____.
27. RPG is an abbreviation for _____.
28. _____ is a language designed specifically for teaching children how to program.
29. One example of a simulation language is _____.
30. (T or F) Many organizations are beginning to rely heavily on third-party programmers and pre-packaged applications.

Solutions

1. T / page 350
2. the logic to be used in a program / page 353
3. coding the program / page 355
4. machine language / page 356
5. machine / page 356 complexity / page 356
6. symbolic / page 356
7. translated / page 356 run or executed / page 356
8. a program written in a symbolic language / page 356
9. the machine language equivalent of the source program / page 356

10. an object program / page 357
a listing of rule violations or
syntax errors / page 357
a program listing / page 357
11. translator program that
converts an input source
program in a symbolic
language to an output object
program in machine language
/ page 359
12. Assembler language / page 359
13. execution / page 360
14. logic errors / page 360
15. *COmmon Business Oriented
Language* / page 365
16. it can be run on many different
makes and models of
computers / page 365
17. it is especially suited to
handling business-type
problems such as payroll and
accounts receivable / page 365

18. English / page 365
19. F / page 365
20. processing large volumes of
input/output / page 365
mathematical functions
/ page 365
21. *Formula Translator* / page 367
22. mathematical / page 367
input/output / page 367
23. low / page 367
high / page 367
24. Ada / page 368
25. Pascal or Ada / page 369
26. FORTRAN / page 369
COBOL / page 369
27. *Report Program Generator*
/ page 371
28. LOGO / page 373
29. Simula / page 373
GPSS / page 373
30. T / page 375

Key Terms

Ada
APL
Application programmer
Assembler language
BASIC
C
COBOL
Coding a program
Compiler
Debugging
Documentation
Execution
Forth
FORTRAN
High-level programming languages
HIPO chart
Interpreter
Logic error

LOGO
Machine language
Maintenance programmer
Object program
Operating system
Pascal
PL/1
Program flowchart
Pseudocode
RPG
Simulation languages
Source program
Structured programming
Supervisor
Symbolic program
Syntax error
Systems programmer
Translator

Review Questions

1. A programming language designed to fill normal scientific needs, utilizing mathematical formulas, is _____, an abbreviation for _____.
2. A programming language designed to meet the needs of both scientific and commercial computer users is _____, an abbreviation for _____.

3. An advantage of PL/1 programming is _____.

4. A programming language that is ideally suited for creating printed reports from input media is _____, an acronym for _____.

5. A programming language that is most often used for terminal processing is _____.

6. A programming language that is often used for writing control programs, translators, and other advanced programs is _____.

7. COBOL is a relatively easy language to learn because it is _____.

8. A programming language is considered common if it can be _____.

9. PL/1 combines the advantages of _____ and _____.

10. BASIC is a programming language very similar to _____.

11. The UNIX operating system was written in the programming language _____.

12. _____ was developed by the Department of Defense for military applications, communications, and weapons control.

13. A language specifically developed to incorporate structured programming concepts is _____.

14. The language called _____, developed by artificial intelligence researchers in the 1970s, was designed for teaching children how to interact with a computer.

15. One language commonly used for modeling or simulation is _____.

APPLICATION

SOFTWARE DOCUMENTATION A MAJOR PROBLEM

by Frank Clark

On a recent visit to a software company to discuss a new software package, the first question I asked was: What type of manuals or other documentation exist for this package? The manager told me that he had nothing at the time but was "working on it."

Though not a typical situation at present, it demonstrates that the problems of software documentation are getting worse, not better. Two of the most persistent problems are poor writing style and inefficient manual development.

In explaining DP terms, some writing is so brief that it reads like a glossary. Some manuals are so full of coding and flowcharts that businessmen cannot get through them without professional help.

The Other Extreme

Some software houses go to the other extreme. They want to sell their software to everyone, so they set the reading level at about the sixth grade and use the writing style of a comic book.

Inefficient procedures present more serious problems for manual development. The documentation specialist is often the last person to learn about new applications software. He is at the end of the production line—just before the loading dock—and is expected to do his job as quickly as the packaging is done in the warehouse.

Procedures for documentation development must be more efficient. Once management approves a new software proposal, the documentation specialist would work up-front with the project manager or lead programmer to aid in planning documentation development. This should include interviewing the marketing and technical staff to gather all pertinent information on the subject matter of the manual and asking such questions as: Why use this manual? How will the manual be used?

Then the audience level of the manual must be identified. For example, if the user is a technical professional the manual can easily be organized as a reference type of document. If the user is not a technical person, the writing should be tutorial in style.

With the recent structured programming techniques, standards can be set for most applications programs. A major objective of structured programming is to break down large problems into manageable segments. This should also lead to a modular and cost-effective approach to the documentation. The actual writing should be a series of well-defined segments or modules of information, which are specified in the table of contents. In this manner, documentation can begin when individual program segments are being coded and tested rather than when a completed program arrives several months later. In other words, programming and documentation should be done in parallel. This procedure puts the documentation specialist in the mainstream of software development—not at the tail end of an impatient system.

Structured documentation standardizes writing much like structured programming standardizes program code. Many users refer to manuals several times a day. These users should always be able to find information in the same format without wasting a great deal of time searching for it.

In addition, software changes or updates can be made in a limited segment of a manual without the need to reprint an entire publication.

Most companies want their documentation specialists to spend as much time as possible on their word processors. They should only need to assign a liaison person to provide the necessary technical information required to document a new software product.

In small companies, the documentation specialist must often be his own editor, technical illustrator and production manager, responsible for formatting pages and selecting type styles.

As computers become more of a universal utility, documentation of applications software will have to be written as professionally as the programs it is describing.

Source: Computerworld, February 28, 1983, page 13. The author is senior documentation specialist for Documentation Development, Inc. Reprinted with permission.

Questions
1. Understanding Key Terms
   Define the following terms in the context in which they are used in the application:
   a. Software documentation.
   b. Software house.
   c. Structured programming techniques.
2. Software, Hardware, and Systems Concepts
   What criteria would you use to evaluate software documentation? Be specific.
3. Management Considerations
   Suppose you were a manager of an organization and discovered an existing software package that met your needs precisely, but the documentation was weak. Would you acquire the package or not? Explain your answer.
4. Social, Legal, and Ethical Implications
   Should software documentation be written in technical language for application programmers and systems analysts, or should it be written as user-friendly as possible? Explain your answer.

CASE STUDY: McKing's Superburgers, Inc.

1. Programming Languages
   If a minicomputer is located in each restaurant of McKing's Superburgers, which of the following programming languages would you recommend using? Explain your answer.
   a. BASIC
   b. COBOL
   c. FORTRAN
   d. Ada
   e. APL
   f. Pascal
   g. PL/1
   h. RPG
   i. C
   j. Forth
   k. LOGO

2. Application Software
   a. What methods of software acquisition would you recommend for McKing's? Discuss the advantages and disadvantages of each method.
   b. Would you recommend that McKing's hire a full staff of programmers, or would you suggest that the company begin computerizing by hiring consultants? Explain your answer.

THE COMPUTER AD: A Focus on Marketing

Consider the ad entitled "When You Absolutely, Positively Can't Be Late" that appears in Figure 10.25.

1. State the advantages of NATURAL as indicated in the ad.
2. What is meant by the "total transportability" of NATURAL?
3. What is meant by the claim that NATURAL is totally interactive?
4. In order to decide whether to acquire NATURAL as an application package or to have programmers on staff write the application programs, what questions would you ask of the vendor?
5. What message is the advertiser trying to convey with (a) the rabbit's foot, (b) the magnet, and (c) the rather desperate look on the man's face?

Figure 10.25
Marketing computer products. (Courtesy Software AG of North America, Inc.)

Within the image:
- ELEMENTS OF A PROGRAM FLOWCHART
- STRUCTURED PROGRAMING
- PRINT "LIST OF FEMALES"
- PRINT "FIRST NAME," "LAST NAME," "TEL. No."
- READ A TAPE RECORD
- HAS LAST RECORD BEEN
- 1

CHAPTER 11

TOOLS FOR SPECIFYING
PROGRAM LOGIC

CHAPTER OBJECTIVES

To familiarize you with:

- How flowcharts, pseudocode, and HIPO charts are used, with particular emphasis on the first two tools.
- How to read, interpret, and draw the appropriate charts.
- Structured programming concepts.

I. AN INTRODUCTION TO PLANNING TOOLS

One major aspect of the information processing function is the logical flow of programming elements necessary to ensure that data is read and processed properly and used to produce the required output. In fact, the logical flow of elements within a program is the singlemost important aspect of programming.

Various descriptive charts are used by computer professionals to plan the logic that a program is to incorporate. We consider the following three techniques, which are the most commonly used in the information processing field for planning program logic.

Tools Used for Planning Program Logic

1. Program flowcharts.
2. Pseudocode.
3. HIPO charts.

As indicated in the previous chapter, programs that are coded without being properly planned are often more difficult to debug, less efficient, and harder for users and managers to read and assess. Experienced organizations require their programmers to use planning tools to map out program logic before the coding is begun.

The program **flowchart,** which is the traditional tool for planning logic, is discussed first.[1] Pseudocode, which is in a coded format, and HIPO charts are more recent tools developed in an effort to standardize program logic and ensure that programs have a specified structure.

Planning tools are either diagrams or coding that specifies the logical flow of data to be used in a particular program. The relative position of the planning process in the programmer's sequence of activities is indicated in Figure 11.1.

As we see in Figure 11.1, the planning tool is either drawn or coded *before* the program is written to ensure that the instructions will be logically integrated. The concept is not unlike that used by architects, who prepare pictorial representations, called blueprints, prior to the actual design of a building. Blueprints verify and integrate elements of a building before construction. Similarly, flowcharts, HIPO charts, and pseudocode verify and integrate elements of a program prior to coding.

The planning tool is most often developed by programmers to ensure that their interpretation of the logic required in the program is accurate. The resulting flowchart, HIPO chart, or pseudocode is often discussed with the systems analyst and the user to verify that the programmer has perceived the program's requirements correctly and knows how they should be met.

If a programmer misunderstands a sequence of steps to be included in the program, this misunderstanding can frequently be detected by examining the planning tool. Finding the error before coding begins will save hours of debugging and program modification time later on.

---

[1]The systems flowchart, a more general representation of data flow in a system, as a whole, is discussed in Chapter 15.

Detailed Breakdown of Operations	Tool
Analyst formulates problem for programmer	Systems design package
Programmer formulates his or her conception of the problem	Programmer's problem definition
Programmer prepares program flowchart, pseudocode, or HIPO chart to depict logic	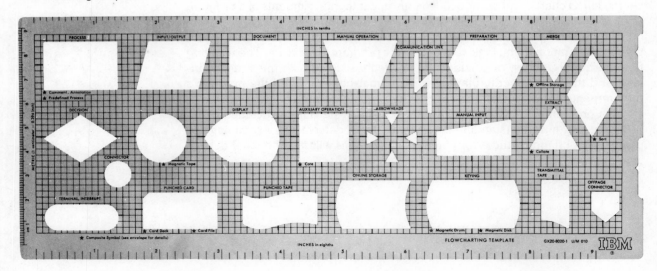
Programmer reviews planning tool with analyst & user	Interview and discussion
Programmer codes the problem	Coding sheet

Figure 11.1
The sequence of programmer activities prior to testing.

II. THE PROGRAM FLOWCHART

A. Elements of a Program Flowchart

Figure 11.2
Flowcharting template.

A standardized tool called a **template** is used to draw the symbols in a program flowchart. This is usually available in plastic or metal. Figure 11.2 illustrates a template, which is used to trace the required flowcharting symbols. These are available at most bookstores and computer shops for a dollar or two.

Most flowcharts can be effectively drawn using the template's five basic symbols, shown in Table 11.1. Note that these symbols conform to information-processing standards and are universally used throughout the computer industry. Thus all information processing personnel and even many users can understand the symbols and the logic used in any flowchart if they are familiar with these basic symbols. Each symbol indicates the specific functions to be included in a particular flowchart.

TABLE 11.1 Major Flowcharting Symbols

	Symbol	Explanation
1.		INPUT/OUTPUT (I/O) symbol This symbol represents any input or output operation as READ NAME, READ A CARD, WRITE A LINE, etc. The specific operation to be performed is indicated by a note inside the symbol.
2.		PROCESSING This symbol indicates any internal computer processing, that is, any series of data transfer or arithmetic operations. We may have, for example, ADD AMOUNT TO TOTAL or COMPUTE TAX = .05 × SALES or TOTAL = X + Y + Z or MOVE INPUT TO OUTPUT
3.		DECISION This symbol is used to test for a logical comparison. Basically, it is used when we want the computer to ask a question. Examples of decision tests include: (a) IS AMOUNT OF SALES GREATER THAN 100.00? (b) IS AMOUNT OF SALES LESS THAN AMOUNT OF CREDIT? (c) DOES SEX FIELD = 'M'? (d) IS TOTAL = ZEROS?
4.		CONNECTOR This symbol denotes a cross references point indicating where the flowchart should continue. It is used to indicate a change in the normal flow of data.
5.		TERMINAL This symbol is used to denote the starting or ending point of a program.

Let us consider an example. Assume that we have a file of records on a tape, each with the format shown in Figure 11.3. The code field in each tape record will contain either a "1" to denote a male or a "2" to denote a female. We would like the computer to process this file and produce a report that lists the names and telephone numbers of females only. An example of the desired output is shown in Figure 11.4. We assume that the records on the tape are already in alphabetical sequence by last name.

The logic for this problem consists of the following steps.

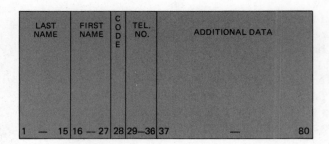

Figure 11.3
Sample record format.

Figure 11.4
Sample output.

Program Logic

1. Read a record from the tape.
2. Determine if the record pertains to a female (i.e., determine if the code field is equal to 2).
3. If the code field is not equal to 2, then do not process this record any further, since it contains data for a male. Instead, read the next record; that is, go back to Step 1.
4. If the record contains data for a female (code is equal to 2), then print out the following fields: first name, last name, telephone number.
5. Go back to Step 1 to read the next record.

The flowchart depicting this logic is illustrated in Figure 11.5. Notice how much simpler it is to represent the logic of this problem by a flowchart rather than with the use of a narrative as above.

The following points should also be noted about flowcharts.

Flowcharting Conventions

1. Each symbol denotes a type of operation. We will focus on the following main operations:
   a. Input/output.
   b. Processing.
   c. Decision.
   d. Transfer or branch.
   e. Terminal.
2. A note is written inside each symbol to indicate the specific function to be performed.
3. The symbols are connected by flowlines; flowcharts are read from top to bottom and left to right.

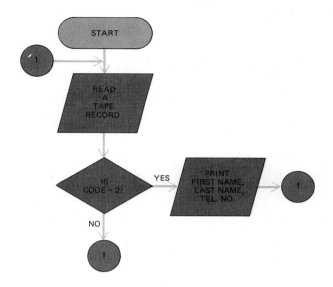

Figure 11.5
Sample flowchart.

4. A sequence of operations is performed until a terminal symbol designates the end of the run, or a branch connector transfers control to another part of the flowchart.

Interpreting the Flowchart in Figure 11.5

1. A tape record is read.
2. If CODE = 2, first name, last name, and telephone number are printed and a branch to the entry point called ① occurs.
3. If CODE is not equal to 2, a branch to the entry point called ① occurs.
4. The sequence of steps will be repeated until there is no more data.

Although the flowchart in Figure 11.5 correctly depicts the logic required, it lacks many details that are generally found in flowcharts of typical business problems. For example, reports generally have title and column headings for identification purposes. In addition, many business reports contain some sort of statistical information; that is, they may include a listing of the total number of records processed, the percentage of records that were in error, and so on. We now consider these additional items.

Let us first focus on the method used to produce a report with a title and column headings, as shown in Figure 11.6. Since the title and the column headings appear at the beginning of the report, we can expect that in our flowchart we will print these items at the beginning of our logic flow. Figure 11.7 shows the logic necessary to accomplish this.

Notice the difference between the following steps.

Explanation
The computer is to print variable data—that is, the contents of the input name and telephone number fields.

The computer is to print constant data—the actual words "FIRST NAME", "LAST NAME", "TEL. NO." as column headings. When an entry is enclosed in quotation marks, it refers to a constant.

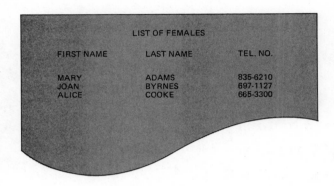

Figure 11.6
Sample output with headings.

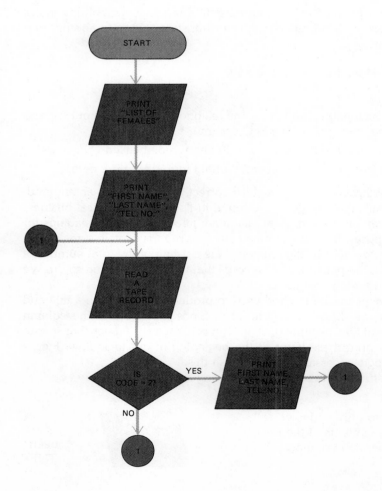

Figure 11.7
Revised sample logic.

End-of-Job Routine

An **end-of-job routine** refers to those instructions that are to be executed when there is no more data to process. For example, let us consider the logic necessary to instruct the computer to print the same report as above but with a message at the end indicating the total number of females that have been printed. This message might appear as:

THE TOTAL NUMBER OF FEMALES IS 576

Since we want this message to print out only when all the records have been processed, we must include in our logic a test to see if the last data record has already been processed. This test is often referred to as the "last record" test and typically appears after the step that reads in an input record, as shown in Figure 11.8.

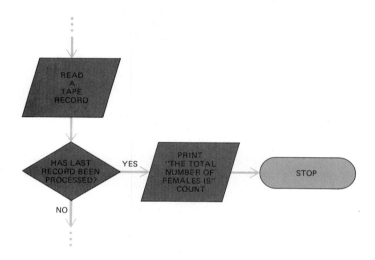

Figure 11.8
Last record test.

Most systems use a special end-of-file indicator when there are no more records to process. This end-of-file indicator is a separate record; it includes special characters in the first positions of the record that will be tested by the computer to see if an end-of-file condition has occurred. Sometimes the programmer designates a record with 999 in the first three positions, for example, as an end-of-file condition. Sometimes, the computer itself can sense an end-of-file record because it contains a special end-of-file indicator.

When data is entered as input on a terminal, the programmer checks for an end-of-file condition by testing one of the data fields to see if it contains a particular value designated to mean that there is no more input. For example, if a NAME field contains the value "LAST" or an AMOUNT field contains 99999, we will assume this to be a "dummy" record used to signal an end-of-file condition. Thus the programmer may instruct the user to enter "LAST" in a NAME field when there is no more data.

The dotted lines in Figure 11.8 indicate that there are other parts of the flowchart that are not shown. Notice that when the last record has already been processed, the computer is instructed to print out the following message: THE

TOTAL NUMBER OF FEMALES IS. We know that this instruction causes a constant to print because the data is enclosed in quote marks. This message is followed by the actual number accumulated in the CPU in the field called COUNT. We will see next how COUNT is established and used in our illustration.

Counting Data Items

In order to print out a count of the number of females, it is necessary for us to establish at the beginning of our logic a special area or field for counting. The purpose of this area is to keep a running total of the number of females as the input records are being processed. In addition to setting up a field in the CPU for counting purposes, we must also make sure that this field is initially set equal to zero. To set up a counting area in the CPU, we can use the symbol shown in Figure 11.9.

Figure 11.9
Setting up a counter.

When drawing a flowchart, we may arbitrarily use any name to designate a field. When you actually write the program, however, you must set up field names according to the rules for each specific programming language.

Consider the operation in Figure 11.9, which will accomplish three things.

IIII▶   **COUNT = 0**

This instruction will:

1. Set aside an area in the CPU for counting.
2. Initialize or clear that area so that it starts out with a value of zero.
3. Provide us with a name, COUNT, by which we can refer to this particular area later on in our program.

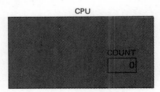

Having now established an area for counting, we must indicate the point in our program where we want to add to this counter. In this program, we want to find the total number of females; each time the computer finds a female record, then, the COUNT field should be incremented by 1. The flowchart segment that indicates this part of the logic is shown in Figure 11.10. Notice that when a "female" record is found, two steps must be performed.

Figure 11.10
Incrementing the counter.

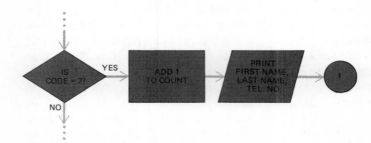

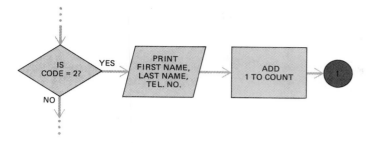

Figure 11.11
Alternative logic for
incrementing the counter.

When CODE = 2

1. Add 1 to the counter, called COUNT, which is keeping a running total of the number of females.
2. Print out the name and telephone number of the female record just read.

Note that the flowchart segment in Figure 11.11 is equally correct, since it also accomplishes the desired logic. That is, in this instance, it makes no difference if we print the output first and then increment COUNT, or if we increment COUNT before printing.

There are frequently several ways to write a flowchart, all of which will result in correct logic. Many times, programmers code the instruction to add one to COUNT in a flowchart as follows:

$$\texttt{COUNT = COUNT + 1}$$

Although this is not a valid equation, it is a valid computer instruction. In fact, in many programming languages this is precisely the type of instruction actually used. Simply stated, the computer does what is indicated to the right of the equal sign first and then stores the result in the field specified at the left. Hence, 1 is added to the current value of COUNT in the CPU and the new total replaces the old value of the field COUNT. In this way, COUNT is incremented by 1.

We are now ready to put together all the segments of the flowchart to accomplish our objectives of first printing a heading and then printing the names and telephone numbers of all females from a tape file; at the end of the report, a count of the total number of females processed will print. Figure 11.12 illustrates this flowchart in its entirety.

To ensure that you understand the fundamental concepts of flowcharting, examine the following illustrative problems and suggested flowcharts.

Example 1

Consider the input and output specifications in Figure 11.13. We wish to read data from a terminal and to print (1) the percentage of students who are female and (2) the total number of students processed.

1. We do *not* have a step at the beginning to print out a title or message, since in this problem we will simply print out two messages, which are produced only after all data has been processed.
2. We have set up two areas to accumulate results—F and T. These names have been arbitrarily chosen and must be used consistently throughout. F

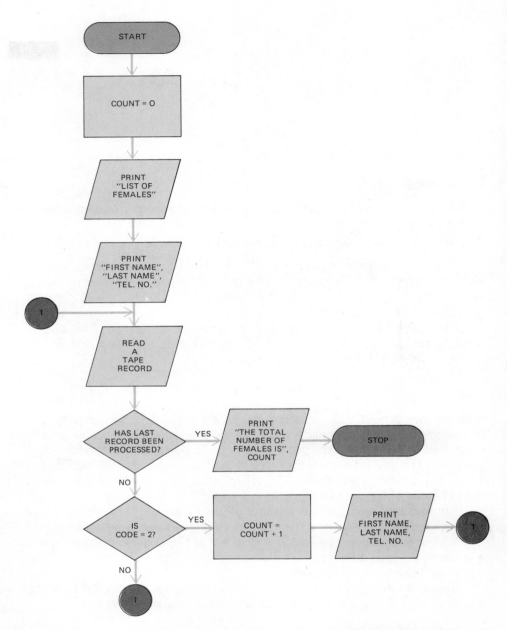

Figure 11.12
Completed flowchart for the first sample problem.

will contain the total number of female students and T will contain the total number of students.

3. The last record or end-of-file condition will be denoted by a SEX CODE of 9. Since valid SEX CODEs are 1 and 2, any other number could have been used to denote an end-of-file condition. We arbitrarily chose 9.

4. Since we need to accumulate the total number of students processed, we increment counter T after a record has been read from the terminal, and we have determined that it is not the last record. That is, for every valid input record entered on the terminal, we add one to T.

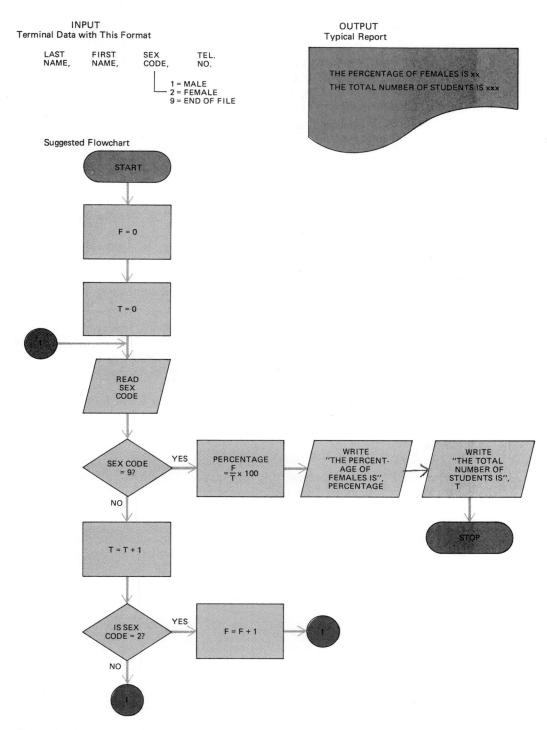

INPUT
Terminal Data with This Format

LAST NAME,	FIRST NAME,	SEX CODE,	TEL. NO.

1 = MALE
2 = FEMALE
9 = END OF FILE

OUTPUT
Typical Report

THE PERCENTAGE OF FEMALES IS xx

THE TOTAL NUMBER OF STUDENTS IS xxx

Suggested Flowchart

START

$F = 0$

$T = 0$

READ SEX CODE

SEX CODE = 9? — YES → PERCENTAGE $= \dfrac{F}{T} \times 100$ → WRITE "THE PERCENTAGE OF FEMALES IS", PERCENTAGE → WRITE "THE TOTAL NUMBER OF STUDENTS IS", T → STOP

NO

$T = T + 1$

IS SEX CODE = 2? — YES → $F = F + 1$ → 1

NO → 1

Figure 11.13
Flowchart for Example 1.

5. After the last record has been read from the terminal, we must indicate how the desired percentage is to be computed. You will recall that the computer does nothing unless it is provided with specific instructions. In this case, we instruct the computer to calculate a percentage by (1) dividing the total number of females by the total number of students, which will produce a decimal number, and (2) then multiplying by 100 to obtain an actual percent. That is, if there are 23% females, we wish to print 23, not .23.

The literal or constant "THE PERCENTAGE OF FEMALES IS" will accompany the actual number. In addition, the literal "THE TOTAL NUMBER OF STUDENTS IS", along with the contents of T, the actual number of records processed, will print.

Example 2

The flowchart in Figure 11.14 illustrates how a payroll report can be produced from input records.

The four input fields may be entered from any input device. If they were entered from a terminal, the user might simply key in the data in response to specific prompts. If, however, the input were entered on disk, tape, or cards, the fields in each record would occupy specific positions:

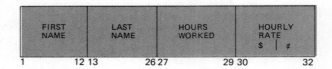

For flowcharting purposes, we simply indicate the fields to be entered as input and ignore the method of input. Flowcharts, then, are drawn so that they are device-independent.

The basic logic for each record that is read in Figure 11.14 is as follows. If HOURS WORKED is in excess of 40, we proceed to the step labeled OVERTIME, where we multiply 40 by RATE, subtract 40 from HOURS WORKED to obtain the OVERTIME-HRS, and then multiply OVERTIME-HRS by 1.5 times the RATE to calculate time-and-a-half for overtime. We then add the regular wages and the overtime wages to obtain GROSS, and branch back to the print sequence. If the HOURS WORKED is not in excess of 40, then we simply multiply HOURS WORKED by RATE to obtain the GROSS. After the GROSS is calculated, we print the person's name and gross salary. For the sake of simplicity, the process of computing payroll deductions for tax purposes has not been included.

Notice that the flowchart in Figure 11.14 is not really complete. Conditions could occur for which we have not provided. Suppose, for example, that a name field was inadvertently omitted, or that HOURS WORKED or RATE was also erroneously blank. What should be done?

To adequately describe a set of procedures, a flowchart must be thorough and include every possible detail by testing for every conceivable contingency. Programmers and users who account for every possible condition will not be plagued later by numerous erroneous results. The revised flowchart in Figure 11.15 is more complete than the preceding one, because it provides for the possibility of blank input fields.

INPUT
Each Record Consists of

| FIRST NAME, | LAST NAME, | HOURS WORKED, | HOURLY RATE |

OUTPUT

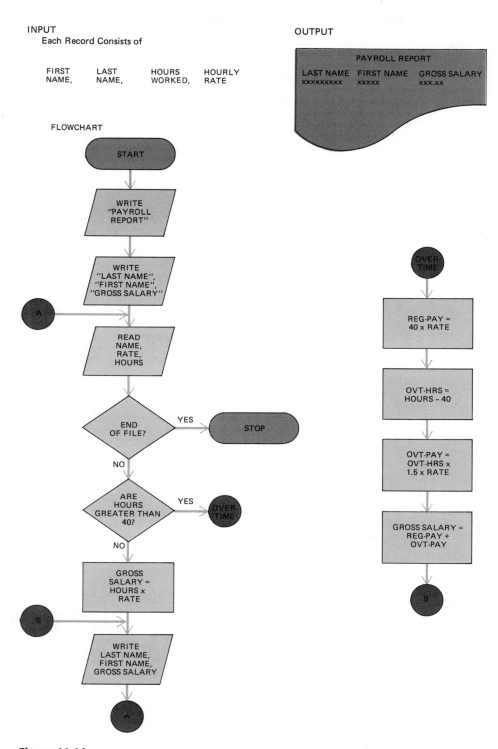

PAYROLL REPORT

LAST NAME	FIRST NAME	GROSS SALARY
xxxxxxxx	xxxxx	xxx.xx

FLOWCHART

Figure 11.14
Flowchart for Example 2.

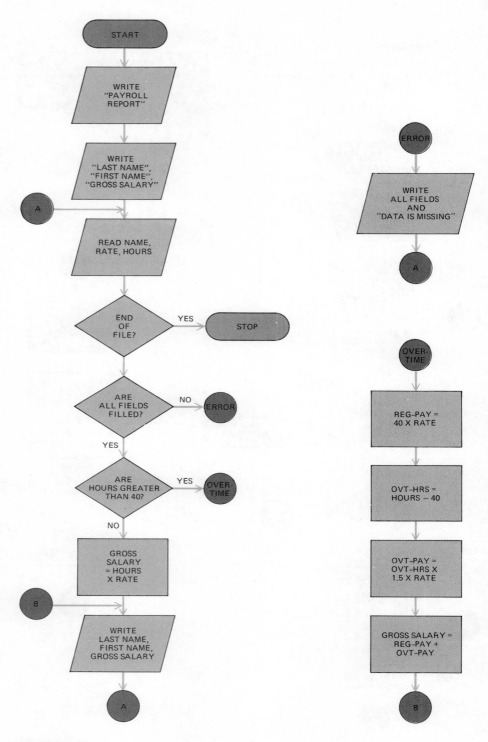

Figure 11.15
Revised flowchart for preparation of a payroll
report after input data has been validated.

Connector Symbols and Branch Points

Observe that the flowchart in Figure 11.15 utilizes the three types of connectors shown in Table 11.2.

TABLE 11.2   Types of Connectors

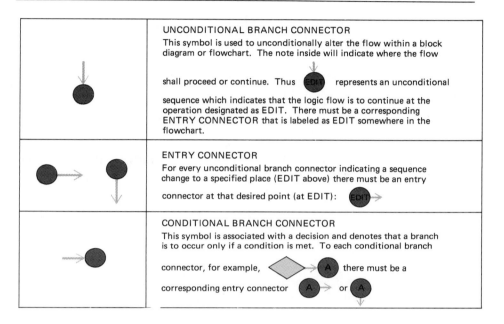

Note that connector symbols may be identified or labeled by any note within the symbol. Some programming languages use a single letter or digit to describe a branch point:

while others use explanatory notation:

Notice, too, that the **unconditional branch** connector is always the *last* element in a sequence. Once we issue an instruction that causes the flow to proceed elsewhere, there is no need for further instructions at that point. The following flowchart excerpt, for example, is invalid and meaningless because it has an unconditional branch followed by an instruction.

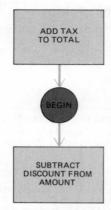

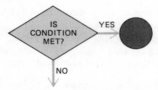

Once an unconditional branch to BEGIN is executed, the instruction following the branch instruction will not be executed.

Keep in mind that the decision symbol and the **conditional branch** connector are always coded together.

This means that *if* a condition is met, then a branch to the entry point indicated should occur. Otherwise, the flow continues with the next sequential step. Every conditional branch connector must have an entry connector associated with it. If →① is a conditional branch instruction, then the entry connector ①→ or ① must be coded in the flowchart. That is, every branch
↓
connector must transfer control to a specified entry point.

Example 3 A Looping Procedure

Suppose we wish to print five output lines for every input record read, for purposes of printing address labels. That is, we wish to perform a print **routine,** or sequence, five times. A sequence of steps to be executed a specified number of times is referred to as a **loop.** See Figure 11.16 for the flowchart depicting this loop procedure.

Generally, for looping operations, we have the following rules:

Loop Rules

General	*Example*
1. Establish a counter with zero contents.	1. SET COUNTER TO 0 (or COUNTER = 0).
2. Perform the operation(s) required.	2. WRITE A LINE.
3. Add 1 to counter. Every time the operation is performed, 1 is added to the counter. Thus the counter reflects the number of	3. ADD 1 TO COUNTER (or COUNTER = COUNTER + 1).

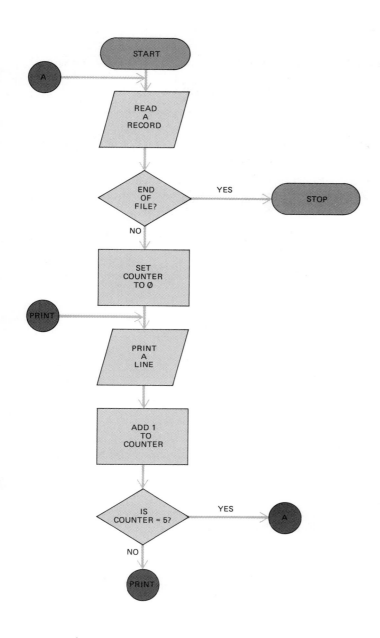

Figure 11.16
Flowchart for Example 3: a looping routine to print five output lines for each input record.

Loop Rules

General	Example
times the operation has been performed.	
4. Test the counter to see if the operation was performed the required number of times.	4. IS COUNTER = 5?
5. Branch if counter equals the required number; otherwise repeat the sequence.	5. Branch to BEGIN if COUNTER = 5; otherwise branch to PRINT.

IN A NUTSHELL

FEATURES OF FLOWCHARTS

1. A flowchart is a pictorial representation of the logic that will be incorporated in a program.
2. A flowchart should be drawn before a program is coded to ensure that all the elements are logically interrelated.
3. Each symbol in a flowchart represents a specific function.
4. The note inside each symbol indicates the specific operation to be performed.
5. Flowcharts are read from top to bottom and left to right unless a branch alters the normal flow.

Self-Evaluating Quiz

1. A flowchart is a diagram that illustrates the _____ of _____ that will be coded in a _____.
2. A sequence of steps in a flowchart consists of _____ connected by _____.
3. The direction of flow in a flowchart is usually from _____ to _____ and _____ to _____.
4. A symbol represents _____.
5. All symbols must be connected by _____; each symbol contains a _____ inside it indicating the specific function to be performed.
6. A flowcharting tool called a _____ contains all the standard symbols used to draw flowcharts.

Identify each of the symbols in questions 7 to 14.

7.

8.

9.

10.

11.

12.

13.

14.

15. Arithmetic operations are coded in _____ symbols.

16. Each symbol can generally be used to code a program _____.

17. If a condition is tested and met, then the _____ indicates where the flow is to continue; otherwise the program proceeds with the _____.

18. When the logic flow is interrupted and is to continue at some step other than the next sequential step, a(n) _____ is said to occur.

19. Consider the following.

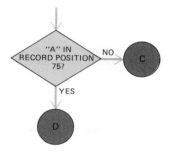

If there is not an A in record position 75, a _____ to _____ will occur.

20. If used, an unconditional branch connector must be the _____ step in a sequence.

21. To every branch connector, there must correspond a(n) _____.

22. (T or F) A branch to one entry point may occur from several different points in a flowchart.

23. A _____ is a sequence of steps to be executed a specified number of times.

24. Consider the flowchart in Figure 11.17. The flowchart depicts the logic for an automobile insurance company procedure. Record position 18 denotes marital status (M = married, S = single, O = other, such as widowed, divorced, separated). Position 19 denotes sex (M = male, F = female; blank denotes that sex is unknown). The procedure or routine determines the total number of individuals who will receive discounts because they are either: (1) female, or (2) married and male. It has been determined by several studies that female drivers and married male drivers have fewer accidents than other people. Because of this fact, this insurance company will issue discounts to those categories of people. With the following input tape records, what will be the contents of TOTAL at the end of all operations?

Tape Record Number	Contents of Position 18	Contents of Position 19
1	M	M
2	M	F
3	S	M
4	M	F
5	O	F
6	M	—
7	S	F
8	M	M

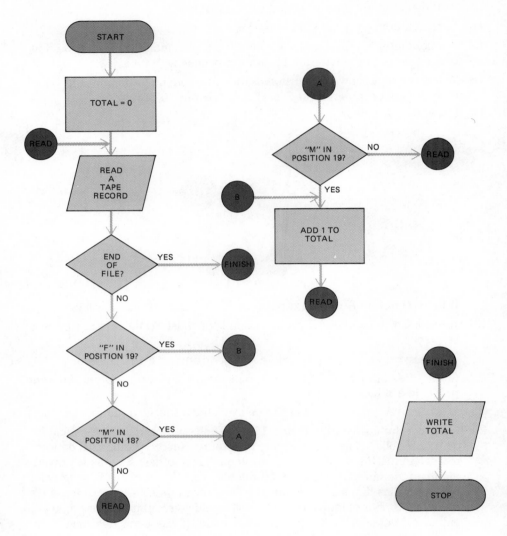

Figure 11.17
Flowchart for Question 24.

Consider the flowchart in Figure 11.18 for questions 25 to 31.

25. For every _(no.)_ records read, 1 line is printed.
26. When there are no more records, a(n) _____ to _____ occurs.
27. At EOJ, _____ is printed that is obtained from the total of all _____.
28. INDEX is a field used as a _____ for _____.
29. After 10 records have been read and added, a branch to _____ occurs.
30. After the data has been printed for each group of 10 records, _____ and _____ must be initialized at zero.
31. Each time a record is read and an amount is added to TOTAL, _(no.)_ is added to INDEX.

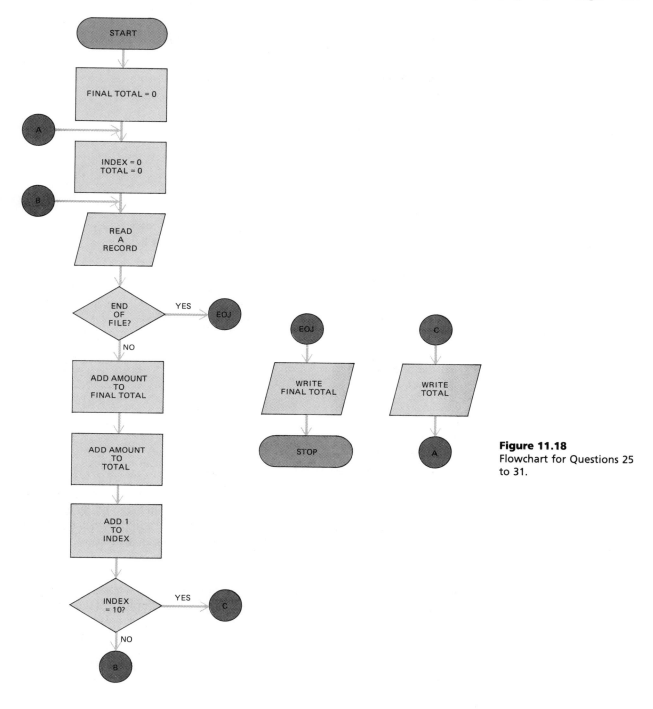

Figure 11.18
Flowchart for Questions 25 to 31.

Solutions

1. order or logical flow
   functions or operations
   program

2. symbols
   flowlines

3. top
   bottom
   left
   right
4. a function (unless a branch occurs)
5. flowlines
   note
6. template
7. processing
8. input/output (I/O)
9. decision
10. unconditional branch connector
11. entry connector
12. entry connector
13. conditional branch connector
14. terminal
15. processing
16. instruction
17. conditional branch connector
   next sequential step
18. branch
19. branch
    C
20. last
21. entry connector
22. T
23. loop
24. 6
25. 10
26. branch
    EOJ
27. a final total
    amount fields
28. counter
    looping
29. C
30. INDEX
    TOTAL
31. 1

B. Illustrative Flowcharting Procedures

At this juncture, you have learned the symbols and some of the techniques that may be used in a program flowchart. You have also been given many examples that show you how to read program flowcharts. This section provides additional examples designed to assist you in learning to draw your own flowcharts.

Example 1

Draw a flowchart that prints the names of all employees whose salary is less than $5000 and creates a tape file of the names of all employees whose salary is greater than $20,000. Assume that there are two input fields, NAME and SALARY, for each input employee record that is entered on a terminal.

The creation of tape files is depicted in a program flowchart in exactly the same way as the creation of print files. Instead of saying WRITE A LINE or PRINT A LINE we may say WRITE A TAPE RECORD.

Try drawing the flowchart on scrap paper. Programmers use either plain paper or a special form called a Flowcharting Worksheet for drawing flowcharts. Once you have completed your flowchart, compare your results with the flowchart in Figure 11.19, which has been prepared on a Flowcharting Worksheet.

Your sequence of symbols should be similar to that of Figure 11.19 but your notes inside the symbols may vary. The translation of these notes into

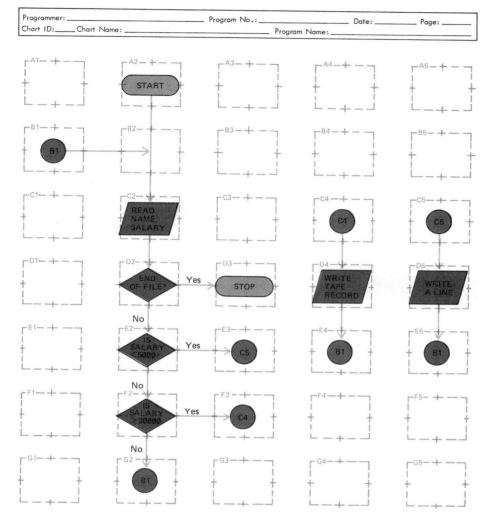

Figure 11.19
Flowchart for Example 1.

proper programming form depends on the programming language used. Thus as long as you convey the correct idea, the actual note may vary.

Note, also, that the mathematical symbols for "less than" and "greater than" are commonly used in flowcharts as they are in actual programs. These symbols are:

Symbol	Meaning
<	Less than
>	Greater than

Example 2

Draw a flowchart to do the following:

1. If a CODE field on a record is 1, AMT is added to TOTAL and the new TOTAL is printed.

2. If the CODE field is 2, AMT is subtracted from TOTAL and the new TOTAL is printed.
3. If CODE is neither 1 nor 2, the error message "INVALID CODE" is printed.

Each record contains values for CODE, AMT, and TOTAL. Your flowchart should look something like the one in Figure 11.20. If your flowchart differs substantially, check the sequence of the illustrated flowchart to make certain you understand the logic flow.

Example 3

Using a loop procedure, draw a flowchart to read in tape records and print the total number of records read. See Figure 11.21 for a solution.

As we have seen previously, by adding 1 to a counter each time a record is read, we can accumulate the total number of records read.

Figure 11.20
Flowchart for Example 2.

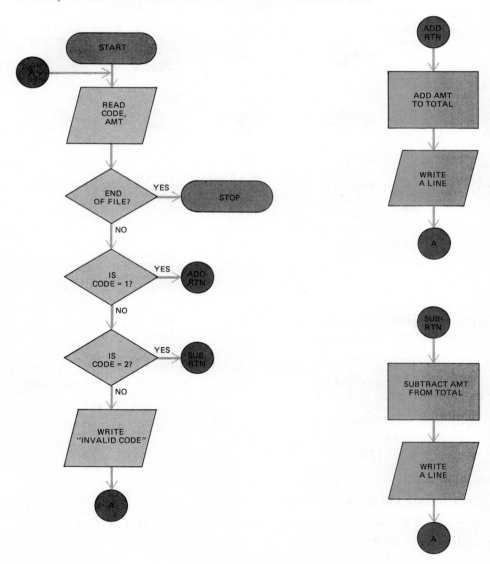

Notice that in the flowchart in Figure 11.21, a single total will print without any reference to the meaning of that number. To prevent any misinterpretation of output, it is considered good programming form to include a constant or literal that explains the meaning of the printed number. Thus, the following would represent a somewhat more meaningful sequence at EOJ.

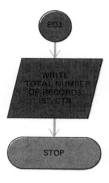

Example 4

Draw a flowchart that will sum the odd numbers from 1 to 101. (*Hint:* start CTR at 1 and add 2 each time. There is no need for input in this problem since we know in advance what our variables are: 1, 3, 5, . . . 101) (see Figure 11.22).

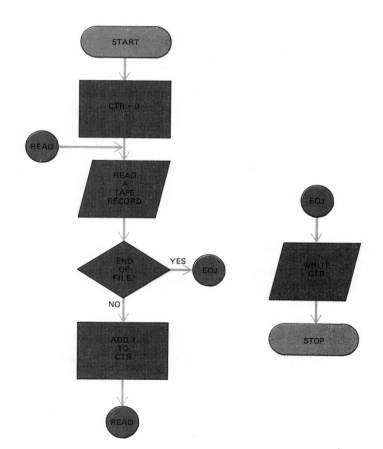

Figure 11.21
Flowchart for Example 3: printing the number of records read.

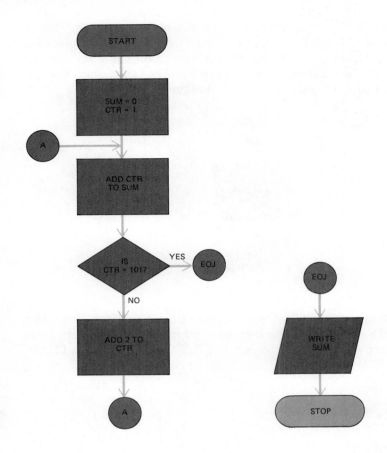

Figure 11.22
Flowcart for Example 4:
summing the odd integers
from 1 to 101.

III. FLOWCHARTING BUSINESS APPLICATIONS

Now that we have noted the basic symbols used to create simple flowcharts, let us study illustrative business applications.

Example 5 A Banking Operation

A banking organization uses magnetic tape to store all transaction data for the week. The tape format is as follows:

ACCOUNT NO.	CUSTOMER NAME	TRANSACTION TYPE (B, W, D)	AMOUNT

Tape records are in sequence by ACCOUNT NUMBER. Each customer has one type "B" record designating the balance on hand at the beginning of the week. This "B" or balance record will be the *first* record for each account or customer. In addition, there may be several "D" (deposit) or "W" (withdrawal) records following a "B" record for a customer, depending on the number of transactions made during the week. Thus, all records for a single customer account will appear together, with the "B" record being the first for the group.

The output of the program will be a printed report with the following information.

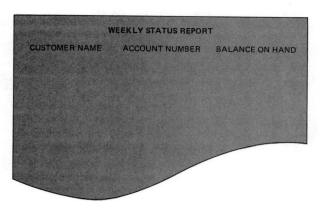

```
BALANCE ON HAND = BALANCE (from "B" record)
                + DEPOSITS (from "D" records)
                - WITHDRAWALS (from "W" records)
```

The flowchart is illustrated in Figure 11.23. Note that the headings are printed first, prior to any tape processing. In some programming languages, information to be printed must first be moved to the print area *before* it is printed; in other languages this MOVE statement is not necessary. We have included the MOVE here for the sake of completeness.

Since the first record read is a "B" record, a branch to NEW-ACCT occurs, where a line is printed. For normal processing this line contains the data for *the previous account.* That is, a "B" record signals the start of a new account and thus the previous account must be printed. For the very first record in the file, however, there is no previous account. Since no data was moved to the print area, a blank line is, in effect, printed at the beginning. The TOTAL area is cleared and data from this new balance record is moved to the print area. Additional tape records are read. Deposits, denoted by "D" records, are added to the TOTAL, and withdrawals, denoted by "W" records, are subtracted from TOTAL. There may be many "D" and "W" records for a specific account, depending on the number of transactions for the week. Processing of withdrawals and deposits continues until a new "B" record for the next customer is read. When this new "B" record is read, the previous data (NAME, ACCOUNT NUMBER, and BALANCE ON HAND) is printed, the print area is cleared, and the data for the new customer is processed.

Each record read is tested for a "B," "D," or "W." If it is a "B" record, it signals a new account, since the first record of an account must contain a "B" record. If it is a "D" or "W" record, the amount is added or subtracted, correspondingly. If it is not a "B," "D," or "W" record, then an error message is printed. It is always good practice to test for valid codes in a program, since input errors may occur.

When there are no more records to be read, a branch to EOJ occurs. At

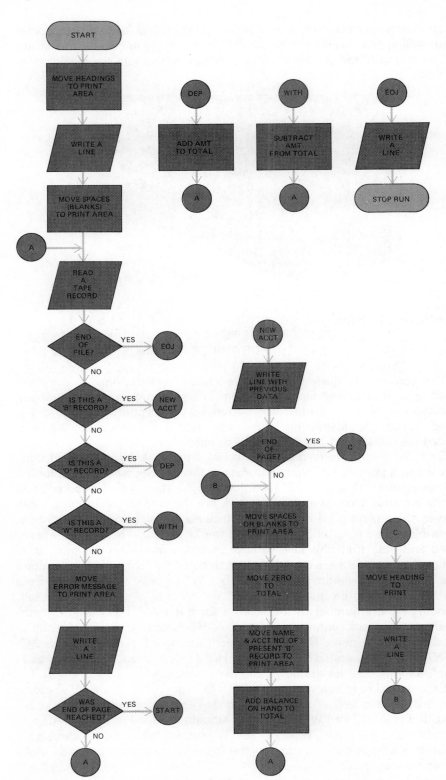

Figure 11.23
Flowchart for Example 5:
illustration of a banking
operation.

EOJ, we must print the *last* account group. Since accounts are printed only when a new account number (a "B" record) is read, the last account must be "forced." That is, the last account group does not have a "B" record following it to signal a print routine. Thus at EOJ, a print routine must be performed.

Note, too, that print programs should test for the end of the page. When the end of a page has been reached, we generally wish to print headings on top of the next page.

Example 6 Simplified Accounts Receivable Billing Procedure

This program will utilize, as input, a master file with information on charge accounts for a particular department store. The input is on tape.

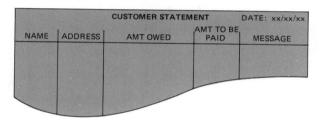

ACCT NO.	NAME	ADDRESS	TYPE OF ACCT	AMT OWED	NO. OF MOS. THAT ACCT IS IN ARREARS

The output is a monthly statement or bill submitted to the customer.

CUSTOMER STATEMENT				DATE: xx/xx/xx
NAME	ADDRESS	AMT OWED	AMT TO BE PAID	MESSAGE

Note that the bills are produced on a series of preprinted continuous forms that already contain headings. The program must merely insert the date and the required information.

The operations to be performed are as follows.

Compilation of Billing Data

If TYPE OF ACCOUNT contains a 1 (regular charge account), the *entire* bill is to be paid each month. In this case, AMT OWED is transmitted to the output field, AMT TO BE PAID, with no interest computed.

If TYPE OF ACCOUNT is a 2 (budget charge account), then 1/12 of AMT OWED + INTEREST CHARGE (1.5% of entire AMT OWED) is recorded on the bill as AMT TO BE PAID.

In each case, NAME, ADDRESS, and AMT OWED are placed directly on the customer statement from the master tape. DATE is stored in the CPU; that is, it was entered by the computer operator from a terminal at the start of the day.

Determination of Charge Status

The field called NO. OF MOS. THAT ACCT IS IN ARREARS denotes the number of months since a payment has been made to an account with a balance due. If two months have elapsed (a 2 is in the field), then a message: RE-

MINDER—YOUR ACCOUNT IS IN ARREARS is to print on the statement. If three months have elapsed (a 3 is in the field), then a message: WARNING—YOUR CHARGE PRIVILEGES HAVE BEEN SUSPENDED is to print.

A separate monthly run of another program provides a listing of all customers who have not made payments in three months. This list is then distributed to sales personnel, who are told not to honor the customer's charge card.

The flowchart is indicated in Figure 11.24.

Figure 11.24
Flowchart for Example 6: Simplified Accounts Receivable billing procedure.

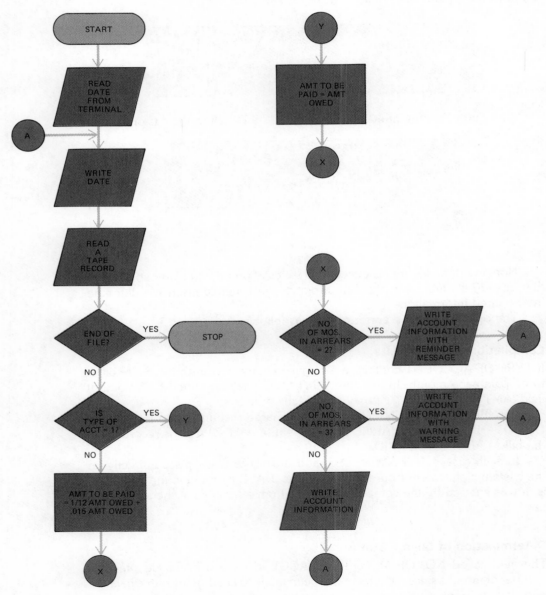

Self-Evaluating Quiz

1. (T or F) A flowchart is read sequentially from top to bottom, unless a branch alters the flow.

2. (T or F) If a programmer draws a flowchart before he or she codes a program, the program will always run flawlessly.

3. (T or F) A flowchart is a group of symbols connected by flowlines that depicts the logic that will be used in a program.

4. (T or F) A flowchart is a standard method of representing the flow of data.

5. (T or F) A terminal symbol is usually the end point in an end-of-job routine.

6. (T or F) A flowchart indicates the steps involved in a program, the sequence or order of these steps, and the number of input records.

7. (T or F) In general, each operation denoted in a flowchart converts to a program step during coding.

8. (T or F) Each decision symbol must be associated with a conditional branch connector.

9. (T or F) There is no standard method for flowcharting.

Use Figure 11.25 to answer questions 10 to 13.

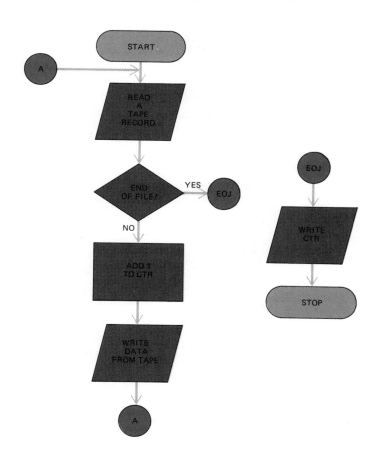

Figure 11.25
Program flowchart for
Questions 10 to 13.

10. (T or F) After each READ instruction, an end-of-file test is performed.
11. (T or F) At the end of the job, CTR will always contain 10.
12. (T or F) For each record read, two lines are printed.
13. (T or F) The program flowchart contains a logically correct set of procedures.

Use Figure 11.26 to answer questions 14 to 16.

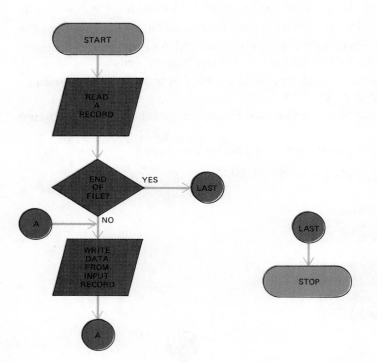

Figure 11.26
Program flowchart for
Questions 14 to 16.

14. (T or F) The program flowchart prints data from a series of input records.
15. (T or F) Only one record is read according to this flowchart.
16. (T or F) Unless the program is terminated by a computer operator, the logic depicted will cause the printing of the same data indefinitely.

Use Figure 11.27 to answer questions 17 to 20.

17. (T or F) The flowchart depicted in Figure 11.27 contains a logically sound set of procedures.
18. (T or F) The total number of drivers (TOTAL) will print if the program written from this flowchart is executed.
19. (T or F) Only two lines print as a result of the logic depicted.
20. (T or F) If a branch to TOTAL1 occurs, there will be no test performed to determine the person's sex.

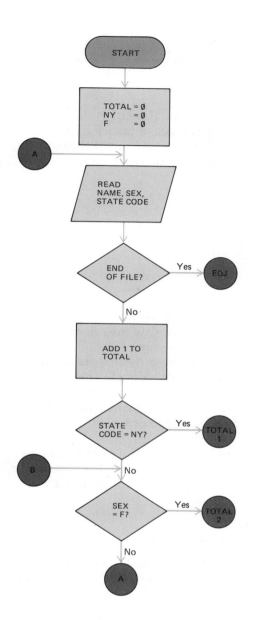

Input Format				
DRIVER NO.	NAME	SEX	STATE CODE	ADDITIONAL DATA

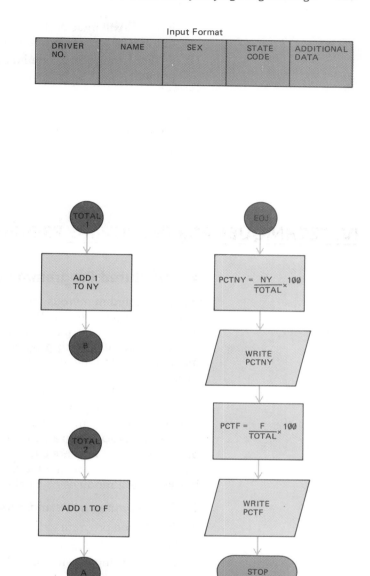

Figure 11.27
Program flowchart for
Questions 17 to 20.

Solutions

1. T

2. F—The chances that it will run smoothly are greater, but no one can guarantee a flawless run.

3. T

4. T—Symbols and flowlines are standard.

5. T

6. F—It does not indicate the number of input records.

7. T

8. T

9. F

10. T

11. F—CTR will indicate the number of records processed.
12. F—For each record, one line is printed.
13. T
14. F—It prints the same input record over and over.
15. T
16. T
17. T
18. F—It is computed but it does not print.
19. T
20. F—After TOTAL1 is performed, a branch to B occurs, where the SEX field is then compared to an 'F'.

IV. TECHNIQUES FOR IMPROVING PROGRAM DESIGN

A. Structured Programming

We have noted numerous times in this text that one of the main problems with computerization is the lack of established standards. One area in which the need for standards is particularly great is in programming.

Until recently, each program was viewed by both programmers and their managers as a unique, individual creation. This perspective made it very difficult to assess the competence of individual programmers, to evaluate their work, or to make modifications to existing programs. As a result, many leaders in the field have been arguing for a less "ego-oriented" approach to programming, one that would be more standardized.

Structured programming is one method to standardize and improve programs so that they are easier to evaluate, debug, and modify. The structured technique consists of modularizing or segmenting each program into distinct blocks. These modules or blocks:

1. Can be written in a standardized way.
2. Enable one program to be written and debugged by a team of programmers.
3. Are used in discussion groups where a team of programmers evaluates the program using a "structured walk-through" of the modules.
4. Can be used or copied in several programs.

To enable each module to function as a stand-alone entity, branches, called "GO TO" instructions in many languages, are to be minimized. Thus, structured programming is sometimes referred to as **GO TO-less programming.** You will see in the next chapter that a branch or GO TO may be replaced by a FOR . . . NEXT loop or GOSUB in BASIC. It can also be replaced by a DO loop in FORTRAN or PL/1, or a PERFORM in COBOL.

B. Top-down Approach

Another way to improve program design is to code structured modules in decreasing order of importance. The first module is referred to as the main module, and this is followed by subordinate segments. This technique is referred to as the "top-down" approach.

C. Pseudocode: A Tool for Depicting Structured Programming Concepts

As we have indicated, a program flowchart is the traditional tool used to depict the logic flow in a program. The flowchart serves two main purposes.

Advantages of Flowcharts

1. Before coding begins, the flowchart assists the programmer in determining the type of logic to be used in a program.
2. The flowchart is a pictorial representation that may be helpful to the user who wishes to examine some facet of the logic in the program.

But despite these advantages, program flowcharts have been the subject of considerable controversy in recent years, mainly for the following reasons.

Limitations of Flowcharts

1. Program flowcharts are cumbersome for the programmer to draw. As a result, many programmers do not draw the chart until *after* the program has been completed, which, of course, defeats one of its main purposes.
2. Flowcharts are no longer completely standardized tools. The newer structured programming and top-down techniques have necessitated changes in the traditional format of a flowchart.
3. It is sometimes difficult for a user to understand the logic depicted in a flowchart. Flowcharts are not, therefore, particularly "user-friendly" tools.

To compensate for some of the shortcomings of program flowcharting, a new tool has been introduced that is specifically designed to depict the logic flow of a structured program. This tool is called **pseudocode.**

As indicated, pseudocode has been designed specifically as a method for facilitating the representation of logic in a structured program. No symbols are used, just words. As with flowcharts, the pseudocode need not indicate *all* the processing details; abbreviations are permissible. However, processing sequences are more easily specified using pseudocode.

The term pseudocode indicates that the technique is a code, similar to that used in a program. The prefix "pseudo" implies that, although this is a code similar to that used in a program, it is merely a *representation of a code* and not a language itself.

The logical control instructions within a structured design are emphasized in pseudocode. Thus the following logical control instructions are always capitalized in a pseudocode representation:

1. PERFORM . . . UNTIL or DO . . . WHILE
   These are used to indicate a sequence or module that will be executed until a specific condition is met. In place of a branch, we use PERFORM . . . UNTIL to indicate that a series of steps is to be repeated until a given con-

dition exists. PERFORM . . . UNTIL is a COBOL expression; the DO loop is used in FORTRAN and PL/1.

2. IFTHENELSE
This is used to test for an individual condition. IF a condition exists THEN perform some operation; ELSE (if the condition does not exist) perform some other operation.

All instructions under the control of the above statements are indented. The end of each sequence is written in pseudocode correspondingly as follows:

1. PERFORM . . . UNTIL   DO . . . WHILE
.   .
{Instructions to be performed}
.   .
.   .
ENDPERFORM   ENDDO

2. IFTHENELSE
.
.
.
ENDIF

A flowchart that indicates the logic flow of a structured program is somewhat different from the flowcharts thus far illustrated. To indicate that a sequence of instructions is to be performed and then control returned to the original sequence, we may use a symbol that designates a PERFORM operation as follows:

To indicate a PERFORM . . . UNTIL, we use the following series of symbols:

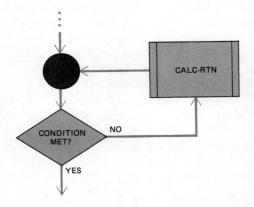

Figure 11.28 indicates the flowchart for a structured program. Note that the flowchart performs the following actions.

1. Files are opened or prepared for processing.

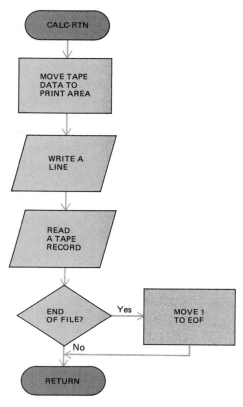

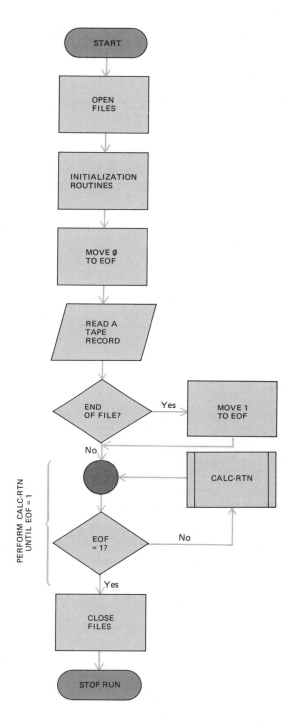

Figure 11.28
Flowchart of a structured program that reads data and prints it until there are no more records.

2. A 0 (zero) is moved to EOF. EOF is a special end-of-file indicator that is initialized at 0 and changed to 1 only *after* the last input record has been read and processed. Thus, EOF is zero throughout the entire sequence except when there are no more records to process.

3. A record is read. If there are no more records, an AT END condition is denoted, and 1 is moved to EOF.

4. A separate routine called CALC-RTN is executed repeatedly until EOF = 1, that is, until there are no more records.

5. When all input records have been processed, the files are deactivated by closing them.

6. The job is terminated by a STOP RUN command.

You will note that there are no branches at all in this flowchart. Control is retained by the main procedure or module. Minimizing the use of branch instructions is one important feature of structured programs.

The pseudocode for this flowchart is as follows.

Initialization operations

Read a tape record; at end move 1 to EOF

PERFORM CALC-RTN UNTIL EOF = 1

    Move tape data to print area

    Write a line

    Read a tape record; at end move 1 to EOF

ENDPERFORM

End-of-job functions

Stop run

Let us consider another illustration. Suppose we have sales records on a tape and we wish to determine the amount of commission to be paid to each salesperson. If sales are greater than $100, commission is equal to 10% of sales; otherwise commission is 5% of sales. The flowchart for this problem is illustrated in Figure 11.29.

To illustrate the logic in this procedure with the use of a pseudocode, we must first specify how the IFTHENELSE procedure is written.

IFTHENELSE Specifications

To indicate the testing of conditions, the following format is used in pseudocode.

IF	(condition)
THEN	(operation to be performed)
ELSE	(operation to be performed if condition is not met)
ENDIF	

The following provides an illustration of the pseudocode specification for the flowchart in Figure 11.29.

Initialization operations

Read a sales record; at end move 1 to EOF

PERFORM CALC-RTN UNTIL EOF = 1

    IF sales greater than 100.00

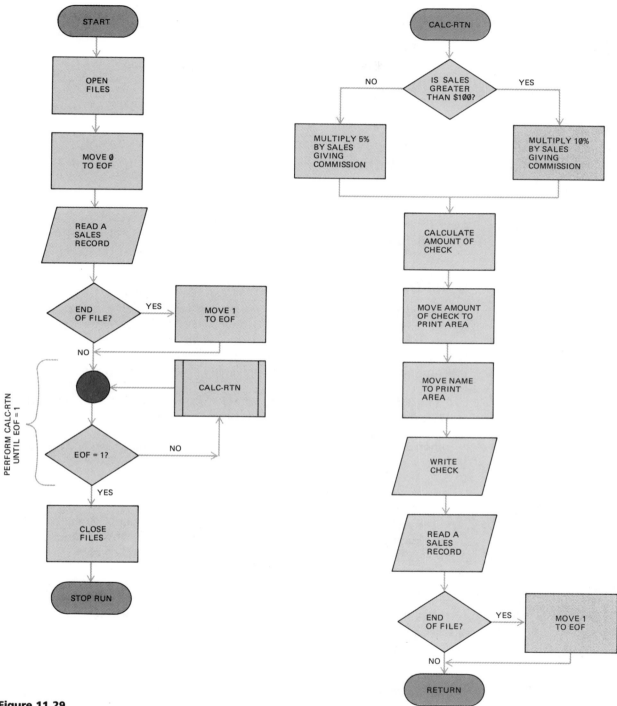

Figure 11.29
Flowchart for sales problem.

THEN

      Multiply 10% (.10) by sales giving commission

ELSE

      Multiply 5% (.05) by sales giving commission

ENDIF

Calculate amount of check = salary + commission

Move amount of check to print area

Move name to print area

Write check

Read a sales record; at end move 1 to EOF

ENDPERFORM

End-of-job functions

Stop run

D. HIPO: A Top-down Structured Design Tool

Structured programs are typically designed using a top-down approach. That is, the main module or procedure is followed by subordinate procedures, in decreasing order of significance. This makes the program easier to read and simplifies the logic as well. **HIPO charts** are ideally suited for representing top-down programming. HIPO is an abbreviation for *H*ierarchy plus *I*nput-*P*rocess-*O*utput.

    Like flowcharts, HIPO is used to graphically represent a system or program. But because it is hierarchical, HIPO is better suited for representing top-down structures in programs.

    We will consider the two facets of HIPO charts: (1) hierarchy and (2) IPO—Input-Process-Output.

1. Hierarchy Segment of HIPO

The hierarchy segment of HIPO is a treelike structure that is similar in design to an organization chart. That is, a HIPO chart, like structured programming itself, is a top-down tool—the main body or module is subdivided into minor-level items in decreasing order of importance.

    The hierarchy segment of HIPO utilizes a boxed entry to represent a specific function (see Figure 11.30).

    Reading in a top-down fashion, we find that the first box represents the system's main operations. Each subordinate box indicates a component of that system, which itself may be subdivided.

    Such a hierarchical chart displays:

(1) The main functions of the system.

(2) The subordinate requirements of each function.

(3) The interrelationship of functions.

HIPO charts make it easy to immediately determine the main components of a system. Moreover, if several programmers have been assigned the task of

Hierarchy Segment

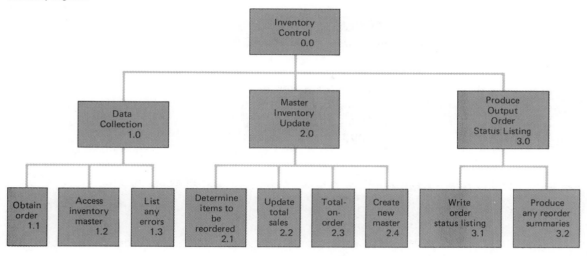

IPO Segment

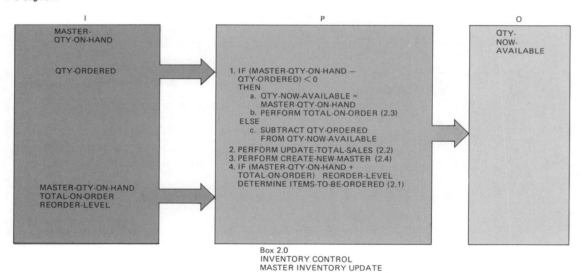

Box 2.0
INVENTORY CONTROL
MASTER INVENTORY UPDATE

Figure 11.30
Illustrative HIPO chart.

programming facets of the system, they can easily see how their programs or
program excerpts will interrelate.

2. IPO Segment

Every box of the hierarchy segment of a HIPO chart has a corresponding IPO
chart (input, process, output).

Thus the IPO charts describe the inputs, processing, and outputs of each
hierarchical block (see Figure 11.30). The process aspect of IPO reads like a
pseudocode description. The IPO charts can then serve as a set of program
specifications for the programmer or user.

CHAPTER SUMMARY

I. Tools used for planning program logic
    A. Program flowchart—a pictorial representation of the logic to be used in a program.
    B. Pseudocode—English-like method for facilitating the representation of logic in a structured program.
    C. HIPO chart—a graphical method of representing top-down structures in programs.
    D. Relationship between pseudocode and HIPO charts.
        1. Both pseudocode and HIPO charts explain the relationships among modules, and both are documentation tools.
        2. Pseudocode specifies the logical control instructions within a structured program.
        3. HIPO charts describe the input, output, and processing of each module.
II. Structured programming—an effort to standardize programs and to improve their reliability
    A. Advantages.
        1. Makes it easier to evaluate programs.
        2. Makes it easier to debug programs.
        3. Makes it easier to modify existing programs.
        4. Enables teams of programmers to work together.
    B. Features.
        1. Modules.
            Each program consists of independent modules, blocks, or segments.
        2. GO TO-less.
            GO TO or branch instructions are minimized.
III. Top-down approach.
    The main module is coded first. This is followed by subordinate modules. Modules are interrelated with PERFORM . . . UNTIL or DO loop coding.

Chapter Self-Evaluating Quiz

1. (T or F) The "last record" or end-of-file test usually appears as the last step in a flowchart.
2. (T or F) When drawing a flowchart, a programmer may arbitrarily use any name to designate a field.
3. (T or F) If the statement T = T + 1 appears in a flowchart, it would be invalid.
4. (T or F) If used, an unconditional branch connector is always the last element in a sequence.
5. A sequence of steps to be executed a specified number of times is referred to as a _____.
6. One main reason why programs have been difficult to evaluate is the lack of _____ in programming.

7. One technique used to help standardize programs is _____.

8. In a structured program, instructions are segmented into _____.

9. Because structured programming minimizes the use of branch instructions, it is sometimes called _____.

10. (T or F) In a top-down program, the main module is coded first.

11. (T or F) Flowcharts are ideally suited for depicting the logic in a structured program.

12. A tool designed to specifically depict the logic flow in a structured program is _____.

13. (T or F) Structured programming usually utilizes a bottom-up approach.

14. HIPO stands for _____.

15. (T or F) A HIPO chart is a top-down design tool.

Solutions

1. F—It typically appears after the step that reads in an input record. / page 393

2. T / page 394

3. F—It is a valid instruction to add 1 to T. / page 395

4. T / page 401

5. loop / page 402

6. standardization / page 420

7. structured programming or top-down programming / page 420

8. modules / page 420

9. GO TO-less programming / page 420

10. T / page 420

11. F—Flowcharts may be used, but they are not ideally suited. / page 421

12. pseudocode / page 421

13. F—Structured programming usually uses a top-down approach. / page 426

14. *hierarchy plus input-process-output* / page 426

15. T / page 426

Key Terms

Conditional branch
Connector
End-of-job routine
GO TO-less programming
HIPO chart
Loop

Program flowchart
Pseudocode
Routine
Structured programming
Template
Unconditional branch

Review Questions

1. A flowchart depicts the _____ that will be used in the program.

2. Each symbol in a flowchart represents a(n) _____.

3. The programmer writes _____ within each symbol.

4. Another name for a flowchart is a(n) _____.

5. For each entry connector in a flowchart there is either a corresponding _____ or a(n) _____.

6. An end-of-job condition usually occurs when _____.

7. An example of what a decision symbol may be used to denote is: _____.

8. In order to perform a looping operation, a(n) _____ must be established with an initial value of _____.

9. The symbol used to denote a processing step is a _____.

10. The symbol used to denote an input step is a _____.

11. The symbol used to denote an unconditional branch connector is a _____.

Use Figure 11.25 to answer questions 12 to 15.

12. The field CTR prints when _____.

13. Each time a record is read, _____ is performed.

14. The purpose of the flowchart is to _____.

15. The number of output lines that print is equal to _____.

Use Figure 11.26 to answer questions 16 to 19.

16. The number of lines that will print is dependent on _____.

17. The data that will print is the same as _____.

18. The end-of-job routine performs a _____.

19. The symbol with the note _____ corresponds to an entry connector.

Use Figure 11.27 to answer questions 20 to 22.

20. The data that prints as a result of these operations is _____.

21. In order to execute the TOTAL1 routine, a record must contain _____.

22. In order to execute the TOTAL2 routine, a record must contain _____.

23. Write a pseudocode to depict the logic in Figure 11.25. First restructure the flowchart so that it includes the structured technique.

24. Write a pseudocode to depict the logic in Figure 11.26. First restructure the flowchart so that it includes the structured technique.

25. If there are several complex programs to be written for one system, a HIPO chart might be a very useful analytical tool. Explain why.

26. Some claim that with structured programming, the attributes that make one a good programmer are no longer the same as they were before this technique was used. Explain why this might be so.

27. Can you think of any reasons why programmers would oppose the use of structured programming?

Flowchart Problems

1. Read in data from a terminal that consists of four test grades for each student. Compute and print each student's average.

2. Read 10 tape records, each containing two amounts. Compute and print the average of all 20 amounts.

3. Find the sum of all even numbers from 2 to 200.

4. Read in four amount fields from a terminal and print the largest. Continue to read sets of four numbers, printing the largest until the first amount field is 9999. In other words, an amount of 9999 signals an end of job.

5. Read a number N from a terminal and find N!, where N! = N × (N − 1) × (N − 2) . . . × 1 (e.g., 5! = 5 × 4 × 3 × 2 × 1 = 120).

6. Read in a series of amount fields and compute the average.

APPLICATION

TO SAVE TIME STRUCTURED PROGRAMS TAKE TIME

by Joe Celko

Several years ago, a bank in the Southeast said that it was going to adopt the newest fad in data processing (DP)—structured programming. The bank propagandized all its people about the wonders to come. It even paid for some formal training classes to show the seriousness of the task.

Nevertheless, the message got crossed up somehow: The programming team managers assumed the "improved programs" produced through structured programming would not require as many compiles during development. They actually implemented a policy of calling programmers on the carpet when they did more than two compiles on the same program.

The first result of the new program, therefore, was that employee morale dropped; and the second was that people ignored the rule altogether.

For the team manager, it made sense to represent the system this way, because the people above him complained when his programmers took up machine resources needed for production work. Therefore, an "improved program" could be assumed by the team manager to be one that reduced his problems with his bosses.

However, the improvements were supposed to come in areas other than office politics. The total time required to develop a correct—and I stress the word "correct"— program should be reduced by using structured techniques. With a structured program, the time used to maintain a program should shrink as well. Moreover, these improvements should be related to the final product, and not merely to the process that made the product.

Line management of the bank had apparently missed the whole point of structured programming. If anything, a structured-programming shop will require many more compiles per program, if you consider the logical results of the structured program development process.

A program is coded from the top down; whenever the programmer does not want to go into the details of a particular part of the process, he inserts a stub. A stub is a block of code that either does nothing but acknowledge that it has been executed or which returns some test values. The stub merely tests the program logic, and is later replaced by real code that performs the intended function. With this type of development, it is clear that the programmer should be recompiling at every level of refinement.

The top-down approach replaced the old three-step or "Wright Brothers" approach to system development, which said: First, put it all together at once. Then, run it and see if it crashes. And, finally, pick up the pieces, patch it up and repeat the previous step until you get off the ground!

Sometimes this approach required only one compile—sometimes, you win the Irish sweepstakes. And sometimes, this approach never got out of the loop between step two and step three. The point is, a line manager cannot tell by looking at the code just how close the programmer currently is to exiting the loop.

Source: Information Systems News, January 9, 1984, page 30. Reprinted with permission.

Questions
1. Understanding Key Terms
   Define the following terms as used in the application.
   a. Programming team manager.
   b. Top-down approach.
   c. Stub.

2. Software, Hardware, and Systems Concepts
   Explain the benefits and disadvantages of structured programming as specified in the application.
3. Management Considerations
   If you were a programming manager, would you require your programmers to adhere to a structured approach? Explain your answer.
4. Social, Legal, and Ethical Implications
   What are some reasons why programmers—as people—might prefer to use a non-structured approach in their programs? Should job satisfaction or preference be a factor in evaluating whether structured techniques are to be incorporated in all programs?

CASE STUDY: McKing's Superburgers, Inc.

One of the programs that will be run in each of McKing's restaurants is a prepared food status program. Every time a customer places an order, the program will update a master file of items that are available at the counter—burgers, french fries, cookies, and so on. The quantity of each item ordered will be subtracted from the total quantity on hand, which will be stored in the master file.

When the quantity on hand of an item is less than or equal to a predetermined stock point, a message will print on a printer in the kitchen that directs the cook to prepare more of that item. The stock point will be denoted as a field in *each* record. It will indicate a minimum quantity on hand for that item; if the amount on hand falls below this point, the cook is directed to prepare more. When an item is prepared in the kitchen and delivered to an inventory bin behind the counter, an entry will be made at the terminal to indicate that the quantity on hand has increased.

See Figure 11.31 for a schematic of the processing involved in this procedure.

1. Draw a flowchart for the procedure described above.
2. Write the pseudocode for the procedure described above.

Figure 11.31
Processing orders at
McKing's Superburgers.

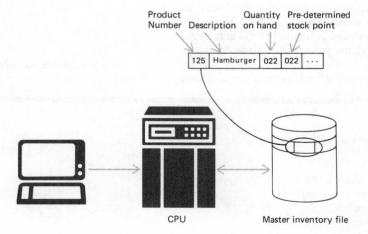

Figure 11.31 (continued)

Types of Detail Transactions

A. Customer Order

Terminal Entries at Order Counter

1. "1"—This is a code that indicates a customer order.
2. Product number—automatically entered when the key representing an item is pressed on the register.
3. Quantity ordered.

Processing:

1. Read corresponding record and compare the quantity ordered by the customer to the quantity on hand.
   a. If the quantity ordered by the customer is less than or equal to the quantity on hand, subtract the quantity ordered.
   b. If the quantity on hand is less than the predetermined stock point, print a message in the kitchen to prepare more of the item.
   c. If the quantity ordered is greater than the quantity on hand, print a message in the kitchen to prepare more of the item.

B. Addition to Food at the Counter

Terminal Entries in Kitchen

1. "2"—This is a code that indicates addition to prepared food at the counter.
2. Product number automatically entered when the key representing an item is pressed on the register.
3. Quantity added to food at the counter.

Processing:

Read corresponding record and add quantity entered to quantity on hand.

CHAPTER 12

PROGRAMMING IN BASIC

CHAPTER OBJECTIVES

To familiarize you with:

- Interacting with a terminal or micro.
- Rules for coding in BASIC.
- Logical control procedures in BASIC.
- How to write elementary and intermediate programs in BASIC.

I. AN OVERVIEW

A. Why Learn BASIC?

The BASIC language is considered the most suitable for a first-level introduction to programming because:

Features of BASIC

1. It is relatively easy to learn.
2. It is relatively easy to code.
3. It can be programmed on a terminal; that is, it provides the student with an ability to interact directly with a computer.
4. It is the most commonly used programming language for mini- and micro-computer systems.

B. The Two Facets of Programming in BASIC

Because a BASIC program is most frequently entered into a computer system via a keyboard on a terminal or micro, there are two aspects to learning how to program in this language:

1. Interacting with the terminal or micro.
2. Programming in BASIC.

Note that neither of these facets is as standardized as one would like. Here again, the lack of overall standards in the computing field results in some difficulties for potential programmers.

1. Each computer system has its own **protocol** or method used to access the system. This protocol is dependent on the type of security required at the specific installation, the access modes available, the programming languages used, etc.
2. The BASIC programming language is relatively standard but there are numerous versions that offer additional options. That is, a simple program written in BASIC for one system can usually be run on any other system with a BASIC interpreter or compiler. Many minis and micros, however, allow the use of numerous additions to the standard. These are called **enhancements**. There are various types of extended BASIC that are available depending on the mini or micro used. Although the versions are not 100% standardized, they are very similar. We will, however, focus on the standard version of BASIC in this chapter. Appendix A discusses many of the enhancements that are available.

Interacting with the terminal or micro requires some knowledge of the *systems software* used. Programming in BASIC requires knowledge of *application software*.

C. Summary of the BASIC Language

The following is a summary of BASIC features discussed in Chapter 10:

IIII➡ **Summary**

1. BASIC was specifically developed for use in a time-sharing environment.
2. BASIC is usually entered into a computer system on a terminal or on a micro or mini in an interactive mode.
3. BASIC is an abbreviation for *Beginner's All-purpose Symbolic Instruction Code.*
4. BASIC is a relatively simple language to learn and code.
5. Although a BASIC program is most often keyed into a computer on a terminal or a micro, it can first be entered on punched cards or tape in a batch mode and then compiled, if desired.
6. All programs must first be coded and then translated. These programs must then be tested with sample data to ensure their accuracy.
7. In BASIC, test data, like instructions, is usually entered on the terminal or micro (or on punched cards in batch mode).

II. INTERACTING WITH A COMPUTER SYSTEM USING A TERMINAL

Actually accessing the computer system via the terminal or micro is usually the most awesome aspect for beginners. Note, however, that although it may take some practice to understand the **log-on procedures** or system commands required, it is virtually impossible for you to damage the system (a fear expressed by many novices), unless of course you physically abuse it.

Since the log-on procedures and system commands vary depending on the system, your instructor will provide you with the precise specifications for your system. This unit focuses on typical methods for interacting with a computer.

A. Type of Computer

BASIC programs can be entered and run on virtually any computer that has a BASIC compiler or interpreter. These computers fall into two categories: (1) minis or micros and (2) mainframes that can be accessed with the use of a terminal. Entering and running on the former requires far less in the way of system commands than the latter. This is because there are fewer options available to the user of a mini or micro; hence the commands to access the BASIC compiler or interpreter are simple.

Regardless of the computer used, system-dependent commands for entering the program and translating it will be required. This section simply provides an overview.

1. Mini or Micro

Some micros have their BASIC translator hard-wired as ROM, which means that BASIC is available to the user as soon as the system is turned on. You simply begin entering the BASIC program without having to call in the translator. This is obviously the easiest method of interaction. After entering a program to be compiled, for example, the user simply types RUN to have it translated and executed.

Other micros and minis have their BASIC compiler or interpreter stored with the operating system. Each operating system has its own method for entering programs and calling in translators. The following is an example of how the user might interact with the system to enter BASIC and then compile it when the CP/M operating system is used.

I. Entering a BASIC Program

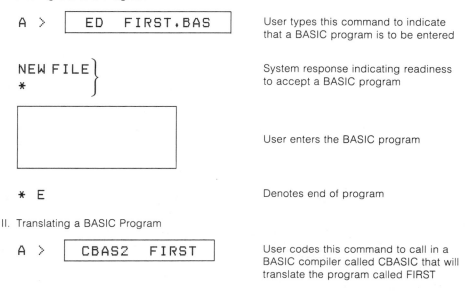

A > | ED   FIRST.BAS | User types this command to indicate
                                that a BASIC program is to be entered

NEW FILE   System response indicating readiness
*   to accept a BASIC program

                                User enters the BASIC program

* E   Denotes end of program

II. Translating a BASIC Program

A > | CBAS2   FIRST | User codes this command to call in a
                                BASIC compiler called CBASIC that will
                                translate the program called FIRST

2. Mainframe

Typically a user will enter a BASIC program on a mainframe using a terminal in an interactive mode. Some older batch-oriented systems, however, still use punched cards to enter programs.

When terminals and a mainframe are used to enter BASIC programs, there will be numerous users running programs at the same time. In such instances, the users must identify themselves to the system. The computer then determines if each one has authorization to use the system. After gaining access to the system, a user must then indicate his or her intention to enter a BASIC program.

B. Logging On to a Mainframe

1. Gaining Access

Identifying yourself or gaining access to a mainframe is called logging on. Note that log-on procedures are usually not required for micros.

The following are typical methods for accessing a CPU.

a. Dialing Up the CPU Using a Telephone   Some terminals use telephone lines for "calling up" a CPU. Along with the terminal, there is a telephone and an acoustic coupler or modem for digital-to-analog transmission. If your system requires a dial-up, you will be given the appropriate telephone number by your instructor.

b. Turning on Hard-Wired Terminals That Are Linked Directly to a CPU If each terminal is linked by cable to a CPU, the terminal can simply be turned on to gain access to the mainframe.

2. Steps for Logging On

Once you have gained access via a terminal, you must indicate:

1. Your authorization code.
2. Your intention to enter a BASIC program.

These procedures are part of *job control* and are dependent on the protocol established at your installation.

The following are examples of typical log-on procedures. The boxed entries are supplied by the user.

```
%E222 PLEASE LOGON
/ LOGON CSA010,AZ129
% E223 LOGON ACCEPTED FOR TEN 2202, ON 04/11/86 AT 1434, LINE 050,
 ***HOFSTRA UNIVERSITY COMPUTING FACILITY***
   ***UNIVAC 90/60 MOD 2---VS/9 VER 3.5***
/  EXEC BASIC
% P500 LOADING VER# 009 OF BASIC.
BASIC 09, NEW OR OLD
*  NEW
NEW PROGRAM NAME-- STERN
READY
```

```
HELLO
RSTS V7.0-07 18-NOV-86 13:51
# 147,1
PASSWORD:  STERN2
PLEASE ENTER YOUR ID CODE:  S1563
YOUR ID CODE HAS BEEN VALIDATED. WELCOME TO RSTS/E V7.0!
WOULD YOU LIKE TO CREATE A NEW FILE (TYPE NEW), OR
      RETRIEVE AN OLD FILE (TYPE OLD) →  NEW
NEW FILE NAME -  NEW PROG1 BASIC
READY
```

Figure 12.1 illustrates how terminals may be used for entering BASIC programs.

In summary, consult your systems manual or your instructor to determine how to log on and then enter a BASIC program.

3. Transmitting a Log-On Message or an Instruction to the CPU

Most terminals have a standard keyboard for typing instructions. The printing

1. Hardwired system

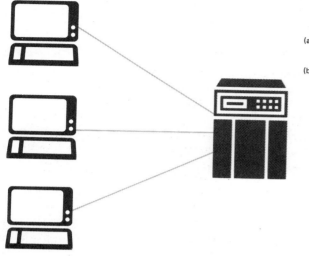

(a) Terminals have direct access to the CPU via cables.

(b) Turning on the terminal provides immediate access to the CPU.

2. Dial-up system

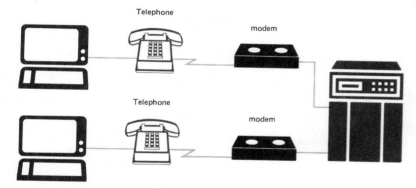

(a) User dials up or keys telephone number of the system and places telephone on the modem.

(b) When the connection is made, a high-pitched signal will be transmitted from the CPU to the telephone.

Figure 12.1
How terminals may be used to enter BASIC programs.

of these instructions and the computer's responses vary; in some cases it is a visual display, in other cases it is a typewritten printout.

After gaining access, the programmer types any message or any BASIC instruction and then depresses a control key to indicate the end of the line; usually this is a RETURN key. On some systems, however, the user must hold down both the CONTROL key and the letter C, for example, to indicate the end of the line.

Only after the control key has been depressed will the line be transmitted to the CPU. This enables the user to take as long as necessary to key in each line.

C. Correcting Typographical Errors

Typographical errors may occur during log-on procedures or during the coding of the BASIC program itself. In either case, the same rules apply.

1. Backspacing

If a key has been depressed incorrectly, it is possible to backspace or override the specific character before the line is transmitted to the CPU.

◀ How Backspacing is Performed on Some Systems

Examples

1. DEL or ERA key—depressing the DEL (delete) or ERA (erase) key on many CRTs deletes the character entirely.

2. ← key: each ← backspaces one character.

3. @ key: each @ backspaces one character; for example, LOGG@ON is transmitted as LOGON.

2. Correcting or Deleting a Line

Suppose you notice that you have made a mistake *after* you transmit a line to the CPU. That is, you have already depressed the control key.

If you made a mistake in your log-on procedure, the computer will respond by asking you to retype your response. Hence, you simply retype the line.

If you made a mistake in a BASIC instruction, you do the same thing: retype the line. You will discover that all BASIC instructions require line numbers. The last line entered with a particular line number will be the only one stored. If the following lines are entered, each line 30 will replace the previous one. Thus, only 30 PRINT D will be stored.

```
30 PRNT D
30 PRINTT D
30 PRINT D
```

Example

Coding	Explanation
10 PPPRINT "HI THERE"	(*Note:* PRINT is spelled incorrectly.)
10 PRINT "HI THERE"	(Simply retype to correct the spelling.)

The last instruction numbered 10 will replace the previous one in which PRINT was spelled incorrectly. Typing a line number by itself will eliminate that line from the program. Thus typing 10 by itself will delete line number 10.

3. Inserting a Line in a BASIC Program

As noted, all BASIC instructions require line numbers. If you have inadvertently omitted an instruction, you can enter it, even out of sequence, by giving it an appropriate line number.

Suppose that while entering a program, you type:

```
20 LET D = A + B - C
30 PRINT D
```

Line 10, which was to read values for A, B, and C, was inadvertently omitted. The omitted line (line 10) can be typed directly *after* line 30, but it must contain its appropriate line number indicating where it belongs in the sequence of instructions. Thus, the following sequence is valid.

```
20  LET D = A + B - C
30  PRINT D
10  INPUT A,B,C
```

The computer automatically executes BASIC statements in sequence *by their line numbers*, regardless of the order in which they are typed. If you need to add an instruction between lines 20 and 30, give it an appropriate line number such as 25.

Summary

1. BASIC instructions begin with line numbers.
2. Programs are coded in line number sequence.
3. Line numbers should be 10, 20, 30, etc. to allow for insertions.

D. Running a Program

Once the program has been entered, it must be tested and debugged. Sample data is used to determine if the program's logic produces the correct results.
    To run or execute a program, type in a *system command*:

RUN

Example

```
10  INPUT A, B, C
20  LET D = A + B - C
30  PRINT D
40  GO TO 10
50  END
RUN
?1, 2, 3
0
?2, 2, 1
3
```

Note: The appropriate method to terminate the run will be discussed shortly.

E. Listing a Program

Programs should be "proofread" for typographical mistakes and logic errors before they are run. It often becomes difficult to proofread a program, however, if there have been many changes made as the instructions have been entered. Consequently, before we type RUN, we often type LIST first to have the computer print out a "clean" copy of the program with all changes made. It should be noted that LIST has no line number since it is a system command.

Using the LIST command, we may check the program before it is executed. For example, consider the following, which is a two-line program that prints the message HI THERE. We use quotation marks around messages to be printed:

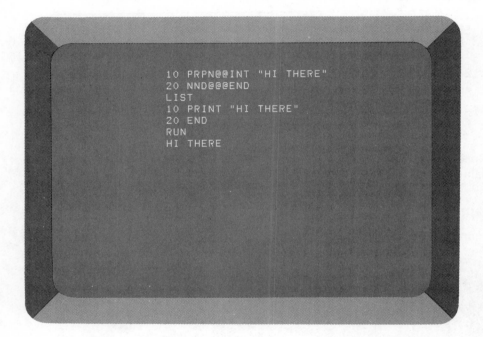

```
10 PRPN@@INT "HI THERE"
20 NND@@@END
LIST
10 PRINT "HI THERE"
20 END
RUN
HI THERE
```

Each @ indicates that a typographical error was made. The LIST command permits us to read the program before we run it.

There is another use for the LIST command. If a BASIC program has been stored on a tape or disk and a user wants to run it, he or she may want it to be listed out first. With a listing, the user can review the logic used. He or she can then make any modifications that may be deemed necessary. If, as an example, the above program had been previously stored as PRT, the following entries could be used.

```
EDIT PRT BASIC
LIST
```

EDIT indicates that the BASIC program called PRT is to be entered if it is not on file or to be retrieved if it already exists. LIST then prints the stored program.

It is a good idea to LIST a program before you RUN it to check for typographical errors. If you detect an error, simply rekey the line using the same line number. If a line has been omitted, enter it with a line number that would place it in proper sequence.

F. Saving a Program

After a program has been entered and executed, the programmer may wish to save it for future processing. To do so, you must usually type in SAVE with the name of the program.

Example

```
SAVE TEST1
```

The computer will store the program called TEST1 on its auxiliary storage medium. In this way, you can call for this program whenever you need to by typing in a system command such as:

```
LOAD TEST1
```

Note once again that many of these rules will vary slightly from one system to the next. Running, listing, saving, and loading programs require knowledge of systems software. Actual BASIC programming is called application programming and is discussed in the next section.

Advice for First-Time Terminal Users

Ask your instructor or computer center aides how to:

1. Access the system.
2. Log-on.
3. Transmit a line.
4. Access the BASIC compiler or interpreter.
5. Delete a character or backspace.
6. Delete a line.
7. If possible go back to a previous line and make direct changes. (*Note:* You can always retype the entire line.)
8. Store or save programs.
9. Load previously stored programs.
10. Create test data.
11. Erase files.

Self-Evaluating Quiz

1. The first step generally required to establish contact with a mainframe via a terminal is to _____.
2. Users must usually enter a(n) _____ to identify themselves to the system.
3. Once a line has been typed, a(n) _____ must be keyed to transmit the line to the CPU.
4. After the program has been typed, the user must request the computer to _____ the program with test or sample data.
5. To correct a typographical error before the line has been transmitted, you may _____.
6. One use of LIST is to instruct the computer to _____ so that _____.
7. To correct a line in BASIC after the line has been transmitted, simply _____.

Solutions

1. log on (dial up the system or turn on the switch)
2. authorization code
3. end-of-line indicator such as RETURN
4. execute or run—usually achieved by typing RUN
5. use a delete or erase key to backspace to the point of the error and type the rest of the line from that point on

6. print a "clean" listing of the program with all typographical errors corrected; the final listing is easier to read by the user
7. retype the line with the same line number

III. A REVIEW OF PROGRAMMING

Before coding a program in BASIC, a programmer should use a planning tool such as a flowchart to depict the logical flow of data in a program. See Figure 12.2 for a sample flowchart.

After a flowchart has been prepared and the programmer is satisfied that it is correct, the program is coded and entered into the CPU. Assume the program is executed and a CRT is used for entering data:

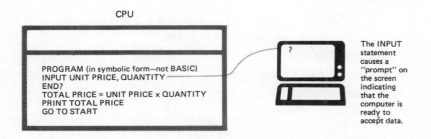

CPU

```
PROGRAM (in symbolic form—not BASIC)
INPUT UNIT PRICE, QUANTITY
END?
TOTAL PRICE = UNIT PRICE x QUANTITY
PRINT TOTAL PRICE
GO TO START
```

The INPUT statement causes a "prompt" on the screen indicating that the computer is ready to accept data.

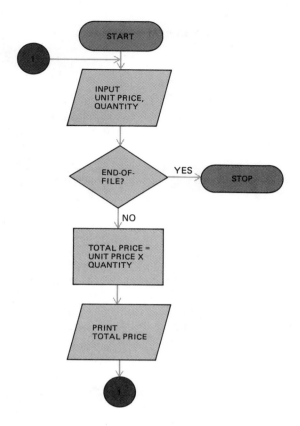

Figure 12.2
Sample flowchart.

If the program calls for input to be entered, the computer will **prompt** the user to respond with data. The prompt on the screen indicating that the computer is ready to accept data can be a ?, underline, blinking square, or cursor, etc. depending on the system. The computer waits for the user to enter data—in this instance, unit price and quantity —before continuing. Usually the RETURN key must be pressed to transmit the data to the CPU:

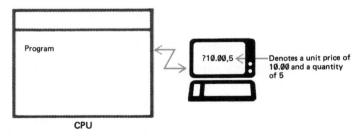

When the user hits return, this is what happens:

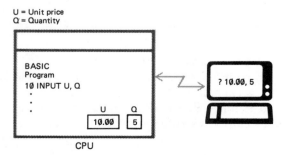

After calculating the results, the computer responds as follows:

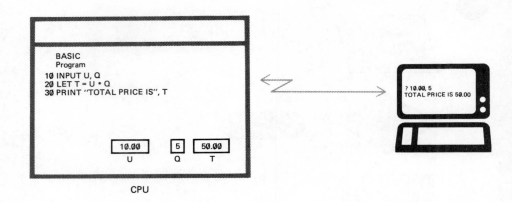

Thus when a program is run, each INPUT command causes a prompt. When the user responds and hits return, the results are transmitted to the CPU and stored in the corresponding fields, in this case U for unit price and Q for quantity. The calculations are then performed and each PRINT results in an output message.

A. An Overview

As previously noted in Chapter 4, programming in any language consists of three basic types of instructions.

Types of Instructions

Operation	Function
Input	Reads data into the computer. The data is considered *variable* because its contents are not known when we are writing the program.
Processing	Processes data by performing arithmetic operations or logical tests on the data.
Output	Produces information that results from the processed data.

Let us begin by examining some simple instructions in BASIC.

Simple Instruction Set in BASIC

Type of Instruction	BASIC Format	Example
Input	INPUT (field names)	INPUT A,B,C
Processing	LET (field name) = arithmetic expression	LET D = A+B+C
Output	PRINT (field name)	PRINT D

In the above sample, we enter into the computer three numbers, called A, B, and C. We add them and store them in a field called D. Then we print the sum stored in D. A, B, C, and D are variable field names. Using the above instructions, we can enter any numbers for A, B, and C and obtain the correct result in D. The variable field names can be used to store integer or decimal

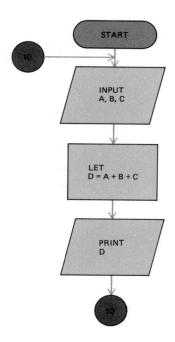

Figure 12.3
Flowchart to print the sum of three numbers.

values. Thus, 10, 36, and -5.2, for example, are valid entries. The variables cannot, however, contain a comma. Thus 1000 is a valid variable but 1,000 is not.

Note, however, that a computer program is rarely written for operating on only one set of data. Computers are usually employed for processing large volumes of data.

Thus, we would normally want to repeat the above sequence of steps for not one group of three numbers, but numerous groups of numbers. To do this, we must give each instruction a line number usually coded 10, 20, 30, and so on. After printing, we simply instruct the computer to repeat or GO TO the line number associated with the first instruction. See Figure 12.3 for the flowchart. The following is the BASIC program.

```
10 INPUT A, B, C
20 LET D = A + B + C
30 PRINT D
40 GO TO 10
```

On most computers, BASIC programs must end with an END statement to signal the computer that there are no more instructions. Thus our first complete BASIC program is as follows.

```
10 INPUT A, B, C
20 LET D = A + B + C
30 PRINT D
40 GO TO 10
50 END
```

To run this program on your computer, type in RUN. Here is a sample of the results you might get.

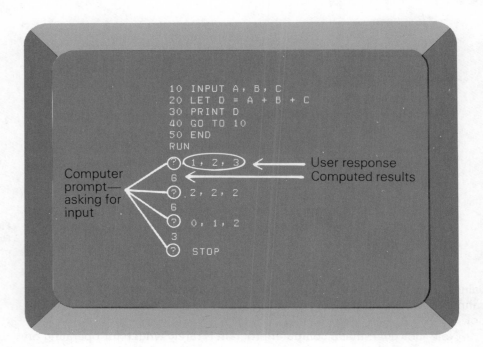

On most systems, the word STOP forces an end of job. Well-designed BASIC programs include a test for the end of data. That is, it is not generally desirable to force an end of run by typing "STOP" as we did above, although it usually works. Later on, when you become more familiar with the BASIC language we will include appropriate tests for the end of data.

B. Fundamental Rules for BASIC Programs

Rules

1. Every instruction must begin with a line number. (Typically line numbers are coded in multiples of 10, that is, 10, 20, 30, etc. to allow insertions in case an instruction was inadvertently omitted.)
2. Instructions are executed in line number sequence unless a GO TO is encountered.
3. On most computers, programs must end with an END statement.
4. Numeric variable names can be represented by a letter or a letter followed by a digit (e.g., A, A1, B6, etc.).
5. Arithmetic operations are coded with the following symbols in a LET statement.

Symbol Used	Operation
+	Addition
−	Subtraction
*	Multiplication
/	Division
**(or ↑ or ∧)	Exponentiation

6. Numeric constants can be used in arithmetic statements.

```
10 LET D = .05 * C
```

7. To branch to a different place in a program, we use a GO TO statement.

Using the seven basic rules described above, we can code a wide variety of programs.

Example 1

For a series of input data that indicate Celsius temperatures, write a program to calculate Fahrenheit temperatures (Fahrenheit = 9/5 Celsius + 32).

```
10 INPUT C
20 LET F = 9/5 * C + 32
30 PRINT F
40 GO TO 10
50 END
```

The values 9, 5, and 32 are considered **numeric constants**. Since the fraction 9/5 could be written as 1.8, line 20 above could also be coded as:

```
20 LET F = 1.8 * C + 32
```

The following is a schematic of how this program works after it has been entered.

a. Entering the Data   When the CPU executes the INPUT command, it activates the CRT and, with a prompt, it asks for input—a Celsius temperature.

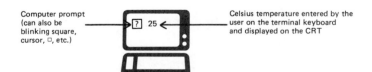

Computer prompt (can also be blinking square, cursor, □, etc.)   →   ? 25   ←   Celsius temperature entered by the user on the terminal keyboard and displayed on the CRT

b. Processing   The CPU executes the program with a value of 25 for Celsius temperature.

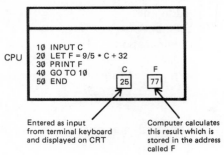

CPU

```
10 INPUT C
20 LET F = 9/5 * C + 32
30 PRINT F
40 GO TO 10
50 END
```

C = 25
F = 77

Entered as input
from terminal keyboard
and displayed on CRT

Computer calculates
this result which is
stored in the address
called F

c. Displaying the Results   The CPU transmits the results to the CRT with the PRINT F command.

? 25
77

Example 2

For each input field representing a total, called T, calculate a price, called F, that allows a 3% discount.

```
10  INPUT  T
20  LET F = T - .03 * T
30  PRINT  F
40  GO TO 10
50  END
```

Note that any quantity T minus .03 of T = .97T. Thus line 20 could be coded as:

```
20 LET F = .97 * T
```

Example 3

Two input fields are to be entered, representing hours worked, called H, and hourly rate, called R. Calculate total wages, called W, for each group of input fields.

```
10  INPUT  H, R
20  LET W = H * R
30  PRINT  W
40  GO TO 10
50  END
```

As illustrated below, the user of this program will enter data for which output information will print. When there is no more data, the user will type STOP.

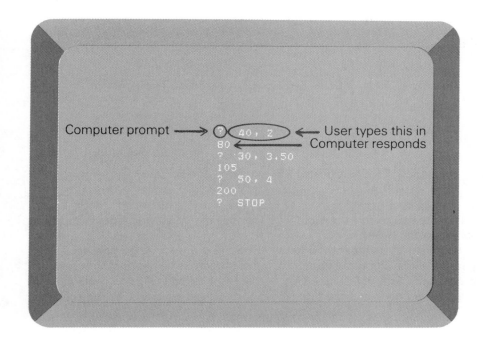

Note again that typing STOP to force an end is used here for simplicity. Later on, we will include appropriate end-of-data tests.

Note that BASIC is a free-style language, which means that any spacing between words and expressions is permissible. This freedom is one main advantage of BASIC over languages like COBOL.

C. Variations on a Theme

Before adding additional instructions to our examples, let us first consider ways in which we can supplement or vary existing instructions.

Note that in addition to computer prompts, we may print alphanumeric messages that make a program more user-friendly. An alphanumeric message is one that may include any combination of letters, digits, and symbols such as %, $, and so on.

1. We can give the user directions by printing a message before the INPUT command.

2. Along with printing the result, we may print a message identifying what the result is.

Each PRINT command results in one line of display.

We code **alphanumeric constants** in BASIC by enclosing them in quotation marks. For example,

```
10 PRINT "HI THERE, I'M YOUR FRIENDLY COMPUTER"
```

will cause the computer to print the following when statement 10 is executed.

```
HI THERE, I'M YOUR FRIENDLY COMPUTER
```

A print statement can print variables, constants, or a combination of both:

```
10 PRINT "THE TOTAL IS ",T
```

We leave a space after the word "IS" so that the value of T does not appear adjacent to the S of IS.

In a PRINT statement the items to be printed on a single line have been separated with a comma. This may result in numerous blanks or spaces between the constants and the actual data, because each variable or constant to be printed on a line is allotted a fixed number of spaces. Consider the following example:

```
THE TOTAL IS     100.00
```

To reduce the spacing between the literal THE TOTAL IS and the amount of 100.00, we may use a semicolon (;) in place of the comma. The semicolon ensures that the data will appear adjacent to the constant.

Example

Print the Fahrenheit temperatures for Celsius temperatures read in as input. Make this as user-friendly as possible.

```
10 INPUT C
20 LET F = 9/5 * C + 32
30 PRINT "FAHRENHEIT TEMPERATURE IS ",F
40 GO TO 10
50 END
```

This program will result in the following after typing RUN.

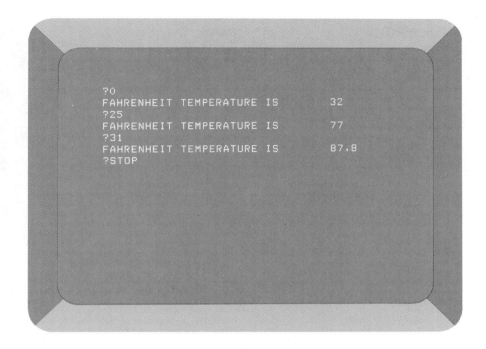

```
?0
FAHRENHEIT TEMPERATURE IS        32
?25
FAHRENHEIT TEMPERATURE IS        77
?31
FAHRENHEIT TEMPERATURE IS        87.8
?STOP
```

If we really want to be specific, we can substitute the following for line 30.

```
30 PRINT "FAHRENHEIT TEMPERATURE FOR ",C," IS ",F
```

Note again that, on many systems, STOP as an input field will cause the program to terminate the run.

Printing alphanumeric constants makes the output more meaningful. These constants can also be used for prompting the user, or explaining what input should be supplied in order to obtain meaningful output.

```
10 PRINT "ENTER A CELSIUS TEMPERATURE"
20 PRINT "I WILL THEN COMPUTE FAHRENHEIT TEMPERATURE"
30 INPUT C
40 LET F = 9/5 * C + 32
50 PRINT "FAHRENHEIT TEMPERATURE IS ",F
60 GO TO 10
70 END
```

This set of instructions will result in the following dialogue between user and computer when the program is run. The data entered by the user appears after the "?".

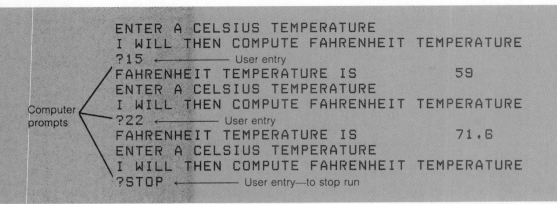

```
                  ENTER A CELSIUS TEMPERATURE
                  I WILL THEN COMPUTE FAHRENHEIT TEMPERATURE
                  ?15 ←─────── User entry
                 /FAHRENHEIT TEMPERATURE IS            59
                / ENTER A CELSIUS TEMPERATURE
               /  I WILL THEN COMPUTE FAHRENHEIT TEMPERATURE
 Computer  <──┤   ?22 ←─────── User entry
 prompts       \  FAHRENHEIT TEMPERATURE IS            71.6
                \ ENTER A CELSIUS TEMPERATURE
                 \I WILL THEN COMPUTE FAHRENHEIT TEMPERATURE
                  ?STOP ←─────── User entry—to stop run
```

If we want to print the instructions only once at the beginning, line 60 should be changed to:

10 GO TO 30

With the change in instruction 60, we would have:

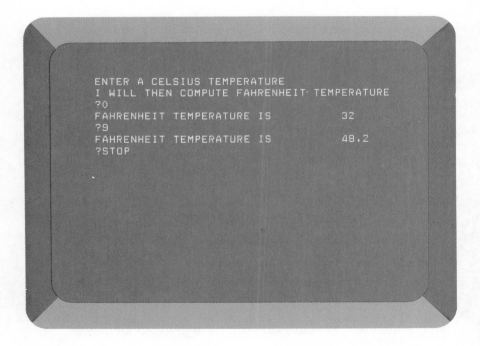

```
ENTER A CELSIUS TEMPERATURE
I WILL THEN COMPUTE FAHRENHEIT· TEMPERATURE
?0
FAHRENHEIT TEMPERATURE IS            32
?9
FAHRENHEIT TEMPERATURE IS            48.2
?STOP
```

Prompting the user of a program with a set of instructions issued at the beginning is considered a user-friendly technique.

Printing Blank Lines   The following will print a blank line:

```
10 PRINT
```

To double space between printed entries, we typically use the above PRINT before or after a PRINT statement that includes data and/or constants to be printed.

1. Hierarchy of Arithmetic Operations

The sequence in which arithmetic operations is performed may affect the results of a computation. Consider the following:

```
10 INPUT B, C, D
20 LET A = B - C * D
30 PRINT A
40 GO TO 10
50 END
```

Suppose B = 10, C = 5, and D = 2. Will the computer perform:

```
B - C * D = 10 - 5 x 2
```

as
(a) $(10 - 5) \times 2 = 10$
or
(b) $10 - (5 \times 2) = 0$

Clearly, if the computer performs the subtraction operation *first* and then the multiplication, the result will be different from that obtained by performing the multiplication first.

The following represents the hierarchy rules used by computers.

Hierarchy Rules

1. Exponentiation is performed first.
2. Multiplication and division are performed next.
3. Addition and subtraction are performed last.
4. Use of parentheses overrides all hierarchy rules.

If an instruction has two or more operations on the same level, they are executed in sequence from left to right.

Let us look again at our previous illustration:

```
20 LET A = B - C * D
```

According to the above rules, the multiplication is performed first and then the subtraction. That is, we have

```
10 - 5 * 2 = 10 - 10 = 0
```

The traditional hierarchy rules can be superseded with the use of parentheses. Thus to obtain B − C multiplied by D, we code:

```
20 LET A = (B - C) * D
```

Example 1

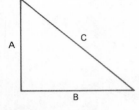

Find the value of the hypotenuse of a right triangle, where the other two sides are entered as input.

Recall that $C = \sqrt{A^2 + B^2}$. Square roots can be calculated in BASIC by raising an expression to the .5 power or by using the special function SQR.

```
10 PRINT "ENTER TWO SIDES OF A TRIANGLE"
20 PRINT "I WILL COMPUTE THE HYPOTENUSE"
30 PRINT
40 INPUT A, B
50 LET C = (A ** 2 + B ** 2)**.5
60 PRINT "THE HYPOTENUSE IS ",C
70 PRINT
80 GO TO 40
90 END
```

After typing RUN, the results will print as:

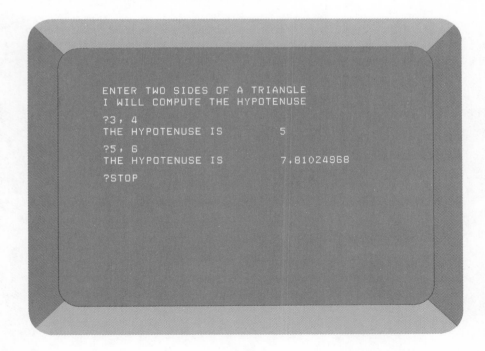

```
ENTER TWO SIDES OF A TRIANGLE
I WILL COMPUTE THE HYPOTENUSE

?3, 4
THE HYPOTENUSE IS          5

?5, 6
THE HYPOTENUSE IS          7.81024968

?STOP
```

The use of the parentheses is necessary to obtain the appropriate order of operations. Line 50 could also be replaced by using the SQR function:

```
50 LET C = SQR (A**2+B**2)
```

Do not be concerned about the use of a mathematical equation in the above. It is used simply to illustrate a point, not to remind you of high school geometry.

Example 2

Read in three exam grades for every student in a class and calculate the average grade for each student.

```
10 PRINT "ENTER THREE EXAM GRADES"
20 PRINT
30 INPUT E1, E2, E3
40 LET A = (E1 + E2 + E3)/3
50 PRINT "THE AVERAGE IS ",A
60 GO TO 20
70 END
```

The results will be:

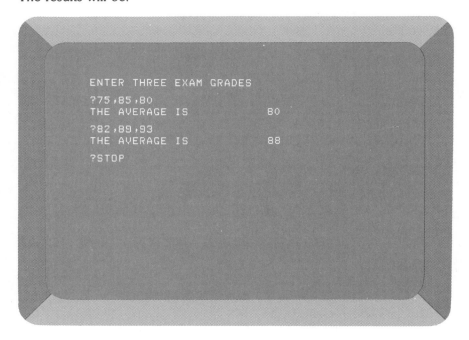

```
ENTER THREE EXAM GRADES
?75,85,80
THE AVERAGE IS          80
?82,89,93
THE AVERAGE IS          88
?STOP
```

Here, again, the parentheses are required for obtaining the proper order of evaluation. The following is incorrect:

```
40 LET A = E1 + E2 + E3 / 3
```

Based on the hierarchy rules, only E3 would be divided by 3 if the parentheses were omitted.

In summary, when we want an operation or a series of operations to be performed first, we enclose them in parentheses.

Example 3

Read in a principal amount, a rate of interest, and the number of periods of investment.

Compute the principal and interest earned after N periods of investment using the formula:

$P(1 + R)^N$ = principal + interest earned

```
 5 PRINT "ENTER PRINCIPAL AMOUNT, YEARLY RATE, NO. OF YEARS"
10 INPUT P1, R, N
20 LET P = P1 * (1 + R) ** N
30 PRINT P
40 GO TO 10
50 END
```

Self-Evaluating Quiz

1. Indicate the difference between the following statements.

```
10 PRINT 8 + 5
10 PRINT "8 + 5"
```

Indicate the result in each of the following cases:

```
2. 10 LET C = 4 + 2/(5 - 3)
3. 10 LET D = (4 + 2)/(5 - 3)
4. 10 LET E = 4 * 5 + 2
```

Indicate the error in each of the following:

```
5. 10 LET C = 2A + D
6. 10 LET A + E = G
7. 10 LET T% = .05 * F
8. 10 PRINT "THE ANSWER IS , F
```

Write a BASIC statement to perform each of the following:

9. $A = \dfrac{3 + C}{D + 7}$

10. $S = \dfrac{(T - 3)^2 - R}{6}$

Solutions

1. *Statement*   *Printed Result*
   ```
   10 PRINT 8 + 5
   10 PRINT "8 + 5"
   ```
                                       13
                                       8 + 5

2. $4 + (2/2) = 4 + 1 = 5$
3. $6/2 = 3$
4. $(4 * 5) + 2 = 20 + 2 = 22$
5. $2 * A$ as follows: `LET C = 2 * A + D`
6. Only a variable name may be used after the word LET:

   `LET G = A + E`

7. T% is not a valid numeric variable on most systems; could be T or T1.
8. Quotation marks are missing.

   `10 PRINT "THE ANSWER IS ", F`

9. `LET A = (3 + C)/(D + 7)`
10. `LET S = ((T - 3) ** 2 - R)/6`

2. Entering Alphanumeric Data Called String Variables

Thus far, we have used an INPUT statement to enter numeric variables. Recall that the rule for entering numeric variables is as follows.

Rule

Numeric variable name: a single letter
                          or
            a letter followed by a digit
            (e.g., A, A1, A9, etc.)

E1, T, N are all valid numeric variable names. But suppose we want to enter alphanumeric data such as a person's name, address, sex, or other information. We must use a string variable. The rule for a string variable name is as follows.

Rule

String variable name: Variable name followed by $
                      (a letter or a letter plus a digit,
                      and $; e.g., A$, N$, A1$, etc.)

Example 4

Read as input a student name and three exam scores. Print the student's name and the average.

```
10 PRINT "ENTER STUDENT NAME AND 3 EXAM SCORES"
20 PRINT
30 INPUT N$, E1, E2, E3
40 LET A = (E1 + E2 + E3) / 3
50 PRINT N$, "HAS AN AVERAGE OF ",A
60 GO TO 30
70 END
RUN

ENTER STUDENT NAME AND 3 EXAM SCORES

?GEORGE WASHINGTON, 80, 70, 75
GEORGE WASHINGTON   HAS AN AVERAGE OF 75
?THOMAS JEFFERSON, 90, 95, 85
THOMAS JEFFERSON    HAS AN AVERAGE OF 90
?STOP
```

D. REM Statement

Note that a line number, followed by REM, followed by anything else, will be treated as a remark or comment in the program. For example:

```
5 REM THIS PROGRAM CALCULATES FAHRENHEIT TEMPERATURE
7 REM FROM CELSIUS TEMPERATURES
```

could be added to the previous program for clarification or as a comment. This also makes a program listing more user-friendly. The remark or note will print *as part of the program*; there is no need for quotation marks at all.

REM statements may be coded anywhere within the program before the END statement. The computer ignores REM statements during execution but prints them as part of the program listing.

Do not confuse REM statements with PRINT. REM is a comment placed within the program. PRINT causes data and constants to print *as output* when the program is executed.

E. Other Uses of the LET Statement

A LET statement can be used, as noted, to perform an arithmetic operation and place the result in the variable field indicated. For example:

```
20 LET E = F - G
```

causes G to be subtracted from F and the result placed in E.

Note, however, that the LET statement does two things.

LET Statement Functions

1. Performs the calculation indicated on the right of the = sign.
2. Moves the result into the variable name specified on the left of the = sign. (Note that the element following the word LET must be a variable name, *not* an arithmetic expression; that is, LET B + C = A is *not* valid.)

Consider the following:

```
10 INPUT E
20 LET E = E + 1
```

Line 20 is an expression that is not a correct mathematical equation but that is, nevertheless, a valid BASIC statement. It performs the following:

1. 1 is added to E.
2. The result is placed in E.

Thus if E were read in as 10, 1 would be added and 11 would be placed back into E. That is, the effect of the statement

```
LET E = E + 1
```

is to add one to E.

We can use this type of expression to obtain a running total. To accumulate the sum of all transaction amounts read in, we code:

```
10 LET S = 0
20 INPUT T
30 LET S = S + T
   .
   .
   .
100 GO TO 20
```

This enables us to accumulate a running total of all amount fields. As we will see in the next section, to print this total we must instruct the computer to go to a PRINT statement after all records have been processed.

Example 5

For all salaries read in as input, provide for a $100 raise and print the new salaries.

```
10 INPUT S
20 LET S = S + 100
30 PRINT S
40 GO TO 10
50 END
```

Note that the following would produce the same results.

```
10 INPUT S
20 LET T = S + 100
30 PRINT T
40 GO TO 10
50 END
```

The LET statement can also be used to move a value into a field. For example:

```
10 LET A = 10.3
```

results in A containing 10.3.

Example 6

Our Celsius-Fahrenheit problem could be coded slightly differently as follows:

```
10 INPUT C
20 LET A = 1.8
30 LET B = 32
40 LET F = A * C - B
50 PRINT F
60 GO TO 10
70 END
```

Since A and B are always to contain 1.8 and 32, respectively, the following would serve just as well.

```
10 LET A = 1.8
20 LET B = 32
30 INPUT C
40 LET F = A * C - B
50 PRINT F
60 GO TO 30
70 END
```

In fact, the latter is more efficient since A and B are computed only once at the beginning, instead of each time a value for C is processed. Until the contents of A and B are altered by another LET statement, they remain as 1.8 and 32, respectively.

F. Conditional Statements

1. Format

Thus far we have considered the following:

Summary of Operations

1. Entering numeric and string variables as input.
2. Performing arithmetic operations using the LET statement.
3. Printing numeric and string variables, as well as constants.
4. Unconditionally transferring control in a program to some other point using a GO TO statement.

But a major aspect of programming relates to selectively processing data, depending on the contents of certain fields. That is, we may wish to calculate a commission for sales people with total sales in excess of $1000. Similarly, we may want to grant discounts selectively to customers with solid credit ratings.

To do this, we need to perform a *logical* test. The IF-THEN statement is used to perform such a test. The format of the statement is as follows.

Format of IF-THEN Statement

[line no.]   IF   [a condition exists]   THEN   [statement no. to be branched to]

For instance,

```
10 IF A = 15 THEN 60
```

means "IF A is equal to 15 go to line number 60." If A is not equal to 15, the next statement after line number 10 would be executed.

The conditions that can be specified in an IF-THEN statement are as follows.

Symbols Used in IF-THEN Statements

Symbol	Meaning
=	Equal to
<	Less than
>	Greater than
<=	Less than or equal to
>=	Greater than or equal to
<>	Not equal to

Example 1

Suppose we wish to read in a patient's name and print the message "PATIENT HAS A FEVER" for patients with temperatures in excess of 98.6. If the temperature is not in excess of 98.6, we print nothing.

The flowchart and program for this are as follows.

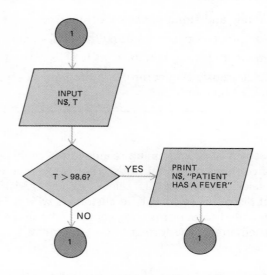

```
10 REM THIS PROGRAM PRINTS NAMES OF PATIENTS
20 REM WITH TEMPERATURES IN EXCESS OF 98.6
30 INPUT N$, T
40 IF T > 98.6 THEN 60
50 GO TO 30
60 PRINT N$, "PATIENT HAS A FEVER"
70 GO TO 30
80 END
```

Note that there are two possible sequences to be performed. For patients with temperatures of 98.6 or less, we have:

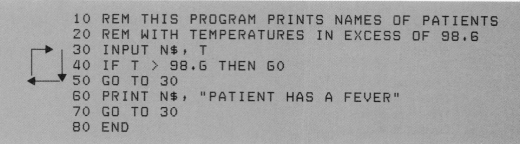

For patients with temperatures greater than 98.6, we have:

```
10 REM THIS PROGRAM PRINTS NAMES OF PATIENTS
20 REM WITH TEMPERATURES IN EXCESS OF 98.6
30 INPUT N$, T
40 IF T > 98.6 THEN 60
50 GO TO 30
60 PRINT N$, "PATIENT HAS A FEVER"
70 GO TO 30
80 END
```

We could have coded the above as follows, without affecting the results.

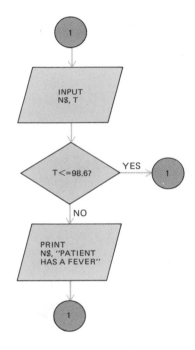

```
10 INPUT N$, T
20 IF T <= 98.6 THEN 10
30 PRINT N$, "PATIENT HAS A FEVER"
40 GO TO 10
50 END
```

2. End-of-File Condition

Thus far we have coded programs that are terminated by typing STOP. This is an artificial end-of-job procedure that is not recommended. It is far more efficient and user-friendly to test for an end-of-file condition and branch to END when it is reached. We use a trailer or dummy record to signal the end of a file.

In the above, a temperature, T, of 999, for example, is not feasible as a real temperature and hence can be used as a value to signal an end-of-file condition:

```
10  PRINT "ENTER NAME AND TEMPERATURE SEPARATED WITH A COMMA"
20  PRINT "ENTER 999 AS TEMPERATURE WHEN THERE IS NO MORE DATA"
30  INPUT N$,T
40  IF T = 999 THEN 80
50  IF T <= 98.6 THEN 30
60  PRINT N$, "PATIENT HAS A FEVER"
70  GO TO 30
80  END
```

Figure 12.4 illustrates the flowchart.

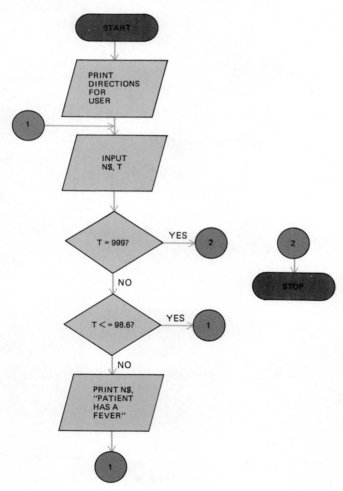

Figure 12.4
Flowchart that incorporates
an end-of-file test.

Example 2

Suppose we wish to count and print the number of entries entered as input. The PRINT statement would be executed at the end of the job, which is signaled by 999 in N. We use C as our counter field and initialize it at 0. In BASIC, it is not necessary on some systems to initialize a field at 0, but it is a useful technique to include, since such initialization is required in other languages. You will recall that incrementing C by 1 each time through a procedure is called keeping a *running total*. At the end of the job, when N is 999, we print the contents of C, which will contain the total number of records processed.

```
10 REM COUNT AND PRINT TOTAL NUMBERS ENTERED
20 LET C = 0
30 INPUT N
40 IF N = 999 THEN 70
50 LET C = C + 1
60 GO TO 30
70 PRINT "TOTAL NO. OF ENTRIES IS ";C
80 END
```

From this point on, all programs should include programmed branches to END or to an end-of-file procedure. The previous use of keying "STOP" is poor programming form and was used just as a convenience before the IF-THEN was introduced.

3. Looping

IF-THEN statements provide the programmer with a significant amount of flexibility and logical control capability. One such capability is **looping**, where we perform a given set of operations until a specific condition is reached.

Example 3

Calculate the sum of all integers from 1 to 100. No INPUT statement is required here, since we already know the variables to be processed.

On first glance, it may seem like the following would be appropriate.

```
10 LET T = 1 + 2 + 3 + ... + 100
20 PRINT T
30 END
```

Note, however, that the dots (...) would need to be replaced with the actual integers and, at best, this would be a tedious task.

Logically, the following would be more appropriate.

Statement	Meaning
10 LET S = 0	Initialize the total, S, to 0
20 LET N = 1	Initialize N to 1
30 LET S = S + N	Add N to S

Statement   *Meaning*
40 LET N = N + 1   Increment N by 1
50 IF N <= 100 THEN 30   If N is less than or equal to 100, repeat steps 30, 40, and 50
60 PRINT S   Print S when N exceeds 100
70 END   End of program

In the above, N varies from 1 to 100 and S is the variable name for the accumulator that will hold the sum of the N integers.

Thus we have:

Number of Times Through the Sequence	Value of N	Value of S
0	1	0 (all variables are initialized to 0)
1	1	1 (0 + 1)
2	2	3 (1 + 2)
3	3	6 (1 + 2 + 3)
.	.	
.	.	
.	.	
100	100	1 + 2 + 3 + ... + 100

We could have coded our summation loop in other ways as well:

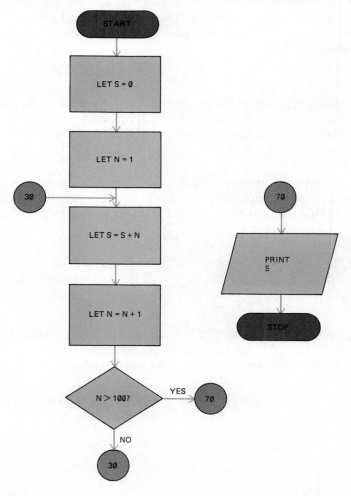

```
 5 REM SUM INTEGERS FROM 1 TO 100
10 LET S = 0
20 LET N = 1
30 LET S = S + N
40 LET N = N + 1
50 IF N > 100 THEN 70
60 GO TO 30
70 PRINT S
80 END
```

This loop procedure enables us to do a wide variety of similar operations, with only minor modifications.

Example 4

Sum all the integers from 1 to 1000.

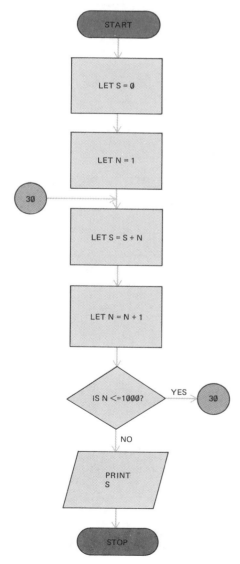

```
 5 REM SUM INTEGERS FROM 1 TO 1000
10 LET S = 0
20 LET N = 1
30 LET S = S + N
40 LET N = N + 1
50 IF N <= 1000 THEN 30
60 PRINT S
70 END
```

Example 5
Sum all the integers from 100 to 2000.

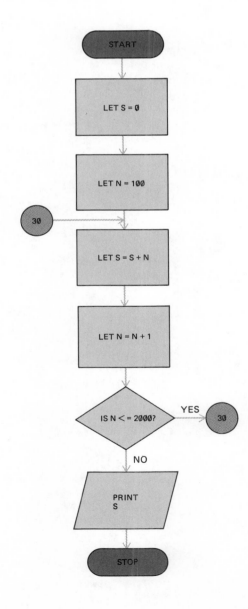

```
 5 REM SUM INTEGERS FROM 100 TO 2000
10 LET S = 0
20 LET N = 100
30 LET S = S + N
40 LET N = N + 1
50 IF N <= 2000 THEN 30
60 PRINT S
70 END
```

Example 6

Sum all the odd integers from 1 to 1001. In this case the integer, N, begins at
1 and is incremented by 2 each time.

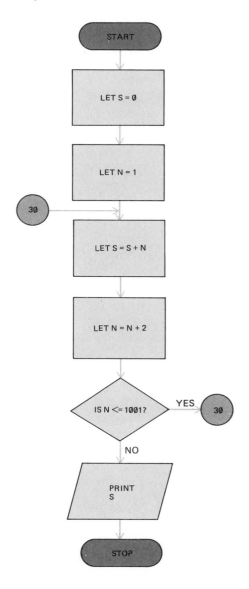

```
 5 REM SUM ODD INTEGERS FROM 1 TO 1001
10 LET S = 0
20 LET N = 1
30 LET S = S + N
40 LET N = N + 2
50 IF N <= 1001 THEN 30
60 PRINT S
70 END
```

Example 7

Read in a value for N. Compute N!, where N! = N × (N − 1) × (N − 2) ... × 1. (N! is called N Factorial.)

For example,

$$3! = 3 \times 2 \times 1 = 6 \qquad 5! = 5 \times 4 \times 3 \times 2 \times 1 = 120$$

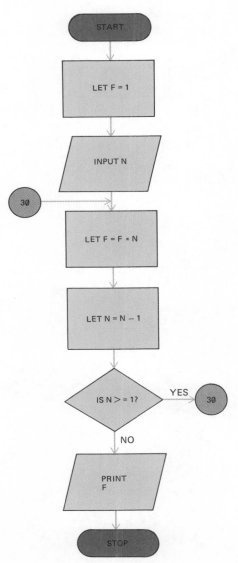

```
 5 REM CALCULATE N FACTORIAL
10 LET F = 1
20 INPUT N
30 LET F = F * N
40 LET N = N - 1
50 IF N >= 1 THEN 30
60 PRINT F
70 END
```

Suppose N = 4; the processing sequence would be as follows.

Number of Times
Through Statement 30   *F*   *N*

Through Statement 30	F	N
1	1	4
2	4	3
3	4×3	2
4	$4 \times 3 \times 2$	1
5	$4 \times 3 \times 2 \times 1$	0

$$F = 4 \times 3 \times 2 \times 1 = 24 \text{ when printed}$$

Looping operations include the following elements. The word "LET" is optional.

Example of a Loop

Sum Odd Numbers 1 to 101

Elements in a Loop

```
10 LET S = 0
```
1. Initialize S, the total, to 0.

```
20 LET N = 1
```
2. Initialize the field that will contain odd numbers.

```
30 S = S + N
```
3. Perform the required operations.

```
40 N = N + 2
```
4. Modify the field containing the odd number.

```
50 IF N <= 101 THEN 30
```
5. Test the field:
   if the operation has been performed the required number of times, you are done; if not, repeat.

```
60 PRINT S
70 END
```

Self-Evaluating Quiz

1. (T or F) The following statement is valid:

   ```
   100 LET X = A * 15,000
   ```

2. Indicate which of the following are valid variable names:

   a. A1   c. AMOUNT   e. Z53
   b. AMT   d. D   f. A$

3. A field name N would represent a(n) _____ field, whereas N$ would represent a(n) _____.

4. Indicate the results if the following is executed:

```
30 LET X = V + W/S - E + C * D
```

where V = 30, W = 10, S = 5, E = 20, C = 3, and D = 6.

5. Indicate the results if the following is executed:

```
20 LET V = W + C ** 2 - E + F/S
```

where W = 20, C = 10, E = 50, F = 20, and S = 5.

6. Write a program to calculate miles per gallon, where G is equal to the number of gallons used and T is equal to the number of miles traveled. Read in both variables as INPUT.

7. Write a series of statements to proceed to line 90 if A is between 98.2 and 100.6 including the end points. If A is not between these two points, proceed to line 190.

8. Write a series of statements to find the largest of three numbers A, B, C, and place the result in H; then proceed to line 200. Assume that A, B, and C have been read in and that this coding is only an excerpt, or part of, a larger program.

9. Write a program to read in a sales amount. If sales amount is greater than $500, allow a 5% discount. If sales amount is between $200 and $500 allow a 3% discount. Otherwise allow a 2% discount.

10. Calculate weekly wages based on input of hourly rate and hours worked. For employees who have worked more than 40 hours, pay them time-and-a-half for overtime. An hours-worked figure of 99 denotes the end of the job.

Solutions

1. F—Numbers cannot contain commas.

2. a, d—Only a single letter, or a letter followed by a digit can be used for a variable name. Note that some computers allow more alphabetic characters in a name but rules vary from one computer to another.

3. variable or numeric
   string variable or alphanumeric field

4. 30

5. 74

6.
```
10 INPUT G,T
20 IF G = 99 THEN 60
30 LET M = T/G
40 PRINT "NO OF MILES PER GALLON IS ", M
50 GO TO 10
60 END
```

7.
```
10 IF A > 100.6 THEN 190
20 IF A < 98.2 THEN 190
30 GO TO 90
```
          or
```
10 IF A <= 100.6 THEN 30
20 GO TO 190
30 IF A >= 98.2 THEN 90
40 GO TO 190
```

8.
```
10 LET H = A
20 IF B > H THEN 50
30 IF C > H THEN 70
40 GO TO 200
50 LET H = B
60 GO TO 30
70 LET H = C
80 GO TO 200
```

9.
```
 10 INPUT S
 20 IF S = 9999 THEN 120
 30 IF S > 500 THEN 80
 40 IF S > = 200 THEN 100
 50 LET T = S - .02 * S
 60 PRINT "NET SALES WITH DISCOUNT IS ", T
 70 GO TO 10
 80 LET T = S - .05 * S
 90 GO TO 60
100 LET T = S - .03 * S
110 GO TO 60
120 END
```

10. The following program corresponds to the flowchart on the next page.
```
  5 REM CALCULATE WEEKLY WAGES USING TIME-AND-A-HALF
  7 REM FOR OVERTIME
 10 INPUT H, R
 15 IF H = 99 THEN 100
 20 IF H > 40 THEN 60
 30 LET W = H * R
 40 PRINT W
 50 GO TO 10
 60 LET H = H - 40
 70 LET W = 40 * R + (H * R * 1.5)
 80 PRINT W
 90 GO TO 10
100 END
```

We could save a step by coding line 80 as

```
80 GO TO 40
```

and omitting line 90. Since lines 80 and 90 duplicate lines 40 and 50, we
can simply code GO TO 40 and save a step.

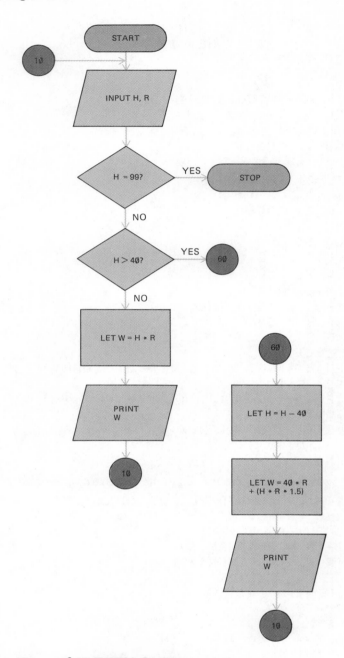

Insert 12.29
Flowchart for Question 10.

G. Other Uses of IF-THEN Statements

1. More on Accumulating a Running Total

Another main use of IF-THEN statements is for performing a summary function *after* all data has been read and processed. In order to do this, we must first read all the data. Thus, after each input instruction, we test to determine whether the data has been completely read; if it has, then we proceed to a separate routine. To do this, we end our data items with a "dummy" entry, signifying the end of the file.

That is, suppose we wish to compute weekly wages based on hours worked and hourly rate; ignore overtime pay in this example. In addition, we want to print the total wages paid for *all* employees, at the end.

A total is incremented for each record. This is called a **running total**. We indicate to the computer that if an hours-worked field is entered as 99, this is a trailer or dummy entry and means we are out of data. At that point, we print the total. Thus, we have:

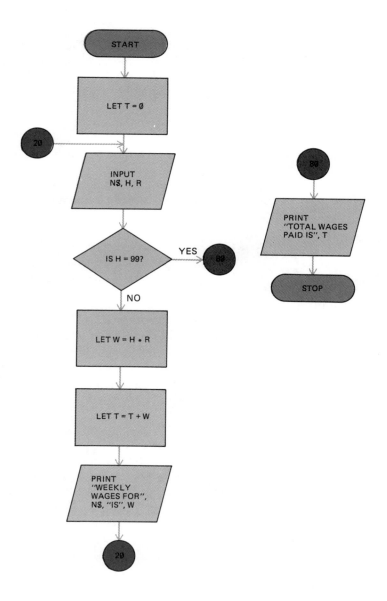

```
 5 REM COMPUTE WEEKLY WAGES FOR EACH RECORD AND
 7 REM A FINAL TOTAL WAGES FOR ALL RECORDS
10 LET T = 0
20 INPUT N$, H, R
30 IF H = 99 THEN 80
40 LET W = H * R
50 LET T = T + W
60 PRINT "WEEKLY WAGES FOR ", N$, " IS ", W
70 GO TO 20
80 PRINT "TOTAL WAGES PAID IS ", T
90 END
```

Line 30 will cause a branch to 80 only when we enter 99 for hours worked. We would do so only at the end of the job. That is, the last record would contain 99 for hours worked (H).

Line 50 computes total wages by adding all the weekly wages, W, each time they are computed.

Example 1

Read three grades for each student. Print an average for each student and a class average.

To print a class average, we must determine the number of student records processed. To determine the number of records processed we code:

```
10 INPUT E1, E2, E3
20 LET C = C + 1
```

Each time an INPUT statement is executed, C is incremented by 1. C will always indicate the number of input records processed.

An exam grade of 0 will denote an end-of-data condition. The following program corresponds to the flowchart on the next page.

```
  5 REM PRINT STUDENT AVERAGES AND A CLASS AVERAGE
 10 LET C = 0
 15 LET T = 0
 20 INPUT E1, E2, E3
 30 IF E1 = 0 THEN 90
 40 LET C = C + 1
 50 LET A = (E1 + E2 + E3) / 3
 60 PRINT "THE STUDENT AVERAGE IS ", A
 70 LET T = T + A
 80 GO TO 20
 90 LET T1 = T/C
100 PRINT "THE CLASS AVERAGE IS ", T1
110 END
```

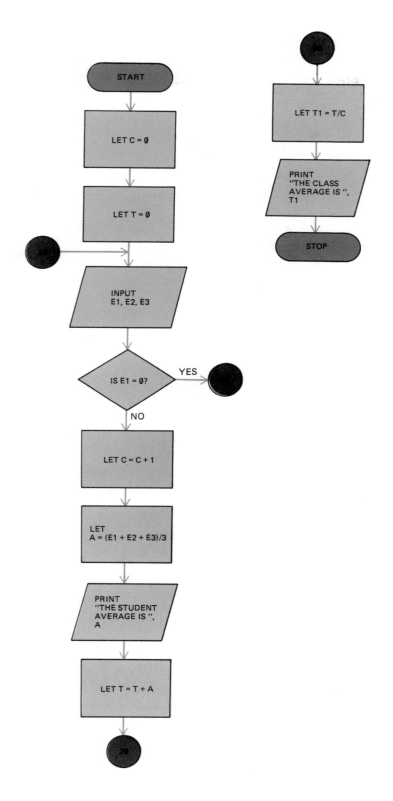

2. Using a String Variable in a Conditional Statement

All IF-THEN statements thus far coded compare numeric variables to numeric constants. Suppose, however, we wish to read in names, birth dates (month and year), and sex (M for male, F for female). In this instance we want to print the birth dates of people who are female. That is, we need to compare a string variable, sex, against an alphanumeric literal "F". Note that the literal "F" is enclosed in quotes. If we erroneously compared a sex field S to F, the computer would assume that F was a variable name.

```
 5 REM PRINT THE BIRTH DATE OF ALL FEMALES
10 INPUT N$, M, Y, S$
20 IF M = 99 THEN 70
30 IF S$ = "F" THEN 50
40 GO TO 10
50 PRINT "THE BIRTH DATE IS ",M,"/",Y
60 GO TO 10
70 END
```

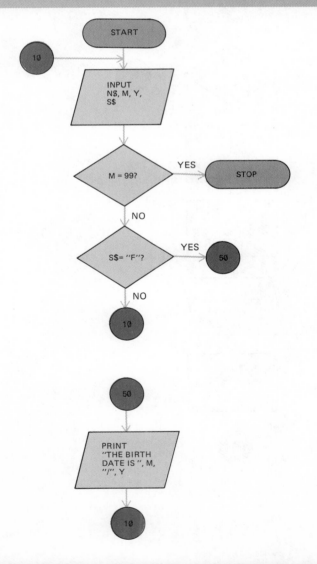

Modifying the above program, suppose instead we want to print the total number of females born in April. The end of the run will be denoted by "LAST" in the name field.

```
  5 REM PRINT THE TOTAL NUMBER OF FEMALES BORN IN APRIL
 10 LET C = 0
 20 INPUT N$, M, Y, S$
 30 IF N$ = "LAST" THEN 90
 40 IF M <> 04 THEN 20
 50 IF S$ = "F" THEN 70
 60 GO TO 20
 70 LET C = C + 1
 80 GO TO 20
 90 PRINT "THE TOTAL NO. OF FEMALES BORN IN APRIL IS ",C
100 END
```

Note that when using an INPUT statement to enter values to be used as string variables on a terminal or micro, it is not necessary to enclose the contents in quotes; that is, name and sex in the above example would be entered during execution, without quotes.

H. Summary

The following program illustrates all of the concepts thus far considered.

Example

Data records for an insurance company are read in with the following items:

    Name
    Sex (M = male, F = female)
    Birth date (MO, YR)
    State (1 for NY)

Print:

```
% DRIVERS FROM NY
% DRIVERS UNDER 25
% DRIVERS WHO ARE FEMALE
```

Hint: Assume the current year to be 1986; thus anyone born after 1961 is considered to be under 25. A SEX code of "Q" is used to signal the end of the file.

```
1 REM THIS PROGRAM COMPUTES % OF DRIVERS FROM NY,
3 REM % OF DRIVERS UNDER 25, % OF DRIVERS WHO ARE FEMALE
5 REM S = STATE CODE (1 FOR NY), M = MONTH OF BIRTH DATE,
```

```
   6 REM Y = YEAR OF BIRTH DATE, T1 = NO OF DRIVERS FROM NY,
   7 REM T2 = NO OF DRIVERS UNDER 25, T3 = NO OF FEMALE DRIVERS
  10 LET T = 0
  20 LET T1 = 0
  30 LET T2 = 0
  40 LET T3 = 0
  50 INPUT N$, S$, M, Y, S
  60 IF S$ = "Q" THEN 170
  70 REM Q IN SEX FIELD DENOTES END OF JOB
  80 LET T = T + 1
  90 REM T KEEPS COUNT OF THE NUMBER OF RECORDS
 100 IF S <> 1 THEN 120
 110 LET T1 = T1 + 1
 120 IF Y <= 61 THEN 140
 125 REM ASSUME CURRENT YEAR = 86 FOR ABOVE
 130 LET T2 = T2 + 1
 140 IF S$ <> "F" THEN 50
 150 LET T3 = T3 + 1
 160 GO TO 50
 170 LET T1 = T1 / T * 100
 180 PRINT "% DRIVERS FROM NY IS ", T1
 190 LET T2 = T2 / T * 100
 200 PRINT "% DRIVERS UNDER 25 IS ", T2
 210 LET T3 = T3 / T * 100
 220 PRINT "% DRIVERS WHO ARE FEMALE IS ", T3
 230 END
```

Self-Evaluating Quiz

Indicate the errors in each of the following:

1. 10 IF Q => 70 THEN 100

2. 10 IF P EQUALS 20 THEN 100

3. 10 IF M > 7 THEN BRANCH TO 200

4. Code a program to read in a value for A and print the absolute value of A. The absolute value of any number is its displacement from 0. Thus the absolute value of −3 is equal to 3; the absolute value of 25 is equal to 25. Let an input value of 999 signal the end of the run.

5. Read in a set of student exam grades, one per line. Print the average. A value of 999 indicates the end of data.

6. Each set of input contains a student's name and four grades for the student. Determine the average and print a grade based on the average as follows.

Average	Grade	Average	Grade
90 +	A	60 to 69	D
80 to 89	B	< 60	F
70 to 79	C		

A name of "LAST" signals the end of the job.

7. A membership society charges dues that depend on each member's salary and years of membership as follows:

Years of Membership	Percent of Salary
1–3	3%
4–6	4%
More than 6	7%

Write a program to enter salary and years of membership. Have the computer compute the dues in each case. Make the program as user-friendly as you can.

Solutions

1. Symbols used should be $>=$, not $=>$ (although the latter form may work on your particular system).

```
10 IF Q >= 70 THEN 100
```

2. EQUALS is not valid in BASIC

```
10 IF P = 20 THEN 100
```

3. THEN BRANCH TO 200 is not the proper form. 10 IF M $>$ 7 THEN 200 is the standard form. 10 IF M $>$ 7 THEN GO TO 200 is permitted on many systems as well.

4. The following program corresponds to the flowchart on the next page.

```
10 INPUT A
20 IF A = 999 THEN 80
30 IF A < 0 THEN 60
40 PRINT "THE ABSOLUTE VALUE OF ", A, "IS",A
50 GO TO 10
60 PRINT "THE ABSOLUTE VALUE OF ", A, "IS",-A
70 GO TO 10
80 END
```

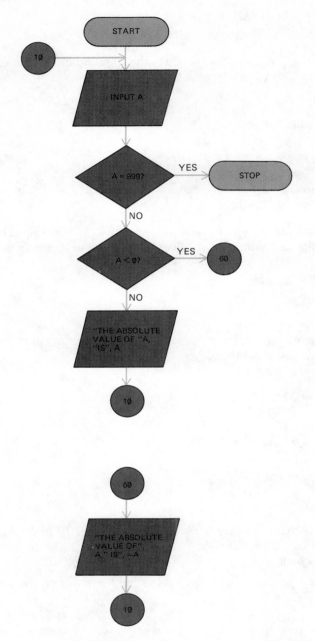

5.

```
2 LET C = O
4 LET T = O
10 INPUT E1
20 IF E1 = 999 THEN 60
30 LET C = C + 1
40 LET T = T + E1
```

```
50 GO TO 10
60 PRINT "AVERAGE IS", T/C
70 END
```

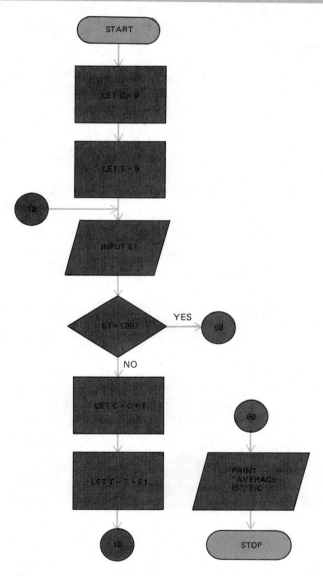

6. The following program corresponds to the flowchart on page 489.

```
10 INPUT N$, E1, E2, E3, E4
20 IF N$ = "LAST" THEN 190
30 LET T = (E1 + E2 + E3 + E4) / 4
40 IF T >= 90 THEN 110
```

```
 50 IF T >= 80 THEN 130
 60 IF T >= 70 THEN 150
 70 IF T >= 60 THEN 170
 80 LET G$ = "F"
 90 PRINT N$, "GRADE IS", G$
100 GO TO 10
110 LET G$ = "A"
120 GO TO 90
130 LET G$ = "B"
140 GO TO 90
150 LET G$ = "C"
160 GO TO 90
170 LET G$ = "D"
180 GO TO 90
190 PRINT "THAT'S ALL FOLKS!!"
200 END
```

7.

```
 10 PRINT "ENTER SALARY AND YEARS OF MEMBERSHIP"
 20 PRINT "ENTER 99,99 WHEN YOU ARE DONE"
 30 INPUT S, Y
 40 IF S = 99 THEN 150
 50 IF Y < 4 THEN 110
 60 IF Y < 7 THEN 130
 70 LET T = .07 * S
 80 PRINT "THE YEARLY DUES ARE "; T
 90 PRINT
100 GO TO 10
110 LET T = .03 * S
120 GO TO 80
130 LET T = .04 * S
140 GO TO 80
150 END
```

Practice Problems

(May be assigned as homework.)

1. Write a program to input the number of miles traveled and the number of gallons of gas used. In each case, compute the number of miles per gallon. Include prompts and messages to make the program user-friendly.

2. Write a program to print the total number of transactions entered as input and the total amount for all the transactions. Include prompts and messages to make the program user-friendly.

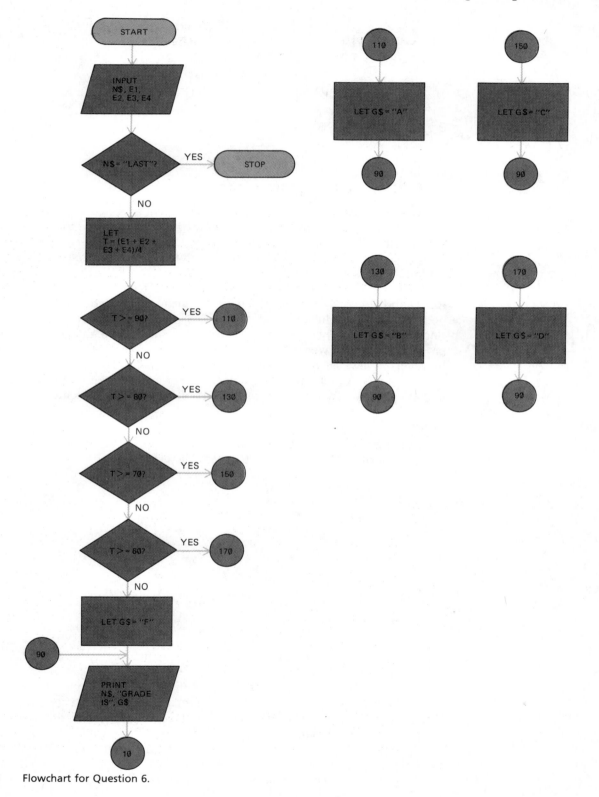

Flowchart for Question 6.

3. Write a program to produce a multiplication table as follows:

```
MULTIPLICATION TABLE
      1X      2X      3X      4X      5X
1      1       2       3       4       5
2      2       4       6       8      10
3      3       6       9      12      15
4      4       8      12      16      20
5      5      10      15      20      25
```

I. READ and DATA Statements

Thus far we have considered the INPUT statement as a data entry command. This statement is used when we do not know what input will need to be processed in advance or at the time the program is coded.

Sometimes, however, we have some complex processing to perform where we know precisely what data we want to operate on. In such a case, we use READ and DATA statements in place of the INPUT command. Note that with READ and DATA statements, the data is actually *part of the program*; there is no need to enter additional data when RUN is typed. Moreover, in many instances there is no need for a trailer record. That is, on many computers the program terminates when there is no more data in a DATA statement. It is best, however, to always include a trailer record; this will avoid error messages on many systems. A trailer record may include, for example, all 9's in a particular numeric field, where a test for 9's is made after the READ statement.

Example

Suppose that for every set of values of X and Y, we would like to calculate the square root of $X^2 + Y^2$. Consider the following program.

```
 5 REM FIND THE SQUARE ROOT OF TWO NUMBERS SQUARED
10 READ X, Y
20 LET A = SQR (X ** 2 + Y ** 2)
30 PRINT A
40 GO TO 10
50 DATA 3, 4
60 DATA 5, 7
70 END
```

The READ statement directs the computer to get a value for X and a value for Y from a DATA statement. The first time the READ instruction is executed, the computer will get the values from the *first* DATA statement. Thus X will contain 3 and Y will contain 4. SQR is a function that finds the square root of $(X^2 + Y^2)$. After the desired calculations are performed and the answer is printed out, the computer goes back to statement 10 again. The computer is told to get *another* set of values—one for X and one for Y. Since the values in the first DATA statement have already been used, the computer knows automatically that it must get the data from statement 60, the next DATA statement.

When the computer goes back to statement 10 for the third time, it finds no data to read in. A message, such as "OUT OF DATA" will then usually be printed by the computer.

It would have been equally valid to have a DATA statement such as the following.

```
50 DATA 3, 4, 5, 7
```

Here, only one DATA statement is used. The first READ causes only the first two values in statement 50 to be used since only two variables are listed in the READ statement. The second time the READ is executed, the next two values in the DATA statement are used. As many items of data as can fit on one line may be used in this form of the DATA statement.

Since they do not affect the logic of the program at all, DATA statements may be placed anywhere, but placing them directly before the END statement makes the program easier to read. The following sequence of instructions is therefore valid.

```
10 READ X, Y
20 DATA 3, 4
30 DATA 5, 7
40 LET A = SQR (X ** 2 + Y ** 2)
50 PRINT A
60 GO TO 10
70 END
```

Thus we see that DATA statements can appear anywhere throughout the program and that they can have any one of a number of formats.

The examples just discussed illustrate how numeric data can be included within a program. Alphanumeric data can also be included in DATA statements, although the rules vary slightly, depending on the computer on which the program is run. Some BASIC translators require alphanumeric data to be enclosed in quotes, as illustrated in the following program excerpt:

```
10 READ N$, S
       .
       .
       .
180 DATA "JAMES PARKS", 10250
190 DATA "ANNE STONE", 13175
200 END
```

Statement 10 instructs the computer to get the values from a DATA statement for two fields—N$, a string variable representing name, and S, a numeric field representing salary. You will recall that when forming a string variable name we use a letter followed by a dollar sign. The rule for forming numeric field names or variables is to use a letter or a letter followed by a digit.

The same program run on a computer where the BASIC translator does not ordinarily require quotes around string variable data would appear as follows:

```
10 READ N$, S
    .
    .
    .
180 DATA JAMES PARKS, 10250
190 DATA ANNE STONE, 13175
200 END
```

Notice that the comma in a DATA statement is only used to separate fields of data. It may not be included within numeric data. That is, the number 10,250 must be entered as 10250. The following DATA statement is therefore interpreted by the computer as having four numeric values.

```
145 DATA 723,12735,123,128.17
```

The four values in this statement are (1) 723, (2) 12735, (3) 123, and (4) 128.17.

Self-Evaluating Quiz

1. An INPUT statement is used when _____.
2. To include data as part of a program, we use _____ and _____ statements.
3. How many values for D will print out in the following program?

```
10 READ A, B, C
20 LET D = A * B - C
30 PRINT D
40 GO TO 10
50 DATA 10, 5, 20, 30, 8, 50, 60, 20, 100
60 DATA 30, 40, 50, 20, 10, 100, 40, 60
70 END
```

4. Write a program, using READ and DATA statements, to read in a code field and an amount. If the code is "A", calculate and print T, tax, as 4.5% of the amount. If code is "B", calculate and print T, tax, as 3.7% of the amount. If code is "C", calculate and print T, tax, as 2.2% of the amount. If code is "D", this designates the end of the job. Use this procedure for the following values.

Code	Amount	Code	Amount
C	5200	B	625
A	463	C	42
B	8211	D	−99
B	3372		
A	495		

5. Code a program to read the names and weights for each of several individuals and print only the names of those people who weigh less than 120 pounds or more than 250 pounds. Use READ and DATA statements.

6. Revise the above program to read in for each person his or her weight and height (in inches). Print the name of any person (1) whose weight is less than 120 pounds and height is less than 64 inches, or (2) whose weight is greater than 250 pounds and height is greater than 74 inches. Print the total number of names on the report at the end. Terminate the program when a weight of 999 is entered.

7. Code a program to read in amount fields and to print the average amount after all input has been read. Assume that an amount of 999.99 signals an end-of-job condition. Use an INPUT statement.

Solutions

1. the input entered is not actually part of the program.

2. READ
   DATA

3. five—We will get an "OUT OF DATA" message when the computer goes through the READ statement the sixth time. There is no value for C.

4.

```
 10 READ C$, A
 15 IF C$ = "D" THEN 150
 20 IF C$ = "A" THEN 70
 30 IF C$ = "B" THEN 100
 40 LET T = .022 * A
 50 PRINT T
 60 GO TO 10
 70 LET T = .045 * A
 80 PRINT T
 90 GO TO 10
100 LET T = .037 * A
110 PRINT T
120 GO TO 10
130 DATA "C", 5200, "A", 463, "B", 8211
140 DATA "B", 3372, "A", 495, "B", 625, "C", 42
145 DATA "D", -99
150 END
```

5.

```
10 READ N$, W
20 IF W < 120 THEN 50
30 IF W > 250 THEN 50
40 GO TO 10
50 PRINT N$
60 GO TO 10
70 DATA "JOAN CONNORS", 125, "MARK DORBS", 275
80 DATA "KATHY FRANKS", 118, "ROBERT PETERS", 185
90 END
```

6.

```
10 LET T = 0
20 READ N$, W, H
30 IF W = 999 THEN 140
40 IF W < 120 THEN 70
50 IF W > 250 THEN 90
60 GO TO 20
70 IF H < 64 THEN 110
80 GO TO 20
90 IF H > 74 THEN 110
100 GO TO 20
110 LET T = T + 1
120 PRINT N$
130 GO TO 20
140 PRINT T
150 DATA "JOAN CONNORS", 125, 59
160 DATA "MARK DORBS", 275, 65
170 DATA "KATHY FRANKS", 118, 62
180 DATA "ROBERT PETERS", 185, 64
190 DATA "LAST", 999,999
200 END
```

7.

```
10 LET T = 0
20 LET N = 0
30 INPUT A
40 IF A = 999.99 THEN 80
50 LET T = T + A
60 LET N = N + 1
70 GO TO 30
80 LET V = T / N
85 PRINT V
90 END
```

IV. ADVANCED CONCEPTS IN BASIC

A. FOR and NEXT Statements

1. FOR ... NEXT and Looping

a. Loops   Recall that a loop is a sequence of instructions that is to be repeated a fixed number of times. Let us reconsider a problem that illustrates how a loop is performed. Suppose we wish to compute the amount of money we will accumulate at the end of one, two, and three years if we bank a specified amount at a given rate of interest. Assume that all money (principal and interest) remains in the bank and is compounded annually. The following general formula is useful for solving problems involving compound interest.

$$P_n = P_o (1 + r)^n$$

When n is 1, P_n is equal to the total amount of money after 1 year of investment of an initial amount (P_o) at a given rate of interest (r). When n is 2, P_n is equal to the total amount after two years of investment. When n is 3, P_n is equal to the total amount after three years of investment.

Let us begin with an illustration that focuses on compound interest for this three-year period.

The input to be entered consists of a principal amount (P_o) and interest rate (r). The number of years to be invested (n) will be predefined as 3.

The output will consist of a chart indicating the value of the principal plus interest for each of three years of investment. The following provides an example of the displayed input and output.

```
ENTER PRINCIPAL AMOUNT:
?  2000
ENTER INTEREST RATE (E.G., 8% AS 8.0):
?  10.0

INVESTMENT CHART FOR 2000.00 AT 10.0% INTEREST
    YEAR         AMOUNT
      1          2200.00
      2          2420.00
      3          2662.00
```

We will now write a program that computes the total, where values of P (principal) and R (rate of interest) are to be entered as input. We are interested in the results when n equals 1, 2, and 3.

(1) Method 1—Without Loops

```
10 PRINT "ENTER PRINCIPAL AMOUNT:"
20 INPUT P
30 PRINT "ENTER INTEREST RATE (E.G., 8% AS 8.0):"
```

```
 40 INPUT R
 50 PRINT
 60 PRINT "INVESTMENT CHART FOR ";P;" AT ";R;"% INTEREST"
 70 PRINT "    YEAR      AMOUNT"
 80 LET R = R / 100
 90 LET A = P * (1 + R) ** 1
100 PRINT "      1         ";A
110 LET B = P * (1 + R) ** 2
120 PRINT "      2         ";B
130 LET C = P * (1 + R) ** 3
140 PRINT "      3         ";C
150 END

*RUN
ENTER PRINCIPAL AMOUNT:
?450
ENTER INTEREST RATE (E.G., 8% AS 8.0):
?9.0

INVESTMENT CHART FOR 450 AT 9.0% INTEREST
     YEAR      AMOUNT
       1       490.50
       2       534.64
       3       582.76
```

Notice that lines 90 through 140 have many similarities. Lines 90, 110, and 130 utilize the same basic formula with only one modification each time the calculation is performed—the value of the exponent is either 1, 2, or 3. Lines 100, 120, and 140, which print the output, are likewise very similar, except that each message indicates a different year—either 1, 2, or 3.

Notice that one routine could be established, instead of three separate routines, to compute the three values. This one routine could utilize a variable exponent N, for example, which begins as 1 and is incremented by 1 each time until it exceeds 3. That is, a loop can be established to be executed three times, varying N from 1 to 3.

(2) Method 2—Using a Loop

```
10 PRINT "ENTER PRINCIPAL AMOUNT:"
20 INPUT P
30 PRINT "ENTER INTEREST RATE (E.G., 8% AS 8.0):"
40 INPUT R
50 PRINT
60 PRINT "INVESTMENT CHART FOR ";P;" AT ";R;"% INTEREST"
70 PRINT "    YEAR      AMOUNT"
80 LET R = R / 100
85 LET N = 1
90 LET A = P * (1 + R) ** N
```

```
100 PRINT "        ";N;"           ";A
110 IF N = 3 THEN 140
120 LET N = N + 1
130 GO TO 90
140 END
```

Notice that this program utilizes a conventional loop. The sequence of instructions that is to be repeated begins with line 90. Lines 90 and 100 are executed for the *first* time with a value of N equal to 1. At line 110, the computer performs a test to see if the sequence should be repeated. Since N is not equal to 3 the first time the statement is executed, the computer proceeds automatically to the next line, where 1 is added to N, so that it now equals 2. With N equal to 2, the computer is then instructed at line 130 to go back to line 90 and process the sequence of instructions again.

(3) Method 3—Using the FOR and NEXT Instructions   We have seen from the previous solutions that we wish to perform a series of operations using a variable N that begins as 1 and is incremented until it reaches 3. The FOR and NEXT statements provide some flexibility in dealing with this type of problem.

The FOR statement establishes a variable and specifies the range in which it is to vary. Thus for our problem we would have:

```
FOR N = 1 TO 3
```

with an appropriate line number.

The statements to follow will be executed, for the first time, with N equal to 1. The NEXT statement essentially instructs the computer to repeat these steps with N at the next value (N = 2). Our NEXT statement would read as:

```
NEXT N
```

with an appropriate line number. NEXT N, then, acts as a GO TO (line number), which transfers control back to the beginning of the loop with a new value for N.

This procedure will be repeated until N equals 3 and all the instructions have been performed for that value. Then the program will continue with the statement directly following the NEXT statement.

Let us now consider this most effective method for handling loops.

```
10 PRINT "ENTER PRINCIPAL AMOUNT:"
20 INPUT P
30 PRINT "ENTER INTEREST RATE (E.G., 8% AS 8.0):"
40 INPUT R
50 PRINT
```

```
 60 PRINT "INVESTMENT CHART FOR ";P;" AT ";R;"% INTEREST"
 70 PRINT "     YEAR      AMOUNT"
 80 LET R = R / 100
 85 FOR N = 1 TO 3
 90     LET A = P * (1 + R) ** N
100     PRINT "      ";N;"          ";A
110 NEXT N
120 END


*RUN
ENTER PRINCIPAL AMOUNT:
?450
ENTER INTEREST RATE (E.G., 8% AS 8.0):
?9.0

INVESTMENT CHART FOR 450 AT 9.0% INTEREST
    YEAR      AMOUNT
     1        490.50
     2        534.64
     3        582.76
```

The statements within the FOR ... NEXT loop, on line numbers 90 and 100, are indented for ease of reading.

The FOR statement in line 85 indicates that the sequence of instructions up to the NEXT statement (line 110) is to be repeated three times, with N = 1 the first time, N = 2 the second time, and N = 3 the last time through the loop.

The NEXT statement (line 110) causes the field N, specified in the FOR statement (line 85), to be automatically incremented to the next value each time the sequence has been executed.

The FOR statement used in the above program will initialize N at 1 and result in N being incremented by 1 until it equals 3, at which point the loop would be executed for the last time.

2. FOR ... NEXT with Variable Delimiters

Let us now modify our program so that we enter principal, rate, *and* number of years of investment. Consider the following example:

```
ENTER PRINCIPAL AMOUNT:
?2000
ENTER INTEREST RATE (E.G., 8% AS 8.0):
?10
ENTER NO. OF YEARS OF INVESTMENT:
?5
```

```
INVESTMENT CHART FOR 2000.00 AT 10% INTEREST
     YEAR         AMOUNT
      1           2200.00
      2           2420.00
      3           2662.00
      4           2928.20
      5           3221.02
```

Suppose INPUT J is used to enter the number of years of investment. In this instance, N in our FOR ... NEXT loop must vary from 1 to J.

It is valid to use a FOR ... NEXT loop with a variable delimiter. That is, the loop may vary from 1 to J, where J is a variable entered as input:

```
 10  PRINT "ENTER PRINCIPAL AMOUNT:"
 20  INPUT P
 30  PRINT "ENTER INTEREST RATE (E.G., 8% AS 8.0):"
 40  INPUT R
 50  PRINT
 60  PRINT "ENTER NO. OF YEARS OF INVESTMENT:"
 70  INPUT J
 80  PRINT "INVESTMENT CHART FOR ";P;" AT ";R;"% INTEREST"
 85  PRINT "     YEAR        AMOUNT"
 90  LET R = R / 100
100      FOR N = 1 TO J
110      LET A = P * (1 + R) ** N
120      PRINT "      ";N;"          ";A
130      NEXT N
140  END


*RUN
ENTER PRINCIPAL AMOUNT:
?450
ENTER INTEREST RATE:
?9.0
ENTER NO. OF YEARS OF INVESTMENT
?10
INVESTMENT CHART FOR 450 AT 9.0% INTEREST
     YEAR         AMOUNT
      1            490.50
      2            534.64
      3            582.76
      4            635.20
      5            692.37
      6            754.69
      7            822.61
      8            896.64
      9            977.34
     10           1065.31
```

3. Using the STEP Value

Suppose that we wish to initialize N to 10 and increment N by 10 each time rather than by 1. That is, we wish N to assume the values 10, 20, 30, and so on, until N equals 100. We wish to compute the interest after 10, 20, 30, etc. periods of investment. The FOR statement is specified as:

```
FOR N = 10 TO 100 STEP 10
```

The STEP may be omitted when we want the variable to be incremented by 1. In the above, we initialize N to 10 and "step" it or increment it by 10 each time the succeeding operations are performed until N is equal to 100.

4. Examples

Consider these examples of FOR ... NEXT instructions. We have coded Examples 1 and 2 previously without FOR ... NEXT instructions.

Example 1

Sum the odd numbers from 101 to 1001 using a FOR ... NEXT loop.

```
10 LET T = 0
20 FOR N = 101 TO 1001 STEP 2
30     LET T = T + N
40 NEXT N
50 PRINT "THE SUM OF ODD NUMBERS FROM 101 - 1001 IS ";T
60 END
```

Example 2

Read a value for M. Find M!, where M! = M × (M − 1) × (M − 2) ... × 1. Use FOR ... NEXT instructions.

```
10 LET T = 1
20 INPUT M
30 FOR N = 1 TO M
40     LET T = T * N
50 NEXT N
60 PRINT "M IS "; M
70 PRINT "M! = "; T
80 GO TO 10
90 END
```

Note that line 30 could have been coded as:

```
30 FOR N = M TO 1 STEP -1
```

It is possible to code FOR ... NEXT loops within FOR ... NEXT loops. Consider the following.

Example 3

There are 10 math classes in College ABC. Each class has 25 students. Each line of input has a student's average. Write a BASIC program using FOR ... NEXT loops to print the 10 class averages.

```
10 FOR I = 1 TO 10
20 LET T = 0
30 FOR J = 1 TO 25
40 INPUT G1
50 LET T = T + G1
60 NEXT J
70 PRINT "CLASS AVERAGE FOR CLASS ";I;" = ";T/25
80 NEXT I
90 END
```

B. ON-GO TO Statements

Many BASIC translators allow the programmer to use the ON-GO TO statement, which is also known as the computed GO TO. The computed GO TO can be used to replace several IF statements. Consider the following program excerpt:

```
10 INPUT A, C, F
20 IF A = 1 THEN 110
30 IF A = 2 THEN 145
40 IF A = 3 THEN 65
    .
    .
    .
```

Lines 20 through 40 could be replaced with an ON-GO TO statement:

```
20 ON A GO TO 110, 145, 65
```

If A is equal to 1, then a branch or transfer is made to the *first* line number indicated, in this case line number 110. If A is equal to 2, then a branch is made to the *second* line number, which is line number 145. If A is equal to 3, then a branch is made to the *third* line number, line number 65.

The general form of the ON-GO TO statement is:

```
ON (expression) GO TO (line number),..., (line number)
```

ON-GO TO instructions are commonly used in programs that utilize menus. Consider the following desired interaction between a user and a program.

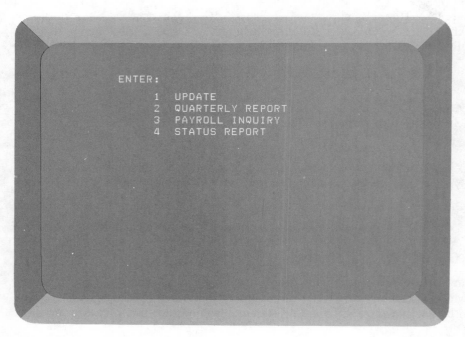

In response to a prompt of ? or [], the user keys in 1, 2, 3, or 4 depending on the program excerpt desired.

To accomplish this in a program, each of the four procedures is coded and tested. Suppose that

1. The UPDATE procedure begins on line 150.
2. The QUARTERLY REPORT procedure begins on line 1270.
3. The PAYROLL INQUIRY procedure begins on line 2510.
4. The STATUS REPORT procedure begins on line 3820.

The following coding excerpt will execute the proper procedure.

```
 10  PRINT "ENTER: "
 20  PRINT "     1     UPDATE"
 30  PRINT "     2     QUARTERLY REPORT"
 40  PRINT "     3     PAYROLL INQUIRY"
 50  PRINT "     4     STATUS REPORT"
 60  PRINT
 70  INPUT N
 80  IF N > 4 THEN 100
 85  IF N < 1 THEN 100
 90  ON N GO TO 150, 1270, 2510, 3820
100  PRINT "ERROR IN INPUT"
110  GO TO 70
```

It should be noted that if the value of the expression is not an integer, it will automatically be *truncated to an integer*. Thus, if we have the statement

```
80 ON A + B GO TO 115, 117, 23
```

and A equals 1.3 and B equals .8, a branch to line 117 will be made, since A plus B equals 2.1, which is truncated to 2. Truncation means that the number is reduced to its integer value (2.1 becomes 2, 3.6 becomes 3, etc.).

Using ON-GO TO to Assign Letter Grades Depending on Numeric Averages

Read In Assume numeric grades can vary from 0 to 99. We will assign letter grades as follows:

Numeric Grade Read In	Letter Grade Assigned
0–59	F
60–69	D
70–79	C
80–89	B
90–99	A

Let us consider grades 60–99 first. For numeric grades 60–99, we may divide the grade by 10, which will give us values from 6–9.9. If we subtract 5 from this quotient, we will have values from 1–4.9 as follows.

Numeric Grade Read In	Value of Q	Value of T
READ G	LET Q = G/10	LET T = Q−5
60–69	6.0–6.9	1.0–1.9
70–79	7.0–7.9	2.0–2.9
80–89	8.0–8.9	3.0–3.9
90–99	9.0–9.9	4.0–4.9

The following instruction can be used to print the appropriate letter grades.

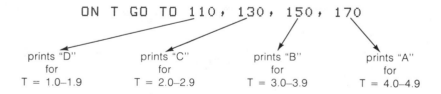

```
ON T GO TO 110, 130, 150, 170
```

| prints "D" for T = 1.0–1.9 | prints "C" for T = 2.0–2.9 | prints "B" for T = 3.0–3.9 | prints "A" for T = 4.0–4.9 |

For a grade less than 60, we print "F". The full program for this procedure is as follows.

```
10 REM THIS PROGRAM PRINTS LETTER GRADES
20 REM FOR EACH STUDENT NAME AND AVERAGE
30 REM READ IN NAME AND AVERAGE
40 READ N$, G
```

```
 50 IF G < 60 THEN 90
 60 LET Q = G / 10
 70 LET T = Q - 5
 80 ON T GO TO 110, 130, 150, 170
 90 PRINT N$;"'S GRADE IS F"
100 GO TO 40
110 PRINT N$;"'S GRADE IS D"
120 GO TO 40
130 PRINT N$;"'S GRADE IS C"
140 GO TO 40
150 PRINT N$;"'S GRADE IS B"
160 GO TO 40
170 PRINT N$;"'S GRADE IS A"
180 GO TO 40
190 DATA "STEWART", 83, "TED", 90
200 DATA "NANCY", 46, "ROBERT", 62
210 END
```

Using the above data, we would have output as follows:

```
STEWART'S GRADE IS B
TED'S GRADE IS A
NANCY'S GRADE IS F
ROBERT'S GRADE IS D
```

Note: Rounding features of some machines may affect results.

Self-Evaluating Quiz

1. Indicate what will print in the following sequence.

```
10 LET X = 0
20 FOR J = 1 TO 4
30    LET X = X + 5
40 NEXT J
50 PRINT X
60 END
```

2. What are the results in the following?

```
10 FOR J = 1 TO 9 STEP 2
20      PRINT J
30 NEXT J
40 END
```

3. Write a program using the FOR ... NEXT to calculate the sum of all even numbers from 2 to 2000.

4. Write a program using the FOR ... NEXT to multiply A by B using successive additions. That is, to obtain the product of A × B, simply add A to a total field B times.

Solutions

1.
Value of J	Value of X
1	5
2	10 (5 + 5)
3	15 (10 + 5)
4	20 (15 + 5)

} Intermediate results

X = 20 at end

2. The following will print:

```
1
3
5
7
9
```

3.
```
10 LET T = 0
20 FOR I = 2 TO 2000 STEP 2
30     LET T = T + I
40     NEXT I
50 PRINT T
60 END
```

4.
```
10 LET T = 0
20 FOR I = 1 TO B
30     LET T = T + A
40     NEXT I
50 PRINT T
60 END
```

C. Arrays

Thus far we have focused on independent variables that are stored as distinct fields. Frequently we wish to store a series of items as a list or a table. The list or table is referred to as an **array** and each item is referenced with a **subscript**. A subscript is a number that indicates the position of a particular value in the array (see Figure 12.5).

There are many types of problems where it is convenient, and sometimes necessary, to store all the input data with a subscripted variable before further processing is performed. Consider the following program, where each student in a particular course has taken six exams. The six exams are to be averaged by the computer.

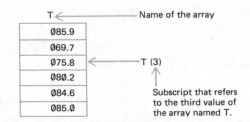

Figure 12.5
Example of an array and
subscripts.

```
10 INPUT E1, E2, E3, E4, E5, E6
20 LET A = (E1 + E2 + E3 + E4 + E5 + E6) / 6
30 PRINT A
40 GO TO 10
50 END
```

This oversimplified program allows the instructor to sit at the terminal, enter
a particular student's grades, and then get the average printed out before proceeding to the next student.

Notice that six different variable names were used in lines 10 and 20: E1,
E2, E3, E4, E5, and E6. Suppose the instructor had given 12 exams. We may
run into several problems when writing the program. First, we cannot use variable names such as E10, E11, and E12, since a variable name on many systems
can only consist of a letter, or a letter and one digit after it. Even if we could
choose meaningful variable names, it becomes tedious and inefficient to code
a series of variables as above. Consider the following:

```
10 INPUT E1, E2, E3, E4, E5, E6, E7, E8, E9, T1, T2, T3
20 LET A = (E1+E2+E3+E4+E5+E6+E7+E8+E9+T1+T2+T3) / 12
```

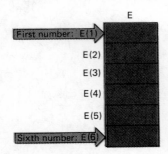

Figure 12.6
List or one-dimensional
array consisting of six exam
grades.

One way to simplify the program is to use an array for storing the exam
scores and a subscripted variable for accessing each of them. Consider again
the problem where six exam scores are to be entered for each student. Suppose
we want the computer to set up a *list*, or *one-dimensional array*. The term one-
dimensional array simply means that the data can be visualized as being stored
in one column within the computer. The name of the list will be E. It will have
six slots or cells into which the numbers can be placed. After the data is stored
in the list, we can refer to any specific item by indicating the appropriate position
in the list with the use of a subscript. The values in the list can then be referred
to as E(1), E(2), E(3), E(4), E(5), and E(6). E(1) refers to the first number in
the list called E, E(2) refers to the second number, and so on. Figure 12.6
illustrates how the list just described can be visualized inside the computer.

Our instructions to read in the scores and average them might then be as
follows.

```
10 INPUT E(1),E(2),E(3),E(4),E(5),E(6)
20 LET A = (E(1)+E(2)+E(3)+E(4)+E(5)+E(6))/6
```

Although these instructions illustrate the use of a subscripted variable, we have not saved anything by doing it this way. However, it may have occurred to you that we might use the FOR and NEXT statements to facilitate our programming. The following instructions simplify the coding:

```
10 LET T = 0
20 FOR J = 1 TO 6
30      INPUT E(J)
40      LET T = T + E(J)
50 NEXT J
60 PRINT T / 6
70 GO TO 10
80 END
```

Line 10 sets up a variable T to accumulate the total of each student's grades. Line 20 indicates that the subsequent lines, 30 and 40, are to be repeated six times, with J varying from 1 to 6, in increments of 1. Lines 30 and 40 process the Jth value of E; that is, the first time through the loop, the first value of E, or the first exam grade, is entered as input and stored in the first slot of the list called E(1). This value is then added to the current value of T, which is zero. Line 50 increments J by 1 and the loop is repeated. The second time through, the second exam grade is entered and stored as E(2), and so on. After all six grades have been entered and accumulated, the computer goes to line 60 automatically, where the accumulated total for all exams for the student just processed is divided by 6, and the answer is printed out. The process is then repeated for the other students.

It should now be apparent why subscripted variables are so useful. Regardless of how many values are to be read into a particular list, essentially the same simple instructions can be used. However, there is one additional instruction that is necessary *if the subscript will exceed 10*: the dimension statement (DIM). Its purpose is to explicitly tell the computer how much room to reserve for an array when it is known that there will be subscripts greater than 10. The BASIC translator automatically reserves enough room to allow for a subscript up to 10 whenever a subscripted variable is encountered during translation. If we know, for example, that there will be 12 grades entered for each student, we will need a dimension statement such as

```
10 DIM E(12)
```

at the beginning of the program. This statement explicitly tells the computer to reserve enough room for a list called E to allow for a subscript up to 12. As a rule, we will use the DIM for all arrays, to clarify the procedure.

To alter the above program so that it reads in 20 exam grades and computes an average, we add the DIM statement and simply change two parameters as follows:

```
10 DIM E(20)
20 LET T = 0
30 FOR J = 1 TO  20    ←—— Delimiter is changed
40      INPUT E(J)
50      LET T = T + E(J)
60 NEXT J
70 PRINT T /  20    ←—— Divide by 20 to obtain average
80 END
```

1. Using an Array to Store Totals

Suppose there are five salespersons for COMPANY ABC. They are each assigned salesperson numbers 1, 2, 3, 4, 5. At the end of the month, we enter as input every sale made by the salespersons as follows:

```
ENTER SALESPERSON NUMBER (1-5):
?
ENTER SALES AMOUNT:
?
```

The input is entered randomly; that is, the first entry may be for salesperson 4, the next for salesperson 1, and so on. There are numerous entries for each salesperson. A salesperson number entered as 9 will signal the end of the job. After all the input is entered, we wish to print the total sales for each salesperson in sequence:

```
            MONTHLY SALES REPORT

SALESPERSON     TOTAL AMOUNT OF SALES
    1
    2
    3
    4
    5
```

The program could be coded as follows.

```
10 FOR J = 1 TO 5
20      LET T(J) = 0   ←—— Initializes five amount fields at 0
30 NEXT J
40 PRINT "ENTER SALESPERSON NUMBER (1-5, 9 FOR EOJ
50 INPUT S
```

```
 60 IF S = 9 THEN 110
 70 PRINT "ENTER SALES AMOUNT:"
 80 INPUT A
 90 LET T(S) = T(S) + A
100 GO TO 40
110 PRINT "      MONTHLY SALES REPORT"
120 PRINT "SALESPERSON         TOTAL AMOUNT OF SALES"
130 FOR J = 1 TO 5
140      PRINT "      ";J;"           ";T(J)
150 NEXT J
160 END
```

2. Using an Array to Store a Table

Suppose we wish to compute BALANCE DUE for each customer record read in. The customer record includes customer name, amount of sales, and sales district. Sales district varies from 1 to 5. The sales tax is dependent on the sales district. Since sales tax itself changes from time to time, we would *not* enter it as a constant. Rather, we would begin our program by entering the tax rates for each of the five sales districts and storing them in an array:

T Array

$T(1) \longrightarrow$ _____   (sales tax for district 1)
$T(2) \longrightarrow$ _____   (sales tax for district 2)
$T(3) \longrightarrow$ _____   (sales tax for district 3)
$T(4) \longrightarrow$ _____   (sales tax for district 4)
$T(5) \longrightarrow$ _____   (sales tax for district 5)

We enter sales tax for the five districts in this array or table before the customer records. Sales tax rates are entered as variable data not as constants because they may change; it is better to change data entered as variables than to modify constants in a program. After entering the sales tax rates, we enter our customer records and depending on the sales district, we "look up" the corresponding sales tax rate from the array:

```
 10 REM THIS PROGRAM CALCULATES EACH CUSTOMER'S BALANCE
 20 REM WHICH INCLUDES SALES TAX
 30 FOR J = 1 TO 5
 40      PRINT "ENTER SALES TAX RATE FOR DISTRICT ";J
 50      INPUT T(J)
 60 NEXT J
 70 PRINT "ENTER CUSTOMER NO. - 9999 FOR END OF JOB"
 80 INPUT C
 90 IF C = 9999 THEN 180
100 PRINT "ENTER BALANCE DUE"
110 INPUT B
120 PRINT "ENTER SALES DISTRICT (1-5)"
130 INPUT S
```

```
140 REM B * T(S) IS THE CALCULATED TAX
150 LET F = (B * T(S)) + B
160 PRINT "CUSTOMER ";C;" OWES ";F
170 GO TO 70
180 END
```

Figure 12.7
Storing a table in an array.

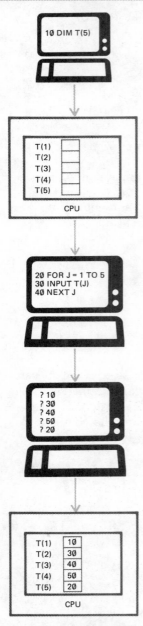

Figure 12.7 is a schematic of how a table is stored in an array.

In this chapter we have provided you with enough information for writing simple and intermediate level BASIC programs. More advanced topics in BASIC are discussed in Appendix A.

CHAPTER SUMMARY

I. The nature of BASIC
  A. BASIC—an abbreviation for Beginner's All-purpose Symbolic Instruction Code.
  B. Every instruction must begin with a line number.
  C. On most computers, programs must end with an END statement.
  D. Numeric variable names can be represented by a letter or a letter followed by a digit (e.g., T, T1).
  E. String variable names for representing alphanumeric data can consist of a letter or a letter plus a digit, followed by a $ (e.g., L$, N1$).
  F. An alphanumeric constant is enclosed in quotation marks (e.g., 10 PRINT "SALES REPORT").

II. The hierarchy of arithmetic operations
  A. Exponentiation (** or ↑).
  B. Multiplication (*) and division (/).
  C. Addition (+) and subtraction (−).
  D. The use of parentheses overrides all hierarchy rules. If an instruction has two or more operations on the same level, they are executed in sequence from left to right.

III. Sample statements
  A. REM—for including a remark or comment.
     (5   REM THIS IS A PAYROLL PROGRAM.)
  B. LET—to perform an arithmetic operation.
     1. 10   LET T = 0 (Initializes a field to zero.)
     2. 50   LET T = T + 1 (Adds 1 to T.)
     3. 75   LET S = S + T (Used to accumulate a running total.)
  C. IF-THEN—to perform a logical test (e.g., 150   IF A = 99 THEN 250).

a. Symbols	Meaning	Symbols	Meaning
=	Equal to	<=	Less than or equal to
<	Less than	>=	Greater than or equal to
>	Greater than	<>	Not equal to

     b. End-of-file condition—typically signaled with a trailer or dummy record. A test can be performed right after an input record is obtained. For example,

```
20 INPUT A, B, C
30 IF C = 999 THEN 200
```

     c. The IF-THEN is very useful for looping procedures.
     d. A string variable in a conditional must be enclosed in quotes (e.g., 30   IF S$ = "F" THEN 70).
  D. INPUT—used to obtain data at the time the program is executed. (A prompt signals the user to enter data.)
  E. READ and DATA—used when the data is included as part of the program.
  F. FOR and NEXT—for coding loops.
  G. ON-GO TO—to replace several IF statements (e.g., 90   ON N GO TO 150, 1270, 2510, 3820).

IV. Arrays
A. Array—a list or a table of data stored in the computer.
B. Each item in an array is referenced with a subscript [e.g., T(1) and E(J)].
C. A DIM (dimension statement) is necessary if the subscript will exceed 10. Its purpose is to explicitly tell the computer how much room to reserve for an array. For example,

```
15 DIM E(12)
```

D. Uses.
1. To store totals.
2. To store tables.

Chapter Self-Evaluating Quiz

1. (T or F) A major advantage of writing a program in BASIC and entering it on a micro is that it does not have to be translated.
2. (T or F) Instructions in BASIC can have sequential line numbers such as 1, 2, 3, and so on.
3. (T or F) An INPUT command will prompt the user to respond with data.
4. (T or F) The instruction 10   PRINT is not valid since it does not indicate what is to be printed.
5. In the following instruction, what operation will be performed first?

```
20 LET X = A - B / C - C * D
```

6. (T or F) A REM statement can be used to produce headings on a printed report.
7. (T or F) The symbols <> in an IF statement mean "not equal to."
8. To include data as part of a program, we use _____ and _____ statements.
9. Write a FOR statement varying X so that it assumes all the odd numbers from 1 to 99.
10. Indicate how many times the loop will be executed with the following statement and what values X will assume.

```
10 FOR X = -5 TO 8 STEP 3
   .
   .
   .
50 NEXT X
```

11. Write a routine, using one INPUT statement and the FOR and NEXT statements, to read in 20 class grades and to then determine and print a class average.

12. A subscript is used to indicate _____ in a list or one-dimensional array.

13. The purpose of a dimension (DIM) statement is to _____.

14. Write a program using FOR-NEXT statements to read in the weights of 11 students and print the average. The weights will be supplied in one DATA statement. Store all the data in a list before proceeding with the calculations.

Solutions

1. F—The program must be translated by a BASIC compiler or interpreter. / page 438

2. T—It is recommended, however, that line numbers such as 10, 20, 30, etc, be used to allow for insertions. / page 443

3. T / page 447

4. F—It will cause a blank line to print. / page 457

5. B/C—page 457

6. F—A REM statement is a comment placed *within* the program. It is ignored during execution. / page 462

7. T / page 465

8. READ / page 490
   DATA / page 490

9. FOR X = 1 TO 99 STEP 2 / page 500

10. five times: X = −5, X = −2, X = 1, X = 4, X = 7 / page 500

11.

```
10 LET F = 0
20 FOR N = 1 TO 20
30      INPUT E
40      LET F = F + E
50 NEXT N
60 PRINT "AVERAGE GRADE IS", F / 20
70 END
```

/ page 501

12. the position of a particular value
    / page 506

13. tell the computer exactly how much room to reserve for a subscripted variable
    / page 507

14.

```
10 DIM W(11)
20 LET T = 0
30 FOR I = 1 TO 11
40     READ W(I)
50     LET T = T + W(I)
60 NEXT I
70 PRINT T / 11
80 DATA 123,175,186,110,134,142,147,189,122,201,184
90 END

*RUN
155.727
*
```

/ page 508

Key Terms

Alphanumeric constant	Numeric variable name
Array	Prompt
Enhancements	Protocol
Hierarchy of operations	Running total
Log-on procedures	String variable name
Looping	Subscript
Numeric constant	

Practice Problems

1. Write a program to read in five amounts from a terminal, one per line, calculate and print their average, and then repeat the process. Stop when an amount is equal to 99999.

2. Write a program to calculate the commission for each sales amount read in from a terminal. If the sales amount is greater than $5000, the commission is computed as 5 percent of the sales amount. If the sales amount is not greater than $5000 but is greater than $500, then the commission is 3% of the sales amount. If the sales amount is $500 or less, then the commission is zero. Print each sales amount and the corresponding commission. Stop when the sales amount is 99999.

3. Write a program to calculate the F.I.C.A. (Social Security) tax on each salary read in from a terminal.

$$F.I.C.A. = 7.05\% \text{ of the salary up to } \$37,800$$

(No tax is computed beyond the first $37,800.)
Print each salary and the corresponding F.I.C.A. tax. Stop when the salary is 99999.

4. Write a program to calculate the wages earned for each employee. The input consists of the following for each employee: name, hours worked,

and hourly rate of pay. Salary is computed as follows.

Wages = rate × hours, for hours ≤ 40
Wages = (rate × 40) + [rate × 1.5 × (hours − 40)], for hours > 40

Print each employee's name and the corresponding wage figure. Stop when rate of pay is 99999.

5. Write a program to read in the following accident data and produce a report with the information shown. Use READ and DATA statements for the input. Supply appropriate messages on the report to identify the results.

Input Data for each driver involved in an accident in past year:
a. Driver's name
b. State code (1 for New York)
c. Sex (M for male, F for female)
d. Birth date (month, year)

Output A report that shows the following results:
a. The percentage of drivers who were male and over 30.
b. The percentage of drivers from New York who are female.

6. Change the output in the above problem as follows. Produce a report that lists the names of all females from New York who were involved in an accident. Indicate the total number of New York drivers involved in accidents, at the end of the report. Assume a fifth field is added with a 1 for accidents, and a 0 for no accident.

7. Write and run a program to determine the most economical quantity of each product for a manufacturing company to produce. The economic order quantity Q may be determined from the formula:

$$Q = \text{square root of } \frac{2RS}{I}$$

The input for each product will consist of:
a. Product name.
b. Total yearly production requirement (R).
c. Inventory carrying cost per unit (I).
d. Setup cost per order (S).

The output should be a report that lists the above data for each product along with the value of Q that has been determined. Include appropriate identifying information. Assume 25 products.

8. Write a program to read in a two-digit decimal number and convert it to a binary number.

9. Write a program to read a five-digit binary number and convert it to a decimal number.

10. Write a program to calculate an attorney's fee. Three fields are read as input:

- Name of Client.
- Type of Fee.
- Amount Recovered.

If type of fee = 1, amount of fee = one-third of the amount recovered.
If type of fee = 2, this indicates a sliding scale; amount of fee will be:

- 50% of the first $1000 recovered.
- 40% of the next $2000 recovered.
- 35% of the next $22,000 recovered.
- 25% of any amount recovered over $25,000.

If type of fee is not a 1 or 2, print "INCORRECT DATA" and stop.

11. Write a program to produce a multiplication tables as follows:

Multiplication Table

	1×	2×	3×	4×	5×
1	1	2	3	4	5
2	2	4	6	8	10
3	3	6	9	12	15
4	4	8	12	16	20
5	5	10	15	20	25

Note: This is the same practice problem assigned previously. In this program, use FOR ... NEXT statements.

12. Use an array to store a six-digit binary number. Write a routine to calculate the decimal equivalent of the binary number.

13. A department store has 25 charge customers with customer numbers 1-25. For each purchase made, enter customer number and amount of charge. Input is entered randomly. There may be numerous entries for each customer. A customer number entry of 99999 signals the end of the job. Print:

```
           CUSTOMER CHARGE REPORT
     CUSTOMER NUMBER     TOTAL AMOUNT CHARGED

           1                   XXXX.XX
           .                      .
           .                      .
           .                      .
           .                      .
          25                   XXXX.XX
```

14. A department store allows a discount to each customer depending on the amount owed. This discount rate varies from month to month and hence is entered before the input data as a table:

```
FOR A MAXIMUM AMOUNT OF        DISCOUNT IS
          1000                   (   )
          5000                   (   )
         10000                   (   )
         99999                   (   )
```

Assume that the maximum amounts are fixed as above. Thus only the four discounts are entered. Then enter customer number and the amount owed. Compute and print the discount amount. A customer number of 99999 signals the end of the job.

15. Using the above problem, assume that the maximum amounts for each discount rate are also variable and must be entered as input. Use *four* discount rates as above.

```
ENTER MAXIMUM AMOUNT AND DISCOUNT
[ ] , [ ]
   .
   .
   .
```

16. Code the problem above, assuming that the number of discount rates themselves are variable.

```
ENTER NUMBER OF DISCOUNTS:
[ ]
ENTER MAXIMUM AMOUNT AND DISCOUNT
[ ] , [ ]
```

17. Complete a program that will print out the yearly book value of a machine based on the straight-line method of depreciation. Depreciation using the straight-line method is calculated by subtracting the salvage value at the end of the life of the machine, from the cost. The balance is divided by the number of years. This quantity (depreciation per year) is then subtracted from the cost on a yearly basis. Your program should appear as shown below. The underlined items will be the input data. An example of your output is shown with sample input data (underlined).

```
DEPRECIATION SCHEDULE
COST OF MACHINE?              11000

SALVAGE VALUE?                1000

YEARS OF LIFE?                 5

YEAR        BOOK VALUE AT END OF YEAR
  1                   9000
  2                   7000
  3                   5000
  4                   3000
  5                   1000
```

a. Clear the screen.
b. Print the heading "DEPRECIATION SCHEDULE."
c. Print the message "COST OF MACHINE?"
d. Input the cost of the machine.
e. Print the message "SALVAGE VALUE?"
f. Input the salvage value.
g. Print the message "YEARS OF LIFE?"
h. Input the years of life the machine is expected to be useful.
i. Print the heading:

```
"YEAR       BOOK VALUE AT END OF YEAR"
```

j. Compute the amount to be depreciated each year.
k. Add 1 to a year counter to keep count of the number of years depreciated.
l. Compute book value for the year by the following formula:
Book value this year = Cost − (depreciation per year × year counter)
m. Print the year counter and book value.
n. If year counter is not equal to years of life, repeat the program from step k.
o. End the program.

CASE STUDY: McKing's Superburgers, Inc.

Using the flowchart or pseudocode you developed in Chapter 11 for McKing's prepared food procedure, write a program in BASIC to accomplish the required logic. Use READ and DATA statements in place of an actual file and then run the program to verify that your logic is correct.

Consider the ad entitled "Hello, Headquarters" that appears in Figure 12.8.

Questions
1. Define the following terms as they are used in the ad:
   a. Programmable function keys.
   b. Modular design.
   c. Electronic mail.
   d. Advanced BASIC.

2. The ad states that after extensive comparison, the IBM Personal Computers' "BASIC language for communication support was [found to be] better." Explain what this means. How might an organization demonstrate that this statement was true?
3. What are "custom applications developed using IBM's Advanced BASIC for sales charts and graphs?"

Figure 12.8
Marketing computer products. (Courtesy IBM.)

*** WANG VS COMMAND PROCESSOR ***

WORKSTATION   0 READY   10:16 AM   FRIDAY   OCTOBER 30,

HELLO   Steve Grohe   EXT 4028

PRESS (HELP) AT ANY TIME TO INTERRUPT YOUR PROGRAM OR TO STOP
PROCESSING OF THE CURRENT COMMAND.

USE THE FUNCTION KEYS TO SELECT A COMMAND:

(1) RUN PROGRAM OR PROCEDURE   (11) ENTER OPERATOR MODE
(2) SET USAGE CONSTANTS   (12) SUBMIT JOB
(3) SHOW PROGRAM COMPLETION REPORT
(4) SHOW DEVICE STATUS

                                      (15) PRINT COMMAND SCREEN
(5) MANAGE FILES/LIBRARIES
(6) MOUNT/DISMOUNT VOLUME   (16) LOGOFF

CHAPTER

13

SYSTEMS SOFTWARE

CHAPTER OBJECTIVES

To familiarize you with:

- What systems software is and why it is used.
- Components of systems software.
- Computer capabilities that can be achieved with systems software.
- Common operating systems.

I. FEATURES OF SYSTEMS SOFTWARE

Thus far, we have considered one type of software referred to as application programs. We have discussed the steps involved in writing application programs and the various languages used.

The second major type of software is called **systems software**. It typically includes the following items:

IN A NUTSHELL

ELEMENTS OF SYSTEMS SOFTWARE

- Operating system.
- Compilers, assemblers, interpreters.
- Input/output control routines.
- Diagnostic routines.
- Job control and accounting routines.
- Report generators.
- Data base management systems.
- Utility programs for file-handling tasks such as sorting and transferring data from one I/O device to another.

The computer system itself operates on application programs under the control of an **operating system**, which is a major part of systems software. The specific characteristics of operating systems are beyond the scope of this text, but there are several features of these systems that are important to understand. See Figure 13.1 for a schematic of how an operating system interfaces with other components of a computer system.

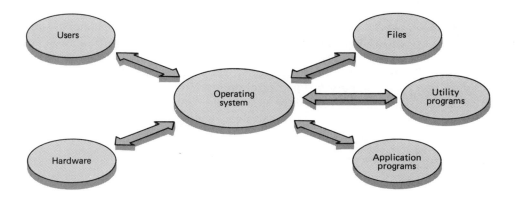

Figure 13.1
Schematic of how an operating system interfaces with other components of a computer system.

A. The Supervisor

The **supervisor** is the control program of the operating system. It coordinates, interrelates, and monitors all aspects of the operating system. As a main software element, it essentially ensures that the computer is operating effectively and efficiently with minimum operator intervention.

Typically the entire operating system consists of a **library** of compilers, assemblers, interpreters, and other programs in addition to the supervisor. They are all stored on an auxiliary storage device such as a disk, called the *system resident device*.

The supervisor is loaded into the main memory before any processing can begin. For computers that operate on a 24-hour basis, the supervisor is always resident in primary storage. Some of the main functions of the supervisor include:

IN A NUTSHELL

FUNCTIONS OF THE SUPERVISOR

1. Controls the processing of data by each application program.
2. Controls the calling of compilers, assemblers, and interpreters needed for translation of source programs.
3. Controls the processing of inquiry-response requests from numerous terminals in a time-sharing or on-line environment.
4. Communicates the requirements of each run to the computer operator via a console terminal.
5. Maintains job accounting information, that is, data on cost, time, date, and scheduling of each run.

In summary, the supervisor is a control program designed to ensure effective computer utilization and to minimize the need for computer operators to constantly monitor the machine's activities. In first-, second-, and even some third-generation computers without operating systems, computer operators were required to restart jobs when errors occurred, to maintain a log of computer activities, and so on. Moreover, with such systems, the ability to automatically process several requests from remote terminals was not feasible. An operating system, then, with a supervisor or control program results in (1) more efficient processing, (2) less need for operator intervention, and (3) the ability to process several requests from different terminals concurrently.

B. Communicating with the Supervisor

A special machine-oriented language designed to enable operators, users, and programmers to communicate their needs to the supervisor and, through it, to the operating system is frequently called a **job control language (JCL)**. A job control language (or simply control language on some systems) is used to perform system commands such as accessing data, programs, and other features of the computer system.

People Who Communicate with the Computer Using a Control Language

1. Data entry operator
   a. A job control language is necessary for indicating which files need to be accessed for inquiry-response purposes, what programs will be used for processing input, and so on.
   b. A job control language is keyed on the terminal by the operator.
2. Programmer
   a. A job control language is necessary for indicating which translator the supervisor should call in for program processing, what devices the program will use, what options the program requires, and so on.
   b. A job control language is entered prior to the program either on a terminal, on cards, or on whatever medium the program itself uses.
3. Computer operator
   A job control language is used to determine how long a specific job has been running, what tapes or disks need to be mounted for specific runs, how many terminals are being used at a specific time, and so on.
4. EDP auditor and DP manager
   A job control language provides job accounting data that is useful in evaluating the system and maintaining proper security.

If a programmer is entering a BASIC program on a terminal, the job control language is also entered on this device as in the following.

```
%E222 PLEASE LOGON
/  LOGON CSA010,A2129
% E223 LOGON ACCEPTED FOR TEN 2202, ON 05.12.86
AT 1434, LINE #050.
  ***HOFSTRA UNIVERSITY COMPUTING FACILITY***
   ***UNIVAC 90/60 MOD 2 ---VS/9 VER 3.5***
/  EXEC BASIC
% P500 LOADING VER# 009 OF BASIC.
BASIC 09, NEW OR OLD
*  NEW
NEW PROGRAM NAME--  STERN
READY
```

Note: Boxed entries are user-supplied.

On the other hand, if the program is entered on cards in batch mode as is sometimes the case with programs in languages like RPG and PL/1, then the job control language would also be entered on cards along with the source program. In either case, the job control language would indicate what translator is needed, what types of files are needed for execution, and so on. Figure 13.2 is a schematic of how an application program interfaces with the operating system.

Figure 13.2
Example of how an
application program
interfaces with the
operating system when it
is being translated.

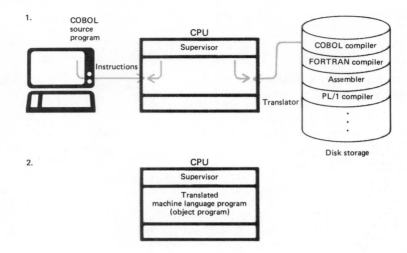

The computer operator, EDP auditor, or DP manager uses a special **console terminal** linked directly to the CPU to communicate with the supervisor. This console is similarly accessed by the supervisor program to indicate the computer's job accounting information for each run. See Figure 13.3 for an example of console terminals.

Figure 13.3
Example of console
terminals. (Courtesy IBM.)

Job Control Language Can Communicate the Following Requirements to the Operating System

System start-up procedures.
Program selection.
Diagnostic messages.
Error correction procedures.
Operating instructions.

Restart procedures.
Overrides.
Inquiry procedures.
Exit procedures.

C. Multiprogramming

1. Running More Than One Program Concurrently

Most modern computer systems, even many micros, usually have the control capability to process more than one program at any given time. That is, several terminals can access the computer practically simultaneously and perform the following:

IN A NUTSHELL

MULTIPROGRAMMING: EXECUTING MORE THAN ONE PROGRAM CONCURRENTLY

1. Some terminals can be used for entering data under the control of a data entry program.

2. Other terminals can be used for making inquiries about a specific data base under the control of an inquiry-response program.

3. Still other terminals and/or local I/O units can be used for entering, debugging, and running other programs concurrently.

All of these operations can be performed practically simultaneously. That is, the processing speed of the computer is so great that it looks to the user as if numerous programs are all running simultaneously even though instructions are executed one at a time. Multiprogramming requires a sophisticated supervisor to coordinate the execution of instructions from numerous programs, and a full-scale operating system.

The ability of a computer to run more than one program concurrently is referred to as **multiprogramming**. Multiprogramming is an essential and integral feature of time-sharing and data communications applications.

Typically there is space reserved in primary storage for the supervisor and there are **partitions** for numerous programs to be run.

Primary Storage

Supervisor
Partition 1—Program 1
Partition 2—Program 2
Partition 3—Program 3
Partition 4—Program 4

Note that although several programs may reside in memory at a given time, the CPU is actually only capable of executing *one instruction at one time*. But the supervisor enables the CPU to execute one instruction from one program, then another instruction from a second program, and so on, so that several programs can all be run concurrently.

2. Overlapped Processing

Computer systems are said to be I/O bound. That is, the slowest operations that they can perform are input/output functions. Thus, while a CPU can process data in speeds measured in nanoseconds, it reads or writes at much slower speeds—characters per second, lines per minute, and so on. If instructions were always executed one at a time in sequence, the slow I/O rate would significantly reduce the overall efficiency of the computer system. In a multiprogramming environment, a slow I/O operation from one program can be executed *at the same time* that arithmetic operations are executed from another. Because instructions can be executed in billionths of a second, the effect is that of executing numerous instructions practically *simultaneously*.

In essence, then, a program is not usually run continuously from beginning to end, when run in a multiprogramming environment. The net effect, however, is to run numerous programs in far less time than it would take to run them consecutively, one after another. Figure 13.4 illustrates how overlapped processing occurs.

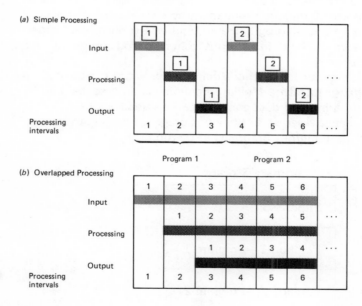

Figure 13.4
Simple processing compared to overlapped processing.

3. Needs of Computers That Operate in a Multiprogramming Environment

There are two additional aspects of the operating system software that must be used to avoid some potential difficulties of multiprogramming.

a. Storage Protection   As noted, multiprogramming enables more than one program to be in the computer at one time. Without any storage protection, the possibility exists that one program, if incorrectly coded, could inadvertently destroy or modify parts of another program and its corresponding data that are in the computer at the same time. This danger might arise especially when a new program is being tested. Most systems have a **storage protection feature** that prevents such dangers. In essence, an application program can only make changes to a single partition. In this way, it may have errors that cause incorrect processing, but it will not adversely affect the processing of other programs.

b. Priority Requirements   Since some application programs must conform to certain schedules, priorities must be established in a multiprogramming environment. Operating system software can be used for establishing priorities, so that the payroll program, for example, will always have priority over test runs. Similarly, on-line requests can be handled in some priority sequence as well, so that a manager's inquiry will be answered before that of a clerk, for example. Moreover, priorities can be assigned to specific terminals, minis, or micros that interface with a mainframe.

D. Multiprocessing

Multiprocessing is the use of two or more central processing units linked together to optimize the handling of data. In a multiprocessing environment, more than one instruction can be executed by the CPUs at the same time. This technique is different from multiprogramming, where one CPU can process different instructions from one or more programs concurrently by interleaving them. With multiprocessing, there is actually more than one CPU; hence instructions from different programs can be executed simultaneously.

A typical application of multiprocessing is the use of a minicomputer to handle scheduling, formatting of data, editing, and summary totals so that the main CPU or mainframe can be used for high-priority or more complex tasks. Figure 13.5 is an example of a large-scale multiprocessing system.

Figure 13.5
Example of a large-scale multiprocessing system. (Courtesy Sperry Corp.)

Sometimes a smaller CPU such as a minicomputer handles input/output operations from a variety of terminals. In this way, the mainframe needs to access only one unit—the minicomputer—rather than each of the numerous terminals. For such applications, the minicomputer is referred to as a **front-end processor**. This front-end processor can establish priorities for each of the terminals, queue the terminal inquiries if the mainframe is "busy," and maintain controls and accounting information.

Minicomputers are used with increasing frequency in a multiprocessing environment to relieve some of the load of a mainframe and to handle input/output scheduling and data entry from remote terminals.

E. Spooling

One function of the operating system is to establish a job queue and to process programs according to a priority system provided by the computing center. Application program output is then generally created on a disk, because disk is a high-speed device; the data is then transferred or *spooled* to the required output form in an off-line operation. This serves to further increase the efficiency of the overall system. Figure 13.6 is a schematic of how **spooling** operates. Figure 13.7 illustrates an actual device called a spooler, which contains the software necessary for performing the spooling operation. Input, as well as output, can be spooled to improve efficiency.

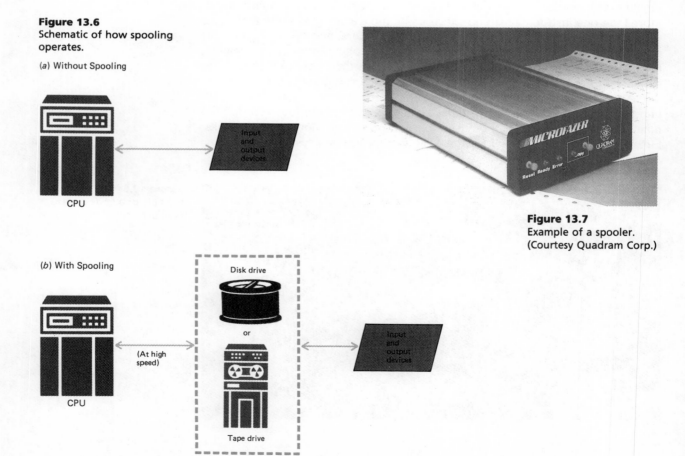

Figure 13.6
Schematic of how spooling operates.

(a) Without Spooling

CPU

Input and output devices

(b) With Spooling

Disk drive

or

Tape drive

CPU

(At high speed)

Input and output devices

Figure 13.7
Example of a spooler.
(Courtesy Quadram Corp.)

F. Virtual Storage

The **virtual storage concept** is an advance in computer technology that permits a computer system to operate as if it had more primary storage capacity than it actually has. This increases the multiprogramming capability of a system.

The virtual storage technique is accomplished by segmenting a program into a series of sections or modules that are stored outside the CPU, typically on a direct-access device such as magnetic disk. Instead of calling the entire program into the CPU at one time to be executed, the control system causes sections of the program to be read in and executed, one at a time. After one section has been executed, another section is brought into the CPU and uses the storage positions occupied by the previous section. This saves considerable storage since a 32K program, for example, might be segmented into 8K blocks that overlay each other. In this way, the 32K program only uses 8K for execution. Figure 13.8 illustrates how virtual storage is achieved.

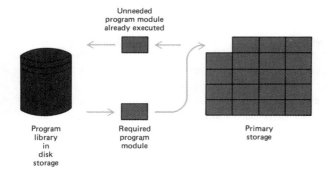

Figure 13.8
The virtual storage concept.

Virtual storage computers have an effective storage capacity far in excess of their actual storage capacity. Without virtual storage capability, several large programs, individually or collectively, might otherwise occupy too much CPU memory to be executed at the same time. Thus one way of facilitating multiprogramming capability is with a virtual storage operating system.

The operating system itself handles the segmentation of programs and swapping of program sections into and out of primary storage.

Many mainframes have virtual storage (VS) operating systems. One main requirement of such a system is an on-line capability and considerable size and speed.

II. WHO SUPPLIES SYSTEMS SOFTWARE?

In the past, the computer manufacturer or vendor supplied the systems software along with the computer system as part of a package. Thus even if the user were able to obtain more efficient systems software, there would be no simple way of contracting with the manufacturer or vendor for the hardware only. Now computer manufacturers and vendors must provide unbundled services. That is, the user can contract for each item of hardware or software separately.

Thus one can obtain a computer system from one vendor and obtain the systems software to control the operations of the hardware from either that vendor or a "software house" that specializes only in software packages.

Manufacturers or vendors generally supply an operating system designed specifically for each machine. An IBM 4341, for example, may use either the IBM OS, DOS, or the MUSIC operating system; the VAX may use VMS, an abbreviation for virtual memory system, and so on.

III. COMMON OPERATING SYSTEMS

Each computer typically has its own operating system. The following are general operating systems that can be used on a wide range of computers.

A. UNIX: An Increasingly Popular Operating System

One of the most popular operating systems available is **UNIX**, which was developed by Bell Labs in 1969. UNIX is a relatively small operating system but is extremely powerful and versatile. It has a very effective text editor that is easily used by noncomputer people. The major advantage of UNIX is that it is an exceedingly user-friendly operating system.

It has been used primarily with computers manufactured by the Digital Equipment Corporation (DEC), most specifically the PDP 11 and the more recent VAX. Many other manufacturers have begun to make UNIX available with their systems as well. UNIX is available for some micros, such as the IBM PC, as well as some mainframes. XENIX is a common micro version of UNIX.

The UNIX operating system is written in a high-level programming language called C. C is a relatively easy language to understand, even for the nonprofessional.

UNIX is a modular operating system that has a great deal of flexibility for integrating modules. It utilizes a hierarchical file system with sophisticated security and protection features.

UNIX was originally provided free to universities by Bell Labs. In 1973, UNIX was first made available to commercial organizations for a licensing fee of $20,000. This annual fee has, in recent years, been drastically reduced so that many vendors are currently selling software that can run with a UNIX operating system.

Figure 13.9 indicates the increased use of UNIX-related EDP expenditures in recent years.

B. CICS and CMS: Communications Monitors

CICS is an abbreviation for IBM's Customer Information Control System. It is a general purpose supervisor and data communications monitor that also provides data base management capabilities. CMS, Conversational Monitoring System, is another IBM innovation that has become very popular in recent years.

CICS and CMS provide an interface with an IBM operating system and application programs written in any one of a number of programming lan-

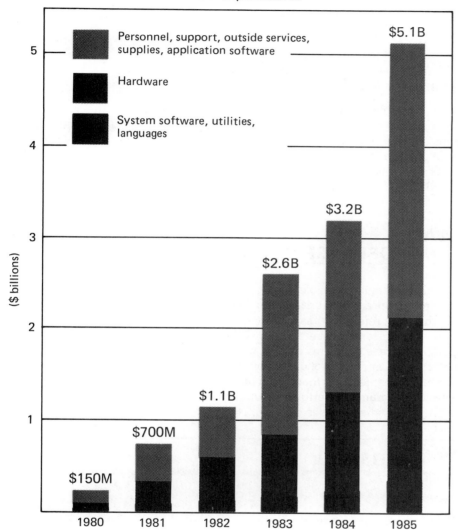

Figure 13.9
UNIX-related EDP expenditures. Expenditures for UNIX and UNIX-like products are expected to top $5 billion by 1985, and may reach $9 billion by 1986. The costs for application software, personnel, and services will account for most money spent on the operating system. (*Source:* Gnostic Concepts, Inc.)

guages, including COBOL, PL/1, RPG, and Assembler Language. Thus, strictly speaking, they are not full operating systems per se.

CICS and CMS can be configured to the needs of each specific installation. They enable systems resources to be distributed to each work station or terminal as needed.

Some of the features provided by CICS and CMS include:

1. Task management—handles priority scheduling, transaction monitoring, and synchronization.
2. Program management—provides multiprogramming capability.

3. Terminal management—handles formatting of data, interfacing with the system, queuing, etc.
4. File and data management—enables authorized users to update files, other users to query files, etc.

C. CP/M, PC-DOS, MS-DOS, and Other Operating Systems for Micros

As mentioned in Chapter 9, CP/M, PC-DOS, and MS-DOS are the most widely used operating systems for micros. UNIX is also widely used. There are literally dozens of other operating systems for micros. Each computer can typically use several different operating systems. The IBM PC, for example, comes with the PC-DOS operating system, although others such as CP/M, MS-DOS, and UNIX or XENIX can be purchased independently.

IV. REVIEW OF FIRMWARE: WHERE HARDWARE AND SOFTWARE MERGE

As already noted, it is possible to acquire as part of a computer system integrated logic circuits on a miniaturized chip that already contain software packages. Such chips are referred to as ROM (read-only memory) or **firmware**.

In small systems where primary storage is limited, the use of ROM is very popular. Whereas programs occupy bytes of main memory, ROM can be built into the system and thus not utilize any user memory. Thus the ROM can contain operating system features that would otherwise need to be programmed, as well as specific programs to perform required functions.

There are several types of ROM.

IN A NUTSHELL

TYPES OF ROM

ROM—read-only memory (standard)
A BASIC compiler for a micro, for example, may exist in ROM (see Figure 13.10).

PROM—programmable read-only memory
ROM that can be programmed by the user or vendor. ROM on a chip allows flexibility for users who would like to produce their own individualized set of functions.

EPROM—erasable programmable read-only memory
ROM on a chip may be erasable; that is, it may be programmed to include a set of functions that can be "erased" or overlaid with another program through a microcode procedure or through electrically erasing the ROM. Figure 13.11 illustrates devices for erasing EPROM chips.

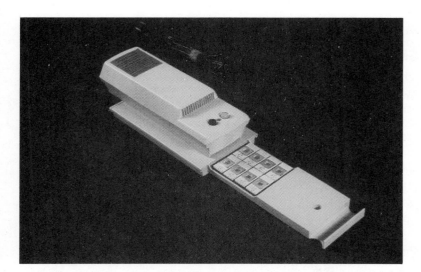

Figure 13.12 provides a brief history of the development of systems software, from its first "generation" in the 1950s to the present.

The Generations of Systems Software

First Generation 1950–1955
Basic Assembly Programs
Basic Utility Programs
Basic Sorting Programs

Second Generation 1956–1964
Macro Assemblers
Fortran Compilers
COBOL Compilers
Report Program Generators
More Utility Programs
Faster Sorting Programs
Basic Operating Systems

Third Generation 1965–1979
Enhancement to Second-Generation
   Programs
Teleprocessing Monitors
On-Line Programming Systems
Data Base Management Systems
Structured Programming Technology
Data Dictionaries

Program Generators
Information Retrieval Programs
Word Processing
Decision Support Systems
Virtual Storage Systems
Performance Measurement Systems

Fourth Generation 1980–1999?
Enhancement to Third-Generation
   Programs
Interactive Applications Development
   Systems
Relational Data Base Management
   Systems
Integrated Data Dictionaries
Integrated Systems Software
Integrated Graphics
Integrated Office Automation
Integrated Mainframe + Personal
Computer Software
Very High-Level Languages

Figure 13.12
History of the development of systems software. (*Source:* Applied Data Research Inc.)

CHAPTER SUMMARY

I. Features of systems software
   A. Systems software includes:
      1. The operating system.
      2. Compilers, assemblers, and interpreters.
      3. Input/output control routines.
      4. Diagnostic routines.
      5. Job control and accounting routines.
      6. Report generators.
      7. Data base management systems.
      8. Utility programs—for file handling, sorting, and transferring data.
   B. The supervisor.
      1. This is the control program of the operating system.
      2. It is loaded into the CPU from the operating system, which is in auxiliary storage.
      3. It controls the processing of each program.
      4. The supervisor minimizes the need for operator intervention.
   C. Communicating with the supervisor.
      1. Job control language is the special language devised for programmers, computer operators, data entry operators, EDP auditors, and DP managers to communicate with the CPU.
      2. Each computer's job control language is different.

D. Additional features of computers.
1. Multiprogramming.
   a. This is the ability to execute more than one program concurrently.
   b. This enables systems to function in a real-time mode using numerous terminals.
2. Multiprocessing.
   a. This is the use of two or more CPUs linked together to optimize the processing of programs and data.
   b. Minis used as front-end processors in conjunction with large mainframes typically operate in a multiprocessing environment.
3. Virtual storage.
   a. This permits a computer system to operate as if it had more primary storage capacity than it actually has.
   b. Programs are segmented and sections are swapped into and out of primary storage by the supervisor.
E. Firmware.
1. Firmware is software that is hardwired.
2. There are standard firmware units as well as programmable firmware units.

Chapter Self-Evaluating Quiz

1. The term _____ denotes those programs usually supplied by the computer manufacturer or software house that are designed to maximize the overall efficiency of the computer.

2. The entire control system is referred to as a(n) _____.

3. The _____ is another name for the specific control program that monitors the overall operations of the computer.

4. The compilers, interpreters, and assemblers used with a computer are typically stored on an auxiliary storage device such as a _____ and are accessed by the _____, as needed.

5. The programmer communicates with the supervisor with the use of a _____ language.

6. The computer operator communicates with the supervisor typically by using a device called the _____.

7. The ability of a computer to run more than one program concurrently is referred to as _____.

8. What is meant by a computer system being I/O bound?

9. Storage protection is an operating system feature used to prevent _____.

10. _____ refers to use of two or more central processing units linked together to optimize the handling of data.

11. (T or F) Virtual storage computers have an effective storage capacity far in excess of their actual storage capacity.

12. _____ refers to hardware that has been pre-programmed or wired to perform specific functions.

Solutions

1. systems software / page 523
2. operating system / page 523
3. supervisor / page 524
4. disk / page 524
   supervisor / page 524
5. job control / page 524
6. console terminal / page 526
7. multiprogramming / page 527
8. The slowest operations that can be performed are input/output functions. / page 528
9. accidental access by a program to another program's partition of memory / page 529
10. Multiprocessing / page 529
11. T / page 531
12. Firmware or ROM / page 534

Key Terms

CICS
Console terminal
Firmware
Front-end processor
Job control language (JCL)
Library of programs

Multiprocessing
Multiprogramming
Operating system
Partition
Spooling
Storage protection feature

Supervisor
Systems software
UNIX
Virtual storage concept

Review Questions

I. True or False

1. (T or F) The terms hardware and software refer to the input/output devices within a computer system.
2. (T or F) Software can be obtained from the computer manufacturer or from "software houses."
3. (T or F) The control program within a computer system can minimize programmer and operator effort, if utilized properly.
4. (T or F) The supervisor is called into the computer by each application program.
5. (T or F) The supervisor is always supplied by the computer manufacturer.
6. (T or F) Each computer system is supplied with its own supervisor.
7. (T or F) The supervisor is part of a larger control system that is typically stored on a high-speed input/output device such as a disk.
8. (T or F) One of the purposes of a supervisor is to minimize operator intervention.
9. (T or F) When a source program requires translation prior to execution, the supervisor must call in the compiler or translator.
10. (T or F) It is possible for a supervisor to retrieve specific programs from a library of programs stored on a high-speed input/output device.
11. (T or F) On most modern computers, it is possible to run several programs concurrently.
12. (T or F) Multiprogramming is made possible by a sophisticated control system.
13. (T or F) For most commercial applications, it is the calculations that require the most computer time.
14. (T or F) Job control language enables the programmer to communicate with the supervisor.
15. (T or F) All computers use the same job control language.

16. (T or F) Job control language specifies system commands.
17. (T or F) During the execution of any program, the supervisor is always maintained in the Central Processing Unit.
18. (T or F) Spooling maximizes the efficiency of input/output operations.
19. (T or F) PC-DOS and CP/M are popular operating systems for microcomputers.
20. (T or F) UNIX is an operating system that can be used with micros or mainframes.

II. Fill in the Blanks

1. A _____ feature of an operating system prevents one program from inadvertently destroying or modifying another program in the computer.
2. The term used to describe the set of programs designed to achieve maximum utilization of the computer is called _____.
3. This set of programs can be supplied by _____ or by _____.
4. The _____ is a special control program that must be in the CPU in order for programs to be run.
5. If a program needs to be compiled, the _____ program calls in the required compiler.
6. The entire control system that is typically stored on a high-speed device, such as disk, is sometimes referred to as a(n) _____.
7. Two major functions of a supervisor are to _____ and to _____.
8. A computer that has the control capability of allowing the simultaneous processing of more than one program at a time in the same CPU is said to have _____ ability.
9. A computer generally performs _____ operations much slower than processing operations; because of this, it is said to be _____ bound.
10. A job control language is used to facilitate communication between _____ and _____.
11. When the supervisor communicates with the operator, it prints messages on the _____.
12. JCL is an abbreviation for _____.
13. When data to be printed is transmitted from the CPU to a disk and then to the printer in an off-line mode, this is referred to as _____.
14. Two popular operating systems for microcomputers are _____ and _____.
15. When programs are actually part of the hardware, we call this _____.

APPLICATION

SIGNS OF UNIX SUPPORT SEEN COMING FROM IBM[1]

By John Gallant
and Paul Gillin

IBM's announcement of a Unix-based operating system for its Personal Computer was a powerful endorsement of the multiuser microcomputer and programmer workstation concepts. The debut of the Personal Computer Interactive Executive (PC/IX) also signaled IBM's corporate strategy to compete in a Unix world, according to analysts contacted last week by *Computerworld*.

IBM's introduction of PC/IX [CW, Jan 16], along with the release of the PCjr and the XT/370 was another step in the industry giant's strategy to blanket the low-end computer market, according to Richard McMahon, president of Acton, Mass.-based AMT Computer Consultants, Inc. "This is also a good forerunner of a larger strategy," McMahon explained. "It could very well be part of an overall game plan to support Unix across the entire line."

"We're all waiting for the other shoe to drop," agreed David Fiedler, editor of "Unique," a newsletter for Unix users. "When IBM says it will support Unix through its entire product line, that will be the really important announcement."

In fact, one observer was puzzled by IBM's decision to release PC/IX before making its anticipated announcement of Unix on a 4300 series superminicomputer. "I was hoping IBM would put its cards on the table and just announce its Unix policy," said Robert Marsh, president of Plexus Computer, Inc. and a director of USR/Group, a Unix users group.

Observers agreed that IBM's PC/IX announcement will bring order to an operating system that until now has lacked a strong vendor endorsement. "The move certainly legitimizes Unix," McMahon said. "It is now available for business applications, where before it was mostly geared to the scientific community. It means there will be wider acceptance of Unix.

Fiedler said the PC/IX announcement gained additional importance because it came just before AT&T introduced its own Unix-based micro.

However, Marsh said the IBM announcement is more of a Big Blue effort to establish a market presence than to throw down the gauntlet in front of AT&T. "There are a whole slew of companies with versions of Unix ready to jump, and IBM is trying to establish its position early before there's a lot of momentum in the other direction," he said.

McMahon said PC/IX makes the concept of a programmer workstation "quite a bit more viable."

[1]*Computerworld*, January 23, 1984, page 6. Copyright © 1984 by CW Communications/Inc., Framingham, MA 01701. Reprinted with permission.

Questions
1. Understanding Key Terms
   Define the following terms as they are used in the application.
   a. UNIX-based operating system.
   b. Multiuser microcomputer.
   c. Programmer workstation.
2. Software, Hardware, and Systems Concepts
   a. Explain the statement: "IBM's announcement of a UNIX-based operating system for its Personal Computer was a powerful endorsement of the multiuser microcomputer and programmer workstation concepts."
   b. What is meant by IBM's strategy to "blanket the low-end computer market"?
3. Management Considerations
   a. Why do you think that IBM has not "put its cards on the table and just announce its UNIX policy"? Is this good management strategy?
   b. As a manager, how would you assess the features of UNIX as a potential operating system for your computer?
4. Social, Legal, and Ethical Implications
   Some professionals believe that an organization should acquire the most popular operating system and not dwell on technical advantages and disadvantages. Do you agree or disagree? Explain your answer.

CASE STUDY: McKing's Superburgers, Inc.

McKing's is currently evaluating the specific vendor proposal that recommended a minicomputer for each restaurant.

1. What type of device is likely to be the system resident device?
2. Will an individual McKing's restaurant need multiprogramming capability? Explain your answer.
3. Would you recommend that a mini be used as a front-end processor in each individual McKing's restaurant? Explain your answer.
4. What type of firmware, if any, might be used at a particular restaurant?

THE COMPUTER AD: A Focus on Marketing

Consider the ad entitled "Natural On-line Applications Development System: It Makes Users Friendly" that appears in Figure 13.13.

Questions
1. Define the following terms as they are used in the ad:
   a. Applications development.
   b. On-line, interactive system.
   c. Plug-compatible mainframes.
2. In your own words explain the nature of the interactive system called NATURAL.
3. How does NATURAL relate to an operating system?
4. Is NATURAL a system that can be used with any computer or operating system? Explain your answer.

Figure 13.13
Marketing computer products. (Courtesy Software AG of North America, Inc.)

MODULE
5

THE WORLD OF INFORMATION SYSTEMS

CHAPTER 14

OFFICE AUTOMATION AND COMMON DATA COMMUNICATIONS SYSTEMS

CHAPTER OBJECTIVES

To familiarize you with:

- The elements of office automation systems.
- The future of office automation and its social impact.
- Point-of-sale systems as used in retail establishments.
- Electronic funds transfer systems as used in the banking industry.

I. OFFICE AUTOMATION

A. Objectives

Broadly defined, **office automation** refers to the use of computers and information processing techniques for performing and managing typical office functions. Frequently data communications lines are used to help automate the office by transmitting messages and data from one location to another.

Note that approximately 30% of the work force have jobs that directly focus on performing and administering office functions. Moreover, the predictions are that there will be a 10% shortage of white collar workers to manage office activities in the near future. Thus, there is both a need and a great impetus for improving the quality of office services through automation.

The major objectives of office automation, then, are as follows.

1. To enable managers to spend less time on clerical work and more time on managing.

Managers and administrators are often unable to complete their tasks because of frequent interruptions that occur during a normal business day. These interruptions result from the need to answer telephone calls, attend conferences, travel to inter-office meetings, respond to the mail, and so on. See Figure 14.1 for an estimate of the amount of time managers spend on clerical and other non-managerial activities. If these activities could be made more efficient, it would give administrators more time to actually make decisions; in addition, they would be better able to perform their management functions.

2. To provide improved information to office workers.

Both managers and their staff need information or reports that are more (a) timely and accurate, (b) readily available, and (c) user-friendly.

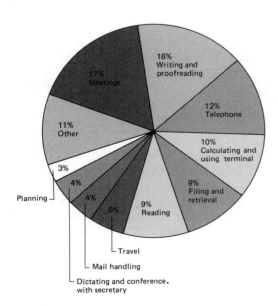

Figure 14.1
Analysis of the time spent by managers on clerical and non-managerial activities. Managers and professionals spend a majority of their time processing and exchanging information. (*Source:* IBM Office System Sales Seminars.)

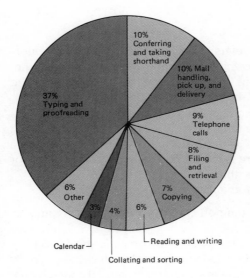

10%
Conferring
and taking
shorthand

10% Mail
handling,
pick up, and
delivery

9%
Telephone
calls

8%
Filing
and
retrieval

7%
Copying

37%
Typing and
proofreading

6%
Other

3%

4%

6%

Calendar

Collating and sorting

Reading and writing

Figure 14.2
Analysis of the time spent
by secretaries on clerical
and non-managerial
activities. Secretaries
provide a wide variety of
information processing
services for their managers.
(*Source:* IBM Office System
Sales Seminars.)

3. To reduce the clerical activities of secretaries, enabling them to serve as
office managers.

Secretaries as well as managers spend too much of their time on clerical
activities such as typing, filing, copying, taking messages, scheduling meetings,
and handling mail. See Figure 14.2 for an estimate of the amount of time
secretaries spend on clerical and other non-managerial activities. If these activities were automated, secretaries would have more time to efficiently manage
the flow of information into and out of the office. This would enable more
information to be processed and would result in more effective handling of the
information as well.

B. Typical Components of Office Automation Systems

The specific components of an office automation system designed to achieve
the above objectives include the following.

1. Word Processing

The term **word processing** refers to computer-aided preparation of documents. Word processors maximize the efficiency of document preparation, distribution, storage, and copying.

With a word processor or a word processing system, a user can type a
rough draft of a report or document. Word processing provides **text editing**
capabilities that enable the user to automatically perform the following before
obtaining a "clean" printout:

Text Editing Capability of Word Processing Systems

Deleting characters.

Inserting characters.

Underlining and/or printing bold face.

Automatic carriage return.

Automatic paging.

Moving or copying paragraphs.

Automatic margins.

Global searches to find and/or replace words or phrases.

Spelling checks with the use of a stored dictionary (optional).

Performing mathematical functions (optional).

Most word processing systems are designed to be as user-friendly as possible. Menus are supplied on a screen which provide instruction as to how to enter data and make changes. See Figure 14.3 for a sample "help" menu. With these "help" menus, a user can learn how to use a typical word processor in a matter of hours.

With text editing, a rough draft of a letter, report, or other document can be prepared, printed, filed, and changed at any time.

```
        A:TEST.DOC  PAGE 1  LINE 1  COL 1              INSERT ON
                              MAIN MENU
 *  *  Cursor Movement  *  *    |   * Delete *   |   *  Miscellaneous  *    |   *  Other Menus  *
^S  char left   ^D  char right  |  ^G  char     | ^I   Tab    ^B   Reform  |  (from Main only)
^A  word left   ^F  word right  | DEL  chr lf   | ^V   Insert On or Off    | ^J   Help    ^K  Block
^E  line up     ^X  line down   | ^T   word rt  | ^L   Find/Replace again  | ^Q   Quick   ^P  Print
 *  *    Scrolling              | ^Y   line     | RETURN End paragraph     | ^O   Onscreen
^Z  line up     ^W  line down   |               | ^N   Insert a RETURN     |
^C  screen up   ^R  screen down |               | ^U   Stop a command      |

 L----!----!----!----!----!----!----!----!----!----!----!----!----!----!--------R
 ■
```

Figure 14.3
Example of a 'help' menu.
(Courtesy MicroPro.)

Mailing lists are also prepared using word processors. Similarly, personalized direct mail documents to customers are commonly prepared by word processors; for this purpose, a name file is merged with a text to produce a letter or document that appears to have been individually prepared.

Many word processing systems can also provide final copy disk output to be used for driving photocomposition equipment so that books and newspapers prepared in-house can be automatically typeset.

As noted above, most word processing systems have dictionaries that can be used for checking spelling. These dictionaries can be expanded to include words that have specific use within a particular organization. Figure 14.4 illustrates how a word processor highlights spelling errors.

Most word processing systems have a keyboard for entering data and a CRT for displaying the entered data on a screen. A printer is essential for providing hard copy output. In addition to a CPU, a word processing system typically has an auxiliary storage unit such as a hard disk or floppy disk for storing the program and the data. There have been numerous advances in word processing equipment, so that some systems can even accept handwritten copy as input. Others have voice recognition devices that can interpret the spoken word. In this way, a user can dictate a letter or document; in addition changes can be made to a draft or document verbally.

MEMO

```
TO: ALL DEPARTMENT MANAGERS
SUBJECT: IBM DISPLAYWRITER SYSTEM

YESTERDAY, AN IBM MARKETING REPRESENTATIVE
DESCRIBED THE BENEFITS OF THE DISPLAYWRITER.

THE REP SAID THAT THIS SYSTEM HOLDS REVISIONS
AND REPETITIVE TYPING TO A MINIMUM, CHECKS THE
SPELLING  ACCURRACY  OF APPROXIMATELY
50,000  COMMONNLY  USED WORDS AND QUICKLY
 TRAASMITS  INFORMATION OVER ORDINARY TELEPHONE
LINES. SO, IT HAS THE POTENTIAL FOR IMPROVING
OUR PRODUCTIVITY.

THE DISPLAYWRITER SEEMS TO BE  EASU  TO USE AND
ECONOMICAL. AND, AS OUR NEEDS GROW, WE CAN
UPGRADE THIS SYSTEM INSTEAD OF REPLACING IT.
```

Figure 14.4
Example of how a word
processor highlights spelling
errors.

There are two broad categories of word processing systems.

a. Stand-Alone Systems   A **stand-alone word processor**, with its own CPU,
functions independently and is used primarily for typing correspondences and
reports. The stand-alone system may include the following elements:

- Typewriter-keyboard.
- CRT.
- Central processor—usually a micro- or minicomputer.
- Storage unit—hard disk, floppy disk, cassette tape, or magnetic card.
- Printer.

Figure 14.5 illustrates a stand-alone word processing system.

   A personal or microcomputer can function as a stand-alone word processing system, and be used for other tasks as well. Many word processing programs
are available that enable the micro to be used in this way. These include WordStar,

Figure 14.5
Stand-alone word
processing system. (Courtesy
CPT, Inc.)

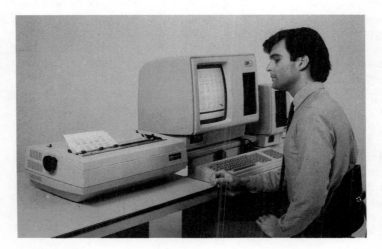

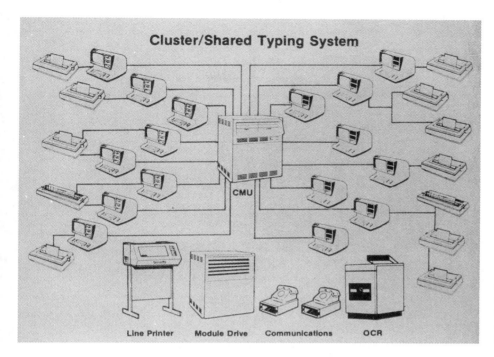

Figure 14.6
Schematic of a shared-logic word processing system. (Courtesy Lanier Business Products, Inc.)

Scripsit, Easywriter, and many others. Most of these software packages are available for several hundred dollars or less; in fact, some microcomputers are sold as a package that includes free word processing software.

There are also stand-alone dedicated word processors manufactured by companies like NBI and Lanier that have advanced word processing capabilities; these are typically used exclusively or predominantly for office automation functions. Dedicated word processors are more expensive than micros but their cost is decreasing at an average rate of 20% per year.

b. Shared-Logic Systems   A **shared-logic word processing system** is a computer network that can have numerous typewriter terminals controlled by a single mainframe or minicomputer. With a shared-logic system, documents produced at one station can be transmitted to other stations as necessary. Thus, in addition to performing the normal word processing functions that decrease the time required to prepare documents, a shared-logic system can serve as a communication tool to transmit interoffice reports and messages. It can also store documents in one central location. See Figure 14.6 for a schematic of a shared-logic word processing system.

Figure 14.7 provides an analysis of the major suppliers of word processing systems.

2. Electronic Mail

Electronic mail, like word processing, is an innovation that may well revolutionize the office. With the use of terminals or computers, and data communications lines, it is possible to transmit copies of a document or message to one or more locations in a matter of minutes or even seconds. Figure 14.8 provides examples of how electronic mail transmission typically functions.

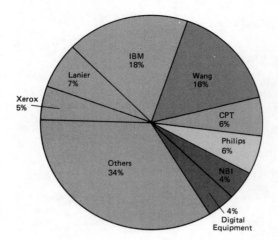

IBM
18%

Wang
16%

Lanier
7%

Xerox
5%

CPT
6%

Philips
6%

Others
34%

NBI
4%

4%
Digital
Equipment

Figure 14.7
An analysis of the major
suppliers of word processing
systems.

The types of electronic mail systems that have been developed include the following.

a. Electronic Message Systems   An **electronic message system** makes it possible for offices to transmit and receive documents without using external mailing organizations such as the post office or special messenger services. It is also possible to leave messages for particular individuals. One arrangement is to have a terminal at each manager's desk with access to an electronic mail system. When a manager is away, his or her machine is turned off and messages and documents "queue up." When he or she returns, the terminal is turned on and messages are transmitted, either in sequence or according to some preestablished priority code. The manager may also be able to "scan" a summary of the messages before selecting the desired sequence in which messages are to be transmitted.

Users can respond to messages, save them, delete them, copy them to other people, respond to them directly, and so on. Electronic message systems have great potential not only for office workers but for individuals in other application areas as well.

b. The Post Office Moves Away from Electronic Mail   **E-COM**, an abbreviation for Electronic Computer Originated Mail, was an experimental mailing system undertaken by the U.S. Post Office. Its objective was to provide a type of electronic mail service to a wide variety of users. There were several hundred customers, and it was anticipated that there would be several million messages transmitted annually.

There were numerous locations within the United States that functioned as "serving post offices." Messages generated at a user terminal were transmitted across telephone lines to a serving post office, which converted the message to hard copy and delivered it. The post office was committed to delivering such messages within 48 hours, either by hand delivery or by electronic transmission from the receiving post office to the intended recipient.

(a)
```
User ID: 40000,7776
Password: ▓▓▓▓▓▓▓▓
Code ? ▓▓▓▓▓▓▓▓
InfoPlex 1B(36) -- Ready at 10:53 EDT 23-Sep-85
on TO6CST 0 Text Files Pending

/COMPOSE
[ Ready ]

To: Purchasing Dept.

From: Marge Vinton
      Marketing Services

Subject: Purchase of Supplies

The following office supplies should be ordered
for Marketing Services and charged to account
576A37.
Thank you.

    2 dozen felt tip Pens (red)
    1 dozen No. 3 Pencils
    2 dozen manila file folders (triple cut)

/STORE PURCH
Subj?: Office Supplies, Marketing Services
Dept.

Text file 31-177 stored at 10:55 EDT 23-Sep-85

/BYE

Off at 10:55 EDT 23-Sep-85
```

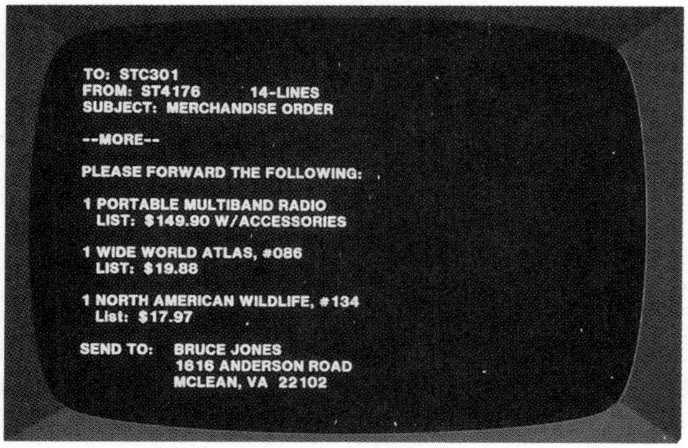

```
TO: STC301
FROM: ST4176       14-LINES
SUBJECT: MERCHANDISE ORDER

--MORE--

PLEASE FORWARD THE FOLLOWING:

1 PORTABLE MULTIBAND RADIO
  LIST: $149.90 W/ACCESSORIES

1 WIDE WORLD ATLAS, #086
  LIST: $19.88

1 NORTH AMERICAN WILDLIFE, #134
  List: $17.97

SEND TO:  BRUCE JONES
          1616 ANDERSON ROAD
          MCLEAN, VA  22102
```

(b)

Figure 14.8
(a) Example of electronic message system dialogue. (Courtesy CompuServe.)
(b) Electronic mail using a service organization called The Source. (Courtesy Source Telecomputing Corp.)

The Department of Housing and Urban Development had projected a savings of $10,500 per year by using E-COM to distribute mortgage insurance premium notices. Private organizations were seeing some savings in mailing promotionals and other material. But, in the end, E-COM failed and was abandoned because the overall anticipated savings never materialized. Thus, it is left to private organizations to provide electronic mail alternatives.

c. Use of Facsimile Equipment   **Facsimile equipment** provides the ability to transmit not only messages, but the contents of actual documents including company logos, graphics, signatures, and images, as well as plain text. The disadvantage of facsimile equipment, however, is a comparatively slow rate of transmission as compared to other methods of electronic transmission. On the average, 250 words may be transmitted at a rate from 2 to 6 seconds using standard facsimile devices (see Figure 14.9).

Figure 14.9
Example of a facsimile device. (Courtesy Xerox Corp.)

3. Types of Electronic Message Systems

Of the three types of electronic mail alternatives described above, electronic message systems are the most popular. There are several types of electronic message systems.

a. Intra-Office Network   This is a network contained within a single location. Local area networks are used extensively for internal communications within a given building or within several buildings that are in close proximity to each other.

b. Subscriber Service   Organizations such as The Source and CompuServe make electronic mail services available to subscribers. They typically require the user to link a terminal, personal computer, or other system to a modem in order to dial up or phone the service. In addition to providing other special functions, these companies serve as a clearinghouse for groups of organizations in much the same way as a post office serves as a clearinghouse. They store all messages until the receiving subscriber logs on and checks his or her mail. For subscriber services to be effective, both the person or organization transmitting a message and the person or organization receiving the message must subscribe to the same service.

c. Point-to-Point Configuration for Inter-Office and Intra-Office Mail   This is a system in which the transmitting station and the receiving station are directly linked to one another either by cable or telephone. For intra-office transmission, each user has access to one central facility. For inter-office transmission, central computer facilities of each office are linked for electronic message switching.

This technique eliminates the need for a service or subscriber organization. One main disadvantage, however, is the potential problem of lack of compatibility between the transmitting organization and the receiving organization. If the software used to transmit or receive messages is not compatible, the text will be undecipherable.

d. Telex   There is a large base of subscribers who have been using Telex services for many years. This makes Telex a viable alternative to other subscriber services and the post office for transmitting messages to a wide variety of organizations.

IN A NUTSHELL

ELECTRONIC MESSAGE SYSTEMS

The biggest stumbling block to electronic message systems in the past has been cost, but costs are falling rapidly. By the late 1980s, it is possible that electronic mail will be even cheaper than postage. Hewlett-Packard, for example, currently has a system in which 25 million messages are transmitted annually for an average cost of less than 5¢ per message.

A second stumbling block is lack of compatibility among divergent technologies.

4. Professional Workstations

As we have noted, office automation is not only intended for clerical workers but for managers or "knowledge workers" as well. It has been estimated that 75% of a manager's time is spent disseminating information. Reducing this percentage will provide professionals with more time for their managerial and decision-making tasks.

In many offices, each manager or executive has a terminal or a microcomputer that serves as a **professional workstation**. The main objective is to minimize clerical and communication functions of managers, so that they can focus on their professional responsibilities.

In addition to word processing and the transmission of electronic messages, one main function of a professional workstation is assisting managers in the preparation of a budget. There are numerous programming packages available that will enable a manager to "plug in" specific budgetary values and have the computer determine the overall effect of proposed changes. This is often referred to as "what if" analysis. It is extremely useful in saving time and in helping to predict the best course of action in different situations. VisiCalc, CalcStar,

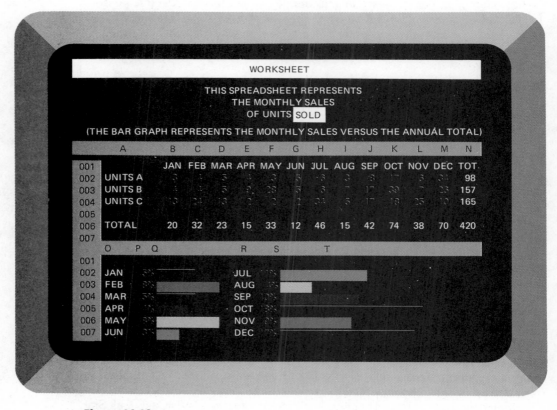

Figure 14.10
Sample spreadsheets.

and SuperCalc are **electronic spreadsheet** packages that enable people to make projections not only about budgets but about other business tasks as well. Figure 14.10 illustrates displays produced by electronic spreadsheets.

In general, a professional workstation may be used for the following functions:

IN A NUTSHELL

FUNCTIONS OF A PROFESSIONAL WORKSTATION

1. Word processing.
2. Electronic mail.
3. Electronic spreadsheets.
4. Accessing data from a mainframe and obtaining reports or answers to inquiries.
5. Accessing major on-line retrieval services that provide useful information for the manager.
6. Providing administrative support such as scheduling meetings, maintaining calendars, maintaining "tickler" or reminder files, maintaining automated telephone directories, performing electronic filing, and so on.

See Figure 14.11 for an analysis of the growing market for professional workstations.

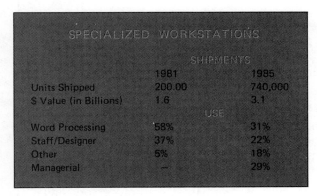

Figure 14.11
The growing market for professional workstations.
[*Source:* Gnostic Concepts (Data Resources Inc.)]

5. Telephone Switching Systems

With the use of advanced computerized telecommunications equipment, it has become possible for a telephone switching system to help improve the overall efficiency of office work. Some examples of computerized functions that can be performed by a telephone switching system include:

Computerized Functions Performed by a Telephone Switching System

Storing phone numbers.

Automatic dial-up.

Teleconferencing.

Forwarding calls.

Automatic call-back when lines are busy.

Distributing calls—queuing incoming calls so that the caller waits for the next available open line.

All of these services can be provided within an advanced data communications network used for both voice and data transmission.

6. Teleconferencing

Traditionally, conferences have been viewed as the most desirable form of group communication. There are, however, some problems associated with conferences:

Problems Associated with Attending Conferences

Travel expenses are high.

Time is lost in travel.

Face-to-face meetings are often unstructured.

"What if" information is often not available.

Group communication is sometimes subject to misunderstanding.

Teleconferencing is the use of electronic transmission of messages in place of face-to-face meetings for communication. Teleconferencing has the following advantages:

IN A NUTSHELL

ADVANTAGES OF TELECONFERENCING

1. Discussions with the use of electronic transmission are efficient and inexpensive.
2. Recording of messages is automatic.
3. Multiple users are easily accommodated.
   a. Subcommittees of large conferences can be organized.
   b. Ballots for voting on various issues can be transmitted and tabulated.
4. Access to other resources such as data bases, word processors, and so on can be automatic.

C. The Social Implications of Office Automation

The technology for achieving an automated office has been available for several years now. Yet the actual development of automated offices has lagged. The main reason for this unrealized potential is resistance. Many secretaries, as well as managers, are not comfortable with the concept of computers in the office and thus are resisting their use.

The word processor, however, which is one aspect of office automation, has become increasingly popular largely because it is now very user-friendly. In addition, many office workers are beginning to view the professional workstation as a useful tool for a wide variety of applications. The fully automated office, then, appears to be slowly evolving.

Another reason why office automation has not developed as quickly as some people have predicted is because of the potential implications for the work force in general. Many workers believe that automated offices will reduce the number of employees in an organization. This fear certainly will inhibit effective utilization of computers by those who are worried that they may lose their jobs or that their responsibilities might be diminished. Social researchers believe that these fears must be addressed and allayed before a fully automated office can become a reality.

Thus the fear of mass unemployment is one major social implication of computers in the office. Another implication has more positive overtones. Computers are a useful tool for expanding the work environment, enabling some employees to work at home without the need to travel into the office a full five days a week, or more. Combined with the expectation that office automation will mean (1) more meaningful information distributed to office workers, and (2) less need to spend time on mundane, clerical functions, this benefit is helping to make computers more widely accepted as office tools.

In summary, integrated office automation consists of:

1. Communications—data, voice, and text.
2. Information retrieval.
3. Analytical tools.
4. Text preparation.
5. Personal support tools—scheduling, electronic calendar, and electronic mail.

LOOKING AHEAD

Office Automation

1. There is a growing need for proper planning to ensure:
   a. An understanding of office automation products available.
   b. Proper integration of elements within the office.
   c. Appropriate organizational support strategies.
2. Voice input systems will become increasingly popular.

   Office workers will be able to dictate messages, letters, and reports, and obtain output from a word processor.
3. Teleconferencing will become increasingly popular.
   This will significantly minimize the cost and time for travel.
4. More shared-logic systems with high-powered capabilities will become available.
5. More professional workstations will be used by managers.

D. Information Resource Management

In recent years, companies have begun to recognize the fact that information is a fundamental resource of the firm that should be administered by a central coordinator just like any other resource. Many executives support the concept of a separate information resource organization supervised by **information resource management**. The concept is to keep the information resource task separate from data processing; thus it should be coordinated and supervised by a separate management group.

LOOKING AHEAD

Information Resource Management (IRM)

1. Information resource management should supervise the flow of information within an organization; traditional management tools and techniques should be applied to the supervision of this information flow.

2. Organizations need an IRM manager who will oversee information needs and office automation; the IRM and the DP functions should be supervised by different individuals.

3. Traditional techniques such as inventory analysis, cost accounting, and budgeting can be applied to the management of information itself.

4. Policies on acquisition and control of personal computers and professional workstations for managers or knowledge workers, as well as secretaries, should be coordinated through the IRM organization.

Self-Evaluating Quiz

1. The term _____ describes the use of computers and information processing techniques to operate and manage the office.

2. (T or F) One main objective of office automation is to reduce the decision-making authority of managers.

3. (T or F) Office automation is designed to reduce the clerical activities of both office workers and office managers.

4. The term _____ refers to computer-aided preparation of documents.

5. (T or F) Most word processors permit users to move or copy paragraphs or inserts from one area of a document to another.

6. (T or F) In general, automatic spelling checks provided by dictionaries that are part of word processors have not been very successful.

7. (T or F) With text editing, a rough draft of a letter, report, or other document can be prepared, printed, and changed at any time.

8. Word processors typically use a _____ for data entry, a _____ for displaying output, and a _____ for hard-copy output.

9. A _____ word processor has its own CPU and functions independently for typing correspondences and reports.

10. (T or F) A standard microcomputer can serve as a word processor.

11. A word processing system that has numerous stations linked to one CPU is called a _____ system.

12. The term _____ refers to the transmission of messages, reports, and mail over data communications lines.

13. (T or F) The post office no longer offers an electronic mail service.

14. When a manager or "knowledge worker" has a micro or terminal at his or her desk for retrieving data, sending messages, and performing calculations, the device is called a _____ .

15. A software package called a(n) _____ enables a user with minimum computer background to prepare budgets, profit-loss statements, and so on.

Solutions

1. office automation
2. F—One main objective is to provide managers with more time for decision-making.
3. T
4. word processing or text editing
5. T
6. F—They have been very successful.
7. T
8. keyboard (although voice entry and scanners may also be used)
   CRT
   printer
9. stand-alone
10. T
11. shared-logic
12. electronic message system or electronic mail
13. T—E-COM (Electronic Computer Originated Mail) failed.
14. professional workstation
15. electronic spreadsheet

II. POINT-OF-SALE (POS) SYSTEMS

One main consumer-oriented application of data communications equipment and terminals is the **point-of-sale (POS) system**. Broadly defined, a point-of-sale system uses computers in retail establishments to enter data at the actual location where a sale is transacted. The following describes the major POS applications in use today:

Main POS Applications

	Features			
Area	Inventory Control	Rapid Cash Transaction Reporting	Accounts Receivable	Illustrative Figure
Supermarkets	X	X		14.12
Fast-food restaurants	X	X		14.13
Department stores	X		X	14.14
Hotels		X	X	14.15

Figure 14.12
POS system in a supermarket. (Courtesy IBM.)

Figure 14.13
Bar/restaurant control system. (Courtesy NCR.)

Figure 14.14
POS system in a department store. (Courtesy NCR.)

Figure 14.15
Guest accounting control system. (Courtesy NCR.)

Point-of-sale systems at supermarkets, fast-food restaurants, department stores, and hotels usually use **electronic cash registers** that perform the following functions. See Figure 14.16 for an example of an electronic cash register.

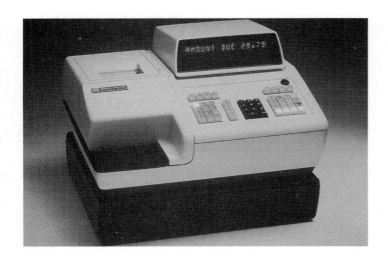

Figure 14.16
Electronic cash register. (Courtesy General Instruments.)

Functions of an Electronic Cash Register

Automatic price look-up.

Automatic extensions (unit price × number of items).

Automatic tax calculation.

Automatic discount calculation.

Automatic voiding of transactions.

Automatic processing of credits or returns.

In department stores, fast-food restaurants, hotels, and supermarkets, electronic cash registers function as point-of-sale terminals for entering the data. These electronic cash registers or POS terminals can store keyed data in some machine-readable form such as disk or tape, or they can immediately transmit the data to a mainframe for on-line file processing and management.

POS systems are used for the following purposes:

IIII➡ **Why POS Systems Are Used**

1. Automatic computations at the point of sale.
2. Data collection.
3. Data communications—transmission of data to a central location.
4. Transaction control—preparation of bills, invoices, and internal reports.
5. Inventory control.
6. Automatic credit authorization.

A POS system has the following advantages:

IN A NUTSHELL

ADVANTAGES OF A POS SYSTEM

1. Minimizes the risk of operator errors.
2. Serves as an automatic data entry device for computer processing.
3. Can be used to immediately update inventory records and customer accounts.
4. Can be used to verify a customer's credit status before an item is charged.
5. Can be used in conjunction with an electronic funds transfer system, discussed below, to automatically transfer funds from a customer's bank account to a store's account.
6. Provides management with on-line information about inventory, salesperson productivity, sales analysis, and so on.

In addition to, or instead of, electronic cash registers, many POS systems have data entry devices which serve as terminals to accept data that is either keyed in manually or that is read by a bar code reader.

Typically, in supermarkets and some retail stores, the operator or clerk is required to use a device called a wand to scan a bar code that contains inventory data. The wand will automatically transmit data to the terminal or electronic cash register. In other cases, a laser beam scans the bar code and then transmits the data to an electronic cash register. Bar code readers are just one type of input device known as an *optical scanner*. The other types of optical scanners have been discussed in Chapter 5.

Most supermarket products have a bar code stamped on them identifying both the product and the manufacturer. This code is called the **Universal Product Code (UPC)**.

The UPC consists of a series of bars of differing widths and with different-sized spacing between them. Most items have bars that represent 10 numbers, the first 5 identifying the manufacturer and the last 5 identifying the product. Figure 14.17 shows a scanning device used for "reading" a Universal Product Code.

The UPC on a supermarket product is typically scanned or read by a bar code reader. Some department stores have inventory tags with bar codes that are also read by bar code readers.

As noted, some POS terminals require the operator to key in the item identification data and the price. Others can automatically scan the bar code, using either laser beams, a wand, or a light pen. A scanning device saves the operator the need for entering the product code and even the price. That is, the POS terminal can "look up" the price of each item from a computerized table, reducing the risk of errors and increasing efficiency. It also enables stores to run sales or increase prices without having to manually change the price of each item.

Figure 14.17
Bar code reader. (Courtesy MSI Data Corp.)

When POS systems were first implemented in supermarkets, many consumers objected to the elimination of individual prices on items. Even though unit pricing for each item increases costs, it provides the consumers with a useful method for verifying prices charged. To protect the consumer, numerous states have passed laws requiring unit pricing on all consumer goods. In many other states that do not have such laws, unit pricing has been retained to help promote customer goodwill.

The success of the Universal Product Code in identifying supermarket items scanned by POS terminals has prompted many department stores to use bar codes to identify their stock or inventory. These bar codes can indicate vendor, style, color, size, department, store, and price of each item. Special electronic cash registers with bar code readers are used to automatically scan the tag on each item. This saves the operator the keying time that would otherwise be necessary. Data that is entered this way may be stored and then used for inventory and accounting purposes in either an interactive or a batch mode.

Types of POS Systems

1. Interactive system.

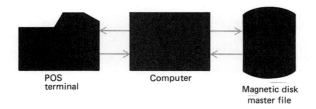

POS terminal   Computer   Magnetic disk master file

Key Features
    a. Immediate update.
    b. Immediate verification.
    c. Inquiry ability.

2. Key-to-storage POS system using batch processing.

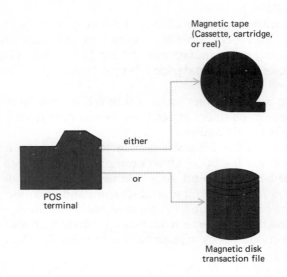

Magnetic tape
(Cassette, cartridge,
or reel)

POS
terminal

either

or

Magnetic disk
transaction file

Key Features

a. At fixed intervals, a transaction file on tape or disk may be used to update the master file in a batch mode.
b. Updating is not immediate.
c. Less expensive than interactive systems.

III. ELECTRONIC FUNDS TRANSFER (EFT) SYSTEMS

A. Introduction

An **electronic funds transfer (EFT) system** is one in which computers are used by banks to enter data at the point of a transaction and to automatically update banking records.

EFT systems can operate within a single branch office, or in a network linking all branch offices to one large central banking facility. EFT systems can also be used in conjunction with point-of-sale systems to automatically transfer funds from a customer's bank account each time a purchase or transaction is made.

The ultimate aim of EFT is the complete and integrated electronic transmission of banking information. Since an EFT system would eliminate the need for any transmittal of paper such as checks or even cash, its ultimate objective is sometimes referred to as "The Cashless Society."

Currently, banks process 70 billion checks annually at an approximate cost of 20¢ per check. The expectation is that improved EFT systems can reduce this cost by 35%. This would result in substantial savings for the banking industry, savings the industry hopes to pass on, at least in part, to the consumer.

B. Implementation of EFT

A fully integrated electronic funds transfer system is a long way from being realized, if indeed it could ever become a reality. Several aspects of banking have, however, been successfully automated.

1. Automatic Teller Machines

Automatic teller machines at bank branch offices and other locations serve as terminals to facilitate the processing of deposits and withdrawals. Approximately 15,000 of these EFT terminals are in use today. They can provide 24-hour banking service. An automatic teller machine may be located in the lobby of a bank, in an office building, or even in an apartment house. If a customer wishes to withdraw cash, he or she inserts a plastic bank identification card into the terminal and keys in a personal identification number that serves as a password. Once the computer verifies the password, it displays a message on the terminal screen directing the customer to indicate the type of transaction (e.g., withdrawal) and the amount involved. After this data is entered, the computer ascertains if there are sufficient funds in the account, and if so, the money is automatically supplied to the customer. Figure 14.18 illustrates a teller machine utilized for this purpose.

Figure 14.18
Automatic teller machine.
(Courtesy NCR.)

2. Interactive EFT-POS Operations for Credit Verification and Automatic Funds Transfer

Interactive EFT-POS operations typically involve the immediate electronic transfer of money at the point at which a sale occurs. In order to pay for merchandise in a store, for example, a customer presents to the salesperson his or her bank card, typically referred to as a "debit card." This card is inserted into an EFT terminal that is directly linked to the customer's bank. The customer ordinarily keys in his or her personal identification number or code. If there are sufficient funds in the customer's account, they are immediately transferred electronically to the store's bank account. This procedure is unlike the use of existing bank credit cards in that the transaction results in an immediate and automatic debit to the customer's existing account and an automatic credit to the store's account.

3. Preauthorized Banking

Preauthorized banking is an EFT innovation that enables deposits and payments to be made electronically. Typical applications include:

1. The direct deposit of funds such as payroll checks, social security payments, and stock dividends to an individual's bank account.
2. The direct payment by the bank of a customer's regular expenses such as mortgage and car payments.
3. The use of a Touch-Tone telephone by a customer to authorize the bank to pay certain bills directly or to transfer money from one bank account to another.

4. Automated Clearinghouse Procedures

An automated clearinghouse application uses an electronic network to facilitate the exchange of funds among financial institutions that are involved with the check-clearing process. These procedures would otherwise take many days and result in inefficient exchanges of paper.

5. Check Guarantee Services

A check guarantee service enables a retail establishment to have direct communication with the customer's bank for check-cashing purposes. The bank guarantees the check used to pay for goods and services if, of course, there are sufficient funds in the account.

LOOKING AHEAD

When the idea for electronic funds transfer was conceived, many financial experts, as well as computer professionals, predicted that the technology would ultimately lead to a cashless and checkless society. They believed that EFT would have even more profound effects on the economy and consumer purchase power than the introduction of the credit card in the 1950s.

But, for many reasons, this prediction has not yet been borne out. There are, in fact, many who now believe that EFT will never have the profound effect on the economy once predicted.

It is interesting to note that, despite the current uses of electronic banking, the financial system in this country relies more heavily today on cash and checks than in the past. The potential for a "cashless society" is no more imminent or likely than it was a decade ago.

Despite the fact that EFT systems have not been fully realized, there are, however, some basic advantages to the EFT innovations described above. These include:

IN A NUTSHELL

ADVANTAGES OF EFT

1. Convenience.
   Electronic banking saves time and enables the elderly and infirm to bank at home. Others too busy to travel to a bank also benefit.

2. Reduced paperwork.
   Pressures on the Post Office may eventually be reduced. With fewer checks being processed by mail, the burden on the Post Office is expected to lessen somewhat.

3. Reduced need for cash.
   Because there is less need to carry cash, there is less fear of robberies, counterfeiting, and so on. This increases personal security.

4. Potential for decreasing the cost of banking.
   As the amount of paperwork is decreased with the use of direct deposits and payments through preauthorized banking, costs will eventually be reduced.

The opponents of EFT point to the following disadvantages:

1. Fear of invasion of privacy.
   The late Supreme Court Justice William O. Douglas, in his dissent in the California Bankers Association Case several years ago, best summarized the privacy problem as follows:

   A person is defined by the checks he writes. By examining them the [government] agents get to know his doctors, lawyers, creditors ... and so on ad infinitum .... [T]hese ... items will ... make it possible for a bureaucrat—by pushing one button—to get in an instant the names of 190 million Americans who are subversive or potential and likely candidates.[1]

2. Since the cost of converting to EFT is high, it may reduce competition in the banking sector. That is, banks that cannot afford electronic systems may not be able to compete for customers who like the conveniences that EFT systems afford.

3. Fear of reduced control over personal finances.
   a. The canceled check, for example, has traditionally been a customer's proof of payment. With a fully implemented EFT system, the canceled check would no longer be used.

---

[1]*California Bankers Association v. Schultz*, 416 U.S. 30, 85.

    b. Stop payments would not be feasible since a customer's account is automatically debited when a transaction is made.

    c. There would be no check "float"—that is, the period between the time a check is cashed and the actual transfer of funds by the bank. Currently this two- to three-day delay on the average provides consumers with some leverage they would not have with EFT.

IV. THE INTERNATIONAL ISSUE RELATING TO DATA COMMUNICATIONS: TRANSBORDER DATA FLOW

With the great proliferation of data communications both in the United States and abroad, the potential for invasion of privacy, security leaks, and other loss of confidentiality is great.

Laws have been passed in more than 20 countries to deal with such problems when information flows across national boundaries. **Transborder data flow**, then, is governed by legislation at the national level. While these laws are important for preserving individual rights, they present a potential threat to the world economy by constraining trade.

Spain, for example, requires money to be deposited in escrow before data files can be transmitted electronically to another country. Sweden requires a government agency to approve any transmission of personal data outside the country. Hence, trading with these countries can be costly and have bureaucratic and political problems associated with it.

CHAPTER SUMMARY

  I. Office automation
    A. Intended for both managers and office workers.
    B. Components:
      1. Word processing.
        a. Preparation, distribution, storage, and copying of documents and reports.
        b. Automated and personalized mailings.
        c. Either stand-alone or shared-logic systems.
        d. Either standard micros or dedicated systems used exclusively for word processing.
      2. Electronic mail.
        a. Supplied by a subscriber service, a network, facsimile equipment, or the postal service.
        b. Used for transmitting messages, reports, and documents.
      3. Professional workstations.
        a. Used by office managers and secretaries.
        b. For word processing, electronic mail, "what if" analysis, accessing data bases, and automated administrative functions.

4. Telephone switching systems.
For storing telephone numbers, automatic dial-up, forwarding calls, automatic call-back, and so on.
5. Teleconferencing.
Use of electronic transmission for communication.
II. Point-of-sale (POS) systems
A. For supermarkets, fast-food establishments, department stores, and hotels.
B. For inventory control, transaction reporting, and accounts receivable.
C. Equipment:
1. Bar code reader or key device for entering data.
2. Electronic cash register for price look-up, calculations, and credit verification.
3. Data may be stored locally or transmitted to a host computer.
III. Electronic funds transfer (EFT) systems
A. Typical components.
1. Automatic teller machines.
2. Interaction with POS systems for credit verification and transmission of funds.
3. Preauthorized banking.
4. Automated clearinghouse procedures for check-clearing.
5. Check guarantee services.
B. Advantages.
1. Convenience.
2. Reduced paperwork.
3. Reduced need for cash.
4. Decreased banking costs.
C. Disadvantages.
1. Fear of invasion of privacy.
2. Only the largest banks will be able to absorb the initial costs of EFT.
3. EFT reduces control over personal finances.

Chapter Self-Evaluating Quiz

1. Office automation is designed to automate clerical functions performed by _____ and _____.
2. The term *word processing* refers to _____.
3. (T or F) In order to use electronic mail, each recipient of electronic mail would need to have his or her own computer.
4. A subscriber service such as CompuServe can be used for electronic transmission of _____ from one office to another.
5. Managers who require immediate access to a central data base and access to an electronic message system should consider the acquisition of a _____.

6. The term _____ is the use of electronic transmission in place of face-to-face meetings for communication.

7. (T or F) Office automation, in general, has progressed faster than generally expected because of almost universal acceptance by office workers.

8. (T or F) Information resource management is generally viewed as a DP function to be supervised by the DP manager.

9. A _____ system is one that uses computers in retail establishments to enter data at the actual point where a sale is transacted.

10. Four major application areas for point-of-sale systems are _____, _____, _____, and _____.

11. Three main uses for point-of-sale systems are _____, _____, and _____.

12. One typical data entry device of a point-of-sale system is a(n) _____.

13. (T or F) A point-of-sale system can be used for automatic credit authorization.

14. Data entered into a point-of-sale system may be keyed or scanned using a _____.

15. The bar code used to identify grocery products or other consumer goods is called the _____.

16. (T or F) With the use of a point-of-sale system, there is no need for individual pricing of items.

17. (T or F) The elimination of individual item pricing has been met with almost universal acceptance by consumers.

18. A(n) _____ system is one in which computers are used by banks to enter data at the point of transaction and to automatically update banking records.

19. (T or F) Most banks have fully integrated electronic funds transfer systems in operation.

20. (T or F) There are some opponents to EFT who believe that a fully integrated system may result in an invasion of an individual's privacy.

Solutions

1. office managers / page 547 clerical workers and secretaries / page 548

2. computer-aided preparation of documents / page 548

3. F—In actuality, while computers are most common, terminals may be used in their place. / page 551

4. messages / page 554

5. professional workstation / page 555

6. teleconferencing / page 558

7. F—Office automation has progressed slower than originally anticipated because of resistance. / page 558

8. F—Information resource management should be viewed as separate from DP management. / page 560

9. point-of-sale (POS) / page 561

10. supermarkets / page 561 fast-food restaurants / page 561 department stores / page 561 hotels / page 561

11. inventory control / page 561
    transaction reporting
    / page 561
    accounts receivable
    / page 561
12. electronic cash register
    / page 563
13. T / page 564
14. bar code reader / page 564
15. Universal Product Code
    / page 565
16. T—Unless it is required by a
    state law. / page 565

17. F—There is considerable
    resistance to elimination of item
    pricing. / page 565
18. electronic funds transfer (EFT)
    / page 566
19. F—Some aspects have been
    implemented but there are no
    fully integrated EFT systems.
    / page 567
20. T / page 569

Key Terms

Electronic cash register
Electronic funds transfer (EFT) system
Electronic mail
Electronic message system
Electronic spreadsheet
Facsimile equipment
Information resource management
Office automation
Point-of-sale (POS) system

Professional workstation
Shared-logic word processing system
Stand-alone word processor
Teleconferencing
Text editing
Transborder data flow
Universal product code (UPC)
Word processing

Review Questions

I. True-False Questions

1. (T or F) Office automation has great potential for both managers and secretaries.
2. (T or F) With office automation, secretaries would have more time to manage the flow of information within the office.
3. (T or F) In general, office automation has not progressed as quickly as was originally anticipated, largely as a result of employee resistance.
4. (T or F) With a fully automated office, managers would be expected to type their own reports.
5. (T or F) It is possible to use a standard micro for both word processing and transmitting messages.
6. (T or F) A major problem with most word processing systems is that they are not user-friendly.
7. (T or F) Information resource managers should be responsible for ordering and coordinating the use of professional workstations.
8. (T or F) Teleconferencing is one method that can reduce the time and cost associated with travel to meetings.
9. (T or F) Electronic message systems are used exclusively for transmitting messages among employees within a given organization.
10. (T or F) Electronic spreadsheets enable users to manipulate numbers to see what effect specific changes would have on the overall picture.

11. (T or F) Point-of-sale systems are used exclusively for reading the Universal Product Code on items.

12. (T or F) All point-of-sale systems are used for maintaining customer account records.

13. (T or F) POS systems can be used in conjunction with EFT systems for credit verification.

14. (T or F) Automated teller machines enable users to make bank deposits or withdrawals 24 hours a day.

15. (T or F) Many countries have rigorous laws regarding the transmission of data across national borders.

II. Fill in the Blanks

1. One objective of office automation is to provide managers with more time for _____.

2. Another objective of office automation is to provide secretaries with more time for _____.

3. The two types of word processing systems are _____ and _____.

4. Most word processing systems display _____ on a screen that provide instructions as to how to enter data and make changes.

5. Devices called _____ provide the ability to transmit text as well as graphics, company logos, signatures, and so on.

6. An example of a subscriber service that may be used for electronic message transmission is _____.

7. Four functions that can be performed by a professional workstation are _____, _____, _____, and _____.

8. Data entry devices for a point-of-sale system may be a _____ or a _____.

9. The bar code used on supermarket products is called the _____.

10. Four functions provided by an electronic cash register are _____, _____, _____, and _____.

11. Four advantages of point-of-sale systems are _____, _____, _____, and _____.

12. One potential disadvantage of point-of-sale systems is _____.

13. EFT is an abbreviation for _____.

14. Four components of EFT systems are _____, _____, _____, and _____.

15. Three potential disadvantages of EFT systems are _____, _____, and _____.

APPLICATION

WANG CHIEF SEES TODAY'S MICROS OBSOLETE BY '90[1]

by Bruce Hoard

Many of today's *stand-alone microcomputers* will be obsolete by 1990, the president of Wang Laboratories, Inc. said here last week at the Office Automation Conference (OAC '83), sponsored by the American Federation of Information Processing Societies, Inc. John Cun-ningham attributed the approaching obsolescence of stand-alone personal computers to a growing need for *multifunction workstations* by professional managers.

"The craze for [personal computers] has caused a bottom-up approach to their usage, rather than a top-down approach that would fit [personal computers] into larger business goals," Cunningham declared.

The low cost of personal computers has led many users to buy first and think later about how to use them, he added. While admitting personal computers offer benefits, he said the value of some of their applications is overrated.

Current stand-alone personal computers will be obsolete by 1990 because as more attention is given to the professional and the manager it will be recognized that they need a multifunction workstation more than a personal computer, he claimed. "In other words, users need a definite set of applications," Cunningham said. "As office automation gains ground with professionals and managers, many of today's stand-alone [personal computers] will turn out to be a shortsighted investment."

When implemented without proper planning, stand-alone personal computers end up with no resource sharing, communications or networking capabilities or *upgradability* to the "advanced functions that characterize office automation."

The continued growth of personal productivity systems for workers at all levels of the office may be endangered by unwise investments and lingering disappointments in today's personal computer, Cunningham said.

The multifunction workstation will supersede the stand-alone micro, he claimed. Eventually, professional,

managerial, and administrative and secretarial workstations will perform all the basic tasks for which they were acquired. Multifunction workstations will also be able to communicate, handle electronic mail, access internal and external data bases, and do graphics and word processing, he declared.

Cunningham said office automation is a "five-year-old who has learned several important early lessons." Its growth could be stunted if technology is implemented with faulty expectations and if people close their minds to new ideas about productivity and cost justification, he added.

Cunningham warned against office automation cost justification based solely on quantifiable measures. He said it is the quality and effectiveness of a memo's content or the timing of a telephone call that are ultimately important.

"The true function of office automation is to enhance the performance of a cooperative office team by helping it to achieve the overall business goals of an organization," Cunningham commented.

[1]*Computerworld*, February 28, 1983, page 16. Copyright © 1983 by CW Communications/Inc., Framingham, MA 01701. Reprinted with permission.

Questions
1. Understanding Key Terms
   Define the following terms in the context in which they are used in the application:
   a. Stand-alone microcomputer.
   b. Multifunction workstation.
   c. Upgradability.
2. Software, Hardware, and Systems Concepts
   a. Indicate some of the ways in which microcomputers can be used as stand-alone units.
   b. Indicate some of the ways in which microcomputers can be used as multifunction workstations.
   c. Indicate some of the ways professionals and managers might best use microcomputers.
3. Management Considerations
   a. If you were a vice president and several of your managers asked for microcomputers, how would you determine whether it would be functional to have them as multifunction workstations as opposed to stand-alone units?
   b. Indicate why the article suggests that stand-alone personal computers might be approaching obsolescence. Prepare a counter-argument to refute this suggestion.
4. Social, Legal, and Ethical Implications
   Indicate the ways in which personal computers may, as the article suggests, be overrated. Do not confine your answer to business applications.

CASE STUDY: McKing's Superburgers, Inc.

1. Point-of-Sale System
   a. What will be the major functions of the electronic cash registers at McKing's?
   b. Will the Universal Product Code have any applicability at each individual McKing's restaurant?
   c. Which of the following types of point-of-sale systems would be most appropriate for McKing's? Explain your answer.
      1. On-line system.
      2. Key-to-storage system using batch processing.

2. Office Automation
   In addition to a point-of-sale system for each restaurant, management at McKing's is considering a vendor proposal that recommends an office automation system for the main office. Explain how any of the following applications might be used:
   a. Word processing.
   b. Electronic mail.
   c. Facsimile transmission.
   d. Electronic spreadsheets.

THE COMPUTER AD: A Focus on Marketing

Consider the ad entitled "Extend Your Reach" that appears in Figure 14.19.

Questions
1. Knowledge-Index is a subscriber service. What questions would you ask a salesperson to determine whether it is suitable for use?
2. Some services charge different rates depending on the time of day. What are the advantages and disadvantages of price differentials?
3. What data bases would be most useful for personal computer users?

Use your personal computer to reach Knowledge Index, and you've tapped into a wealth of information on business, personal money management, education, consumer products, medicine, current affairs, computers. And much more.

It's a special service for personal computer users from Dialog, the world's leading online information retrieval service. Now, the same information used by thousands of corporations, libraries and professionals is available to you nights and weekends at special low rates.

Knowledge Index offers you millions of summaries of articles, books, reviews, reports, and news items. Plus unique databases like Micro-computer Index and International Software Database. You can even order complete documents and software packages right from your terminal.

A one-time initiation fee of only $35 gets you your password, a complete, self-instructional user manual, and two free hours of Knowledge Index—a value of over $50! One low cost—40¢ a minute—covers it all, and a typical inquiry takes only a few minutes. There is no monthly minimum—you pay only for what you actually use.

So, use Knowledge Index to extend your reach. Call or write for complete information.

KNOWLEDGE-INDEX
A Service of Lockheed Dialog.

3460 Hillview Avenue, Palo Alto, CA 94304 • 800/528-6050 x 415 (in Arizona 800/352-0458 x 415)

Figure 14.19
Marketing computer products. (Courtesy Lockheed Dialog.)

CHAPTER 15

SYSTEMS ANALYSIS AND DESIGN

CHAPTER OBJECTIVES

To familiarize you with:

- The steps involved in systems analysis and design.
- The pitfalls that systems analysts should avoid.
- The ways in which analysts could maximize the efficiency and effectiveness of computerized systems.
- The tasks involved in a feasibility study and in capacity planning.

I. INTRODUCTION

A. What Is a Business System or Application?

A **business system** or application is an organized method for accomplishing a business function. An accounts receivable business system, for example, serves to store and record information on money owed by customers. In most organizations, many business systems such as the accounts receivable function have been computerized to maximize the efficient flow of information, while other business systems have remained largely manual.

A **systems analyst** is a computer specialist who makes recommendations for the overall computerization of business systems. This involves much more than programming; in fact, the programming function is typically relegated to a programmer who is supervised by the analyst.

The analyst begins by studying current procedures and designs. Then he or she designs more efficient and economical systems to better accomplish the tasks performed by the existing set of operations. The analyst and the user must work closely in both the analysis and design of business systems in order to achieve this basic objective. In fact, the most frequent cause for the failure of computerized business systems to meet their objectives is inadequate communication between the analyst and the user.

The following lists the basic skills that will help to make an analyst effective at his or her job:

Skills of the Systems Analyst

1. Strong user orientation.
2. Self-starter—has an ability to work even with poorly defined objectives.
3. Keen understanding of organizational flow, company goals, and objectives.
4. Ability to determine in advance the impact of a system on user departments.
5. Planning and control (project management) skills.
6. Behavioral sensitivity to the impact of a system on individuals.
7. In-depth knowledge of user departments.
8. Cost consciousness and ability to estimate and adhere to costs and schedules.
9. Leadership ability, administrative experience, political sensitivity.
10. Technical skills (programming, systems, data base design, telecommunications, etc.).

Most colleges offer upper-level courses in systems analysis and design and there are textbooks devoted entirely to this subject. It is not our intention, therefore, to provide an in-depth discussion, but only to introduce you to the subject.

B. The First Step in Analysis and Design

An analyst's job begins when he or she is called on by the management of an organization to study an existing set of procedures and to seek ways to improve it or to redesign it so it is more efficient. There are two main reasons why management would request the services of an analyst:

1. A current set of procedures to accomplish a specific task does not exist, but management or the operating staff would like to implement a computerized one. If there is no set of procedures, for example, to evaluate the hiring and promotion policies of a company, management may call on a systems analyst to design an automated set of procedures.

2. A current set of procedures (either manual or computerized) to accomplish a specific task exists, but management is dissatisfied with it and wants a revised one. If the payroll system, for example, is slow and has a high error rate, management may request a redesign.

Some objectives of a new design might include:

IN A NUTSHELL

OBJECTIVES OF COMPUTERIZED BUSINESS SYSTEMS OR APPLICATIONS

1. Lower costs.
   a. Reduction in clerical operations.
   b. Savings in space required for files, personnel, and equipment.
   c. Reduction in redundant or overlapping files.
   d. Less duplication of operations.
   e. Detection of problems before they become too costly to correct.
   f. Reduction in the routine, clerical aspects of top management jobs.
   g. Reduction in the amount of paperwork generated.
   h. Better coordination of functions performed by different departments.

2. Faster response time.
   a. Improved ability to react to changing external conditions.
   b. Faster turnaround time for processing jobs.

3. Improved accuracy.
   a. Lower error rate.
   b. More accurate forecasts.
   c. More confidence in the system.

4. Improved information for management.
   a. Higher-quality information.
   b. Faster response time.
   c. Ability to develop alternative management plans.

C. An Overview of Steps Involved in Analysis and Design

Regardless of whether the analyst is called on to develop a system that is completely new or to revise an existing one, the tasks involved are exactly the same.

They include the following:

Tasks of Systems Analysis and Design

1. PLANNING

   Developing a plan or course of action.

2. ANALYSIS AND DESIGN

   a. Analyzing the existing business system or set of procedures to determine the basic problem areas.

   b. Designing a new system that will operate more efficiently and effectively than the existing one.

   c. Supervising the programming and testing procedures.

3. IMPLEMENTING THE NEW SYSTEM

   Implementing the new system so that there are no major transitional or conversion problems.

4. OPERATING THE NEW SYSTEM

   Making certain the new system functions properly.

These four elements are known as the **system life cycle** (see Figure 15.1). The term "life cycle" is used when referring to a system because all designs are best viewed as dynamic or subject to change. That is, a system will need to be continually revised to better meet new and changing objectives. Thus, even after an analyst has designed a new system, modifications or "fine tuning" will be necessary from time to time to ensure that the system continues to function even if objectives and goals change.

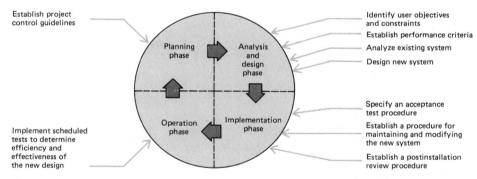

Figure 15.1
The system life cycle.

Note that the new design usually involves the computerization of some facet of the business system. The analyst is, after all, an information processing professional who views the computer as a tool that can be used to make business systems more efficient. There are isolated instances, however, in which an analyst designs a new business system *without* recommending the use of computers, because he or she feels that the cost is, in a particular case, unjustified.

You will recall that the systems analyst may be:

1. A staff employee within the organization.

2. An outside consultant who makes recommendations to management.

In either case, the analyst's role is essentially *advisory*—he or she makes recommendations. The decision to proceed with a new business system rests with management.

The *analysis and design phase* is the most critical aspect of the analyst's job. This phase requires management approval at two points. After an existing set of procedures and objectives has been analyzed, the analyst prepares a report to management called the **problem definition**. This document indicates the difficulties or problem areas in the current system, and, in a general sense, it outlines the features that the analyst will redesign to eliminate these problem areas.

If management concurs, the analyst begins to design a new set of procedures. Before the new system is implemented, however, management must give its approval of this new design and its proposed cost as well.

Figure 15.2 provides an in-depth flowchart of steps involved in the system life cycle, with particular emphasis on the systems analysis and design phase.

Figure 15.2
Flowchart of the steps involved in systems analysis and design.

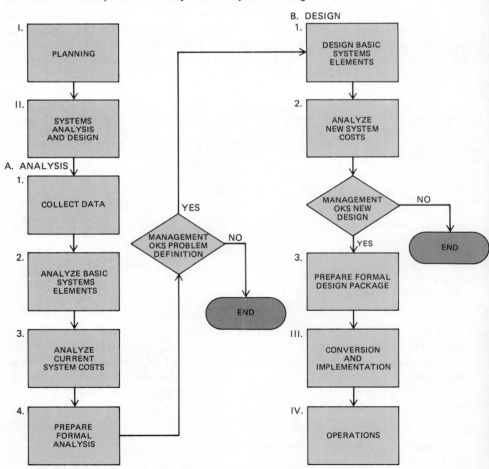

II. THE PLANNING OF BUSINESS SYSTEMS

The need to carefully organize and plan the steps involved in systems analysis and design is critical. Although it is not always feasible to pinpoint accurately the time and personnel that will be needed to perform any task, initially establishing a plan could be very useful for interrelating the various components and for keeping a record of progress as well. Since an analyst works with users, programmers, and the computer operations staff in any design, control of the project requires a well-designed plan before any analysis or design is begun.

III. THE ANALYSIS AND DESIGN OF BUSINESS SYSTEMS

A. Systems Analysis

Before undertaking the design of a new system, the analyst must fully understand the precise requirements of that design and the basic problem areas that have caused management to be dissatisfied with existing procedures. The following steps are systematically undertaken to provide an analysis of an existing business system.

1. Data Collection

To obtain an adequate understanding of the current objectives, existing procedures, and basic problem areas, the analyst must collect data in a systematic way. The methods used for data collection include:

IN A NUTSHELL

DATA COLLECTION TECHNIQUES

1. Studying procedures or operations manuals if there is an existing system—this helps to determine how the existing system, in principle, was designed to function.
2. Evaluating current forms and their distribution—this helps to isolate what data is required from the system and who requires it.
3. Interviewing managers and the operating staff—if the analyst is sensitive to the needs and fears of the user, this technique can prove to be the most important one in the data collection phase.
4. Observing users as they perform their jobs—this will provide some insight into basic problem areas.
5. Preparing, distributing, and evaluating questionnaires—this supplements information obtained from interviews and observations.

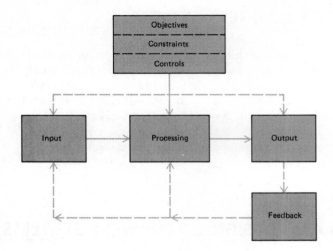

Figure 15.3
Fundamental structure of a business system in terms of its seven elements.

2. Defining a Business System in Terms of Its Basic Elements

Analysis of a system is performed according to a set of procedures that is designed to be as scientific and objective as possible. Figure 15.3 illustrates (1) the elements used to analyze a system and (2) how these elements relate to one another. We discuss each of the elements in depth. When designing a new system, one must evaluate and redesign each component, as required.

a. Objectives The systems analyst must be aware of exactly what the user requires from a specific system. That is, management's goals or objectives must be known and fully understood. For example, one of a company's objectives for a new design might be to establish a computerized accounts receivable system so that a customer can walk into a branch store and have a clerk immediately determine the customer's balance at any time, based on on-line computer records.

After reviewing the objectives of a current system with the user, the systems analyst may quite possibly recommend a modification to these objectives. Because the analyst has specialized expertise in information processing, he or she may be aware of computer capabilities that can be utilized to provide more efficient performance at a lower cost. To say to management, for example, "I can provide you with 95% of what you want for 50% of the cost" is a very persuasive argument for modifying existing objectives.

b. Constraints The analyst and the user must both recognize any limitations or **constraints** that may exist when designing a computerized system. There are several common constraints that usually affect most systems being computerized. These are legal, budgetary, and equipment constraints, as discussed below.

(1) Legal. Many systems have legal requirements to which they must adhere. For example, in a payroll system, the company is required by law to withhold various taxes such as federal, state, Social Security, and local. In addition, a W-2 withholding form must be sent to each employee at the end of the year. The analyst may wish, for example, to redesign the W-2 form; federal and local governments, however, have dictated what the form should look like, how many copies there should be, and when they must be sent to employees. Hence, the form cannot be modified at all. The user must make the analyst aware of all legal constraints under which the system is to operate since these cannot be altered.

(2) Budgetary.   Often the management of a company imposes a budgetary constraint on the analyst, limiting the time, and hence money, that can be expended in analyzing and designing a new system. Management may say, for example, that the new computerized accounts receivable system must be operational within one year and should not cost more than $100,000 to design. The analyst must therefore work with the user to achieve a functional system within the allotted time and cost.

(3) Equipment.   Computer equipment or hardware devices that are employed within the company represent another type of constraint. Systems analysts generally attempt to utilize the computer configuration that is currently available at the company although small acquisitions are always possible. Any additional equipment not currently utilized in the company that the analyst considers a requirement for the system must be justified from a cost standpoint. If a major change in equipment is being considered, the analyst must perform a feasibility study to determine whether a change to the existing computer system is justifiable. This study is considered later on in this chapter.

c. Output   After considering general requirements and limitations, the analyst studies the output that the system produces. It is the user's job to inform the analyst of all current output forms and any additional output required from a new design. The analyst is likely to recommend new or revised reports that can be readily obtained from a computerized system.

Output, however, constitutes more than just reports. For example, it is usually necessary to save information in the form of updated files that can be used for producing reports in the future or for making inquiries. The user must therefore make the analyst aware of how output information is currently stored for future processing.

d. Processing   After studying the existing output, the analyst must analyze the processing, or types of operations that are currently performed in order to obtain the desired results. All procedures that are followed and the ways in which various computations are made must be understood.

e. Input   All input data that serves as the basis for desired outputs must be studied. The analyst will typically seek answers to questions such as the following, to ensure that the desired information about inputs is obtained.

Checklist for Understanding Current Input Needs

1. Where does all data used for processing originate?
2. How often is each type of input generated?
3. If there are codes or abbreviations used for input, does the analyst have complete lists of these?
4. What happens to input documents after they have been processed?

f. Controls The user must familiarize the analyst with the ways in which errors are minimized under the current system. That is, the methods used to control or check errors must be specified. With knowledge of these **çontrols**, the analyst can then incorporate them in the computerized system, and perhaps suggest some controls for the new design with which the user may not be familiar. Chapter 17 discusses controls in detail.

g. Feedback It is essential that the analyst be made aware of how errors in the current system are handled once they are discovered. This is called **feedback**.

Even with the use of many controls, it is still possible for errors to occur. The user must therefore explain all current procedures for adjustments and corrections when feedback procedures indicate that errors have occurred.

For example, in a payroll system, what happens when a paycheck is issued for an incorrect amount? Suppose, for example, that the check is in excess of the correct amount. The procedure may call for the check to be voided and a new one issued. In addition, however, appropriate adjustments must be made to the employee's year-to-date figures for earnings, federal tax withheld, Social Security tax deducted, and so on.

3. Analysis of Current Systems Costs

While the analyst is studying a particular system, he or she will be collecting data on the existing operating costs. This information will be useful later for comparing present costs with the costs of a proposed design. Management often will not approve a proposed system unless it will result in a savings in operating costs. Another reason for analyzing current costs is that many systems have specific elements that are disproportionately expensive and it is useful for the analyst to pinpoint these.

The analyst will probably want to compare the current systems costs to expenditures in previous years. In this way, he or she can determine how well growth factors have been accommodated in the system.

The user may thus be called on to supply appropriate cost data to the analyst. The major costs that must be considered are labor, equipment, material, supplies, and overhead associated with the current system.

4. Formal Analysis

a. Problem Definition The problem definition is the formal document prepared by the analyst, which defines in detail all aspects of the current system, including costs, and the fundamental flaws in the system that impede the achievement of its stated objectives. In essence, it highlights those areas that the analyst will improve in a new design for the system.

Generally, the analyst works closely with the user in preparing the problem definition since the user is most familiar with the current system and will be able to pinpoint any errors or misunderstandings. Similarly, the user might have some pertinent suggestions or comments on items overlooked.

Thus the problem definition contains a formal analysis of the present system. This document is used to provide management with the analyst's understanding of the system and its basic problem areas. All data obtained in this problem definition represents a joint effort of both the analyst and the user. On the basis of this problem definition, management will decide whether or not to have the analyst proceed with a new design.

b. Tools for Depicting a System: Systems Flowcharts and Data Flow Diagrams   One tool used by analysts to depict elements in a system is called a **systems flowchart**. This diagram is used to indicate the features of the existing system and is an integral part of a problem definition. It is also used to depict the flow of information in the new design.

The systems flowchart, like its more detailed counterpart, the program flowchart, depicts the relationships between inputs, processing, and outputs, in terms of the system as a whole. It is a general representation of the information flow within the total system. Figure 15.4 illustrates the symbols commonly used in systems flowcharts. They are drawn using a flowchart template, which typically has both systems and programming symbols.

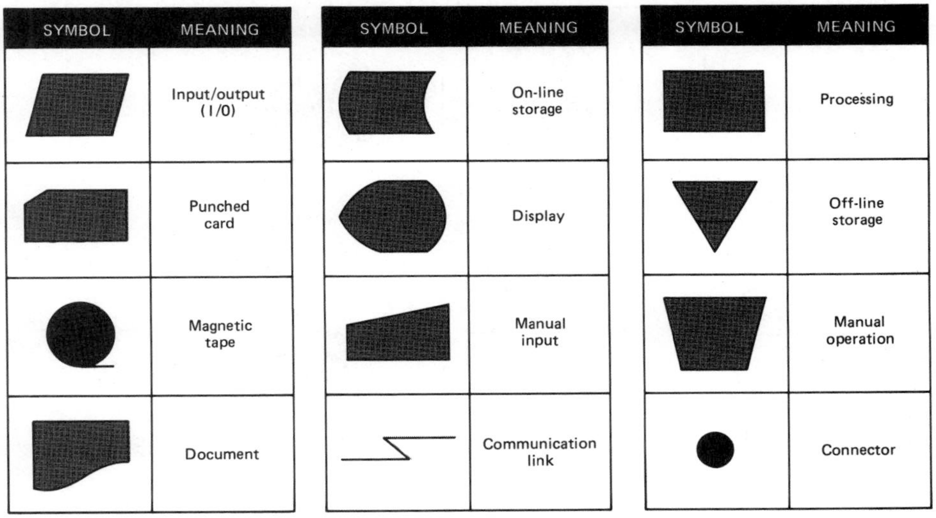

SYMBOL	MEANING	SYMBOL	MEANING	SYMBOL	MEANING
	Input/output (I/O)		On-line storage		Processing
	Punched card		Display		Off-line storage
	Magnetic tape		Manual input		Manual operation
	Document		Communication link		Connector

Figure 15.4
Systems flowchart symbols.

Example

Figure 15.5 on page 590 illustrates a sample systems flowchart for a payroll system. Payroll change forms indicating new employees and changes in position are keyed into input records, sorted, and used to update a master payroll tape. In addition to the updated payroll tape, the payroll checks and a payroll report are generated by the computer.

Note that it is relatively easy for management to understand the overall processing involved by reading a systems flowchart.

There are also structured systems design tools such as **data flow diagrams** for depicting systems elements (see Figure 15.6 on page 591). Other structured design tools also exist.

There are also computer programs that can be used for creating flowcharts and data flow diagrams (see Figure 15.7 on page 590).

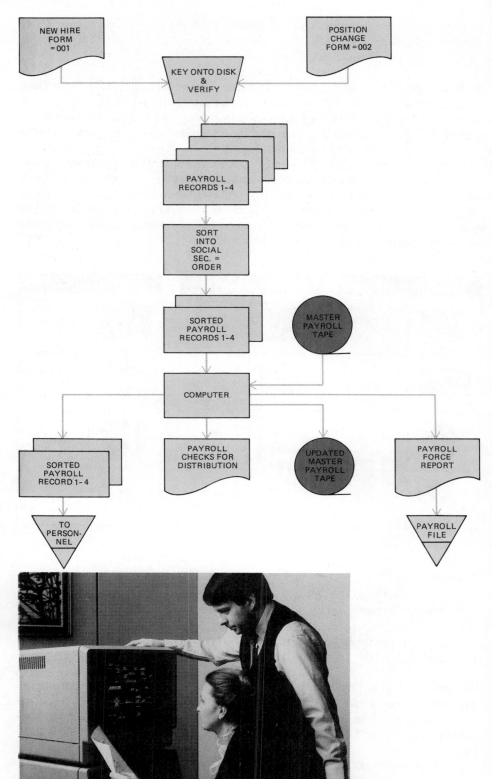

Figure 15.5
Sample systems flowchart for a payroll system.

Figure 15.7
A computerized system that interactively creates and updates structured systems design charts in a real-time environment. (Courtesy McAuto/McDonnell Douglas—St. Louis.)

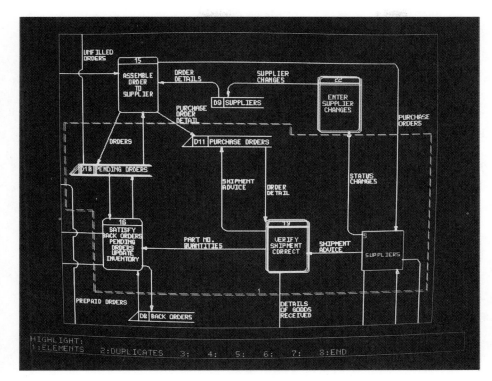

Figure 15.6
Close-up of a data flow diagram that a systems analyst might use for depicting input-processing-output. This illustration was computer-produced. (Courtesy McAuto/McDonnell Douglas—St. Louis.)

5. Management OK as a Prerequisite for a New Design

After a system has been analyzed and the formal problem definition and planning tools prepared, the analyst presents his or her analysis and ideas for a new design to management for its approval. Once the analysis is approved, the analyst can begin the formal design work by systematically redesigning each of the systems elements described above.

Self-Evaluating Quiz

1. Before an analyst can design a new system that will alleviate system flaws, he or she must _____.
2. The seven basic elements of any system are _____, _____, _____, _____, _____, _____, and _____.
3. The term _____ is used when referring to a system because all designs are best viewed as dynamic or subject to change.
4. A constraint is a(n) _____ imposed on a system.
5. Two common types of constraints are _____ and _____.
6. To determine the economic possibility of acquiring new equipment to handle business tasks, a(n) _____ study must be performed by the analyst.
7. (T or F) Control procedures are built into systems to minimize errors.
8. Three basic methods for collecting data are _____, _____, and _____.
9. Procedures manuals generally indicate how a system, in principle, _____.
10. The single most effective method of collecting data is usually the _____.

11. Two tools commonly used to depict elements in a system are _____ and _____.

12. The _____ is the formal document prepared by the analyst, which defines in the utmost detail all aspects of the current system.

Solutions

1. study the present system in depth

2. objectives
   constraints
   outputs
   processing
   inputs
   controls
   feedback

3. life cycle

4. limitation or restriction

5. legal
   budgetary
   equipment

6. feasibility

7. T

8. studying procedures manuals
   evaluating forms
   interviewing employees
   making observations
   using questionnaires

9. should function

10. interview

11. systems flowcharts
    data flow diagrams

12. problem definition

B. Systems Design

Designing each business system independently as discussed here is referred to as the "traditional systems approach." An alternative method of design is to (1) determine the needs of the company *as a whole,* (2) establish a company-wide data base that is accessible to *all* departments, (3) provide *integrated* information to top-level management, and (4) then design subsystems to satisfy each user's requirements. This is referred to as the Management Information Systems (MIS) approach and will be considered in the next chapter.

As noted in Figure 15.3, there are seven basic elements of a system. These seven elements of an existing system must be analyzed to determine problem areas; similarly, the same seven elements must be systematically redesigned in a new system.

1. **Objectives**
2. **Constraints**   } These elements are modified as necessary.
3. **Outputs**

Some outputs are produced at fixed intervals and others are produced as needed, on demand. Payroll checks and accounts receivable bills, for example, would be created periodically or at fixed intervals, using a master file as input. Other reports, such as status reports or special studies, could be produced on-line as a response to an inquiry.

Frequently, existing systems produce numerous reports that are actually unnecessary or only needed in rare instances. The analyst must determine which reports are required on a regular basis, which can be eliminated entirely or condensed, and which can be generated only when needed.

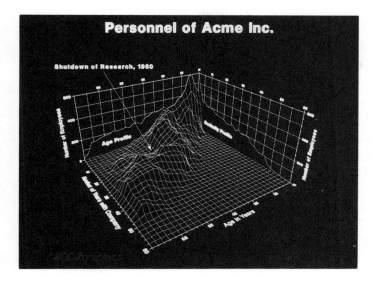

Figure 15.8
The use of graphics in place of lengthy reports: one method a systems analyst could use for providing management with an analysis of the personnel at the company based on years of service. (Courtesy ISSCO.)

Increasingly, graphics output is seen as an alternative to printed reports because it is better able to provide summary data in a concise, meaningful way (see Figure 15.8).

Periodic output may be classified as follows.

Output: In Graphic or Report Form

Detail output—each record from a file is printed as output.

Summary output—data records are grouped and summary totals are printed.

Exception output—only those items that are not within a predefined range are printed (e.g., overdrawn accounts, accounts in arrears, etc.).

Where possible, summary and exception output should be provided in place of detail data since they generate less paper and can often provide more meaningful analyses for the user.

4. File Processing

There are frequently three types of processing programs used in a system. They perform the following functions:

a. Edit Procedures   Each file that is processed by the system must be *edited,* or checked for errors. The analyst indicates to the programmer the types of error control procedures to be incorporated in a program that edits a file.

b. Update or File Maintenance Procedures   Updating a file is the process of keeping it current. Some files are updated periodically, at fixed intervals in a batch mode. Other files are updated as changes occur, directly, in an on-line mode (see Figure 15.9).

Analysts determine which mode would best satisfy the needs of the user. They indicate to the programmer the tasks to be performed for an update. The programmer then codes the update or file maintenance program.

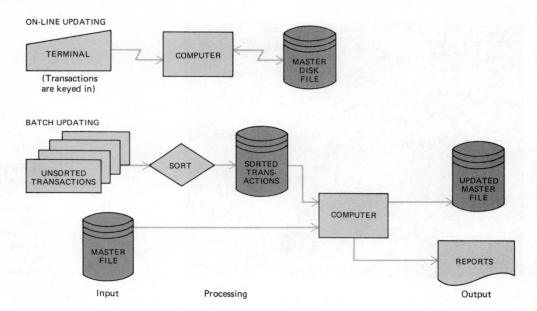

Figure 15.9
Types of updating.

c. Reporting Output is generated by a separate program that uses master files as input and produces detail, summary, or exception reports on a periodic or demand basis.

5. Inputs

If input is to be redesigned, each input form must be determined, new file types must be selected, new formatting provided, and new fields added, when necessary, to input data.

There are several types of files that are typically established when designing a system. Among the most common are:

1. Master file—contains the main body of information for the system.
2. Transaction file—contains data that will be used to update the master file.

a. Selection of a File Medium for Each Master File Tape and disk are traditional file media that are selected by the analyst for master files. The selection of file media is based on:

IN A NUTSHELL

FACTORS IN SELECTING FILE MEDIA

1. Cost.
2. Speed of device.
3. Volume.
4. Projected growth.
5. Current hardware.
6. Type of processing.

The relative merits of each file type have been outlined in Chapters 5 through 7. The user should be aware of the file media selected by the analyst for the input files and should be advised as to the reasons why the analyst chose the specific types.

b. Design of Files   Once the file type has been chosen for each file, the analyst must structure, organize, and design the file as efficiently as possible.

The user who must work with the analyst should pay particular attention to the following file design items, which will directly affect processing.

1. *Field size.* Each field within a record must be long enough to accommodate the largest data item. A NAME field in a payroll file, for example, must generally be large enough to accommodate the employee with the longest name.

2. *Coded fields.* To conserve space on a file and to facilitate the processing of data, the analyst often uses coded fields of data. ACCOUNT NUMBER, for example, in place of CUSTOMER NAME, may become a new design item in a file. Generally either or both may serve as key fields. Thus if a user knows one but not the other, the computer can still access the corresponding record.

   If coded fields are employed by the analyst in the file design, the user must make certain that they are adequate and will be used effectively. It should be ascertained that the length of the coded field is adequate enough to handle all items—both for the present and in the near future. For example, an accounts receivable department that currently has 986 customers should use an ACCOUNT NUMBER field of at least four positions (0001 to 9999) to ensure that it is large enough to allow for future growth. The current controversy over increasing the zip code from five digits to nine digits is a result of inadequate planning when the zip code used by the postal system was first designed.

3. *Positioning of Data within a Record.* Generally, the analyst arranges a record format so that the keying operations are facilitated. Key fields such as ACCOUNT NUMBER, SOCIAL SECURITY NUMBER, and INVENTORY NUMBER should be easily identifiable at the beginning of the record. Most often, the critical fields appear first in a record.

c. Creation of Transaction Files   Master files must be maintained, or kept current, in order to be useful for the system. Changes to the master file occur periodically and are used to update the master file. The change records become a *transaction file.* This file may contain:

Illustrations of Transaction Data

1. Items received or sold—used to update an inventory file.
2. Promotions, raises, changes to employees' records—used to update a payroll file.
3. Customer payments—used to update an accounts receivable file.

The file design considerations discussed previously are relevant here as well.

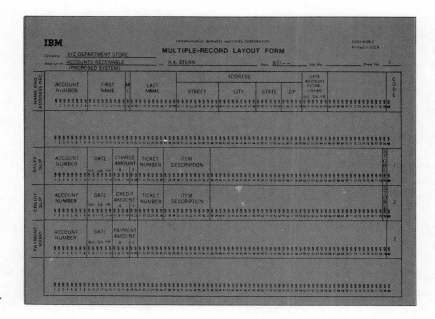

Figure 15.10
Sample record layout form.

Figure 15.10 illustrates a sample layout form, which the analyst uses to depict the record format for each file. This form is used by programmers when they code their programs; it becomes part of the formal documentation as well. Master files, transaction files, and others are all described using layout forms.

6. Controls and Feedback

These must be carefully designed for all new systems. In fact, many systems fail because of inadequate control procedures.

After all the elements of a system are designed, the analyst supervises the programmers, who must then code and debug the update procedures, edit procedures, output procedures, control procedures, and so on. There are usually several programs required in the design. The analyst has project control responsibilities, which means he or she must monitor the progress of the programmers and make certain they are interpreting the design correctly.

C. Obtaining Management's Approval as a Prerequisite for Implementing the New Design

1. Presenting the Elements of the New Design to Management

Once the entire set of procedures has been designed and the programs written, the analyst again makes a presentation to management. This presentation includes:

1. A detailed description of the new system.
2. An analysis of the actual design costs and the recurring or operating costs of this new system.
3. A plan for converting to the new system.

If management approves the new design, then the analyst can continue with the final phase of conversion and implementation.

A major factor in obtaining management's approval is the ability of the analyst to demonstrate that the new design will result in a cost benefit. Thus **cost-benefit analysis** is an integral part of the analyst's job.

2. Justifying the New Design from a Cost Standpoint

The purpose of cost-benefit analysis is to determine the monetary impact of a new design on the company as a whole. This study must be presented to management in order to obtain a final approval.

In presenting the new design to management, the analyst must indicate the costs associated with the new system and compare these costs to those associated with the existing system. Presumably the new design will result in a monetary benefit after the new design costs have been amortized or absorbed.

The costs associated with a new design can generally be evaluated as follows.

Non-Recurring Systems Development Costs

- Hardware (Use of the computer for testing, debugging, and conversion)
- Personnel
  Systems analysts
  Programmers
  Operators for testing

- Overhead
- Supplies

Recurring Systems Costs

- Equipment
- Operations

- Overhead
- Supplies

Cost-benefit analysis consists of determining the monetary advantages to be derived from the new design. These include:

IN A NUTSHELL

MONETARY ADVANTAGES OF A NEW SYSTEM DESIGN

1. Tangible benefits.
   a. Cost savings benefits.
      Reduced labor force.
      Fewer error correction
      procedures needed.
   b. Operational benefits.
      Faster turnaround.

2. Intangible benefits.
   Improved customer relations.
   Better ability to handle growth.
   Greater responsiveness.

There are numerous quantitative methods that can be used to evaluate cost factors and to present management with a relatively reliable method of determining the impact of the new system on the company as a whole from a cost standpoint. Graphs are frequently used effectively for this purpose.

IV. IMPLEMENTING AND OPERATING THE NEW SYSTEM

A. Conversion from the Existing System to the New Design

Converting to a new system includes:

▕▐▐▐▶ **Conversion Procedures**

1. Establishing schedules and error control procedures.
2. Supervising a pilot operation.
3. Training existing staff to use the new design.
4. Informing the computer staff of systems requirements.

   The **conversion** and **implementation** procedures once again require analysts to be sensitive to the needs of the operating staff and users. After all, these people will now be required to deal with computerized procedures and many of them will be somewhat fearful or even resistant. It is the analyst's responsibility to understand this resistance, to allay fears, and to ensure a smooth transition.

B. Documentation: Ensuring That There Is a Written Record

Once the system is functioning properly, the analyst must provide a total record of the precise procedures and techniques used in the system. This record is called a **documentation package** and is typically developed throughout the design stage and finalized after the conversion is completed. It is similar to a procedures manual in that it describes all the facets of the new design. In this way, a formal document exists that can be consulted if there is a problem or a need to make changes. Once the documentation package is written, the user need not consult the analyst if some point needs clarification; rather, he or she can go directly to the documentation package. See Figure 15.11 for a sample list of elements in a documentation package.

LOOKING AHEAD

Trends in Systems Analysis

1. Systems studies are focusing increasingly on the functioning of the total organization as opposed to individual applications.
2. Tools and techniques used by the systems analyst are becoming more powerful, cost effective, and modular.
3. Increased emphasis is being placed on the management of data.
4. Systems designs are required to be user-friendly.
5. More attention is being given to humanistic attributes such as intuition and creativity, as opposed to scientific methodologies, in determining and correcting basic problem areas of existing systems.
6. Less attention is being given to technical elegance and more attention is being given to actual usefulness in design.

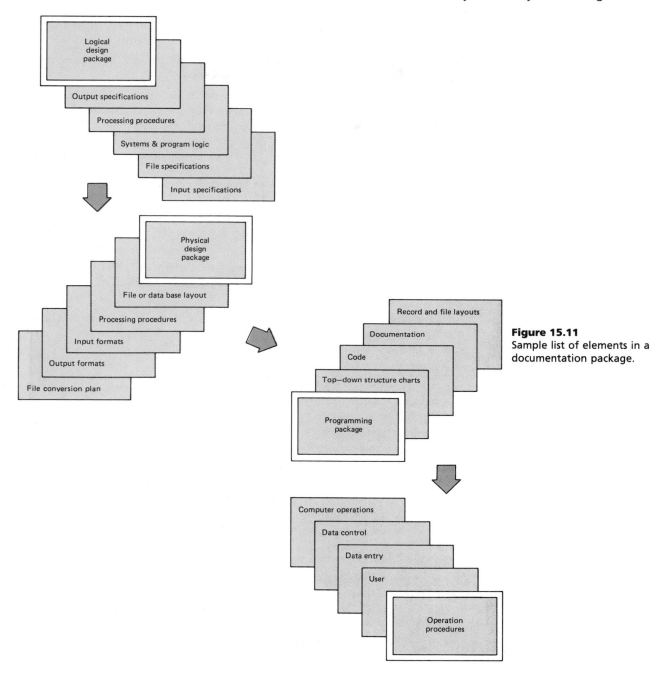

Figure 15.11
Sample list of elements in a documentation package.

Self-Evaluating Quiz

1. The _____ must work closely with the user when creating a new systems design.
2. The processing steps involved in a new design are best illustrated by diagrams such as _____ and _____.
3. The new files are described on _____ sheets.

4. Once all the elements for a new design have been prepared and integrated, the analyst must prepare a _____ of the proposed system.

5. One major reason for converting to a new design, at least from management's perspective, is that it eventually will save _____.

6. Initially, costs of the proposed system will include _____, _____, and _____ expenses, which must be assimilated before a comparison between present and proposed system costs can be evaluated.

7. In addition to saving the company money, a new design may have _____ cost benefits.

8. An example of an intangible cost benefit is _____.

9. Elements included in non-recurring systems development costs are _____, _____, _____, and _____.

10. Elements included in recurring systems costs are _____, _____, _____, and _____.

11. Once the analyst has fully designed a system by integrating all of the above elements, he or she must prepare a formalized, detailed record called the _____, describing that design.

12. After the system has been designed and approved and programming effort has been completed, the analyst must develop a _____ procedure to ensure a smooth transition from the old system to the new.

Solutions

1. systems analyst
2. systems flowcharts
   data flow diagrams
3. record layout
4. cost analysis
5. money
6. design; programming; conversion
7. intangible
8. improved production planning
   better customer service

9. systems design costs
   programming costs
   training costs
   conversion costs
10. personnel costs
    overhead costs
    equipment costs
    supply costs
11. documentation package
12. conversion

V. PROJECT MANAGEMENT: SUPERVISING THE OVERALL INTEGRATION OF A NEW DESIGN

Project management refers to the overall supervision of a systems project by the analyst. This encompasses:

1. Scheduling of systems design elements.
2. Supervising programming activities.
3. Training the staff in the new system.

4. Implementing the new system.

The following is a series of tongue-in-cheek—although realistic—"laws" of project management based on the experiences of those who have had to manage systems projects:[1]

1. A carefully planned project will take only twice as long to complete as expected.
2. A project will progress to 90% completion, then remain 90% complete forever.
3. If project content is allowed to change freely, the rate of change will soon exceed the rate of progress.
4. When things appear to be going better, you have overlooked something.
5. Any attempt to debug a system will simply add new bugs.
6. No major project was ever developed on time and within budget; your project will not be the first.

To minimize some of the experiences outlined above, planning and scheduling are important components of project management. The systems analyst who is responsible for overseeing a systems project should develop a work plan identifying each task that must be performed. He or she should then develop a schedule that takes into consideration (1) desired completion dates and (2) task dependencies—which tasks must be completed before the next ones are begun.

In addition to planning and scheduling, project management includes project control as well. Programs and resource expenditures must be continually monitored; comparison of actual progress against planned progress must be frequently made to determine if any corrective measures are necessary. Corrective measures may include:

1. Increasing the efficiency of project tasks being performed.
2. Re-evaluating original expectations or objectives.
3. Changing original schedules.

Better project management can be achieved if the analyst bears in mind the words of Frederick P. Brooks, Jr. in *The Mythical-Man Month*, which has become a classic book:

> More projects have gone awry for lack of calendar time than for all other causes combined. Why is this cause of disaster so common?
>
> First, our techniques of estimating are poorly developed. More seriously, they reflect an unvoiced assumption which is quite untrue, i.e. that all will go well.
>
> Second, our estimating techniques fallaciously confuse effort with progress, hiding the assumption that men and months are interchangeable.
>
> Third, because we are uncertain of our estimates, we are too willing to merely revise original schedules.

[1] William R. Synnott and William H. Gruber, *Information Resource Management* (New York: Wiley), 1981.

Fourth, schedule progress is poorly monitored. Techniques proven and routine in other...disciplines are considered radical innovations in [systems development].

Fifth, when schedule slippage is recognized, the natural (and traditional) response is to add manpower. Like dousing a fire with gasoline, this makes matters worse, much worse. More fire requires more gasoline; thus begins a regenerative cycle which ends in disaster.[2]

VI. COMMON PROBLEMS WITH COMPUTERIZED BUSINESS SYSTEMS

Despite the systematic approach used by analysts in designing new systems, there are frequently major problems encountered in new designs. We consider below some of the major reasons why computerized business systems sometimes fail to meet their objectives.

A. Lack of Proper Integration among Systems within a Company

Because each system is designed independently when using a traditional systems approach, there is frequent duplication of effort within the company as a whole, and a lack of integration among systems. As a result, top-level management is sometimes unable to obtain a total view of company-wide operations. Management Information Systems minimize this problem, but they, too, have inherent disadvantages such as cost and excessive time required for design.

B. Lack of Standardization

Since each system functions independently, there are typically no company-wide standards regarding computer applications. It is then difficult to assess the effectiveness and efficiency of each design. This problem, too, can be minimized by an integrated approach to systems design.

C. Ineffective Communication between the Analyst and Users

As we have seen, efficient systems design requires appropriate communication between the analyst and the users. Users consist of both managers and the operating staff. If communication is poor, the system will be flawed, and the users will not follow the established structure. This will soon lead to a design that is not properly utilized.

To minimize this problem, users should be knowledgeable in information processing, and analysts should have significant business expertise. Indeed, some experts have suggested that the analyst and the user both be held responsible for the new design.

Numerous studies have been undertaken to pinpoint specific areas that delay implementation of a system or result in user dissatisfaction. Figure 15.12 illustrates the results of one such study.

[2] Frederick P. Brooks, *The Mythical Man-Month* (Reading, Mass.: Addison-Wesley), 1975, page 14.

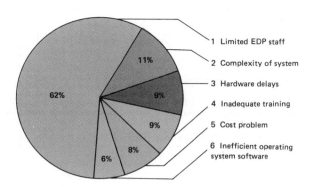

Mainframe Industry Survey

1 Limited EDP staff

2 Complexity of system

3 Hardware delays

4 Inadequate training

5 Cost problem

6 Inefficient operating system software

Figure 15.12
Causes for delays in implementing new systems. (*Source: Datamation.*)

D. Inadequate Controls

Even the best systems eventually become unreliable if proper controls are not implemented. These controls must do the following.

Purpose of Controls

1. Minimize input errors.
2. Reduce the risk of sabotage.
3. Minimize the risk of deliberate manipulation of the system for personal gain.

Chapter 17 considers systems controls in depth.

LOOKING AHEAD

1. Users will begin to satisfy more and more of their own information processing needs.

2. Users will be provided with an increasing supply of powerful tools and techniques for satisfying their own needs.

3. Communication skills will continue to be emphasized in organizations, in an effort to improve the interaction between users and computer professionals.

VII. FEASIBILITY STUDY: DETERMINING WHETHER A NEW COMPUTER SHOULD BE ACQUIRED

As previously noted, systems analysts typically design new business systems using the computer equipment that is available to the organization. Sometimes, however, either the analyst or management believes that a new computer system, or additional peripherals or I/O devices, are needed to maximize the efficiency of the system. If additional equipment is necessary, a **feasibility study** must be undertaken to determine the equipment that would best meet the needs of the company as a whole. Thus, in addition to performing systems analysis and design, the analyst is sometimes required to participate in a feasibility study if the need arises.

When an entirely new computer system is deemed necessary by management, then a major feasibility study is undertaken. This study must determine the needs of the company as a whole. On the basis of this study, management will select the most suitable equipment. A major feasibility study might be undertaken for the following reasons.

IN A NUTSHELL

REASONS FOR UNDERTAKING A MAJOR FEASIBILITY STUDY

1. To replace manual operations.
   Small companies are acquiring micros, minis, and mainframes with increasing frequency to perform operations currently performed manually.

2. To replace an existing computer system.
   A current system may become obsolete, inadequate, unresponsive, and so on.

3. To replace a time-sharing operation.
   A company that rents time on a large computer may decide that it is less costly and more efficient to acquire its own system.

4. To replace the services provided by a service bureau.
   A service bureau that provides access to a computer system as well as providing computer professionals to design, program, and operate the system may be ideal initially, especially for a company with no computer staff, but the user organization may eventually decide to acquire its own system.

When the acquisition of a new computer system is being considered, management usually selects specific individuals to serve on a feasibility team or committee. The committee usually consists of the following:

Feasibility Committee

1. A representative from each department.
   This person will indicate his or her department's computational needs.

2. A company executive.
   This person chairs the committee and makes certain that it acts in the interest of the company as a whole and that it receives appropriate cooperation from all departments.

3. A senior systems analyst.
   This person has the technical expertise to make recommendations and to evaluate proposals that will be made by computer manufacturers and vendors.

4. An outside consultant.
   This person is an expert on current computer systems. He or she may be a paid consultant who can objectively evaluate the computational needs of the company. Or the consultant may be a representative of one of the ven-

dors—that is, computer manufacturers or leasing companies; although such a representative may be biased, he or she knows a significant amount about computer systems. Moreover, there is no charge for the services of a vendor representative.

Once assembled, the feasibility committee proceeds as follows.

Functions of a Feasibility Committee

1. Perform a needs analysis and review options available.
2. Prepare a request for proposal (RFP).
   If a new computer system is considered to be justifiable, a document is prepared that lists the functional specifications required of the proposed system. Included in the RFP are such items as performance criteria, anticipated volume, estimated file sizes, programming languages required, and the installation schedule. The RFP is sent to several vendors.
3. Evaluate the bids made by vendors and make a selection that is passed on to management.
4. If the selection is approved, devise an installation plan.
   Once approval is obtained, devise a plan to prepare for the installation of the computer system.

   Let us consider each of the above functions in more depth.

A. Perform a Needs Analysis

The first step in a feasibility study is to evaluate in depth the current and anticipated computational needs of each department. Particular attention is paid to the ways in which a computer system could improve the productivity of the company as a whole.

To be considered cost-effective, a computer installation should eventually result in a savings after the initial systems costs have been absorbed. Cost factors to be considered in determining feasibility are:

IN A NUTSHELL

COST FACTORS

1. Cost of designing computerized systems.
2. Cost of programming effort.
3. Rental, leasing, and/or purchase costs of computer hardware and software.
4. Cost of training company personnel to use computer inputs and outputs.
5. Cost of supplies.
6. Cost of operating a computer facility.
7. Cost associated with installing the computer, for example, the construction of an air-conditioned room for the system.

The current cost of processing data must be compiled and then compared to the projected computer costs. Note that often it is necessary to project present costs into the future to determine what the costs would be one to three years hence under the present system, allowing for normal growth trends. Very often, an existing system, if continued indefinitely, would require extensive revision anyway. These revision costs should be included along with present system costs, so that a fair comparison to a completely revamped, computerized system can be made.

If, after a cost comparison is completed, there appears to be a savings in the end by installing a computer, then the company can prepare a list of requirements and criteria to be fulfilled by a computer system. Observe that the savings need not be in the near future. Sometimes, the savings obtained by installing a computer system takes many years to be realized.

If a new computer system cannot be justified, the feasibility committee may recommend a redesign of forms or procedures. Or, a service bureau that can perform company operations with a computer for a fixed fee could be investigated. The distinct advantage of contracting with a service bureau is that the initial cost outlay is greatly reduced. Note, however, that the company would have no computer system of its own; virtually everything is owned and operated by the service bureau. If the company decides to install a computer at a future date, it must buy or rent the programs and procedures from the service bureau, or must develop new ones on its own.

B. Prepare a Formal Request for Proposal from Vendors

If a computer system is considered feasible, then the committee prepares a request for proposal (RFP) that will ask vendors to indicate specific facts about their computer systems and to respond to particular requests. Among the types of questions that would be asked are:

⫸ Questions to Be Answered in Vendor Proposals

1. Equipment specifications.
   a. What is the basic configuration of the system recommended?
   b. What optional equipment is available?
   c. Does the system have time-sharing capability?
   d. What provisions are made for equipment maintenance?
   e. Is there any emergency back up?
   f. What are the power, air conditioning, and humidification requirements?
   g. What is the estimated delivery date?
2. Software specifications.
   a. Describe the features of the operating system.
   b. What programming languages are available?
   c. What application packages are available?
3. Cost.
   a. What are the rental, leasing, and purchase prices of hardware and software?
   b. What is the cost of maintenance?

4. Support.
   a. What type of training is available?
   b. What type of vendor support is provided for installation?
   c. What type of support will be provided for maintenance?

These are general questions that would usually be asked by a feasibility team. There are frequently many more questions asked as well that relate to the specific needs of each company.

C. Evaluate the Bids Made by Vendors and Make a Selection

Once the bids are received from vendors, they must be carefully evaluated by the feasibility committee. The cost of operating each proposed computer system is the most important factor in rating competitive bids. However, intangible factors such as the computer manufacturer's reputation, anticipated installation date, support to be provided, and so on, must also be considered.

On the basis of the responses to the RFPs, the feasibility team then decides on a specific computer system. It must also determine whether the system should be purchased, leased, or rented. Figure 15.13 indicates the main advantages and disadvantages of these three methods of acquisition. Figure 15.14 indicates the overall cost of leased, rented, or purchased systems as a function of time.

PURCHASE		
Advantages	1.	Tends to be the cheapest method of acquisition.
	2.	Provides the user with a sizeable tax credit.
Disadvantages	1.	There is the possibility that equipment obsolescence could leave the user with outdated hardware.
	2.	Large capital investment.
	3.	Maintenance is not included.
LEASE		
Advantages	1.	Tends to be cheaper than rental.
	2.	There is an obligation on the part of the manufacturer or its agent to support the system for a fixed period of time.
	3.	Purchase options are available.
	4.	May or may not include maintenance.
Disadvantages	1.	Even if dissatisfied, the user is obligated to retain the equipment for the life of the lease.
RENTAL		
Advantages	1.	Provides the user with the most flexibility.
	2.	Provides the best protection against equipment obsolescence.
Disadvantages	1.	Tends to be expensive.
	2.	Provides very little protection against increases in cost.
	3.	Usually leaves servicing of the equipment as an additional cost.

Figure 15.13
Methods of computer acquisition.

Once the committee has reviewed all the bids, it should make its recommendation to management in writing. The recommendation would highlight the reasons why a particular system and method of acquisition were chosen.

Figure 15.14
Total outlay for acquiring constant computer power. (*Source:* Chris Mader, *Information Systems,* Second Edition, page 370.

D. Devise an Installation Plan

When a company finally signs a contract with a vendor, it may have to wait a year or longer before delivery is actually made. The feasibility committee should map out a plan to ensure a smooth transition from current operations to new computerized ones. A typical plan includes the following items.

1. *Establish an Information Processing or Information Systems Department or Re-evaluate the Existing One.* This necessitates the hiring of computer and data entry operators, programmers, systems analysts, and managers. Some employees may be transferred from other departments and may be trained for new positions in the Information Processing department.

2. *Design one or two business systems in their entirety for the new computer.* Even though the computer has not yet arrived, it is possible to design business systems and to write required programs and have them tested. Often a computer manufacturer has test centers available for running programs for clients who have not yet received their computer. If this opportunity is not available, programs can usually be tested by renting computer time from other companies. In this way, systems and programming efforts for specified applications can be completed even before the new computer arrives. Thus, there need be no delay in implementing new designs. In some short-sighted organizations, these phases are not even begun until the computer is delivered and, as a result, the equipment remains idle for many months.

From the above discussion, one can easily realize why feasibility studies sometimes take two or more years to complete. These studies are the foundation for tremendous change within a company.

E. A Review of Some Options Available

Many of the main computer manufacturers and other vendors make systems available to users along with a wide variety of services such as:

- Training.
- Maintenance.
- Software support.

Until 1969, manufacturers were able to make their systems available as a package that included *all their services* such as training, maintenance, supplies, and so on. As a result of an antitrust suit against IBM, manufacturers were ordered to unbundle, or to make available *on an itemized basis,* each of the services they offer. This unbundling order enabled smaller manufacturers, vendors, and special software houses to compete with IBM and other large manufacturers for each specific service provided. Sweeping changes occurred in the EDP field as a result of this ruling, enabling smaller organizations that specialize in one or two services to compete with the very large companies.

IN A NUTSHELL

On January 1, 1970, IBM unbundled its software. This marked the beginning of an entirely new software industry.

Today the software industry grosses approximately $10 billion annually and is represented by more than 2500 companies marketing tens of thousands of programs and packages.

The following represent some equipment and services that can be provided by smaller vendors, even if a company acquires a mainframe from a major computer manufacturer.

1. Plug-Compatible Machines (PCMs)

It is now feasible for small manufacturers and vendors to supply hardware that is compatible with the mainframes or CPUs of the larger manufacturers. Organizations like IBM, DEC, and others must permit their CPUs to operate with peripheral equipment that is plug-compatible. Thus, a Control Data Corporation disk drive that is plug-compatible with an IBM 4341 may prove less costly and more beneficial for specific users.

As a result, there are numerous companies that specialize in providing one type of hardware such as printers, terminals, or tape drives. If these devices are less costly and more powerful than those supplied by the CPU manufacturer, the user may decide to acquire plug-compatible devices.

2. Original Equipment Manufacturers' (OEMs) Products and Services

Most EDP organizations find it difficult to keep abreast of recent PCM developments. Specialized organizations called OEMs (**original equipment manufacturers**) purchase systems and devices in bulk at wholesale prices. They then supply customized configurations to EDP users that are:

- Relatively inexpensive.
- More powerful.
- Better suited to individual user needs.

OEMs have become even more popular in recent years largely as a result of the growth in minis and smaller computer systems. Major manufacturers have developed small computer and minicomputer systems that are relatively inexpensive. However, because of their tremendous overhead, these companies cannot provide support to the users at a reasonable cost. These major manufacturers sell their systems primarily to OEMs, which serve as their agents. OEMs buy in bulk at wholesale prices and serve as intermediaries or distributors. They provide software and hardware support and services to users at a cost that is frequently lower than if the user bought directly from the manufacturer. For example, the Digital Equipment Corporation relies heavily on OEMs to distribute their systems whereas IBM, in general, prefers to deal directly with the end user.

3. Turnkey Systems Supplied by OEMs and Other Vendors

When a manufacturer or its agent supplies a computer system that includes, as a package, the hardware, software, and firmware necessary for processing a specific application, this package is called a turnkey system. The client or user is required to simply "turn the key" to make the system operable. It is an entirely self-sufficient system where the user is not required to have any information processing knowledge at all.

OEMs will purchase hardware in bulk from computer manufacturers at wholesale prices and then provide packaged turnkey systems designed specifically to satisfy the needs of individual users. Typically such users do not have any in-house computer capability and use the turnkey system as a "black box."

The advantages and disadvantages of turnkey systems are as follows.

Advantages

1. Turnkey systems may provide users with computer capability without the cost of program and system development.
2. Frequently, these systems including software are cheaper than purchasing just the hardware from the major manufacturer.

Disadvantages

1. Turnkey systems are designed to satisfy the needs of many users—hence they may be somewhat inflexible and not precisely what the user had in mind.
2. These systems make users very dependent on the turnkey systems support facilities.

4. Service Bureaus and Facilities Management Organizations That Supply Computer Time and Services

A *service bureau* is a company that supplies computer processing facilities to user organizations. It may, for example, provide terminals on site at the user organization for on-line processing, using communication lines to access the service bureau's hardware and software. Sometimes service bureaus provide data pickup, where the data is taken by messenger to the service bureau to be processed and the output hand-delivered to the user.

Service bureaus offer the latest in mainframe equipment and often have a computer staff generally able to satisfy the needs of a wide variety of user organizations. For companies that need considerable computer capability but cannot afford a mainframe, contracting with service bureaus is a viable alternative. With the increased power of minicomputers and microcomputers, however, many firms that once depended on service bureaus for their computing needs now have acquired minis and micros for in-house computing.

Facilities management organizations are those companies that are called on to maximize the efficient use of a user organization's in-house computer. Facilities managers serve as consultants who determine if the current equipment is suitable for the user's needs, if some hardware could be consolidated, if additional hardware is needed, if centralized data processing is more cost-effective than decentralized, and so on.

The major objective of facilities management is to optimize a company's computer services and to produce a cost savings if feasible.

5. Specialized Software

Customized and general purpose software is currently available from numerous organizations.

VIII. CAPACITY PLANNING

In the past, computer services at an organization would continue to be utilized until bottlenecks and crisis situations forced management to begin to think about upgrading the system. At that juncture, the company would attempt to determine what additional services to acquire and, once a decision was reached and a contract signed, it would often take many months before the new system was fully operational. In the interim, the organization would continue to suffer from inefficient computerization, often at great expense to the company as a whole.

Capacity planning refers to the balancing and monitoring of existing computer workloads and the forecasting of future workloads through analytical modeling. With capacity planning, a company is constantly monitoring its computer facilities and can more adequately predict what will be needed in the future and when it would be more appropriate to fill those future needs. Capacity planning is becoming an extremely important aspect of managing information resources.

Capacity planning has two main objectives:

Objectives of Capacity Planning

1. To get the most efficient and effective use of current computer resources.
2. To forecast and plan for the computing needs of the future.

Systems analysts trained in capacity planning techniques can help to make computer equipment at a company function more efficiently and effectively.

CHAPTER SUMMARY

I. Analyzing an existing system
   A. Management directive.
      1. Management asks the analyst to study a given system because there is some dissatisfaction with its operations.
      2. The analyst serves in an advisory capacity.

    B. Components studied by the analyst.
      1. Objectives.   4. Processing.
      2. Constraints.   5. Inputs.
      3. Outputs.   6. Controls and feedback.
    C. Methods used by the analyst to collect data.
      1. Study manuals and forms.   3. Make observations.
      2. Interview key personnel.   4. Use questionnaires.
    D. The analyst prepares a problem definition indicating major flaws and current costs.
    E. If management gives its OK, the design phase can begin.
II. Designing the new system
    A. The analyst has project control responsibilities—supervises all programmers, users, and operators working on the new design.
    B. Elements in the new design are the same as those in the existing system.
      1. Objectives.   4. Processing.
      2. Constraints.   5. Inputs.
      3. Outputs.   6. Controls and feedback.
    C. The analyst prepares conversion and implementation plans and manages the transition from the old system to the new one.
    D. The analyst prepares a documentation package specifying the elements of the new design.
III. Feasibility study
    A. If a new computer system is required, the analyst takes an active role.
    B. Steps involved in undertaking a feasibility study.
      1. Prepare needs analysis for all users.
      2. Request bids from vendors.
      3. Evaluate bids and make a selection.
      4. Prepare an implementation plan.
IV. Capacity planning
    A. An integral part of the analyst's job is to assess the current computer equipment and predict when a new one will be needed.
    B. If capacity planning is not undertaken before an immediate need arises, companies frequently must continue with outdated or inefficient equipment for months or even years until new equipment is selected and delivered.

Chapter Self-Evaluating Quiz

1. The most frequent cause for the failure of computerized business systems to meet their objectives is _____.
2. (T or F) Analysts determine what systems require redesign.
3. (T or F) A problem definition is prepared after a new system has been designed.
4. (T or F) The interview method is typically considered the most effective method for collecting data on an existing system.
5. (T or F) Typically an analyst studies the output of a system first so that he

or she knows what is *required* before attempting to analyze the processing steps and input involved.

6. A systems flowchart depicts the relationships between _____, _____, and _____ in a system.

7. A _____ file contains the main body of information for a system, and a _____ file contains data that will be used to update that file.

8. (T or F) A programmer must structure, organize, and design each file in a system as efficiently as possible.

9. (T or F) Preparing a cost-benefit analysis for a proposed system is usually the responsibility of a cost accountant.

10. The typical feasibility committee consists of a _____, _____, _____, and _____.

11. (T or F) The tasks involved in a feasibility study are similar to those in systems analysis and design.

12. Bids from _____ must be compared during a feasibility study.

13. (T or F) A feasibility study may indicate that it is cheaper, in the long run, to use a service bureau than to establish a computer center.

14. The term _____ refers to the forecasting of future computer needs.

15. (T or F) Capacity planning can reduce the amount of inefficiency that results during the transition from an old computer system to a new one.

Solutions

1. inadequate communication between the analyst and the user / page 581

2. F—Analysts are assigned to study given systems by management. / page 581

3. F—Documentation is prepared after a new system is designed; the problem definition is prepared *before* the new design is undertaken. / page 584

4. T / page 585

5. T / page 587

6. inputs / page 589
   processing / page 589
   outputs / page 589

7. master / page 594
   transaction / page 594

8. F—This is the job of the systems analyst. / page 595

9. F—It is the responsibility of the systems analyst. / page 597

10. user department representative / page 604
    company executive / page 604
    senior systems analyst / page 604
    outside consultant / page 604

11. T / page 605

12. computer vendors / page 605

13. T / page 606

14. capacity planning / page 611

15. T / page 611

Key Terms

Business system
Capacity planning
Constraints
Controls
Conversion

Cost-benefit analysis
Data flow diagram
Documentation package
Feasibility study
Feedback

Implementation
Original equipment manufacturer (OEM)
Problem definition
Project management

System life cycle
Systems analyst
Systems flowchart

Review Questions

I. True-False Questions

1. (T or F) An experienced systems analyst can generally computerize a system in less than a week.

2. (T or F) The user must work closely with the systems analyst to achieve an effectively computerized business system.

3. (T or F) Once a computerized system is operational, it is relatively easy to make modifications to it.

4. (T or F) Before a new system can be designed, the current system must be completely analyzed.

5. (T or F) The major reasons that the analyst studies the current system are to understand the operations required and to find the existing problem areas.

6. (T or F) The systems analyst's role is essentially advisory.

7. (T or F) A new design must be based on current systems objectives, which cannot be altered in the revised system.

8. (T or F) It is possible that current constraints are unrealistic and severely limiting with respect to the objectives of the system.

9. (T or F) Legal constraints can generally be modified in the new system.

10. (T or F) A systems design will generally include revisions in output so that more meaningful reports are produced.

11. (T or F) If an analyst suggests a new form of output in the systems design, then the user should not question it since the analyst is more qualified to decide what is best for the system as a whole.

12. (T or F) A systems analyst should design a total system, utilizing computer equipment where applicable, and not necessarily following the current method for performing operations.

13. (T or F) A systems analyst should always design his or her system utilizing computer equipment to replace all manual operations.

14. (T or F) A systems flowchart depicts the relationships between inputs, processing, and outputs for the system, as a whole.

15. (T or F) If the department manager concurs, the systems analyst is free to redesign all inputs to a system; there is no need to check with the operating staff.

16. (T or F) The documentation supplied by the user describes the new systems design in detail.

17. (T or F) The documentation can be the user's tool for evaluating the new design.

18. (T or F) The systems analyst must supply a conversion procedure to ensure a smooth transition from the old system to the new one.

II. Fill in the Blanks

1. An analyst must evaluate the manner in which a current system meets its _____.

2. Common constraints that usually affect most systems being computerized are _____, _____, and _____.

3. The way in which errors are minimized is through the use of _____ procedures.

4. An organized method for accomplishing a business function is referred to as a _____.

5. Suppose, in the current system, a payroll check is incorrectly computed. The procedures used to correct the error are part of _____.

6. The methods for collecting data on an existing system are _____, _____, and _____.

7. The analyst learns from the _____ how a specific system should function.

8. The analyst learns from _____ how a specific system actually functions.

9. Often, management will not approve the design of a new system unless it can show a _____ of operating costs.

10. Before the analyst can design a new system, he or she must _____.

11. The basic inadequacies of the present system are formalized in the _____.

12. Generally, the fields that are positioned at the beginning of a record are _____.

13. _____ and _____ procedures must be integrated in a new design to ensure that the proposed system will function properly and to pinpoint any minor flaws so that they may be corrected before they become major ones.

14. Once all elements for the new design have been prepared and integrated, the analyst must prepare a _____ analysis of the proposed system.

15. It is usually necessary for the systems analyst to justify a new design from a _____ basis to convince management that it is viable.

16. A _____ is a company that supplies computer processing facilities to user organizations.

17. The first few years in which a new design has been implemented are usually very costly because _____.

18. Once the analyst has fully designed a system by integrating all of its basic elements, he or she must prepare a formalized detailed record called the _____, which describes that design.

19. The analyst must prepare a _____ procedure to ensure a smooth transition from the old system to the new, once the new design has been completed and approved.

20. _____ are devices that can be used with different types of computer systems.

APPLICATION

DP Cost Allocation: A Management Perspective[1]

by Michael J. Hoffman

Each day operating managers and managers of data processing centers are faced with questions concerning the allocation of data processing costs within the organization. Should the cost be accounted for as a "lump sum" corporate overhead figure to be allocated to all cost centers? Should only those departments using the service be responsible for paying the bills? What are the effects of one approach versus the other on data processing costs, control and the goals of the organization itself?

Attitudes of key operating managers will have a direct effect upon the accounting methods used to allocate data processing costs. When data processing is viewed as a powerful cost savings tool, one is less likely to object to having a share of the cost allocated to his or her department. On the other hand, when data processing is thought of as a money-wasting activity that the company has simply because competition has it, one may object to sharing even a small part of the cost.

Chargeout philosophies and methods for DP costs can provide real assistance to user departments in planning future endeavors. Unfortunately, many user managers report that the chargeout system they operate under is either so unfair or difficult to understand they may as well guess at the DP service effect on their bottom line.

Accounting method decisions for the costs of DP services are not a DP or management decision alone. Top level corporate and user management must be involved.

Overall organizational goals will influence the cost recovery methods significantly. As the DP service grows from infancy to maturity, several changes in method may evolve. Allocation of costs over the entire organization may be used in the early stages to promote use of the service for capacity utilization. Education of the user community in benefits to be realized may be achieved.

Proliferation of DP applications and steeply increasing costs throughout the organization will signal need for control. The individual managers using the service will come to realize the potential benefits of the service and see it as a resource to be controlled for maximum benefit.

Chargeout systems based upon actual usage of the resource will help with control. The chargeout system must be in a form that is usable by the non-data process-

ing manager. It must be tied to the business which it serves.

The chargeout system must be fair to all users. It must be understandable in order to use it as a control device. Chargeout systems must be stable as well as flexible to change with the rapid DP evolution. The system is not an end in itself. It is a tool to be managed not the reverse. The cost of a chargeout system must not exceed the benefits it derives.

[1]*Journal of Systems Management*, January 1984, page 16. Reprinted with permission.

Questions
1. Understanding Key Terms
   Define the following terms as they are used in the application:
   a. Operating manager.   b. User management.   c. Chargeout system.
2. Software, Hardware, and Systems Concepts
   Indicate the ways in which data processing costs can be distributed within a company. State the advantages and disadvantages of each.
3. Management Considerations
   If you were an executive of a company, would you advocate a chargeout system? Explain your answer.
4. Social, Legal, and Ethical Implications
   Do you think that a chargeout system increases or decreases negative user perceptions of computers and computer professionals? Explain your answer.

CASE STUDY: McKing's Superburgers, Inc.

1. Systems Elements
   For the order-entry system at each restaurant, identify and discuss each of the following elements.
   a. Objectives.   c. Inputs.   e. Outputs.   g. Feedback.
   b. Constraints.   d. File processing. f. Controls.
2. Feasibility Study
   Should any of the following options be considered by McKing's management when it is evaluating the feasibility of a computerized order-entry system? Explain your answers.
   a. Use of plug-compatible machines.
   b. Use of OEM equipment.
   c. Use of a turnkey system supplied by an OEM.
   d. Use of a service bureau.
   e. Use of a facilities management organization.
3. Indicate the cost benefits that could be derived from an automated point-of-sale system.
4. Indicate the intangible benefits that could be derived from an automated point-of-sale system.
5. Prepare a systems flowchart for a proposed point-of-sale system at McKing's.

Consider the ad entitled "Method/1: A Blueprint for Building Systems Success" that appears in Figure 15.15.

Questions
1. Explain in your own words what Method/1 achieves for the user.

2. Would you expect Method/1 to include a framework for systems flowcharts or data flow diagrams? Explain your answer.
3. How does Method/1 assist "in building the vital bridge linking technical design to user understanding and acceptance"?

METHOD/1: A Blueprint for Building Systems Success

Successful systems demand a blueprint and foundation on which to build. METHOD/1 is a proven systems methodology that provides you with this structure for systems success.

METHOD/1 provides a complete framework for the planning, design, implementation and maintenance of your information systems, including guidelines, specific steps and documentation. So, your projects can come in on time within budget, and meet the needs of your users.

It's a planning and design guide that simplifies your systems activities. METHOD/1 provides a basis for maintaining project consistency and control. It also assists you in building the vital bridge linking technical design to user understanding and acceptance.

METHOD/1 includes a training program for all levels of personnel from programmers to systems managers, from users to senior management.

METHOD/1 has been adopted by over a hundred organizations in both the public and private sectors. METHOD/1 is the foundation upon which Arthur Andersen & Co. has developed the world's largest management information consulting practice.

Discover how METHOD/1 can aid you in developing successful information systems, call William Odell at (312) 580-2506. Or, write him at 69 West Washington Street, Chicago, Illinois 60602.

ARTHUR ANDERSEN &CO.

Enter 203

Figure 15.15
Marketing computer products. (Courtesy Arthur Andersen & Co.)

CHAPTER 16

MANAGEMENT INFORMATION SYSTEMS

CHAPTER OBJECTIVES

To familiarize you with:

■ How integrated management information systems differ from traditional systems.
■ The basic features of an integrated management information system.
■ The advantages and disadvantages of MIS.
■ The basic features of decision support systems.
■ Management science techniques used in the design of information systems.

I. MANAGEMENT INFORMATION SYSTEMS: CONCEPTS

A. Introduction

Our discussion of information processing systems has thus far focused on the traditional techniques commonly used to analyze and design conventional systems. This **traditional systems approach** treats each business system as an independent entity; thus, the relationship between business systems is not emphasized. The assumption is that if each department or system within an organization functions efficiently, then the organization as a whole will run smoothly. In other words, the entire organization is viewed as equivalent to the sum of its parts.

In recent years, this traditional systems approach has sometimes been found to be inefficient and even inadequate. We have seen in the last chapter that this conventional approach has been extremely useful in satisfying the needs and requirements of (1) operating staff and managers and (2) middle-level departmental managers. Top-level executives, however, who are responsible for making the most significant company-wide decisions, are frequently not well served by this approach. That is, by treating each system within an organization as an independent entity, the integrated nature of their functions is not put into proper perspective. Broad-based, centralized information is thus difficult for top-level executives to obtain. To be able to inquire about a profit-loss statement or a company-wide sales forecast, for example, may not be feasible, even if each independent system is functioning efficiently. In short, while each system may function well on its own, the needs of the company as a whole are frequently not satisfied by using this traditional systems approach.

A **management information system (MIS)** is designed to facilitate the decision-making process of top-level management as well as middle and lower management. MIS uses a *top-down design* approach. That is, the primary objective is to provide top management with information on the company as a whole. Each business system within the company is treated, then, as a **subsystem**. The methodology used focuses on the total company as one main MIS application. The assumption is that if the entire integrated MIS requirements are met, then the needs of each subsystem will be easily accommodated. Thus the company as a whole is an integrated entity that has goals which are separate from, but also encompass, the collective goals of all the independent subsystems (see Figure 16.1).

If the main objective of an MIS is to provide top-level management with sales forecasts, for example, then summary reports for middle management and detail listings for low-level management can easily be provided as well.

Note, then, that the needs of each subsystem are met through a filtering process. The focus is on top-level management; after its requirements have been satisfied, then the needs of each subsystem can be met (see Figure 16.2) by filtering the data down to lower levels.

MIS systems generate output information in two main ways:

1. Scheduled Reports
   These are listings that are prepared at fixed intervals. They may be:
   a. Individual records or detail listings.

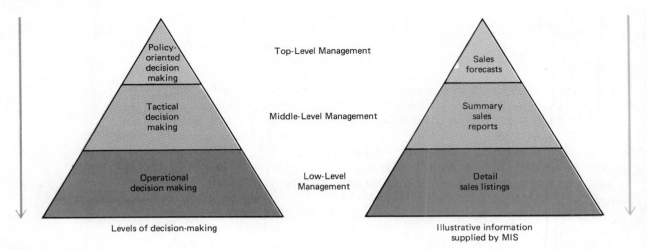

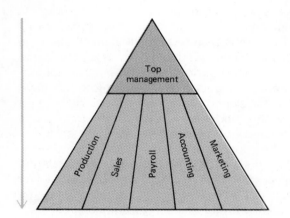

Figure 16.1 (above)
The needs of management in a management information system.

Figure 16.2 (at left)
The needs of each subsystem are met through a filtering process.

  b. Summary reports.

  c. Exception reports—indicating those records that fail to meet established criteria.

2. Responses to Inquiries

  Sometimes management requires specific information or answers to particular questions, not on a continuing basis, but at various intervals. An MIS application must provide the user with the ability to obtain answers to any relevant questions whenever the need for such answers arises.

  In order to provide responses to inquiries, an MIS must function in an on-line environment. Terminals are made available at strategic locations so that management can query the system as required.

  MIS output may be specified in the form of graphs that provide overall company-wide analyses. Figure 16.3 illustrates the types of data that can be provided in graphic form by an MIS.

  Before considering the requirements of MIS, let us review some of the main distinctions between an MIS and traditional systems.

MIS Approach	Traditional Systems Approach
• Integrated. • Each set of procedures is treated as a subsystem. • Focuses on needs of top-level management. • Avoids duplication of effort.	• Non-integrated; frequently results in duplication of effort. • Each system is treated as an independent entity. • Focuses on the needs of middle- and low-level management and the operating staff.

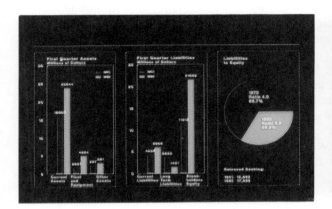

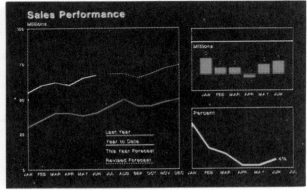

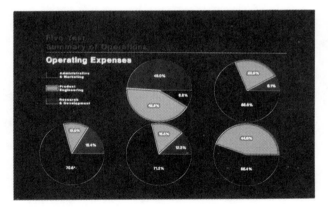

Figure 16.3
Use of graphics output to display the types of analysis typically required by top-level management for decision-making purposes. (Courtesy ISSCO.)

B. Computing Requirements for MIS

When an MIS is used in a company, each department has computerized subsystems that are part of, or subordinate to, an overall company-wide system. That is, we no longer refer to departmental systems that function autonomously, but we consider instead that each subsystem will interact to result in a more efficient total company-wide system.

The typical components of an MIS include the following.

1. On-Line Data Base

One of the prominent features of the MIS concept is a **data base**. Rather than establishing unique files for each subsystem, all subsystems can access data from one central storage medium maintained by a computer system. This storage medium contains data required by *all* subsystems. In this manner, data does not need to be duplicated by each system requiring it. It can be retained in one centralized location, and then accessed by each subsystem as required. Figure 16.4 shows how data is conventionally stored on files in traditional systems as compared to how data can be stored utilizing one central data base. For demonstrating the fundamental concept, two systems, payroll and personnel, are used as illustrations.

Figure 16.4 illustrates one of the many features of a management information system—efficiency. Suppose we are considering an automobile manufacturer that employs approximately 100,000 people. With the conventional manner of designing systems (the traditional systems approach), 100,000 records would be required in the payroll file. Similarly, 100,000 records would be required in a personnel file. With an MIS, a *single data base* incorporating all personnel and payroll information for each employee would be far more efficient.

Another obvious advantage of the data base concept is the elimination of duplication of effort. For example, it is not necessary to update two separate files with the same data, since all data is maintained in one central place. In this way, an MIS can effectively increase profits by also optimizing customer service and by decreasing the time required for processing individual items. In addition,

Figure 16.4
Comparison of a data base to conventional file storage. (*a*) Traditional systems approach using files. (*b*) MIS design using a data base.

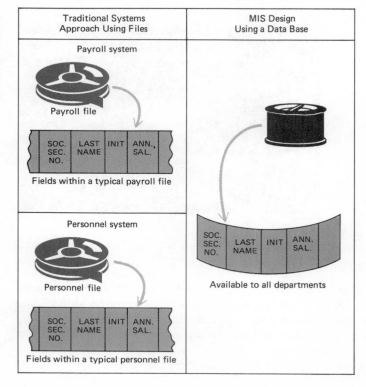

MIS projects help to standardize the decision-making process. The computer is used to produce results that are obtained by integrating data from all subsystems.

a. Methods of Organization in a Data Base: Lists, Trees, and Networks   In this text we have discussed three main methods of file organization that are typically used with conventional files: sequential, indexed, and direct.

A data base that contains many different types of records for numerous applications is usually very large. Moreover, this central data base is frequently made accessible to a wide variety of users for answering inquiries and for on-line updating. In such instances, the three methods of file organization considered in Chapter 7 are not sufficient.

When an integrated data base is to be used for on-line inquiry and/or updating, the following types of data bases may be employed: (1) a **relational data base**, in which entities are linked to one another using *chains*, *pointers*, and *lists* to interrelate items; (2) a **hierarchical data base**, in which entities are linked to one another in a hierarchical fashion; we will focus on *tree structures* to establish hierarchy; and (3) a **network data base**, where a combination of hierarchical and relational links exists between entities.

b. Relational Data Bases Using Chains, Pointers, and Lists   The concept of **chaining** associates records that have some element or attribute in common based on the record content and *not* the physical location of the record. All payroll records of employees with a job title of "programmer," for example, may be chained. A chain represents a logical path through a data base by linking groups of records together for purposes of inquiry or updating.

A **pointer** is a technique that will allow the accessing mechanism to locate or "point to" a specific record or entity in a data base. Each employee record with a job title of "programmer" will point to the next record with that job title.

Suppose we wish to locate, or access, all programmers within a central employee file. Figure 16.5 demonstrates one method of linking all programmers within the employee file. Even though the file itself is in sequence by social security number, data relating only to programmers can easily be obtained. An asterisk (*) denotes the last record in the file with the given attribute, that is, a title equal to programmer.

Note that several pointers could be used for each record so that numerous chains can be established, each for a different purpose. There could be a chain linking employees with 10 or more years of service, a chain linking employees who earn a given salary on a specific level, and so on. The pointers established depend on the needs of the organization.

A simple **list** or chain is a set of data with pointers indicating the physical location of records with a specific attribute. For example, consider a file with records containing the data shown in Figure 16.6a. Figure 16.6b illustrates how a simple list can be established with a pointer indicating all employees from Seattle. Figure 16.6c shows a Name pointer that points to the next record in alphabetical sequence by Name.

To insert a new record into a list is a simple matter. We simply change the pointer in the preceding record to point to the inserted record which, in turn, would point to the next record in sequence with the specific attribute.

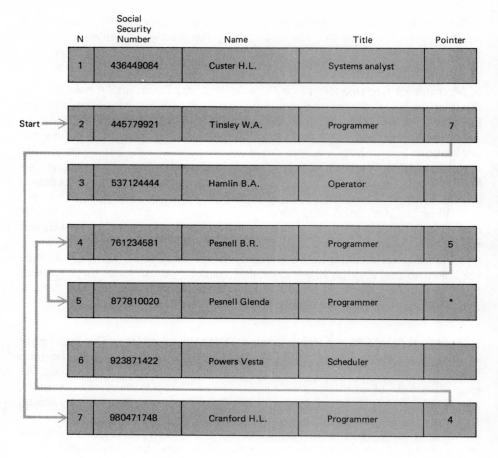

Figure 16.5
Simple chain structure that associates programmers in an employee file. (*Source:* John G. Burch, Jr., Felix R. Strater, and Gary Grudnitski, *Information Systems: Theory and Practice,* (New York: Wiley), page 220.)

In a simple list, the last record contains an end of list indicator. A *ring list* is a list that has the last record point to the *first* record in the group. This makes it possible to locate any record in a given group regardless of the starting point.

There are numerous extensions of lists. An *inverted list* has a basic record that points to more detailed information as needed. In this way, it is not necessary to access all the data for a given record unless it is all needed. Figure 16.7 illustrates how an inverted list is used in data bases.

c. Hierarchical Data Bases Using a Tree Structure   A tree organization permits records to be organized and accessed hierarchically. For each item, a record is considered a main or header record that references a series of subordinate data items or records. The header record points to all subordinate data items. Figure 16.8 illustrates a **tree structure** used in data bases.

d. Network Data Bases   The most comprehensive form of logical data organization is the network data base. Any data element in a network may be related to any other data element. A record or entity may have any number of pointers into it and leaving it. A data element may be a member of several different groups and thus may have more than one header record. Figure 16.9 illustrates a network structure used in data bases.

Physical Address	Employee Name	Division Office	Job Title	Age
07	Adams	Boston	Programmer	32
12	Brown	Seattle	Analyst	40
10	Zebo	Detroit	Programmer	29
04	Cook	Seattle	Operator	24
60	Moore	New York	Accountant	37

(a)

Physical Address	Employee Name	Division Office	Job Title	Age	Seattle Pointer
07	Adams	Boston	Programmer	32	
→ 12 (Entry point)	Brown	Seattle	Analyst	40	04
10	Zebo	Detroit	Programmer	29	
04	Cook	Seattle	Operator	24	
60	Moore	New York	Accountant	37	

(b)

Physical Address	Employee Name	Division Office	Job Title	Age	Seattle Pointer	Name Pointer
→ 07 (Entry point)	Adams	Boston	Programmer	32		12
12	Brown	Seattle	Analyst	40	04	04
10	Zebo	Detroit	Programmer	29		
04	Cook	Seattle	Operator	24		60
60	Moore	New York	Accountant	37		10

(c)

Figure 16.6
(a) File of data. (b) Establishing a simple list with a pointer indicating all employees from Seattle. (c) Adding a Name pointer that points to the next record in alphabetical sequence by name. (*Source:* John G. Burch, Jr., Felix R. Strater, and Gary Grudnitski, *Information Systems: Theory and Practice,* (New York: Wiley), page 224.)

Search Parameter	Physical Address
Name:	
Adams	07
Brown	12
Cook	04
Moore	60
Zebo	10
City:	
Boston	07
Detroit	10
New York	60
Seattle	04, 12
Job title:	
Accountant	60
Analyst	12
Operator	04
Programmer	07, 10
Age:	
21–30	04, 10
31–40	07, 12, 60

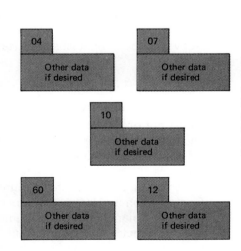

Figure 16.7
Use of an inverted list in a data base. (*Source:* John G. Burch, Jr., Felix R. Strater, and Gary Grudnitski, *Information Systems: Theory and Practice,* (New York: Wiley), page 225.)

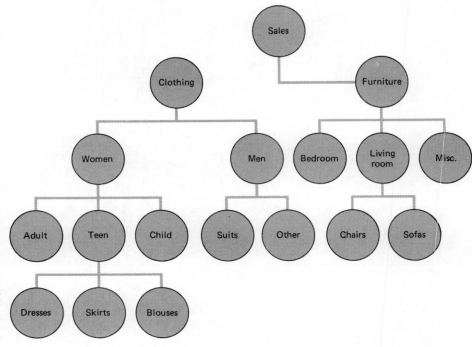

Figure 16.8
Use of a tree structure as conceived by a sales analyst. (*Source:* John G. Burch, Jr., Felix R. Strater, and Gary Grudnitski, *Information Systems: Theory and Practice,* (New York: Wiley), page 229.)

In Figure 16.9, each record that contains an ''E'' serves as an entry point to the data base. A user may enter the inventory product master record and access order, shipment, and price information, plus the typical information contained in the inventory product master record itself (e.g., quantity on hand of a particular product).

The customer credit data record contains basic information about each customer. For each customer, there may be several shipping and billing locations. This information can be retrieved and can point to appropriate ''bill to'' and ''ship to'' records. These records contain shipping and billing names and addresses and other data relevant to that customer's billing and shipping activities.

Networks have the most sophisticated order and arrangement of entities in a data base.

2. Conversational or Interactive Processing Mode

Data must not only be current in a management information system, but also immediately accessible in user-friendly form, in order to provide management with reliable and timely information needed for planning and for decision-making purposes. As a result of this requirement, a conversational or interactive processing mode is an essential feature.

Conversational or interactive processing is necessary to update files on-line and to provide management with immediate responses to inquiries. The ability of an MIS to provide timely information in this way depends, to a large extent, on the methods used to organize data within a file. If, for example, a listing of all employees with an MBA degree is required, the information can easily be provided if the data base has been properly organized and structured. There

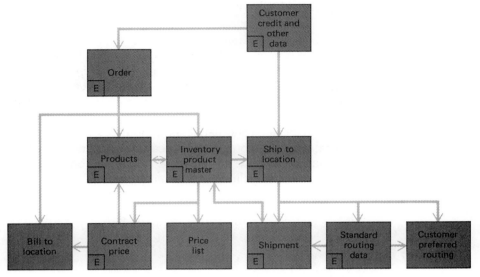

Figure 16.9
Example of a network structure. (*Source:* John G. Burch, Jr., Felix R. Strater, and Gary Grudnitski, *Information Systems: Theory and Practice,* (New York: Wiley), page 231.)

are numerous methods for organizing and structuring a data base—the method to be selected will, of course, depend on the overall needs of the specific organization.

Figure 16.10 illustrates how a data base is used for responding to inquiries in a management information system.

3. Data Communications Equipment

In order to provide managers at remote locations with conversational or interactive processing capability, data communications equipment is typically utilized. Remote terminals using telephone lines or cables, for example, can transmit data instantaneously to the computer so that information in the data base can be updated or accessed immediately. Inquiries by management, requesting either specific reports or isolated items of information, can be transmitted directly to the computer, with responses being returned over communication lines.

Figure 16.10
A centralized data base used for statewide law enforcement in Wisconsin. (Courtesy Teletype Corp.)

4. A Central Processing Unit (CPU) with a Sophisticated Operating System

To adequately process data in an MIS environment, a CPU with a sophisticated supervisor and control system is needed. The control system provides the computer with the capability to handle on-line real-time needs, incorporating the use of data communications equipment. In addition, this supervisor usually enables the computer to operate in a multiprogramming environment. You will recall that with multiprogramming cabability, the computer can process several inquiries at the same time, typically from managers using different terminals.

Frequently, MIS operates in a distributed data processing environment where there is one main CPU; numerous users have access to the data base using a network of terminals, micros, or minis linked to a mainframe.

In summary, we have seen that some of the basic features of a management information system include:

Features of MIS

1. An on-line data base.
2. Interactive capability.
3. Data communications equipment.
4. A CPU with a sophisticated operating system.

C. Features of MIS Software

1. Data Base Management System

For each company to design all of the software features required of management information systems would be extremely costly and time consuming. A typical MIS application for a medium-sized organization takes from three to five years of systems design and programming effort, with the cost sometimes running into millions of dollars.

There are numerous vendors that offer standard **data base management systems (DBMS)** software packages that may be used as part of an MIS. The suppliers of DBMS packages include computer manufacturers as well as independent software houses.

A DBMS, then, is a package that provides users with software needed to implement an integrated management information system. DBMS includes the software necessary for storage, retrieval, inquiry, and reporting from a data base. DBMS packages for mainframe and mini use range from tens of thousands of dollars to well over $100,000. Simplified DBMS packages can also be acquired by micro users for several hundred dollars.

DBMS packages make a central data base available to:

- Programmers who write application programs.
- Users who make inquiries.
- The physical operating system.

Each user will have different access rights or privileges; some will be permitted to simply make inquiries about some aspects of the data base; others will be

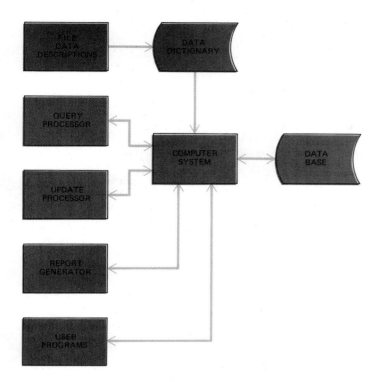

Figure 16.11
Generalized data base
management system.

allowed to access the entire data base; still others will be permitted to make
changes (Figure 16.11 describes a generalized data base management system
for mainframe use).

The DBMS provides software for:

1. Integrating the data so that it can be readily available for any anticipated
   need.
2. Avoiding duplications in the data base.
3. Accessing and updating the data base efficiently.
4. Enabling the data base to be maintained separately from the programs that
   access it.

Figure 16.12 provides a list of criteria used for evaluating DBMS packages.

2. Query Language

Most data base management systems enable the user to access the data base
using a **query language**. A query language is a high-level language that requires little or no programming expertise to be used. User requests are specified
in this query language; the data base is then searched, the requested data is
accessed, calculations are performed if necessary, and the information is then
transmitted to the user.

There are numerous query languages that are available with data base
management systems, most of them using English words and expressions to
indicate user needs. Many systems are menu-driven enabling users to simply
select the data requested.

1. Data integrity.
   Does the DBMS protect against data corruption, erroneous data entry, unauthorized access, etc.?
2. Physical data protection.
   Is it feasible to restart or recover in case of damage or breakdown? Can you back up a data base to a prior restart or entry point?
3. Data security.
   Does the DBMS provide for specific read or write access to each individual item? Are there methods used for protecting the data from unscrupulous users?
4. Data independence.
   Can the data base structure be modified without changing programs?
5. Data integration.
   Does the DBMS eliminate data redundancy?
6. Performance.
   Does the DBMS allow for concurrent multi-user access with appropriate controls? Is response time adequate even with multi-users on-line?
7. Ease of use.
   Can programs be written in any language? Are instructions short and simple?
8. Query reporting system.
   Can queries be made in English-like sentences?
9. Portability.
   Does DBMS run under the more popular operating systems such as UNIX, OS, VMS for mainframes, or CP/M, MP/M, CP/M-86, MS-DOS for micros, and so on?
10. Support.
    Are professional training seminars, product updates, and enhancements readily available?
11. Documentation.
    Is the manual describing the features and access methods of the DBMS easy to understand?

Figure 16.12
Criteria for evaluating
DBMS packages.

Because data bases are being accessed with increasing frequency by users who are not familiar with computer terminology, query languages have become very important in an MIS environment and are likely to become increasingly more so in the future.

An example of a query language appears in Figure 16.13.

3. Data Dictionary

Since all user departments will have access to one centralized data base, it is essential that a standardized method of referring to data items be established. A **data dictionary** provides a standardized method of describing the data items stored in the data base.

The data dictionary is the single source for all information and documentation about the information processing function.

The data dictionary usually includes a set of controls that requires passwords for access to sensitive or vital data (see Figure 16.14).

SIMPLIFIED QUERY LANGUAGE

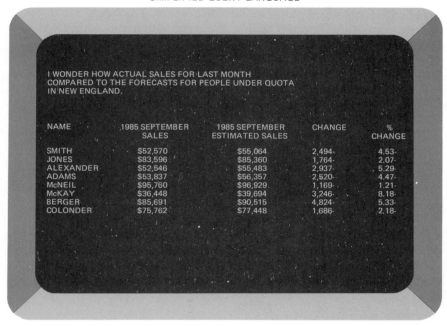

I WONDER HOW ACTUAL SALES FOR LAST MONTH
COMPARED TO THE FORECASTS FOR PEOPLE UNDER QUOTA
IN NEW ENGLAND.

NAME	1985 SEPTEMBER SALES	1985 SEPTEMBER ESTIMATED SALES	CHANGE	% CHANGE
SMITH	$52,570	$55,064	2,494-	4.53-
JONES	$83,596	$85,360	1,764-	2.07-
ALEXANDER	$52,546	$55,483	2,937-	5.29-
ADAMS	$53,837	$56,357	2,520-	4.47-
McNEIL	$95,760	$96,929	1,169-	1.21-
McKAY	$36,448	$39,694	3,246-	8.18-
BERGER	$85,691	$90,515	4,824-	5.33-
COLONDER	$75,762	$77,448	1,686-	2.18-

Figure 16.13
An example of a query
language. (Courtesy
Artificial Intelligence Corp.)

Figure 16.14
Use of a data dictionary.

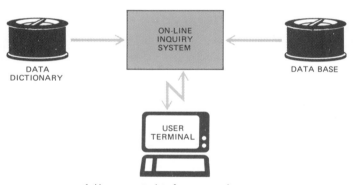

1. User requests data from a record.
2. System locates record via data dictionary.
3. Record is retrieved from data base.
4. Record is displayed on user terminal.

LOOKING AHEAD

1. Relational data base technology will grow in overall popularity.

2. High-level query languages will become more user-friendly for inquiry and reporting purposes.

3. Data base technology will improve in overall performance and efficiency.

D. Data Base Administrator as Coordinator

The use of DBMS packages within an MIS environment has resulted in the need for another computer specialist within the information processing environment—the **data base administrator**.

The data base administrator is the person responsible for maintaining the data base and for making certain that data resources are effectively administered. Figure 16.15 illustrates who the data base administrator interacts with within the information processing community.

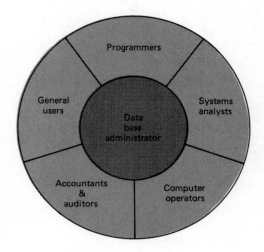

Figure 16.15
Interaction of a data base administrator with others within the information processing community.

The data base administrator is also responsible for designing appropriate security controls and for preventing unauthorized use of the data base. He or she assists the systems analysts and programmers who need to make use of the data base for various applications.

The data base administrator is also responsible for ensuring that an MIS functions efficiently.

E. Limitations of Some Existing MIS

Management information systems have extensive potential and capability for the decision- and policy-makers in a large company. Note, however, that not all MIS projects undertaken thus far have met with success.

There are several reasons why MIS systems sometimes fail to provide management with the type of information it requires.

1. Inadequate Communication Between Information Processing Professionals and Users

In many instances, the task of planning, designing, and implementing a management information system has been left to a computer specialist who is sometimes unskilled in the area of management and thus poorly equipped to understand the requirements of such a system. In addition, users, including top-level management, are frequently unfamiliar with information processing concepts and thus are unable to specify their needs clearly enough.

2. Greatly Underestimated Costs

The task of planning, designing, and implementing a vast and complex management information system has often been underestimated. The systems analyst often gives management time and cost estimates that are unrealistically low. This is because analysts are sometimes enthusiastic about undertaking such projects and thus tend to minimize the difficulties associated with their design.

3. Difficulty in Establishing Priorities

It has been difficult to establish priorities for ensuring that the most critical information needs of department executives will be effectively met. Unfortunately, when priorities are to be established, power plays and politics become major factors. Thus it is often the most influential executive, and not the executive with the greatest need, who has priority for using the system.

4. Security and Control Problems

It is difficult to maintain complete security of any information system. The problem of security is, however, compounded when a single, comprehensive data base is made available to a wide variety of user departments. That is why most data base management systems limit access to individual data items or entries.

Data base security requires the protection of all information maintained in the data base. This security requires the data to be free from errors resulting from inadvertent as well as deliberate changes or mistakes. The need for security is, in part, related as well to issues of privacy. A bank's data base, for example, must be secure enough to guarantee each depositor's right of privacy. Regardless of whether a system's security can be violated as a result of a criminal act or a simple accident, it is imperative that an MIS include appropriate hardware and software controls to prevent any misuse. Figure 16.16 lists different types of security precautions commonly employed. See Chapter 17 for an in-depth discussion of security and control procedures that are available.

Category	Procedure
External	Security clearance of personnel EDP audit Program controls User ID and passwords
Physical environment and hardware	Fire and flood protection devices Hardware monitors
Data	Backup files Encryption of data
Software	Monitoring use Access control through user ID Software monitors
Communication lines	Encryption, or "scrambling," of transmitted data

Figure 16.16
Security precautions for a management information system.

5. Inadequate Standards

If query languages and data dictionaries were all designed using an industry-wide standard, some of the problems encountered by individual users would be minimized. Although there are numerous packages available, there are no universal standards that have been accepted by the computing field, in general. As a result, packages developed for one system are not easily transferred to another. When a new computer system is acquired, then, considerable modifications of existing packages are often needed, resulting in errors and inadequacies.

6. Continually Changing Needs of Management

Since it can take several years to design, program, and implement an MIS project, it is conceivable, indeed likely, that management's needs and priorities may change during this period. Changes in input and output requirements, for example, can drastically affect the design of the data base and lead to substantial re-programming effort. Depending on the magnitude of the changes, and on how much time and effort has already been expended on a project, management may decide to accept a less-than-ideal system for the sake of expediency.

F. Decision Support Systems: A New Direction for MIS

There are three main objectives of an MIS.

IN A NUTSHELL

OBJECTIVES OF AN MIS

Item	Function
Decision-oriented reports	Printed and displayed output that facilitates the decision-making process
Hierarchical information	A data base that provides top-down or structured information
Decision support components	These help predict the potential outcome of a management decision that is being considered, before it is actually implemented

---

We have discussed the first two items in some depth. **Decision support systems** (DSS) use mathematical models to predict the outcome of several alternative courses of action within an information system.

Suppose, for example, a manager receives a report indicating the various terms of a loan that Banks A, B, and C are willing to provide. A decision support system can determine which loan will be most cost-effective for the organization in the long run, based on the company's predicted growth pattern.

DSS can also be used for determining the best course of action in more complex situations. For example, a decision support system can be used to predict the results of several proposed sales promotionals being considered. This analysis provided by a DSS is then used by management for selecting one or more of the proposed sales promotions also.

The two main benefits of DSS are:

Benefits of DSS

1. To assist the decision-maker in performing "what if" analyses.
2. By decreasing the time needed for performing "number-crunching" operations, DSS increases the time decision-makers have for using their professional expertise to actually achieve their major goals.

Note that the intention of DSS should not be to totally automate the decision-making process, but to *assist* management in making decisions. That is, many managers resist DSS because they fear that computerized support will usurp their powers. But decision support systems can only be effective if they are developed as management tools, to augment or enhance management's decision-making capability.

Top management has often expressed the need to use a computer as a personal tool that can enhance the decision-making process. These executives want the ability to ask the computer "what if" a specific course of action is taken and to obtain a reasonable answer. That is, management would like to query the system and have it forecast or predict results based on present conditions. In fields like financial planning, sales forecasting, and budget planning, such query ability would greatly improve the computer's applicability.

On a far more simplified level, electronic spreadsheets facilitate "what if" analyses; that is, you can alter a budgetary item, for example, and have the computer generate all new computations based on the change. This, of course, would only be a minor aspect of an overall decision support system.

Thus, decision support systems have been designed to provide top management with individual access to a computer, enabling the manager to ask "what if" and, based on the response, to make appropriate decisions.

"What if" analysis requires the development of a model of some aspect of the present system. Management queries result in the manipulation of this model. Based on probabilities assigned to alternative courses of action, the computer selects the alternative most likely to produce the desired outcome (see Figure 16.17).

To be effective, decision support systems must be capable of meeting the needs of an individual manager, as well as being flexible and easy to use. The goal is to provide generalized and specific models, data bases, and other computer-based support to the decision-maker at the executive level. Clearly such systems have great potential for management, but they require design specifications that must be precise and highly versatile.

II. MANAGEMENT SCIENCE TECHNIQUES USED IN INFORMATION SYSTEMS

We have focused on the general tasks involved in the design of management information systems. There are several technical features associated with these tasks that should be mentioned. Management science is a discipline that employs mathematical and scientific tools for assisting management in its decision-making function. These tools are particularly effective in the design of decision support systems. Such tools include the following.

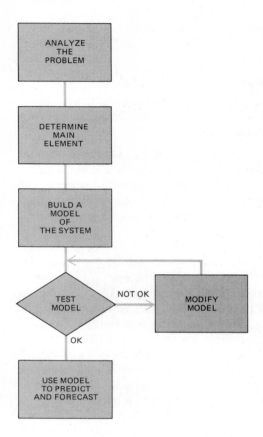

Figure 16.17
Use of a model for "what
if" analyses.

A. Operations Research

Operations research is a mathematical technique that is most often emphasized in graduate management science programs. It involves the use of a computer to develop mathematical expressions that define complex interrelationships among data elements within an organization.

B. Simulation and Model Building

Simulation is an operations research technique in which a representation or model of a system is developed that can be manipulated and studied in order to better understand the behavior of the actual system itself, and to make predictions about the system.

There are, in essence, two basic kinds of models used. There is the *physical model*, such as a model airplane that is flown in a wind tunnel to simulate actual flight conditions. The other kind of model is the one of primary interest to the businessperson, the *conceptual* or *mathematical model*, which can be described by an analyst in mathematical terms and then programmed by a programmer.

The technique of simulation affords managers the opportunity to ask the computer "What would happen if I were to do this?" thus allowing them to test the effectiveness of decisions without actually implementing them. In this manner, the computer can *simulate* the conditions the manager intends to impose on a system and can then predict the corresponding results. Simulation, then, is a common technique used in decision support systems.

Listed below are some typical applications to which simulation can be applied in business.

IN A NUTSHELL

SIMULATION APPLICATIONS

1. How much should the sales force in a department store be increased in order to adequately handle customer demands at peak times?
2. By how much will the addition of a specific number of new machines in a manufacturing plant alleviate current production backlogs?
3. How will a specific change in policy of the Inventory Control department reduce inventory investment and, at the same time, maintain adequate availability of merchandise to meet consumer demands?
4. How will the company's profit picture be affected by specific proposed capital expenditures?
5. How will a change in a department store's credit policy affect sales?
6. How will the addition of a new branch office affect the company's total profits?

Simulation is an extremely powerful technique that is becoming more widespread as a management science tool for several reasons.

1. It uses the computer to *simulate time*. The computer can represent in minutes events that would take an actual time span of days, months, or years. Thus, a manager can see immediately what the effects of a particular policy might be over an extended period of time.

2. It is often prohibitively expensive, especially in terms of financial risk, time spent, and human resources, for management to implement a particular decision on the chance that it may be successful. The use of simulation can increase the likelihood that a simulated decision found to be successful will, in actual practice, be a prudent one.

3. In many business structures, the interrelationships among the various subsystems are extremely complex. As a result, it is not possible to use simple relationships to determine the effects of specific decisions. If management varies some facet of one system, for example, the effects on all other systems may not be easy to determine. By using simulation, one can define more precisely the possible effects of a major policy decision.

4. Special high-level programming languages have been developed for writing a program that will perform simulation experiments. These programming languages include the following, just to mention a few of the more common ones:

   a. GPSS—General Purpose Systems Simulator
   b. DYNAMO

c. GASP—General Activity Simulation Program

d. SIMSCRIPT

With the use of these languages, the programmer or analyst need only supply a series of system specifications in order for the computer to perform a simulation. Thus, simulation today has become more widespread because of software availability.

5. Simulation is used in many companies as a training tool for management, to enable managers to enhance their decision-making skills. Managers often participate in **management games**, a technique whereby business leaders experiment with a hypothetical company to see if they can pinpoint problem areas and to see whether various suggested decisions made by them to alleviate problems would be effective if implemented. With the use of management games, business leaders learn to make more effective decisions.

C. Advanced Statistical Techniques

Statistical packages that utilize stochastic processes, Monte Carlo techniques, linear programming methodology, and so on, have become extremely useful for the information processor. These techniques are taught in many business and management science programs.

CHAPTER SUMMARY

I. Comparison of the traditional systems approach to the MIS approach

MIS	*Traditional Systems Approach*
A. Each system is treated as a subsystem within an integrated organization.	A. Each system is treated as an independent entity.
B. Specifically designed to satisfy the needs of top-level management.	B. Specifically designed to satisfy the needs of middle- and lower-level management and the operating staff.
C. Needs of lower-level management and operating staff are satisfied through a filtering process.	

II. Requirements of management information systems
   A. On-line data base—one major storage medium is used rather than separate files for separate systems.
   B. Conversational or interactive processing capability—for inquiry-response reporting.
   C. Data communications facilities—terminals or workstations are placed in managers' offices for immediate accessibility to the data base.
   D. A central processing unit (CPU) with a sophisticated operating system.

III. Features of MIS
   A. Data base management system—software package to provide storage, retrieval, inquiry, and reporting from a data base.

B. Data dictionary—provides descriptive information about the data items stored in the data base.
  IV. Personnel: the data base administrator—person responsible for maintaining the data base and for making certain that data resources are effectively administered.
   V. Why MIS applications sometimes fail
      A. Inadequate communication between information processing professionals and users.
      B. Greatly underestimated costs.
      C. Inability to establish proper priorities.
      D. Security and control problems.
      E. Inadequate standards.
      F. Continually changing needs of management.

Chapter Self-Evaluating Quiz

1. MIS is an abbreviation for _____.
2. MIS provides management with _____.
3. (T or F) Traditional systems analysis focuses on the top-down approach.
4. (T or F) With an MIS approach, the needs of each subsystem are met through a filtering process.
5. With an MIS approach, output can be obtained as scheduled reports or as _____.
6. A data base of a management information system is _____.
7. Data communications is typically used with MIS to provide _____.
8. (T or F) Fully integrated management information systems are usually very costly.
9. DBMS is an abbreviation for _____.
10. Data base management systems permit the user to access the data base with a nontechnical, user-oriented _____ language.
11. A _____ provides descriptive information about the data items stored in the data base.
12. The computer professional responsible for maintaining the data base is called a _____.
13. Management information systems have sometimes failed because of communication problems between _____ and _____.
14. (T or F) MIS designs require even more stringent controls than traditional systems.
15. (T or F) When designing an MIS, it is important that the integrated system be flexible enough to meet the changing needs of an organization.

Solutions

1. Management Information Systems / page 621
2. an integrated approach to the total company in order to facilitate the decision-making process / page 621

3. F—MIS designs focus on a top-down approach. / page 621
4. T—First the needs of management are met and then the operating needs of each subsystem are satisfied via a filtering process. / page 621
5. responses to inquiries / page 622
6. a central storage medium containing data required of all subsystems / page 624
7. conversational or interactive capability / page 629
8. T / page 630
9. data base management system / page 630
10. query / page 631
11. data dictionary / page 632
12. data base administrator / page 634
13. management or users information processing professionals / page 634
14. T—With MIS, the integrating elements of an organization can provide the opportunity for serious computer crimes. / page 635
15. T / page 636

Key Terms

Chaining
Data base
Data base administrator
Data Base Management System (DBMS)
Data dictionary
Decision support system (DSS)

Hierarchical data base
List
Management game
Management information system (MIS)
Network data base
Pointer
Query language

Relational data base
Simulation
Subsystem
Traditional systems approach
Tree structure

Review Questions

I. True-False Questions

1. (T or F) Most companies with computers have fully integrated management information systems in operation.
2. (T or F) An MIS provides management with current information that is obtained from computerizing the interaction of the various departments within a company.
3. (T or F) In a company that has implemented an MIS, departmental systems usually function autonomously.
4. (T or F) A data base means that each subsystem shares a centralized store of data.
5. (T or F) There are data base management systems available for microcomputers.
6. (T or F) A knowledge of BASIC is essential in order for a manager to access a data base from a terminal.
7. (T or F) Some management information systems have failed because they could not meet the changing needs of management.
8. (T or F) Many MIS projects have failed because they have utilized batch processing techniques rather than on-line processing.
9. (T or F) A typical data base management system for a medium sized organization with a mainframe will sell for less than $2000.

II. Fill in the Blanks

1. A management information system provides management with current information that is obtained from computerizing _____.

2. A _____ refers to one vast file of data that contains all information needed by the various subsystems within the company.

3. Two major advantages of a management information system are _____ and _____.

4. A conversational or interactive capability is essential for a management information system because _____.

5. Conversational or interactive capability is achieved by the use of _____.

6. A multiprogramming environment is usually an essential characteristic of a management information system since it allows _____.

7. Several years are often required for the development of a management information system because _____.

8. Two major reasons why some companies do not undertake MIS projects are _____ and _____.

APPLICATION

THE POLITICS OF SYSTEMS[1]

by Samuel H. Solomon

Mr. Peters, vice president of information systems at XYZ Industries, had just finished telling a guest about the major systems in development for various departments in the firm. In particular, the marketing information system was a source of great pride because it was to be completed the next month both on time and within budget.

Just then, Peters received an interoffice memorandum from the marketing department announcing the formation of a Decision Support Systems group. Peters tried to disguise his surprise and confusion as he read the memo; then he escorted his visitor to the door and contemplated his next move. Surprise turned to anger as he thought about the "successful" system about to be installed in this user's department. This was the first time Peters had heard of the project. He wasn't even sure what the director of marketing meant by the term "decision support system."

This hypothetical case may seem extreme, but it's representative of the problems many dp managers face as they struggle with the issues surrounding information systems. Peters had made sound purchases, was managing his people well, and was delivering the kind of MIS support XYZ seemed to want. Still, he was blind-sided by the DSS memo. The fact is that his failure was not technical or even managerial, at least in any traditional sense. It was a matter of politics.

The seeds were planted the day Peters joined the firm. The assurances of Johnson, senior vice president for administration, that Peters would really control information systems, and would have access to the right people, seemed adequate. But Peters allowed himself to be hired at the wrong level, by the wrong person. He went about his job without a clear-cut commitment from top management to an information systems plan, and thus was never entirely sure who his customers were or how they should be served. He didn't realize just how often systems and project decisions seemed to the other department heads to be pie-in-the-sky. It was a loss for XYZ as well as for Peters.

The very combination of the two words—politics and systems—may strike terror in the hearts of technically oriented computer professionals who just want to get the job done. Yet, politics is the means by which most important decisions are made. While corporations can't handle issues via a two-party system, corporate politics can nevertheless create an atmosphere for debate and consensus. Furthermore, harnessing political forces is the only sure way to succeed in establishing a system organization. The dp manager's political manifesto is roughly this: system successes have relatively little to do with completing the documentation and handover phase of the project. Managing the organizational process to support information systems and technology is the single most important success factor.

Peter Keen nicely summed up the situation in an issue of *Communications of the ACM* when he wrote that "information systems development is an intensely political as well as technical process; organizational mechanisms are needed that provide MIS managers with authority and resources for negotiation. The traditional view of MIS as a staff function ignores the pluralism of organizational decision making and the link between information and power. Information systems increasingly alter relationships, patterns of communication, and perceived influence, authority, and control. A strategy for implementation must therefore recognize and deal with the politics of data and the likelihood, even legitimacy, of counterimplementation.''

DP at a Critical Stage

Data processing is now reaching a critical stage in its political development. MIS departments are saddled with outdated information systems and support organizations based on an architecture of the '60s and the '70s. System "usurpers," both within and outside the firm, have arisen to meet the demands of a changing business environment. During the '70s, the threat originated from timesharing firms; in the 80's, we see microcomputer retailers marketing information systems directly to end users. In addition, software vendors, consulting firms, and self-proclaimed systems experts are diluting MIS's authority. Users, supported by increased computer awareness and the power of desktop computing, are demanding, and in many cases assuming, direct control of their dp requirements.

[1]*Datamation,* December 1983, page 212. Reprinted with permission of *Datamation*® magazine, © by Technical Publishing Company, a Dun & Bradstreet Company (all rights reserved).

Questions
1. Understanding Key Terms
   Define the following terms as used in the applications.
   a. Decision Support Systems group.
   b. MIS as a staff function.
   c Desktop computing power.
2. Software, Hardware, and Systems Concepts
   Explain the following statements that appear in the application:
   1) He [Peters] didn't realize just how often systems and project decisions seemed to other department heads to be pie-in-the-sky.
   2) Explain the major points make by Peter Keen in his *Communications* article that is quoted here.
3. Management Considerations
   It is claimed in this applications that a vice president of information systems must have a clear-cut commitment from top management in order to perform his or her job properly. Explain why this is so.
4. Social, Legal, and Ethical Implications
   What are some of the consequences, both positive and negative, to businesses of having a staff of users who are, in general, computer literate?

CASE STUDY: McKing's Superburgers, Inc.

McKing's is considering a vendor proposal for a management information system that would operate in a distributed data processing environment. The system would focus on the order-entry and prepared food inventory control facets of McKing's operations.

1. Indicate (a) the kinds of scheduled reports and (b) the types of responses to inquiries that would be most useful to management.
2. Indicate how a relational data base using chains could be utilized.
3. Indicate how a hierarchical data base using a tree structure could be utilized.
4. Would McKing's need on-line real-time capability for its management information system? Explain your answer.
5. Would a decision support system have applicability at McKing's? Explain your answer.
6. If you were part of McKing's management, what concerns would you have relative to the development of a management information system?

THE COMPUTER AD: A Focus on Marketing

Consider the ad entitled "ADABAS: Data Base Management System" that appears in Figure 16.18.

Questions
1. Define the following terms as they are used in the ad:
   a. Relational-like system.
   b. On-line data dictionary.
   c. On-line inquiry language.
   d. Batch report writer.
   e. Host language interface.
   f. Inverted list architecture.
2. What does it mean to state:
   a. "For quick changes, ADABAS can't be beat?"
   b. "It is unnecessary to predefine data relationships or data access methods?"
3. Suppose you were a manager considering the acquisition of ADABAS. Prepare a list of questions you would ask of the sales representative.

Figure 16.18
Marketing computer products. (Courtesy Software AG of North America, Inc.)

MODULE
6

THE HUMAN FACTOR IN COMPUTING

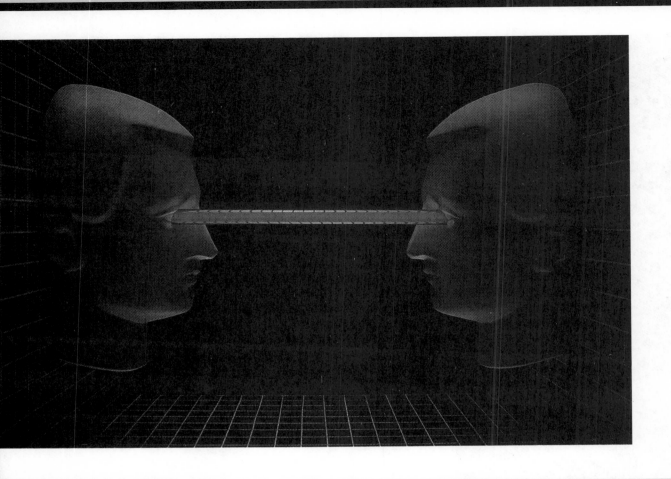

CHAPTER 17

OBSTACLES TO OVERCOME: MAKING THE COMPUTER SECURE, PRIVATE, AND USER-FRIENDLY

CHAPTER OBJECTIVES

To familarize you with:

- The need for security, control, and audit procedures for computerized systems.
- The variety of computer crimes that can and have been committed.
- The issue of privacy that has arisen in connection with computerized systems.
- The types of human errors that can occur with computerized systems.
- Controls and auditing procedures for ensuring the integrity, security, and privacy of computer data.
- The user's responsibility for ensuring that systems are designed that are secure, private, and user friendly.

I. INTRODUCTION

A. The Need for Security, Control, and Audit Procedures

Three fundamental concepts must be considered when a computerized system is designed.

1. Computers, by themselves, do not usually make mistakes. It is *human error* that is responsible for most computer-generated mistakes.
2. Computerized systems are particularly vulnerable to criminal acts. In fact, the average loss from a computer crime has been estimated at over $400,000, whereas the average bank robbery, for example, nets approximately $10,000. Some overzealous computer enthusiasts, called **hackers,** make a hobby out of accessing and even changing information in sensitive data bases. These hackers cause a great deal of problems for banks, hospitals, government agencies, and so on.
3. Threats to security include not only deliberate acts but natural disasters, such as fire, flood, and other so-called "acts of God."

Thus, it is not sufficient for a user to simply *assume* that a system designed by computer professionals will always function as intended. A computerized system may not function properly as a result of a variety of intentional as well as unintentional acts on the part of individuals who will have access to the system. Moreover, failures could result from occurrences beyond the control of any individual.

The success of a system design may well depend on the ability of the computer professional (usually the systems analyst) *and* the user to foresee not only the most likely types of human errors and natural disasters that may occur, but also the types of criminal acts that could conceivably compromise the integrity or soundness of the system. Since it is not possible to anticipate every conceivable situation, the analyst should design audit procedures to check for errors on a regular basis.

A computerized system typically consists of three major components:

1. The design of the functional elements of the system, such as the type of processing to be used (e.g., on-line, batch, real-time), the types of files to be used (e.g., magnetic disk, magnetic tape, etc.), the layouts for all inputs and outputs, and so on.
2. The design of security and control procedures to ensure the integrity of the system and the production of timely, accurate, and useful outputs.
3. The design of audit procedures to enable auditors to verify that the system is, in fact, accomplishing its stated objectives.

Organizations have begun to recognize that the design of these components is not the sole responsibility of the systems analyst. The user and other computer professionals, such as auditors and managers, *must* work closely with the analyst to ensure that all facets of the system have been carefully designed and integrated and that they are monitored appropriately.

Designing the security and control procedures for a system is generally a more difficult task than designing the other functional elements of the system because it is necessary to build in elements that will protect against the "unknown" as well as the "known."

The design of audit procedures is necessary to provide checks on the overall performance of the system and to indicate how effectively it is operating.

In this chapter, we will provide insight into the kinds of problems that must be anticipated when a new system is designed and implemented, and we will explore commonly used security, control, and audit procedures for minimizing these problems.

When a system is being designed, the systems analyst should always remember *Murphy's law*, which states, in broad terms, that *if* it is feasible for something to go wrong, it *will* eventually go wrong. Hence all conceivable controls should be designed to detect such errors.

B. The User's Responsibility

1. Working Actively with the Systems Analyst

We have already discussed the fact that a communication gap frequently exists between the systems analyst and the user. The result is that computerized systems are sometimes unreliable, exceedingly costly, and not what management or the operating staff really wanted. Moreover, the actual task of computerizing the system can result in such fear and resistance on the part of both the operating staff and management that the system is not trusted and therefore not effectively utilized.

To bridge this communication gap, it is imperative that (1) the user become familiar with the requirements of computerization and that (2) the systems analyst become more attuned to the needs of the business in which he or she is employed. The user cannot simply entrust the computerization of a system to an analyst and wait for it to be fully designed and programmed before becoming involved. The user must be *actively* involved with the systems analyst from the inception of the design through the programming and implementation stages.

Interaction between the analyst and the user is essential for the following reasons.

1. The user works with the system on a daily basis and thus knows not only the intricate details of how it operates, but also its problem areas and vulnerable points. These facts must be adequately communicated to the systems analyst so that proper corrective measures and controls can be built into the new system. Since the systems analyst generally does not have as much expertise as the user on the intricate details of a particular business system, effective communication between these employees is essential.

2. You will recall that the systems analyst is a staff person, or an advisor. Consequently, he or she can only *recommend* changes to a system and cannot simply enforce a change unless it has been approved. Thus, it is the analyst's job to "sell" the user on the design so that full support is achieved. It is the user's responsibility, then, to assess the effectiveness of an analyst's proposal, and, if found to be satisfactory, to approve the design so that the required programming and implementation can be performed. Determining if a proposal is satisfactory means evaluating not only if objectives will be met, but if they will be met efficiently and effectively, within budgetary constraints.

3. Once the system's components have been programmed, and before it is implemented, the user must ascertain that the new system runs properly. A pilot run of the system with test data supplied by the user is one method for determining if the system works as intended. The test data should be comprehensive and include typical errors as well as data that might depict the kinds of intentional abuses that can be anticipated.

By working closely with the analyst, the user will ensure not only that the system will perform as intended but also that errors and intentional abuses and/or misuses of the system will be detected and prevented *before* irreparable harm is done. It is always best to prevent errors rather than to try to correct them once they occur.

2. Establishing Realistic Goals

The user must have a realistic understanding of the amount of design and programming effort that will be required for a particular system. The following two "laws" of economics applicable to computerization shed light on elements to be considered in order to set realistic goals.

a. The Law of Diminishing Returns   Basically, the **law of diminishing returns** states that as we add resources to a system (in general terms), the resulting benefits will continue to increase, but only up to some point. Once that point has been reached, continued input of resources will not lead to a corresponding increase in benefits. Instead, the benefits will begin to diminish in relation to the amount of input that is required.

In the computer field, this principle means, in effect, that at some point in time, the magnitude of the benefit to be gained from using additional resources (people, time, money, and equipment) to add features to a computerized system will not be as great as one might expect by examining the cost involved to attain those added features.

Suppose a system with certain control procedures can be designed at a cost of $50,000 to detect and prevent 95% of the anticipated errors and intentional abuses of the system. In order to achieve a system that will detect 96% of the errors and abuses, it may cost $150,000. To detect 97%, it may cost $350,000, and so on. Figure 17.1 illustrates the concept of the law of diminishing returns.

In this example, to improve the level of error detection from 80% to 95% only costs an additional $10,000. However, to increase the level 1% from 95% to 96% will cost an additional $100,000. This example illustrates the law of diminishing returns. From a purely economic standpoint, after a level of error detection of 95% has been attained, the benefits diminish in relation to the added costs that must be expended to achieve a better system. In general, it would not be cost-effective to increase the level of error detection beyond this point unless there were some overriding need to do so.

b. Pareto's Law   Vilfredo Pareto, a nineteenth-century Italian economist, studied income distributions in many economic systems. From his studies, he concluded that, as a general rule, a minority of the population controlled the majority of the wealth. Today, **Pareto's law** has been generalized to apply to a

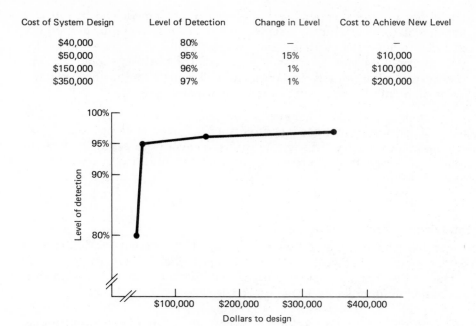

Cost of System Design	Level of Detection	Change in Level	Cost to Achieve New Level
$40,000	80%	—	—
$50,000	95%	15%	$10,000
$150,000	96%	1%	$100,000
$350,000	97%	1%	$200,000

Figure 17.1
Illustration of the law of diminishing returns.

variety of systems. In the computer field, Pareto's law suggests that for a given system, only a minority of the components within the system will have a significant effect on particular outputs to be obtained. The analyst and user should determine what those components are and focus on them. Such an approach is far more effective than giving each component the same weight.

Thus, the law of diminishing returns, coupled with Pareto's law, tells us that there is a point where the user and the systems analyst should stop looking for improvements to a system or procedure because the amount of resources spent in searching for those improvements will far outweigh the benefit gained. It may be possible to find this point by specifically seeking out and concentrating on the few, critical aspects of a system that are responsible for the major problems within the system.

3. Establishing a User-Friendly System

If a system is not specifically designed so that it is user-friendly, it is likely that the system will not function as intended.

Computer professionals, for example, often design systems that provide technical or concise messages on CRT screens that are intended to guide the user as to what data is to be entered. A message to a data entry operator such as

```
ENTER EMPLOYEE'S NAME AND CODE
```

is hardly adequate. Is the employee's full name to be entered? If yes, is last name to be entered first? Is the employee's middle name, or just his or her middle initial to be included? Are commas to be used to separate the name? What code is to be entered, and what are possible values for the code? The following message is clearer, and thus more user-friendly.

```
ENTER EMPLOYEE'S LAST NAME, FIRST NAME, MIDDLE
      INITIAL, SEX CODE (1 = FEMALE, 2 = MALE)
SEPARATE EACH ENTRY WITH A COMMA:
```

To make the message even more user-friendly *and* less prone to errors, perhaps the sex code should have the alphabetic values of F for female and M for male.

Sometimes, the user is in a position to approve what a systems analyst recommends. Thus, users should realize that there is no such thing as a sacred procedure or set of codes that cannot be changed to make the system easier to use. Although some changes may prove to be too costly, every option should be explored.

C. The Effects of Computerization on Workers

The user as well as the systems analyst must be aware of the possible negative effects of computerization on workers and how computer errors and abuses or misuse can result.

The computer is often viewed as a dehumanizing machine. Many workers tend to feel alienated by the computer, especially when many aspects of their jobs are automated. This dissatisfaction can easily lead to an employee's frustration and result in either indifference or dislike of one's job, or the intentional misuse of the computer in order to retaliate.

On the other hand, computerization can also have positive effects on workers. By being able to give fast and accurate responses to customer inquiries on inventory status, for example, salespeople can get increased job satisfaction and even greater commissions. Computerization can reduce tedious clerical work and provide the opportunity for workers to be more creative.

II. COMPUTER CRIME AND INVASION OF PRIVACY

A. Computer Crime

Since many organizations depend on computers and only a few really know how to use a computer, the opportunity for computer crime is great.

Computer crime is the act of stealing, embezzling, or otherwise defrauding an organization with the use of a computer. Note that many such crimes frequently go either undetected or unreported. It has been estimated that there are 200,000 computer crimes a year, with only a handful likely to be prosecuted. Often, when an organization finds that a computer crime has been committed and discovers the perpetrator, it refuses to bring criminal charges against the individual involved. There are two primary reasons for a company's unwillingness to disclose the crime:

1. The adverse publicity received by the company may destroy consumer confidence in the organization. This is especially true for a bank, for example.

2. Frequently, the organization actually hires the perpetrator as a computer security consultant to make the computer system secure! After all, the perpetrator is intimately familiar with the weaknesses in this area.

The following examples will highlight some of the more infamous computer crimes that have been uncovered in recent years.

Example 1

Background   The Equity Funding Corporation dealt in mutual funds and insurance policies. The company's shares were traded on the stock market.

Nature of the Crime   The chairman of the board and some of the executive officers of the company used terminals to enter insurance policies on nonexistent people. By entering bogus data over a period of *years*, they greatly increased the company's apparent assets. Of the 97,000 insurance policies maintained by the computer, almost two-thirds were for fictitious policies with a face value of $2.1 billion! As a result of the company appearing to be more profitable than it actually was, the stock of Equity Funding was greatly inflated; consequently, the officers, who were large shareholders, were able to sell their shares at considerable profits.

Another aspect of the crime involved a practice known as reinsurance. The company would sell computerized lists of some of their insurance policies to other insurance companies (reinsurers), a procedure commonly used to spread insurance risks. The computer printouts, however, contained data on fictitious as well as real insurance policies. The officers of Equity Funding themselves paid premiums to the reinsurers. They then submitted false documentation to show that some of the fictitious people who were insured had died. As beneficiaries of these policies, the officers received over $1 million in insurance proceeds!

Why the Crime Went Undetected for Years   Auditors consistently accepted computer printouts that listed policyholders as being beyond reproach.

How the Crime Was Uncovered   A former employee of the company revealed the scheme. Twenty-two people were convicted of various crimes as a result of this fraud.

Example 2

Background   An individual on Long Island used a microcomputer in his home to generate bogus bills that were sent to small municipal governments around the country.

Nature of the Crime   The bills were for services and supplies that were never rendered. Each bill averaged about $400. When a bill was not paid, the individual's microcomputer, which maintained approximately 60,000 records on disk, generated a second notice. In most cases, the municipalities paid after receiving the second notice. In this way, the individual who developed this scheme received over $1 million.

Why the Crime Went Undetected for Over a Year   Municipalities routinely paid the relatively small bills without determining if they were legitimate or not. Compared to bills for thousands of dollars typically received from most suppliers, these bills were considered "insignificant," that is, not worth the time to check their validity.

How the Crime Was Uncovered   One municipality became suspicious when it was billed for the identical amount ($508) by two "different" suppliers. In this instance, the perpetrator had inadvertently double-billed. The individual involved was convicted of grand larceny.

Example 3

Background   An individual opened a checking account at a New York commercial bank. He received preprinted checks that had magnetic ink characters on the bottom indicating the account number and the bank. He had a printer illegally make up another set of checks that were identical to those he had received, with only one alteration—the magnetic ink characters were changed to refer to a bank on the West Coast. However, the checks still had the name of the New York bank printed on them.

The perpetrator was aware of the fact that once a check has been deposited in a bank, it typically takes from three days to two weeks for that check to clear, depending on whether it is a local or an out-of-state check. The perpetrator also knew that a depositor must be notified within that time period if the check has "bounced." If no notice is given, the depositor can draw against the check after the required time period.

Nature of the Crime   The perpetrator used the altered checks to open an account at another bank. After each check was deposited, it was processed by the Federal Reserve check-clearing system, where MICR (magnetic ink character reader) sorters routed the check to the West Coast bank, based on the identifying magnetic ink characters encoded on the bottom. The check was rejected by that bank's computer, since there was no account at the bank with the number appearing on the check. Since the check had a New York bank name on it, an operator would send the check back to New York where it was put into the computer system to be processed. Naturally, the check was again re-routed to the West Coast, which took additional time for processing. This delay, due to circular routing, is what the perpetrator counted on to "kill" time. Eventually, in the absence of any notice that the check had "bounced," the perpetrator was able to draw on the check that he had deposited. The net result was that he received over $1 million by processing numerous checks in this manner. He or she has never been caught!

Why the Crime Went Undetected Until It Was Too Late   Computer equipment, in this case MICR devices, processes over 100,000,000 checks written daily in the United States. This type of fraud had not been anticipated. Consequently, appropriate controls had not been built into the check-clearing system.

How the Crime Was Uncovered   From constant routing back and forth across the country, one of the bogus checks became so frayed that it could not be processed by the MICR equipment. An operator examined the check and noticed the discrepancy between the encoded bank number and the printed name of the bank.

We will see later in this chapter controls that can be used to detect and prevent such computer crimes.

B. The Privacy Issue

The privacy issue has attained great significance in recent years as computers have transcended virtually *every* facet of our personal and professional lives.

This development has coincided with the widespread use of electronic funds transfer systems, point-of-sale systems, and the development of data bases of every kind by government agencies and private companies.

The balance between an individual's right to privacy, on the one hand, and the public's "need to know" is indeed a very delicate one.

With the proliferation of data banks in existence, there are several potential threats to an individual's privacy that must be (1) recognized, (2) assessed, and (3) prevented, when establishing computer systems and networks.

1. There is the possibility that those who have authorization to access the data banks will misuse or abuse their authority.

2. Another potential threat is that outsiders who have no authorization to access the information will find a way to penetrate a particular system in order to retrieve, modify, delete, or add information.

3. There is always the possibility that one or more weaknesses in the design of a particular system will result in the unintentional disclosure of information.

The methods for protecting an individual's privacy will be discussed later in this chapter.

The following examples illustrate how a person's right to privacy can be compromised by computerized systems.

Examples

1. An individual discovered that his name was in Canada's Crime Information System as a possible criminal. His name and identification had been used by an armed robber. The individual was *not*, however, successful in having his name removed from the system. Since funding was not available to re-evaluate *all* of the records in the file, as was required by the government regulations in effect, it was not possible to re-evaluate just his record.

2. In an effort to report on the long-term effects of abortions, government researchers examined the medical records of 48,000 women who had had abortions. This investigation was undertaken without the consent of the women. Inadvertently, some of the women's names were disclosed in a preliminary report.

3. A study of the practice of 34 of the nation's largest banks revealed:
   a. Most of them do not inform customers of routine disclosure of customer information to government agencies, even though this is required by federal law.
   b. Most of them release information to non-governmental inquirers, such as creditors, without any legal document such as a subpoena.

The privacy issue has taken on a new dimension in the 1980s, as home information systems are becoming a reality. It has been estimated that by the end of this decade:

1. 15 to 20 million cable TV viewers could have access to two-way, or interactive, systems. (Recall the concept of *videotex* that was discussed in Chapter 9.)

2. 10 to 15 million microcomputers are expected to be in use, with many of these being used as home computers.

As a consequence of this expected growth in the use of cable TV and home computers, it is projected that a variety of relatively new consumer services will become *fully* developed. Along with this development will emerge numerous privacy issues. The following list provides a sample of the kinds of consumer services that have already been made available as pilot projects, and are expected to be further developed.

1. Home banking, allowing consumers to transfer funds, check account balances, etc., from their homes.
2. Shop-at-home services, allowing consumers to ascertain the availability and price of various goods at particular stores, and then order these through their home systems.
3. Information services, whereby consumers can access a variety of data bases containing information on numerous topics such as the stock market, developments in medicine, and so on.
4. Opinion polling, whereby consumer opinions are solicited concerning a range of national and local issues.
5. Interactive home study courses.

There are several potential threats to privacy involved with these home information systems. The following represent just some of the possibilities.

1. The operator of the information system might use personal data supplied by subscribers, without their knowledge or permission. For example, lists of subscribers with certain habits or traits could be sold to a variety of advertisers, employers, credit agencies, and so on.
2. Information of a confidential nature supplied by subscribers might be intentionally or unintentionally revealed to those not authorized to receive such information. This threat might easily arise in applications such as home banking and consumer polling.

Numerous federal and state laws have been enacted to deal with the issue of privacy. The following two federal laws are typical of the legislative attempts that have been made to prevent the erosion of an individual's privacy. The Privacy Act of 1974, for example, is concerned with data banks of personal information that are maintained by federal agencies. The act provides that an agency can release information only with the individual's written consent or through a legal process such as a court order. In addition, an individual has the right to inspect his or her personal information in a data bank and must be given the opportunity to have erroneous information corrected. The Right to Financial Privacy Act of 1979 deals with the type of personal information that federal agencies can obtain from financial institutions. The act contains procedures that generally require prior notice to be given to people before personal information can be released.

Although various federal and state laws have made tremendous inroads toward protecting an individual's privacy, there is still much work that needs to be done in this area.

C. Controls for Ensuring the Security and Privacy of Data

The value of information to an organization must be carefully assessed by management so that an appropriate level of security is implemented. Recognizing that no system is foolproof, in an absolute sense, users nevertheless find it possible to incorporate various procedures to minimize the probability of security violations. This section explores some of the more commonly used security procedures that have been used to prevent computer crime.

1. Physical Access Controls

This typically involves the use of physical controls—that is, guards, alarms, detection devices, and so on. The following partial list suggests some additional techniques that are available and are being employed in varying degrees by some computer centers to prevent unauthorized access to *both* hardware and software.

1. Sign-in logs.
2. Use of badges.
3. Use of keys to unlock on-site terminals that are hardwired (directly connected to the computer).
4. Use of security guards.
5. Fire, smoke, and burglar alarms.
6. Use of fingerprints and voiceprints for identification.
7. Use of shredding machines to destroy verification lists that are produced by the computer. After files are created or updated and it is determined that the computer's records are accurate, verification lists need to be destroyed.
8. Use of backup files on media such as magnetic tape or disk. These can be stored in fireproof vaults in case it is necessary to re-create files that have been lost, stolen, or accidentally destroyed.

See Figure 17.2 for an example of a physical access control.

2. Separation and Rotation of Functions within the Information Processing Department

It is essential that the various functions normally performed by the information processing department be performed by *different* individuals. This separation of duties is necessary to minimize the risk of unauthorized and fraudulent use and/or modification of data as well as programs. The basic premise is that the separation of duties will require two or more perpetrators within the department to commit a fraud. This factor will make the probability of detection greater than if one person alone were involved. When access to a computer is restricted, it is extremely difficult for one person to perform all the necessary steps involved in perpetrating a fraud, from programming through data entry and computer operation. The analyst and user should keep this in mind when defining tasks for a new system. For sensitive areas, it is wise to segment a task into two or more independent jobs to be performed by different people.

Thus, it is advisable to have various information processing functions such as the following performed by different people:

1. Systems analysis and design.
2. Application programming.
3. Maintenance programming.
4. Systems programming.

Figure 17.2
Example of a physical access control. (Courtesy Laminex Access Control Systems.)

5. Data entry.
6. Computer operations.
7. Input control.
8. Output control and distribution.

In addition to the separation of duties, it is advisable to have duties rotated randomly among individuals within each group from time to time. This arrangement is likely, for example, to thwart the collusion of a particular data entry operator who enters only payroll data and a programmer who works exclusively on payroll programs.

3. Designing Controls During the Systems Development and Programming Stages

a. Systems Design Controls   It must always be remembered that a systems analyst is a staff person—an advisor. As we have seen, this means that the analyst can only *recommend* that a computerized system be designed in a particular way. If the analyst cannot sell the user on the design, then it cannot be implemented.

We have seen that it is imperative that the user *approve in writing* any design project that is given the "go ahead" for development. This requirement for written approval itself provides three major controls:

1. It forces the user to review carefully the analyst's understanding of the user's needs and the detailed workings of the system being designed. Any misconceptions on the part of the analyst can thus be detected *before* the design specifications are finalized, the programs are written, and the new system is implemented.

2. It serves as a form of control over unauthorized changes to a system by computer personnel. It is more difficult for unauthorized individuals to gain access to and to modify various aspects of the system *without* being detected by the analysts and programmers who, in fact, have authorization to work on the system.

3. It serves as a form of control over unauthorized changes to a system by the user and/or other noncomputer personnel. It is likely that unauthorized changes by these individuals will be detected by the systems analysts and programmers who have the responsibility for the design and implementation of the system, if instructions are included in the program to detect unauthorized use.

b. Controls on Programs   Programmers, if they are so inclined, are in a unique position to commit computer frauds. They not only know the specific logic used in the programs they have written, they also have knowledge of various file names, authorization codes, and passwords. This knowledge can be used for unauthorized access to the computer system to retrieve, modify, add, or delete records, as well as steal funds.

There are several controls that can be used to minimize the possibility of programmer fraud during the programming stage. The following list indicates some of the more common programming controls.

1. Relatively large programs that are being written should be segmented into small modules, with several programmers assigned different segments or modules to code. This technique of segmenting a large program into modules is one of the major features of structured programming. Two major objectives are accomplished as a result:
    a. It is easier to detect a programming fraud since several programmers are working with the same program. In this kind of environment, programming a fraud into the system would require the collusion of two or more programmers, thereby increasing the chance of being detected.
    b. It is easier to debug programs that have been written in modular form. This fact creates a control over the quality of the programs.

2. Logs should be kept of those programs that are tested, when the tests are performed, and the duration of each test. Many operating systems have the ability to maintain this type of log automatically. These logs minimize the risk that programs will be altered under the guise of a "test run."

3. A programmer should only have the ability to access programs and files that he or she is working on during the development stage, on a "need to know" basis. Once his or her programs have been tested and have been turned

over to the operations staff, the programmer should no longer have free access to the programs unless approved modifications are required. This limited access can be controlled through the restricted use of authorization codes, passwords, JCL (job control language) codes, and so on. These codes can be deactivated by the operating system once the programmer has completed the programming phase.

4. Thorough documentation for all completed programs, including program listings and runs with sample data, should be maintained, preferably under the control of the programming manager.

c. File Conversion Controls   When an existing computerized system is modified or an entirely new one is designed, it is likely that existing files will require changes in (1) record layouts and/or (2) the media on which they are stored. The process of changing the format of a file is referred to as file conversion. It is essential that controls be incorporated during this process to ensure the integrity of the new files. Typical controls include:

1. Comparing record counts and batch totals of key fields before and after conversion to verify that all of the data has been correctly converted.
2. Comparing and checking randomly selected records before and after conversion.
3. Testing the system with the new files to verify that all aspects of file conversions have been successfully completed.

d. Controls to Regulate Changes to Systems and Programs   The controls that have been indicated are applicable not only during the systems design and programming stages but also whenever modifications are required after a new system is in operation. In the latter case, it is also essential that:

1. All changes be approved in writing by both the user and the information processing department.
2. Logs be maintained indicating information such as the nature of each change, the person who requested the change, the date the change was incorporated in the system, and the analysts and programmers who worked on the changes.
3. All documentation, including new program listings and runs with test data, be updated to reflect the changes.

4. Data Communications Security

Because of the proliferation of data base systems that can be accessed with terminals via telephone lines and other communication links, special security precautions must be utilized to maintain the integrity of such systems. The need for controlling access to data bases from remote locations is especially acute, in light of the following factors:

1. Many companies use terminals in a time-sharing environment to access a central computer through the use of a regular telephone line.
2. Many individuals have acquired their own microcomputers or terminals for use in their homes. With an interface, these microcomputers can be converted into on-line devices that can access remote data bases.

3. We can expect further development of the use of on-line terminals by employees in their homes to perform various work functions without traveling to a work place. Word processing functions, for example, can be performed by employees working at home with on-line terminals.

Executives could also utilize on-line terminals from their homes to supervise and to communicate with various managers in the company. Reducing the need for employees to travel to their offices would help to alleviate our energy and transportation problems and would change the concept of how and when people perform their jobs as well. The notion of a new "cottage industry" (sometimes called "telecommuting"), with workers operating from their homes, has been considered by many to be the onset of a new Industrial Revolution.

In summary, there is no question that users and analysts must carefully consider data communications security when designing a system that can permit remote access to a central computer.

a. Terminal Control Features   The following list indicates some of the commonly used control features that are often designed into the terminal itself, depending on the intended use of the terminal and the kind of security that is desired.

1. The terminal may be designed with a lock so that the unit can only be used with a key that is in the possession of an authorized user.
2. The terminal may be designed with a magnetic card or badge reader so that the unit can only be operated when an authorized card or badge is inserted.
3. Some operating systems have been designed to actually lock the keyboard of a terminal if unauthorized use of the terminal is detected. The keyboard is thereby deactivated until a security officer unlocks it.
4. The terminal may have its own identification code built into the unit so that the operating system can recognize the terminal when it is used. The system can be designed so that only certain terminals can be used to access specific files and programs.
5. The terminal may be designed to encipher and decipher data transmitted in cryptographic form. This will be discussed later in this section.

b. User Identification and Authentication   User identification is the means by which terminal users identify themselves to the computer system, typically with an account number or some other unique code.

Authentication is the process by which a user's identity is verified. There are several major ways to authenticate a user's identity.

1. Require the user to enter either a password or answers to a specific sequence of personal questions. The password is typically from four to eight characters and should be changed periodically. To prevent unauthorized observation of a password by someone other than the user, the system should either (1) suppress printing of the password on the terminal or (2) conceal it by superimposing other characters, such as asterisks, when it is entered.
2. Require the user to insert some physical item in the terminal, such as a key, magnetically encoded card, or badge.

3. Have the computer system perform a comparison of some physical attribute of the user with a copy that has already been stored in the system. Some systems have already been developed for comparing such characteristics as fingerprints, voiceprints, and signatures.

c. Authorization   We have just seen that user identification and authentication are designed to establish a user's identity with a computer system. Once a user has gotten past that stage, the system must then ascertain the precise limits of the user's authorization to access programs, files, and the system's resources. A user, for example, may have "read only," "write only," or "read and write" capability when accessing files. In addition, certain users may only be allowed access to a particular file when the staff that controls that file is on duty. If, for example, a company's Personnel department does not work after 5:00 P.M., then no access to the personnel file should be allowed after that time unless a special code or password approved by the department head has been issued.

d. Encryption   When operating in a data communications environment, it may be necessary to use various **encryption** or "scrambling" techniques that will render computer data unintelligible when interceptions, such as wiretaps, occur. This is a major method used to preserve the privacy of data and to protect it from any tampering. See Figure 17.3 for an example of an encryption device.

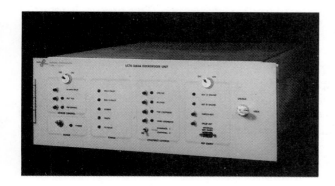

Figure 17.3
Data encryption device.
(Courtesy Linkabit Corp.)

Many banks, for example, use encryption for transmitting data in their Electronic Funds Transfer (EFT) Systems. Typically, there are two encryption keys (encoding procedures) required—one key is used at the point of transmission to encode the data to be transmitted. The other key is used at the destination point to convert the encrypted transmission to an understandable and usable format. These keys are changed daily and are themselves divided into segments, with each segment being stored in a different vault. Thus, it is extremely unlikely that a perpetrator who intercepted a transmission could readily understand or make use of the data.

There are a variety of encryption systems that exist, but there is a federal standard that has been developed to facilitate transmission of encrypted data among different computer systems. In 1976, the National Bureau of Standards provided this encryption standard for federal agencies. That encryption algorithm was developed and patented by IBM and is referred to as the Data Encryption Standard.

The **Data Encryption Standard (DES)** is a coding algorithm designed to scramble information so that it will be unintelligible if it is intercepted during transmission. Like all encryption systems, there must be a key that controls the conversion of scrambled information back into an unscrambled, and therefore, intelligible form.

The use of DES, which has become the standard for encrypting information in this country, can be understood by the following diagram.

```
                        Key                 Key
                         ↓                   ↓
         Cleartext→ DES→ Ciphertext →DES→ Restored Cleartext
```

Basically, DES operates as follows.

1. 64 bits (8 bytes) of information are processed by DES at a time. When first entered, the 64 bits, which are still in an intelligible form, are referred to as cleartext.

2. A 64-bit *key* is used to "scramble" the information, producing 64 bits of ciphertext. This process is referred to as encryption.

3. When the ciphertext is to be "unscrambled" at the receiving end, the same 64-bit key is used to produce intelligible information. This process is referred to as decryption.

5. Disaster Prevention

It is critical that every company have plans to prevent disasters from interfering with its information processing operations. The potential disasters include fire, water leaks, earthquakes, tornados, and sabotage. The following will provide insight into the types of measures that can be used to prevent or minimize the effects of a disaster.

▐▐▐➡ Measures for Disaster Prevention

Disaster Threat	Sample Preventive Measures
Fire	1. Locate the computer system in fire resistant buildings.
	2. When not in use, store tape and disk files in a fire-proof vault.
	3. Use non-combustible furniture, rugs, etc. in the computer room.
	4. Have fire extinguishers strategically located.
	5. Do not permit smoking in the computer room.
Water leaks and floods	1. Place hardware above the floor level, for example, on a platform.
	2. Have an adequate drainage system for the floor installed.
	3. Place electrical wiring above the floor level to prevent shortages that may be caused by water.

Disaster Threat	*Sample Preventive Measures*
Natural disasters (earthquakes, tornados, etc.)	1. Locate the computer system in a building that has been designed to withstand natural disasters. 2. Make sure the building has proper grounding. 3. Have an alternate site in case the main location is destroyed or badly damaged, as discussed below.
Sabotage	As discussed previously, 1. Employ physical access controls, such as sign-in logs, use of badges, fingerprint or voice identification, etc. 2. Separate and rotate the functions within the information processing department.

It is hoped that the use of disaster prevention measures will, in fact, minimize the possibility of a computer center being incapacitated because of a disaster. It is good policy, however, to have disaster recovery plans in case a disaster does occur. In this connection, it should be noted that there are disaster recovery firms that provide temporary services for companies that have experienced a computer disaster. Two types of services that are offered are:

1. "Hot sites"—a fully equipped computer center, including security, fire protection, etc.
2. "Cold sites"—an empty shell or location into which a company can place its own computer equipment. This is feasible, for example, if the company has made advance arrangements with its hardware vendor for quick delivery of a system in case of an emergency.

Based on the above discussion, you should now understand and be less impatient with your computer center for requiring you to adhere to rigorous rules for utilization.

D. Software Protection

Numerous controversies have arisen over the years concerning the legal protection of computer software. Suppose, for example, that a programmer working for Company A writes a payroll program and then leaves the company. If he or she takes a copy of the program and then uses that program in Company B, what legal rights does Company A have? Micro software suppliers have even more pervasive problems. For example, what prevents an individual or organization from purchasing a software package that costs several hundred dollars and freely distributing it to others at no cost?

Over the years, a variety of legal techniques have been used to provide software protection and legal redress, including use of common law copyrights, trade secret laws, and the doctrine of unfair competition. Perhaps the most significant protection afforded software has come about as a result of the most recent Copyright Act passed by Congress.

The *Copyright Act of 1976* that became effective January 1, 1978 has eliminated some of the controversies for programs that are registered with the Copyright Office. It is important to recognize, however, that *ideas* are not protected. It is the *expression* of the ideas that may be copyrighted. Thus, for example, if a programmer develops an algorithm for sorting records into ascending sequence using what is referred to as a "bubble" sort, it is the *actual instructions* that are protected. The *idea* of a bubble sort can be used by anyone else without copyright infringement.

Note that the legislative history that describes how Congress developed the Act mentions both computer programs and data bases as types of works to be protected.

Although the Copyright Act provides protection for the life of the author plus 50 years, there are two major problems that may arise, thereby deterring companies from registering their software.

1. What is the practicality of copyrighting a program that will be undergoing periodic revisions? Take, for example, a tax program designed for accountants to be used in preparing income tax returns. Since the tax laws change each year, the program must also be updated to reflect the latest revisions.

2. By depositing software with the Copyright Office, unique algorithms and logic will be available for review by the general public. One possible solution would be to deposit object programs (in machine language) instead of source programs (in a high-level language). There are certain legal disadvantages to depositing object code, but these are beyond the scope of this book. (For example, it may be more difficult for a company to obtain a preliminary injunction to stop another party from using the program.)

The Copyright Act provides the following remedies for infringement of software copyrights.

1. Court injunctions can be granted to prevent an unauthorized user from using protected software.

2. The copyright owner can bring a lawsuit to recover actual damages incurred. Although it may, at times be difficult to prove, actual damages would include lost sales, royalties, or profits that are attributable to copyright infringement. (In the case of a software house, the question of proof is relatively easy, since one of the purposes of the software house is to sell software.)

3. The copyright owner is entitled to recover any profits the infringer has made as a consequence of the infringement. Here, again, it is a question of proof.

4. In a lawsuit, the successful party may be awarded court costs *and* reasonable attorney fees. (It is unusual for legal fees to be awarded in lawsuits.)

5. A criminal penalty for infringement may be imposed. The penalty can consist of a fine not exceeding $10,000 or imprisonment for not more than one year, or both.

Although such measures are certainly a deterrent, the problem of copying software, particularly micro software, remains. Many developers have built into their programs protective measures that make it difficult, for example, to copy full programs or to list them in their entirety. Such software techniques are becoming increasingly popular and sophisticated as methods to prevent infringement of copyright.

The above discussion has been intended to introduce the concept of software protection. Numerous books have been written on this subject (see Appendix D.)

LOOKING AHEAD

1. A copyright bill that covers semiconductor chips has a good chance of being passed by Congress.

2. A concept of 'limited copyright protection' in place of the current all or nothing philosophy (either a work may be copyrighted or not) will be implemented.

3. Algorithms—currently viewed as ideas and not copyrightable—will be protected under new laws.

4. A company will be permitted to use another company's chip design if a royalty is paid.

III. MINIMIZING HUMAN ERRORS

A. Types of Human Errors

It is not uncommon to find that computers are being blamed for a variety of mistakes in computer-generated output. "The computer made a mistake!" is commonly given as the reason for an assortment of errors. Computers, by themselves, do not usually make mistakes. Recall that central processing units utilize parity bits designed to:

1. Detect if the computer has malfunctioned while it is processing data.

2. Stop the processing and print a message on the console terminal that alerts the operator to the fact that a malfunction has occurred. It is then typically necessary to call the vendor to have a customer engineer come to correct the problem.

Hardware errors, then, rarely go undetected. Thus, no matter how complicated a particular calculation may be, we can be virtually assured that the computer will always produce the correct result—if there is no human error involved.

The user and the systems analyst must anticipate that human errors can be introduced into a system from a variety of sources. Every system must be designed so that:

1. The likelihood of errors occurring in the first place is minimized.

2. Errors are detected and adequate procedures implemented so that the integrity of records in files and data bases is not affected.

The following sample of "computer mistakes" indicates how widespread and catastrophic human errors can be when computers are involved.

Examples

1. During the past year, $85 million was improperly paid by the Social Security Administration to deceased Social Security recipients.

   The Explanation The computer had not been programmed to match death records against beneficiary files.

2. 61 prospective lawyers who recently took the New York State Bar exam received notifications that were incorrect: 26 who had been notified that they had passed, actually failed; 35 who had been told they had failed, actually passed.

The Explanation The computerized grading program incorrectly weighted the various parts of the exam.

3. A woman who submitted a Medicare claim for $20 to be reimbursed for a cane found that the government was sending her monthly checks for 40 cents each to pay her claim.

The Explanation Previously, Medicare paid for monthly cane rentals because "that always came up cheaper, according to the computer's program, than the total purchase price." When rentals were eliminated, the computer was not reprogrammed correctly.

4. Recently, in a newspaper listing of stock prices on the New York Stock Exchange (NYSE), no stocks beginning with a J were listed.

The Explanation The following was printed where these stocks would normally be listed:

"J" on strike
Due to some kind of bug in our computer, the "J's" in the NYSE won't print. We hope to settle the matter tomorrow.

5. The city of East Baton Rouge, Louisiana, was notified by the local electric company that it had been underbilled for two years because of a computing error by the utility.

The Explanation The number 10 had been used by the computer instead of the number 100 as a code for determining the city's cost. In addition, the error was compounded by a mistake in recording the meter reading. The last digit of the reading was dropped altogether.

6. Several years ago, a computer system operated by the North America Air Defense Command "decided" that the Soviet Union had launched a nuclear missile attack against the United States. As a result, six F-101 fighters and four F-106 interceptors were immediately airborne. It took *six* minutes for the Pentagon to realize that there was no attack.

The Explanation "Computer error."

We will briefly discuss some of the major types of human error that any effective systems design will attempt to minimize.

1. Errors in Input Data

The quality of output from a computerized system is a direct function of the quality of the input data that was used to generate it. It is therefore essential that input data be *validated* before it is processed.

It is not usually possible to determine if all input fields contain *correct* data. It can, however, be determined if the data meets certain prescribed criteria. For example, consider an Hours Worked field in a particular time card that contains the number 45, designating the number of hours a particular employee has worked during the past week. It is not possible for the computer to determine that the number is erroneous and should, in fact, be 42 for that employee. However, if the field contains 98, it is reasonable to suspect that there is an error. In such a case, the record would not be processed in the normal way but "flagged" as a potential error. This is one example of where an **exception report** would undoubtedly prove useful for reviewing questionable input data before it is processed. That is, a listing of all records that did not contain data within established limits would be printed for checking purposes.

There are numerous other ways in which input data can be validated. The following list suggests some of the more common problems that must be considered.

1. Do numeric fields, in fact, contain numeric data? If a numeric field contains non-numeric data, an interrupt in the program will occur when that field is used in a calculation.
2. Does the data appear in the proper format? For example, a Date field may be required to be entered in the format MMDDYY, where M represents month, D represents day, and Y represents year.
3. Do coded fields contain only valid codes?
4. Do key fields that identify each record contain the necessary data?
5. Are specified fields within established limits?
6. Has data been entered in the proper sequence?

The above are considered **validity checks**, which are routines designed to:

1. Ensure that the data conforms to certain requirements.
2. Minimize the processing of erroneous input.

Although these routines will be written by programmers, it is the systems analyst and the user who determine which validity checks are to be performed and the specific requirements of each.

Realistically, it may not always be possible to validate *all* input data. Suppose, for example, that employee records have the following fields:

Field	Positions
Employee Number	1-5
Last Name	6-17
First Name	18-29
Sex Code	30
(1 = Female)	
(2 = Male)	
Other Data	31-100

If an input record is entered with a sex code of 3, for example, this can easily be detected as an error. What happens, however, if an input record is entered for an employee named Leslie Barnes, with a sex code of 2? It is not possible, based solely on the data in the input record, to validate the sex code, since Leslie can be a female's name as well as a male's.

2. Systems Design Errors

As we have seen, a major reason why computerized systems frequently fail to meet their required objectives is because of a communication gap between the systems analyst and the user. The systems analyst is well versed on computer capabilities and the technical features of hardware and software but may have very limited knowledge of how the various business areas, such as accounts receivable, accounts payable, and so on operate within the company. The user, on the other hand, is an expert in his or her business area, but may have little or no knowledge of computers. Herein lies a major reason for a communication gap between the analyst and the user, a gap that often leads to misunderstandings on the part of the analyst as to exactly what is required from the computerized system.

The lack of certain details and/or a misunderstanding of how certain procedures function can easily lead to errors in the design of the system, errors that may not be picked up until after the system has been implemented.

A case in point will demonstrate how critical it is for the analyst to understand all details of a system from the earliest stages of the design phase.

Background   The president of a major company recently received a paycheck produced by a new computerized payroll system. The amount of the check was correct; however, on the stub, the amount for Year-to-Date Earnings was listed as $0. It is significant to note that the paycheck was produced in July and that the president's previous paychecks from January through June had all contained correct Year-to-Date Earnings' figures. Why did something suddenly go wrong in July?

The Explanation   After a thorough investigation, it was discovered that when the system was designed, and subsequently programmed, it was *assumed* by the analyst that the largest annual salary for anyone in the company was $99,999.99, a number requiring *five* integer positions. The analyst included these five integers in the design specifications that were eventually transmitted to the programming staff. As it happened, the assumption was incorrect; the president in particular earned $200,000 per year. As of July 1, the Year-to-Date Earnings for this individual were $100,000, thus requiring *six* integer positions to print out the amount. Based on the analyst's specifications, the programmer had only allowed for a maximum of *five* positions, thereby causing the amount of $100,000 to be truncated to 0.

It is important to note in this example that the user must also bear part of the responsibility for the error. In this case, the user (payroll manager) did not work closely enough with the analyst during the design phase to ensure that this type of error would not occur. In addition, after the programs were written, the user did not supply adequate test data which should have been designed to detect this type of error.

3. Programming Errors

Programs for business applications typically contain hundreds, and often thousands, of instructions. It is relatively simple for errors in logic to occur in a program. Moreover, each system design typically includes numerous programs where the output from one program is used as input by another. Test data for each of these programs must be precise and complete.

B. Control Procedures for the Handling of Data

We will now discuss controls that can be used to detect and prevent human errors as opposed to deliberate misuse. It should be noted, however, that many of the controls discussed here serve both purposes.

1. Input Controls

We have already seen in Chapter 5 how certain controls such as data verification and programmed checks for reasonableness can be used to ensure that input transactions are complete and accurate. We will now briefly discuss additional design considerations and controls that are frequently used as well.

1. Source documents should be designed so that they are easy to complete in an accurate manner. For example, preprinted boxes can be used for each digit of an account number, each character of a name, and so on.

2. Source documents that will be converted into machine-readable form by a keying process with a device such as a keypunch machine, key-to-tape encoder, etc., should have the starting column or position number preprinted next to each field.

3. For source documents that will require a keying operation, the fields on the form should be located in the sequence in which they will be entered. This will help minimize keying errors that may result from eye fatigue, visual transposition of data, and so on.

4. For source documents with multiple copies, the destination of each copy should be printed on the appropriate form. The use of color-coded copies should be considered to facilitate the distribution process.

5. A list of individuals who are empowered to complete each form should be established by the user.

6. Before a user department forwards a batch of source documents to the computer center for processing, both batch totals and item counts should be determined by the user. A **batch total** is the total obtained by adding up the values in a particular field on all documents in the batch. An **item count** is simply a count of the number of documents in the batch. Figure 17.4 illustrates how these controls can be used to ensure that all input data is properly accounted for throughout the various stages of processing.

2. Processing Controls

We have already seen that some controls, such as batch totals and item counts, that are used during the data entry process are also used during the processing phase. There are also other controls, such as edit procedures, that may be implemented.

An **edit procedure** is the process of validating a file of data to ensure that records do not contain obvious omissions, inconsistencies, or errors.

Keep in mind that the specific edit procedures required for an application are determined by the analyst and are verified by the user. The following are edit procedures that commonly are used.

a. Field Test   A **field test** is used to determine if specific data fields have valid formats.

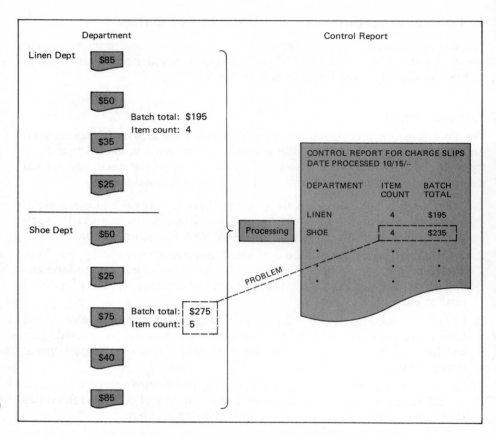

Figure 17.4
Example of the use of batch totals and item counts.

An amount field, for example, in an input record must be numeric. If it is not, then an error has occurred, and unless the field is corrected or omitted, erroneous processing will occur. An arithmetic operation performed on numeric fields that erroneously contain non-numeric data will typically cause a program interrupt.

Depending on the nature of the numeric field, we may *reject* an erroneously coded numeric field or we may simply fill it with zeros on the validated file. If, for example, an ACCOUNT NUMBER field contains non-numeric data and this is the key field on the master file, then we must reject the record.

Similarly, some fields such as FIRST NAME, DESCRIPTION, and CITY should contain only alphabetic data. The edit routine should check to determine that they do, in fact, contain strictly alphabetic data. Here again, we may reject records with erroneously coded alphabetic fields or we may simply fill the field with spaces.

b. Code Test   As we have seen, a **code test** can often be used to determine if a coded field is valid.

Suppose we have a sales record that is keyed in from a terminal with the following fields:

Salesperson's Number
Salesperson's Name

Branch Office

Sales Amount

Suppose, too, that there are currently five branch offices, coded 1 to 5. An edit program should incorporate a routine to determine if the field called BRANCH contains a number from 1 to 5. If it does not, an error condition must be noted. Either the record will be rejected because branch office is a key field, or the field will be flagged as erroneous, so that a future correction can be made.

c. Missing Data Test   For most records, key data fields are required for processing. For example, a payroll record must typically contain a Social Security number (or employee number) and annual salary. If either of these fields is missing, then the record should be rejected since it would not be usable in a payroll file update. Similarly, an accounts receivable record with a missing account number or amount is equally useless.

For data fields that are *not* critical, missing information may be merely noted on a listing or else filled with some compensating data.

d. Reasonableness Test   During processing, a test for reasonableness can be made to check for errors. As an example, in a payroll system for workers paid on an hourly basis, a test for reasonableness might be employed as follows. Suppose the highest hourly rate for any employee in the company is $10 per hour and the hours worked usually does not exceed 60 hours per week. Overtime starts after 40 hours. Therefore, a limit check of $700 per week for gross pay is reasonable, calculating overtime at time-and-one-half ($40 \times 10 + 20 \times 10 \times 1.5$). If, during processing, gross pay for an individual turned out to be $900, the corresponding payroll check should not be processed until further investigation is made. We would probably want the input data pertaining to that employee to be printed in an exception report.

3. Output Controls

The analyst must design output controls to:

1. Verify the accuracy of the output.
2. Ensure that output is retained for a fixed period of time and then disposed of properly after it is no longer needed.

There are several major controls that can be used to verify the accuracy of the output. We will discuss many of these in the next section on auditing. For now, however, we mention two of the controls that are commonly used. One is to perform a *random sampling* of the output to ascertain that the input transactions used to generate the selected output were properly processed. Another control is to check and verify *every* item listed on an exception report.

In designing output and determining retention cycles, the analyst must consider legal requirements as well as the company's needs. The same considerations are true for input records as well. Figure 17.5 illustrates record retention guidelines established by the accounting firm of Coopers and Lybrand for selected types of source documents and outputs.

Type of Record	Retention Period (in years)
Accounting	
Auditors' reports	Permanent
Cash projections	2
Credit memos	3
Depreciation records	3
Employee payroll records (W-2, W-4, annual earning records, etc.)	4
General journal	Permanent
General ledger	Permanent
Inventory lists	3
Invoices	
Sales and cash register tapes	3
Purchases (merchandise)	3
Purchases (permanent assets)	3
Payroll journal	4
Payroll tax returns	4
Pension/profit sharing	
Plan and trust agreement	Permanent
Financial statements	Permanent
Actuarial reports	Permanent
IRS approval letter	Permanent
Associated ledgers and journals	Permanent
Personnel files	3
Production and sales reports	3
Timecards and daily time reports	3

Source: Coopers & Lybrand.

Figure 17.5
Sample record retention guidelines.

In addition to the retention of records, there is a need for backup files, as previously discussed. A backup file serves a control function, in the event that master files are lost, stolen, or damaged.

It should be noted that the user must indicate what procedures are to be used so that sensitive records are destroyed after their retention time has expired. For example, shredding devices are typically used to destroy source documents and computer printouts that are no longer needed and are considered to contain sensitive data.

IV. AUDITING PROCEDURES

Although entire books have been written on the subject of auditing in a computer environment, in the next few pages we will provide an overview of typical auditing procedures that are used. Frequently, specific controls are built into the new system during the design phase to facilitate the auditing process. Before we discuss these controls, however, we will provide some perspective on the auditing function itself.

A. The Auditing Function

There are two main categories of auditors:

1. **Internal auditors**, who audit the operating procedures performed within the company.
2. **External auditors**, who render professional opinions on financial statements of a company to outside groups, such as stockholders.

We focus here on the internal auditing function, since the entire chapter has been devoted to the security and control of procedures performed within a company. The major objectives of an auditor typically include:

1. Ensuring that adequate controls have been implemented to detect and prevent computer crime and human error.
2. Reviewing the reliability, efficiency, and cost-effectiveness of the system being audited and the financial reports produced by it.

To accomplish these objectives effectively, the auditor should be completely independent of the user department as well as the systems analyst working on the system. In many companies, therefore, internal auditors report directly to the company's board of directors.

We will now briefly consider some of the tools used by auditors.

B. Sample Audit Tools

1. Tags and Snapshots

This procedure essentially involves (1) identifying selected transactions with special tags, or codes, and then (2) observing these tagged transactions as they flow through the various phases of the system.

The tag can consist of a separate field in an input record which has a code designating that the record has been tagged. Alternatively, one of the regular fields in the record can be designed to incorporate a special character to serve as a tag. For example, a minus sign can be used as a tag when it is coded in the low-order position of a numeric field such as SOCIAL SECURITY NUMBER.

Once a record has been tagged, the computer can be programmed to take a "snapshot" or print out the status of that record at various times during normal processing. For example, an auditor might want to examine a particular record in a master file both before and after it has been updated to ascertain if the updating procedure has been properly performed.

2. Tracing

In connection with the above technique, an auditor may want to trace the specific instructions executed during the processing of a tagged record. The purpose in doing this is to verify the logic used for processing selected transactions. Note that some programming languages have instructions to facilitate tracing.

3. Test Data

This auditing tool simply involves the use of input transactions specially prepared by the auditor, where the auditor knows in advance what results should be produced. The objective is to see how the system handles the data. To fully test out the system, the auditor's input records should include *every* type of data conceivable, including blank fields, erroneously completed fields, as well as valid data.

4. Integrated Test Facility

This technique allows the auditor to integrate fictitious records into the master file or data base *without* the user or the Information Processing staff being aware of their existence. These records can then be processed with transactions supplied by the auditor, who can monitor the system as often as desired.

CHAPTER SUMMARY

I. The need for security, control, and audit procedures
   A. Computers, by themselves, do not usually make mistakes. Most computer-generated mistakes are attributable to human error.
   B. Computerized systems are particularly vulnerable to criminal acts.
   C. Threats to security include not only deliberate acts but natural disasters, such as fire, flood, and other so-called "acts of God."
   D. The user's responsibility in the development of a new system.
      1. To work actively with the systems analyst from inception of a new design through programming and implementation stages.
      2. To ensure that realistic goals are established.
      3. To ensure that a user-friendly system is developed that has appropriate security, control, and audit procedures.
II. Computer crime and invasion of privacy
   A. Computer crime is the act of stealing, embezzling, or otherwise defrauding an organization with the use of a computer.
   B. Many computer crimes go undetected or unreported.
   C. The privacy issue has attained new significance with:
      1. The widespread use of electronic funds transfer systems, point-of-sale systems, and the great proliferation of data bases.
      2. The development of consumer services available to those with home computers, such as home banking, shop-at-home services, information services, and opinion polling.
   D. Controls for ensuring the security and privacy of data.
      1. No system is foolproof, in an absolute sense.
      2. One can get whatever degree of protection one wants (short of perfection) if one is willing to pay for it.
      3. Every company should have plans to prevent disasters such as fire, floods, earthquakes, and sabotage from interfering with its information processing operations.
III. Minimizing human errors
   A. The user and the systems analyst must anticipate that human errors can be introduced into a system from a variety of sources.
   B. Every system must be designed so that:
      1. The likelihood of errors occurring is minimized.
      2. Errors are detected and adequate procedures implemented so that the integrity of data bases is not compromised.
IV. The need for auditing procedures
   A. The major objectives of auditing procedures include:
      1. Ensuring that adequate controls have been implemented to detect and prevent computer crime and human error.

Chapter Self-Evaluating Quiz

1. (T or F) It is human error that is responsible for most computer-generated mistakes.
2. (T or F) Systems analysts should simply ignore a user's fear of or resistance to computers since there is not much he or she can do about it anyway.
3. (T or F) Typically a systems analyst can design the necessary computer control procedures for an application without the need to consult a user.
4. (T or F) A pilot run of a new system with test data supplied by the user is one method for determining if a system works as was originally intended.
5. (T or F) It is always expedient to continue to improve a system no matter what the cost.
6. (T or F) Computer crimes sometimes go unreported to the police because companies are afraid of adverse publicity.
7. (T or F) The Equity Funding case illustrates how inadvertent misuse of computers can cause problems for a company.
8. (T or F) The use of computers can, if not controlled, lead to invasion of an individual's privacy.
9. (T or F) The widespread use of computers in the home has led to increased concern over issues relating to individual privacy.
10. (T or F) To date, no federal laws have been passed to protect an individual's privacy from unauthorized access of a data base by a computer.
11. Examples of methods used for controlling physical access of a computer are _____, _____, and _____.
12. (T or F) Rotating functions within a computer center can minimize unauthorized access to a data base.
13. (T or F) Typically programmers should have access to all files and data bases maintained by a company.
14. The term _____ is used to describe scrambling techniques used to make computer data unintelligible in the event of a wiretap.
15. Threats to the security of a computer system include natural disasters such as _____.

Solutions

1. T / page 651
2. F—Systems analysts should attempt to dispel fears if they expect users to effectively utilize a new design. / page 652
3. F—The user should typically be involved. / page 652
4. T / page 653
5. F—The "law of diminishing returns" applies to systems design: improving a system beyond a certain point may simply prove to be too costly. / page 653

6. T / page 655

7. F—The Equity Funding case illustrates deliberate misuse of computers, not inadvertent misuse! / page 656

8. T / page 658

9. T / page 658

10. F—The Privacy Act of 1974 and the Right to Financial Privacy Act of 1979 have some protective clauses. / page 659

11. badges
    keys
    sign-in sheets
    security guards
    alarms

fingerprints and voiceprints / page 660

12. T—It becomes increasingly difficult for individuals to learn how to access data bases and/ or modify programs without others knowing about it. / page 660

13. F—Programmers should have access to files and data bases on a "need to know" basis. / page 662

14. encryption / page 665

15. fire / page 666
    flood / page 666
    earthquake / page 667

Key Terms

Batch total	Edit procedure	Hacker	Validity check
Code test	Encryption	Item count	
Computer crime	Exception report	Law of diminishing returns	
Data Encryption Standard (DES)	Field test	Pareto's law	

Review Questions

I. True-False Questions

1. (T or F) The design of security and control procedures should be the sole responsibility of the systems analyst, who has special expertise in this area.

2. (T or F) Once a new system has been programmed and implemented, the user should ascertain that it runs properly in a pilot run.

3. (T or F) Test data for a pilot run of a new system should be supplied by the programmer who wrote the programs.

4. (T or F) The law of diminishing returns indicates that there is a point where the user and the systems analyst should stop looking for improvements to a system.

5. (T or F) The majority of computer crimes go either undetected or unreported.

6. (T or F) Most computer crimes are successful because of the development of user-friendly systems.

7. (T or F) Now that it has been revealed, it is unlikely that the type of computer fraud that was committed in the Equity Funding Corporation would ever be repeated in another company.

8. (T or F) It is imperative that the user approve in writing any design project that is given the "go ahead" for development.

9. (T or F) For control purposes, it is better to have a large program written by one programmer rather than several individuals.

10. (T or F) Encryption is a major method used to preserve the privacy of data when a company operates in a data communications environment.

11. (T or F) It is possible, but expensive, for a programmer to have his or her ideas copyrighted.

12. (T or F) It is not usually possible to determine if all fields in an input record contain correct data.

II. Fill in the Blanks

1. _____ error is responsible for most computer-generated mistakes.
2. The systems analyst is a (staff/line) person who can only recommend changes to a system.
3. The (programmer/systems analyst/user) is the best person to supply test data for a pilot run of a new system.
4. Two primary reasons for a company's unwillingness to disclose a computer crime are _____ and _____.
5. A _____ file serves a control function in the event that a master file is lost, stolen, or damaged.
6. _____ is a major method used to render computer data unintelligible when interceptions, such as wiretaps, occur in a data communications environment.
7. _____ is the means by which a terminal user's identity is verified.
8. It is possible to get copyright protection for the _____ that are used in a program but not the _____.
9. Central processing units utilize _____ bits to detect if the computer has malfunctioned.
10. It is essential that input data be _____ before it is processed.
11. Edit procedures that are commonly used to validate a file of data include _____, _____, _____, and _____.

APPLICATION

DP DISASTERS HURT ENTIRE FIRM[1]

By Lel F. Somogyi

Disasters in the computer room affect not only the DP operation, but the rest of the company as well. A corporation's cash flow can be interrupted, its position in the marketplace can be hurt, customer and employee relations can be strained and a firm's purchasing power can be jeopardized.

While there is no way to prevent many disasters, the risks and implications of a significant disruption of DP services cannot be ignored.

Planning is the key to survival in any contingency program. The goal is to get critical applications running as quickly as possible regardless of the reason the system is not working. For example, there can be hardware damage resulting from a fire, explosion or power failure.

But also remember that a system can be rendered helpless by other factors. For example, a data communications failure could make vital data inaccessible.

But contingency planning involves more than just finding innovative ways of getting the hardware back on-line. There are many issues to consider. For example, how much money will a firm lose if a critical application is lost? What happens if that application is down for an extended period of time?

Function at Many Levels

A contingency plan can function at many levels. It is up to the DP executive to determine which steps a firm should take to protect its data. This decision should include an economic justification of various contingency planning alternatives and integrate top management and user views.

A good contingency plan must also hold provisions to test and refine the plan.

There should be a framework for maintaining the plan. This involves training personnel in how to recover successfully from a disaster.

Gaining top-level, corporatewide support for a disaster recovery plan is probably the strongest guarantee for success.

Three Basic Steps

To do this, there are three basic steps that help define the overall impact of the DP operation on the rest of the company.

■ The first step is to evaluate thoroughly the costs and benefits of a contingency plan. This involves input from the DP department as well as from the users of the system.

■ Next, the DP executive must determine which applications are most critical to the firm's operation. This involves a priority analysis of applications and a determination of the operating requirements for each of the key applications.

This phase also includes an analysis of the risks and benefits of various recovery alternatives.

■ The last step involves the actual development of a contingency plan. This plan should be developed by the DP personnel so that they are familiar with its structure. The final step also involves testing the contingency plan to make sure it works and training personnel in how to cope with disaster.

At the conclusion of each of these phases, an interim report of observations, findings and recommendations should be released to management for review and comments before proceeding to the next phase.

In this way, management involvement is maintained, and there is a higher potential for a workable contingency plan.

The main reason a contingency plan fails is because the firm chose a technical solution before adequately understanding the management requirements of the organization.

[1]*Computerworld,* January 9, 1984, page 59. Copyright © 1984 by CW Communications/Inc., Framingham, MA 01701. Reprinted with permission.

Questions
1. Understanding Key Terms
   Define the following terms as they are used in the application.
   a. Contingency plan.
   b. Disaster recovery plan.
   c. Priority analysis of applications.
2. Software, Hardware, and Systems Concepts
   What are some of the potential risks to a company if a disaster occurs in the computer room?
3. Management Considerations
   The following is stated: "Gaining top-level, corporatewide support for a disaster recovery plan is probably the strongest guarantee for success." Why is this so?
4. Social, Legal, and Ethical Implications
   a. What are some of the social factors that might influence a company's decision regarding whether or not to implement a disaster recovery plan?
   b. Under what circumstances would it be more prudent for an organization to invest more in a disaster prevention plan than a recovery plan?

CASE STUDY: McKing's Superburgers, Inc.

Management at McKing's is considering the proposal for a distributed data processing system.

1. Indicate whether you would recommend use of the Data Encryption Standard at McKing's. Explain your answer.

2. Would the use of the audit procedure known as an integrated test facility prove beneficial to McKing's? Explain your answer.

3. What control procedures would you recommend to ensure that only authorized users at each restaurant can gain access to the central computer?

4. What physical access controls would you recommend for use at the central computer facility?

5. What disaster prevention techniques would you recommend for the central computer facility?

THE COMPUTER AD: A Focus on Marketing

Consider the ad entitled "Computer Security is a Terminal Problem" that appears in Figure 17.6.

Questions

1. Why does the ad suggest that a computer system's most vulnerable point is the terminal? Do you agree? Explain your answer.
2. Based on the ad, are there any specific requirements for a computer system for which the acquisition of GUARDIAN is being considered?
3. The ad states that GUARDIAN "limits access, monitors and records all on-line activities and provides reports in plain English." Suppose you are a manager of information processing. Prepare a list of specific questions you would ask to determine how valid the above claims are.

Computer security is a terminal problem.

All the locks, checkpoints and guards in the world can't protect your computer system at its most vulnerable point, your terminals. Anybody who sits down at a keyboard can strike right at the heart of your system. That's why you need GUARDIAN.

GUARDIAN is the flexible CICS security software specially designed to protect the on-line portion of your computer system. It limits access, monitors and records all on-line activities and provides reports in plain English. Start defending your most vulnerable area. Call today for more information about GUARDIAN.

ON-LINE SOFTWARE INTERNATIONAL

Fort Lee Executive Park
Two Executive Drive, Fort Lee, NJ 07024
(201) 592-0009 • Toll Free (800) 526-0272

Figure 17.6
Marketing computer products. (Courtesy On-Line Software International.)

CHAPTER 18

THE COMPUTER PROFESSIONAL

CHAPTER OBJECTIVES

To familiarize you with:

- Professional opportunities in the computing field and in related areas.
- The availability of jobs and typical salary ranges.
- How to obtain the job you want.
- Resume and interview preparation.
- The pros and cons of certification in the computer field.
- Ethical issues faced by computer professionals.
- The major computer societies.

I. CAREER OPPORTUNITIES

A. Entry-Level Programming Positions and Typical Requirements

Most college graduates who have majored in the computing field begin their careers as programmers.

Programming positions can be classified as follows:

Programming Positions

1. **Maintenance programmers**—modify existing programs to make them more current or more efficient.
2. **Application programmers and programmer analysts**—write, debug, and document full programs for specific business jobs.
3. **Scientific programmers**—write, debug, and document full programs for specific scientific applications.
4. **Systems programmers**—develop operating system components designed to maximize the efficient use of the computer system.

Many organizations initially hire entry level programmers for maintenance work so that they can learn firsthand the need for well-documented, logical programs. Maintenance programming also helps the novice understand the types of programs typically coded at the organization. Since maintenance work tends to get tedious unless you have an interest in "troubleshooting," most maintenance programmers become application programmers after a short time.

Application programmers generally have a long-range objective in the management area. Scientific and systems programmers, on the other hand, are usually computer science majors who have long-range interests in maximizing their command of operating systems and computer systems, and becoming more specialized programmers.

Entry-level programming jobs usually require the following:

IN A NUTSHELL

TYPICAL REQUIREMENTS FOR ENTRY-LEVEL PROGRAMMERS

1. College degree.
2. Programming experience.
3. Personal attributes—logical mind, interest in problem solving, good communication skills.
4. Programmer aptitude test.

---

1. College Degree

Depending on the company, its requirements, and the salary offered, the degree sought might be one of the following. Note, however, that there is great variation in the names of degree programs in the computing field.

1. A four-year degree: Bachelor of Science (B.S.) in computer science or Bachelor of Business Administration (B.B.A.) in information processing.

2. A two-year degree: Associate's degree (A.A.S. or A.S.) in computer science or business data processing.

In general, four-year college graduates can expect higher-paying, more responsible programming positions, but there are many good jobs available for two-year graduates as well. A student's grade point average, particularly in computing courses, is viewed by most organizations as a major factor in evaluating job applicants.

2. Programming Experience

This is the "Catch 22" for many graduates. Some organizations require entry-level programmers to have some business or programming experience. If most organizations in a particular location have this requirement, it becomes nearly impossible for students to acquire the needed experience.

But the situation is rarely insurmountable. Many students find it possible to earn extra money and gain experience by working in their college's computing center and/or working part time for local firms or for their instructors who have consulting jobs. This provides the needed experience that many companies require.

3. Personal Attributes

Generally, organizations interview their potential employees before making a job offer. Personal characteristics of the job applicant that are typically sought vary widely, but most organizations look for a logical mind and a demonstrated interest in problem solving. As emphasized in this text, many organizations believe that communication barriers between users and computer professionals account for a large number of failures in computerization. As a result, they are intent on hiring individuals who are articulate, sensitive, good listeners, and able to communicate.

The interview is generally used by companies to determine if a prospective candidate has the personal attributes desired. Courses in business writing and public speaking could be useful for providing these needed communication skills.

4. Programmer Aptitude Test

Many companies believe that a programmer aptitude test will help them determine the suitability of an individual for a programming position. These tests generally measure logical ability, reading comprehension, and sometimes communication skills. Figure 18.1 illustrates some of the questions found on typical programmer aptitude tests.

Note that, in general, people with graduate degrees (M.B.A., M.S., and so on) are generally considered over-qualified for entry-level programming positions. Sometimes, however, individuals with these degrees are hired as programmers, with the understanding that there will be a brief "break-in" period in an entry-level job, to be followed by a promotion within a short time.

1. Indicate the next letter in the following sequence.
   a   dd   c   ff   e   hh
   (a) g   (b) i   (c) f   (d) j   (e) k
   The answer is (a).
2. Which figure has the most in common with the one shown?

Sample figure

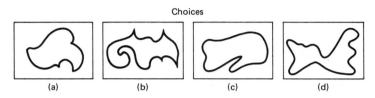

Choices

(a)   (b)   (c)   (d)

The answer is (b). (Note that both figures have *two points on the top*.)

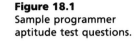

Figure 18.1
Sample programmer
aptitude test questions.

B. The Next Step

After working as a programmer or in some other entry-level position for one to
two years, some people are ready for a move. Because the computing field is
not really standardized, there are various paths that can be taken after one has
had some programming experience. The following are typical options available
to a programmer:

The Next Step

1. The lateral move.
2. The technical path.
3. The management path.
   a. Programming manager.
   b. Systems analyst and then systems manager.
   c. DP operations manager.
   d. Data base administrator.
   e. EDP auditor.
   f. Manager of a user department or data processing liaison for a user de-
      partment
   g. Director of information systems.
4. Going into business or consulting.
5. Teaching.

1. The Lateral Move

Many programmers seek "greener pastures" at other organizations after they
have gained experience. As we will consider later in this chapter, there are many
more jobs for experienced programmers than there are professionals to fill them.
Hence, most programmers find that they can obtain higher-paying jobs in prime
locations with numerous benefits, after they have gained some experience. Many
choose a career path in which they change jobs every few years to earn higher
salaries and to learn from new experiences.

2. The Technical Path

Frequently, programmers, particularly those with a computer science orientation, seek opportunities to expand their technical skills. After gaining some experience, they are interested in positions in software engineering, compiler design, operating system design, computer graphics, sophisticated data communications design, systems programming, and so on. These jobs tend to be filled by highly skilled, experienced programming professionals.

3. The Management Path

Many programmers view the computer primarily as a tool to facilitate management decision-making. This tends to be particularly true of people with business or B.B.A. degrees, or those with extensive business experience. For these professionals, promotion to management is a primary goal. There are numerous management positions available for skilled computer professionals with good communication skills. (You may wish to review the sample organization charts in Figures 2.13 and 2.14 for summaries of how typical companies organize their computer staff.)

a. Programming Manager   The first step in management for many computer professionals is to supervise other programmers as a **programming manager**.

b. Systems Analyst and Then Systems Manager   Recall that a **systems analyst** is responsible for analyzing existing business procedures, determining the problem areas, and designing more efficient computerized procedures. Some companies use the term **programmer analyst** to describe a systems analyst who may also do some programming.

In many organizations, a systems analyst supervises the work of programmers and works closely with top management to determine the organization's overall needs. Hence, even though technical responsibilities are part of the job, the position of systems analyst is considered a management-level job. In general, the more business experience systems analysts have, the more attuned they will be to the needs of specific departments and to the company as a whole.

The typical career path for many college graduates, then, is to begin as a programmer, gain experience in numerous application areas, and then advance to a position of systems analyst.

Sometimes people with Master's degrees will be hired as systems analysts directly from graduate schools, or as junior analysts where they begin as interns and are slated to advance to the conventional systems analyst positions in a short time.

After serving as a systems analyst, the computer professional could advance to **systems manager**. A systems manager is the individual who oversees the activities of all systems analysts. A person with systems experience and good management and communication skills is apt to be promoted to a systems manager.

c. DP or Operations Manager   After gaining considerable experience, a computer professional may be promoted to the position of **DP or operations manager**. In this position, one assumes responsibility for the overall functioning of the computer and data entry operations. This is a job with general operating responsibilities in which the manager directly supervises the data entry operators, control staff, and computer operators. The operations manager has overall responsibility for the efficient and effective utilization of the computer equipment. The security and integrity of the computer system is his or her responsibility as well. Assessing the efficiency of existing equipment and making recommendations for new acquisitions are also part of the job.

It is also possible for a member of the operating staff itself to be promoted to operations manager. In this instance, the individual may not have had actual programming or systems experience.

d. Data Base Administrator

A **data base administrator** is the individual responsible for organizing and designing the data base and all other data used by the organization. Control of the use, security, and integrity of the data base is the responsibility of this professional. Some programmers and analysts typically report to a data base administrator for creating, modifying, and updating data bases.

Typically, a programmer or analyst with several years of data base experience and good communication skills may be promoted into this position.

e. EDP Auditor

An **EDP auditor** is an individual with accounting and computer expertise who assesses the overall effectiveness and integrity of the computer system. The EDP auditor is also responsible for detecting if there have been efforts to misuse the system or defraud the company with the use of a computer.

An EDP auditor may be a Certified Public Accountant (CPA) as well as a computer professional.

f. Manager of a User Department or Data Processing Liaison for a User Department

As user departments in an organization become more computerized, there is a great need for computer expertise within these departments themselves. Since one main reason why computerized systems fail is poor communication between users and computer professionals, a computer professional within the user area could help bridge this communication gap. As a result, increasing numbers of organizations are hiring programmers and analysts to serve as department managers or technical liaisons with the computer staff.

g. Director of Information Systems

The **director of information systems** is usually the highest-level position in a computer organization. Typically it is a vice presidential position, but this varies considerably, depending on the organization. The director of information systems has overall responsibility for all computer operations and the entire staff of programmers, analysts, and other computer professionals.

The director of information systems has usually had considerable experience on numerous levels in computing and demonstrated management and technical skills.

4. Going into Business or Consulting

Many experienced programmers are eager to form their own consulting organizations. They may begin by doing freelance programming and systems work, troubleshooting for clients, or developing packages that they then sell or lease to customers.

The advantage of establishing your own company or consulting practice is that you are working for yourself. In addition, the potential income may be very great. But the disadvantages are that there is great risk and there is considerable instability.

5. Teaching

Even though teaching jobs traditionally pay less than positions in the computing field, many people find the experience rewarding.

Most colleges will accept adjunct or part-time faculty who have either a Bachelor's or Master's degree with some experience in computing. Permanent, full-time positions at many universities require a Ph.D. degree, while others require a Master's degree.

Because salaries are relatively low compared to industry, and because numerous years of education are required for a Ph.D., there has been a serious dearth of qualified faculty with Ph.D. degrees. This situation represents a serious problem for the academic community, but it is also a unique opportunity for individuals who prefer the advantages of a teaching career.

To indicate the variety of job descriptions and job requirements for the positions described above, Figure 18.2 illustrates typical job offerings in a recent edition of a New York newspaper.

C. Other Computer-Related Entry-Level Positions

1. Operations Staff

There are numerous opportunities available in the following areas:

1. Data entry operator.
2. Word processing operator.
3. Computer operator.

Frequently, an entry-level position as an operator does not require a college degree or any experience. In some instances, however, training and experience will mean higher salaries initially and more responsibility.

These positions are ideal for some individuals with limited college background or for those who are working their way through school.

After gaining some experience as an operator, an individual could be promoted to operations management or to a position as a programmer.

2. Marketing or Sales

Many college graduates find that they have an interest in computing but are not suited for, or interested in, technical positions. There are numerous jobs available in the sale and marketing of computers and application packages.

Marketing or sales positions are available in organizations that manufacture peripherals (I/O devices), mainframes, micros, or minis, in addition to companies that sell software.

Figure 18.2
Typical job offerings in the computer field.

D. Average Salaries of Computer Professionals

Note that salaries vary widely among organizations and depend generally on the following:

Factors Influencing Salaries

1. Type of organization.
2. Specific responsibilities.
3. Geographic location.
4. Number of years of experience.

Sometimes specific benefits provided by a company will mean salaries are not as high as are offered by other organizations. Benefits used to attract employees include grants of micros, travel opportunities, long vacation periods, and so on.

Figure 18.3 is a chart illustrating average salaries for computing professionals.

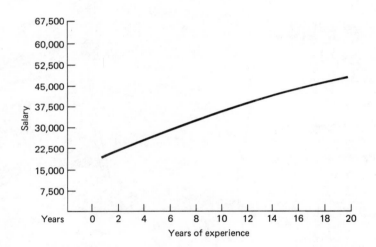

Figure 18.3
Average salaries for computing professionals.

II. GETTING YOUR FIRST JOB

A. Where to Look

1. The Placement Office at Your School

Most schools have placement offices for matching the needs of local businesses with their graduates. This is a good place to begin the search for a position, since most organizations that have contacted the placement office are familiar with the degree requirements and course offerings at the school. Moreover, scheduled campus interviews can make your search easier.

2. College Placement Books

There are a wide variety of books published that list companies that hire entry-level people directly from school. Your placement office or library should have several of these publications.

Many graduates obtain numerous job offers by simply mailing resumes to a wide variety of organizations listed in the handbook.

3. Newspaper Ads

Most frequently, newspaper ads focus on positions for experienced personnel. Sometimes, however, ads will be placed for entry-level people as well.

4. Placement Agencies

There are both benefits and disadvantages associated with registering with placement agencies. Successful placement usually depends on the quality of the agency. Reputation is one way of determining the quality of an agency. Thus, ask others who have used the agency about their experiences or ask the agency for the names of some of their clients whom you can contact.

In almost all instances, the company pays the agency's fee so there is usually no financial obligation on the part of the applicant. The agency should be able to:

1. Pinpoint your strengths and weaknesses.
2. Make recommendations for improving your image.
3. Set up interviews in which the potential employer is looking for someone with your qualifications.
4. Provide you with background information on the potential employer.

B. The Resume

The resume is the document that formally describes your credentials to a company. There is no standard way to prepare a resume, but guidelines do exist. The resume should be typed and segmented into specific sections such as the following.

1. Identifying Information

Centered at the top of the resume should be your name, address, and telephone number.

2. Career Objectives

Indicate the type of position you are currently seeking. You may also include your long-range career objectives as well.

3. Personal Background

Include items that will describe you to a potential employer. The following are typically included but can be omitted if you desire.

Birth date.

Citizenship.

Marital status.

Number of children (and ages).

Health.

4. Educational Background

Include post-high school education, degrees, graduation dates, major, grade point average, awards, honors, and relevant extra-curricular activities. In addition, it is advisable to include a list of computer courses you have taken, programming languages you have learned, and computers with which you have had experience.

5. Relevant Work Experience

Work experience should be listed chronologically, beginning with your most current position. Indicate dates, job titles, and responsibilities. Emphasize "hands-on" experiences, where appropriate. Include major projects you may have completed as a student.

6. Other Work Experience

Include, chronologically, non-computer-related jobs you have held, indicating dates, job titles, and responsibilities.

7. Certification and Membership

If you hold a **Certificate of Data Processing (CDP)** or you are a **Certified Computer Professional (CCP)**, this should be clearly indicated. Membership in professional organizations should also be included since this demonstrates a commitment to computing. We will discuss issues relevant to certification and membership later in this chapter.

8. References

It is useful to include a list of people who can attest to your expertise in the computing field. These may include professors, employers, and supervisors.

Keep in mind that before potential employers make an offer, they typically check references. This means either requesting letters of recommendation or actually telephoning one or more references and asking pertinent questions. Thus, you should ask permission before including an individual as a reference.

Figure 18.5
Sample cover letter for a resume.

```
                                              Home
                                              Address
                                              Date

Address of
organization

To Whom It May Concern:

    Enclosed you will find a copy of my resume which I am submitting in response to
your advertisement which appeared in _____ on _____. Please
note that I am applying for the position of _____.
    I can be reached at the above address or by phone at _____ during
business hours and _____ in the evening.
    References and other material will be supplied to you on request.
    I look forward to hearing from you.

                                              Sincerely yours,
```

Nancy Stern
4 Main Street
Anywhere, USA 48732

PERSONAL	Social Security No.	Birthdate	Married Yes No	Citizen Yes No	Number of Dependents	Maximum Percent Travel Desired	Health
	355-24-2121	12/29/51	X	X	3 (ages 4, 8, 10)	10	Excellent

POSITION DESIRED
   Systems Analyst

TECHNICAL BACKGROUND
   Programmer analyst for 3 years with large banking firm

PROGRAMMING LANGUAGES
   COBOL on IBM 4341

REFERENCES

	Name	Company	Position	Telephone
1.	John Marley	University of Louisville	Professor	(502) 893-3304
2.	Don Wood	Touche Ross, Inc.	Partner	(312) 589-6200
3.	John Sterling	U.S. Senator	Ohio	(513) 812-5069

EDUCATION

	Educational Institution	Field of Study	Degree	No. of Years	Year Degree Received	Average Grades
1.	University of Illinois	Computer Science	BS	4	1982	3.4
2.	Northwestern University	Finance	MBA	2	1984	3.2

CLUBS
   Computer Club, Yearbook Committee

LICENSES,
CERTIFICATION,
MEMBERSHIPS   1. CPA Illinois   2. Phi Beta Kappa   3. Member, ACM

OTHER INTERESTS
         1. Republican Party State Chairman   2. Chamber of Commerce   3. Oriental languages
         4. Karate tournament

LOCATION PREFERENCE   Northeast

Figure 18.4
Sample resume.

As a general rule, do not include any information pertaining to salary requirements. This is best left to the interview.

Since there is no universally accepted standard format for resumes, you may choose to make some alterations to the above to highlight significant facts about yourself. See Figure 18.4 for a sample resume.

If you are mailing your resume to potential employers, include a cover letter indicating that your resume is enclosed, and stating the position for which you are applying. Your cover letter may also include the best time to reach you by telephone. See Figure 18.5 (at left) for a sample cover letter.

C. The Interview

If a company believes there is a possible match between your qualifications and its needs, you will be contacted for an interview.

The interview is of great significance in:

1. Determining whether an applicant will fit in well in the organization.
2. Determining whether the position available is of serious interest to the applicant.

Thus, an interview has a dual role. It is not simply a technique that potential employers use to make their decision. It is also a technique *you* should use for determining if the available job is one that you are apt to find challenging and interesting.

1. Preparing for the Interview

Learn as much as you can about the company, its products, its financial position, potential for growth, etc. before the interview. The information can be learned from a variety of sources such as the company's annual report. See Figure 18.6 for a list of recommended resources to use before the interview.

---

1. Annual reports from companies to which you are considering applying. These provide a great deal of information on the current status of the company, its philosophy, and objectives.
2. *Peterson's Guide to Engineering, Science, and Computer Jobs*
   A comprehensive reference on current openings in over 1200 companies. Lists employers according to size, type of organization, and training programs. The Guide may be obtained from Box 2123, Princeton, NJ. As of this writing it is priced at $12.00.
3. The June issue of each year's *Datamation*
   Each June, *Datamation* publishes a salary survey for numerous EDP professions.
4. *Source EDP*
   This organization publishes an Annual Salary Survey for EDP professionals.
5. J. Daniel Couger and Robert A. Zawacki, *Motivating and Managing Computer Personnel* (New York: Wiley), 1980.
   This book provides a comprehensive view of the difficulties faced by computer professionals as well as the problems associated with managing computing professionals.
6. Jack French, *Up the EDP Pyramid* (New York: Wiley), 1981.
   This book explores the various career options available to computer professionals.

Figure 18.6
Preparing for the interview.

Dress appropriately. When in doubt, a conservative suit is appropriate. Makeup should be minimal. Being punctual for the interview is, of course, essential.

2. Communicating with the Interviewer

Answer all questions honestly and succinctly. Be prepared for the following types of questions.

1. "What are your career objectives and goals?"
Be specific. Include both your immediate and long-range career objectives and goals.

2. If you are currently employed, "Why are you changing jobs?"
Indicate the reasons, relevant to your career objectives. To indicate that money is the primary reason for changing jobs would probably not make an appropriate impression. Do not dwell on personality conflicts that may exist at your present job.

3. "Tell me about yourself."
Don't be tempted to ramble. Focus on your "career" self.

4. "What do you know about the company?"
The more you know, the more impressed the interviewer will be.

5. "Do you have any other offers?"
Indicate that you are looking, but it is probably wise to be vague about your options.

6. "Would you be willing to relocate?"
Answer this question honestly. Otherwise you might be wasting your time as well as the interviewer's time.

In general, remember that the primary purpose of the interview, from the company's perspective, is to determine the personal attributes of the applicant. The following are typical attributes sought by interviewers:

Intelligence.

Innovation.

Honesty.

Respect for others.

Enthusiasm.

Potential for remaining with the company.

The checklist in Figure 18.7 provides additional guidelines that should prove helpful in preparing for the interview.

3. Using the Interview to Help You Decide About the Job

The interviewer may be a company executive, computer manager or supervisor, or personnel officer. If the interviewer is a personnel officer, he or she will generally not be able to assess your professional skills; on the other hand, he or she has expertise to determine whether your personal attributes fit the "company image." If the interviewer is a computer manager, he or she will generally be more interested in your professional expertise. If the interviewer is a company executive, he or she will probably be able to assess both your personal attributes and your computer qualifications.

It is perfectly acceptable, indeed encouraged, that you ask the following questions:

a. Information About the Company   Even if you learned something about the company before the interview, ask for an "insider's view."

b. Specific Job Responsibilities   Do not assume that a title "says it all." Frequently, for example, the title "systems analyst" is used when the job descrip-

---

Checklist for Interviews

1. Be on time for the interview—it reflects favorably on you.
2. Shake hands firmly.
3. Speak clearly and crisply. Don't use slang. Avoid "yup/nope," "you know." Don't ramble; make your point concisely.
4. Bring your resume and point to various items on it where appropriate.
5. Listen most of the time. Try not to interrupt or cut off the interviewer.
6. Maintain eye contact. This suggests that you have confidence in yourself.
7. Ask about whether you will need to travel and the approximate percentage of travel required.
8. Ask about the company's policy on overtime—will you need to work weekends, second and third shifts, and so on.
9. Be serious, be cheerful, smile. No wisecracks, no lies.
10. Avoid complaints about your current boss, company, salary, and so forth.
11. Don't smoke, chew, eat, or drink during the interview.
12. Avoid exaggerations or bragging.
13. Ask for the job if you want it: "I hope you consider me."
14. Remain calm, don't fidget.
15. Know yourself—objectives, goals, career strengths.
16. Know your weaknesses and have answers ready for questions such as:
    Why are you leaving your current position?
    Why were you fired?
    Why did you change jobs?
    Why did you have a low grade point average?
17. Ask questions, for example, on the following subjects:
    Company product
    Company financial data
    Company stock and ownership
    Company growth and record
    Company plants and size
    Company competition
    Company customers
    The DP plans and budget

Source: Jack French, *Up the EDP Pyramid* (New York: Wiley), 1981, pages 101–102.

Figure 18.7
Checklist for interviews.

---

tion really involves programming. Be sure you understand exactly what functions you will be performing and what your specific responsibilities will be. Determine what sort of training you will receive, how closely you will be supervised, and what decision-making responsibilities you might have.

c. Potential for Promotion   What is the typical period an employee in this job position waits for promotion?

d. Fringe Benefits   In addition to the standard medical, pension, and life insurance benefits, determine whether the company will pay your tuition for an advanced degree, whether you can take information processing seminars, whether you will receive bonuses, and so on.

e. Salary   There is no *specific* rule about salary negotiations. Note, however, that most companies have a standard salary for entry-level positions. Hence, when applying for your first job, it is probably best to wait until the interviewer discusses money. For higher-level positions, it is probably best to indicate your salary requirements during an interview, since this might be a negotiable item.

Note that although you may regard salary as a critical factor, it should be viewed as only one aspect, albeit a major one, of an overall package. To accept a position solely on the basis of the "highest offer" may be a mistake. Job satisfaction and promotion potential are viewed by many professionals as more important than salary.

D. The Employment Outlook

The need for computer professionals has always been great, with the demand typically exceeding the supply in almost all areas of the United States and on virtually all levels. The expectation is that this trend will continue through the 1990s. Indeed, there is evidence to suggest that the need for computer professionals will grow at an even faster rate than it has in the past.

The Federal Bureau of Labor Statistics estimates that the number of computer professionals employed in 1990 will be 50% greater than in 1980. During the same period, overall employment growth is expected to increase only 20%. As a result, many people believe that the computer field is virtually recession proof.

The reasons for this increased need for computer professionals are as follows.

1. The use of computers has been expanding greatly in many organizations.
2. More and more small businesses purchase computers but do not have the expertise to use them—they need to hire or contract with computer professionals.
3. The need for computer professionals has, in the past, been limited almost entirely to computer departments. With increasing frequency, user departments are hiring computer professionals to computerize decentralized operations and to serve as liaison with a centralized computer department.

Even currently, the need for qualified professionals is so great that companies offer new employees not only high salaries but certain "perks" such as (1) bonuses, frequently paid at the time of hire, (2) microcomputers for personal use, (3) flexible hours and the use of terminals for communicating with the office from home, (4) a greater-than-usual allowance for vacation time. With such "perks," any qualified computer professional can expect to find job prospects booming both currently and in the years ahead.

In addition, some companies offer "bounties" to third parties who are instrumental in finding a qualified professional who satisfies the company's needs.

LOOKING AHEAD

1. Job satisfaction will become increasingly important to computer professionals as a major criterion for accepting a position.
2. Managers and executives will need to take a more active role in determining how they can best retain computer professionals.
3. Computer professionals will begin their training at an earlier age and will thus enter the job market with substantial expertise.
4. Programmers will be the employees most in demand in the next few years.
5. Six out of 10 new jobs in the United States will be computer related.
6. Demand for programmers will increase at an average annual rate of 18.7%.

III. CCP AND CDP: CERTIFYING COMPUTER PROFESSIONALS

A. The Issues

It is an extremely difficult task to assess the skill and proficiency of any professional. In some fields such as medicine, law, and education (at certain levels), a license is required in order to be a practicing professional. The license is granted by a government agency and requires an applicant to possess specific educational credentials and to pass an examination. In such fields, one cannot practice without the license.

In other fields, such as accounting and engineering, there are certificates that a professional may have, but the certification is not absolutely required to practice in the field. It is simply a credential that attests to the individual's competency, but there are many professionals who practice without it. Usually, individuals can earn the certification if they pass an examination. In accounting, the CPA, or certified public accountant, has passed a series of tests that demonstrate his or her proficiency. Similarly, in engineering, the PE, or professional engineer, is an individual who has passed a rigorous engineering examination in his or her specialization. One may be a practicing accountant or engineer without this certification, but having it is a credential that demonstrates a high degree of skill in one's field.

There has been a great deal of controversy in recent years as to whether computer professionals should be *licensed*, that is, required to pass specific exams to practice, or whether they should be *certified*, that is, given the opportunity to pass exams as a way of achieving an added credential. Most computer professionals believe that certification is more appropriate than licensing.

There are currently two organizations that certify computer professionals: the Data Processing Management Association (DPMA) and the Institute for Certification of Computer Professionals (ICCP).

B. The Certificate in Data Processing (CDP)

Beginning in 1962, the DPMA (Data Processing Management Association) made available a Certificate in Data Processing (CDP) to individuals with college training and experience in the field, who could pass a rigorous exam. This certification program was taken over in 1973 by the Institute for Certification of Computer Professionals.

C. The Certified Computer Professional (CCP)

Since 1973, the Institute for Certification of Computer Professionals (ICCP), sponsored by eight computer organizations, has established a certification program with the following objective:

> ICCP is a non-profit organization established for the purpose of testing and certifying knowledge and skills of computing personnel. It is a coordinated, cooperative, industry-wide effort.
>
> A primary objective is the pooling of resources of constituent societies so that the full attention of the information processing industry will be focused on the vital tasks of development and recognition of qualified personnel.
>
> The Institute will foster, promote and encourage development and improvement of standards of performance and good practice. It will become an authoritative source of information for employers, educators, practitioners and public officials.[1]

Unlike the CDP, CCP eligibility requirements are as follows:

> Although any interested individual may take this examination, it is intended for senior-level programmers. No specific educational or experience requirements must be met in order to take the examination, but a candidate who does not have broad experience will find the examination extremely difficult to complete successfully.[2]

Collectively, both the CDP and CCP certifications are held by fewer than 10% of the active computer professionals. The number is small because of the following reasons.

1. The computing field is relatively new, as compared to other professional fields.
2. There is still considerable controversy over what specific technical expertise and training are required of a computer professional.
3. Many managers or users who are responsible for hiring computer professionals are not aware of these certifications, and do not believe them to be important.

Many computer societies, however, have actively promoted these examinations for their members and there is some evidence that these certifications will become increasingly important in the years ahead.

---

[1]Brochure, *Institute for Certification of Computer Professionals.*

[2]Ibid.

IV. ETHICS IN COMPUTING

All professions have a code of ethics which broadly indicates the conduct expected of a professional. Ethical conduct goes beyond adhering to laws and requires the professional to follow standards that may not be covered by specific legislation.

We have already seen that there are numerous illegal uses of computers which must be controlled if businesses are to continue to prosper with increased computerization. But many unethical activities not specifically addressed by current laws must also be controlled. These include the following:

1. To what degree should a computer professional be responsible for his or her design or program?
   a. If, for example, the system or program results in invasion of privacy and an analyst or programmer was aware of this potential, is he or she personally responsible?
   b. If, for example, a system produces erroneous results, is the computer professional ethically responsible?
   c. Is it reasonable to expect software packages to be totally free of errors?

2. Do computer professionals have the right to utilize their organization's computer equipment whenever they desire?
   a. Should computer professionals be permitted to use computers for game playing, printing "Snoopy calendars," and so on?
   b. Should computer professionals be permitted to use computers to place them in an advantageous position (e.g., in gambling casinos)?
   c. If a time-sharing facility is available, does a programmer have the right to use it for non-job-related activities?
   d. Should a programmer copy a software package for his or her own personal use without appropriate permission?

3. Should computer professionals take some social responsibility for the ways in which their products are utilized?
   a. If, for example, a computer system is to be used to replace a labor force, is this, at least in part, the computer professional's responsibility?
   b. Is it the computer professional's responsibility to ensure the integrity of a system and to protect it from invasion of privacy, even if these are not part of the system's objectives?

There are, of course, no simple answers to any of these questions. Moreover, many very ethical people have argued against the need for computer professionals to be totally responsible for their work. They claim that the way a system is used may not be under the computer professional's control. Just as Alfred Nobel cannot be held accountable for the immoral use of his invention of dynamite, computer professionals should not be held accountable for programs that are used illegally or unethically.

As the debate over these ethical issues goes on, there are many leaders in the field who believe that a code of ethics is of primary importance. As computers become prevalent and as their unethical use increases, more and more citizens will call on their government to pass laws that will clearly specify the legal responsibility of computer specialists. Leaders in the computer field insist that it would be far better for professionals to police themselves, before the government finds it necessary to pass laws.

It is difficult, however, to control unethical practices. Certifying agencies require candidates to agree to adhere to their Codes of Ethics, Conduct, and Good Practice. See Figure 18.8 for a selected section of codes enumerated by the Institute for Certification of Computer Professionals. It must be recognized, however, that merely because a computer professional has been certified does not guarantee that he or she will adhere to the ethical standards established.

Figure 18.8
Selected Codes of Ethics, Conduct, and Good Practice of the ICCP.

2.2: **Social Responsibility:** One is expected to combat ignorance about information processing technology in those public areas where one's application can be expected to have an adverse social impact.

2.5: **Integrity:** One will not knowingly lay claims to competence one does not demonstrably possess.

2.8: **Protection of Privacy:** One shall have special regard for the potential effects of computer-based systems on the right of privacy of individuals whether this is within one's own organization, among customers or suppliers, or in relation to the general public.

Because of the privileged capability of computer professionals to gain access to computerized files, especially strong strictures will be applied to those who have used their positions of trust to obtain information from computerized files for their personal gain.

Where it is possible that decisions can be made within a computer-based system which could adversely affect the personal security, work, or career of an individual, the system design shall specifically provide for decision review by a responsible executive who will thus remain accountable and identifiable for that decision.

3.1: **Education:** One has a special responsibility to keep oneself fully aware of developments in information processing technology relevant to one's current professional occupation. One will contribute to the interchange of technical and professional information by encouraging and participating in education activities directed both to fellow professionals and to the public at large. One will do all in one's power to further public understanding of computer systems. One will contribute to the growth of knowledge in the field to the extent that one's expertise, time, and position allow.

3.5: **Discretion:** One shall exercise maximum discretion in disclosing, or permitting to be disclosed, or using to one's own advantage, any information relating to the affairs of one's present or previous employers or clients.

V. MAJOR COMPUTER SOCIETIES

There are numerous societies to which many professionals belong. These societies provide members with journals and general information about the field. They also sponsor key activities in the computing field. We will briefly consider three of the most common, all of which offer student memberships:

1. **Association for Computing Machinery (ACM)**
   11 West 42 St.
   New York, NY 10036

Founded in 1947, the ACM is the oldest and largest computing society. It has over 50,000 members, publishes seven major periodicals, and has over 30 special interest groups in a wide variety of computing subjects. See Figure 18.9 for an ACM application for membership that can be xeroxed and filled out by students.

ACM STUDENT MEMBERSHIP APPLICATION

Association for Computing Machinery, P.O. Box 12114, Church Street Station, New York, N.Y. 10249, (212) 869-7440. Telex: 421686

STUDENTS: Join the Association for Computing Machinery (ACM) for only $15 and receive the following benefits:

- Free subscription to *Communications of the ACM*, ACM's monthly flagship journal which publishes highly readable articles, special reports and debates.
- $5 dues credit that may be applied toward a subscription to either *Computing Surveys, Computing Reviews* or the *Journal of the ACM*.
- Free copy of the ACM *Graduate Assistantship Directory*.
- Special student member rates when joining any of ACM's Special Interest Groups or attending any ACM conferences, symposia and workshops.
- Student Members receive a special membership dues rate when converting to Voting Membership at the first renewal period after graduation.
- Student Members can take advantage of the Employment Register sponsored by ACM's annual Computer Science Conference, as well as the ACM's Student Chapter-sponsored summer Employment Register.

Purposes of ACM

1. To advance the sciences and arts of information processing including, but not restricted to, the study, design, development, construction, and application of modern technology, computing techniques and appropriate languages for general information processing, storage, retrieval, transmission/communication, and processing of data of all kinds, and for the automatic control and simulation of processes. **2.** To promote the free interchange of information about the sciences and arts of information processing both among specialists and the public in the best scientific and professional tradition. **3.** To develop and maintain the integrity and competence of individuals engaged in the practice of information processing.

I hereby affirm that I subscribe to the purposes of ACM (as indicated above) and understand that my membership is not transferable. I enclose a check, bank draft or money order in the full amount.

Signature _____

Please print: **date**

Name _____

Address _____

City/State/Zip _____

Dues: Circle appropriate amount.

Student members 15.00

    Student member with $5 dues credit. Students who subscribe to *Journal of the ACM, Computing Surveys,* or *Computing Reviews* are entitled to a $5 dues credit. If you wish to subscribe to any one of the above, circle the $10 dues and the appropriate subscription rate for the journal selected in the "Publications" section 10.00

Student Member: You must be registered in an accredited educational institution on a full-time basis—A Faculty Member must certify your full-time status.

Institution _____

Faculty Member's Signature _____

                                                         date

Publications: Circle appropriate rate(s)

Computing Surveys (quarterly) 103	$10.00
Journal of the ACM (quarterly) 102	12.00
Computing Reviews (monthly) 104	19.00
Collected Algorithms, Initial Vols. I, II, III & 1 yr's quarterly updating supplements 105	75.00

Transactions on: (all quarterlies)

Mathematical Software/TOMS 108	18.00
Database Systems/TODS 109	18.00
Programming Languages and Systems/TOPLAS 110	18.00
Graphics/TOG 112	24.00
Office Information Systems/TOOIS 113	20.00
Computer Systems/TOCS 114	20.00

Overseas Members: If you'd like to join ACM please write ACM Headquarters for an Overseas Membership Application.

For Office Use: ▢▢▢▢▢▢ **J**

Special Interest Group Membership:

Circle appropriate rate(s), SIG Membership includes a Newsletter subscription.

Code	Acronym	Student
001	**SIGACT** (Automata and Computability Theory)	$ 5.00
032	**SIGAPL** (APL)	5.00
002	**SIGARCH** (Computer Architecture)	10.00
003	**SIGART** (Artificial Intelligence)	6.00
004	**SIGBDP** (Business Data Processing and Management)	5.00
005	**SIGBIO** (Biomedical Computing)	5.00
006	**SIGCAPH** (Computer and the Physically Handicapped, Print)	5.00
029	**SIGCAPH** (Cassette Edition)	5.00
030	**SIGCAPH** (Both Print and Cassette Editions)	9.00
007	**SIGCAS** (Computers and Society)	4.00
026	**SIGCHI** (Computer and Human Interaction, formerly SIGSOC)	10.00
008	**SIGCOMM** (Data Communication)	10.00
010	**SIGCPR** (Computer Personnel Research)	4.00
011	**SIGCSE** (Computer Science Education)	5.00
012	**SIGCUE** (Computer Uses in Education)	7.00
013	**SIGDA** (Design Automation)	3.00
033	**SIGDOC** (Documentation)	2.00
015	**SIGGRAPH** (Computer Graphics)	10.00
016	**SIGIR** (Information Retrieval)	3.00
018	**SIGMAP** (Mathematical Programming)	7.50
019	**SIGMETRICS** (Measurement & Evaluation)	5.00
020	**SIGMICRO** (Microprogramming)	6.00
014	**SIGMOD** (Management of Data)	3.00
021	**SIGNUM** (Numerical Mathematics)	5.50
027	**SIGOA** (Office Automation)	3.00
022	**SIGOPS** (Operating Systems)	4.00
035	**SIGPC** (Personal Computing)	5.00
023	**SIGPLAN** (Programming Languages)	11.00
037	**SIGPLAN**-AdaTEC (SIGPLAN Tech. Comm. on Ada)	10.00
038	**SIGPLAN**-FORTREC (SIGPLAN Tech. Comm. on Fortran)	3.00
036	**SIGSAC** (Security, Audit and Control)	4.00
024	**SIGSAM** (Symbolic & Algebraic Manipulation)	3.00
025	**SIGSIM** (Simulation)	2.00
031	**SIGSMALL** (Small Computing Systems and Applications)	4.00
034	**SIGSOFT** (Software Engineering)	4.00
018	**SIGUCCS** (University and College Computing Services)	5.00

Payment Information:

Payment must accompany application. Please make checks payable to ACM Inc., and mail this application to: ACM, P.O. Box 12114, Church Street Station, New York, NY 10249.
Prices effective 4/84.
Prices subject to change.   **Total Amount: $**_____

Figure 18.9
ACM membership application form. (Courtesy ACM.)

2. **Data Processing Management Association (DPMA)**
505 Busse Highway
Park Ridge, IL 60068

With over 24,000 members in the United States, Canada, and abroad, the **Data Processing Management Association (DPMA)** is the largest computer management professional association. The purpose of the DPMA is to engage in education and research activities designed for self-improvement of its members.

3. **The Computer Society of the Institute of Electrical and Electronics Engineers (IEEE)**
P.O. Box 639
Silver Springs, MD 20901

The **Institute of Electrical and Electronics Engineers (IEEE)** has many societies, in addition to the Computer Society. The aim of the Computer Society is to advance the theory and practice of computer and information processing technology.

Both students and active professionals find computer societies an excellent vehicle for learning about advances in the field and for communicating with other professionals.

CHAPTER SUMMARY

I. Job opportunities
   A. Entry positions in the programming field.
      1. Types.
         a. Application—programming in business application areas.
         b. Maintenance—modifying existing programs.
         c. Scientific—programming in scientific or technical areas.
         d. Systems—writing operating systems.
      2. Typical requirements.
         a. College degree—junior or four-year college.
         b. Some programming experience is helpful.
      3. Interviewers look for job applicants with a logical mind, good communication skills, enthusiasm, and so on.
   B. Job opportunities for those with experience.
      1. More technical programming positions in software engineering, computer graphics applications, and so on.
      2. Programming management.
      3. Systems analyst.
      4. Other positions.
         a. Operations manager.
         b. Data base administrator.
         c. EDP auditor.
      5. The top position is director of MIS.

II. Certifying computer professionals and ethical issues
   A. CDP—Certificate in Data Processing.
   B. CCP—Certified Computer Professional.
   C. Ethics.
      1. One reason why certification is important is that there are codes of ethics established by certifying agencies.
      2. There is a great need for standards and codes of ethics in the computing field mainly because the opportunity exists for professionals to gain unauthorized access to computers.

Chapter Self-Evaluating Quiz

1. A _____ programmer is responsible for modifying existing programs to make them more current or efficient.

2. A _____ programmer is responsible for writing and modifying operating systems.

3. (T or F) Most companies seek programmers who have a logical mind but since programmers are creative people they need not possess good inter-personal skills.

4. (T or F) Some companies ask job applicants to take a test in order to evaluate their skills.

5. The two main promotion opportunities for programmers are _____ and _____.

6. A programmer interested in a promotion into management may seek a job as a _____.

7. The title of the person who has overall responsibility for the operation of the computer center and the activities of the entire computer staff is _____.

8. The four major sources of job opportunities for people interested in jobs in the computing field are _____, _____, _____, and _____.

9. (T or F) In general, a resume should include the salary requirements of the job applicant.

10. (T or F) A job applicant should answer an interviewer's questions honestly, even if the answer may jeopardize his or her chances for getting the job.

11. If an individual is required to pass an exam to practice in a discipline, we call this _____.

12. If an individual has the option of taking a special test in order to obtain an added credential, the credential is usually called _____.

13. The two certificates in the computer field are called _____ and _____.

14. (T or F) Certifying agencies usually have a code of ethics they ask members to follow.

15. Two major computer societies are _____ and _____.

Solutions

1. maintenance / page 687
2. systems / page 687
3. F / page 688
4. T / page 688
5. management opportunities
   / page 690
   technical opportunities—
   compiler design, software
   engineering, and so on.
   / page 690
6. programming manager
   / page 690
   systems analyst / page 690
   operations manager / page 690
7. director of information systems
   (or a similar title) / page 691
8. placement office in school
   / page 694
   college placement publications
   / page 694
   newspaper ads / page 695
   placement agencies / page 695
9. F / page 697
10. T / page 698
11. licensing / page 702
12. certification / page 702
13. CDP—Certificate in Data
    Processing / page 703
    CCP—Certified Computer
    Professional / page 703
14. T / page 705
15. ACM (Association for
    Computing Machinery)
    / page 705
    DPMA (Data Processing
    Management Association)
    / page 707
    The Computer Society of the
    IEEE (Institute of Electrical and
    Electronics Engineers)
    / page 707

Key Terms

ACM (Association for Computing
   Machinery)
Application programmer
CCP (Certified Computer Professional)
CDP (Certificate in Data Processing)
Data base administrator
Director of information systems
DPMA (Data Processing Management
   Association)
EDP auditor

IEEE (Institute of Electrical and
   Electronics Engineers)
Maintenance programmer
Operations manager
Programmer analyst
Programming manager
Scientific programmer
Systems analyst
Systems manager
Systems programmer

Review Questions

I. True-False Questions

1. (T or F) Most college graduates who have majored in computing obtain entry-level positions as programmers.
2. (T or F) An application programmer is one who develops programs for improving the overall quality of the operating system.

3. (T or F) An application programmer who is interested in a career in management should focus on becoming a systems programmer first.

4. (T or F) Having a college degree will generally not improve your chances of obtaining a good job as an entry-level programmer.

5. (T or F) An individual with programming experience is apt to be considered more qualified for a job in the computing field than one who has not had any experience.

6. (T or F) In general, the need for good communication skills is not applicable in the computing field; one is only required to have good technical skills.

7. (T or F) A high score on a programmer aptitude test is generally the most important criterion that an organization uses in determining whether or not to hire an individual.

8. (T or F) Programmers who are interested in seeking a new job should determine first whether they wish to pursue a technical career path or a management career path.

9. (T or F) In some companies systems analysts supervise programmers; in other companies systems analysts are in an area or department separate from programming and do not have direct managerial responsibilities.

10. (T or F) An M.B.A. is a useful degree to have if one wishes to pursue a career path in management.

11. (T or F) An EDP auditor is the individual responsible for organizing and designing a company's data base.

12. (T or F) Most data entry operators and computer operators have college degrees.

13. (T or F) In general, your resume should indicate the salary you are seeking.

14. (T or F) A job applicant should prepare for an interview by learning something about the company beforehand.

15. (T or F) Most forecasts indicate that the job market for computer professionals will dry up considerably within the next few years.

II. General Questions

1. Indicate the major distinctions among the following:
   a. Application programmer.
   b. Maintenance programmer.
   c. Scientific programmer.
   d. Systems programmer.

2. If you were a personnel director, what personal attributes would you look for when hiring an entry-level programmer? Explain your answer.

3. If you were a VP in a large organization, would you ask your director of MIS to hire entry-level programmers or would you ask your personnel director to do the hiring? Defend your position.

4. If you were a personnel director, would you use a programmer aptitude test?

5. Prepare a resume that you might use if you were applying for an entry-level position as a programmer.

6. Suppose you have been a COBOL programmer for three years. Indicate what steps you would take if you were seeking a position as a systems analyst. What questions would you ask an interviewer in order to determine if a job opening would appeal to you?

7. If you were a personnel director responsible for hiring a DP manager, would you give preference to candidates with a certificate in data processing? Explain your answer.

8. Indicate in your own words the differences between licensing and certifying professionals in any field.

9. Do you think a systems analyst should be held accountable if a system he or she designed is easily accessed by unauthorized users?

10. Indicate some reasons why it is important for computer professionals to belong to professional societies.

APPLICATION

INTERVIEW FORMAT GAUGES PERSONAL CHARACTERISTICS[1]

NEW YORK—The aptitude test given to prospective programmer trainees at Chemical Bank here evaluates technical programming skills, "but there were some other things we needed to know about people," recalled Eleanor F. Miley, assistant vice-president for technical training. So, together with a group of managers in the bank's Systems Development Department and the bank's Personnel Research Department, Miley developed the format for a structured interview.

The group came up with 35 characteristics or skills and classified these in seven dimensions, which appear on the evaluation sheet used by the interviewers. These are communication, self-motivation, flexibility regarding work hours, working under pressure, teamwork, perseverance and adaptability.

Because they needed a consistent way of measuring each individual candidate against these dimensions, they developed descriptions under each category called "anchors." These descriptions are based on a scale of one to five. For example, if the person being interviewed displays difficulty in communicating clearly, the interviewer gives him a "1" under communication.

The 45-minute interviews are conducted by three people who represent the technical training and systems development groups. They must reach a consensus on each applicant, so they score each applicant individually and then work together on a joint evaluation.

"Without this particular structure, it would have been chaos," Miley said.

[1] *Computerworld*, February 7, 1983, page 8. Copyright © 1983 by CW Communications/Inc., Framingham, MA 01701. Reprinted with permission.

Questions
1. Understanding Key Terms
   Define the following terms as used in the application:
   a. Aptitude test.
   b. Communication.
   c. Systems development group.
2. Software, Hardware, and Systems Concepts
   If you were interviewing an applicant for a programming position, indicate which of the following you would regard as essential. Explain your answer.
   a. Experience with the specific computer system you have.
   b. Knowledge of the specific programming language(s) you use.
   c. Experience in the same type of business as yours.
3. Management Considerations
   Suppose you interview an applicant for a programming position. He has excellent technical skills but is not a good communicator. Under what conditions would you consider hiring him? Under what conditions would you immediately eliminate him from consideration?
4. Social, Legal, and Ethical Implications
   What questions would you ask an applicant to determine whether he or she would act ethically and responsibly when dealing with sensitive data?

CASE STUDY: McKing's Superburgers, Inc.

Chapter Questions

1. What criteria would you use for hiring programmers for McKing's?

2. What specific personal attributes should the programmers have?

3. What experience would you look for when hiring systems analysts for McKing's?

4. What experience should the director of information systems have?

5. Would you recommend that previous business experience be a job requirement for the professional computing staff? Explain your answer.

THE COMPUTER AD: A Focus on Marketing

Consider the ad entitled "LocalNet Networks Make Industry Managers Downwardly Mobile" that appears in Figure 18.10.

Questions
1. Explain the meaning of the ad's title.
2. Do you think managers should think *first* about acquiring computers as professional workstations for (a) themselves or (b) their employees? Explain your answer.
3. Suppose you were a manager who was interviewing candidates for a position as technical liaison with the computer group. Would you consider an individual who has a personal computer to be more appropriate for the job than one who does not? Explain your answer. Remember that there is no definitive "right or wrong" answer to this question. The persuasiveness of your arguments—pro or con—is the critical component here.
4. Explain the meaning of the phrase: "a single LocalNet cable distributes the power of four computers from busy R & D labs to executive corner offices."

Figure 18.10
Marketing computer products. (Courtesy Sytek, Inc.)

CHAPTER 19

COMPUTERS
IN OUR FUTURE

CHAPTER OBJECTIVES

To familiarize you with:

- The potential effects of increased computerization, in the years ahead.
- The technological advances most likely to have the greatest impact in the future.
- The social issues that continue to be raised by increased computerization.

I. PREDICTIONS ABOUT THE FUTURE ARE OPINIONS, NOT DEFINITIVE STATEMENTS

This chapter is designed to highlight developments that currently appear to have great potential for business, education, and society in general. Some of the areas that are highlighted here have already begun to have considerable impact; others are still too embryonic to have had any discernible effect.

Focusing on the future in this chapter also brings together some of the more significant innovative concepts that have been emphasized throughout the text in numerous chapters and with various perspectives. We will, for example, review critical issues such as those relating to micros, data communications, anticipated advances in specified technological areas, and so on.

But basically this chapter includes some predictions about the ways in which computers and information processing are likely to impact society in the years ahead. Predictions should always be viewed as considered opinions, not definitive statements of "truth." We have based our predictions on our own perceptions and experiences in the computing field and have made the assumption that "the past is the best predictor of future performance." It might be interesting for you to follow events and developments, as they occur, in the months and years ahead to determine how accurate we are in our predictions. You may find that we overstate the importance of some developments, understate the importance of others, or prove to be incorrect in some of our analyses. As future computer professionals and users, you should learn to view predictions about the future as opinions that you are free to evaluate yourselves and make judgments about.

II. MICROS IN OUR FUTURE

A. A General Overview

It is entirely appropriate that we begin our predictions about the future with a discussion of the profound effects we believe micros will continue to have on business, education, and society in general. Throughout this text, we have seen how micros are currently being used effectively as word processors, intelligent terminals, professional workstations, data communications units, personal computers in the home, and so on.

There is little doubt that the trend toward cheaper micros with increased computing capability will continue. Initially, micros were developed as 4-bit machines with limited storage and slow processing speeds. Currently, 8-bit and 16-bit micros dominate the market; moreover, both have considerable software available in numerous application areas. Evidence suggests that within the next few years the new 32-bit micros will have computing power roughly equivalent to many current minis and superminis and they will dominate the micro market. Thus, we believe that the current trend of making sophisticated computers accessible to larger and larger segments of the population will continue.

B. Micros in Business

Despite these trends in the micro market, considerable controversy surrounds their use. Within the business sector specifically, there is concern about rampant and indiscriminate acquisition of these computers by users. Many information processing directors and other computer professionals strongly believe that all computer acquisitions should be coordinated from one central department to ensure that whatever systems are acquired are compatible, cost-effective, and appropriately distributed where they are most needed.

This controversy over the need for a coordinated policy for acquiring micros is really part of a larger issue that has been considered throughout this text in numerous forms: the communication gap between users and computer professionals. Many users believe they are able to evaluate how well basic hardware will meet their specific needs without having to seek assistance from a professional computer staff; on the other hand, computer professionals tend to believe that users, in general, are inadequately prepared to make judgments concerning computers, even micros, and their applicability to business.

We believe that one aspect of this specific communication gap will slowly resolve itself in the years ahead. Users will undoubtedly become increasingly computer literate and no longer need to rely on experts for solving basic computational problems.

But the need for coordinating computer acquisitions, even on the micro level, is a more critical issue for companies in general. Organizations should develop a consistent policy regarding the purchase of any equipment, but most specifically computers. Such a policy would minimize:

1. Extraneous or unnecessary purchases by determining if several users could share systems.
2. The cost of computers, by encouraging bulk orders at discount prices.
3. The possible acquisition of the wrong type of equipment; a coordinator with specific expertise would be best able to recommend the most appropriate devices.
4. The acquisition of incompatible equipment that cannot interface with the mainframe.

It may well happen that a coordinated policy is administered by a separate information resources department and *not* by the information processing department. Many organizations now have a technical liaison staff that is responsible for bridging the communication gap between users and computer professionals; such a technical liaison group might be better able to coordinate acquisition of micros for user groups than an information processing department that sometimes tends to be viewed with hostility.

Thus, one controversial area regarding micros in business relates to the need for coordination of computer acquisitions within businesses. There is also controversy over whether micros will, in the future, simply augment mainframes in the years ahead as they are currently doing, or whether they will replace them entirely.

There is little doubt that by the year 1990, there will be more micros in businesses than mainframes. Figure 19.1 gives one analysis. This prediction should not be particularly surprising since a company is apt to have numerous

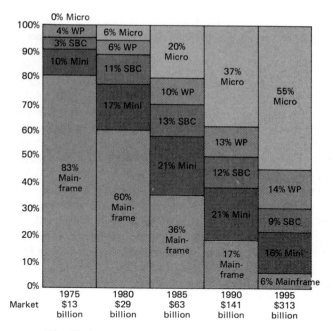

WP = Word processor
SBC = Small business computer

Figure 19.1
An analysis of the computer market.

micros with only one or two mainframes. In our opinion, however, it is unlikely that micros will be used to replace mainframes. The main focus of micros in business is to be user-friendly and flexible enough for small applications; that is, these computers are not designed to have the kind of power typically required of mainframes. Thus, in our opinion, the sum of computer power provided by many micros is not likely to equal the integrated, cost-effective, high-level computer power of a sophisticated mainframe. Moreover, there will always be a need for a centralized system to coordinate and integrate the flow of data at most medium-sized and large companies.

Thus, while the number of micros will undoubtedly continue to grow in the years ahead, we believe they will continue to supplement traditional mainframe power, not replace it. Moreover, interfaces between micros and mainframes will serve to greatly enhance the overall computer power in most organizations.

C. Micros in the Home and Classroom

The use of micros in the home and classroom is another controversial subject. Many knowledgeable people believe that consumer-oriented micros are likely to be a fad similar to the overrated and once highly touted CB radio. There are those who believe that many personal computer manufacturers will continue to lose money and there will be a significant shakeout in the marketplace. Thus, while there are currently more than 150 microcomputer manufacturers, a shakeout is likely to leave a handful of larger manufacturers in what may become a diminishing home market.

It is our opinion that micros in the home and classroom will continue to have great appeal and applicability, and will *not* be simply a fad. We believe that the number of homes with micros will increase from the current 5% to well over 50% by the year 2000. Figure 19.2 represents what we regard as realistic

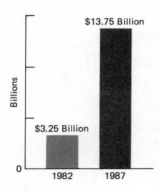

Figure 19.2
Expenditures for micro
hardware and software.

expectations for the growth of hardware and software in the next few years. As micros increase in power and decrease in cost they will become even more attractive for home and school use.

Consider the average home with the following products: (1) an electric typewriter at an average cost of $300, (2) an encyclopedia at an average cost of $600, (3) educational and entertaining games for both children and adults at an average cost of $600. In a relatively short time, we anticipate that for the same total $1500 cost, a computer will be able to provide word processing services on a letter-quality printer, an encyclopedia on a disk or access to an encyclopedia from a centralized data base, and access to hundreds of educational and entertaining games. When this computer becomes available for $1500, virtually no home will be without one—indeed the average student may not be able to exist without one. In addition, for the same cost, this home computer will be able to provide access to numerous external data bases for information, shopping, communications, and so on. Moreover, schools will offer course material on disk, require homework to be handed in on disks, and even provide tests on disks.

In addition, students will want to purchase computers to attain greater flexibility in their studies. Texts and other published material will be widely available on disk. Just as many students today purchase books rather than using library materials for greater flexibility, we will find that the ability to use disks at home or in dormitories as well as at school will mean that more and more students will own their own computers.

The microcomputer revolution, then, has in our opinion, only just begun.

III. COMPUTERS AND THE WORLD OF COMMUNICATIONS

A. AT&T Information Systems and Other Suppliers of Communication Facilities

As we have already indicated, the use of computers along with data communications devices has great potential for:

1. Electronic mail and message systems.
2. Teleconferencing.
3. Videotex and teletext.
4. Accessing data bases through subscriber services.
5. Networking and distributed data processing.

Major technological advances will be forthcoming not only from computer vendors but from suppliers of communication facilities. AT&T, recently divested of the Bell operating companies, will focus on supplying needed communication services to home, school, and business users. Similarly, other suppliers of data communications systems such as MCI, Rolm, ITT, GTE, and so on, will compete with AT&T Information Systems in providing inexpensive, flexible, and sophisticated data communications facilities.

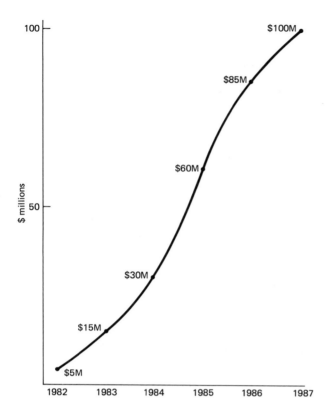

Figure 19.3
The market for local area networks. (*Source:* The Yankee Group.)

Local area networks will increase in popularity, making communications more effective among users in close proximity to each other. A recent study of local area networking in factories shows that the market will grow from $15 million in 1983 to over $100 million by 1987 (see Figure 19.3). We believe that local area networks as well as other more widespread networks will make micros and other computers even more useful for business, home, and educational use. Moreover, future, more sophisticated networks will enable many traditionally incompatible computers to communicate effectively with each other in ways that are currently not possible.

B. Teletext and Videotex

Teletext and videotex ventures such as *Time*'s teletext service and Knight-Ridder's Viewtron have great potential for providing customers with access to large information bases and for enabling users to bank and shop at home. TVs, as well as terminals or micros, will be used for displaying text and obtaining other useful information.

Despite the speed and convenience that these services provide, cost remains a serious drawback. Access to large data bases costs from $35 per hour to as much as $150 per hour. Even at $35 per hour, the cost is still relatively high for the average consumer, although businesses appear to be less concerned with the expense.

Videotex has the potential for spreading rapidly in a wide variety of application areas. Consider the following:

IN A NUTSHELL

VIDEOTEX: OFF AND RUNNING

Currently, Travelhost offers a videotex service to guests in several hotels throughout the country. Using a terminal connected to a TV set in your hotel room, you have immediate access to the following services:

Airline schedules

United Press International news

Stock exchange information

Electronic mail

Games

Local restaurants—reviews and menus

On-line shopping

Local job opportunities

The user pays for the service with the use of a credit card number that must be entered before the connection to the system is made. Current cost for the service is $20 per hour from 9 A.M. to 5 P.M. and $7 per hour at other times.

A second area of potential applicability for videotex is electronic publishing. Electronic publishing provides news services, magazine copy, and even books displayed on a screen for subscribers. Whether or not users will find displayed text a useful application area remains to be seen.

Moreover, there is considerable controversy over whether or not this service will be welcomed by the consumer. Studies to determine user interest tend to be inconclusive. Videotex and teletext are application areas that are seen as having potential, but the actual future impact is very difficult to predict.

IV. FIFTH GENERATION COMPUTERS: WILL THE UNITED STATES BE ABLE TO SUSTAIN ITS TECHNOLOGICAL LEAD IN THE COMPUTING FIELD?

There is considerable concern on the part of the computer industry and on the part of the U.S. government as to whether U.S. companies will be able to maintain their technological lead in computing. Many experts are particularly concerned about the Japanese ability to manufacture computer parts at very low cost. Of even more concern, is the Japanese focus on a new generation of computers that some believe will catapult them into a dominant position within the next decade.

Japan is focusing on developing its so-called "fifth generation computers" by 1990. If realized, these machines will have the following characteristics:

1. Integrated circuits with a minimum of 1 million transistors per semiconductor chip.

2. The ability to communicate with users in a natural language; spoken, written, and graphic languages will be accepted with the ability to translate among the three.

3. The ability to actually accumulate knowledge so that the system appears to "learn and infer"; this enables a system to answer vague and unanticipated requests and to make decisions to augment human decisions.

4. Simplified programming with the use of more structured design that will help users define their own problems and be able to generate reliable programs to solve them.

5. A variety of sizes from portable to supercomputer that can operate within a network structure.

The fifth-generation computers will draw heavily on artificial intelligence for knowledge-based applications. The main objective is to rely less heavily on existing software which currently depends on professional skills and expertise.

Thus far, Japan has achieved a high level of quality in their hardware but their software has lagged behind. The Japanese hope that by 1990 they will have a 30% share of the world market in computers and an 18% share of the U.S. market. Because of the Japanese success in other high-technology areas, many U.S. manufacturers are concerned about the possibility that Japan will achieve its goal.

We believe that the Japanese predictions may be overly optimistic and that their goals will not be realized for quite some time, if at all. We also believe that many U.S. manufacturers will begin to pool their research and development projects in an effort to overcome the Japanese threat; this cooperative effort, if it is realized, will itself have very positive effects on the U.S. computing field, both for manufacturers as well as for users.

V. FUTURE TECHNOLOGICAL GROWTH

Because the computing field is so highly competitive, we can expect technology to continue to develop rapidly with new and exciting innovations being marketed virtually all the time. Among the new technologies that have great potential for the future are:

1. One million-bit chip—for increased computer capacity, speed, and flexibility.
   Currently the largest chips available store from 256 to 512K bits of random access memory. By 1990, it is anticipated that 1 million bits of random access memory will be available on a single chip. Figure 19.4 illustrates advances in chip technology.

2. Magnetic bubble memory.
   Today, semiconductor memory remains the most cost-effective type of

Figure 19.4
Use of laser techniques to reduce the size of computer chips. (Courtesy Battelle Columbus Laboratories.)

memory available for computers. It is anticipated, however, that by 1990 non-volatile magnetic bubble memory as well as cache memory may prove to be less costly than semiconductor memory. If this occurs, these memories may become at least as popular as semiconductors.

3. Floppy tape—to compete with floppy disk for flexible storage.
4. Floppy disk and hard disk with greater capacities.
5. Microfloppies roughly three inches in diameter for use in homes and schools.
6. Erasable laser and optical disks with the ability to store hundreds of megabytes of data on a disk similar in size to a microfloppy.
7. Voice systems that enable users to speak into a device and have the voice patterns translated into computer signals. Figure 19.5 illustrates an audio word processing workstation with great potential for office use. The operator speaks the words rather than types them. A typed copy is produced. The computer can even repeat words for verification before typing a final copy. Figure 19.6 illustrates a simple calculator with voice output. Such

Figure 19.5
Audio work processing workstation. The operator speaks the words instead of keying them. The system can repeat them to make certain that it "understood" correctly. (Courtesy Wang Laboratories, Inc.)

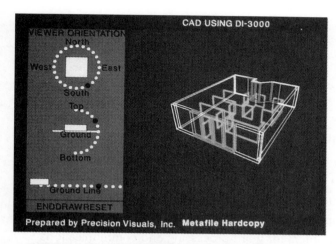

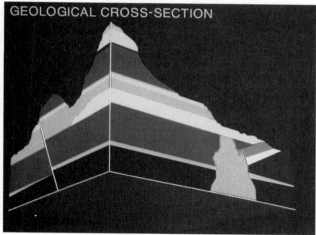

Figure 19.6 (above)
Compuvoice calculator.
(Courtesy Panasonic Corp.)

Figure 19.7 (at left)
Expanded use of color
graphics. (Courtesy Precision
Visuals, Inc.)

devices are becoming widely used in the home, largely as a result of the decrease in the price of electronic circuitry.

8. Ergonomically designed equipment such as terminals with:
   a. Touch-sensitive screens.
   b. Glare-reducing displays.
   c. Brightness controls.
   d. Fully detachable keyboards.
9. Easier and more illustrative use of color graphics (see Figure 19.7).
10. Computerized telephone systems with great flexibility and computer power (see Figure 19.8).

Figure 19.8
Displayphone. (Courtesy
Northern Telecom.)

VI. COMPUTERS AS A CULTURAL FORCE

There are two primary ways that computers can be used in business and in society, in general: (1) for obtaining information efficiently and effectively and

(2) for providing services that might not otherwise be feasible without a tool that can process vast amounts of data at high speeds. But computers also have the potential for making widespread and significant changes to social, political, and economic institutions as well. We will consider some of the changes that have already begun to occur as a result of computerization.

A. The Changing Nature of the Workplace

The ways in which many people perform their jobs have been profoundly affected by the computer. The following have been considered in this text:

1. Users in large organizations are increasingly dependent on computer output.
2. Managers rely on computers for decision-making.
3. Office workers use computers for word processing and communications.

Moreover, people who are computer literate have begun to acquire their own computers or workstations that provide them with great flexibility in the performance of their jobs. With the use of a computer that has data communications capability, an employee has access to his or her company's software and data base; in addition, he or she can also interact with other workers from virtually any location. As a result, workers can perform many of their tasks at home or indeed anywhere away from the office—a concept known as telecommuting.

This factor can result in significant changes to the ways in which traditional Monday-to-Friday, 9-to-5 jobs are performed. Working conditions can be more flexible, thereby resulting in:

1. Greater job satisfaction.
2. Staggered hours and days that can ease burdens on people, mass transportation, energy needs, and so on.
3. Better use of the existing work force. Housebound people such as those with small children or with physical handicaps can be employed to perform specific tasks directly from their homes.

Futurist Alvin Toffler coined the phrase "the electronic cottage" to describe his prediction that movement of workers from factories and offices back into the home will occur on a large scale in the years ahead. We concur with this prediction.

B. The Changing Nature of Businesses

It is possible that computers will provide a competitive edge most particularly to large companies. This may mean that small businesses will be unable to compete effectively in many industries. That is, small companies may simply be unable to offer the same services provided by organizations that have extensive data bases and highly sophisticated means of accessing them.

A large law firm, for example, has the capability of preparing a case using numerous legal data bases and other resources typically not available to small firms or sole practitioners that are on tight budgets. Such capability could well mean that the smaller organizations will not be able to survive in the information age. That is, the benefits derived from dealing with small businesses may simply be insufficient if services offered by large organizations are viewed as substantially superior. Consider the services offered by large banks and large retail establishments. These organizations can provide credit services, for example, that could not be offered by small concerns. Thus, the smaller banks and stores may find themselves unable to compete in the years ahead.

C. The Computer as an Integrated Social Tool

With increasing frequency, computers are being used in the following areas, just to name a few.

1. For the Handicapped
   There are computerized devices for the electronic reading of books to the visually impaired (see Figure 19.9). Similarly, voice-activated wheelchairs have great promise for the future (see Figure 19.10).

Figure 19.9 (at left)
Computerized book reading with a Kurzweil machine: an ideal tool for the visually impaired. (Dan McCoy/ Rainbow.)

2. For Law Enforcement Agencies
   Computers are used in patrol cars to make inquiries using the National Crime Information Center and Motor Vehicle data bases (see Figure 19.11). Similarly, facsimile devices are used to speed fingerprint analyses from Washington, D.C. to local police stations (see Figure 19.12).

Figure 19.10 (above)
A voice-activated wheelchair. (Dan McCoy/ Black Star.)

Figure 19.11 (at left)
Computer as an integral part of a patrol car. (Courtesy Digital Equipment Corp.)

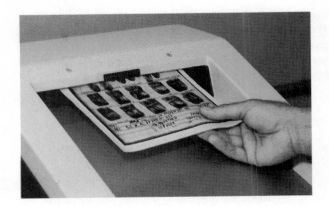

Figure 19.12
Use of a facsimile system in law enforcement. (Courtesy Litton Industries.)

3. For Sports Analysis
   Computers may be used to study tidal conditions before a yacht race (Figure 19.13) or to provide biomedical information regarding the physical condition of people engaged in athletic activities (Figure 19.14).

Figure 19.13
Use of a computer to study tidal conditions before a yacht race. (Mathew Naythons/Black Star.)

Figure 19.14
Computerized biomedical studies in sports. (Andy Levin/Black Star.)

4. For Agriculture
   Computers are also being used in farming to keep track of livestock (see Figure 19.15).

Figure 19.15
Farmer keeping track of
livestock. (David Burnett/
Contact-Woodfin Camp.)

5. For Homemaking Activities
   From systems that retrieve and store recipes (Figure 19.16) to shopping at
   home electronically (Figure 19.17) to robots that can walk your dog (Figure
   19.18), the potential is for far greater consumer use of computers in the
   years ahead.

Figure 19.16
Using a computer to
retrieve recipes. (Tony
Korody/Sygma.)

Figure 19.17
Shopping at home
electronically. (Courtesy
Viewdata Corp. of America,
Inc.)

Figure 19.18
Robots can even walk your dog! (Faverty/Liaison.)

D. The Changing Nature of the Home and Society in General: Is Overdependence on Computers a Realistic Fear?

First, we have seen how computers can affect education both in the home and in the classroom. We have also seen how information systems for obtaining news and other information from a centralized data base can be used. Paying bills, shopping, and buying tickets are all possible applications of computer processing using data communications (see Figure 19.19).

Microelectronics is also used to save energy in homes and offices. Computerized thermostats are currently widely used for energy control. Similarly, computerized fire detection systems and integrated home monitor and security systems are now common (see Figures 19.20 and 19.21).

Figure 19.19 (below)
Home information system. (Courtesy Bell Labs.)

Figure 19.20 (above, center)
Computerized fire detection system. (Courtesy Firetek/ McNeil Pharmaceutical.)

Figure 19.21 (above, right)
Integrated home monitor and security system. (Courtesy NEC.)

Yet despite the numerous advantages mentioned, many sociologists are concerned that we are becoming a society that is overdependent on computers and that this overdependence could someday adversely affect our safety and our economy.

The threat of nuclear disasters as a result of a computer error or computer crime is the subject of many films and books. Similarly, the threat of a war caused by a computer "bug" in our national defense system has been the subject of many suspense stories. It should come as no surprise to learn that such threats are indeed very real. Reliance on computers can—and sometimes has—resulted in an overdependence that could adversely affect the lives of many people. Unless control systems become more sophisticated, the potential for disaster will remain.

There are other less life-threatening breakdowns that could have serious effects on our economy as well. A computer error in one of the stock exchange systems or a banking system could profoundly affect our entire economy. Similarly, court dockets are filled with cases of businesses that have filed suit against computer vendors for problems that resulted in a loss of business or even in bankruptcy. Here, again, these cases demonstrate an overdependence on computers that profoundly affected the firms involved.

Sophisticated student users sometimes called "hackers" have been able to break computer codes in their schools and change grades or otherwise disrupt a computer system. These and other cases point to the ease with which computer codes can be broken, and the fact that the potential for doing damage is great.

All of these misuses suggest that there is a need for more sophisticated control and security measures and for a careful evaluation of the potential dangers of overdependence on computerization.

E. The Development of a Society That Is Functionally Computer Literate

As computers continue to be used in homes, businesses, and schools, it is becoming increasingly evident to many people that they need to be computer literate in order to function effectively in society. Undoubtedly the next generation will be far more computer literate than the previous ones. We can expect that by the year 2000 virtually every student will have had at least one course in computers and that most of them will be able to communicate effectively with a micro or mainframe. Computers may well become as much a part of our society as the automobile. In such an environment, careers in computing will remain as recession-proof as they have in the past. Moreover, those without any knowledge in this field will find themselves technically deficient in a wide variety of application areas.

F. The Changing Nature of Communications in General

As noted, workers increasingly communicate with one another via terminals. Similarly, students spend more time than ever interacting with a computer and less time interacting with teachers or their peers. Consumers have begun to place orders for all sorts of products by interfacing with a computer rather than by traditional, face-to-face communication with a salesperson. Employees can now communicate with one another using teleconferencing techniques that rely heavily on computers. Figure 19.22 shows how a system can accept data from a computer and then project the information on screens in one or more locations. Use can also be made of computer-generated graphics, thereby allowing last-minute changes to presentations that would otherwise be impossible with slides and graphs prepared in advance.

Such use of computers has the potential for improving efficiency as well as for improving the overall quality of life. But the substitution of computerized communication for interpersonal communication can have adverse affects on

Figure 19.22
Electronic projector for teleconferencing. This system can accept data from a computer. (Courtesy GE.)

society as well, if it is not carefully controlled and monitored.

There are many people who argue for a national policy on computers that will focus on such potential social changes. Other people believe that the marketplace should decide what changes will occur, and that no overall policy is necessary.

Regardless of your beliefs on this and other issues, you—as future computer professionals and users—should be aware of the potential for change inherent in the widespread use of computers. Moreover, regardless of whether you believe such changes will, in the end, be positive or negative, one thing is very clear: working with computers in the years ahead promises to be challenging, exciting, and most rewarding.

LOOKING AHEAD

Smart Card Technology Takes Off

1. A smart card, which closely resembles a credit card, contains an embedded microcomputer.

2. It is designed to store information in a secure fashion.

3. It has great potential in numerous application areas such as in banking as debit cards, for drivers licenses and passports, for recording data for pacemakers, as hotel door keys, and as ski lift tickets.

4. Experiments have been undertaken with smart cards used with pay telephones.
   a. You buy a card with a predefined monetary balance.
   b. With each phone call, you insert the card in the phone and the appropriate amount is deducted from the card's balance.
   c. When the balance reaches 0, the user discards the card.

CHAPTER SUMMARY

I. Predictions are opinions, not hard facts.

II. Micros: a major component in our future—in homes, businesses, and the classroom.
Increased use of micros is not without controversy.
   A. Some companies want a specific policy regarding the use, acquisition, and distribution of micros.
   B. Some companies are considering replacing mainframes with a series of micros, but this is not, in general, the norm. Most companies will continue to use micros to supplement existing mainframes.
   C. Some predictions indicate that the use of micros in the home is nothing more than a fad. We believe there will be a shakeout—with fewer micro manufacturers controlling more of the market. The market will, however, continue to grow.

III. Videotex and teletext have great potential but their future remains uncertain, mainly because there is no way of accurately predicting whether people will respond favorably to these services.

IV. Computer manufacturers in the United States face an imminent threat from the Japanese for control of the computer industry in the 1990s.

V. Technological innovations will continue to provide cheaper, faster, and more versatile equipment.

VI. Computers have great potential as a cultural force in our society and could result in profound changes in society. Some of these changes may be very positive while others may produce negative effects if they are not closely monitored and controlled.

Chapter Self-Evaluating Quiz

1. (T or F) The authors believe that users in a corporate setting should be free to purchase any micros they desire.

2. (T or F) The authors believe that micros in business will ultimately replace mainframes.

3. (T or F) The authors believe that the use of micros in the home is just a fad and that people will ultimately lose interest in them.

4. (T or F) The authors believe that the microcomputer revolution, is for all practical purposes, over.

5. (T or F) Local area networks will increase in popularity in the future.

6. (T or F) Videotex and teletext provide users with access to large information bases.

7. A major drawback to the widespread use of teletext and videotex services has been _____.

8. (T or F) The Japanese development of a so-called "fifth-generation" of computers poses a threat to the U.S. computer industry.

9. (T or F) Voice systems that enable users to speak into a computer device

and have voice patterns transmitted into computer signals, have great potential for the future.

10. (T or F) Predictions about the potential impact of computers on society are largely negative in orientation.

Solutions

1. F—We believe there should be some coordinated company-wide policy regarding the acquisition of micros. / page 718

2. F—We believe micros will continue to supplement mainframes in business, not replace them. / page 719

3. F—We believe micros will have great potential for home use. / page 719

4. F—We believe it has just begun. / page 720

5. T / page 721

6. T / page 721

7. cost / page 721

8. T / page 723

9. T / page 724

10. F—Some are negative and some are positive. / page 731

Review Questions

You may use any of the resources described in Appendix D to help you answer these questions.

1. Report on some innovative technological development in computing discussed in this chapter.

2. Provide a brief evaluation of the status of some technological development described in this chapter.

3. Discuss some current controversy regarding computer utilization that is not considered in this chapter.

4. Provide a brief evaluation and update on the status of some controversy that has been described in this chapter.

5. Do you think the communication gap between computer professionals and users is widening or narrowing? Explain your answer.

APPLICATION

TELECOMMUTING BANNED BY SERVICE UNION BOARD[1]

by Marguerite Zientara

WASHINGTON, D.C.—Telecommuting—thought by many to be the solution to child care needs, wasted gasoline and handicapped workers—has been banned by the Service Employees International Union (SEIU) here.

The ban, passed by SEIU's executive board a year ago, is being fought by the Center on National Labor Policy, Inc., a public interest law firm in North Springfield, Va.

Although telecommuters in the U.S. now number only a few hundred, the University of Southern California's Center for Future Research has predicted that in 10 years there could be 5 million people working at computer terminals in the home, in jobs ranging from DP to accounting.

SEIU, however, a union of 780,000 consisting of mostly clerical and health workers, passed the ban on computer homework "because we feel other kinds of homework are used to take advantage of workers and that it would be better for people to stay in the permanent and regular work force," explained Jackie Ruff, executive director of District 925 of SEIU.

Citing the home-based garment industry, Ruff noted, "I'm sure you've seen articles explaining that, in fact, the people who are doing the homework don't have any benefits, vacation, job security and so on, and are directly substituting for people who would have those more decent working conditions were they employed directly by an employer."

A different possible motivation emerges from the Center on National Labor Policy's point of view. "I think basically [the union passed the ban] because it's difficult to organize people who work at home," suggested Jon Imbody, public relations director for the center.

Advocates of telecommuting cite cost savings in commuting and child care, more time with one's children, flexible work schedules, increased productivity, better attendance and higher quality work.

On the question of the child care benefits of telecommuters, Ruff explained, "One of the things we work toward is some kind of assistance for child care. So we feel the way to deal with child care and working mothers is to pay them enough so they can afford it on their own, and for employers and government funding in some way to help support child care."

"We don't think the way to do it is to take somebody and say 'We're not going to give you health insurance or any other benefits, and we're going to pay you the least we can get away with'," she added.

Acknowledging that saving fuel and reportedly higher productivity rates are not the union's central concerns, Ruff said, "Our real concern is that people we represent be able to have a decent, fair standard of living, so if our members are saying they can't afford to commute to work, we try to see if through collective bargaining we can get wages that will allow them to commute."

The Center on National Labor Policy is coordinating groups and associations interested in telecommuting and other homework, with an eye toward petitioning the Labor Secretary and Vice-President who is in charge of the Regulatory Task Force, to have the ban lifted.

Among the groups the center is working with are the National Alliance of Home-Based Business Women, the National Association for Cottage Industry and the National Homeworkers Extension Council.

"Right now it's just a matter of knocking on a lot of doors and getting a lot of support and convincing people in the administration that it's an issue worthy of their consideration," Imbody said.

"We've talked to a lot of people in the Labor Department, and right now we're focusing on the White House and the Regulatory Task Force," he said. "It seems to be the kind of thing that the more people who find out about it, the better our chances are."

[1] *Computerworld*, July 11, 1983, page 7. Copyright © 1983 by CW Communications/Inc., Framingham, MA 01701. Reprinted with permission.

Questions
1. Understanding Key Terms
   Define *telecommuting* as it is used in the application.
2. Software, Hardware, and Systems Concepts
   What are the advantages and disadvantages of telecommuting as discussed in the article?
3. Management Considerations
   Based on your understanding of the issues, would you be "for" or "against" telecommuting if you were an executive of a large corporation? Explain your answer.
4. Social, Legal, and Ethical Implications
   Do you think the union has valid grounds for arguing against telecommuting? Be specific.

CASE STUDY: McKing's Superburgers, Inc.

1. Trends
   Consider the following trends. Answer the questions and indicate what impact the trends may have on McKing's decision to computerize its order-entry and inventory control systems.

a. Industry emphasis is on structured programming techniques. Should this be encouraged at McKing's?
b. Application packages, custom-designed software, and turnkey systems are becoming increasingly popular. Should these be investigated as alternatives to writing application software?
c. The cost of software is increasing over time. What suggestions do you have for minimizing the impact of these higher costs?
d. The cost of hardware is decreasing over time. What suggestions do you have for gaining maximum benefit from this decrease?

2. The Future
a. Is it feasible for the concept of telecommuting to have any applicability at McKing's?
b. Once the order-entry and inventory systems are implemented, what systems would you recommend be considered next for computerization?

Systems Study

You have answered a series of questions throughout the book on the following aspects of the proposed system for McKing's.

1. Objectives of the point-of-sale system.
2. Constraints.
3. Inputs.
4. Outputs.
5. Types of processing.
6. Costs.
7. Controls.
8. Implementation considerations.

Extract material from all of the information provided and integrate your answers to the questions asked. The resulting information will form the basis of a systems study. The systems study should specifically include the following:

1. Introduction—a description of what the computerized system should achieve.
   —the objectives of the system—both long-term and short-term.
2. Narrative—a description of the way the system will function.
   —indicate any potential bottlenecks that you foresee.
3. Processing—a description of the processing; include systems flowcharts, data flow diagrams, program flowcharts, pseudocode and HIPO charts where appropriate.
4. Layouts of input and output—include a Printer Spacing Chart for each printed report.
   —include a CRT layout for any displayed output.
   —describe master files and transaction files.
5. Implementation plan.
6. Controls.
7. Cost-benefit analysis—justify the system from a cost standpoint.

THE COMPUTER AD: A Focus on Marketing

Consider the ad entitled "You Don't Switch Voice Calls This Way Any More. Why Should You Do It For Data?" that appears in Figure 19.23.

Questions

1. One could say that the ad implies that "new is better." Explain why. Do you agree or disagree with this point of view?
2. Define the following terms as they are used in the ad:
   a. PABX networking.
   b. Contention.
   c. Computer ports.
3. In your own words, indicate how "inter-PABX networking" differs from the old "switchboard" method of transferring voice calls?
4. The ad states that "local networking" provides "proven technology at low cost per port, without special cables or compatibility problems." Indicate when the use of special cables instead of PABX networking may be more cost-effective and efficient. What sort of compatibility problems is the ad referring to?

Figure 19.23 Marketing computer products. (Courtesy MICOM.)

APPENDIXES

ADDITIONAL TOPICS IN BASIC PROGRAMMING

I. PRINT OPTIONS

One of the main purposes of using computers for information processing is to produce reports or printed output. This output should be as clear and meaningful as possible and should be designed to precisely satisfy user needs.

Two special features are typically employed to make output user-friendly, or easy to interpret by the user:

1. Headings should be included that help identify the overall output report and the specific fields that are to be printed.
2. Output fields should be **edited** so that they include symbols such as dollar signs, commas, minus signs, etc. to make them as readable as possible.

Headings and edited fields are utilized regardless of whether output is printed on a hard-copy report or displayed on a CRT screen. In either case, it is imperative that the programmer make the output meaningful and clear. In addition to printing headings to identify output, there are other options available for making information easier to read and interpret.

A. The TAB Option

Headings consisting of alphanumeric constants or literals are placed in specific locations on an output line to identify the report and the output fields. Consider the following CRT output. We are assuming a CRT screen width of 75 positions for the purpose of this example.

```
                     STUDENT  GRADES

   LAST  NAME        FIRST  NAME            GRADE

   ABRAMS            JOAN                    85
   BARNES            ALAN                    95
   COHEN             BARBARA                 90
      .                  .                    .
      .                  .                    .
      .                  .                    .
```

In order to center the heading, we want the S in the word STUDENT to start in position 31. This was determined as follows.

1. The output line can contain 75 characters.
2. The title STUDENT GRADES contains 15 characters, including two spaces between the words STUDENT and GRADES.
3. To center the title, we would like to have an equal number of spaces on either side of the alphanumeric constant. This means that we should have 30 spaces on either side of the heading:

$$
\begin{array}{l}
75 \text{ positions on the line} \\
\underline{-15 \text{ characters in title}} \\
60 \text{ spaces left} \\
60/2 = 30 \text{ spaces on either side of title}
\end{array}
$$

Thus, we will start the heading in position 31.

The TAB option can be used in the PRINT statement to obtain the output in the specific locations desired. For example, consider the following statement:

```
20 PRINT TAB(31);"STUDENT GRADES"
```

This will cause the alphanumeric constant to begin in position 31. Note that a semicolon separates the TAB option from the actual heading or literal to be displayed or printed.

The starting positions for the column headings LAST NAME, FIRST NAME, and GRADE are also computed so that each of these field headings is evenly spaced across the line. A Printer Spacing Chart or CRT Layout Form is useful in helping the programmer establish suitable margins.

The following program excerpt illustrates how the TAB option can be used to obtain the results discussed above.

```
10  PRINT
20  PRINT TAB(31);"STUDENT GRADES"
30  PRINT
40  PRINT TAB(18);"LAST NAME";TAB(44);"FIRST NAME";TAB(71);"GRADE"
50  PRINT
    .
    .
    .
120 PRINT TAB(18);L$;TAB(44);F$;TAB(73);G
130 END
```

In line 120 we include the TAB for spacing the Name and Grade fields to be printed. The TAB for G (Grade) was set at 73, which means that it will be centered under the column heading ''GRADE,'' which prints in positions 71-75.

Before the TAB option is utilized, the programmer must ascertain the size of the terminal screen or printer on which the output will appear. Typical line sizes range from 40 to 132 print positions per line, depending on the device used. TAB is an option used for printing graphics as well.

B. The PRINT USING Statement[1]

Consider the following program.

Program 1

```
10  READ A
20  IF A = 9 THEN 60
30  PRINT A
40  GO TO 10
50  DATA 12.75,8.60,125000.50,9
60  END
RUN
12.75
8.60
125000.50
```

The results would be more readable if they were printed as follows.

```
    12.75
     8.60
125,000.50
```

In the latter case, notice that:

1. The numbers are aligned on the decimal point.
2. A comma has been inserted in the last number for ease of reading.

We will see how these results can be accomplished with the PRINT USING statement.

Two of the major purposes of the PRINT USING statement are to provide the following:

Purposes of the PRINT USING Statement

1. To provide proper alignment of results.
2. To edit the results.

   Editing means making the results more meaningful by adding characters such as dollar signs, commas, and asterisks for readability.

Before we discuss the PRINT USING statement in detail, note that the form of this statement varies slightly from one version of BASIC to another. Check the BASIC language manual for the system you are using to determine the precise requirements for your program. We will note major differences from one version to another in the discussion that follows.

The general form of the PRINT USING statement is

```
PRINT USING  [string expression(s), list]
```

[1]Note that this statement is not available on all micros; for the IBM PC, a semi-colon must separate all items.

where the string expression indicates the format to be used when printing the item(s) in the list. (TRS 80 BASIC requires a semicolon, rather than a comma, to separate the string expression(s) and the list.)

We now consider some of the commonly used string expressions to illustrate how alignment and editing of results can be obtained.

1. Aligning Numeric Fields

a. Aligning Integer Fields The symbol # is used in the string expression of the PRINT USING statement to indicate that a numeric field is to be printed *right-justified*, with leading or leftmost positions filled with blanks. This will ensure that all data is printed with units positions aligned properly. Consider the following:

```
30 PRINT USING "######",A
```

The values for A will print as follows:

Value of A (with prompt)	PRINT USING String Expression	Printed Results
?1234	"######"	1234
?26	"######"	26
?374	"######"	374
?26873	"######"	26873
?987261	"######"	987261

The string expression "######" indicates that the value of the variable can be from 1 to 6 digits. If A had a value greater than six digits such as 1234567, it would print with an error sign such as ***** or perhaps %1234567. Without the PRINT USING, results would print left-justified, as indicated in the column marked "Value of A" above.

b. Aligning Fields with Decimal Places If the number to be printed contains a decimal point, we include the decimal point in the string expression:

```
30 PRINT USING "######.##",A
```

Consider the following examples:

Value of A (with prompt)	PRINT USING String Expression	Printed Results
?12.75	######.##	12.75
?8.60	######.##	8.60
?125000.50	######.##	125000.50
?14.7685	######.##	14.77
?87.67	######.##	87.67
?-6.48	######.##	-6.48
?-.25	######.##	-0.25

If A has three or more decimal positions, the use of the decimal point in the PRINT USING statement will mean that the results will be **rounded** to two decimal points rather than truncated. Thus if A has a value of 12.755, it will print as 12.76.

Note that the values for A can have as many as six integers. Note, too, that if A has only decimal positions, it will print with a zero before the decimal point. Thus, .25 would print as 0.25.

The following program illustrates the use of the "#" and "." symbols for obtaining proper alignment in Program 1.

```
10  READ A
20  IF A = 9 THEN 60
30  PRINT USING "######.##",A
40  GO TO 10
50  DATA 18.758,7.352,125000,.2,9
60  END
RUN
      18.76
       7.35
 125000.00
       0.20
```

When the last value, 9, is read, the program is terminated.

2. Inserting Commas in Numeric Fields

If we want one or more commas to print with a number, we can simply include these commas in the string expression of the PRINT USING statement.

```
30  PRINT USING "#,###,###.##",A
```

If A has a value of 1052000.50 it will print as 1,052,000.50. Commas will print only if the value of A has enough significant positions; otherwise the commas will be suppressed. Thus, if A has a value of 532.50, for example, it will print without the commas as ƀƀƀƀƀƀƀ532.50, where ƀ denotes a blank.

The following will indicate the results of some examples of the PRINT USING where commas are to be printed:

Value of A	PRINT USING String Expression	Printed Result
4872.83	###,###.##	4,872.83
873586.487	###,###.##	873,586.49
287.05	###,###.##	287.05
31.621	###,###.##	31.62
2876543.92	###,###.##	%2876,543.92

Note: The symbol % in the last example indicates that the field is too long. The string expression allows for a maximum of six integers.

When a field is too large for the PRINT USING string expression, it may print with a % to indicate a size error or it may print as all asterisks (*) depending on your system.

3. Inserting Dollar Signs in Numeric Fields

If we want a dollar sign to print along with the contents of a field, we include the dollar sign in the PRINT USING statement.

```
10 PRINT USING "$#,###.##",A
```

If A contained a value of 3546.23, it would print as $3,546.23.
    Consider the following examples:

Value of A	PRINT USING String Expression	Printed Results
28.73	$#,###.##	$ 28.73
4872.26	$#,###.##	$4,872.26
927.163	$#,###.##	$ 927.16
.06	$#,###.##	$ 0.06

4. Using a Floating Dollar Sign

Sometimes printing a dollar sign as above is not sufficient. If A contained 1.93, for example, the output would print as follows.

```
$    1.93
```

In the above, there are too many blanks separating the dollar sign from the first significant character. By including two dollar signs at the beginning of the string expression of the PRINT USING statement, we can ensure that the dollar sign prints adjacent to the first significant character. The use of two dollar signs will cause the $ to **float**, or print *next to the first significant digit* of the number. Consider the following program:

```
10 READ A
20 IF A = 9 THEN 60
30 PRINT USING "$$#,###.##",A
40 GO TO 10
50 DATA 5200.50,325.55,85320.75,9
60 END
RUN
 $5,200.50
   $325.55
$85,320.75
```

Examine the last value of A to be printed. Notice that the position occupied by the second dollar sign in the string expression of the PRINT USING statement can be replaced with a digit, if required. The first dollar sign can never be replaced with a digit. Thus, the string expression "$$#,###.##" can permit *five* integers or a number as large as 99999.99 to be printed out as $99,999.99.

Consider the following examples.

Value of A	PRINT USING String Expression	Printed Results
28.73	$$#,###.##	$28.73
4872.26	$$#,###.##	$4,872.26
927.163	$$#,###.##	$927.16
.06	$$#,###.##	$0.06
87263.27	$$#,###.##	$87,263.27

5. Printing Numbers with Asterisks

We sometimes want numbers to print with leading asterisks instead of spaces. This is known as asterisk fill. This minimizes the possibility of someone tampering with the amount. That is, $**15.23 is more difficult to change, on a check for example, than $ 15.23.

We can include two asterisks(**) at the beginning of the string expression in the PRINT USING statement to accomplish asterisk fill. For example, if A has a value of 25.75, the following statement:

```
30 PRINT USING "***,###.##",A
```

will cause *****25.75 to print out. Any output where numeric values should be protected from changes should use asterisk fill or floating dollar signs.

The following points should be noted about the use of the asterisk in the string expression.

1. Nonsignificant commas, if designated in the string, will be replaced with asterisks, as shown in the above example.

2. The two asterisks may be replaced with digits, if the field to print is large enough. For example, with the above PRINT USING statement, if A has a value of 850750.35, it will print as 850,750.35, without any asterisks.

3. Asterisks preceding a dollar sign will result in the printing of leading asterisks and a floating dollar sign.

Consider the following examples:

Value of A	PRINT USING String Expression	Printed Results
8712.34	***,###.##	**8,712.34
27.45	***,###.##	*****27.45
283.05	***,###.##	****283.05
26.32	**$#,###.##	****$26.32

6. Printing Plus and Minus Signs

If a field is negative, a minus sign will print to the left of the number, unless otherwise specified. For example, if E has a value of -25.59, the statement:

```
30 PRINT USING "###.##",A
```

will cause A to print as -25.59. However, we may want the minus sign printed to the right of the number, as is sometimes desired in financial reports. To accomplish this, we place a minus sign to the right of the string expression in the PRINT USING statement as follows:

```
30 PRINT USING "###.##-",A
```

If the value of the field is positive, a blank instead of the minus sign will appear in the output.

The use of the minus sign in the string expression will cause a negative number to print with the appropriate sign. *No* sign will print if the number is signed positive or unsigned.

To print a plus or minus sign depending on the value of the field, we use a plus sign in the string expression. This results in the following:

➡ Use of Plus Sign in String Expressions

1. Minus sign will print for negative numbers.
2. Plus sign will print for positive and unsigned numbers.

   Consider the following illustrations:

Value of A	PRINT USING String Variable	Printed Results
-142	###-	142-
142	###-	142
+142	###-	142
-142	###+	142-
142	###+	142+
+142	###+	142+

7. Printing String Variables and Constants

Thus far, we have been considering variations of the PRINT USING statement for editing and printing numeric fields. In order to print string variables and constants, we can designate the size of the field by using the backslash character (\) in the PRINT USING statement. Each \ allows for one character to print. Each space between the backslashes also allows one character to print. Consider the following PRINT USING statement, with two blanks between the slashes:

```
20 PRINT USING "\  \","NAME"
```

This statement will enable the four characters in the word NAME to print. Each slash and each space allows for a character to print. If the string expression had been written as ''\\'', only NA would print out. Similarly, to print the contents of a string variable, we could write

```
50 PRINT USING "\   \",B$
```

Instead of the backslash character (\), some versions of BASIC use one of the following symbols:

1. For TRS-80 BASIC: a percentage symbol (%) is used. For example:

```
20 PRINT USING "%   %";"NAME"
```

2. For systems using BASIC-PLUS-2: the letter L, with the first L in a string preceded by a single quote is used. For example:

```
20 PRINT USING "'LLLL","NAME"
```

3. For systems using CBASIC:
   a. String constants with a forward slash (/) is used. For example:

```
20 PRINT USING "/   /","NAME"
```

   b. String variables with one ampersand (&) to print a field of any length is used. For example:

```
30 PRINT USING "&",A$
```

4. Other systems use a # sign in place of /.

Note, then, that there are some differences in the format of PRINT USING statements, depending on the compiler used.

The PRINT USING results in output that is left-justified. For example, if B$ had the values of ABC, AB, ABCD, each time the PRINT USING was executed, the following will print:

```
ABC
AB
ABCD
```

Consider the following examples. We will use the backslash character in these examples.

```
10 PRINT USING "string expression",A$
```

Data in Field	PRINT USING	Printed Results
ABCDEF	"\ \"	ABCDEF

Note: Above accommodates
six characters (4 blanks
and 2 backslashes)

ABCDEF	"\ \",A$	ABCDE
ABCD	"\\",A$	AB
AB	"\ \",A$	AB

Alphanumeric data is left-
justified when PRINT USING
is executed

8. Using More Than One String Expression in a PRINT USING Statement

We often find it necessary to print out a combination of numeric fields and string variables or constants on a particular line. The following example illustrates how two or more string expressions can be specified in a single PRINT USING statement.

```
150 PRINT USING "\   \ ##,###","THE NUMBER IS ",N
```

Notice that the string expressions are simply written in the order in which they will be used, with at least one space being left between each string expression.
    The results will print as follows:

```
THE NUMBER IS        58,726
```

9. Using Semicolons to Separate Items in a PRINT Statement

We have seen that we may use commas or semicolons to separate items in a PRINT statement. When commas are used to separate items, each item prints in separate zones across the page as follows.

```
10 PRINT 1,2,3
RUN
1                 2                 3
```

The actual number of characters in each zone varies from system to system, but 18 characters is not an uncommon number for each zone.
    To print the items more compactly, we may use a semicolon instead of a comma to separate fields in a PRINT statement:

```
10 PRINT 1;2;3
RUN
1  2  3
```

II. LIBRARY FUNCTIONS

There are functions available in BASIC to call in pre-programmed routines that may be used as part of the program. For example, suppose we wish to determine the integer portion of a number A. The following instruction will store that integer portion in the variable labeled T.

```
LET T = INT(A)
```

INT ( ) is a library function that may be used in any BASIC program to obtain the integer value of a variable. Consider the following examples:

```
10 LET T = INT(A)
```

Initial Value of A	Result in T	Initial Value of A	Result in T
3.7	3	−7.23	−8
4.16	4	6.0	6

Notice that the computer returns the integer value that is less than or equal to the number. The instruction using INT ( ) calls in the routine for determining the integer portion of a number.

Example

Read in a number N. Determine if it is odd or even.

```
10 INPUT N
20 IF N = 99999 THEN 100
30 LET T = N/2
40 LET Q = INT(T)
50 IF N = 2 * Q THEN 80
60 PRINT "THE NUMBER ";N;" IS ODD"
70 GO TO 10
80 PRINT "THE NUMBER ";N;" IS EVEN"
90 GO TO 10
100 END
```

In addition to the INT function, there are numerous other library functions available. As we have seen, the function **SQR** can be used to determine the square root of a number.

```
5 REM THE FOLLOWING CALCULATES THE HYPOTENUSE OF
7 REM      A RIGHT TRIANGLE
10 INPUT A,B
20 LET C = SQR(A ** 2 + B ** 2)
30 PRINT C
40 END
```

You may recall that the square root of a number is the same as raising the number to the .5 power. Thus, in the above the results printed will be exactly the same as the following:

```
20 LET C = (A**2 + B**2)**.5
```

ABS ( ) is a library function for calculating the absolute value of a number. Thus one solution for determining the absolute value of A is as follows.

```
10 INPUT A
20 IF A = 999 THEN 60
30 LET T = ABS(A)
40 PRINT "THE ABSOLUTE VALUE OF ";A;" IS ";T
50 GO TO 10
60 END
```

Common library functions include the following.

Common Library Functions

Function	Meaning
SQR (T)	Finds the square root of T
INT (T)	Finds the integer portion of T
ABS (T)	Finds the absolute value of T
SGN (T)	Finds the sign of T:

if T = 0, SGN (T) = 0
if T < 0, SGN (T) = −1
if T > 0, SGN (T) = +1

Function	Meaning
EXP (T)	Finds the value of e (2.71828183) raised to the T power
LOG (T)	Finds the logarithm of T
SIN (T)	Finds the sine of T
COS (T)	Finds the cosine of T
TAN (T)	Finds the tangent of T
RND (T)	Finds a random number

We will discuss the random number generator next because it has such widespread use, especially for model building and for game programs.

III. OTHER BASIC PROGRAMMING CONCEPTS

A. RND as a Random Number Generator

The **RND** library function is a commonly used function, particularly for coding a game or building a model where **random numbers** are frequently utilized. The coding of the RND function varies somewhat from system to system. Depending on the system, you may use the following:

1. LET Y = RND

2. LET Y = RND (T), where T is any integer, or where T must be either 0 or 1. On some systems, then, RND is defined as a value greater than or equal to 0 but less than 1 (e.g., a positive fraction). On others, RND(T) generates any random number.

Example

The following program prints a simulated roll of dice using a random number generator. Each value of X and Z should be a number from 1 to 6 just as would be obtained from throwing two dice.

```
10 REM   STORE THE RESULTS FROM TWO DICE
15 REM   WHERE RND (0) PRODUCES A RANDOM NUMBER
20 REM          FROM 0 TO 1
25 LET Y = RND(0)
30 LET X = INT(6 * Y + 1)
40 LET T = RND(0)
50 LET Z = INT(6 * T + 1)
60 PRINT X,Z
```

The above program excerpt will work properly on systems that generate a random number from 0 to 1 with the use of RND (0).

If Y is the random number from 0 to 1, then 6*Y will be a number from 0 to 5.9999. 6*Y + 1 will be a number from 1 to 6.9999. INT (6*Y + 1) will then produce an integer from 1 to 6. Statements 40 and 50 produce a second random number from 1 to 6 in Z.

Example

Code the program for a Mastermind game, where the player must guess four of the computer-generated numbers from 1 to 6 and place them in the proper sequence as selected by the computer. No doubles are permitted (see Figure A.1).

Figure A.1
Mastermind program.

```
10 PRINT "THIS IS MASTERMIND"
12 PRINT
14 PRINT
15 PRINT "TO START, PICK 4 NUMBERS FROM THE DIGITS 1-6"
18 PRINT                              "NO DUPLICATES"
23 PRINT "X MEANS RIGHT POSITION, RIGHT INTEGER"
25 PRINT "I MEANS RIGHT INTEGER, WRONG POSITION"
26 PRINT " - MEANS WRONG NUMBER"
28 PRINT
110 FOR I = 1 TO 4
120 LET A(I) = 0
130 NEXT I
140 FOR I = 5 TO 8
150 LET A(I) = INT(RND(1) * 6 + 1)
160 IF A(I) = A(I-1) THEN 150
```

Figure A.1 (continued)

```
170 IF A(I) = A(I-2) THEN 150
180 IF A(I) = A(I-3) THEN 150
190 IF A(I) = A(I-4) THEN 150
200 NEXT I
210 LET N = 0
220 LET N = N + 1
230 PRINT
240 LET M = 0
250 INPUT B
260 LET B = B/1000
270 FOR I = 1 TO 4
280 LET A(I) = INT(B)
290 LET B = (B-A(I))*10
300 IF I = 3 THEN B = B + .0005
310 NEXT I
320 FOR I = 1 TO 4
330 LET J = I + 4
340 IF A(I) <> A(J) THEN 380
350 PRINT "X";
360 LET M = M + 1
370 LET A(I) = 17
380 NEXT I
390 IF M = 4 THEN 550
400 FOR I = 1 TO 4
410 FOR J = 5 TO 8
420 IF A(I) <> A(J) THEN 470
430 IF J = I + 4 THEN 470
440 PRINT "I";
450 LET M = M + 1
460 GO TO 480
470 NEXT J
480 NEXT I
490 IF M = 4 THEN 220
500 LET M = M + 1
510 FOR I = M TO 4
520 PRINT "-";
530 NEXT I
540 GO TO 220
550 PRINT
560 PRINT "YOU DID IT IN ";N;" MOVES"
570 GO TO 110
```

Example

Write a drill-and-practice module to help elementary school students learn their multiplication tables. Use RND to obtain numbers at random (see Figure A.2).

```
 10 DIM A$(10)
 20 FOR I = 1 TO 10
 30 READ A$(I)
 40 NEXT I
 50 LET I = 1
 60 PRINT "HI, WHAT'S YOUR NAME?"
 70 INPUT N$
 80 PRINT "NICE TO MEET YOU";N$
 90 PRINT "WOULD YOU LIKE TO PLAY AN ARITHMETIC GAME?"
100 INPUT Y$
110 IF Y$ = "YES" THEN 130
120 GO TO 510
130 PRINT "GOOD, LET'S GET STARTED"
140 PRINT "JUST TYPE IN YOUR ANSWERS UNTIL"
150 PRINT "YOU WANT TO STOP - THEN TYPE - 1"
160 PRINT
170 LET C = INT(RND(1) * 9)
180 LET D = INT(RND(1) * 9)
190 PRINT "HOW MUCH IS ";C;" X ";D;"?"
200 INPUT Z
210 IF Z = -1 THEN 360
220 IF V = 0 THEN Y = Y + 1
230 IF Z = C * D THEN 280
240 PRINT "YOU MADE A MISTAKE, TRY AGAIN"
250 IF V = 0 THEN X = X - 1
260 LET V = 1
270 GO TO 200
280 LET V = 0
290 PRINT A$(I)
300 PRINT
310 LET X = X + 1
320 LET I = I + 1
330 IF I = 11 THEN I = 1
340 GO TO 170
350 PRINT "NICE PLAYING WITH YOU";N$
360 PRINT "YOUR SCORE IS ";X;" RIGHT OUT OF ";Y;" QUESTIONS"
370 GO TO 510
380 DATA "EXCELLENT, LET'S TRY ANOTHER"
390 DATA "DON'T LOOK NOW BUT YOUR BRAINS ARE SHOWING!"
400 DATA "YOU ARE REALLY A WHIZ KID"
410 DATA "EINSTEIN MUST HAVE BEEN YOUR BROTHER!"
420 DATA "DO THEY GIVE NOBEL PRIZES IN BRAINS??"
430 DATA "BRILLIANT, BRILLIANT!!"
440 DATA "KEEP IT UP!"
450 DATA "WHAT A REFINED MIND!"
460 DATA "I AM VERY IMPRESSED!"
470 DATA "WOW!!"
510 END
```

Figure A.2
Drill-and-practice program.

B. Subroutines

A **subroutine** is a series of instructions that is executed from different points in a program. Instead of coding the set of instructions each time it is needed, it is possible to code a *single routine* and then call it in and execute it whenever it is required. This is performed with the use of the **GOSUB** statement, which has the following form:

(line number)   GOSUB   (line number)

Each time the GOSUB statement is encountered, control is transferred to the line number indicated. The statements beginning at that line number are then executed until a RETURN statement is encountered at the end of the routine branched to. Control then returns to the statement immediately following the GOSUB statement.

Example
Consider the following:

```
10  _____
20  _____
30  _____
40  GOSUB 1000
50  _____
60  _____
70  _____
80  GOSUB 1000
90  _____
100 _____
110 _____
120 _____
1000 _____
1010 _____
1020 _____
1030 RETURN
        ⁺
        ⁺
1040 END
```

The steps between 1000 and 1030 are executed when the GOSUB command is encountered.

After the RETURN, control passes to the statement after the GOSUB.

After the GOSUB in line number 40 is executed, lines 1000 through 1030 are performed and control is then returned to statement number 50. After the GOSUB in line number 80 is executed, lines 1000 through 1030 are performed again and control is returned to statement number 90.

Example
Read input consisting of three fields: amount 1, amount 2, and amount 3. Print the word "ERROR" and the specific field that caused an error if any one of the following conditions exists.

amount 1 > 1000
amount 2 < 500
amount 3 = 750

```
 10  INPUT A1,A2,A3
 20  IF A1 = 999 THEN 9999
 30  LET T$ = "AMOUNT 1"
 40  IF A1 < = 1000 THEN 60
 50  GOSUB 1000
 60  LET T$ = "AMOUNT 2"
 70  IF A2 > = 500 THEN 90
 80  GOSUB 1000
 90  LET T$ = "AMOUNT 3"
100  IF A3 <> 750 THEN 120
110  GOSUB 1000
120  GO TO 10
1000 PRINT "ERROR IN ";T$
1010 RETURN
9999 END
```

GOSUB ... RETURN sequences can also be useful for producing results that vary depending on when they are computed in a program. Consider the following:

Example

```
      .
      .
 50  LET A = 1
 60  LET Z = 10
 70  LET S = 1
 80  GOSUB 900
 90      .
  .      .
  .      .
200  LET A = 5
210  LET Z = 20
220  LET S = 5
230  GOSUB 900
        .
        .
900  FOR I = A TO Z STEP S
910  PRINT I
920  NEXT I
930  RETURN
940  END
```

This latter procedure is a useful method for producing graphs or graphics. A fixed routine is coded. The actual output produced will depend on the values of specific parameters when the GOSUB is executed.

GOSUBs are used in structured programs; they modularize a program so that it is easier to read, debug, and modify. Each module or subroutine can be tested independently; for large programs, subroutines may even be written by different people and debugged separately as well.

C. String Functions[2]

You will recall that alphanumeric data can be stored in a field that has a name consisting of an alphabetic character followed by a $. Thus, A$, B$, etc. can be used as alphanumeric field names or string variables.

We can read, print, and compare alphanumeric fields. To compare a field to "ABC", for example, and to branch to statement 50 on an equal condition, we code:

```
10 IF F$ = "ABC" THEN 50
```

When dealing with interactive systems, it is sometimes useful to manipulate string variables in more sophisticated ways. It may be necessary, for example, to separate the field into individual characters for sorting purposes or for specific types of analyses.

BASIC **string functions** enable programmers to modify, compare, analyze, and combine alphanumeric data. Combining alphanumeric data into one string is called **concatenation**. In order for computers to be useful in interactive settings where users may not be particularly computer oriented, we must enable them to enter data that may not be in the precise form we want. With the use of string functions, the BASIC program can analyze the input to see if it contains an appropriate response, and then operate on it as necessary.

Example 1

Suppose you ask a terminal operator for a response of "Y" to indicate Yes and "N" to indicate No. It is possible that the operator will respond with the full word rather than the letter Y or N as requested. The following coding will eliminate any difficulties associated with a terminal response that may not be precisely the one that was requested.

```
10 PRINT "IS THIS THE FIRST OF THE MONTH?"
20 PRINT "ENTER Y FOR YES AND N FOR NO"
30 INPUT A$
40 IF A$ = "Y" THEN 500
50 IF A$ = "N" THEN 700
60 IF LEFT$(A$) = "Y" THEN 500
70 IF LEFT$(A$) = "N" THEN 700
      .
      .
```

[1]Not available on all computers.

The string function LEFT$(A$) enables the programmer to test the leftmost character of A$ to determine if it is a Y or N. In this way, if the terminal operator keyed in the entire word YES or NO or even YEA or NOPE, the program would proceed properly.

Example 2

Suppose you ask the terminal operator to enter an item description. The size of the field is variable and may affect the alignment of output data. It is possible to determine the length of a string variable with the use of the LEN string function. Consider the following:

```
10 PRINT "ENTER ITEM DESCRIPTION AND ITEM PRICE"
20 INPUT D$,P
30 LET T = LEN (D$)
40 IF T > 15 THEN 80
   .
   .
   .
```

Some of the string functions that can be used in BASIC are as follows:

String Function	Purpose	Example
LEN (string)	Determines length of the string	if F$ equals "FRED" LEN (F$) = 4
LEFT$(string, no. of characters)	Determines the leftmost characters in string	LEFT$("NOTHING",2) = NO
RIGHT$(string, no. of characters	Determines the right-most characters in string	RIGHT$("AB",1) = B
string 1 + string 2	Combines or concatenates two strings	"A-" + "OK" = "A-OK"
MID$(string, expression 1, expression 2)	Starts with character at expression 1 until expression 2 is reached	MID$("ABCDE",3,2) = "CD"

Note: When the number of characters is omitted, it is assumed to be 1.

D. Sorting Data

A common business application of computers is sorting data. Data may be sorted into ascending sequence, that is, from lowest value to highest. Similarly, data may be sorted into descending sequence, from highest value to lowest.

Typically, the data to be sorted is placed in an array in unordered fashion and is then rearranged appropriately. One common sorting technique is referred to as the **bubble sort**. Using the bubble sort, two adjacent values in an array are compared. If ascending sequence is desired, then the lower of the two values being compared is placed first, followed by the larger quantity. Because it requires additional storage, the bubble sort is best used when we have a limited number of items.

Using this procedure, two quantities are compared until the entire array has been processed, then the next group of two values within the array are compared. This procedure continues until all entries have been placed in their proper sequence. Note that the bubble sort can be used for sorting either numeric or alphanumeric values. The following is an excerpt from a BASIC program that sorts 15 variables into ascending sequence. Assume the 15 numbers have been read into an array B(15).

```
10 LET A = 0
20 FOR I = 1 TO 14
30 IF B(I) < B(I + 1) THEN 80
40 LET C = B(I)
50 LET B(I) = B(I + 1)
60 LET B(I + 1) = C
70 LET A = 1
80 NEXT I
90 IF A = 1 THEN 10
100 REM THE NUMBERS ARE NOW IN SEQUENCE
    .
    .
    .
```

IV. VERSIONS OF BASIC

Note that we have considered the standard form of BASIC, which can be run on most types and sizes computers. Frequently, the BASIC program is interpreted, rather than compiled, so that any errors are indicated right after the line that contains the syntax errors.

```
10 INPUT A,B,C
20 LET D = A+B+C
30 PRINT D(

SYNTAX ERROR D(
```

There are numerous versions of extended BASIC. In one version, for example, an IF-THEN need not cause a branch; instead, a command could be executed.

```
10 IF C = 0 THEN T = T + 1
```

Moreover, statements can be strung together on a single line, separated only by a semicolon or other delineator, depending on the particular version of extended BASIC.

```
10 INPUT A,B,C; LET D = (A+B+C)/3;PRINT D
```

Some versions of BASIC allow longer variable names. Hence, HOURS or COUNT may be used in place of H or C.

The version of BASIC you have learned will work on all computers. If you check your user manual, however, you may find that there are numerous extensions available to you.

Practice Programs

1. Write a program to calculate the total amount of money it will cost to raise a child from birth to age 18. Assume a cost of $3700 per year and an inflation rate of 8% per year. Space output evenly and neatly across the page. Use the PRINT ... USING option.

2. Read in data consisting of the following fields for each order placed:
   Item Description; Unit Price; Qty Ordered.
   Write a program to print the following for each order:
   Item Description; Total Price; Discount; Net Price.
   Total Price is equal to Qty Ordered times the Unit Price.
   Discount is 2% on orders with a quantity of 20 or less; 5% on orders with a quantity between 20 and 50; 7% on orders with a quantity of 50 or more.
   Net Price is equal to the Total Price minus the Discount.
   Printed output should include headings and edited results.

3. Write a program using the INT function to round a field called A to the nearest integer.

4. Write a program using the TAB function to print a diagonal line of X's across a page:

```
    X
      X
        X
          X
            X
```

5. Write a program using the TAB function to print your last name using X's across the page. For example, the name STERN could be printed as follows:

```
XXXXX     XXXXX     XXXXX     XXXXX     X     X
X             X     X         X     X   XX    X
XXXXX         X     XXXX      XXXXX     X X   X
    X         X     X         X     X   X   XX
XXXXX         X     XXXXX     X     X   X     X
```

6. Write a program that will simulate the tossing of a coin randomly and print the results of each toss—HEADS or TAILS.

7. Write a program to read in values for N and print "INTEGER" if N has an integer value and "NUMBER WITH DECIMAL COMPONENT" if N is not an integer.

PROGRAMMING IN HIGH-LEVEL LANGUAGES: A COMPARATIVE APPROACH

The purpose of this appendix is to familiarize the student with some of the features of the most commonly used programming languages. The following languages are considered.

- COBOL
- FORTRAN
- BASIC
- RPG

We focus on the basic structure of the languages and provide an illustration and in-depth explanation of the same task programmed in each language. This method provides the student with a basic understanding of the advantages and disadvantages of each language. In Chapter 12 and Appendix A BASIC is considered in more detail in an effort to provide the student with enough information so that he or she can actually program in that language.

Programs may be read by a computer in either a batch or an on-line mode. When programs are entered in a **batch mode,** they are normally keyed onto cards, tape, or floppy disk. The computer then translates the program and if there are no major errors it can then execute the program.

When programs are entered in an **on-line mode,** they are entered on a terminal. This mode is generally easier for the programmer. Changes can be made directly to the keyed entries and programs can be stored for future processing. On-line programming, however, usually requires a data communications network that is not always available for simple testing of programs.

BASIC is almost always written using a terminal, whereas programs written in COBOL, FORTRAN, and RPG are entered in either batch or on-line mode.

I. COBOL

A. The Nature of Structured COBOL

COBOL is the most widely used commercial programming language. You will recall that COBOL is an abbreviation for *COmmon Business Oriented Language.* It is a business-oriented language designed specifically for commercial applications. It is also a computer language that is universal, or common to many computers. The universality of COBOL allows computer users great flexibility. A company is free to use computers of different manufacturers while retaining a single programming language. Similarly, conversion from one model computer to a more advanced or newer one presents no great problem. Computers of a future generation will also be equipped to use COBOL.

Thus the meaning of the word COBOL suggests two of its basic advantages. It is common to most computers and it is commercially oriented. There are, however, additional reasons for its being such a popular language.

COBOL is an English-like language. All instructions are coded using English words rather than complex codes. To add two numbers together, for example, we use the word ADD. Similarly, the rules for programming in COBOL conform to many of the rules for writing in English, making it a relatively simple language to learn. It therefore becomes significantly easier to train programmers.

Thus the English-like quality of COBOL makes it easy to **write** programs. Similarly, this quality makes COBOL programs easier to **read.** Such programs can generally be understood by non-data-processing personnel.

With a brief introduction to the language, a student can effectively read a program and understand its nature. COBOL's similarity to English significantly reduces the communication gap between the programmer and the user. Both can work jointly to correct or improve the logic of a COBOL program.

COBOL also lends itself to the structured approach so that programs are easy to read and modify.

B. Basic Structure of a COBOL Program

1. The Coding Sheet

COBOL programs are written on coding or program sheets (Figure B.1). The coding sheet has space for 80 columns of information. Each line of the sheet will be entered on one line of a terminal.

Similarly, each line may be keypunched into one card; the standard COBOL card (Figure B.2) may be used for this purpose.

Thus, for *every line* written on the coding sheet, we may obtain *one punched card or one terminal program line.* The entire program is called the COBOL source program. Note that *all* programming languages utilize specially designed coding sheets, except PL/1 and BASIC, free-form languages that do not require characters to be in any specific positions. Similarly, all source programs consist of instructions keyed from coding sheets, where one line is either (1) keyed into one record or (2) typed on a terminal.

Let us examine the COBOL program sheet more closely. The top of the form has identifying fields such as System, Program, and so on, which are used to maintain control of the coding sheets but which actually have no effect on the program. Only the numbered items become part of the program.

IIII▶   **COBOL Program Sheets**

Item	Meaning	Keyed Into Columns
Sequence	Includes page and line number—optional, with no effect on program	1-6

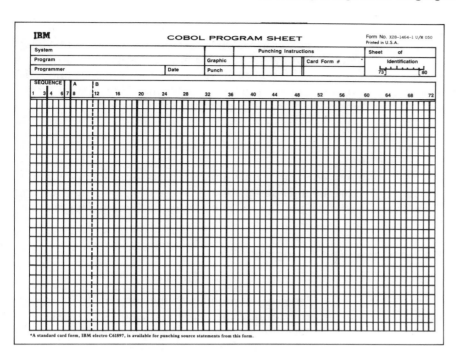

Figure B.1
COBOL coding sheet.

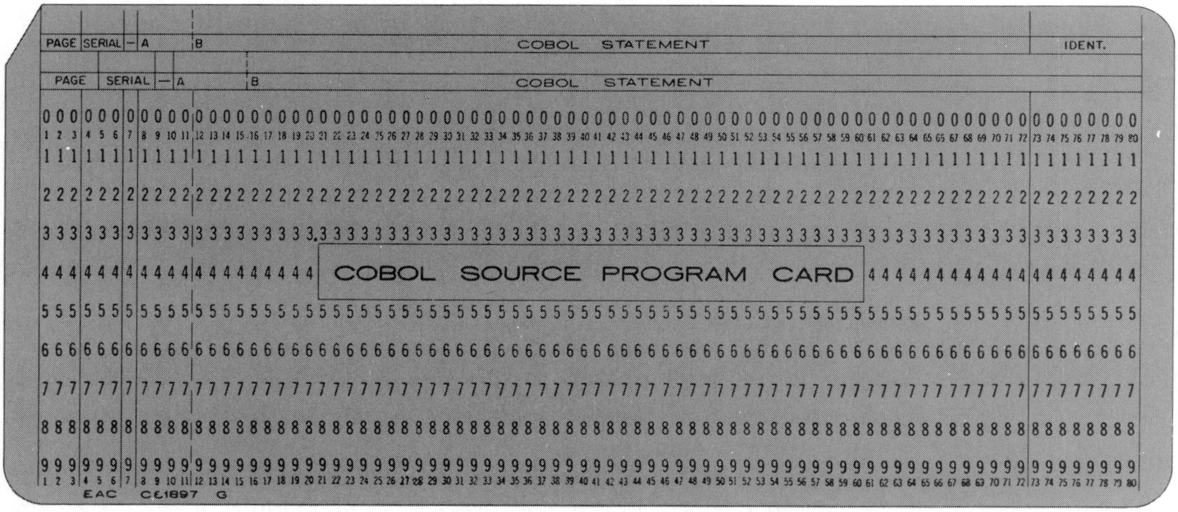

Figure B.2
COBOL source program
card.

Item	Meaning	Keyed Into Columns
COBOL statement	Includes actual instructions	8-72
Identification (upper right corner)	Includes an identifying code, usually a number; optional	73-80

The identification number, positions 73 to 80, and the page and serial number, positions 1 to 6, are optional entries in a COBOL program. Both fields, however, can be extremely useful should the source program be misplaced or lost.

Page and serial (line) numbers on each line are advisable. If page and serial numbers are supplied, it is also an easy task to make insertions in their proper places. Note that some coding sheets preprint the serial numbers to assist the programmer.

2. The Four Divisions

Every COBOL program consists of four separate **divisions.** Each division is written in an English-like manner designed to decrease programming effort and to facilitate the understanding of a program by users. Each of the four divisions has a specific function.

Four Divisions of a COBOL Program

Name	Function
IDENTIFICATION DIVISION	■ Identifies the program to the computer ■ Provides documentary information that assists users in understanding the nature of the program and the techniques it will employ
ENVIRONMENT DIVISION	■ Describes the computer equipment and features to be used in the program
DATA DIVISION	■ Describes input and output formats used in the program ■ Defines constants and storage areas necessary for processing data
PROCEDURE DIVISION	■ Contains instructions and logic flow necessary to create output from input data ■ Coded directly from flowchart, pseudocode, or other planning tool

C. An Illustrative COBOL Program

1. Definition of the Problem

A computer center of a large company is assigned the task of calculating weekly wages for all non-salaried personnel. You recall that, to process data, the input must be in a form that is acceptable or understandable to the computer. Punched cards, magnetic tape, and magnetic disk are common forms of input to a computer system.

Thus the employee data will be received from the Payroll Department in the form of time cards. These time cards will contain three fields as indicated in Figure B.3. For purposes of a COBOL program these fields will be called:

Field	Length
EMPLOYEE-NAME	20
HOURS-WORKED	2
HOURLY-RATE	3 (1 integer, 2 decimal)

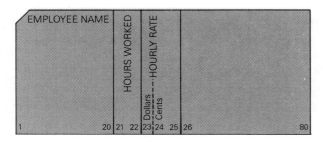

Field	Length
EMPLOYEE-NAME	20
HOURS-WORKED	2
HOURLY-RATE	3 (1 integer, 2 decimal)

Figure B.3
Input card format for sample program.

The three fields of data will be transcribed or keypunched onto a punched card that will be accepted as input to the information processing system.

Card columns 1 to 20 are reserved for each EMPLOYEE-NAME. If any name contains less than 20 characters, the low-order, or rightmost, positions are left blank. Similarly, HOURS-WORKED will be placed in columns 21 to 22 and HOURLY-RATE in columns 23 to 25. The HOURLY-RATE figure, as a dollars and cents amount, is to be interpreted as a two-decimal field. That is, 125 in columns 23 to 25 is to be interpreted by the computer as 1.25. The decimal point is not generally punched into a card used for commercial applications since it would waste a column. We will see that this method of implying or assuming decimal points is easily handled in COBOL.

A deck of employee cards, with the above format, will be keypunched and then read as input to the computer. WEEKLY-WAGES will be calculated by the computer as:

```
WEEKLY-WAGES = HOURS-WORKED X HOURLY-RATE
```

The computed figure, however, *cannot* generally be added to the input record. That is, with card or tape processing we cannot easily create output data on an input record.[1]

We will create, then, an output file that contains all input data in addition to the computed wage figure for each record. The output PAYROLL-FILE will be placed on a magnetic tape with the record format shown in Figure B.4. At a later date, the tape will be used to create payroll checks.

Thus the input to the system will be called EMPLOYEE-CARDS. The computer will calculate WEEKLY-WAGES from the two input fields HOURS-WORKED and HOURLY-RATE. The input data along with the computed figure will be used to create the output tape called PAYROLL-FILE.

---

[1]Disk processing can be used to simply add additional data to input records.

Figure B.4
Output tape format for sample program.

2. The Program

Once the input and output record formats have been clearly and precisely defined as in Figures B.3 and B.4 and the logic has been determined, the program may be written. You recall that a program is a set of instructions and specifications that operates on input to produce output. Figure B.5 is a simplified COBOL program that will operate on employee cards to create a payroll tape file with the computed wages.

Notice that the program is written in an English-like language. Note also that the program is divided into **four major divisions.** The IDENTIFICATION, ENVIRONMENT, DATA, and PROCEDURE DIVISIONS are coded on lines 01, 03, 07, and 22, respectively. Every COBOL program must contain these four divisions in the above order. Each must appear on a line by itself, with no other entries, and must be followed by a period. Punctuation in COBOL is just as important as it is in English.

a. Identification Division.   In this program, the IDENTIFICATION DIVISION has, as its only entry, the PROGRAM-ID. That is, the IDENTIFICATION DI-VISION of this program merely serves to identify the program.

b. Environment Division.   The ENVIRONMENT DIVISION assigns the input and output files to specific devices in the INPUT-OUTPUT SECTION. EM-PLOYEE-CARDS, the name assigned to the input file, will be processed by a card reader. Similarly, PAYROLL-FILE is the output file assigned to a specific tape drive.

c. Data Division.   The DATA DIVISION describes, in detail, the type of files and the field designations within each record. The input and output areas in the CPU are fully described in the DATA DIVISION in the FILE SECTION. The File Description, or FD, for EMPLOYEE-CARDS indicates that identifying labels are not needed and that the card format will be called EMPLOYEE-RECORD. This record includes three input fields called EMPLOYEE-NAME, HOURS-WORKED, and HOURLY-RATE. Each field has a corresponding PICTURE clause denoting the size and type of data that will appear in the field.

Input File: Employee Cards

Field	Picture	Meaning
EMPLOYEE-NAME	A(20)	A—alphabetic field (20)—20 positions
HOURS-WORKED	99	9—numeric field two 9s—two positions *Note:* 99 is same as 9(2).

COBOL Program Sheet

System				Punching Instructions						Sheet	of
Program FIRST SAMPLE PROGRAM			Graphic						Card # Form	Identification	
Programmer N. STERN		Date	Punch							73	80

Sequence		Cont.	A	B	COBOL Statement

```
001 01    IDENTIFICATION DIVISION.
001 02    PROGRAM-ID. SAMPLE.
001 03    ENVIRONMENT DIVISION.
001 04    INPUT-OUTPUT SECTION.
001 05    FILE-CONTROL.    SELECT EMPLOYEE-CARDS ASSIGN TO READER.
001 06                    SELECT PAYROLL-FILE ASSIGN TO TAPE-1.
001 07    DATA DIVISION.
001 08    FILE SECTION.
001 09    FD  EMPLOYEE-CARDS  LABEL RECORDS ARE OMITTED.
001 10    01  EMPLOYEE-RECORD.
001 11        05  EMPLOYEE-NAME        PICTURE A(20).
001 12        05  HOURS-WORKED         PICTURE 9(2).
001 13        05  HOURLY-RATE          PICTURE 9V99.
001 14    FD  PAYROLL-FILE    LABEL RECORDS ARE OMITTED.
001 15    01  PAYROLL-RECORD.
001 16        05  NAME-OUT            PICTURE A(20).
001 17        05  HOURS-OUT           PICTURE 9(20).
001 18        05  RATE-OUT            PICTURE 9V99.
001 19        05  WEEKLY-WAGES        PICTURE 999V99.
001 20    WORKING-STORAGE SECTION.
001 21    01  EOF                     PICTURE 9    VALUE 0.
001 22    PROCEDURE DIVISION.
001 23        OPEN INPUT EMPLOYEE-CARDS, OUTPUT PAYROLL-FILE.
001 24        READ EMPLOYEE-CARDS AT END MOVE 1 TO EOF.
001 25        PERFORM WAGE-ROUTINE UNTIL EOF = 1.
001 26        CLOSE EMPLOYEE-CARDS, PAYROLL-FILE.
001 27        STOP RUN.
001 28       ROUTINE.
001 29        E EMPLOYEE-NAME TO NAME-OUT.
001 30        HOURS-WORKED TO HOURS-OUT.
001 31        OURLY-RATE TO RATE-OUT.
001 32        Y HOURS-WORKED BY HOURLY-RATE GIVING WEEKLY-WAGES.
001 33        YROLL-RECORD.
001 34        OYEE-CARDS AT END MOVE 1 TO EOF.
```

Figure B.5
Simplified COBOL program for creating a payroll tape file.

Meaning

positions
assumed decimal point after
, 125 will be interpreted
s 1.25)

does not appear on
t is nonetheless implied.

Similarly, the output file called PAYROLL-FILE does not use labels and has a record format called PAYROLL-RECORD. PAYROLL-RECORD is subdivided into four fields, each with an appropriate PICTURE clause. The first three fields, NAME-OUT, HOURS-OUT, and RATE-OUT will be taken directly from each input record, using a MOVE statement. The last field, WEEKLY-WAGES, with three integer, or dollar, positions, and two decimal, or cents, positions, must be computed. Since HOURS-WORKED has two integer positions and HOURLY-RATE has one such position, *three* integer positions are needed for the product of these two fields.

If any constants or work areas were required in the program, they, too, would be described in the WORKING-STORAGE SECTION of the DATA DIVISION. Notice that a field called EOF with a VALUE of 0 has been defined in this program. We will see how this field is used in the PROCEDURE DIVISION.

d. Procedure Division.   The PROCEDURE DIVISION contains the set of instructions or operations to be performed by the computer. Each instruction is executed in the order in which it appears, unless a PERFORM statement alters the sequence. The first PROCEDURE DIVISION entry is:

```
OPEN INPUT EMPLOYEE-CARDS, OUTPUT PAYROLL-FILE,
```

This instruction accesses the files and indicates to the computer which file is input and which is output.

The next instruction in the PROCEDURE DIVISION is:

```
READ EMPLOYEE-CARDS AT END MOVE 1 TO EOF,
```

This is an instruction that causes the computer to read **one** data into storage. If there are no more cards to be read when this statement is ted, a "1" will be moved to the field called EOF; otherwise EOF remains ed. In most instances, the first attempt to read a card causes data to b ted from a single record to storage and the next instruction to be ex

The next instruction is the following:

```
PERFORM WAGE-ROUTINE UNTIL EOF = 1,
```

This instruction will cause all the statements specified wi labeled WAGE-ROUTINE (beginning on line 28) to be until EOF = 1. A quick glance at the statements within dicates that the instructions will be executed until there which time a "1" is moved to EOF.

Once EOF = 1, the statement to be executed nex following the PERFORM. That is, PERFORM WAGE-R 1 causes execution of WAGE-ROUTINE until there ar point control returns to the statement following the P on lines 26 and 27, CLOSE and STOP RUN, are e have been processed at WAGE-ROUTINE.

The first instruction, OPEN, activates the files. The next instruction, READ, reads a single record. At WAGE-ROUTINE, the first record is processed and subsequent records are read and processed until there are no more input records. Then the CLOSE, which deactivates the files, and the STOP RUN are executed and the program is terminated. The five steps—OPEN, READ, PERFORM, CLOSE, and STOP—represent the main body or main module of the PRO-CEDURE DIVISION. The PERFORM statement is used in all structured COBOL programs to ensure that control is always retained in the main module.

Let us look more closely at the instructions to be executed at the WAGE-ROUTINE paragraph. First, EMPLOYEE-NAME of the *first* card, which was read with the READ statement on line 24, is moved to NAME-OUT of the output area. HOURS-WORKED and HOURLY-RATE of this first card are also moved to the output area. WEEKLY-WAGES, an output field, is then calculated by multiplying HOURS-WORKED by HOURLY-RATE.

After the data has been moved to the output area, a WRITE command is executed. This WRITE command takes the information in the output area and places it on magnetic tape.

The above set of instructions will process the *first* card and create one tape record. The READ statement is then executed and data from another card is transmitted to storage.

The sequence of instructions within WAGE-ROUTINE is executed under the control of the PERFORM statement on line 25. That is, execution of WAGE-ROUTINE instructions will be repeated until EOF = 1, which will only occur after all cards have been processed. Hence, after the second card has been read, WAGE-ROUTINE will be executed again, the input data moved, the cal-culation performed, a tape record written, and a third card read. This sequence continues until there are no additional cards available for processing, at which point the instruction on line 26, the CLOSE, is executed.

Figure B.5, then, represents a sample COBOL program in its entirety. This program will run on any commercial computer with only slight modifications possibly required in the ENVIRONMENT DIVISION. Since this division indicates the computer equipment utilized in the program, it is frequently machine-de-pendent, that is, non-standard.

Figure B.5 is an illustration of the program coded by the programmer. These sheets must then be keyed on a terminal, or transcribed into a machine-readable form (cards, tape, etc.) and then run on the computer.

Figure B.6 is a sample program listing as prepared by a computer from the source program during compilation or translation into the machine-language equivalent.

An analysis of the program reveals several essential points. The English-like manner and the structural organization of a COBOL program make it com-paratively easy to learn. Similarly, the ease with which a COBOL program may be read by users with only minimal exposure to the language makes it a distinct asset to most information processing installations. Note, however, that COBOL, unlike the remaining languages we consider, is very wordy, requiring much writing. Other languages are more compact, with fewer rules and words to be coded by the programmer.

```
00101   IDENTIFICATION DIVISION,
00102   PROGRAM-ID, SAMPLE,
00103   ENVIRONMENT DIVISION,
00104   INPUT-OUTPUT SECTION,
00105   FILE-CONTROL, SELECT EMPLOYEE-CARDS ASSIGN TO READER,
00106                 SELECT PAYROLL-FILE ASSIGN TO TAPE-1,
00107   DATA DIVISION,
00108   FILE SECTION,
00109   FD   EMPLOYEE-CARDS   LABEL RECORDS ARE OMITTED,
00110   01   EMPLOYEE-RECORD,
00111        05   EMPLOYEE-NAME        PICTURE A(20),
00112        05   HOURS-WORKED         PICTURE 9(2),
00113        05   HOURLY-RATE          PICTURE 9V99,
00114   FD   PAYROLL-FILE    LABEL RECORDS ARE OMITTED,
00115   01   PAYROLL-RECORD,
00116        05   NAME-OUT             PICTURE A(20),
00117        05   HOURS-OUT            PICTURE 9(2),
00118        05   RATE-OUT             PICTURE 9V99,
00119        05   WEEKLY-WAGES         PICTURE 999V99,
00120   WORKING-STORAGE SECTION,
00121   01   EOF                       PICTURE 9 VALUE 0,
00122   PROCEDURE DIVISION,
00123        OPEN INPUT EMPLOYEE-CARDS, OUTPUT PAYROLL-FILE,
00124        READ EMPLOYEE-CARDS AT END MOVE 1 TO EOF,
00125        PERFORM WAGE-ROUTINE UNTIL EOF = 1,
00126        CLOSE EMPLOYEE-CARDS, PAYROLL-FILE,
00127        STOP RUN,
00128   WAGE-ROUTINE,
00129        MOVE EMPLOYEE-NAME TO NAME-OUT,
00130        MOVE HOURS-WORKED TO HOURS-OUT,
00131        MOVE HOURLY-RATE TO RATE-OUT,
00132        MULTIPLY HOURS-WORKED BY HOURLY-RATE GIVING WEEKLY-WAGES,
00133        WRITE PAYROLL-RECORD,
00134        READ EMPLOYEE-CARDS AT END MOVE 1 TO EOF,
```

Figure B.6
Sample COBOL program listing.

The above COBOL program has been coded using *structured programming* techniques. These techniques are designed to:

IIII➡ **Structured Programming Features**

1. Make the program more readable.
2. Facilitate the debugging process.
3. Simplify the logical control in the program by eliminating GO TO or branch statements.

Note that the first series of steps in the PROCEDURE DIVISION, called the main module, controls the functions of the entire program. All other paragraphs are executed with the use of PERFORM statements that return control to the main module.

Self-Evaluating Quiz

1. The word COBOL is an abbreviation for _____.
2. COBOL is a common language in the sense that _____.
3. COBOL is a business-oriented language in the sense that _____.
4. All COBOL programs are composed of _____.
5. The names of these four divisions in the order in which they must be coded are _____, _____, _____, and _____.
6. The function of the IDENTIFICATION DIVISION is to _____.
7. The function of the ENVIRONMENT DIVISION is to _____.
8. The function of the DATA DIVISION is to _____.
9. The function of the PROCEDURE DIVISION is to _____.

Solutions

1. *COmmon Business Oriented Language*
2. it may be used on many different computers
3. it makes use of ordinary business terminology
4. four divisions
5. IDENTIFICATION
   ENVIRONMENT
   DATA
   PROCEDURE
6. identify the program
7. describe the equipment to be used in the program
8. describe the input, output, constants, and work areas used in the program
9. define the instructions and operations necessary to convert input data to output

II. FORTRAN

FORTRAN is a computer language that, like COBOL, is universal, or common to many computers. The name FORTRAN is an acronym for *FOR*mula *TRAN*-slator, suggesting that this language is particularly suited for writing programs that deal primarily with formulas. FORTRAN is widely used for scientific and engineering applications. Notwithstanding this fact, it is also true that FORTRAN is utilized to program many traditional business applications.

The purpose of this section is twofold.

1. To enable a student to read and understand simple FORTRAN programs.
2. To explore typical business applications that are programmed in FORTRAN.

A. The Nature of FORTRAN

The essence of the FORTRAN language is that most instructions are written in terms of mathematical formulas or expressions. Whereas in COBOL we might say:

```
MULTIPLY HOURS-WORKED BY HOURLY-RATE GIVING WEEKLY-WAGES
```

in FORTRAN we would use the following instruction to accomplish the same result.

```
WAGES = HOURS * RATE
```

Notice that in COBOL the instruction reads like an English sentence, whereas in FORTRAN we have what appears to be an equation.

To demonstrate the nature of this language, we present, in Figure B.7, a simplified FORTRAN program to calculate weekly wages for employees. This program is equivalent to the COBOL program presented at the beginning of this appendix.

Figure B.7
FORTRAN program for sample problem 1.

```
C       THIS PROGRAM ACCOMPLISHES THE SAME THING AS THE
C       COBOL PROGRAM AT THE BEGINNING OF THIS APPENDIX
        DIMENSION NAME(5)
     5  READ (1,100,END=99) NAME,HOURS,RATE
        WAGES = HOURS * RATE
        WRITE (6,110) NAME,HOURS,RATE,WAGES
        GO TO 1
    99  END FILE 6
        STOP
   100  FORMAT (5A4,F2.0,F3.2)
   110  FORMAT (5A4,F3.0,F4.2,F6.2)
        END
```

An explanation of this program is as follows.

Line　*Statement and Explanation*

1st　`C THIS PROGRAM ACCOMPLISHES THE SAME THING AS THE`
2nd　`C COBOL PROGRAM AT THE BEGINNING OF THIS APPENDIX`

The "C" in column 1 of each line indicates that the entry contains only comments to clarify the program for someone reading it. These lines have *no* effect on the logic of the program itself.

3rd   DIMENSION NAME (5)

This instruction is technically necessary, since FORTRAN compilers generally do not allow an alphanumeric field as large as 20 positions to be read in and stored in *one* field. It is therefore necessary in this program to instruct the computer to set up five adjacent fields of four positions each to hold all of the data from the input field (NAME). In this way, we can accommodate our 20-position NAME field.

4th

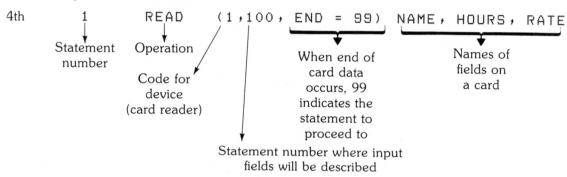

5th   WAGES = HOURS * RATE

This line is a formula to perform the desired calculation. Note the use of the asterisk in place of the multiplication sign.

6th   WRITE (6,110) NAME, HOURS, RATE, WAGES

This is an instruction to tell the computer to write on tape unit 6 the following fields: NAME, HOURS, RATE, and WAGES, which are further described as to field specifications in statement number 110.

7th   GO TO 1

We have a branch back to statement number 1 to repeat the process if there are input records left to process.

8th   99 END FILE 6

This statement is one to which a branch occurs after there are no more records to be processed. That is, the END = 99 in statement 1 causes a branch to statement number 99 after all input records have been processed. The END FILE command in this statement is an instruction that causes the computer to place an end of file indicator on the tape.

9th   STOP

When this instruction is executed, all records have been processed and control is returned to the supervisor.

10th   100 FORMAT (5A4, F2.0, F3.2)

The purpose of the FORMAT statement is to describe the specifications or format of the input or output, in detail. This FORMAT, numbered 100, is associated with the input statement READ (1,100, . . .). The 100 in the READ statement indicates that the FORMAT statement is on line number 100.

In the FORMAT statement, the *first* specification of 5A4 indicates that the first five adjacent groups of four positions each contain alphanumeric (A) data pertaining to NAME, the first field listed in the read statement. That is, columns 1 to 20 in the card contain this data. Since the FORTRAN compiler does not usually allow for an alphanumeric specification larger than four positions, such as A20, we must accommodate large fields by grouping the data in some manner that will yield the desired size. A specification of 10A2, for example, would achieve the same result as the specification used above. However, a different statement—for example, DIMENSION NAME (10)—would have to be put at the beginning of the program.

The next specification is the F, or floating-point, specification, which indicates the length of the field *on the card* and the number of decimal positions. In this case, the F2.0 indicates that the second field (HOURS) will be two positions long with no (0) decimal positions. The last specification, F3.2, indicates that the third field (RATE) will be three positions long and should be stored as a decimal number with two digits to the right of the decimal point.

Note that in FORTRAN a decimal point may appear in the input or simply be implied. Thus, F4.2 could be appropriate for input of 1234, which would be interpreted as 12.34; also, F4.2 would be appropriate for 1.23, where the decimal point is part of the input.

11th   110 FORMAT (5A4, F3.0, F4.2, F6.2)

This FORMAT describes the output listed in the WRITE statement: WRITE (6,110) NAME, HOURS, RATE, WAGES. We are asking the computer to store NAME, HOURS, RATE, and WAGES on tape for the card just processed. The FORMAT statement describes each of these fields.

The specification 5A4 has the same meaning as in the previous FORMAT. The second specification (F3.0) indicates that HOURS is to occupy three positions on the tape—two integers *and* the decimal point, with no (0) decimal digits after it. Note that the decimal point is *always* included in the output. The next specification of F4.2 indicates that RATE is to occupy four positions on the tape—one integer, the decimal point, and two decimal digits. The last specification of F6.2 describes how WAGES is to be stored. It is to occupy six positions, including a decimal point with two digits to the right. Note that in FORTRAN, unlike COBOL, there is no convenient way of storing a field on tape with an implied decimal point to separate dollars from cents. In FORTRAN, such a field is usually stored with the decimal point actually included.

12th   END

The END statement signifies to the computer that there are no more statements in this program.

Now that we have seen the structure of a FORTRAN program, we discuss some programs that involve slightly more sophisticated logic in order to illustrate some of the common types of FORTRAN statements. As the next illustration, we will read in cards with the weekly sales figures for each salesperson and produce a report that shows commissions that have been earned. The sales cards and the sales report have the formats shown in Figure B.8.

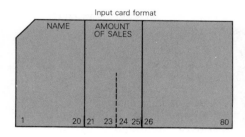

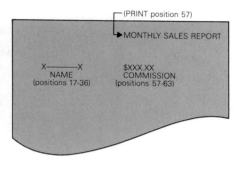

Figure B.8
Input and output formats
for sample problem 2.

```
C       THIS PROGRAM TAKES RECORDS WITH THE WEEKLY SALES
C       FIGURES FOR EACH SALESPERSON, AND PRODUCES A REPORT
C       WHICH SHOWS COMMISSIONS THAT HAVE BEEN EARNED
        DIMENSION NAME(5)
        WRITE (3,5)
    5   FORMAT ('1',56X,'MONTHLY SALES REPORT')
    7   READ (1,10,END=100)NAME,SALES
   10   FORMAT (5A4,F5.2)
        IF (SALES.GT.100.00)GO TO 20
        IF (SALES.GT.50.00)GO TO 30
        COMMIS = 000.00
        GO TO 40
   20   COMMIS = SALES * .03
        GO TO 40
   30   COMMIS = SALES * .02
   40   WRITE (3,50) NAME,COMMIS
   50   FORMAT ('0',16X,5A4,20X,'$',F6.2)
        GO TO 7
  100   STOP
        END
```

Figure B.9
Coding for sample
problem 2.

Figure B.9 shows the coding for this program.

This program points out some interesting features of FORTRAN not encountered in Figure B.7.

1. The first WRITE instruction tells the computer to print out a specified heading. Notice that there are no field names indicated next to the WRITE statement. However, the associated format, statement number 5, tells the computer what to do. The first specification, '1', is a code for carriage control
   purposes that tells the computer to begin the report on the first line of a new
   page. The next specification, 56X, tells the computer to skip 56 positions on
   the first line and then begin the heading (between quotation marks) in the
   57th print position.
2. After the READ instruction and the associated FORMAT statement, we tell
   the computer that IF SALES are greater than (.GT.) 100.00, a branch to
   statement 20 should be executed. If it is not, the computer automatically
   goes to the next instruction, which, in this case, is another test.

3. Statement 40 instructs the computer to write out the values for NAME and COMMIS in accordance with the specifications in statement 50. This statement, shown below, is explained as follows.

```
50 FORMAT ('0', 16X, 5A4, 20X, '$', F6.2)
```

The first specification, '0', is a code for carriage control purposes that tells the computer to double space before printing the line. The 16X tells the computer to skip the first 16 print positions on the line and then print the NAME field, which is a 20-position alphanumeric (A) field. After the NAME field, 20 positions are skipped (20X), a dollar sign is printed, and right next to the dollar sign, COMMIS will print out with three integers, a decimal point, and two decimal positions.

B. Comparison of FORTRAN and COBOL

At this point, we can make several observations about FORTRAN as compared to COBOL.

1. COBOL is a more structured language than FORTRAN, in the sense that COBOL has four DIVISIONS (IDENTIFICATION, ENVIRONMENT, DATA, and PROCEDURE) that *must* be included in every program in the sequence specified. FORTRAN, on the other hand, is more flexible. There are no particular statements that must be included.

2. A program in FORTRAN, being generally more mathematical in nature, may not be as easy for a user to understand as one in COBOL, which is similar to English. The following comparison dramatizes this point.

```
COBOL                        FORTRAN

IF SALES-AMT IS                  IF (SALES .GT. 100.00) GO TO 20
GREATER THAN 100.00          .
MULTIPLY .03 BY SALES-       .
AMT GIVING COMMISSION.       .
                             20 COMMIS = SALES*.03
```

Notice, for example, that the code .GT. in FORTRAN is not as easy to read as the words GREATER THAN in COBOL. That is, it requires prior familiarity with a code rather than simple understanding of English.

3. In FORTRAN, each field name can consist of a maximum of 6 characters, whereas in COBOL the maximum is 30 characters. This limitation often results in abbreviated field names in FORTRAN that may not be as self-explanatory for the user as corresponding names in COBOL. For example, in COBOL we might call a field YEAR-TO-DATE-GROSS-EARNINGS or perhaps Y-T-D-GROSS-EARN. In FORTRAN, the best we can do is something like YTDGRS.

4. From the examples presented in FORTRAN, you may have noticed the amount of effort required by the programmer to code FORMAT statements that precisely specify what the input or output looks like. In COBOL, with the aid of PICTURE clauses, it is usually easier to describe input or output

specifications. However, although FORTRAN is considered to be cumbersome in the area of input/output specifications, it is much easier to code arithmetic operations in this language. That is, arithmetic instructions are less verbose and easier to write than in COBOL. In addition, FORTRAN enables the programmer to include complex mathematical functions that cannot be included in a COBOL program. In some business applications, such as sales forecasting, or inventory control, there is often the need to use higher mathematics such as trigonometric functions. For instance, a formula might require the computer to find the cosine of a particular angle. In FORTRAN, we can easily write an instruction such as:

```
Y = COS(X)
```

and the FORTRAN compiler, or translator, will recognize what is meant by the operation "COS." In COBOL, this cannot be done very easily, since the COBOL compiler is not equipped to recognize the code COS, or most other mathematical functions.

   Although a programmer can write instructions that will allow the COBOL compiler to compute the cosine, this job obviously takes more effort than using FORTRAN, where it can be performed with the use of a function. It is possible to write part of a program in COBOL and part in FORTRAN assuming that the computer has both compilers.

C. Understanding More Advanced FORTRAN Programs

In the following paragraphs, we present some additional concepts of FORTRAN that allow the student to more easily understand and review FORTRAN programs for business applications.

1. Mathematical Operations

The following list shows the fundamental mathematical operations and the symbols used in FORTRAN.

Symbol	Operation
**	Exponentiation
*	Multiplication
/	Division
+	Addition
−	Subtraction

   Exponentiation involves raising some number to a power, or multiplying a number by itself a specified number of times. That is, 2^3 is represented as 2**3 in FORTRAN and is calculated as the number 2 multiplied by itself 3 times (2^3 = 2 × 2 × 2 = 8). For example, if a programmer wishes the computer to add A^2 and B^2 to obtain the result X, where A, B, and X are fields, the following instruction would be coded in FORTRAN.

$$X = A**2 + B**2$$

Similarly, the FORTRAN expression:

$$ANSWER = (AMT1 + AMT2 + AMT3)/3.0$$

calculates the average of the three fields—AMT1, AMT2, AMT3. Suppose the parentheses were omitted from the above arithmetic expression. The question is whether this instruction would still calculate the average. That is, the expression:

$$ANSWER = AMT1 + AMT2 + AMT3/3.0$$

might reduce to either of the following two formulas.

$$ANSWER = \frac{AMT1 + AMT2 + AMT3}{3.0}$$

or

$$ANSWER = AMT1 + AMT2 + \frac{AMT3}{3.0}$$

If the parentheses were not included, the average would *not* be calculated properly. ANSWER would, in fact, equal

$$AMT1 + AMT2 + \frac{AMT3}{3.0}$$

The reason has to do with the **hierarchy of operations:** that is, the computer does not necessarily perform operations in the order in which the expression is read. The basic rules of hierarchy are as follows.

Hierarchy Rules

1. Any operations within parentheses, if included, are performed first.
2. In the absence of parentheses, operations are normally performed in the following order.
   I. Exponentiation (**)
   II and III. Multiplication (*) or Division (/), whichever appears first.
   IV and V. Addition (+) or Subtraction (−), whichever appears first.

Exponentiation is performed first. After that, the computer looks at the mathematical expression beginning at the equal sign and proceeds to the right. It finds the next highest operation in the formula according to the hierarchy rules, and then it performs that operation. Therefore, the FORTRAN statement mentioned above is evaluated as follows.

$$ANSWER = \underbrace{AMT1 + AMT2}_{\text{2nd operation}} + \underbrace{AMT3/3.0}_{}$$

Thus, we have:

$$\frac{AMT3}{3.0} + AMT1 + AMT2$$

This explains why parentheses are required to obtain the correct formula for the average. As indicated in the hierarchy rules above, multiplication and division both have equal priority below exponentiation, while addition and subtraction both have equal priority below multiplication and division. It is sometimes best to include parentheses around complex calculations when there is some doubt as to how the computer will evaluate the operations.

2. Understanding Why Equations Are Not Equations

A very common FORTRAN statement is of the following type.

```
N = N + 1
```

This is obviously not a valid equation in the mathematical sense. That is, normally N cannot be equal to 1 more than N. However, the above *is* a valid FORTRAN statement. That is, we set N equal to one more than the original N. Thus, if N = 5 and the FORTRAN statement N = N + 1 is executed, N is then set equal to 6. The FORTRAN statement sets the field on the left side of the = sign equal to the result calculated on the right side.

An arithmetic statement in FORTRAN does the following:

1. Performs all computations that are indicated to the right of the equal sign.
2. Takes the final result and moves it to the field whose name is specified to the left of the equal sign. Therefore, the statement N = N + 1 has the following meaning to the computer.
   a. Add 1 to the current value of the field called N.
   b. Take this result and move it to N. In other words, add 1 to N. The statement N = 0 technically abides by the same rules. Since there are no computations involved, the computer simply takes the result indicated at the right of the equal sign (zero) and moves it to the field called N. In essence, N = (constant) is a data transfer operation that moves the constant to the field name. The above expression is used to initialize counters at zero. If, in a FORTRAN program, the programmer wants the computer to count the number of records processed, we might expect to find the following instructions.

```
N = 0
READ (1,3) NAME, SALES
N = N + 1
```

After every record is read, 1 is added to the field N. Thus, at the end of the run N reflects the number of records read.

Self-Evaluating Quiz

1. The name FORTRAN is an acronym for _____.
2. FORTRAN is widely used for _____ problems.
3. While COBOL uses words such as ADD, MULTIPLY, SUBTRACT, DIVIDE to indicate mathematical expressions, FORTRAN uses _____.
4. COBOL instructions read like sentences, while in FORTRAN instructions read like _____.
5. In business areas such as _____, where advanced mathematical concepts are employed, FORTRAN is most often used.
6. (T or F) The expression X = X + 1, although not a valid mathematical expression, is a valid FORTRAN expression.

Solutions

1. *FOR*mula *TRAN*slator
2. scientific or mathematical
3. mathematical symbols
4. mathematical equations
5. sales forecasting
6. T

III. BASIC

A. The Nature of BASIC

Terminals are an exceedingly popular mode of data entry. In addition to entering input, it is possible to write and debug programs with the use of terminals. Commercial organizations, as well as many colleges and universities, have found programming with the use of terminals to be, in many cases, profitable and efficient.

Some programming languages are better suited for terminal processing than others. Since a terminal is a relatively slow method of data entry, BASIC was designed to require minimum coding or keying. Instructions and data formats are simple and require less programming effort than those of most other languages. Similarly, BASIC was not designed to handle sophisticated routines that are required in other languages. Thus, this language may be learned in a relatively short time.

In short, BASIC is the programming language ideally suited for terminal processing in a time-sharing environment. The term BASIC is an abbreviation for *Beginner's All-Purpose Symbolic Instruction Code*, which, by its very name, suggests the major feature of the language—it is ideal for beginners.

BASIC is becoming an increasingly popular language just as terminals are becoming increasingly popular in information processing environments. BASIC is currently being used extensively for the following applications.

Applications of BASIC

1. College campuses
   Many colleges have acquired terminals connected to their central computer system. Programming with the use of these terminals affords the student the unique learning experience of interacting directly with the computer. Most microcomputers can be programmed in BASIC as well.

2. Businesses
   Increasing numbers of business people are provided with access to terminals connected to mainframes or to minis. These people can learn BASIC in a relatively short period and can then write short programs to extract or otherwise process data that is needed quickly.

3. Engineering or scientific applications
   BASIC is used extensively by engineers and scientists to solve problems and perform calculations that are necessary for their work.

BASIC can be regarded as a simplified version of FORTRAN, similar to the latter in format but without all the intricate or sophisticated options. Both languages utilize mathematical notation and, as such, are generally regarded as somewhat scientific in nature. But, like FORTRAN, BASIC may be used effectively for some business problems. In addition, FORTRAN and BASIC are ideally suited for business applications where mathematical or scientific notations are used, such as sales forecasting and graph plotting.

Note that the programmer communicates *directly* with the computer when coding on a terminal in BASIC. Since such programs are almost always short and simplified, they often contain *data* as well as *instructions*. That is, programs in most other languages are usually written so that they can be run by the operations staff in periodic intervals with voluminous input. A Payroll program written in COBOL, for example, may be implemented so that it will be run on a monthly basis with a large number of records. When a programmer, scientist, or businessperson codes a BASIC program on a terminal, it is often a "one-shot" job. That is, a simple BASIC program is coded merely to obtain an output listing and *not* to be run periodically. It also requires minimal input since the keyboard device is far too slow to transmit a voluminous amount of data.

Note, however, that BASIC can be run on a computer *without* the use of a terminal. Thus a program in BASIC can be compiled and translated and utilized for periodic runs in the same manner as COBOL or FORTRAN programs. Because BASIC is so widely used and is simplified enough to serve as an ideal language for the beginner, we have included an entire chapter on it, Chapter 12, which provides the fundamentals of this programming language. In addition, Appendix A focuses on advanced concepts in BASIC. For now, we simply illustrate a sample program to demonstrate the relative simplicity of BASIC.

B. An Illustrative BASIC Program

We have seen sample COBOL and FORTRAN programs that create a tape from employee time cards. The employee cards have the format indicated in Figure

B.3 and the tape has the format indicated in Figure B.4, where

```
WEEKLY-WAGES = HOURS-WORKED X HOURLY-RATE
```

A simple BASIC program run with the use of a terminal cannot usually accept card input nor can it create tape output unless the terminal system contains a card reader as input and a tape drive as output. Usually, the terminal has only a keyboard and some print or video display. We will, then, examine a BASIC program that reads data in from a terminal, determines WEEKLY-WAGES (W), and prints the results on the same terminal.

```
100 INPUT N$, H, R
105 IF H = 99 THEN 999
110 LET W = H * R
120 PRINT N$, H, R, W
130 GO TO 100
999 END
```

Notice that the BASIC program has significantly fewer steps than the program in the other languages. However, although coding is simplified in BASIC, the form of input and output is somewhat limited.

Notice that BASIC is a free-form language, which means that there are no special positions in which instructions must be entered. We can enter instructions anywhere on the line and need not adhere to any formal rules in this regard.

Line Numbers

The left-hand numbers associated with each instruction are called line numbers. Essentially, any numbers that are positive integers may be used, but it is recommended that the numbers selected not be continuous. That is, if during debugging we discover that an instruction was inadvertently omitted between line 100 and 105, we can key in 101, for example, and the computer will automatically insert the instruction in its proper place. Hence line numbers in BASIC are not merely, as in other languages, for sequencing; they actually are an important part of the program itself. Line number 999 is typically used, as a convention, for the last instruction. Let us examine each instruction more carefully. We begin with an INPUT statement.

```
INPUT N$, H, R
```

After the program has been entered, compiled, and listed, it is ready for execution. An executed INPUT statement causes the computer to request the keying in of some input data. Typically, a question mark or a prompt is printed or displayed, which is a signal to the programmer or user that some data must be entered.

The names of input fields in this sample program are N$, H, and R for name, hours worked, and hourly rate respectively. Note that field names are generally more concise and less informative than in other languages. The dollar sign, $, associated with the name field, N$, establishes it as an **alphanumeric field,** one that may contain letters, digits, or even special symbols. We separate input fields by commas. Hence a sample input entry of name, hours worked, and hourly rate might be:

```
PAUL NEWMAN, 15,9.98
```

Note that the rate, R, may be keyed in *with* the decimal point. For example, 1.25 is a valid entry for rate; that is, the decimal point is coded rather than implied or assumed, as in COBOL.

The following, statement 105, tests for an end-of-data indicator.

```
IF H = 99 THEN 999
```

Statement 105 is a conditional statement. It causes a branch to statement number 999, the end of the job, if H, hours worked, contains "99." Hence, to signal the computer that there is no more input or to cause the computer to terminate the run, we enter a value of H equal to 99. We could have chosen any value, such as -1, that could not be used as a valid number for any employee. The IF statement would then be coded as: IF H $= -1$ THEN 999.

A LET statement follows.

```
LET W = H * R
```

This is an arithmetic statement, with * signifying multiplication, as it does in FORTRAN.

Next, we have a PRINT statement.

```
PRINT N$, H, R, W
```

The name, hours worked, hourly rate, and computed wage figure will print for the input supplied.

We then use a GO TO statement.

```
GO TO 100
```

This statement causes a branch back to statement 100, the INPUT statement, and the series of steps is then repeated. This processing continues until a "99" is keyed in for hours worked, which signals a branch to the END statement.

```
END
```

This statement results in the termination of the run.

Self-Evaluating Quiz

1. (T or F) Terminal devices are ideally suited for high-speed interaction with the computer.

2. (T or F) BASIC is a language that is specifically designed for terminal processing in a time-sharing environment.

3. (T or F) BASIC is ideally suited for programming complex business applications, such as Accounts Receivable and Payroll on large-scale systems.

4. (T or F) Many programs written in BASIC are used only once to obtain an answer to a specific question or problem.

5. (T or F) In BASIC, a statement requires a line number only when a branch will be made to that statement.

6. In the statement 20 IF A = 100 THEN 50, the significance of THEN 50 is _____.

7. An INPUT statement causes the computer to print a _____ to signal the user that _____.

Solutions

1. F—Data entry at a terminal is usually slow.

2. T

3. F—BASIC is frequently used for such applications on small systems, however.

4. T

5. F—Each instruction requires a line number.

6. a branch to statement 50 will occur if A is equal to 100

7. ? or some other prompt; data must be entered

IV. RPG II AND RPG III

A. The Nature of RPG

RPG is an abbreviation for *Report Program Generator*. It is a high-level language in which the programmer codes specifications for a problem and the computer generates a program. That is, coding in RPG does not result in a source program but in a set of specifications that will be used to generate a program. The advantages of RPG include:

1. *Easy to code.* Since RPG consists, basically, of a series of specifications, it is relatively simple to code and is generally regarded as the highest level or least machine-like language offered. Because of the ease with which RPG can be learned, it is used in many colleges and businesses.

2. *Requires minimal storage.* Since RPG consists of only a set of specifications, it requires minimal storage capacity. Thus small-scale computers that do not have adequate primary storage to run large COBOL or PL/1 programs often utilize RPG.

3. *Ideal for report output.* RPG, as a program generator, is used primarily to produce reports or report-like output. Although it may create tape or disk output, it is not as effective a language for handling complex input/output tasks, such as creating non-standard header labels or employing key fields

for indexing. In short, it is an excellent business tool for producing reports and responses to inquiries.

The disadvantages of RPG include:

1. *Cannot easily handle complex logic.* RPG is usually used for simple applications, where complex logic is not required and report-like output is needed. Whenever the logic becomes complicated, the programmer would probably code in a more powerful language such as PL/1, COBOL, or FORTRAN.

2. *Difficult to debug.* Keep in mind that coding in RPG does *not* result in a source program. The coded specifications must be used to *generate* a source program. Thus any logic errors made by the programmer are difficult to find and debug since they require evaluation of a new source program.

Let us consider an information processing installation with a personnel system that is computerized. Suppose the Personnel Department frequently requests special reports that require data from the computerized personnel file. For example, a listing of all employees who are college graduates with degrees in Computer Science may be required one day, while a listing and tabulation of all employees who have been employed at least 10 years may be necessary the next day. RPG is an appropriate language for coding the above types of problems to produce the desired output. It is a relatively simple language and, since no complex computations are required, it is ideal in the above case. Programmers can typically code the problems in a matter of hours and obtain the desired output very quickly. Similarly, users with some exposure to data processing can learn the RPG specifications and code such special programs themselves. This individual programming is often done in large companies where the programming staff is already overburdened or where managers wish to obtain special studies by coding simplified programs.

In short, RPG has real advantages for minicomputers, which are sometimes not large enough to run COBOL, PL/1, or FORTRAN programs, and in companies where reports requiring relatively simple logic are handled.

We will focus on RPG II and RPG III, the two most common forms of RPG. A simple RPG program is coded on four specification forms (see Figure B.10).

RPG Coding Sheets

Name	Description
1. Control and File Description Specifications	Lists the files to be used, the devices they will employ, and special features to be included.
2. Input Specifications	Describes the format of input files.
3. Calculation Specifications	Describes arithmetic and logic operations to be performed.
4. Output Specifications	Describes the format of output files.

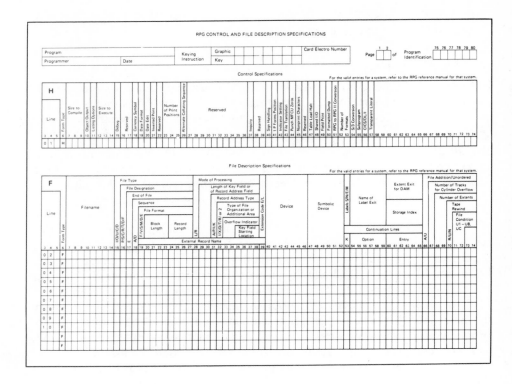

Figure B.10
RPG specification sheets.

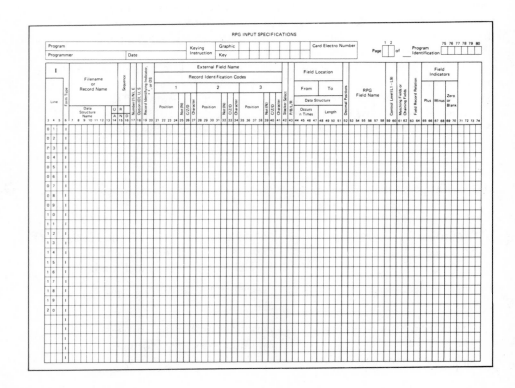

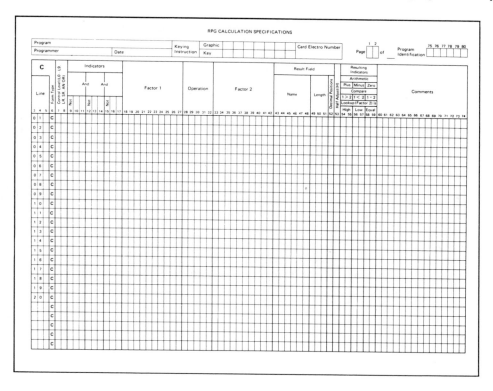

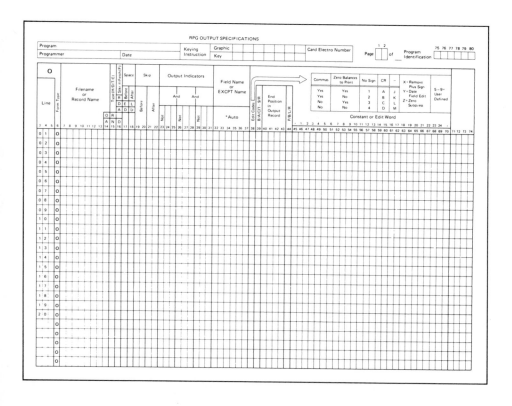

The program created from all the forms comprises the **RPG source program,** which must be translated into machine language before it can be run or executed.

B. Basic Structure of an RPG II Program

RPG programs are generally written on the above four specification sheets, in the order indicated. There are additional sheets, not discussed in the text, which are required for specialized processing.

Note that on the same sheet used for File Description Specifications, there is provision for Control Specifications (see Figure B.10). RPG, for most computers, requires a special line, called a control line, as its first entry. Different versions of RPG have different requirements for this entry. For most installations, all that is required is an H in column 6, denoting a Heading record. Thus control specifications for our illustration will merely have an H in column 6.

Each specification sheet has space for 80 columns of information. As indicated, each **line** of a sheet is keypunched into one punched card or keyed onto one terminal line.

Let us examine the coding sheets more closely.

⫸ RPG Coding Sheets

Item	Meaning	Columns into Which Data is Keyed
Page number (upper right corner)	Used to number coding sheets—optional, with no effect on compiler	1-2 (of each line)
Line number	Pre-numbered except for low-order digit	3-5
Form type	Indicates specifications sheet: F—File Description I—Input Specifications C—Calculation Specifications O—Output Specifications	6
RPG statements	These columns are coded according to established specifications.	7-74
Identification (upper right corner of form)	Identifies the program to the computer—optional entry	75-80

The small numbers 3 to 74 above the rectangular boxes represent the corresponding positions into which the specifications are keyed.

1. Identification

In the upper right-hand corner, there is a provision for a program identification field, labeled as positions 75 to 80. The identification number provided here will be keyed into columns 75 to 80 of *all* lines keyed from this form. Although this identification field is not required for processing, it should be used in case inserts need to be made. This identification field can be **alphanumeric,** consisting of any combination of characters, or **numeric,** consisting of digits only. Any field that can uniquely identify the program is used.

2. Page and Line Numbers

Columns 1 and 2, representing page number, are the same for an entire sheet, and thus are coded only once at the top of the form. Page and line numbers, representing columns 1 to 5 of each line in the RPG program, are not required for processing, but are highly recommended should entries need to be inserted. If a program is out of sequence, the page and line number information is of great assistance for re-sorting.

The remaining data recorded on the top of each form is *not* keyed into the program. It supplies identifying information only, should the coding sheets be misplaced.

3. Form Type

A quick glance at column 6 indicates to which form the entry applies: F for File Description, I for Input, C for Calculation, or O for Output. An asterisk (*) in column 7 of any form is used to designate the entire line as a comment, not to be compiled.

C. An Illustrative RPG Program

Let us program in RPG II the simplified payroll program illustrated in the previous sections in COBOL, FORTRAN, and BASIC. The input card format is indicated in Figure B.3.

The output will be a printed report with the format illustrated in the print layout sheet in Figure B.11. The output, in this case, has been designated as a printed report, rather than as a tape, since RPG is most often used to produce reports. The three input fields will be printed in addition to a WAGES field to be calculated as:

Figure B.11
Output format for sample program.

$$WAGES = HOURS \times RATE$$

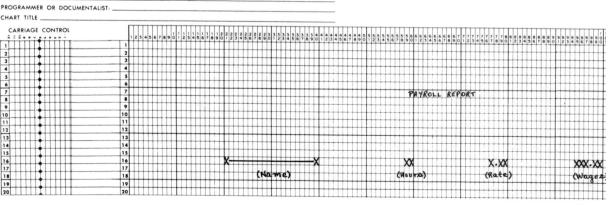

Figure B.12 illustrates the specifications sheets required to code the program in RPG.

We now discuss each of the specification sheets in detail.

1. File Description Specifications Sheet

The File Description Specifications sheet supplies pertinent data on the input and output files utilized. Each file is indicated on a *single* line of this sheet. Since our program consists of two files, an input file and an output file, this File Description Specifications sheet will have *two* lines completed. Notice that there are, however, many programs with more than two files.

7-14: Filename.   Columns 7 to 14 of each line represent the name assigned by the programmer to each of the files. These same file names will be used on the Input and Output-Format Specifications sheets. In our example, CARDS is the name assigned to the input card file and REPORT is the name assigned to the output print file. The file name field, as all alphanumeric fields in RPG, is left-justified. Names begin in the leftmost positions of the field and nonfilled low-order or rightmost positions remain blank.

15: File Type: Input or Output.   Column 15 is simply indicated as an I, for input, or an O for output.

16: File Designation.   Input files require an entry in column 16; output files do not. For input files, the file designation in column 16 must be either P, for primary input form, or S, for secondary input. For single input files, this entry is always P. For multiple input files, one must be designated as P for primary and the other as S, for secondary. An update program, for example, uses a **primary** master input file and a **secondary** detail input file. Output files do *not* have a file designation.

17: End of File.   Column 17, End of File Indicator, contains an E for the input file. This indicates that we want an end-of-file condition to be tested; that is, when there are no more records in our input file, we want this to denote an end-of-file condition.

18: Sequence.   Column 18, Sequence, is an entry that is used for some tape and disk processing.

19: File Format.   Column 19 is the File Format field and for card files is always F, denoting fixed format. This indicates that all records within the file are the same size. V, for variable, is in this field when record sizes are not the same within the file. Print files contain an F in Column 19 since print records are also fixed in length. We may have 80 position headings and 132 position detail records, for example.

20-27: Block and Record Length.   Block Length, columns 20 to 23, and Record Length, columns 24 to 27, are typically 80 for cards and 132 for printed reports. Note that these fields, as all numeric fields in RPG, are right-justified; that is, high-order or leftmost nonfilled positions are left blank.

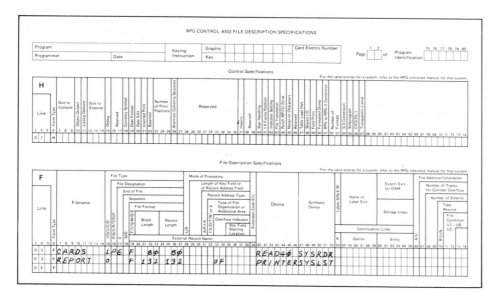

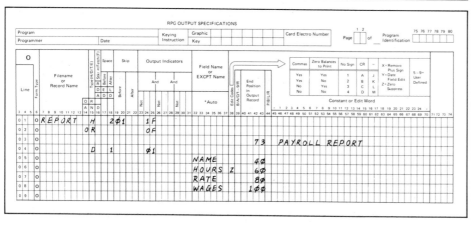

Figure B.12
Coded specification sheets for sample program.

28-32: (omit).   Positions 28-32, representing several fields, are used predominantly for tape and disk processing and are not discussed here.

33-34: Overflow Indicator.   Columns 33 and 34 are required for print files to denote that a page overflow indicator is to be used. That is, if we desire the report to proceed from page to page with the desired headings, we must use an overflow indicator to sense the end of a specified form. Thus print files should have an OF, for overflow, in Columns 33 and 34.

35-39: (omit).   Columns 35 to 39 are not used for simple RPG II programs and thus are not discussed.

40-52: Device and Symbolic Device.   The Device and the Symbolic Device names, columns 40 to 46 and 47 to 52, respectively, are assigned specifically at each information processing installation and thus will vary from one computer center to another. In the above illustration, the input device is READ40 with symbolic name SYSRDR (system reader) and the output device is PRINTER with symbolic name SYSLST (system list device). Programmers must obtain the appropriate entries for these fields from the operations staff at their computer center.

53-74: (omit).   The remainder of the File Description Specifications sheet is not used unless tape or disk processing is required.

2. Input Specifications Sheet

7-14: Filename.   Each input file is described on the Input Specifications sheet. Since our sample RPG program has only one input file, called CARDS, then CARDS is described on this sheet.

15-16: Sequence.   The sequence AA describes the first card record format within the file. If additional types of records existed within the file they would be coded as AB, AC, and so on.

17-18: (omit).   Columns 17 and 18 are not used.

19-20: Record Identifying Indicator.   Columns 19 and 20 represent the Record Identifying Indicator. In our example, indicator 01 is turned on every time a card record is read. This indicator will then be used to determine, for output specifications, when a line is to be printed. If 01 is used in the Output-Format Specifications sheet, then a line will print each time indicator 01 is "turned on," that is, for every card read.

21-41: Record Identification Codes.   Record Identification Codes (21 to 41) are used to test input positions for specific contents. They are not required in this sample program.

42-43: (omit).   Columns 42 and 43 have specialized use and are not discussed here.

44-58: Field Indicators.   Field indicators located in the group of columns from 44 to 58 are used to denote fields within the input record. "Field Location From," columns 44 to 47, denotes the high-order or leftmost position of a field and "Field Location To" denotes the low-order or rightmost position of a field. For numeric fields, column 52 must be completed to denote the number of decimal or fractional positions. For alphanumeric fields, it is left blank.

Thus we have for CARDS:

Columns	Field Name	Field Type
1-20	NAME	Alphanumeric (no entry in 52)
21-22	HOURS	Numeric—integer with no decimal positions (0 in 52)
23-25	RATE	Numeric with two decimal positions (2 in 52)
		(428 in columns 23-25 of an input card would be treated as 4.28 by the computer)

59-74: (omit).   Positions 59 to 74 of this sheet have specialized use and are not discussed here.

3. Calculation Specifications Sheet

Any arithmetic or logic operation is defined on the Calculation Specifications sheet.

7-8: Control Levels.   Since no control levels are used here, columns 7 and 8 are blank.

9-17: Indicators.   Since we wish to perform a multiplication operation (HOURS × RATE) for *all* input records, we use indicator 01, which is "turned on" for all input cards. This is the only indicator required.

18-48: Operation and Result Field.   Factor 1, HOURS, is multiplied (MULT) by Factor 2, RATE, to produce a resultant field called WAGES. For other operations we may use:

- ADD
- SUB
- DIV
- COMP (compare), etc.

49-52: *Field Length and Decimal Position.* The field length for the resultant numeric field, WAGES, is 5 (column 51) including 2 decimal positions (2 in column 52).

53: *Half Adjust.* Column 53, Half Adjust, is used for rounding. That is, when we wish the computer to round the results to the nearest position, we use this field.

54-59: *Resulting Indicators.* The Resulting Indicators in Columns 54 to 59 are turned on only for compare (COMP) operations.

60-74: *Comments.* Any comments in columns 60 to 74 may be included. These are printed on the listing but do not affect processing. We may also include entire lines as comments by utilizing an asterisk (*) in column 7 of *any* sheet.

4. Output Specifications Sheet

7-14: *Filename.* The output file REPORT is described here.

15: *Type.* Three types of records may be included.

- Heading (H)
- Detail (D)
- Total (T)

Since we only have Heading and Detail records, only H and D types (column 15) have been included.

16: *Stacker Select.* This field is appropriate only for punched output, where output data cards can fall into several pockets or stackers.

17-22: *Space and Skip.* These options are appropriate only for printed output. A printer can be made to space 1, 2, or 3 lines either *before* or *after* it writes a line. The 2 in Space After of our illustration indicates that *after* the Heading line is printed, we wish to space the form 2 lines. Only the digits 1, 2, or 3 may be used in *either* column 17 or 18.

The Skip option for printed output is used to position the form at a specific line. A 01 in either Skip field is a code for skipping to the beginning of a new page. In our illustration, we skip to a new page *before* printing.

Thus the output file REPORT has a heading record (H), which requires skipping to a new page *before* printing, and spacing of the form two lines *after* printing.

23-31: *Output Indicators.* The Output Indicator 1P (columns 24 and 25) implies that we wish to print the H record (Heading) on the first page (1P). If any other condition also requires the printing of this record, then we code OR on the next line in columns 14 and 15 and the corresponding condition. The notation OF in columns 24 and 25 indicates that we also wish to print a heading on an overflow, or end-of-page condition.

In short, we are indicating that we wish the H or heading type record to print on the first page *or* when the end of a page is reached. In either case, we skip the paper to a new page, print the heading, and then advance the paper two lines.

In most print applications, we want headings to print on the first printed page. Also, when we have reached the end of a page, we want the program to skip to a new page and print new headings. In this way, each individual page of the continuous form has a heading so that, when the report is separated into individual sheets, each can be identified.

32-70: Field Delineators.   The heading PAYROLL REPORT is to print with the last character in position 73 (print layout sheet, Figure B.11).

The detail line, D, prints when indicator 01 is on, which is for all cards. Each time a detail line prints, the form is spaced 1 line (after printing). Since each input card turns on indicator 01, a detail line will print for each input card.

Four output fields print:

Printing of Output

Field Name	Print Positions (sheet indicates last print position)
NAME	21-40
HOURS	59-60
RATE	77-80 (decimal point prints on output and therefore counts as a position)
WAGES	95-100 (here, too, decimal point appears on output)

The first three fields are directly transmitted from the card record. Note that these input and output fields have the same names. NAME requires no editing. HOURS requires zero suppression (Z in column 38) to eliminate leading zeros and also the standard plus sign generated by the computer. RATE requires a decimal point to print after the first integer position. Recall that, to save space on a card, decimal points are often not coded. They are **implied** or **assumed** in input records. The output document, however, must have these decimal points for readability. Hence the Edit Word, columns 45 to 70, is used. WAGES, obtained from the calculations, requires the printing of a decimal point, after the first three integer positions. Thus, '⌑⌑⌑.⌑⌑' is the Edit Word.

If, in addition we wish to suppress leading or nonsignificant zeros, we include a zero in the low-order integer position. Thus if WAGES contained an Edit Word of '⌑⌑0.⌑⌑' then 003.42 would print as 3.42 instead of 003.42. If we also desire a dollar sign to print out, we would include the following Edit Word: '$⌑0.⌑⌑'.

The above four specification sheets will result in a complete RPG II program that performs the required operations. Notice that there is no visible step-by-step logic displayed in the specifications. When the sheets are coded so that they conform to the RPG II rules, however, then a program is compiled that contains the step-by-step logic.

Self-Evaluating Quiz

1. RPG II is an abbreviation for _____.
2. The coding sheets used for writing an RPG II program are called _____ sheets.
3. One common form of output for an RPG II program is a _____.
4. (T or F) Small-scale computers that do not have adequate storage to run large COBOL or PL/1 programs often utilize RPG II.
5. (T or F) RPG II is best suited for programs with complex logic.
6. The four specifications forms that may be used in an RPG II program are _____, _____, _____, and _____.
7. Each line for every form is keyed into a single _____ or _____ on a terminal, which is then part of the _____.

Solutions

1. *Report Program Generator* II
2. specifications
3. printed report
4. T
5. F

6. FILE DESCRIPTION; INPUT; CALCULATION; OUTPUT
7. card; line; RPG II source program

Summary

This appendix has considered four of the most common programming languages in use today—COBOL, FORTRAN, BASIC, and RPG. There are numerous other languages as well, but the majority of businesses with computer facilities utilize one or more of the above.

The objective of this appendix is not to teach you how to program in each of these languages—that would require considerably more discussion. Rather, the purpose is to provide you with a basic understanding of each language's features and how they compare with each other. By illustrating a program in each of the four languages that provides a solution to the same problem, you can see some of the ways in which these languages are best utilized.

BASIC is perhaps the most popular language for teaching students how to program, for numerous reasons.

Why BASIC

1. It is easy to learn and code.
2. It is ideally suited for interactive processing using terminals.
3. It is ideally suited for mini- and microcomputer systems.

Chapter 12 and Appendix A then, provide an in-depth discussion on BASIC programming.

Review Questions

Compare and contrast the programming languages discussed in this appendix
with respect to the following items.

1. English-like features.
2. Applicability to scientific problems.
3. Applicability to business problems.
4. Format requirements.
5. Simplicity.
6. Features available.

A CLOSER LOOK AT COMPUTER NUMBERING SYSTEMS AND DATA REPRESENTATION

In Chapter 4, we included a brief discussion of the binary numbering system and the method used by a computer to represent data. A review of part IV, Data Representation, within Chapter 4 will provide details on:

1. Binary Representation
2. Determining the Decimal Equivalent of a Binary Number
3. Determining the Binary Equivalent of a Decimal Number
4. Representation of Characters in Storage

This discussion of numbering systems in Chapter 4 indicates:

1. Why the binary numbering system is ideal for representing data in a computer.
2. The ways in which binary numbers can be converted into decimal numbers.
3. The ways in which decimal numbers can be converted into binary numbers.
4. The methods used to represent data in memory using the binary numbering system.

This appendix provides a more thorough discussion of numbering systems and data representation.

I. MORE ON BINARY NUMBERS

Thus far, we have seen that binary numbers are ideally suited to computer processing since they can be used to represent the on-off state of circuits. An "on" condition in storage can be indicated by a 1; an "off" condition by a 0.

We have learned how to convert numbers from binary to decimal by utilizing the positional values and how to convert from decimal to binary.

This section considers the addition and subtraction of binary numbers as they are handled by the computer.

A. Addition of Binary Numbers

The addition of binary numbers follows a series of simple rules:

▐▐▐▶ **Addition of Binary Numbers**

For each position beginning with the rightmost:

1. $1 + 0 = 1$
2. $0 + 1 = 1$
3. $0 + 0 = 0$
4. $1 + 1 = 0$ with a carry of 1 to the next position.

Example 1 $10_2 + 11_2 = (?)_2$

Binary   *Decimal*

$$\begin{array}{r} 10 \\ +\ 11 \\ \hline 101 \end{array} \qquad \begin{array}{r} 2 \\ +\ 3 \\ \hline 5 \end{array}$$

Units position: $0 + 1 = 1$
2's position: $1 + 1 = 0$ with carry of 1
4's position: carry of $1 +$ zero (nothing) $= 1$

Thus, we have 101_2 as the sum.

Example 2 $1101_2 + 1010_2 = (?)_2$

Binary   *Decimal*

$$\begin{array}{r} 1101 \\ +\ 1010 \\ \hline 10111 \end{array} \qquad \begin{array}{r} 13 \\ +\ 10 \\ \hline 23 \end{array}$$

Notice that in each example we checked our solution by converting the binary numbers to decimal and then determining if the decimal sum was equal to the binary total. If not, then an error was made in the binary addition.

B. Subtraction of Binary Numbers

The process of binary subtraction is somewhat more complicated than that of addition. Note that a computer does not perform simple subtraction in the manner that we customarily perform it. It performs subtraction by a series of negative additions. In this way, the same addition mechanisms can be used for subtraction as well.

▐▐▐▶ **Subtraction of Binary Numbers (General Rule)**

1. **Complement** the subtrahend (number to be subtracted) by converting all 1's to 0's and all 0's to 1's.

2. Proceed as in addition.

3. Cross off the high-order or leftmost digit (a 1 when the number is positive) and add this 1 to the total (called end-around-carry).

Example 3 $1101_2 - 1000_2 = (?)_2$

Binary   Decimal

1101	13	Minuend
-1000	-8	$-$ Subtrahend
	5	Difference

1. Complement the subtrahend or number to be subtracted.
   Complement of 1000 = 0111 converting all 0's to 1's and all 1's to 0's.

2. Proceed as in addition using the complemented value as the factor to be added.

$$\begin{array}{r} 1101 \\ +\ 0111 \\ \hline 10100 \end{array}$$

3. Cross off high-order 1 and add it to result.

$$\begin{array}{r} \cancel{1}0100 \\ +\ \llcorner\!\!\rightarrow 1 \\ \hline 0101 \end{array}$$

Answer is 0101_2 or 101_2 since leftmost 0 has no value.
Since $101_2 = 5_{10}$, the binary subtraction solution is correct.

Example 4 $11101_2 - 11000_2 = (?)_2$

Binary   Decimal

11101	29
$-\ 11000$	-24
	5

1. Complement the subtrahend.
   Complement of 11000 = 00111.

2. Proceed as in addition.

$$\begin{array}{r} 11101 \\ +\ 00111 \\ \hline 100100 \end{array}$$

3. End-around-carry:

$$\begin{array}{r} \cancel{1}00100 \\ +\ \llcorner\!\!\rightarrow 1 \\ \hline 00101 \end{array}$$

This procedure for subtraction, which is the method used by the computer, is called **complementation and end-around-carry.**

In the above examples, notice that the subtrahend, or number to be subtracted, was always smaller than the number to be subtracted from. If, however, the subtrahend is larger than the minuend, or number being subtracted from, we must modify Step 3 in the rules for subtraction.

Subtraction of Binary Numbers (If subtrahend larger than minuend)

1. Complement the subtrahend (number to be subtracted) by converting all 1's to 0's and all 0's to 1's.

2. Proceed as in addition.

3. Complement the result and place a negative sign in front of the answer.

Example 5

Binary	Decimal
11000	24
−11101	−29
	− 5

1. Complement the subtrahend.
   Complement of 11101 = 00010.

2. Proceed as in addition.

$$
\begin{array}{r}
11000 \\
+00010 \\
\hline
11010
\end{array}
$$

3. Complement the result and add negative sign.
   Complement of 11010 = 00101.
   Answer = -00101_2 or -5_{10}.

Example 6

Binary	Decimal
1101	13
−11001	−25
	−12

1. Complement the subtrahend.
   Complement of 11001 = 00110.

2. Proceed as in addition.

$$
\begin{array}{r}
1101 \\
+00110 \\
\hline
10011
\end{array}
$$

3. Complement the result and add negative sign.
   Complement of 10011 = 01100.
   Answer = -1100_2 or -12_{10}.

Self-Evaluating Quiz

1. The addition of 1 + 0 or 0 + 1, in binary, results in _____.
2. The addition of 1 + 1, in binary, results in _____.
3. The method used by the computer for subtraction of binary numbers is called _____.

4. $\begin{array}{r} 11011 \\ +10011 \\ \hline \end{array}$

5. $\begin{array}{r} 11111 \\ +11011 \\ \hline \end{array}$

6. $\begin{array}{r} 111 \\ +101 \\ \hline 110 \end{array}$

7. $\begin{array}{r} 11011 \\ -10011 \\ \hline \end{array}$

8. $\begin{array}{r} 111011 \\ -110001 \\ \hline \end{array}$

9. $\begin{array}{r} 010110 \\ -110001 \\ \hline \end{array}$

Solutions

1. 1
2. 0 with a carry of 1
3. complementation and end-
   around-carry
4. 101110 (27 + 19 = 46)
5. 111010 (31 + 27 = 58)
6. 10010 (7 + 5 + 6 = 18)

7.
```
    11011
  + 01100          27 − 19 = 8
   ̷100111
   └──→1
    1000
```

8.
```
    111011
  + 001110         59 − 49 = 10
   ̷1001001
   └──→1
    ̷1̷010
```

9.
```
    010110
  + 001110
    100100          complement = 011011;
```
answer = −11011; (22 − 49 = −27)

II. OCTAL NUMBERS

Only on specially constructed engineering or scientific computers are pure binary codes utilized. On these computers, alphanumeric input is automatically converted by the computer to binary, all operations are performed, and the data is then converted back to alphanumeric form as output. All displays of storage images and addresses are in binary.

Pure binary representation has, however, one distinct disadvantage. It requires many more positions for data than any other numbering system. To represent the two-digit decimal number 86, for example, we must use seven binary digits (1010110). Thus most commercial computers **group** binary numbers in an effort to conserve storage. IBM, specifically, utilizes the hexadecimal or base 16 numbering system. This system is discussed in the next section.

Here we discuss the **octal** numbering system, or base 8 system, used by other computer manufacturers. We see that this numbering system can be used to represent *three* binary digits as a single octal number. In this way, we can significantly reduce the number of digits required to represent any number and still maintain the binary concept. That is, we can still utilize the on-off electrical impulse concept of binary numbers to represent numbers.

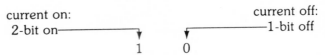

Note here that while some computer specialists and users are unfamiliar with binary, octal, and hexadecimal numbering systems, knowledge of these concepts can be very helpful in debugging programs, understanding how a computer operates, and selecting computer equipment.

A. Representing Numeric Data with Octal Numbers

The octal numbering system uses the eight digits 0 to 7 to represent any number. The decimal numbers 0 to 7, respectively, are represented by the corresponding octal numbers 0 to 7. The decimal number 8 is equal to 10 in the octal code. In the decimal numbering system, each positional value is a factor of 10; in the binary numbering system, each positional value is a factor of 2. In the octal numbering system, as you might expect, each positional value is a factor of 8.

Positional Values

. . .	8^2	8^1	8^0	In exponential form
. . .	64	8	1	In decimal form

In the octal numbering system, as in all such systems, we write numbers in sequence until all digits in a specific position are exhausted. Then we initialize the given position with 0 and add 1 to the next position. Consider the following pattern in the octal numbering system:

Decimal	Octal
0	0
1	1
2	2
.	.
.	.
.	.
7	7	$7_8 + 1_8 = 10_8$
8	10
9	11
.	.
.	.
.	.
15	17	$17_8 + 1_8 = 20_8$
16	20
.	.
.	.
.	.
23	27	$27_8 + 1_8 = 30_8$
24	30
.	.

Decimal	Octal	
.	.	
.	.	
.	.	
63	77	$77_8 + 1_8 = 100_8$
64	100	
65	101	
.	.	
.	.	
.	.	
71	107	$107_8 + 1_8 = 110_8$
72	110	

B. Determining the Decimal Equivalent of an Octal Number

To determine the decimal equivalent of any octal number we multiply the positional value by the appropriate digit and add the results.

Example 1 $(725)_8 = (?)_{10}$

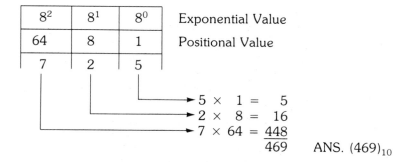

8^2	8^1	8^0	Exponential Value
64	8	1	Positional Value
7	2	5	

$$5 \times 1 = 5$$
$$2 \times 8 = 16$$
$$7 \times 64 = \underline{448}$$
$$469 \quad \text{ANS. } (469)_{10}$$

Example 2 $(1436)_8 = (?)_{10}$

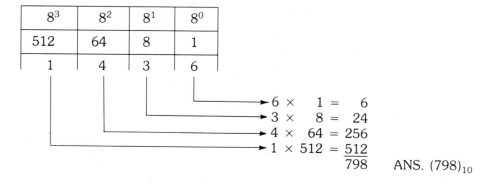

8^3	8^2	8^1	8^0
512	64	8	1
1	4	3	6

$$6 \times 1 = 6$$
$$3 \times 8 = 24$$
$$4 \times 64 = 256$$
$$1 \times 512 = \underline{512}$$
$$798 \quad \text{ANS. } (798)_{10}$$

In summary, to find the decimal equivalent of an octal number, we multiply each digit by its positional value.

Self-Evaluating Quiz

Find the decimal equivalent of the following octal numbers.

1. $125_8 = (?)_{10}$
2. $236_8 = (?)_{10}$
3. $1213_8 = (?)_{10}$
4. $1419_8 = (?)_{10}$

Solutions

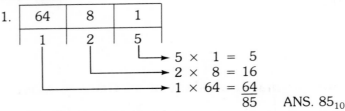

1.

64	8	1
1	2	5

$5 \times 1 = 5$
$2 \times 8 = 16$
$1 \times 64 = \underline{64}$
85 ANS. 85_{10}

2.

64	8	1
2	3	6

$6 \times 1 = 6$
$3 \times 8 = 24$
$2 \times 64 = \underline{128}$
158 ANS. 158_{10}

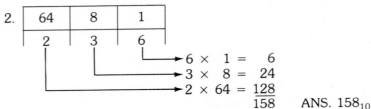

3.

512	64	8	1
1	2	1	3

$3 \times 1 = 3$
$1 \times 8 = 8$
$2 \times 64 = 128$
$1 \times 512 = \underline{512}$
651 ANS. 651_{10}

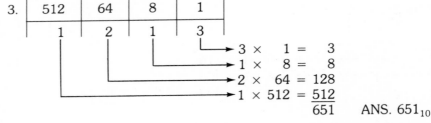

4. This is a trick question! It should have occurred to you that 1419_8 is not a valid number since octal numbers use digits 0 to 7 only. Since 1419 contains a "9" it is invalid.

C. Determining the Octal Equivalent of a Decimal Number

1. The Remainder Method in General

There is a technique called the **remainder method** that may be used to convert a decimal number to any other numbering system. The technique is as follows.

▐▐▐➡ **Remainder Method for Converting Decimal Numbers into Any Other Base**

1. Divide the decimal number by the base (for a binary equivalent, we divide by 2).

2. Indicate the remainder, which will be either 0 or 1 in the case of binary division.

3. Continue dividing into each quotient (result of previous division) until the divide operation produces a zero quotient or result.

4. The equivalent number in the base desired is the numeric **remainders** reading from the last division to the first.

Several examples will serve to clarify this procedure.

Example $(38)_{10} = (?)_2$

Remainder

1. Begin by dividing the number by the base 2.

3. Divide previous result, 19, by base.

$2\,\overline{)\,38}$ $\quad$19	0	2. Indicate the remainder.
$2\,\overline{)\,19}$ $\quad$9	1	4. Indicate the remainder.
$2\,\overline{)\,9}$ $\quad$4	1	.
$2\,\overline{)\,4}$ $\quad$2	0	.

indicates the end ———▶ $2\,\overline{)\,2}$ $\quad$1

$2\,\overline{)\,2}$ 0

$2\,\overline{)\,1}$ $\quad$0   1

———resultant binary number reads from bottom to top (100110)

When the divide operation produces a quotient or result of zero, then the process is terminated. The binary equivalent, reading from the last division to the first is:

$$(38)_{10} = (100110)_2$$

Using the remainder method for converting from decimal to binary, we find it a more efficient procedure to perform the first divide operation at the bottom of the work sheet and work up. The following is exactly equivalent to the example above.

Remainder

2 $\overline{)\,1}$ $\quad$0	1	
2 $\overline{)\,2}$	0	
2 $\overline{)\,4}$	0	
2 $\overline{)\,9}$	1	
2 $\overline{)\,19}$	1	
2 $\overline{)\,38}$	0	

In this way, the result is read from top to bottom: $(100110)_2$.

Example $(67)_{10} = (?)_2$

To find the binary equivalent by determining the combination of positional values can be a long and arduous procedure when the numbers are large. Instead we may use the remainder method.

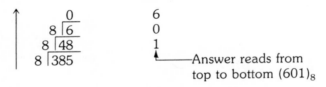

Thus the result, reading from top to bottom, is: $(1000011)_2 = (67)_{10}$.

2. The Remainder Method with Octal Numbers

To find the **octal** equivalent of a **decimal** number, we again may use the remainder method, this time dividing by the base 8.

Example 1 $(385)_{10} = (?)_8$

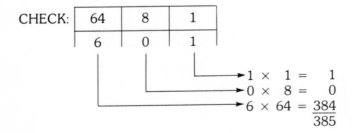

To check our work we should determine if our octal number 601 is equal to the decimal 385:

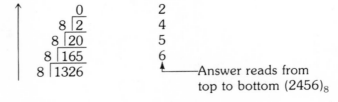

Example 2 $(1326)_{10} = (?)_8$

Thus, to convert from the decimal numbering system to any other system, we may use the remainder method, using the base of the latter as a divisor. To convert a decimal number to an octal number, we divide by 8, using the remainder of each division to produce a solution.

Self-Evaluating Quiz

Find the octal equivalent of the following decimal numbers.

1. $221_{10} = (?)_8$
2. $143_{10} = (?)_8$
3. $206_{10} = (?)_8$

Solutions

1.
$$\begin{array}{r} 0 \\ \hline 8\,|\,3 \\ \hline 8\,|\,27 \\ \hline 8\,|\,221 \end{array}$$
   3
   3
   5   ANS. 335_8

2.
$$\begin{array}{r} 0 \\ \hline 8\,|\,2 \\ \hline 8\,|\,17 \\ \hline 8\,|\,143 \end{array}$$
   2
   1
   7   ANS. 217_8

3.
$$\begin{array}{r} 0 \\ \hline 8\,|\,3 \\ \hline 8\,|\,25 \\ \hline 8\,|\,206 \end{array}$$
   3
   1
   6   ANS. 316_8

D. Converting Octal to Binary and Binary to Octal

At the beginning of this section, we learned that octal numbers are used to represent data in place of binary numbers on many computers. Binary numbers are uniquely suited for computers since each position can be represented as a 1 or 0, that is, an on- or off-state of an electrical current. Such numbers, however, are often cumbersome to deal with, since many binary numbers are required to represent relatively small decimal numbers. To represent 26, for example, we must use *five* binary digits, 11010. To make more efficient use of computer storage, we can group binary numbers in some pattern. The octal numbering system can be represented as a group of *three* binary digits, or bits. That is, any three binary digits can be represented as a single octal number.

Example 1 $(100111)_2 = (?)_8$

4	2	1	4	2	1
1	0	0	1	1	1

       4   7

ANS. $(47)_8$

In short, we subdivide binary numbers into groups of threes, with the positional value of each group represented as 4 2 1. We then determine the octal equivalent.

Example 2 $(11011)_2 = (?)_8$

This number does not contain two complete groups of three. You will recall, however, that 11011 is the same as 011011, since high-order or leading zeros do not change the value of a number. 011011 does contain two complete groups:

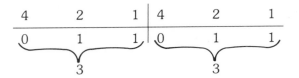

ANS. $(33)_8$

Note that a computer usually uses the binary numbering system since each circuit in storage can be represented as on or off depending on whether an electrical current or impulse is present. Data on many such computers can be represented for display purposes on memory dump printouts in the **octal system.** In this way, the computer can easily print out data by combining binary numbers into groups of threes. This is a relatively simple conversion and requires far less circuitry than converting binary numbers into **decimal** numbers for display purposes. Thus if a storage position contained 11111110, and the computer were asked to display this position, it would be a simple task to display it in the octal system:

$$
\begin{array}{ccc}
011 & 111 & 110 \\
3 & 7 & 6
\end{array}
$$

In short, many computers utilize the octal numbering system for displaying memory printouts to programmers and operators. That is, data that is currently in the computer can be accessed by a programmer or operator if he or she can read the octal code. Such memory images are usually displayed when an error has occurred.

Computers accept normal alphanumeric or decimal codes and print reports or write other forms of output in decimal, as well; but instead of converting binary numbers to **decimal,** which can be very cumbersome because of the number of digits involved, they convert to **octal** first and then to decimal.

Example 1 $(110111110011011)_2 = (?)_{10}$

To use the normal method of multiplying the digit by its positional value is, indeed, cumbersome.

16384	8192	4096	2048	1024	512	256	128	64	32	16	8	4	2	1	
1	1	0	1	1	1	1	1	0	0	1	1	0	1	1	1

2
8
16
128
256
512
1024
2048
8192
16384

ANS. $(28{,}571)_{10}$

It would be far simpler to determine the octal equivalent of the above and then to determine the decimal number from the octal number.

a. Convert to octal

110	111	110	011	011
6	7	6	3	3

b. Convert from octal to decimal

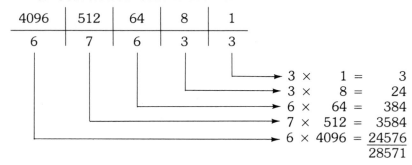

4096	512	64	8	1
6	7	6	3	3

$$3 \times 1 = 3$$
$$3 \times 8 = 24$$
$$6 \times 64 = 384$$
$$7 \times 512 = 3584$$
$$6 \times 4096 = 24576$$
$$28571$$

ANS. $(28571)_{10}$

Thus, to simplify conversions, many computers utilize the octal numbering system. In fact, most operations could be performed in the octal system, to further simplify computer procedures.

It is just as simple as the above to convert from octal back into binary. Thus a computer can convert a number from binary to octal, perform the required operations, and convert back again into binary. To convert from an octal number to a binary number, we merely represent each octal number as three binary numbers, as shown below.

Example 2 $(725)_8 = (?)_2$

7	2	5
421	421	421
111	010	101

ANS. $(111010101)_2$

Example 3 $(302)_8 = (?)_2$

3	0	2
011	000	010

$= (011000010)_2$ or $(11000010)_2$ since the high-order 0 has no significance.

E. Addition and Subtraction of Octal Numbers

Thus far we have seen the conversions required from any octal, binary, or decimal number to any of the other systems. Let us now see how to perform the arithmetic operations of addition and subtraction of octal numbers.

To add two octal numbers, we proceed as we do in the decimal system, keeping in mind, however, that if any addition produces an octal number in excess of 7, we must utilize the next position: $8_{10} = 10_8$, $9_{10} = 11_8$, and so on.

Example 1 $(73)_8 + (24)_8 = (?)_8$

$$\begin{array}{r} 73 \\ + \ 24 \\ \hline 117 \end{array}$$

ANS. $(117)_8$

Example 2 $(243)_8 + (745)_8 = (?)_8$

$$\begin{array}{r} 243 \\ + \ 745 \\ \hline 1210 \end{array}$$

ANS. $(1210)_8$

We should check our work by converting each of the octal numbers into the decimal system to determine if, in fact, the addition is correct.

To subtract in the octal numbering system, we may use the complementation and end-around-carry method used in the subtraction of binary numbers: $(715)_8 - (603)_8 = (?)_8$

$$\begin{array}{r} 715 \\ -603 \\ \hline \end{array}$$

1. Complement the subtrahend: 174 is the complement of 603
   603 + (its complement) = 777
   (*any no.*) + (its complement) = 777
2. Proceed as in addition

$$\begin{array}{r} 715 \\ + \ 174 \\ \hline 1111 \end{array}$$

3. End-around-carry

1111
└→1
112   ANS. $(112)_8$

F. Illustration of Use

It is very useful to be able to perform arithmetic operations in the octal numbering system when utilizing a machine that employs this code. Suppose, for example, that a computer program has a "bug" or error in it. While the program is running, a computer display indicates the following.

PROGRAM CHECK INTERRUPTION 5721

This implies that at storage position 5721 there is an error.

It is possible to find this error on a program listing that indicates storage positions of each instruction. The address of the instruction often cannot, however, be determined directly. In many cases, the program listing indicates each instruction address in relative terms; that is, relative to the loading point of the program. The computer must relocate each program at the time of execution to allow room for the supervisor and any other necessary programs or subroutines. Thus while the program listing may denote instructions from storage positions 0000 to 3653, which are the available numbers at compile time, the computer may actually place the program in storage positions 3012 to 6665. For many computers, these addresses are noted on program listings and displayed in the octal numbering system. Thus to find the instruction at 5721, we must first subtract the starting address of the program, 3012. Since the program **listing** begins at 0000 we must find the **absolute** error point, which is determined by subtracting the actual or relocated starting address from the actual program error point.

    5721
  − 3012

1. Complement the subtrahend: 4765 is the complement of 3012

2. Proceed as in addition

      5721
    + 4765
     12706

3. End-around-carry

    12706
    └──→1
     2707

Thus 2707 on the program listing would be the point where the error may be found.

In short, for computer purposes, we can think of the octal numbering system as a shorthand method for representing binary numbers. Since each group of three binary numbers can be used to represent a single octal number, a computer can eliminate much of the cumbersome processing of binary numbers by representing some of its internal computer codes in the octal system.

Self-Evaluating Quiz

1. The octal numbering system has a base of _____, using numbers _____.
2. The major advantage of octal numbers for computers is _____.
3. The use of binary numbers by computers is advantageous because _____.
4. Binary numbers for display purposes, however, are often _____.
5. Three binary numbers may be used to represent _____.
6. One octal number may be used to represent _(no.)_ binary digits or bits.
7. $(8975)_{10} = (?)_8$
8. $(7099)_{10} = (?)_8$
9. $(7576)_8 = (?)_8$
10. $(6607)_8 = (?)_{10}$
11. $(111011111)_2 = (?)_8$
12. $(11110000110)_2 = (?)_8$
13. $(7552)_8 = (?)_2$
14. $(66051)_8 = (?)_2$
15. $(1111111011111111)_2 = (?)_{10}$
    HINT. Convert first to the octal system.
16. Suppose you are helping to debug a program run on an octal computer that has an error at storage location 7562. The program listing has instructions that have absolute addresses beginning at 0000. The program has been relocated to start at 3300. Find the absolute error point that can then be found on the program listing.

Solutions

1. 8; 0 to 7
2. they may be used to represent binary numbers by combining them into groups of threes
3. each binary digit or bit can be used to represent the on (1) or off (0) state of a circuit
4. cumbersome because many digits are required to represent relatively small decimal numbers
5. a single octal number
6. three

7. $(8975)_{10} = (?)_8$

```
                0    Remainder
         8  |2       2
         8  |17      1
         8  |140     4
         8  |1121    1
         8  |8975    7
```

ANS. $(21417)_8$

8. $(7099)_{10} = (?)_8$

```
                0    Remainder
         8  |1       1
         8  |13      5
         8  |110     6
         8  |887     7
         8  |7099    3
```

ANS. $(15673)_8$

9. $(7576)_8 = (?)_{10}$

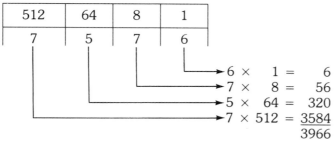

512	64	8	1
7	5	7	6

$$6 \times 1 = 6$$
$$7 \times 8 = 56$$
$$5 \times 64 = 320$$
$$7 \times 512 = \underline{3584}$$
$$3966$$

ANS. $(3966)_{10}$

10. $(6607)_8 = (?)_{10}$

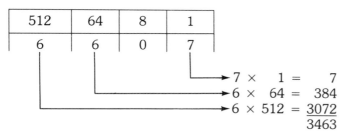

512	64	8	1
6	6	0	7

$$7 \times 1 = 7$$
$$6 \times 64 = 384$$
$$6 \times 512 = \underline{3072}$$
$$3463$$

ANS. $(3463)_{10}$

11. $(111011111)_2 = (?)_8$

111	011	111
7	3	7

ANS. $(737)_8$

12. $(11110000110)_2 = (?)_8$

011	110	000	110
3	6	0	6

ANS. $(3606)_8$

13. $(7552)_8 = (?)_2$

7	5	5	2
111	101	101	010

ANS. $(111101101010)_2$

14. $(66051)_8 = (?)_2$

6	6	0	5	1
110	110	000	101	001

ANS. $(110110000101001)_2$

15. $(11111111011111111)_2 = (?)_{10}$
   a. Convert to octal first

011	111	111	011	111	111
3	7	7	3	7	7

$(377377)_8$

   b. Convert from octal to decimal

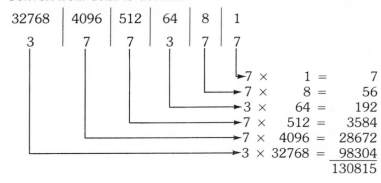

32768	4096	512	64	8	1
3	7	7	3	7	7

$$
\begin{aligned}
7 \times 1 &= 7 \\
7 \times 8 &= 56 \\
3 \times 64 &= 192 \\
7 \times 512 &= 3584 \\
7 \times 4096 &= 28672 \\
3 \times 32768 &= \underline{98304} \\
&\,130815
\end{aligned}
$$

16.
$$
\begin{array}{r}
7562 \\
-3300 \\
\hline
4262
\end{array}
$$

or using complementation and end-around carry:
   I. complement subtrahend: 4477 is the complement of 3300
   II. add 4477 + 7562 = 14261
   III. end-around-carry

$$
\begin{array}{r}
\cancel{1}4261 \\
\llcorner\!\!\rightarrow 1 \\
\hline
4262
\end{array}
$$

III. HEXADECIMAL NUMBERS

A. Representing Numeric Data with Hexadecimal Numbers

We have seen that a computer uses binary numbers rather than decimal numbers to perform arithmetic operations. This is logical because the two binary numbers 1 and 0 can be made to correspond to the on-off state of computer circuits.

Note, however, that it is not feasible for the computer to utilize an entire storage position or byte to represent one binary digit. Binary numbers utilize many positions to represent relatively small numbers. While the decimal number 23 would use two storage positions, one for the 2 and one for the 3, its binary equivalent 10111 would utilize *five* storage positions. Thus to have the computer store a single binary digit in one storage position would make inefficient use of large storage capacity.

As we have seen in the previous section, the computer can group together *three* binary digits to produce a single digit in the octal or base 8 numbering system. In this section we will see that *four* binary digits can similarly be grouped together to produce a digit in the base 16 or **hexadecimal** numbering system. In computers that represent data in base 16, each storage position can store two hexadecimal digits with each such digit corresponding to four binary digits.

   In base 10 there are 10 unique digits 0 to 9; in base 2 there are 2 unique digits 0 to 1; in base 8 there are 8 unique digits 0 to 7. In base 16, as you might expect, there are 16 unique digits. Since the decimal system uses only 10 individual digits, the remaining 6 are represented as letters A to F.

Hexadecimal	Decimal
0	0
.	.
.	.
.	.
9	9
A	10
B	11
C	12
D	13
E	14
F	15

B. Determining the Decimal Equivalent of a Hexadecimal Number

Note that while the decimal numbering system has only *10* digits 0 to 9, the hexadecimal numbering system requires 6 more individual characters to represent numbers 10 to 15. Arbitrarily, the letters A to F were selected to represent these numbers.

   To determine the next number after F in the hexadecimal system (or 15 in decimal) we must utilize another position. That is, $(10)_{16} = (16)_{10}$. Further, $1A_{16} = 26_{10}$, $1B_{16} = 27_{10}$, and so on. Since the hexadecimal numbering system has a base of 16, each positional value can be expressed as a factor of 16.

$\cdots$	16^3	16^2	16^1	16^0
$\cdots$	4096	256	16	1

To determine, then, $(10)_{16}$ in base 10 we have:

16	1
1	0

$0 \times 1 = 0$
$1 \times 16 = 16$ ANS. $(16)_{10}$

We use the same method as previously discussed to convert from any numbering system to the decimal system: multiply each digit by its positional value and then obtain the sum or total. Do not become confused by the use of hexadecimal digits A to F. When performing any arithmetic operation, merely convert hexadecimal digits to their decimal counterpart.

Example 1 $(AF)_{16} = (?)_{10}$

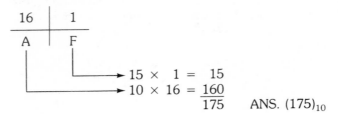

15 × 1 =   15
10 × 16 = 160
         175   ANS. $(175)_{10}$

Example 2 $(B6A)_{16} = (?)_{10}$

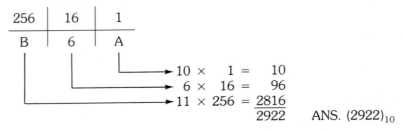

10 ×   1 =   10
 6 × 16 =   96
11 × 256 = 2816
          2922   ANS. $(2922)_{10}$

Self-Evaluating Quiz

Find the decimal equivalent of the following hexadecimal numbers.

1. $(2E)_{16} = (?)_{10}$
2. $(A23)_{16} = (?)_{10}$

Solutions

1.

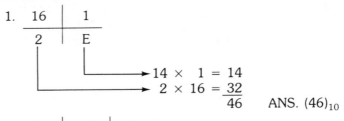

14 × 1 = 14
 2 × 16 = 32
         46   ANS. $(46)_{10}$

2.   156 | 16 | 1
      A | 2 | 3

 3 ×   1 =   3
 2 × 16 =   32
10 × 256 = 2560
          2595   ANS. $(2595)_{10}$

C. Determining the Hexadecimal Equivalent of a Decimal Number

To convert from the decimal numbering system to the hexadecimal system we use the remainder method, dividing by 16.

Example 1 $(382)_{10} = (?)_{16}$

Remainder in
Hex.

	1
	7
	E

16 ⌐1
16 ⌐23
16 ⌐382

0

————Reading from top to bottom

ANS. $(17E)_{16}$

Example 2 $(1583)_{10} = (?)_{16}$

Remainder in
Hex.

0

16 ⌐6
16 ⌐98
16 ⌐1583

6
2
F

ANS. $(62F)_{16}$

Self-Evaluating Quiz

Find the hexadecimal equivalent of the following decimal numbers.

1. $(132)_{10} = (?)_{16}$ 2. $(214)_{10} = (?)_{16}$

Solutions

1.   0   8   2.   0   D
   16 ⌐8   4   16 ⌐13   6
   16 ⌐132   16 ⌐214   ANS. $(D6)_{16}$
              ANS. $(84)_{16}$

D. Addition and Subtraction of Hexadecimal Numbers

Arithmetic operations in hexadecimal are similar to those in other numbering systems. Perform the operation on each column decimally, convert the decimal number to hexadecimal, and proceed.

Example 1 $(BAD)_{16} + (431)_{16} = (?)_{16}$

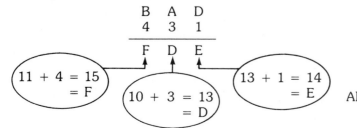

B A D
4 3 1
—————
F D E

11 + 4 = 15
    = F

10 + 3 = 13
    = D

13 + 1 = 14
    = E   ANS. $(FDE)_{16}$

Example 2 $(CBA)_{16} + (627)_{16} = (?)_{16}$

$$
\begin{array}{ccc}
 & C & B & A \\
+ & 6 & 2 & 7 \\
\hline
1 & 2 & E & 1
\end{array}
$$

$12 + 6 = 18_{10}$
$= 12_{16}$

$10 + 7 = 17_{10} = 11_{16}$ (carry 1)

ANS. $(12E1)_{16}$

Keep in mind that the carrying of hexadecimal numbers to the next position is performed in exactly the same manner as in the decimal numbering system. A sum of 16 results in a carry of 1 $(10_{16} = 16_{10})$.

Example 3 $(83E)_{16} + (F6F)_{16} = (?)_{16}$

$$
\begin{array}{rccc}
 & 8 & 3 & E \\
+ & F & 6 & F \\
\hline
1 & 7 & A & D
\end{array}
$$

$14 + 15 = (29)_{10} = (1D)_{16}$ (carry 1)

ANS. $(17AD)_{16}$

We can subtract hexadecimal numbers by again converting every digit to decimal for each position and then converting the difference obtained back to hexadecimal. Note that the system of borrowing from or exchanging with the next position results in an exchange of 16 rather than 10.

Example 4 $(26)_{16} - (7)_{16} = (?)_{16}$

$$
\begin{array}{rcl}
26 & & 1 \quad\quad (16 + 6) \\
- \ 7 & = & - \quad\quad\quad\quad 7 \\
\hline
 & & 1 \quad\quad\quad F
\end{array}
$$

(16 borrowed from 2nd position)

ANS. $(1F)_{16}$

On some computers, specifically the IBM line, computer printouts *of storage locations* and their contents are specified in hexadecimal. While the normal program output is printed decimally, any program specifications are indicated in hexadecimal. Thus programmers are required to understand positional numbering theory to assist in computer processing.

When errors or "bugs" exist in a program or when programmers wish to pinpoint the contents of specific storage locations for testing purposes, they must be able to perform hexadecimal arithmetic.

Memory **dumps,** or displays of storage contents, are often given in hexadecimal. Thus a programmer may be advised that a program began at hexadecimal location 28E6 and that an error occurred at location 3EF2. The program listing has the address of each instruction, but only in relative terms, that is, from address 0000 on with no relation to where the program began. Thus to obtain the absolute error point and to find the corresponding instruction, the starting point, 28E6, must be subtracted from 3EF2 to obtain the absolute error point.

```
       E 16 ⎤
   3 E F  2 ⎦
 − 2 8 E  6
 ──────────
   1 6 0 C     Absolute Error Point
```

In order to extract items from storage, then, the average programmer must understand hexadecimal arithmetic.

E. Converting from Hexadecimal to Binary and from Binary to Hexadecimal

At the start of this section, we indicated that hexadecimal numbers are used by some computers because they effectively reduce four binary digits to a single digit in base 16. That is, we can represent any four binary digits by a single hexadecimal digit.

Given any binary number, regardless of its size, we can convert it to a hexadecimal number by dividing it into groups of four digits and representing each group with a single hexadecimal digit.

Example 1 $(1101001101110111)_2 = (?)_{16}$

8421	8421	8421	8421
1101	0011	0111	0111
D	3	7	7

ANS. $(D377)_{16}$

Example 2 $(101101111)_2 = (?)_{16}$

0001	0110	1111
1	6	F

ANS. $(16F)_{16}$

Note that when the binary number does not consist of a multiple of four digits, it can be enlarged by using high-order or nonsignificant zeros. That is, 11 is the same as 0011, which has four digits. Because of the simple relation between binary and hexadecimal digits, the computer can represent data in hexadecimal, by still maintaining the binary (on-off state) configuration.

Notice also that it is sometimes easier to determine the **decimal** equivalent of a **binary** number by first finding its hexadecimal equivalent. A large binary number requires numerous calculations to determine the positional values and then to convert to decimal. The conversion process is simpler from hexadecimal to decimal, and, since we can easily represent binary numbers as hexadecimal numbers, the double conversion often simplifies the operation.

Let us consider the binary number in Example 2 directly above.

$(101101111)_2$

Suppose we wish to find its decimal equivalent. We can use the standard method by determining each positional value and then adding all "on" positions. Or we can convert the number to hexadecimal and obtain 16F as in the example. Then we can convert:

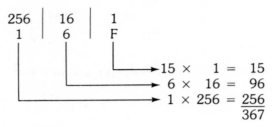

ANS. $(367)_{10}$

Often we find that the time it takes to convert large binary numbers to the decimal numbering system is significantly reduced by performing the intermediate conversion to hexadecimal.

Self-Evaluating Quiz

1. $(8E6)_{16} = (?)_{10}$
2. $(9FC)_{16} = (?)_{10}$
3. $(1387)_{10} = (?)_{16}$
4. $(8365)_{10} = (?)_{16}$

5. $\quad$ 8EC
    $+$ DE2

6. $\quad$ 9CC
    $+$ DEE

7. $\quad$ 9CE
    $-$ 8DF

8. $\quad$ AEC
    $-$ 932

9. $(11011111110111)_2 = (?)_{16}$
10. $(111111101111)_2 = (?)_{16}$

Solutions

1. $(8E6)_{16} = (?)_{10}$

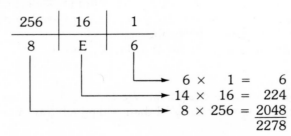

ANS. 2278

2. $(9FC)_{16} = (?)_{10}$

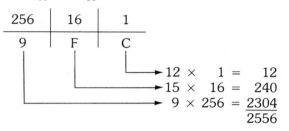

256	16	1
9	F	C

$$12 \times 1 = 12$$
$$15 \times 16 = 240$$
$$9 \times 256 = \underline{2304}$$
$$2556 \qquad \text{ANS. 2556}$$

3. $(1387)_{10} = (?)_{16}$

Remainder in Hex.

$$
\begin{array}{rl}
 & 0 \\
16 & \overline{\smash{)}5} \\
16 & \overline{\smash{)}86} \\
16 & \overline{\smash{)}1387}
\end{array}
\qquad
\begin{array}{l}
5 \\
6 \\
B
\end{array}
\qquad \text{ANS. 56B}
$$

4. $(8365)_{10} = (?)_{16}$

Remainder in Hex.

$$
\begin{array}{rl}
 & 0 \\
16 & \overline{\smash{)}2} \\
16 & \overline{\smash{)}32} \\
16 & \overline{\smash{)}522} \\
16 & \overline{\smash{)}8365}
\end{array}
\qquad
\begin{array}{l}
2 \\
0 \\
A \\
D
\end{array}
\qquad \text{ANS. 20AD}
$$

5. $\begin{array}{r} 8EC \\ +DE2 \\ \hline 16CE \end{array}$

6. $\begin{array}{r} 9CC \\ +DEE \\ \hline 17BA \end{array}$

7. $\begin{array}{r} 9CE \\ -8DF \\ \hline EF \end{array}$

8. $\begin{array}{r} AEC \\ -932 \\ \hline 1BA \end{array}$

9. $(11011111110111)_2 = (?)_{16}$

0011	011▶	1111	0111
3	7	F	7

ANS. $(37F7)_{16}$

10. $(111111101111)_2 = (?)_{16}$

1111	1110	1111
F	E	F

ANS. $(FEF)_{16}$

IV. REPRESENTATION OF CHARACTERS IN STORAGE

We have seen that with a combination of on-off bits, or binary digits, it is possible to represent any number. Many computers group binary numbers in an effort to conserve storage so that data may be represented internally in the octal numbering system, where three binary numbers are grouped, or in the hexadecimal numbering system, where four binary numbers are grouped.

Most computer systems use some variation of the binary representation to store all characters including letters and special symbols. We shall discuss two widely used computer codes to familiarize the student with the principles involved.

A. The Binary Coded Decimal or BCD Code

Binary Coded Decimal or BCD is a computer code, or method of data representation, that was very common on early computers. It is still frequently used, particularly as a means of coding data on external media such as tapes and 96-column cards.

Each storage position can be viewed as in Figure C.1. Every character is represented as a series of "on-off" bits in bit-positions BA8421.

The digit portion of this code is already familiar to you since it includes the characters 8-4-2-1 or 2^3-2^2-2^1-2^0. Each decimal digit 0 to 9 can be represented by some combination of 8-4-2-1 "on" bits.

Zones are "off" for digit representation. Hence each decimal digit is represented as follows in BCD.

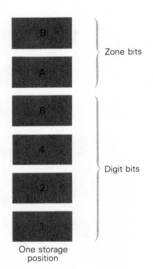

Zone bits

Digit bits

One storage position

Figure C.1
Structure of the BCD code in each storage position.

Decimal Digit	BCD Configuration						Bit Configuration	
	B	A	8	4	2	1		
1	0	0	0	0	0	1	1	bit
2	0	0	0	0	1	0	2	bit
3	0	0	0	0	1	1	2-1	bits
4	0	0	0	1	0	0	4	bit
5	0	0	0	1	0	1	4-1	bits
6	0	0	0	1	1	0	4-2	bits
7	0	0	0	1	1	1	4-2-1	bits
8	0	0	1	0	0	0	8	bit
9	0	0	1	0	0	1	8-1	bits
0	0	0	1	0	1	0	8-2	bits

The representation for digits 1 to 9 is the standard binary representation. Zero, you will note, has a bit-configuration of 8-2. You might have expected zero to be represented as all zeros but that is the configuration for a blank character. To distinguish between a blank and a zero, the 8-2 or 001010 BCD representation is used for the latter.

Zones B and A are used to represent the Hollerith zones 12-11-0. You will recall that the Hollerith zones are used as follows.

$$12 + \text{digits 1 to 9} = \text{A to I}$$
$$11 + \text{digits 1 to 9} = \text{J to R}$$
$$0 + \text{digits 2 to 9} = \text{S to Z}$$

In BCD we have the following.

Zone	B-A bits	
12	B – A	on
11	B	on
0	A	on

Hollerith codes are then directly convertible to BCD codes. The zone portion converts as above and the digit portion is represented in binary form. Hence, the BCD configuration in one storage position for the letter A, which is 12-1 in Hollerith, is

B	A	8	4	2	1
1	1	0	0	0	1

or B-A-1

The BCD configuration for the letter C, which is 12-3 in Hollerith, is:

B	A	8	4	2	1
1	1	0	0	1	1

or B-A-2-1

Similarly, the BCD configuration for the letter N, which is 11-5 in Hollerith, is:

B	A	8	4	2	1
1	0	0	1	0	1

or B-4-1

B. Parity

There is one more element necessary to complete the BCD Code, an element called a **parity** or check bit denoted as C. The purpose of this bit is to provide an internal check on the validity of the character represented. There exists a slight possibility, although it is very slight indeed, that the computer could lose or gain a bit during processing; that is, a circuit might accidentally go off or on. To prevent such an occurrence from going unnoticed, computer codes generally include an extra **parity** or **check bit.** Using BCD, we employ the check bit to ensure that there are always an odd number of bits on in a particular position. Hence, E, which is represented by the four bits BA41, would require an additional bit so that it has an odd number of bits on. Thus E is represented in its complete BCD form as CBA41, where C is the check bit. The letter D, which is represented by BA4, already uses an odd number of bits. Hence the check or parity bit would be off in this case. Figure C.2 illustrates how a sample punched card would be represented in storage in BCD.

Most computers that use BCD codes are generally classified as odd-parity machines, since there must always be an odd number of bits on at a given time. If the computer gains or loses a bit during processing, the bit configuration would be invalid since there would then be an even number of bits on, an occurrence that would automatically stop the machine.

You might well ask, at this point, what happens if two bits, instead of one, are inadvertently turned on or off in a storage position. That would still leave

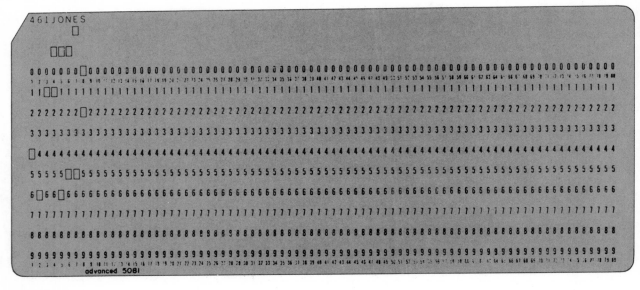

Figure C.2
Punched card data and its
BCD equivalent in storage
positions 801 to 808.

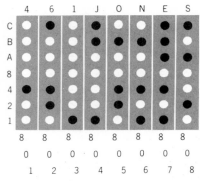

NOTE: Odd-parity machine.

an odd number of bits and the machine would not recognize an error. It is true, in fact, that the computer is capable of recognizing only a *single* error for each position, a possibility that itself can best be described as remote. The possibility of *two* errors in a single position is, however, so unlikely that it is not even provided for. Thus, a parity system detects practically all possible transmission errors.

Some machines are called even-parity computers, meaning that an even number of bits is required in a given position at all times. The principle is exactly the same as described above with the check bit being used to ensure an even number of bits on at a given time.

As a summary, examine Table C.1, which provides the BCD configuration for numbers, letters, and some of the more common special characters.

C. The EBCDIC Code

More recent computers often use an internal computer code that is an extension of the BCD code described above. It is called EBCDIC, which means *Extended*

Table C.1 BCD Code for Numbers, Letters, and Selected Special Characters

Character	C	B	A	8	4	2	1	Character	C	B	A	8	4	2	1
0	C			8		2		A		B	A				1
1							1	B		B	A			2	
2						2		C	C	B	A			2	1
3	C					2	1	D		B	A		4		
4					4			E	C	B	A		4		1
5	C				4		1	F	C	B	A		4	2	
6	C				4	2		G		B	A		4	2	1
7					4	2	1	H		B	A	8			
8				8				I	C	B	A	8			1
9	C			8			1	J	C	B					1
								K	C	B				2	
blank	C							L		B				2	1
—		B						M	C	B			4		
&	C	B	A					N		B			4		1
$	C	B		8		2	1	O		B			4	2	
*		B		8	4			P	C	B			4	2	1
.		B	A	8		2	1	Q	C	B		8			
								R		B		8			1
								S	C		A			2	
								T			A			2	1
								U	C		A		4		
								V			A		4		1
								W			A		4	2	
								X	C		A		4	2	1
								Y	C		A	8			
								Z			A	8			1

Binary Coded Decimal Interchange Code and is pronounced eb-ce-dick. Using the BCD Code, it is possible to represent 64 characters. Using EBCDIC, it is possible to represent 256 characters. The additional characters that can be represented in EBCDIC include lowercase letters (as well as uppercase or capital letters), many additional special symbols, graphic symbols, and control characters.

With the EBCDIC Code, each storage position consists of eight bits. On many machines, including most IBM systems, a single storage position consisting of eight bits is called a **byte.**

Each byte is divided into a zone portion, consisting of four bits, and a digit portion consisting of four bits, producing what is referred to as the zoned decimal format.

Zone	Digit

Byte

There are no BA bits in EBCDIC as in BCD. Instead, the zone portion of the byte is represented in exactly the same manner as the digit portion.

BYTE

Zone				Digit			
8	4	2	1	8	4	2	1

The digit portion is used in exactly the same manner as described for BCD. For the zone portion, a 12-zone is represented as 8-4, an 11-zone as 8-4-1 and a 0-zone as 8-4-2.

Thus the letter A, in Hollerith, a 12-zone and a 1-punch, is:

Zone   Digit

8	4	2	1	8	4	2	1	Positional Value
1	1	0	0	0	0	0	1	Bits

Byte

The 12-zone corresponds to 1100, a 12 in binary, and the 1 is 0001. A hexadecimal printout of this byte would be C1 (8 + 4 in the hexadecimal system is a C). That is, the zone and digit portions are treated independently for printout purposes.

The letter T corresponding to 0-3 punches is represented as:

Hex. Printout	Zone				Digit				Character
E3	8	4	2	1	8	4	2	1	T
	1	1	1	0	0	0	1	1	

0-zone   3-digit

In a hexadecimal printout, the T would be represented as E3. Numeric characters are also represented in this form. For **unsigned** numbers, all zone bits are on. Thus we have 1111 as the zone portion of all numbers. The number 8 then is represented in a byte as:

Zone				Digit			
8	4	2	1	8	4	2	1
1	1	1	1	1	0	0	0

Actual value   +   8
Hexadecimal representation   F   8

The 1111 in the zone portion of a byte is used to denote an unsigned number that is assumed to be positive. The selection of 1111 was based on the fact that it would make unsigned numbers the highest in the collating or sorting sequence. Note that an unsigned 5 in a hexadecimal printout of storage would read as F5.

A definitive positive sign is denoted by 1100 (hex C) and a minus sign by 1101 (hex D).

The following chart summarizes the representation of the zone portion of characters in EBCDIC and hexadecimal.

Summary of Zone Representation

Hollerith	EBCDIC	Hexadecimal
12	1100	C
11	1101	D
0	1110	E
No zone	1111	F
(unsigned numbers)		

Note that, as indicated in the previous section, each group of four bits or binary digits can be used to represent a single hexadecimal digit. Thus a short-hand method for representing characters in EBCDIC is to represent them as *two* hexadecimal digits. Since each hexadecimal digit is used to represent four binary digits, two hexadecimal digits are needed to represent one byte or eight bits.

E6 in hexadecimal represents the EBCDIC code for W:

Zone				Digit			
1	1	1	0	0	1	1	0

0-zone   6-digit

This is equivalent to 0–6 in Hollerith or the letter W.

F5 in hexadecimal represents the zoned decimal format in EBCDIC for a positive 5:

Zone	Digit
F	5
1111	0101

All unsigned numbers in zoned decimal format are represented hexadecimally with an F followed by a digit.

Table C.2 provides a summary of the EBCDIC representation of numbers and letters.

The EBCDIC code also has provision for a parity or check bit called a **P-bit** in this system.[1] Many third-generation computers are **even-parity** ma-

---

[1] See page C-27 for a further discussion of the check bit.

TABLE C.2   EBCDIC and Hollerith Codes for Numbers and Letters

Character	EBCDIC		Hollerith
	Zone	Digit	
A	1100	0001	12-1
B	1100	0010	12-2
C	1100	0011	12-3
D	1100	0100	12-4
E	1100	0101	12-5
F	1100	0110	12-6
G	1100	0111	12-7
H	1100	1000	12-8
I	1100	1001	12-9
J	1101	0001	11-1
K	1101	0010	11-2
L	1101	0011	11-3
M	1101	0100	11-4
N	1101	0101	11-5
O	1101	0110	11-6
P	1101	0111	11-7
Q	1101	1000	11-8
R	1101	1001	11-9
S	1110	0010	0-2
T	1110	0011	0-3
U	1110	0100	0-4
V	1110	0101	0-5
W	1110	0110	0-6
X	1110	0111	0-7
Y	1110	1000	0-8
Z	1110	1001	0-9
0	1111	0000	0
1	1111	0001	1
2	1111	0010	2
3	1111	0011	3
4	1111	0100	4
5	1111	0101	5
6	1111	0110	6
7	1111	0111	7
8	1111	1000	8
9	1111	1001	9

chines. Hence the P-bit is used to ensure that an even number of bits is always on. EBCDIC is thus a nine-bit code. Figure C.3 illustrates how sample punched card data would be represented in storage in EBCDIC.

As noted in Chapter 4, ASCII is still another popular code used in many computers.

We have, by no means, exhausted all the variations on computer codes. To do so would require a text for that purpose only. Rather, we have provided the principles used in most computer codes. Other codes are merely variations on this theme and after reading the fundamentals in this appendix you would require only a minimal amount of effort to understand them.

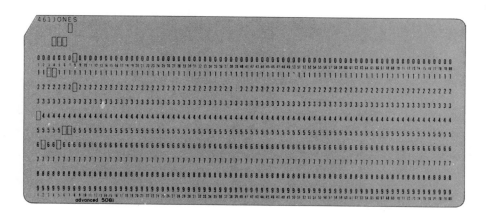

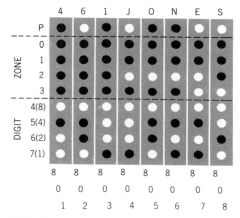

Figure C.3
Punched card data and its EBCDIC equivalent in storage positions 801 to 808.

NOTE: Even-parity machine.

Self-Evaluating Quiz

Find the BCD code for the following. Use Table C.1 if necessary. There is no need to memorize configurations.

1. A
2. 8
3. 5
4. T
5. K

Find the EBCDIC code for the following. Use Table C.2 if necessary. There is no need to memorize configurations.

6. A
7. 8
8. 5

9. T
10. K

Solutions

1. BA1
2. 8
3. C41 (C is the check bit)
4. A21
5. CB2

	Zone	Digit	Hex.
6.	1100	0001	C1
7.	1111	1000	F8
8.	1111	0101	F5
9.	1110	0011	E3
10.	1101	0010	D2

Review Questions

1. $721_8 = (?)_2$
2. $677_8 = (?)_{10}$
3. $101101_2 = (?)_{10}$
4. $423_{10} = (?)_8 = (?)_2$
5. $E27D_{16} = (?)_{10}$
6. $1739_{10} = (?)_{16}$
7. $110110_2 + 11101_2 = (?)_2$
8. $11110_2 - 11001_2 = (?)_2$
9. $8FC_{16} + 9EE_{16} = (?)_{16}$
10. $E8FD_{16} = (?)_2$
11. Find the BCD Code for the following.
    a. 7
    b. Q
    c. F
    d. V
12. Find the EBCDIC Code for the following.
    a. 7
    b. Q
    c. F
    d. V
13. Determine the decimal equivalents of the following binary numbers.
    a. 1001111
    b. 11100
    c. 110011

14. Determine the binary equivalents of the following decimal numbers.
   a. 234
   b. 435
   c. 333

15. Add the following binary numbers and indicate the sum in binary form. Check your work by converting each number back into decimal form.
   a. 11101111 + 1111101111
   b. 111111011101 + 1111011
   c. 1110111 + 111111

16. Determine the decimal equivalents of the following hexadecimal numbers.
   a. 6FFE
   b. 70FD
   c. 67EE

17. Determine the hexadecimal equivalents of the following decimal numbers.
   a. 10678
   b. 16745
   c. 2345

18. Add the following hexadecimal numbers. Check your answers.
   a. 45EE + FE34
   b. 3355 + FDE2
   c. 897F + 5FFF

19. Represent the following in EBCDIC form.
   a. G
   b. M
   c. −3
   d. +6
   e. W
   f. D

A GUIDE TO RESOURCES AND JOURNALS IN THE COMPUTING FIELD

This book provides a broad overview of information processing concepts and applications. As a result, there are many topics that are treated very sparsely. Students may find that:

1. There are topics presented about which more information is desired.
2. A topic has been assigned by an instructor for a paper and source material relating to the topic must be found.

The following pages provide a bibliographic review of journals, books, proceedings, and other sources relating to specific computer topics.

The review has been categorized as follows:

I. Books and Journals by Subject
   The subjects chosen for this review are those most likely to spark student interest or most likely to be topics assigned as papers. The focus in this section is on standard texts that provide an in-depth survey or analysis of the subject matter. Books tend to be comprehensive and general enough to retain their timeliness. Journal articles, on the other hand, tend to be specific in nature and provide state-of-the-art information; hence they become obsolete rather quickly. Thus, this section will include the names of journals that specifically relate to each subject. Units II and III provide information on journals in general.

II. Periodicals Specifically Related to Computers and Information Processing
   These include many of the more informative and interesting journals on computing. These periodicals contain articles that relate to all of the topics discussed in this text. To obtain state-of-the-art knowledge about any topic, scan the recent issues of these journals; you are certain to find pertinent information.

III. General Periodicals
   These journals frequently include nontechnical but relevant articles on computers.

IV. Prominent Computer Societies

V. Suggested Term Paper Topics

Note that when using any source you should pay particular attention to the date. An article on robotics, for example, that has a 1969 date of publication is best viewed as historical and should *not* be used as a source on current developments.

I. BOOKS AND JOURNALS BY SUBJECT

Artificial Intelligence

Banerji, Ranan, *Artificial Intelligence: A Theoretical Approach* (Amsterdam: North Holland), 1980.
 Provides an analysis of heuristics by focusing on several studies at a number of research centers.

Barr, Avron, Edward A. Feigenbaum, and Paul R. Cohen, *The Handbook of Artificial Intelligence*, 3 vols. (Los Altos, CA: William Kaufmann, Inc.), 1981.
 An overview of the subject.

Bellman, Richard, *An Introduction to Artificial Intelligence: Can Computers Think?* (San Francisco, CA: Boyd and Fraser), 1978.
 This is a comprehensive, classic book on AI.

Dreyfus, Hubert L., *What Computers Can't Do* (New York: Harper & Row), 1972.
 A philosophical evaluation of the problems inherent in artificial intelligence research. Although it is a dated book, the issues are still relevant.

Feigenbaum, Edward A. and Pamela McCorduck, *The Fifth Generation: Artificial Intelligence and Japan's Computer Challenge to the World* (Reading, MA: Addison-Wesley), 1983.
 A discussion on the Japanese "threat" and the need for an American response. An important book on the subject.

Greenwood, Richard D. and Ignatius Brodzinski, *Artificial Intelligence: Tools, Techniques and Applications* (New York: Harper & Row), 1984.

Krueger, Myron W., *Artificial Reality* (Reading, MA: Addison-Wesley), 1983.
 An optimistic view of an environment run by computer systems.

McCorduck, Pamela, *Machines Who Think* (San Francisco, CA: W. H. Freeman), 1979.
 A history of AI.

Michie, Donald, *On Machine Intelligence* (New York: Wiley), 1974.
 A well-written account of the main ideas of AI. It includes a collection of articles written for the nonspecialist by Michie, who is regarded as one of the leading authorities on AI in Great Britain.

Simon, Herbert A., *The Science of the Artificial*, 2nd ed. (Cambridge, MA), 1981.
 A classic in its field.

Weizenbaum, Joseph, *Computer Power and Human Reason* (San Francisco, CA: W. H. Freeman), 1976.
 A refreshing view of the problems inherent in AI research from the point of view of an insider.

Journals Specifically Related to Artificial Intelligence
American Journal of Computational Linguistics (quarterly).
American Society for Cybernetics—Forum (quarterly).
Artificial Intelligence: An International Journal (monthly).

Basic Programming

Albrecht, B. et al., *What to Do After You Hit Return* (Menlo Park, CA: People's Computer Co.), 1975.

Albrecht, R. L., L. Finkel and J. R. Brown, *BASIC for Home Computers* (New York: Wiley), 1978.

Albrecht, R. L., *BASIC: A Self Teaching Guide*, 2nd ed. (New York: Wiley), 1978.

Note: Albrecht has authored and coauthored an entire series of BASIC self-teaching guides for a wide variety of computers including micros, published by Wiley and others. All of them are quite good.

Clark, James F. and William O. Drum, *Basic Programming: A Structured Approach* (Cincinnati, OH: South-Western Publishing Co.), 1983.

Graham, Neill, *Programming the IBM Personal Computer: Fundamentals of BASIC* (New York: Holt, Rinehart and Winston), 1984.

Kemeny, John G. and Thomas E. Kurtz, *BASIC Programming*, 3rd ed. (New York: Wiley), 1980.

Kittner, M. and B. Northcutt, *Basic BASIC: A Structured Approach* (Menlo Park, CA: Benjamin/Cummins), 1984.

Marateck, Samuel L., *BASIC Programming*, 2nd ed. (New York: Academic Press), 1982.

One of the most thorough books on BASIC.

Osborne, Adam, Gordon Eubanks, Jr., and Martin McNiff, *CBASIC: A User's Guide* (New York: McGraw-Hill), 1983.

An in-depth view of CBASIC, a very popular version of BASIC for micros.

Price, Wilson T., *Programming the IBM Personal Computer: Business BASIC* (New York: Holt, Rinehart and Winston), 1984.

Shelly, Gary and Thomas Cashman, *An Introduction to BASIC Programming* (Fullerton, CA: Anaheim Press), 1982.

A four-color, elementary introduction to BASIC programming.

Silver, Gerald A. and Myrna Silver, *Basic Programming for Microcomputers* (New York: Harper & Row), 1984.

Computers: From the Past to the Present

Annals of the History of Computing (Arlington, VA: AFIPS Press).

This is a quarterly publication that focuses on the history of computing. It includes articles by computer pioneers as well as by historians.

Austrian, Geoffrey, *Herman Hollerith* (New York: Columbia University Press), 1982.

An interesting and well-documented biography of Hollerith.

Burks, Arthur W., Herman H. Goldstine, and John von Neumann, "Planning and Coding Problems for an Electronic Computing Instrument," Part 1 (reprinted in John von Neumann, *Collected Works*, Vol. 5, ed. A. H. Taub), Oxford, 1963.

Encyclopedia of Computer Science and Engineering, 2nd ed., edited by Anthony Ralston (New York: Van Nostrand Reinhold), 1983.

300 contributors
500 entries

700 charts, tables, illustrations
5000-term index

Evans, C., *The Micro Millennium* (New York: Viking Press), 1979.
A broad and entertaining overview of computer development.

Fishman, Katherine Davis, *The Computer Establishment* (New York: Harper & Row), 1981.
This is a journalist's view of the growth of computers with specific attention to IBM. It focuses on how IBM came from behind to eventually dominate the computing field.

Goldstine, Herman H., *The Computer from Pascal to von Neumann* (Princeton, NJ: Princeton University Press), 1972.
This book considers the history of digital and analog calculating devices as well as those computers with which the author was involved: ENIAC, EDVAC, and John von Neumann's Institute for Advanced Study computer.

Goldstine, H. H. and J. von Neumann, ''Planning and Coding Problems for an Electronic Computing Instrument,'' Parts 2 and 3 (reprinted in John von Neumann, *Collected Works*, Vol. 5, ed. A. H. Taub), Oxford, 1963.

Hodges, Andrew, *Alan Turing: The Enigma* (London: Burnett Books), 1983.

Kidder, Tracy, *The Soul of a New Machine* (Boston: Little Brown), 1981.
This Pulitzer-prize winning book focuses on the development of the Data General Corporation.

Lukoff, Herman, *From Dits to Bits* (Portland, OR: Robotics Press), 1979.
This work is an autobiography written by a computer pioneer who worked on ENIAC and UNIVAC.

Metropolis, N., ed., *A History of Computing in the Twentieth Century* (New York: Academic Press), 1980.
This volume contains a series of papers presented by computer pioneers at a 1976 History of Computing Conference at Los Alamos, New Mexico.

Morrison, P. and E. Morrison, eds., *Charles Babbage and His Calculating Engines: Selected Writings by Charles Babbage and Others* (New York: Dover Publications), 1961.
This book includes material on Babbage's life and his two engines.

Randell, Brian, ''An Annotated Bibliography on the Origins of Computers,'' *Annals of the History of Computing*, Vol. 1, No. 2, October, 1979.
Includes the most extensive bibliography of historical sources currently available.

Randell, Brian, *The Origins of Digital Computers: Selected Papers*, 2nd ed. (Berlin: Springer-Verlag), 1982.
This book contains 32 original papers and manuscripts relating to the origins of digital computers, as well as an extensive bibliography.

Redmond, Kent D. and Thomas M. Smith, *Project Whirlwind* (Bedford, MA: Digital Press), 1980.
This book discusses the intellectual and sociological factors influencing the development of M.I.T.'s first electronic digital computer.

Sobel, Robert, *IBM: Colossus in Transition* (New York: Times Books), 1981.
This is an ''outsider's'' view of the corporate giant.

Stern, Nancy, *From ENIAC to UNIVAC* (Bedford, MA: Digital Press), 1981.
This book discusses the development of the ENIAC, EDVAC, BINAC, and UNIVAC as well as the academic, governmental, and commercial forces that influenced their development.

Wexelblatt, Richard, ed., *History of Programming Languages* (New York: Academic Press), 1982.
 This work is based on the proceedings of the History of Programming Languages Conference held in Los Angeles on June 1-3, 1978 and sponsored by the ACM Special Interest Group on Programming Languages (SIGPLAN). It presents a record of the early history of 13 languages, including ALGOL, APL, APT, COBOL, BASIC, FORTRAN, GPSS, JOSS, JOVIAL, LISP, PL/1, SIMULA, and SNOBOL.

MIT Press, Reprint Series on the History of Computing.
 Reprints older, important documents on the history of computing.

The Digital Museum in Boston, MA and The Charles Babbage Institute at the University of Minnesota have more information on the history of computers.

Computers and Automation

Brooks, Frederick P., *The Mythical Man-Month* (Reading, MA: Addison-Wesley), 1975.
 A classic in its field.

Simon, Herbert A., *The New Science of Management Decision* (New York: Harper & Row), 1960.
 A classic work on management science.

Tomeski, Edward A. and Harold Lazarus, *People-Oriented Computer Systems: The Computer in Crisis*, 2nd ed. (New York: Basic Books), 1983.
 This book focuses on how and why computer systems have failed people and organizations, and what can be done to make these systems better serve society.

Winner, Langdon, *Autonomous Technology: Technology Out-of-Control as a Theme in Political Thought* (Cambridge, MA: M.I.T. Press), 1977.
 An ideological critique of technology as it affects political systems.

Computers and the Future

Ellul, Jacques, *The Technological Society* (New York: Knopf), 1974.
 A famous humanist's analysis of our technical civilization and the effect of an increasingly standardized culture on the future of man.

Martin, James, *The Wired Society* (Englewood Cliffs, NJ: Prentice-Hall), 1978.
 A work that focuses on the effects that the technology of communication is likely to have on society in the not-so-distant future.

Toffler, Alvin, *Future Shock* (New York: Bantam), 1971.
 A sociological view of the effects of technology on society.

Toffler, Alvin, *The Third Wave* (New York: Morrow), 1980.
 The book focuses on what the author describes as the "third wave" of change in history, the first being the agricultural revolution and the second being the industrial revolution. It provides an analysis of the forces that are influencing society.

Journals Specifically Related to Computers in the Future

Abacus (quarterly).

Computers and the Humanities

Bateman, Wayne, *Introduction to Computer Music* (New York: Wiley), 1980.
This book focuses on how digital computers may be used to generate new and interesting musical sounds.

Ernst, D., *Electronic Music* (New York: Macmillan), 1977.

Higgins, D., *Computers for the Arts* (New York: Abyss Publications), 1977.

Hiller, L. A. and R. A. Baker, *Computer Cantata* (New York: Theodore Presser), 1968.

Hiller, L. A. and L. M. Isaacson, *Experimental Music* (Hightstown, NJ: McGraw-Hill), 1959; *Illiac Suite for String Quartet* (New York: Theodore Presser), 1957.
Two classic works in the field.

Leavitt, Ruth, ed., *Artist and Computer* (New York: Harmony Press), 1974.
A series of articles written by people who have experimented with computer art.

Morgan, Christopher P., *The Byte Book of Computer Music* (Petersborough, NH: Byte), 1979.
This book is designed for people who wish to experiment with computer music.

Journals Specifically Related to Computers and the Humanities

Computer Graphics and Art (monthly).
Computers and the Humanities (quarterly).

Computers in Education

Bork, Alfred, *Personal Computers for Education* (New York: Harper & Row), 1984.

Coburn T. et al., *Practical Guide to Computers in Education* (Reading, MA: Addison-Wesley), 1982.

Davisson, W. I. and F. J. Bonello, *Computer-Assisted Instruction in Economic Education: A Case Study* (Notre Dame, IN: Univ. of Notre Dame Press), 1976.
An analysis of one CAI project.

Ellis, Allen, *The Use and Misuse of Computers in Education* (Hightstown, NJ: McGraw-Hill), 1974.

Jackson, ed., *Teaching Informatics Courses* (New York: North Holland), 1982.

Oettinger, Anthony G., *Run, Computer, Run* (Cambridge, MA: Harvard University Press), 1969.
This is a classic work that summarizes the basic issues relating to CAI.

Rockert, J. F. and M. S. Scott-Morton, *Computers and the Learning Process in Higher Education* (Hightstown, NJ: McGraw-Hill), 1975.
An in-depth view of computers used at the university level.

Seidel, Robert J. and Martin Rubin, eds., *Computers and Communications: Implications for Education* (New York: Academic Press), 1977.
A sociological and technological evaluation of CAI.

Journals Specifically Related to Computers in Education

ACM (Association for Computing Machinery) Bulletins
ACM SIGCUE (quarterly)
AEDS Journal and AEDS Monitor (quarterly).
The Computing Teacher (quarterly)
Educational Computer Magazine (bimonthly).
Journal of Computers in Mathematics and Science Teaching (quarterly)
PLATO Password (quarterly).
T. H. E. Journal (monthly)

Computers in the Sciences and Medicine

Colleen, M. F., ed., *Hospital Computer Systems* (New York: Wiley), 1974.
   This is a collection of papers on the use of computers in hospitals.
Perkins, W. J., ed., *Biomedical Computing* (Baltimore, MD: University Park
   Press), 1977.
   This is a collection of technical articles that describe the state of biomedical
   computing.

Data Communications

Fitzgerald, Jerry, Ardra Fitzgerald, and Warren Stallings, *Business Data Communications and Basic Concepts, Security and Design* (New York: Wiley),
   1984.
Loomis, Mary, *Data Communications* (Englewood Cliffs, NJ: Prentice-Hall),
   1983.
McNamara, John E., *Technical Aspects of Data Communications* (Bedford, MA:
   Digital Press), 1980.

Electronic Funds Transfer

Bequai, August, *The Cashless Society* (New York: Wiley), 1981.
   A book about EFT at the crossroads.
Chorafas, M., *Money: The Bank of the 80's* (New York: Petrocelli), 1982.
   A futuristic approach.
Colton, K. and K. Kraemer, *Computers and Banking: Electronic Funds Transfer
   Systems and Public Policy* (New York: Plenum Publishing Co.), 1980.
   A series of articles focusing on EFT.
Communications of the ACM, December 1979 issue.
   The entire issue consists of a series of papers devoted to the impact of EFT
   on society.

Flowcharting

Boillet M. et al., *Essentials of Flowcharting* (Dubuque, IA: W. C. Brown), 1982.
McIverney, Thomas F. and Andre J. Vallee, *A Student's Guide to Flowcharting*
   (Englewood Cliffs, NJ: Prentice-Hall), 1973.
Shelly, Gary B. and Thomas J. Cashman, *Introduction to Flowcharting and
   Computer Programming Logic* (Fullerton, CA: Anaheim Publishing), 1972.
Stern, Nancy B., *Flowcharting: A Self-Teaching Guide* (New York: Wiley), 1975.

Impact of Computers on Society (general)

Abshire, Gary, M., ed., *The Impact of Computers on Society and Ethics: A Bibliography* (Morristown, NJ: Creative Computing), 1980.
Contains 1920 alphabetic entries of books, magazine articles, news items, scholarly papers, and other works dealing with the impact of computers on society and ethics. Covers 1948 through 1979.

Bitter, Gary, *Computers in Today's World* (New York: Wiley), 1984.

Graham, Neill, *The Mind Tool*, 3rd ed. (St. Paul, MN: West Publishing Co.), 1983.

Hopper, Grace and Steven L. Mandell, *Understanding Computers* (St. Paul, MN: West Publishing Co.) 1984.

Sanders, D. *Computers in Society*, 3rd ed. (New York: McGraw-Hill), 1980.

Silver, Gerald A., *The Social Impact of Computing* (New York: Harcourt Brace Jovanovich), 1979.

Stern, Robert A. and Nancy Stern, *Computers in Society* (Englewood Cliffs, NJ: Prentice-Hall), 1983.

Job Control Language

Ashley, Ruth and Judi N. Fernandez, *Job Control Language: A Self-Teaching Guide* (New York: Wiley), 1978.

Brown, Gary DeWard, *System/370 Job Control Language* (New York: Wiley), 1977.

Shelly, Gary B. and Thomas J. Cashman, *OS Job Control Language and DOS Job Control Language* (Fullerton, CA: Anaheim Publishing), 1977.

Management Information Systems

Bradley, James, *Introduction to Data Base Management in Business* (New York: Holt, Rinehart and Winston), 1983.

Burch, John G., Jr., Felix R. Strater, and Gary Grudnitski, *Information Systems: Theory and Practice*, 2nd ed. (New York: Wiley), 1979.

Date, C., *An Introduction to Database Systems*, 2nd ed. (Reading, MA: Addison-Wesley), 1983.

Kroenke, David, *Database: A Professional's Primer*, 2nd ed. (Chicago, IL: SRA), 1982.

Lucas, Henry, *Information Systems Concepts for Management*, 2nd ed. (New York: McGraw-Hill), 1982.

McCleod, Raymond, Jr., *Management Information Systems*, 2nd ed. (Palo Alto, CA: SRA), 1982.

Martin, James, *An End User's Guide to Data Base* (Englewood Cliffs, NJ: Prentice-Hall), 1981.

Senn, James A., *Information Systems in Management*, 2nd ed. (Belmont, CA: Wadsworth), 1981.

Sprague, Ralph H., Jr. and Eric D. Carlson, *Building Effective Decision Support Systems* (Englewood Cliffs, NJ: Prentice-Hall), 1982.

Thierauf, Robert, *Decision Support Systems for Effective Planning and Control* (Englewood Cliffs, NJ: Prentice-Hall), 1982.

Ullman, Jeffrey D., *Principles of Database Systems* (New York: Computer Science Press), 1982.

Wetherbe, James, *Computer-Based Information Systems* (Englewood Cliffs, NJ: Prentice-Hall), 1983.

Personal Computing

Ahl, David, ed., *Basic Computer Games* (Morristown, NJ: Creative Computing), 1979.
  A listing of numerous games in BASIC that can be played on a microcomputer. There have been numerous versions of this publication.
Ashley, Ruth and Judi Fernandez, *CP/M: A Self-Teaching Guide* (New York: Wiley), 1981.
DeVaney, Chris and Richard Summe, *IBM's Personal Computer* (Indianapolis, IN: Que Corp.), 1982.
Goldstine, Larry, *IBM Personal Computer* (Englewood Cliffs, NJ: Prentice-Hall), 1983.
McGlynn, Daniel R., *Personal Computing: Home, Professional and Small Business Applications*, 2nd ed. (New York: Wiley), 1982.
  This book provides a basic introduction to personal computers, their capabilities and limitations.
Mogan, Thom, *CP/M User's Guide* (New York: McGraw-Hill), 1981.
Osborne, A., *An Introduction to Microcomputers* (New York: Osborne Associates), 1976.
  A technical work on the features and circuitry of microprocessors.
Perricone, Susan B. and Charles R. Schneider, *A Ten Step Guide to Selecting Your Small Business Computer System* (New York: Harper & Row), 1984.

(There are literally thousands of books on this subject; most are available at local bookstores.)

Journals Specifically Related to Personal Computing

BYTE
70 Main Street
Peterborough, NH 03458

Creative Computing
P. O. Box 789-M
Morristown, NJ 07960

Dr. Dobb's Journal of Computer Calisthenics and Orthodontia
Box 310
Menlo Park, CA 94025

Interface Age
P.O. Box 1234
Cerritos, CA 90701

Personal Computing
Hayden Publishing Co., Inc.
50 Essex St.
Rochelle Park, NJ 07662

(There are hundreds of such journals available at local bookstores and computer stores.)

Privacy and Security

Buck, *Introduction to Data Security and Controls* (Reading, MA: QED), 1982.

Goldstein, R. C., *The Cost of Privacy* (Brighton, MA: Honeywell), 1975.

Hsiao, David K., Douglas S. Kerr, and Stuart E. Madnick, *Computer Security* (New York: Academic Press), 1979.
  Provides a review of recent research in computer security together with a critical assessment of this research.

Parker, D. B., S. Nycum, and O. S. Oura, *Computer Abuse* (Springfield, VA: National Technical Information Service), 1973.
  Includes case histories of computer abuse.

Parker, D., *Computer Security Management* (Reston, VA: Reston), 1981.

Parker, Donn, G., *Crime by Computer* (New York: Scribners), 1976.

Wessel, Milton R., *Freedom's Edge: The Computer Threat to Society* (Reading, MA: Addison-Wesley), 1974.
  Discusses the effect of computerized data bases on individual privacy.

Westin, A. and M. Baker, *Databanks in a Free Society* (New York: Quadrangle Books), 1972.

Westin, A. F., *Privacy and Freedom* (New York: Atheneum), 1967.
  An authoritative, though somewhat dated study of privacy problems.

Software and Operating Systems

Deitel, Harvey, *Operating Systems*, (Reading, MA: Addison-Wesley), 1983.

Frank, Werner L., *Critical Issues in Software* (New York: Wiley), 1983.

Myers, Glenford J., *Software Reliability: Principles and Practices* (New York: Wiley-Interscience), 1976.

Thomas, Rebecca and Jean Yates, *A User Guide to the UNIX System* (New York: McGraw-Hill), 1982.

Structured COBOL Programming

Feingold, Carl, *Fundamentals of Structured COBOL Programming*, 4th ed. (Dubuque, IA: W. C. Brown), 1983.

Spence, J. Wayne, *COBOL for the 80's* (St. Paul, MN: West Publishing), 1982.

Stern, Nancy and Robert A. Stern, *Structured COBOL Programming*, 4th ed. (New York: Wiley), 1985.

Welburn, Tyler, *Structured COBOL* and *Advanced Structured COBOL* (Palo Alto, CA: Mayfield Publishing), 1983.

Structured Techniques

DeMarco, Tom, *Structured Analysis and Systems Design*, 2nd ed. (Englewood Cliffs, NJ: Prentice-Hall), 1982.

Gane, Chris and Trish Sarson, *Structured Systems Analysis: Tools and Techniques*, 2nd ed. (Englewood Cliffs, NJ: Prentice-Hall), 1982.

Yourdon, Edward, *Managing the Structured Technique*, 3rd ed. (Englewood Cliffs, NJ: Prentice-Hall), 1983.

Yourdon, Edward, *Structured Walkthroughs*, 3rd ed. (Englewood Cliffs, NJ: Prentice-Hall), 1983.

Systems Analysis, Design, and Control

Awad, Elias M., *Systems Analysis and Design* (Homewood, IL: Richard D. Irwin), 1979.

Biggs, Charles L., Evan G. Birks, and William Arkins, *Managing the Systems Development Process* (Englewood Cliffs, NJ: Prentice-Hall), 1980.

Burch, John G., Jr., and Joseph L. Sardinas, Jr., *Computer Control and Audit: A Total Systems Approach* (New York: Wiley), 1978.

Cortada, James W., *Managing DP Hardware: Capacity Planning, Cost Justification, Availability, and Energy Management* (Englewood Cliffs, NJ: Prentice-Hall), 1983.

Couger, J. Daniel, M. A. Colter, and R. W. Knapp, *Advanced Systems Development/Feasibility Analysis* (New York: Wiley), 1982.

Davis, William, *Structured Systems Analysis* (Reading, MA: Addison-Wesley), 1983.

Enger, Norman L., *Documentation Standards for Computer Systems*, 2nd ed. (Fairfax, VA: The Technology Press), 1980.

Fitzgerald, Jerry, Ardra Fitzgerald, and Warren Stallings, *Fundamentals of Systems Analysis*, 2nd ed. (New York: Wiley), 1984.

Gore, Marvin and Stubbe, John, *Elements of Systems Analysis*, 3rd ed. (Dubuque, IA: William C. Brown), 1983.

Kindred, Alton R., *Data Systems and Management*, 2nd ed. (Englewood Cliffs, NJ: Prentice-Hall), 1980.

Thierauf, Robert J. and George W. Reynolds, *Systems Analysis and Design: A Case Study Approach* (Columbus, OH: Charles E. Merrill), 1980.

The Computer Profession

Couger, J. Daniel and Robert A. Zawacki, *Motivating and Managing Computer Professionals* (New York: Wiley), 1980.

French, Jack, *Up the EDP Pyramid* (New York: Wiley), 1981.
A job-hunting manual for computer professionals.

Greenbaum, Joan M., *In the Name of Efficiency* (Philadelphia, PA: Temple University Press), 1979.
This book looks at the origins and techniques of modern management science and its use in the data processing work place.

Kraft, Philip, *Programmers and Managers, the Routinization of Computer Programming in the United States* (New York: Springer-Verlag), 1977.
This book considers the interrelationships between programmers and managers.

Parker, Donn B., *Ethical Conflicts in Computer Science and Technology* (Arlington, VA: AFIPS), 1979.
This book considers the ethical problems and conflicts generated by scientific and technological developments as they affect both the technological community and society in general.

Sheiderman, Ben, *Software Psychology: Human Factors in Computer and Information Systems* (Cambridge, MA: Winthrop), 1980.
This book considers motivational, stylistic, and language design factors influencing programmers. It also describes current research techniques and indicates practical guidelines for programming and systems design.

Weinberg, Gerald, *The Psychology of Computer Programming* (New York: Van Nostrand), 1971.

This book was one of the first to consider the human element in computer programming. It considers in detail the actual behavior and thought processes of programmers as they carry out their daily activities.

Yourdon, Edward, *Techniques of Program Structure and Design* (Englewood Cliffs, NJ: Prentice-Hall), 1975.

Focuses on the structured approach to programming and systems analysis.

II. PERIODICALS SPECIFICALLY RELATED TO COMPUTERS AND DATA PROCESSING

This list is by no means exhaustive, but it does include some of the best-known journals in the field.

Mostly for Mainframes

Publication: *AFIPS Conference Proceedings*
Organization: American Federation of Information Processing Societies, 1899 Preston White Drive, Reston, VA 22091
Frequency: Annually
Orientation: These proceedings include a wide variety of articles in many different subject areas. The articles are based on papers presented at the annual National Computing Conference.

Publication: *Communications of the ACM* (Association for Computing Machinery)
Organization: ACM
Address: 11 West 42nd Street, New York, NY, 10036
Frequency: Monthly
Orientation: Computer science publication. Focuses on topics such as computer architecture, artificial intelligence, operating systems, programming languages, social impact of computers, management science, operations research.

Publication: *Computer*
Organization: IEEE Computer Society
Address: IEEE Computer Society, 5855 Naples Plaza, Suite 301, Long Beach, CA 90803
Frequency: Monthly
Orientation: For technical and computer science people, technology-oriented, some attention to social applications.

Publication: *Computer Decisions: The Management Magazine of Computing*
Organization: Hayden Publishing Company, 50 Essex Street, Rochelle Park, NJ 07662
Frequency: Monthly
Orientation: This is a relatively nontechnical, management-oriented magazine that focuses on major computer issues such as security, word processing, minicomputers. The articles tend to be of general interest but provide only an introduction to some of the major topics.

Publication: *Computerworld: The Newsweekly for the Computer Community*
Address: 375 Cochituate Road, Framingham, MA 01701
Frequency: Weekly
Orientation: This is a newspaper that addresses itself to events and occurrences in the data processing industry. It is relatively nontechnical and can serve the beginning data processing student as well as the data processing professional. Some of the categories that appear in each issue are: news, editorial, software and services, communications, systems and peripherals, miniworld, and computer industry. This is an excellent source for reviewing the most recent advances in all facets of the computer field.

Publication: *Datamation*
Address: 666 Fifth Avenue, New York, NY 10019
Frequency: Monthly
Orientation: This journal features many interesting articles on the data processing industry. The articles are usually written by top-level DP professionals. Many of the articles are technical in nature, but a large number would be of interest to DP students. Most of the recent advances in the industry are covered in this journal.

Publication: *Data World* (4 volumes)
Organization: Auerbach Publishers, Inc., 6560 North Park Drive, Pennsauken, NJ 08109
Frequency: This is offered by yearly subscription, which includes monthly updates. Most university libraries have subscriptions.
Orientation: This work, like *Datapro*, provides a reference on computer developments that is comprehensive and current. This service provides coverage of the world's most widely used and actively marketed EDP products and services. It indicates vendor information, product specifications and prices, and independent product evaluations. Major topics include general-purpose computers, minicomputers, peripherals, data handling, software and data communications. This work is an invaluable reference.

Publication: *Datapro*
Organization: Datapro Research Corp.
Address: 1805 Underwood Boulevard, Delran, NJ 08075
Frequency: This reference is offered by yearly subscription, which includes monthly updates. Most university libraries have subscriptions.
Orientation: This is a first-rate reference providing a comprehensive and current analysis of the performance of computers, data communications, office systems, software, etc.

Publication: *IBM Systems Journal*
Organization: IBM
Address: Armonk, NY 10504
Frequency: Quarterly
Orientation: Each quarter the journal focuses on a specific area in computing such as graphics, computer-aided design, etc.

Publication: *Infosystems*
Organization: Hitchcock Publication
Address: Hitchcock Building, Wheaton, IL 60187
Frequency: Monthly
Orientation: This is a nontechnical applications-oriented journal that focuses on various uses of DP equipment. Frequently, an entire issue is devoted to a specific application—for example, word processing, computer-aided manufacturing, or micrographics, just to name a few.

Publication: *Interface Age*
Address: P. O. Box 1234, Cerritos, CA 90701
Orientation: This is a monthly magazine for personal and small business computer users, devoted largely to hardware.

Publication: *Journal of Systems Management*
Organization: Association for Systems Management
Address: 24587 Bagley Road, Cleveland, OH 44138
Frequency: Monthly
Orientation: This is a systems-oriented journal that focuses on management concerns. Topics include those relating to systems analysis and design, data base management systems, management information systems, cost-benefit analysis, and human resources management.

Publication: *Mini-Micro Systems*
Organization: A Cahners publication
Address: 221 Columbus Avenue, Boston, MA 02116
Frequency: Monthly
Orientation: The mini-micro articles focus on recent advances in the computing field and tend to be relatively nontechnical. Some of the feature articles, however, are somewhat technical.

Publication: *Security World*
Organization: Cahners Publishing Company, 5 South Wabash Avenue, Chicago, IL 60603
Frequency: Monthly
Orientation: Features issues that are central for the security professional. Includes features on catastrophe protection, methods to prevent and detect crime, security systems, and security personnel.

Publication: *Small Systems World*
Organization: Hunter Publications, 53 West Jackson Boulevard, Chicago, IL 60604
Frequency: Monthly
Orientation: Contains 3 or 4 articles on various computer topics, not necessarily specific to small computer systems. Some articles are general and some are rather technical in nature. There are a relatively small number of pages per issue.

Mostly for Micros

The following are some of the major personal computing journals.
Business Computer Systems
Byte
Compute!
Computer and Electronics
Creative Computing
80 Micro
PC World
Personal Computing
Popular Computing
Softalk

III. GENERAL PERIODICALS

The following periodicals are generally available in most university libraries. They are not specifically computer-related, but they frequently have nontechnical articles relevant to the computing field.
Administrative Management
Business Horizons
Business Week
Dun's Review
Forbes
Fortune
Harvard Business Systems
Management Review
Inc.
Management Science
Modern Office Procedures
Operations Research
Privacy Journal
Scientific American
Sloan Management Review

IV. PROMINENT COMPUTER SOCIETIES

Professional Societies

American Federation of Information Processing Societies (AFIPS)*, 1899 Preston White Drive, Reston, VA 22091

American Institute of Aeronautics & Astronautics, 1290 Sixth Avenue, New York, NY 10019

The American Society for Information Science, 1010 Sixteenth Street, N. W., Second Floor, Washington, DC 20036

American Statistical Association, 806 Fifteenth Street, N. W., Washington, DC 20005

Association for Computational Linguistics, SRI International, 333 Ravenswood Avenue, Menlo Park, CA 94025

* These organizations have constituent societies as members, not individuals.

The Association for Computing Machinery, Inc. (ACM), 11 West 42nd Street, New York, NY 10036

Association for Educational Data Systems (AEDS), 1201 Sixteenth Street, N. W., Washington, DC 20036

Association for Systems Management (ASM), 24587 Bagley Road, Cleveland, OH 44138

Data Processing Management Association (DPMA), 505 Busse Highway, Park Ridge, IL 60068

The Institute of Electrical and Electronics Engineers, Inc. (IEEE), 345 East Forty-Seventh Street, New York, NY 10017

The Institute of Electrical and Electronics Engineers, Inc. (IEEE), Computer Society, 1109 Spring Street, Suite 202, Silver Springs, MD 20910

Instrument Society of America, International Headquarters, 67 Alexander Drive, P. O. Box 12277, Research Triangle Park, NC 27709

International Federation for Information Processing (IFIP)*, Geneva, Switzerland

The Society for Computer Simulation, Inc., P. O. Box 2228, LaJolla, CA 92038

Society for Industrial and Applied Mathematics, 1405 Architects Building, 117 South 17th Street, Philadelphia, PA 19103

Society for Information Display, 654 Sepulveda Boulevard, Los Angeles, CA 90049

V. SUGGESTED TERM PAPER TOPICS

1. Recent advances in new memory devices.
2. Networks: technology and applications.
3. Office automation: will the office of the future ever be realized?
4. The cottage industry: effects of computers on the work environment.
5. Electronic mail: technology and trends.
6. Comparing hierarchical and relational data bases.
7. Structured design methodology: is it really worth it?
8. The impact of computers on individual privacy.
9. Robotics and its effects on unemployment.
10. Recent innovations in artificial intelligence.
11. Computer graphics: technology and applications.
12. Computers and their applications to:

Music	Education
Art	DNA research
Medicine	Energy

13. Micros as workstations for managers.
14. Examine the Japanese computer industry and indicate how it is likely to influence the American computer industry in the next decade.
15. Should the computer professional be certified?
16. What is ANSI and what is its influence on the computer field?

GLOSSARY

Abacus An ancient device used for counting; utilizes the base five numbering system.

ACM (Association for Computing Machinery) The oldest and largest computing society.

Acoustic Coupler Device connected to, or part of, a terminal that enables the terminal to access a CPU, using any standard telephone.

Ada A high-level programming language developed by the Department of Defense; named for Ada Augusta, the Countess of Lovelace; makes extensive use of real-time and structured programming procedures; includes automatic error recovery and fail-safe operations; an easy-to-maintain language.

Aiken, Howard The developer of the first electromechanical relay computer, the Mark I. The computer was constructed at Harvard University and funded in part by IBM.

Alphanumeric Constant Any fixed value used in a program that consists of a combination of letters, digits, and symbols; a heading that is written by a program typically consists of alphanumeric constants.

Alphanumeric Field A data field that can contain any combination of letters, digits, and special characters. Address fields, for example, are alphanumeric because they typically contain letters as well as numbers, and sometimes special characters as well.

Analog Computer A device that measures or processes data in a continuous form.

Analytical Engine A computational device conceived by Charles Babbage in the nineteenth century; similar in concept to modern computers.

APL A high-powered interactive programming language; an acronym for *A Programming Language*; best used with a terminal in an interactive mode; ideally suited for handling complex problems in a free-form style of coding.

Application Program A program written to satisfy the needs of a specific business application. Application programs are written by in-house programmers or by consultants.

Application Programmer The person who writes the programs for a given application; must be familiar with programming concepts in addition to business information processing needs.

Arithmetic-Logic Unit The unit of a CPU that performs arithmetic operations and comparisons.

Array A list of variables used to store a series of items such as a list or a table. A subscript indicates the location of a particular value or entry within the array.

Artificial Intelligence (AI) A field of study that attempts to use computers for tasks traditionally considered to require some form of human intelligence.

ASCII A common computer code used extensively for data communications; an abbreviation for *American Standard Code for Information Interchange*.

Assembler Language A programming language that is very similar to machine language.

Audio Response Unit An output device that transmits messages from a CPU to a user in verbal form; the computer is equipped with various prerecorded key phrases or words that are extracted as required for the purpose of answering specific requests.

Audit Procedures Procedures designed (a) to ensure that adequate controls have been implemented to detect and prevent computer crime and human error, and (b) to assess the reliability, efficiency, and cost-effectiveness of a system.

Augusta, Ada A nineteenth-century computing pioneer who developed theoretical programs for Charles Babbage's Analytical Engine.

Automatic Teller Machine A device that serves as a data entry terminal for the processing of bank deposits and withdrawals.

Auxiliary Storage A separate storage unit that supplements the CPU's primary storage; usually a disk or tape device; same as secondary storage.

Babbage, Charles A nineteenth-century mathematician who designed two computational devices called the Difference Engine and the Analytical Engine; the latter contained many of the concepts used in twentieth-century electronic digital computers. Neither device was completed.

Backup File A copy of a file typically stored on disk or tape; a backup file can be used to re-create the original file in the event that it is damaged, lost, or stolen.

Band Printer A line printer that uses a flexible stainless steel print band photo-engraved with print characters; the most common type of line printer.

Bar Code Reader An optical scanner that reads a bar code such as a Universal Product Code. Bar codes used on grocery items and other products are read by bar code readers.

BASIC A high-level symbolic programming language; an acronym for *Beginner's All-Purpose Symbolic Instruction Code*; a relatively easy programming language to learn; best suited for programming with the use of terminals, minicomputers, and microcomputers.

Batch Processing The processing of data in groups or batches at fixed intervals, as opposed to the immediate processing of data. Files that are maintained using batch processing techniques are actually current only at the time at which they are updated.

Batch Total A control total that is obtained by summing the values of a particular field on all records to be processed in a batch.

Baud Rate The unit of measuring data transmission speeds; usually measured in terms of bits per second.

Binary Numbering System A numbering system that uses a combination of 0's and 1's; ideally suited for use in computers, where 0 represents the "off" state and 1 represents the "on" state.

Bit A contraction for *binary digit*. The term refers to the representation of data in binary form, as a series of on-off or 1-0 digits.

Blocking Combining several logical records into one physical record to conserve space on a magnetic tape or disk and to provide more efficient processing.

Bpi (bits per inch) An abbreviation for bits per inch. Tape densities are measured in bits per inch (bpi), where a density of 800 bpi, for example, is equivalent to 800 characters per inch.

Bus The internal connection used to move data from one part of the computer to another; transmits data from a microprocessor to input/output devices.

Business System An organized method for accomplishing a business function.

Byte The number of bits used to represent a character in a computer code. The most common byte size is eight bits.

C A programming language used to write utilities, operating systems, and application programs for research and business.

Cache Memory A type of high-speed memory used for storing the most frequently referenced data and instructions.

Capacity Planning The balancing and monitoring of existing computer workloads and the forecasting of future workloads through analytical modeling.

Card Reader An input device of a computer system that reads punched card data and transmits it to the CPU.

Cathode Ray Tube (CRT) A terminal device that displays messages on a television-like tube; output is referred to as "soft copy," since it is not produced in a form that can be retained as a permanent record.

CCP (Certified Computer Professional) A certification issued by the Institute for Certification of Computer Professionals; this organization first tests and then certifies the knowledge and skills of computing professionals.

CDP (Certificate in Data Processing) A certificate issued by the Data Processing Management Association to individuals with college training and experience in the field who pass an examination.

Central Processing Unit (CPU) The computer unit that controls the actual operations of the computer system; a CPU consists of primary storage, an arithmetic-logic unit, and a control unit.

Centralized Data Processing The performance of the DP function by a single computer center within a company. Contrast with decentralized and distributed data processing.

Chaining A method of linking records in a data base.

Chain Printer A printer that uses a print mechanism with characters that rotate on a chain.

Character A unit of data consisting of a digit, letter, or special symbol.

Chip A memory device made from a thin wafer of silicon that can hold thousands of integrated circuits.

CICS An abbreviation for IBM's Customer Information Control System; a general purpose supervisor and data communications monitor.

Coaxial Cable Used in place of standard electrical wires for high-quality data transmission; consists of a central cylinder surrounded by a series of wires that can carry data at very high speeds.

COBOL A high-level symbolic programming language; an acronym for *Common Business Oriented Language*; an English-like language; most suited for business-type problems.

Code Test A test to determine if a coded field is valid.

Coding a Program The writing of the set of program instructions.

Common Carrier A company that specializes in offering standard telephone lines called "switched lines" or leased, private lines for data communications.

Compatibility Two systems are compatible when software prepared for one computer can be utilized by another without the need for a rigorous conversion.

Compiler A translator program that produces a machine language equivalent of a high-level symbolic program.

Computer-Assisted Instruction (CAI) An educational technique that utilizes computers for teaching various subject areas; the computer usually prints textual information on a terminal and then asks the student to respond to a series of questions; depending on the accuracy of the responses, the computer will either proceed to a more advanced topic or else repeat the material.

Computer Crime The act of stealing, embezzling, or otherwise defrauding an organization with the use of a computer.

Computer Literate Being able to understand the advantages and limitations of computers in this Information Age and being be able to use a computer as well.

Computer-Managed Instruction (CMI) A technique used to monitor the effectiveness of computer-assisted instruction.

Computer Output Microfilm (COM) Microfilm output from a computer system.

Computer System An integrated series of components consisting of a central processing unit, input, and output devices.

Conditional Branch A branch, or transfer, that occurs in a program or flowchart only when a particular condition is met.

Connector A symbol used in a program flowchart to indicate a branch or transfer to another point.

Console Terminal A computer device used primarily for communication between the computer operator and the supervisor program.

Constant A fixed value that is part of a program; this value does not change during the execution of the program.

Constraints Limitations on the design and operation of a system imposed by management; includes legal, budgetary, and equipment limitations.

Continuous Form The output form generally produced by a computer printer. Although a continuous form can be separated into individual sheets, it is fed through the printer in one continuous sheet to increase speed and facilitate processing.

Control Listing A list of all input used by an organization to manually check data in an effort to minimize data entry errors.

Control Unit The part of a CPU that controls the operations of a computer.

Controls Methods used to minimize system errors; includes, for example, the calculation of batch totals, item counts and limit checks.

Conversion of Systems The process of converting from an existing set of business procedures to a new design devised by the systems analyst to improve efficiency.

Cost-Benefit Analysis A technique used to determine the overall costs of a given system and to compare them to cost factors estimated for the new design; cost-benefit analysis is performed to determine when and if a proposed new design will be cost-effective.

CP/M An operating system used with many microcomputers; an acronym for *Control Program for Microprocessors*.

Cylinder A series of vertical tracks on a magnetic disk pack that is used for storing data. Records on a disk are frequently accessed by addresses that include a cylinder number.

Daisy Wheel Printer A daisy wheel is a mechanism that prints fully formed characters; sometimes daisy wheel printers are referred to as "letter-quality" printers.

Data A collection of raw facts that is entered into a computer system as input, is processed, and transformed into meaningful information.

Data Base The set of data maintained by a company as one single, major collection that can be accessed by individual departments as needed. This data base is much more efficient than storing individual files for each department, a procedure that frequently results in duplication of effort and lack of proper control.

Data Base Administrator The person responsible for maintaining the data base and making certain that data resources are effectively administered; also responsible for designing appropriate security controls and preventing unauthorized use of the data base.

Data Base Management System (DBMS) A software package designed to provide users with a fully integrated management information system. A data base management system includes techniques for creating files, updating files, reporting on file information, and querying files as well.

Data Communications The technology that enables electronic transmission of data from one location or site to another.

Data Dictionary Provides descriptive information about the data items stored in the data base; provides the single source for all information and documentation about the data base.

Data Encryption Standard (DES) A coding algorithm designed to scramble information so it will be unintelligible if intercepted during transmission across data communications lines.

Data Entry Device The device used to convert data from a source document to machine-readable form.

Data Flow Diagram A pictorial representation of the flow of data within a system.

Data Processing Manager The individual responsible for the operations of a computer center.

Data Verification A procedure that minimizes data entry errors; data that has been keyed by an operator is re-keyed to ensure that the second keying procedure matches the original data entered.

Debugging To free a program from errors or "bugs."

Decentralized Data Processing The use and control of independent data processing facilities by individual departments within an organization. With this technique, each department controls its own processing needs. There is, however, some duplication of effort among departments. Contrast with centralized data processing and distributed data processing.

Decision Support System A system which helps predict the potential outcome of a management decision that is being considered, before it is actually implemented.

Dedicated System A computer that is used only for a specific application or type of application.

Density The number of characters that can be represented in an inch of magnetic tape or on a disk track; often expressed as bpi (bits per inch).

Difference Engine A computational device conceived by Charles Babbage in the nineteenth century.

Digital Computer A device that represents quantities as discrete digits.

Direct-Access Feature The method of processing or accessing data independent of the actual location of that data. This method can be used with a direct-access device such as magnetic disk. The term random access is sometimes used in place of direct access. Contrast with sequential access.

Direct File Disk records are accessed by converting a key field, through some calculation, to an actual address that identifies the surface, track, and possibly cylinder or sector number where the record may be found.

Director of Information Systems Usually the highest-level position in a computer organization; typically it is a vice presidential position; person is responsible for all computer operations and the entire staff of programmers, analysts, and other computer professionals.

Disk Drive A direct-access device designed to minimize the access time required to locate specific records; ideally suited for on-line or immediate processing.

Distributed Data Processing (DDP) A method of processing designed to incorporate the benefits of both centralized and decentralized data processing. A minicomputer or terminal is used to process data at individual sites and to transmit it to a central data base; in addition, numerous users have access to a data base using a network of terminals and minis linked to one main CPU. Contrast with centralized data processing and decentralized data processing.

Documentation Package The formal report that describes a new system design in its entirety.

Dot-Matrix Printer A common type of serial printer; uses a grid-like structure for forming a wide variety of characters including graphic symbols.

DPMA (Data Processing Management Association) An organization that certifies computer professionals; the largest computer management professional association.

Drum Printer A line printer that uses a cylindrical steel drum embossed with characters.

EBCDIC See Extended Binary Coded Decimal Interchange Code.

Eckert, J. Presper, Jr. Along with John W. Mauchly, developer of the ENIAC, the United States' first electronic digital computer.

E-COM An abbreviation for Electronic Computer Originated Mail; a type of electronic mail service once operated by the United States Post Office.

Edit Procedure The process of validating a file of data to ensure that records do not contain obvious omissions, inconsistencies, or errors.

EDP Auditor An individual with accounting and computer expertise who assesses the overall effectiveness and integrity of a computer system; responsible for detecting if there have been attempts to misuse the system or defraud the company with the use of a computer.

EDSAC The first operational stored program computer constructed in 1949 at Cambridge University in England.

EDVAC The first computer designed to have stored program capability, but not actually completed until 1951.

Electronic Cash Register A device used in retail establishments to enter data, store it, and transmit it to a CPU for processing.

Electronic Data Processing (EDP) Refers to the processing of data by electronic digital computers.

Electronic Funds Transfer (EFT) System The use of computers in the banking industry to enter data at the point of transaction for automatically updating banking records and, in general, automating banking operations.

Electronic Mail Copies of a document or message are transmitted with the use of terminals or computers and data communications lines to one or more locations in a matter of minutes or seconds.

Electronic Message System An electronic mail alternative that makes it possible for offices to transmit and receive documents without using external mailing services like the Post Office.

Electronic Spreadsheet A programming package that enables people to make projections and to build models; this package is an ideal tool for business applications including sales forecasting, financial analysis, preparation of budgets, inventory control, and so on.

Encryption A scrambling technique which renders computer data unintelligible when interceptions occur; a major method used to preserve the privacy of data and to protect it from any tampering.

End-of-Job Routine The instructions to be executed when there is no more data to be processed; may include, for example, a series of summary or total procedures.

Enhancements Additions to a standard programming language.

ENIAC The United States' first operational electronic digital computer developed by J. Presper Eckert, Jr., and John Mauchly in 1946.

Ergonomics The science of making the work environment safer and more comfortable for employees; one goal of ergonomics is increased job satisfaction for computer users.

Exception Report A listing of records or items that do not fall within pre-established guidelines.

Execution The operating cycle during which a program is actually being processed, or run.

Extended Binary Coded Decimal Interchange Code (EBCDIC) A computer code used to represent characters; most frequently used on IBM and IBM-compatible computers.

Facsimile Equipment Devices that copy documents and transmit them to other locations; provides the ability to transmit not only text but company logos, graphics, signatures, and so on.

Feasibility Study An analysis used to determine the computer equipment that a company should select for its information processing needs.

Feedback Procedures used to ensure that a system is operating effectively; includes procedures to follow if any errors have occurred.

Fiber Optic Cable A technology for transmitting data at high speeds using cables; consists of thin glass fibers that can carry a high volume of data.

Field A group of consecutive storage positions used to represent an item of data. Examples of fields within records include Name, Address, and so on.

Field Test A test used to determine if specific data fields have valid formats; that is, fields designated as numeric should have numeric data, and so on.

File A collection of individual records that is treated as one unit. A payroll file, for example, refers to a company's complete collection of employee records.

Firmware Hardware that has been preprogrammed or wired to perform specific functions. A user can frequently purchase with a computer system some software or program support that is built into the hardware.

Fixed-Head Disk A device that does not have a movable access arm; each track on the disk has its own read/write mechanism that accesses a record as it rotates past the arm.

Fixed-Length Record Term used to describe records, within a file, that are all the same length.

Floppy Disk A storage medium used primarily with micros and minis for storing data and programs; uses direct-access methods of processing; accessing floppy disk information is faster than accessing information from a tape cassette or cartridge; the most popular external storage medium for micros.

Forth A high-powered programming language that is mostly used for real-time control applications and for a wide variety of engineering problems; also used to write operating systems; can be used with some personal computers.

FORTRAN High-level symbolic programming language; an acronym for *Formula Translator*; most suited for scientific or mathematical problems.

Front-End Processor A mini or other device that collects data from a series of terminals and then transmits the entire set of data at high speeds to a mainframe; can sometimes edit, format, and even process the data before transmitting it.

Full-Duplex Line A communication line that permits data transmission both to and from a computer at the same time.

GO TO-Less Programming Another term for structured programming; structured programming enables each module or procedure to function as a stand-alone entity; the technique avoids the use of branches or "GO TO" instructions.

Graphics Display Terminal A cathode ray tube with the ability to display a wide variety of graphics, pictures, and even animated data on a screen, often in color.

Hacker A computer enthusiast who makes a hobby out of accessing and even changing information in data banks.

Half-Duplex Line A communication line that permits data transmission both to and from a computer, but not at the same time.

Hard-Copy Output A permanent record of output from a computer system. Contrast with soft copy or visual display output.

Hardware The actual computer devices that constitute a computer system. Contrast with software.

Hardwired Linkage by cable of an input/output device, such as a terminal, to a CPU; with hardwiring, telephone lines are not necessary for transmitting messages from a remote location to a CPU.

Header Label The first record recorded on a tape or disk for identification purposes.

Hierarchical Data Base A method of organizing data so that major items are grouped together, then subdivided into minor ones.

Hierarchy of Operations The sequence in which operations are performed by the computer; unless otherwise noted a programmed computation would be evaluated such that multiplication is performed before addition.

High-Level Programming Language A symbolic programming language that requires translation using a compiler; easier to code than a low-level language but more difficult for the computer to translate since it typically uses English-like codes instead of machine-like codes.

HIPO Chart An abbreviation for *hierarchy* plus *input-process-output*; a planning tool used to graphically represent a system or program design; utilizes a top-down structure.

Hollerith, Herman A nineteenth-century inventor who, while working for the Census Bureau, developed the concept of a punched card for representing data; he also developed and built electrical tabulating devices that could process punched card data.

Hollerith Code The system of punches used on an 80-column card to represent data; named for Herman Hollerith.

Host Computer The main processor in a network of terminals and CPUs.

IBG (interblock gap) See interblock gap.

IEEE (Institute of Electrical and Electronics Engineers) Computer Society A computing society that serves to advance the theory and practice of computer and information processing technology.

Immediate Processing When terminals are connected to a CPU so that data can be processed as soon as it is transacted; typically the terminals are located at the points where data is generated or transacted.

Impact Printer An output device that functions like a typewriter; it uses a hammer to strike a character against an inked ribbon, which causes an image of the character to be printed.

Implementation The term used to describe the conversion from a manual or existing procedure to a new computerized one.

Indexed File A direct access file that uses an index for looking up the address of disk records.

Indexed Sequential Access Method (ISAM) A method of accessing data on a disk so that on-line processing is facilitated. The disk uses an index to locate records.

Information Data that has been processed so that it is meaningful and useful for managers and operating staff.

Information Processing Producing meaningful information that management can use for decision-making purposes and that the operating staff can use for its day-to-day activities.

Information Resource Management The supervision and control of information processed as if it were a typical organizational resource.

Information System A computerized application that uses hardware and software in an integrated, meaningful way.

Input Incoming data read into a computer system for processing.

Input Unit A device that reads data from a specific form and converts it into electrical pulses, which are then transmitted to an input area in the CPU.

Integrated Circuit Circuits that consist of electronic components on a thin silicon wafer; results in much faster and less expensive processing than if transistors were used.

Intelligent Terminal A programmable terminal that has its own computing ability.

Interblock Gap (IBG) An area of a tape or disk that separates physical records.

Interpreter A translator that converts a high-level symbolic program into machine language; instructions are translated one line at a time into machine language code.

Item Count A count of the number of documents in a batch of source documents that are sent to a computer center for processing; item counts are used for control purposes.

Jacquard, Joseph A nineteenth-century French inventor who used punched holes in a card to drive a weaving loom so that it would weave the required patterns and use specified colors.

Job Control Language (JCL) The machine-oriented language used for communicating with a computer's operating system.

K Equivalent to approximately 1000 bytes of storage.

Key-to-Storage Procedure A procedure that uses a device with a keyboard to convert source documents into a storage medium such as disk or tape.

Laser Memory An alternative type of memory using light energy rather than magnetic fields for storing characters.

Law of Diminishing Returns As resources are added to a system, the resulting benefits will continue to increase, but only up to some point. That is, there is a point at which the benefits will begin to diminish in relation to the amount of input required.

Leibniz, Gottfried A seventeeth-century mathematician who built one of the first calculators.

Letter-Quality Printer An impact printer used to produce clear and easy-to-read output; uses fully formed characters similar to those on a typewriter.

Library of Programs A collection of programs used by an organization for meeting its information processing needs.

Light Pen A device used with CRT terminals to enable users to make changes directly to the data displayed on the screen.

Line Printer A computer output device that prints one line of information at a time. Contrast with serial or page printer.

List A set of data with pointers indicating the physical location of records that have a specific attribute or characteristic.

Local Area Network A transmission medium for terminals and host computers closely linked by a single facility or in nearby facilities.

Logic Error A mistake in a program that will cause erroneous output to be generated; can occur from a mistake in the sequencing and instructions as well as from an improperly coded instruction that does not accomplish what was desired. Contrast with syntax error.

LOGO A programming language developed specifically for teaching children how to interact with a computer; used extensively by artificial intelligence researchers.

Log-On Procedures The procedures used for gaining access to a mainframe.

Loop A sequence of steps in a program or flowchart to be executed a specified number of times.

Machine Language The machine's own internal code for processing data; a program written in machine language requires no translation.

Magnetic Bubble Memory A type of memory that consists of magnetized spots on a thin film of semiconductor material; data can be retained in magnetic bubble memory even if the power is shut off.

Magnetic Core A tiny doughnut-shaped ferrite element that was a main component for representing data or instructions in memory in older computers.

Magnetic Ink Character Reader (MICR) An input device capable of reading characters imprinted with magnetic ink, such as those on bank checks.

Mainframe The traditional computer system used in most medium and large business organizations for (1) information processing in a centralized or distributed mode, and (2) data communications applications where terminals at remote locations transmit data to a central processing unit.

Maintenance Programmer The person responsible for revising and updating existing programs as needed.

Management Game A hypothetical or simulated management situation in which the user makes decisions based on a series of specified criteria.

Management Information System (MIS) A type of integrated system designed to facilitate the decision-making process of top-level management as well as middle and lower management; uses a top-down design approach to storage and retrieval of information.

Mark I An electromechanical computer constructed at Harvard University with IBM funding in 1944, under the direction of Howard Aiken.

Mauchly, John Along with J. Presper Eckert, Jr., the inventor of the United States' first electronic digital computer.

Megabyte (MB) Equivalent to approximately one million bytes of storage.

Memory size The number of storage positions in a computer system.

Menu A method for asking users what requests they have; a user selects the desired item from a series of displayed options.

Microcomputer Small computers that are widely used in homes, schools, and small businesses, and as professional workstations.

Microform A term used to describe all microfilmed output; includes microfiche as well as traditional rolled microfilm.

Microprocessor A computerized control system of a standard computer or other automatic device.

Minicomputer A small computer frequently used to supplement existing computer power in an organization that has a mainframe, or to provide computer power to organizations that could not otherwise afford it; superminis sometimes have as much power as mainframes.

Modem A device that converts digital data signals so that they can be transmitted over communication lines; an abbreviation for modulator-demodulator.

Mouse A push-button control device for interacting with a CRT or computer; eliminates the need to type computer commands using a keyboard.

Moving-Head Disk A disk that has all the read/write heads attached to a single movable-access mechanism. All the read/write heads move together to locate a specific record.

MP/M An operating system for micros that enables several users to run programs concurrently using one CPU; an acronym for Multiprocessing Monitor Control Program; an enhanced version of CP/M.

MS-DOS An operating system developed by Microsoft for use with IBM personal computers and IBM-compatible personal computers.

Multiplexer A device that can collect messages from numerous terminals and transmit them, all at one time, at high speeds over one communication channel; ideal for reducing communication costs and making transmissions more efficient.

Multiprocessing The use of two or more CPUs linked together to optimize the processing of data.

Multiprogramming The ability of a computer system to process numerous programs concurrently.

Nanosecond One billionth (10^{-9}) of a second. Most modern computers can operate on data at speeds measured in nanoseconds.

Network A coordinated system of linked terminals and/or minis and CPUs that may operate independently but also share data and other resources from a central CPU.

Network Data Base A method of data organization that provides users with access to centralized data by relating items according to some set of characteristics or by some hierarchical chain.

Node Each terminal or mini linked to a host CPU in a network.

Nonimpact Printer Printers that use heat or laser technology, or photographic techniques for printing output.

Numeric Constant A fixed numeric value that is part of a program; this value does not change during execution of the program.

Numeric Field An item of data that is typically used in arithmetic operations; e.g., an amount field would be classified as numeric.

Numeric Variable A field in a BASIC program used to enter numeric data; generally represented by a name that consists of a single letter or a letter followed by a digit (e.g., A, A1, etc.).

Object Program The machine language equivalent of a source program. Object programs are the only ones that can be executed by the computer.

Off-Line Operation A procedure that uses devices not directly under the control of a central mainframe; a key-to-storage procedure would be an example of an off-line operation.

Office Automation The use of computers and information processing techniques to process and manage office functions.

On-Line Operation The use of input/output devices directly connected to a CPU either for immediate data entry or for inquiring about the status of a file.

Operating System A series of control programs that enables a computer to automatically handle tasks that would otherwise require manual intervention. These tasks include calling in a compiler, scheduling runs, input/output control, and so on.

Operations Manager A person who supervises the activities of data entry and computer operators.

Optical Character Recognition (OCR) Device An input unit capable of reading typed or handwritten data.

Optical Mark Reader An input unit capable of reading marks coded on documents; frequently used to score tests that are taken by filling in marks on a grid.

Optical Memory A new type of storage using light energy rather than magnetic fields to store characters.

Optical Scanning Device (optical scanner) A type of optical reader that can convert marks, symbols, and characters into electrical signals.

Original Equipment Manufacturer (OEM) Specialized companies that buy computer systems and devices in bulk and supply customized configurations to end-users.

Output Data that has been processed by a computer system; the information that is obtained from a computer system is referred to as output.

Output Unit A device that receives information from the CPU and converts the electronic pulses into an appropriate output form.

Page Printer A printer that can print a full page of information at one time.

Pareto's Law A dictum which states that only a minority of the components within a computer system have a significant effect on the particular output to be obtained.

Parity Bit A check bit used to minimize the risk of computer transmission errors.

Partition A segment of main memory; some computers can run several programs simultaneously by partitioning main memory.

Pascal A programming language named for Blaise Pascal; uses structured programming techniques.

Pascal, Blaise A seventeenth-century mathematician who invented one of the first mechanical calculators.

PC-DOS A disk operating system for the IBM personal computer.

Picosecond One trillionth (10^{-12}) of a second. Some supercomputers can operate on data at speeds measured in picoseconds.

PL/1 High-level symbolic programming language; an acronym for *Programming Language One*; combines the features of FORTRAN, a scientific language, and COBOL, a business language.

Plotter A hard-copy output device that can print graphic data.

Plug-Compatible Machine (PCM) Peripheral equipment that can be used with numerous mainframes or CPUs.

Point-of-Sale (POS) System A computerized system that processes data using terminals at the point where sales are transacted; used to immediately update sales and inventory data.

Pointer A concept that allows an accessing mechanism of a computer to locate or "point to" a specific record or entity in a data base.

Polling The technique used to query terminals, to determine if there are messages to be transmitted.

Primary Storage The main memory of a computer system that is located within the CPU; contrast with auxiliary storage.

Printer Spacing Chart A planning tool that is used by the computer specialist to map out margins and spacing to be used in a computer-produced report.

Problem Definition A formal document prepared by the systems analyst that defines the current system and its basic inadequacies.

Professional Workstation A micro or terminal at a manager's desk; minimizes clerical and communication tasks required of managers and other users, so they can focus on decision-making and administrative duties.

Program A series of instructions that enables a computer to read input data, process it, and convert it to output.

Program Flowchart A planning tool in pictorial form that depicts the logic to be used in a program.

Programmer The computer professional who writes and debugs the program, or set of instructions, that operates on input and converts it to output.

Programmer Analyst A computer professional who performs systems analysis and design tasks as well as programming.

Programming Manager The individual who supervises the programming staff.

Project Management The overall supervision of a systems project.

Prompt A signal from the computer which indicates that it is ready to accept data; typically on a CRT screen the prompt is a ?, underline, blinking cursor, and so on.

Protocol Procedures for gaining access to a computer system.

Pseudocode A planning tool that uses a program-like instruction code for depicting logic flow in a structured program; uses words rather than figures or symbols for representing logic. Contrast with program flowchart.

Query Language An English-like language used to access a data base.

RAM (random-access memory) Memory that is used for storing programs and data.

Read-Only Memory See ROM.

Read/Write Head The mechanism on a magnetic tape or magnetic disk drive that enables the device to read magnetic data and to record magnetic data.

Real-Time Processing The processing of data quickly enough to affect decision-making.

Record A set of related fields treated as a unit. A payroll record on magnetic disk, for example, consists of fields relating to a particular employee; fields in such a record would include Social Security Number, Name, and Address.

Relational Data Base A type of data organization in which entities are linked to one another using chains, pointers, and lists to interrelate them.

Remote Data Entry Entering data via remote terminals; the data is then transmitted to a CPU using data communications linkages.

Remote Job Entry (RJE) Entering programs and data via terminals that are not at the same location as the CPU.

Robotics The design and use of robots.

ROM (read-only memory) The part of computer memory that contains prewired functions; cannot be altered by programmed instructions.

Routine A series of instructions that performs a specific set of operations or procedures.

RPG An abbreviation for *Report Program Generator;* a symbolic language ideally suited for creating printed reports from input media; a minimum of programming effort is required. RPG II and RPG III are the two most current versions of RPG in use.

Running Total When a total is incremented each time a record is processed.

S-100 Bus One of the most common internal connections used in micros to (1) move data from one part of the computer to another and (2) transmit data from the microprocessor to input/output devices.

Scientific Programmer A computer professional who writes programs that are used in scientific applications.

Scroll The method used to display different portions of a text on a CRT.

Secondary Storage A separate storage unit that supplements the CPU's primary storage. Usually stored on disk or tape. Same as auxiliary storage.

Serial Printer A device similar to a typewriter that is used primarily for printing data on terminals; data is printed one character at a time.

Shared-Logic Word Processing System A word processing system in which two or more terminals share the processing capability of a single central processor.

Simplex Line A communication line that permits data transmission in one direction only, that is, either to or from a CPU at a given time.

Simulation A technique in which a representation or model of a system is developed that can be manipulated and studied in order to better understand an actual system and make predictions about the effects of planned changes.

Simulation Language A programming language most commonly used for modeling or simulating applications; enables the programmer to use the computer to simulate "real world" situations and make decisions based on the outcome.

Soft-Copy Output Output from a computer system that

is in the form of a visual display; the display is not retained unless it is linked to a hard-copy printer.

Software Programs that enable the computer system to operate effectively. These include the supervisor, user programs, utility programs, and so on.

Source Document The originating report or document that is either converted to a machine-readable form, or is read directly as input to a computer system.

Source Program A program written in a symbolic programming language; source programs must be translated before they can be executed.

Special-Purpose System A system designed by a manufacturer to satisfy the needs of a specific type of user.

Spooling A technique used to transmit input and output at high speeds to an intermediate device such as disk or tape so that CPU time is not wasted for low-speed operations.

Spreadsheet See electronic spreadsheet.

Stand-Alone Word Processor A text editing and document processing system that functions independently without any linkage to a central CPU.

Stibitz, George A computer pioneer who developed a relay computer at Bell Laboratories in 1939.

Storage Protection Feature A technique that prevents a program from inadvertently destroying or modifying portions of another program.

Stored-Program Concept The use of main memory for storing programs as well as data.

String Variable A field in a BASIC program used to enter alphanumeric data; generally represented by a name that consists of a letter or a letter plus a digit, followed by a $ (e.g., A$, A1$, etc.).

Structured Programming A technique used to standardize and improve programs so they are easier to evaluate, debug, and modify; consists of modularizing or segmenting each program into distinct blocks all executed under the control of a main module.

Subscript An item that is referenced in an array; the number used to indicate the location of a particular value or entry within a list or table.

Subsystem An entity within an integrated management information system.

Supercomputer A high-speed computer with very great processing capability. Supercomputers serve as host processors for local computer and time-sharing networks and in scientific application areas such as weather forecasting.

Supermini A high-powered minicomputer with storage capacity and speed often equivalent to mainframes.

Supervisor A part of the operating system that is stored in the CPU for purposes of controlling the operations of the entire computer system.

Symbolic Program A program written in a form that is easier for the programmer to understand than the machine's own code; requires a translation process before it can be executed or run.

Syntax Error A violation of a programming rule.

System An organized method for accomplishing a business function.

System Life Cycle The planning, analysis and design, implementation, and operation of a new system.

Systems Analysis The techniques used (1) to study operations and costs of an existing set of procedures, and (2) to prepare a formal definition of these procedures in their entirety and of the major problem areas that must be eliminated.

Systems Analyst The computer specialist responsible for analyzing current procedures and designing the most efficient and economical systems or procedures to better accomplish given tasks within a company.

Systems Design The preparation of a new set of procedures that will perform the basic operations of a system more efficiently and effectively than current operations permit.

Systems Flowchart A pictorial representation of a system's procedures and operations; prepared by the systems analyst; depicts the relationship between inputs, processing, and outputs, in terms of the system as a whole.

Systems Manager The individual who supervises the activities of all systems analysts.

Systems Programmer The person who designs programs to maximize the efficiency of the supervisor, and the overall operating system.

Systems Software Systems software includes the operating system, diagnostic routines, input/output control routines, compilers, assemblers, interpreters, and data base management systems.

Tape Cartridge A device similar to magnetic tapes used with minis and micros; stores data and programs that are processed sequentially in a batch mode.

Tape Cassette Similar to a tape cartridge; used with home cassette recorders as well as computers.

Tape Drive A high-speed device that can read data from a magnetic tape and also record data onto one.

Telecommuting The ability of workers to perform their jobs from remote locations using microcomputers and data communications channels.

Teleconferencing The use of electronic transmission in place of face-to-face meetings.

Teleprocessing A term used to describe the use of telephone lines to transmit and process data.

Teletext A one-way system of transmitting graphics onto home and office screens; similar to cable TV facilities.

Template A special plastic or metal tool used to draw the symbols in a flowchart. Each symbol represents a specific operation.

Text Editing The capability to alter, change, and rearrange text on a word processing system in order to obtain a clean printout.

Time-Sharing The term used to describe a central processing unit that is shared by several users, usually with terminals. Small companies that cannot afford to rent or buy their own computers find this technique particularly advantageous.

Touch-Sensitive Screen A CRT that enables users to enter input by touching the screen at specific points.

Track A recording surface on magnetic tape or magnetic disk.

Traditional Systems Approach A technique in which each system within an organization is treated as an independent entity; specifically designed to satisfy the needs of middle- and lower-level management. Contrast with management information system.

Transaction-Oriented Processing The immediate processing of data as it is transacted.

Transborder Data Flow Information that flows across national boundaries.

Translator A program used to convert a source program into machine language; types of translators include compilers, interpreters, and assemblers.

Tree Structure Permits records in a data base to be organized and accessed hierarchically.

Turnaround Document When output from the computer can be reentered as input at some later date, it is called a turnaround document.

Turnkey System A computer that can be used by an organization with no programming or computer expertise; the computer has usually been pre-programmed for specific applications.

Unconditional Branch A branch, or transfer, in a program or flowchart that occurs regardless of any existing condition.

UNIVAC The first commercially developed computer; completed in 1951.

Universal Product Code (UPC) A bar code that appears on virtually all consumer goods; can be read by a scanner; used in point-of-sale systems in supermarkets and other retail establishments.

UNIX An operating system noted for its user-friendly commands.

Update The process of making a file of data current.

User An individual who uses computer-produced output in performing his or her job.

User-Friendly A term used to describe computer-related activities that are easy to interpret by a user.

Utility Program A programming package used to perform a standard function such as sorting, merging, or transferring data from one device to another.

Validity Check A check of input data to ascertain that it is within established limits.

Value-Added Carrier An organization that offers communication channels with added features such as noise-free transmission.

Variable-Length Record Term used to describe records within a file that are of different sizes.

Videotex A two-way system that enables users to receive as well as transmit messages.

Virtual Storage Access Method (VSAM) An efficient method of accessing indexed disk files.

Virtual Storage Concept A technique used to maximize and optimize the storage available in a computer by using overlay techniques.

Voice Recognition Unit A device capable of interpreting the spoken word and transmitting the data to the CPU.

von Neumann, John A mathematician who, in the late 1940s, helped develop the stored program concept used in modern computers.

Wand Reader A hand-held device used to scan or read bar codes or standard characters; typically used in inventory applications.

Wilkes, Maurice The computer pioneer who constructed the EDSAC in 1949; the EDSAC was the first operational stored program computer.

Winchester Disk Drive Provides a higher storage capacity and greater reliability than many other types of disk drives; used primarily with micros.

Word Processing The computer-aided preparation of documents.

Module and Chapter Opening Photo Credits

Module 1 Phototake
Module 2 Stephen Marley
Module 3 Don Carroll
Module 4 Tony Coluzzi
Module 5 Manfred Kage/Peter Arnold
Module 6 Courtesy Texas Instruments, Inc.

Chapter 1 Opener Yoichiro Kawaguchi
Chapter 2 Opener Arthur d'Arazien/Image Bank
Chapter 3 Opener Mitchell Funk
Chapter 4 Opener Steven Dunwell/Image Bank
Chapter 5 Opener Guy Powers
Chapter 6 Opener Ed Young/Joan Kramer Associates
Chapter 7 Opener Rod Turner/Courtesy Tab
Products Co.
Chapter 8 Opener Corning Glass Works
Chapter 9 Opener Peter Menzel/Stock Boston
Chapter 10 Opener Dan McCoy/Black Star
Chapter 11 Opener Dan Lenore
Chapter 12 Opener Dan Lenore
Chapter 13 Opener Courtesy Wang Laboratories, Inc.
Chapter 14 Opener Sepp Seitz/Woodfin Camp
Chapter 15 Opener Stephen Marley
Chapter 16 Opener Gary D. Landsman
Chapter 17 Opener Michel Tcherevkoff
Chapter 18 Opener Charles West/The Stock Market
Chapter 19 Opener Brad Guice

Index